An Introduction to Health Psychology

Val Morrison and Paul Bennett

PEARSON
Prentice
Hall

Harlow, England • London • New York • Boston • San Francisco • Toronto
Sydney • Tokyo • Singapore • Hong Kong • Seoul • Taipei • New Delhi
Cape Town • Madrid • Mexico City • Amsterdam • Munich • Paris • Milan

Pearson Education Limited
Edinburgh Gate
Harlow
Essex CM20 2JE
England

and Associated Companies throughout the world

Visit us on the World Wide Web at:
www.pearsoned.co.uk

First published 2006

ISBN: 978-0-13-099408-0

British Library Cataloguing-in-Publication Data
A catalogue record for this book is available from the British Library

Library of Congress Cataloging-in-Publication Data
Morrison, Val, 1961–
    An introduction to health psychology / Val Morrison and Paul Bennett.
      p. cm.
    Includes bibliographical references and index.
    ISBN 0-13-099408-1 (pbk. : alk. paper)
    1. Clinical health psychology.   I. Bennett, Paul, 1955–   II. Title.
  R726.7.M77 2006
  616′.001′9—dc22

                                   2005048916

10 9 8 7 6 5 4 3 2
10 09 08 07

Typeset in 10.25/12.5pt Sabon by 35
Printed and bound by Mateu-Cromo Artes Graphicas, Madrid, Spain

The publisher's policy is to use paper manufactured from sustainable forests.

CONTENTS

5   Predicting health behaviour   113

6   Reducing risk of disease – individual approaches   147

7   Population approaches to public health   176

LIST OF FIGURES

LIST OF TABLES

LIST OF PLATES

PREFACE

Background to this book

Health psychology is a growth discipline at both undergraduate and post-graduate level; it is also an exciting, challenging and rewarding subject to study, with career opportunities developing within healthcare as well as within academic settings. We wrote this book because we believed that a comprehensive European-focused textbook was required, that didn't predominantly focus on health behaviours, but which gave equal attention to issues in health, in illness, and in healthcare practice and intervention. Furthermore, we feel that for psychologists, textbooks should be led by psychological theory and constructs, as opposed to behaviour- or disease-led. Illnesses may vary, but, psychologically speaking, they share many things in common – for example, potential for life or behaviour change, distress, challenges to coping, potential for recovery, involvement in healthcare and involvement with health professionals. We very much hope that you enjoy what we have put together.

Aims of this textbook

The overall aim of this textbook is to provide a balanced, informed and comprehensive UK/European textbook with sufficient breadth of material for introductory students, but which also provides sufficient research depth to benefit final year students or those conducting a health psychology project. We believe that in addition to covering mainstream health psychology topics such as health and illness beliefs, behaviour and outcomes, topics such as socioeconomic influences on health, biological bases, individual and cultural differences and psychological interventions in health, illness and healthcare, are all essential to the study of health psychology.

With this in mind we began the task of constructing chapters which followed the general principle of issue first, theory second, research evidence third, and finally the application of that theory and findings by means of intervention. For example, if we can describe what associations there are between illness and a particular behaviour such as smoking, and then explore some of the psychosocial explanations of that behaviour by testing theories such as social learning theory, through empirical research, then we can inform those whose aim it is to reduce unhealthy behaviours. Describing, predicting, and then intervening are primary goals of health psychologists.

This text is intended to provide comprehensive coverage of the core themes in current health psychology but it also addresses the fact that many individuals neither stay healthy, nor live with illness, in isolation. The role of family is crucial and therefore we devote a large part of a chapter to the impact of illness on significant others. Neither should Western theorists assume cross-cultural similarity of health and illness perceptions or behaviours, and therefore we include examples of theory and research from non-Westernised countries wherever possible. Throughout this text runs the theme of differentials, whether culture, gender, age/developmental stage, or socio-economic. Furthermore, a whole chapter is devoted to socio-economic differentials in health.

Structure of this textbook

The textbook has been structured into three broad sections. The first, *Being and Staying Healthy*, contains seven chapters, starting with a chapter which considers what we actually mean when we talk about 'health' or 'being healthy' and presents a brief history to the mind–body debate which underpins much of our research. The second chapter describes how factors such as social class, income and even postcode can affect one's health, behaviour and access to healthcare. Many of today's 'killer' illnesses, such as some cancers, heart disease and stroke, have a behavioural component. The third and fourth chapters describe how certain behaviours such as exercise have health-enhancing effects whereas others, such as poor diet or smoking behaviour, have health-damaging effects. Evidence of lifespan, cultural and gender differentials in health behaviours is presented. These behaviours have been examined by health and social psychologists over several decades, drawing on several key theories such as social learning theory and socio-cognitive theory, and in Chapter 5 we describe several models which have been rigorously tested in an effort to identify which beliefs, expectancies, attitudes and normative factors contribute to health or risk behaviour. This section, therefore, presents evidence of the link between behaviour and health and illness, and highlights an area where health psychologists have much to offer in terms of understanding or advising on individual factors to target in interventions. We therefore end with two chapters on intervention. Chapter 6 presents evidence of successful and less successful approaches to changing individual behaviours that increase risk for disease, while Chapter 7 applies the same review and critique to population approaches such as health education and promotion.

The second section, *Becoming Ill*, contains six chapters which take the reader through the process of becoming ill and the factors that may influence whether or not this happens in a given set of circumstances. We start with a whole chapter dedicated to describing biological and bodily processes relevant to the physical experience of health and illness (Chapter 8). This will provide a brief overview of relevant issues to help with reading this text. Chapter 9 describes how we perceive and respond to symptoms, highlighting individual, cultural and contextual factors that influence these processes, and in Chapter 10 presenting to, and communicating with, health professionals is reviewed with illustrations of 'good' and 'not so good' practice. The role of patient involvement in decision making is an important one in current health policy and practice and the evidence as to the benefits of patient involvement is reviewed here. Chapters 11 and 12 take us into the realm of stress, something that very few of us escape experiencing from time to time! We present an overview of stress theories, where stress is defined either as an event, a response or series of responses to an event, or as a transaction between the individual experiencing and appraising the event, and its actual characteristics. We describe in some detail a growing field of study known as psychoneuroimmunology, involving the study of how the mind influences the body via alterations in immunological functioning, which influence health status. Chapter 12 presents the research evidence pertaining to factors shown to 'moderate' the potentially negative effect of seemingly stressful events (for example, coping styles and strategies, social support, optimism). These two chapters highlight the complexity of the relationship between stress and illness. Chapter 13 turns to methods of alleviating stress, where it becomes clear that there is not one therapeutic 'hat' to fit all as we describe a range of cognitive, behavioural and cognitive-behavioural approaches.

In the third section, *Being Ill*, we turn our attention to the impact of illness on the individual and their families across two chapters. In the first of these (Chapter 14), we define and describe what is meant by 'quality of life' and how research has shown it to be challenged or altered by illness. In Chapter 15 we address other illness outcomes such as depression, and acknowledge the importance of family and significant others in patient outcomes. Perhaps unique to this textbook is a large section devoted to the impact of providing care for a sick person within the family and how differing beliefs and expectations of illness between the care-giver and the care-receiver can play a role in predicting health outcomes for both individuals. Chapter 16 addresses a phenomena that accounts for the majority of visits to a health professional – pain – which has been shown to be much more than a physical experience.

Chapter 17 looks at ways of improving health-related quality of life by means of interventions such as stress management training, the use of social support, and illness management programmes.

Finally, Chapter 18, which we have called Futures, closes this book with a summary of some (but not all) areas of achievement where health psychology research can be shown to have 'made a difference'. For example, where health psychology research has been 'successful' in terms of translating research findings into interventions. We close with some thoughts about what the future may hold for health psychology, as a practice, as a profession, and as an informed voice influencing and shaping future health policy and practice.

Acknowledgements

This project has been a major one which has required the reading of literally thousands of empirical and review papers published by health, social and clinical psychologists around the globe, many books and book chapters, and many newspapers to help identify some hot health issues. The researchers behind all this work are thanked for their contribution to the field.

On a more personal level, several key researchers and senior academics also acted as reviewers for our chapters. They provided honest and constructive feedback on every single page. They provided informed suggestions which really have made this a better book than it might otherwise have been! They also spotted errors and inconsistencies that are inevitable with such a large project, and took their role seriously.

Many thanks also to the team at Pearson Education, with several development editors having taken their turn at the helm and guided us through a few bad patches where academic demands and our own research prevented us from spending time on 'the book': originally Jane Powell, then for four years, the wonderfully supportive Paula Parish, and finally David Cox who saw us through the final months where it was hard to believe we had no more time to update, add or remove and basically, we had to submit! Morten Fuglevand, the Acquisitions Editor, is also thanked for his patience and humour and his confidence in the final product which at an early stage led him to secure his company's agreement to 'go colour'. We think it makes a difference and hope you do too. To the design team, photo acquisitions people, cartoonist and publicist, thanks for enhancing our text with some excellent features.

Finally, to those that have made the coffee in the wee small hours while we hammered away at our computers in the North and the South of Wales – our families – heartfelt thanks. To Dave, who put up with my absences, and had to do even more around the house than usual (and that's a lot!), and to Tanya who missed out on some fun outings while Mum worked yet another weekend – my continued love and appreciation. To Gill who stoically coped with my absences during both day and night . . . I think you noticed them! Love and thanks for looking after me.

Val Morrison
Paul Bennett
May 2005

GUIDED TOUR

CHAPTER 1

What is health?

Learning outcomes

By the end of this chapter, you should have an understanding of:

■ key models of thinking about health and illness: the biomedical and the biopsychosocial
■ how health is more than simply the absence of physical disease
■ the domains of health considered important by different populations
■ the role of age and developmental stage in determining health concepts
■ the role of psychology in understanding health and illness
■ the aims and interests of the discipline of health psychology

Image: Alamy/Big Cheese Photo

Learning Outcomes at the start of each chapter introduce the key topics that are covered and summarise what is to be learnt.

---

smokers, nicotine gum aimed at nicotine-dependent participants, and a combination of both approaches. Each group did indeed fare better from the intervention targeted at their particular problem, although only the nicotine-dependent group benefited from the combined intervention. By the one-year follow-up, 50 percent of the nicotine-dependent smokers who received the combined programme were still not smoking, compared with 32 percent who only received the NRT and eleven percent of those who received the problem-focused intervention. Among the habitual smokers, the equivalent rates were 42, 38 and 47 percent.

RESEARCH FOCUS

Steptoe, A., Doherty, S., Rink, E., Kerry, S., Kendrick, T. and Hilton, S. (1999). Behavioural counselling in general practice for the promotion of healthy behaviour among adults at increased risk of coronary heart disease: randomised trial. *British Medical Journal*, 319: 943–8.

The authors note that while the Family heart study and OXCHECK trials only achieved modest improvements in the health of people going through screening programmes, their effectiveness could be improved first by only targeting people at high risk for CHD, and second by providing more behavioural and motivational interventions than the traditional educational methods used in these studies.

Their screening intervention was based on the stages of change model (see main text), with differing types of advice and behavioural interventions given to patients at different stages of readiness to change their behaviour. The intervention was carried out by practice nurses in patients at high risk for CHD. They reasoned that this more targeted approach on people at significant risk for CHD would result in more change than that achieved by the OXCHECK and Family heart study trials.

Participants and methods
Twenty general practices were allocated either to provide the intervention or to act as controls. The practices were matched for the level of social deprivation in the areas they served. Patients entered the trial at each practice if they were identified as having one or more modifiable risk factors for CHD:

■ smoking more than one cigarette per day;
■ high serum cholesterol;
■ being overweight combined with low levels of exercise (fewer than twelve episodes of vigorous or moderate exercise for at least 20 minutes in the previous month).

Patients were excluded if they were receiving drugs related to heart disease or high blood pressure, or already had CHD. They received either behavioural counselling or a minimal treatment control intervention.

Behavioural counselling
One practice nurse from each of the ten intervention practices was trained in behavioural counselling. They were trained to assess patients' readiness to change and to use motivational techniques, goal setting and specific behavioural advice to enable change. The various goals and intervention approaches they used were:

Research Focus boxes provide a summary of the aims and outcomes of current empirical papers. They encourage an understanding of methods used to evaluate issues relevant to health psychology and problems associated with them.

Botha (2000), for example, reported that attenders at a routine diabetes clinic were more likely to be younger, to have access to a car and to have a white collar job than people who did not attend. People with low resources may be affected both by limited access to healthcare resources and by limited means to access them when they are provided.

IN THE SPOTLIGHT

Inequalities of health provision

Health provision involves both provider and user. The 'postcode lottery' suggests that providers are failing to provide equity of care across different parts of the UK, with those in the poorest areas generally receiving less care than those in better-off areas. We have shown how the Scottish Executive demonstrated that while more resources are available for the care of people in more deprived areas in Scotland, these are not sufficient to cope with the serious health needs of the population. Inequalities in the provision of service are not simply evident on a local scale. Whole regions may differ in their health provision. An audit of the prescription of a drug known as herceptin (see www.cancerbacup.org.uk/fund/press/RocheAudit.doc), which can be effective in the treatment of advanced breast cancer, found that 14 percent of women in the Midlands had access to it in 2003. This figure rose to 28 percent in the North and North-east, 33.5 percent in the South-east and East Anglia, and 61 percent in the South-west. These differences were found despite herceptin being recommended for the treatment of women with advanced breast cancer by the government's treatment advisory body (the National Institute for Clinical Excellence – NICE).

But it is not just at a geographical level that there are inequalities in health provision. We show later in this chapter that differential levels of care may be provided within hospitals to patients of different ethnic origins. African American patients, for example, may be offered less curative surgery for CHD than white patients in some hospitals in America. People who are poor may access healthcare less than the better-off. Finally, doctors may select patients to have different treatments as a result of their behaviour – some high-profile doctors have suggested, for example, that smokers should not be offered cardiac surgery as their smoking would prevent their gaining maximum benefit from it. As economic resources become or remain tight across all healthcare systems, inequalities in the provision of healthcare are likely to become more frequent, and perhaps more explicit. But they only make evident what has been the case for many years – albeit with much less publicity.

■ **Socio-economic status as a *relative* issue**

So far, the discussion has considered factors that differ across socio-economic groups that may affect health. Wilkinson (1992) suggested a further factor – that simply knowing you are less well-off than your neighbours may in itself contribute to ill-health. His analysis of levels of ill-health and premature mortality both within and between countries led him to suggest that it is not just *absolute* wealth that determines health: rather, it is *relative* wealth. He drew on evidence that shows only a weak relationship between the absolute wealth of a society and overall life expectancy. More important is the distribution

In The Spotlight boxes present some, often controversial, material to provoke thought such as the postcode lottery in access to healthcare and the MMR debate.

Environmental influences on health behaviour

Behaviour and behaviour change do not occur in isolation from the environment in which they occur. The environment may contribute directly to risk of disease (see Chapter 2). It can also indirectly influence health by influencing the ease with which health-promoting or health-damaging behaviour can be conducted. However keen young single mothers may be to exercise, not having someone to look after their child while they are doing so may prevent them from exercising; asking people to eat healthily at work may not be possible unless they are offered healthy choices in the work canteen; and so on. The health belief model (Becker, Haefner and Maiman 1977; see Chapter 5) provides a simple guide to key environmental factors that can be influenced in order to encourage behavioural change. In particular, the model suggests that an environment that encourages healthy behaviour should:

■ provide cues to action – or remove cues to unhealthy behaviour;
■ enable healthy behaviour by minimising the costs and barriers associated with it;
■ increase the costs of engaging in health-damaging behaviour.

What do YOU think? This next section concerns environmental and social issues that can facilitate or inhibit our health-related behaviour. Before considering this in a relatively theoretical way, consider for a moment your own behaviour. What parts of your life increase the possibility of you behaving in a health-enhancing way? What factors prevent this? Do you have easy access to sports or leisure facilities? If you wanted to, would you feel safe cycling or walking around the area where you live? Does your locality offer easy access to good-quality shops, or does accessing them easily require a car or bus ride? Does this restrict your (or other people's) access to healthy foodstuffs? What about people with fewer resources than you – or with higher demands on their time – single mothers with limited income, for example. How does the environment influence their health choices?

Cues to action

Much of our behaviour is routine, based on habit. Accordingly, we rarely think about change. One strategy to encourage change may therefore simply be to interrupt the sequence of habitual behaviour, allowing or even forcing consideration of new ways to behave. Hunt and Martin (1988), for example, advocated changing the location of more or less healthy foodstuffs on supermarket shelves in order to interrupt routine patterns involving placing the usual food in the trolley and to encourage active consideration of the food choice. Supermarkets already do this to encourage purchasing of special offers and so on – Hunt and Martin suggested that similar tactics could be used to encourage healthy eating.

What do YOU think? boxes ask the reader to pause and reflect on their own beliefs, behaviours or experiences. In this way, material can be contextualised within the reader's own life, helping to promote understanding.

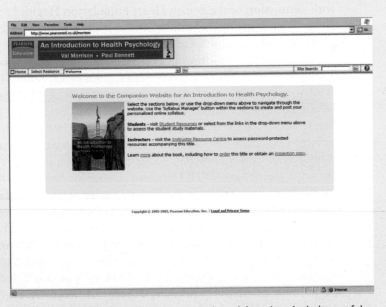

Figure 8.7 Electrical conduction and control of the heart rhythm.

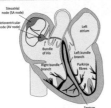

Key terms are defined alongside the text for easy reference and to aid understanding. Some terms are given a further, in-depth, definition in the end of book **Glossary**.

Each chapter is supported by suggested **Further Reading** to direct the reader to further information sources.

The **Companion Website** at www.pearsoned.co.uk/morrison includes useful resources such as multiple choice questions, weblinks, a searchable glossary and flashcards for students, and PowerPoint slides and tutorials for lecturers.

PUBLISHER'S ACKNOWLEDGEMENTS

We are grateful to the following for permission to reproduce copyright material:

Kate Taylor for the cartoons; Table 1.1 from *The Nation's Health*, Department of Health, Crown copyright material is reproduced with the permission of the Controller of Her Majesty's Stationery Office and the Queen's Printer for Scotland; Table 2.2 and Figure 2.1 from *Independent Inquiry into Inequalities in Health*, HMSO (Acheson, D., 1998), Crown copyright material is reproduced with the permission of the Controller of Her Majesty's Stationery Office and the Queen's Printer for Scotland; Figure 2.2 from *Fair Shares for All: Report of the National Review of Resource Allocation for the NHS in Scotland*, Scottish Executive, Crown copyright material is reproduced with the permission of the Controller of Her Majesty's Stationery Office and the Queen's Printer for Scotland; Figure 3.1 from 'Overweight and obesity as determinants of cardiovascular risk' in *Archives of Internal Medicine*, 162, pp. 1867–1872, American Medical Association (Wilson, P.W.F., D'Agostino, R.B., Sullivan, L., Parise, H. and Kannel, W.B., 2002); Table 3.1 adapted from *Alcohol Policy and the Public Good* (Edwards, G. *et al.*, 1994), by permission of Oxford University Press; Table 3.2 from *Report 5*, International Center for Alcohol Policies (1998); Figure 3.3 from BHF coronary heart disease statistics at www.heartstats.org, reproduced with permission of the British Heart Foundation Health Promotion Research Group, University of Oxford; Figure 3.5 from 'Condom use by age and gender' by Kaye Wellings, Julia Field, Anne M. Johnson & Jane Wadsworth from *Sexual Behaviour in Britain: The National Survey of Sexual Attitudes and Lifestyles* (Copyright © Kaye Wellings, Julia Field, Anne M. Johnson & Jane Wadsworth 1994), reproduced by permission of PFD (ww.pfd.co.uk) on behalf of Kaye Wellings, Julia Field, Anne M, Johnson & Jane Wadsworth; Figure 4.1 from 'Young people meeting the MVPA guidelines on physical activity (%)' in *Young People's Health in Context – Health Behaviour in School-aged Children (HBSC) Study: International Report from 2001/2002 Survey*, Copenhagen, WHO Regional Office for Europe, 2004 (Health Policy for Children and Adolescents, No. 4), Figure 3.17, p. 94; Figure 4.2 from 'A family tree of chromosome inheritance', © Dorling Kindersley; Figure 5.3 from http://userpage.fu-berlin.de/~health.hapa.htm, reproduced with permission from Prof. Dr. Ralf Schwarzer of Freie Universität, Berlin; Figures 8.1–8.4 from *Physiology of Behavior*, 8th edition, Allyn and Bacon, Boston, MA (Carlson, N., 2003), copyright © 2004 by Pearson Education. Reprinted by permission of the publisher; Figure 9.1 from 'A symptom perception approach to common physical symptoms' in *Journal of Social Science and Medicine*, 2344, pp. 2343–2354 (Kolk, A.M., Hanewald, G.J.F.P., Schagen, S. and Gijsbers van Wijk, C.M.T., 2003), copyright © 2003 with permission from Elsevier; Figure 9.2 from *Making Sense of Illness: The Social Psychology of Health and Disease* (Radley, A., 1994) reproduced by permission of Sage Publications Ltd; Figure 9.3 from 'Illness cognition: using common sense to understand treatment adherence and effect cognitive interactions' in *Cognitive Therapy and Research*, 16(2), pp. 143–163 (Leventhal,

H., Diefenbach, M. and Leventhal, E., 1992), Figure 1, p. 147, with kind permission of Springer Science and Business Media; Figure 9.4 from 'Determinants on three stages of delay in seeking care at a medical setting' in *Medical Care*, 7, pp. 11–29, Lippincott, Williams & Wilkins (Safer, M.A., Tharps, Q.J., Jackson, T.C. and Leventhal, H., 1979); Table 9.2 from 'Seeking medical consultation: perceptual and behavioural characteristics distinguishing consulters and nonconsulters with function dyspepsia' in *Psychosomatic Medicine,* 62, pp. 844–852, Lippincott, Williams & Wilkins (Cheng, C., 2000); Figure 10.1 from 'Breaking bad news: a review of the literature' in *Journal of the American Medical Association,* 276, pp. 496–502, American Medical Association (Ptacek, J.T.P. and Eberhardt, T.L., 1999); Table 11.1 from 'The social readjustment rating scale' in *Journal of Psychomatic Research*, 11, pp. 213–218 (Holmes, T.H. and Rahe, R.H., 1967), © 1967 Elsevier, Inc., with permission from Elsevier; Figure 11.1 from *Stress and Health: Biological and Psychological Interactions* (Lovallo, W.R., 1997) p. 77, copyright 1997 by Sage Publications, Inc. Reprinted by permission of Sage Publications, Inc.; Figure 11.2 and Table 11.3 from *Stress and Health*, Brooks/Cole (Rice, P.L., 1992), reprinted by permission of the author; Figure 12.1 from *Stress and Emotion: A New Synthesis* (Lazarus, R.S., 1999), pp. 198, reprinted with permission from Free Association Books, London; Figure 12.2 from 'Serum lipid concentrations, hostility, and cardiovascular reactions to mental stress' in *International Journal of Psychophysiology*, 28, pp. 167–79; Figure 12.3 from 'Hardiness and health: a prospective study' in *Journal of Personality and Social Psychology,* 42, pp. 168–177 (Kobasa, S.C., Maddi, S. and Kahn, S., 1982), published by American Psychological Association and adapted with permission; Figure 14.1 from 'Quality of life: a process view' in *Psychology and Health,* 12, pp. 753–767 (Leventhal, H. and Coleman, S., 1997), reproduced with permission from Taylor & Francis, www.tandf.co.uk/journals; Figure 15.1 from 'Positive effects of illness reported by myocardial infarction and breast cancer patients' in *Journal of Psychosomatic Research*, 47, pp. 537–543 (Petrie, K.J., Buick, D.L., Weinman, J. and Booth, R.J., 1999) © 1999 with permission from Elsevier; Figure 15.2 from 'Turning the tide: benefit finding after cancer surgery' in *Social Science and Medicine,* 59, pp. 653–662 (Schulz, U. and Mohamed, N.E., 2004) © 2004 with permission from Elsevier; Figure 15.3 from 'Interpersonal emotional processes in adjustment to chronic illness' in J. Suls and K.A. Wallston (eds) *Social Psychological Foundations of Health and Illness,* (De Vellis, R.F., Lewis, M.A. and Sterba, K.R., 2003), p. 263, reproduced with permission from Blackwell Publishing Ltd; Figure 16.1 from *Biological Psychology: An Introduction to Behavioural and Cognitive Neuroscience* (Rosenzweig, M.R., Breedlove, S.M. and Eiman, N.V., 1996), p. 272, copyright 1996, reprinted by permission of Sinauer Associates, Inc. Publishers.

Alamy/Big Cheese Photo (p. 3); Mark Cowan/Icon/Action Plus (Plate 1.1, p. 7); Mike King/Action Plus (Plate 1.2, p. 24); Hartmut Schwarzbach/Still Pictures (p. 31); Reuters/Corbis (Plate 2.1, p. 36); Nathan Benn/Corbis (Plate 2.2, p. 44); Rex Features/Jon Angerson (p. 59); Royalty-Free/Corbis (Plate 3.1, p. 75); Getty Images (Plate 3.2, p. 77); Mike Hewitt/Action Plus (p. 88); University of Wales Bangor, School of Psychology (Plate 4.1, p. 93); Jacob Silberberg/Getty Images (Plate 4.2, p. 109); Chaloner Woods/Getty Images

(p. 113); Royalty-Free/Corbis (Plate 5.1, p. 118); Alain Dex, Publiphoto diffusion/Science Photo Library (Plate 5.2, p. 144); Neil Tingle/Action Plus (p. 147); Alamy/Medical-on-line (Plate 6.1, p. 154); Royalty-Free/Corbis (Plate 6.2, p. 170); Chris Lisle/Corbis (p. 176); Terrence Higgins Trust (Plate 7.1, p. 183); AFP/Getty Images (p. 209); Lester V. Bergman/Corbis (p. 242); Dr Andrejs Liepins/Science Photo Library (Plate 8.1, p. 218); Eye of Science/Science Photo Library (Plate 8.2, p. 218); Health Screening (UK) Ltd (Plate 9.2, p. 265); Alamy/Image Source (p. 275); John Cole/Science Photo Library (Plate 10.1, p. 288); Ronald Grant Archives (Plate 10.2, p. 291); Bernardo Bucci/Corbis (p. 304); Alamy/Aflo Foto (Plate 11.1, p. 312); Rex Features/Cameron Laird (Plate 11.2, p. 315); Alamy/Peter Bowater (p. 336); Alamy/Steve Hamblin (Plate 12.1, p. 352); Alamy/David Sanger (p. 365); Alamy/The Hoberman Collection (Plate 13.1, p. 368); John Cole/Science Photo Library (Plate 13.2, p. 387); Alix/Science Photo Library (p. 395); Joe Vaughn/ Getty Images (Plate 14.1, p. 400); Jerry Cooke/Corbis (Plate 14.2, p. 402); Alamy/Photofusion (p. 419); Alamy/Agency Photo Network (Plate 15.1, p. 430); Reg Charity/Corbis (Plate 15.2, p. 437); David Mack/Science Photo Library (p. 445); David Cannon/Allsport/Getty (Plate 16.1, p. 454); Will & Deni McIntyre/Science Photo Library (Plate 16.2, p. 473); Alamy/Sandii McDonald (p. 477); Simon Fraser/Coronary Care Unit/Hexham General Hospital/Science Photo Library (Plate 17.1, p. 493); Glyn Kirk/Action Plus (Plate 17.2, p. 502); Alamy/Andrew Fox (p. 507); University of Wales Bangor (Plate 18.1, p. 511); Bananastock/Photolibrary.com (Plate 18.2, p. 525).

In some instances we have been unable to trace the owners of copyright material, and we would appreciate any information that would enable us to do so.

Reviewers

We would also like to express thanks to the original reviewers who have been involved in the development of this book. We are extremely grateful for their insight and helpful recommendations:

Sandra Horn, University of Southampton
Amy Spatz, researcher at Queen Mary, University of London – thanks also to FreshMinds for their coordination of this review
Denise de Ridder, Utrecht University, Netherlands
Fiona Jones, Institute of Psychological Sciences, University of Leeds
Martha C. Whiteman, University of Edinburgh
Dr Mark Forshaw, Leeds Metropolitan University

PART 1

Being and staying healthy

CHAPTER 1

What is health?

Learning outcomes

By the end of this chapter, you should have an understanding of:

- key models of thinking about health and illness: the biomedical and the biopsychosocial
- how health is more than simply the absence of physical disease
- the domains of health considered important by different populations
- the role of age and developmental stage in determining health concepts
- the role of psychology in understanding health and illness
- the aims and interests of the discipline of health psychology

Image: Alamy/Big Cheese Photo

CHAPTER OUTLINE

What do we mean by health, and do we all mean the same thing when we use the term? This chapter considers the different ways in which people have been found to define and think about health: first, by providing an historical overview of the health concept that introduces the debate over the influence of mind on body; and, second, by illustrating how health belief systems vary according to factors such as age and culture. Evidence is provided from studies of both Western and non-Western populations. We also explore the issue of developmental differences in health perceptions and examine whether children define and think about health differently to a middle-aged or elderly person. Against this backdrop of defining health and describing health belief systems, the chapter then introduces the field of health psychology and outlines the domain's key areas of interest. What is health psychology, and what questions can it address?

What is health? Changing perspectives

Stone (1979) pointed out that until we can agree on the meaning of health and how it can be measured we are going to be unable to answer questions about how we can protect, enhance and restore health. The root word of health is 'wholeness', and indeed 'holy' and 'healthy' share the same root word in Anglo-Saxon, which is perhaps why so many cultures associate one with the other: e.g. medicine men have both roles. Having its roots in 'wholeness' also suggests the early existence of a broad view of health that included mental and physical aspects. This view has not held dominance throughout history, as the next section illustrates.

Models of health and illness

One needs first to be clear about what health is. Health is a word that most people will use, but without realising that it may hold different meanings for different people, at different times in history, in different cultures, in different social classes, or even within the same family, depending, for example, on age. Some different, but not necessarily oppositional, views of health are described below.

■ Mind–body relationships

Archaeological finds of human skulls from the Stone Age have attributed the small neat holes found in some skulls to the process of 'trephination' (or trepanation), whereby a hole is made in order for evil spirits to leave the ailing body. Disease appeared to be attributed to evil spirits. However, by the time of ancient Greece the association between mind and body was viewed somewhat differently. The ancient Greek physician Hippocrates (*circa* 460–377 BC) considered the mind and body as one unit but did not attribute illness to evil spirits but to the balance between four circulating bodily fluids (called humours): yellow bile, phlegm, blood and black bile. It was thought that when a person was healthy the four humours were in balance, and when they were ill-balanced due to external 'pathogens', illness occurred. The humours were attached to seasonal variations and to conditions of hot, cold, wet and dry, where phlegm was attached to winter (cold–wet), blood to spring (wet–hot), black bile to autumn (cold–dry), and yellow bile to summer (hot–dry). Furthermore, it was thought that the level of specific bodily humours related to particular personalities: excessive yellow bile was linked to a choleric or angry temperament; black bile was attached to sadness; excessive blood was associated with an optimistic or sanguine personality; and excessive phlegm with a calm or phlegmatic temperament. Interestingly, as far back as Hippocrates, it was suggested that eating healthily would help to preserve the balance of the humours, showing an early awareness of a relationship between nutrition and health (Helman 1978). This humoral **theory** of illness therefore attributed disease states to bodily functions but also acknowledged that bodily factors impacted on the mind.

theory
a general belief or beliefs about some aspect of the world we live in or those in it, which may or may not be supported by evidence. For example, women are worse drivers than men.

This view continued with Galen (*circa* AD 129–199), another influential Greek physician. Galen considered there to be a physical basis for all ill-health (physical or mental) and believed that the four bodily humours not only underpinned the four dominant temperaments (the sanguine, the choleric, the phlegmatic and the melancholic) but that these temperaments could contribute to the experience of specific illnesses. For example, he proposed that melancholic women were more likely to get breast cancer, offering not a psychological explanation but a physical one because melancholia was itself thought to be underpinned by high levels of black bile. This view was therefore that the mind and body were interrelated, but only in terms of physical and mental disturbances both having an underlying physical cause. The mind was not thought to play a role in illness aetiology. This view dominated thinking for many centuries to come but lost predominance in the eighteenth century as organic medicine, and in particular cellular pathology, developed and failed to support the humoral underpinnings. However, Galen's descriptions of personality types were still in use in the latter half of the twentieth century (Marks, Murray, Evan and Willig 2000: 76–7).

In the early Middle Ages (fifth–sixth century), however, Galen's theories lost dominance as health became increasingly tied to faith and spirituality. Illness was at this time seen as God's punishment for misdeeds, or similar to very early views, as the result of evil spirits entering one's soul. Individuals were considered to have little control over their health, whereas priests, in their perceived ability to restore health by driving out demons, did. As the Church was at the forefront of society, science developed slowly. The mind and body were generally viewed as working together, or at least in parallel, but because medical understanding was limited in its development through the prohibition of scientific investigation such as dissection, mental and mystical explanations of illness predominated. Such causal explanations therefore called for treatment along the lines of self-punishment, abstinence from sin, prayer or hard work.

These religious views persisted for many, many centuries, slowly beginning to be challenged by the early fourteenth and fifteenth centuries with the start of a period known as the Renaissance. The Renaissance was a period of 'rebirth', when individual thinking became increasingly dominant and the religious perspective became only one among many. Furthermore, the scientific revolution of the early 1600s led to a huge upsurge in scholarly and scientific study and developments in physical medicine. The explanations for illness therefore became increasingly organic and physiological, with little room for psychological explanations.

During the early seventeenth century, the French philosopher René Descartes (1596–1650), like the ancient Greeks, proposed that the mind and body were separate entities. However, Descartes also proposed that interaction between the two 'domains' was possible, although initially the understanding of how mind–body interactions could happen was limited. For example, how could a mental thought, with no physical properties, cause a bodily reaction (e.g. a neuron to fire) (Solmes and Turnbull 2002)? This is defined as **dualism**, where the mind is considered to be 'non-material' (i.e. not objective or visible, such as thoughts and feelings) and the body is 'material' (i.e. made up of real 'stuff', physical matter such as our brain, heart and cells). The material and the non-material were considered independent. Physicians acted as guardians of the body, which was viewed as a machine amenable to scientific investigation and explanation. In contrast, theologians acted as guardians of the mind, a place not amenable to scientific investigation. The suggested communication between mind and body was thought to be under the control of the pineal gland in the midbrain (see Chapter 8), but the process of this interaction was unclear. Because Descartes believed that the soul left humans at the time of death, dissection and autopsy study now became acceptable to the Church, and the eighteenth and nineteenth centuries witnessed a huge growth in medical understanding. Anatomical research, autopsy work and cellular pathology concluded that disease was located in human cells, not in ill-balanced humours.

Dualists developed the notion of the body as a machine (a **mechanistic** viewpoint), understandable only in terms of its constituent parts (molecular, biological, biochemical, genetic), with illness understood through the study of cellular and physiological processes. Treatment during these centuries became more technical, diagnostic and focused on the body internal, with individuals perhaps more passively involved than previously, when they had been called upon to pray or exorcise their demons in order to return to health. This approach underpins the **biomedical model** of illness.

dualism
the idea that the mind and body are separate entities (cf. Descartes).

mechanistic
a reductionist approach that reduces behaviour to the level of the organ or physical function. Associated with the **biomedical model**.

biomedical model
a view that diseases and symptoms have an underlying physiological explanation.

■ Biomedical model of illness

In this model, a symptom of illness is considered to have an underlying pathology that will hopefully, but not inevitably, be cured through medical intervention. Adhering rigidly to the biomedical model would lead to proponents dealing with objective facts and assuming a direct causal relationship between illness, its symptoms or underlying pathology, and adjustment outcomes. This relatively mechanistic view of how our bodies and its organs work, fail and can be treated allows little room for subjectivity. The biomedical view has been described as reductionist: i.e. the basic idea that mind, matter (body) and human behaviour can all be reduced to, and explained at, the level of cells, neural activity or biochemical activity. Reductionism tends to ignore evidence that different people respond in different ways to the same underlying disease because of differences, for example, in personality, cognition, social support resources or cultural beliefs (see later chapters).

Plate 1.1   Having a physical disability does not equate with a lack of health and fitness, as this paralympian has shown.

Source: Mark Cowan/Icon/Action Plus

■ Biopsychosocial model of illness

What is perhaps getting closer to the 'truth', as we understand it today, is the view of dual-aspect monists: those with this viewpoint would agree that there is one type of 'stuff' (monist) but would suggest that it can be perceived in two different ways: objectively and subjectively. For example, many illnesses have organic underlying causes, but they also elicit uniquely individual responses due to the action of the mind. So, while aspects of reductionism and dualistic thinking have been useful, for example in furthering our understanding of the aetiology and course of many acute and infectious diseases (Larson 1999) such as coronary heart disease and AIDS, we would propose that the role of the 'mind' in the manifestation of, and response to, illness is crucial to the advancement of our understanding of the complex nature of health and illness. Consider for example the extensive evidence of 'phantom limb pain' in amputees – how can pain exist in an absent limb? Subjectivity in terms of beliefs, expectations and emotions interact with bodily reactions to play an important role in the symptom or illness experience (see Chapter 9 in terms of symptom perception, and Chapter 11 in terms of stress reactivity). This text aims to illustrate that psychological and social factors can add to biological or biomedical explanations and understanding of health and illness experiences. This **biopsychosocial** approach is employed in health psychology. Evidence of changed thinking is found in an editorial

biopsychosocial
a view that diseases and symptoms can be explained by a combination of physical, social, cultural and psychological factors (cf. Engel 1977).

in the *British Medical Journal* (Bracken and Thomas 2002) suggesting that it is time to 'move beyond the mind–body split'. The authors note that simply because neuroscience now enables us to explore the 'mind' and its workings by the use of increasingly sophisticated scanning devices and measurements does comment mean we are furthering our understanding of the 'mind' – the thoughts, feelings and the like that make up our lives and give it meaning. They comment that 'conceptualising our mental life as some sort of enclosed world living inside our skull does not do justice to the reality of human experience' (p. 1434). The fact that this editorial has succeeded in being published in a medical journal with a traditionally biomedical stance suggests that Descartes' 'legacy' is finally weakening.

■ Challenging dualism: psychosocial models of health and illness

Historically, there has been tension between those who viewed the mind and body as separate (dualists) and those who saw them as a unit (monists), but increasingly focus has been on the bidirectional relationship between mind and body. Psychology has played a significant role in this altering perspective. A key influence was Sigmund Freud in the 1920s and 1930s, who redefined the mind–body problem as one of 'consciousness'. Freud postulated the existence of an 'unconscious mind' following examination of patients with conversion hysteria. Unconscious conflicts were identified during hypnosis and using free association techniques as the 'cause' of physical disturbances such as the paralysis and loss of sensation seen in some patients, for whom no underlying physical explanation was present (e.g. Freud and Breuer 1895).

Freud stimulated much work into unconscious conflict, personality and illness, which ultimately led to the development of the field of *psychosomatic medicine* as we now know it. Early work asserted that a certain personality would lead to a certain disease (e.g. Alexander's ulcer-prone personality), and while evidence for direct causality has proved limited, these developments in

thinking certainly did set the groundwork for fascinating studies of physio-logical processes that may link personality type to disease (see Chapter 11's discussion of hostility and heart disease associations, for example). However, one limitation to result from this work is that among those adhering to a strict biomedical viewpoint, illnesses with no identifiable organic cause were often considered as nervous disorders or psychosomatic conditions for which medical treatment was often not forthcoming. However, psychologists have highlighted the need for medicine to become more holistic and to consider the role played in the aetiology, course and outcomes of illness, by psychological and social factors. The biopsychosocial model signals a broadening of a disease or biomedical model of health to one encompassing and emphas-ising the interaction between biological processes and psychological and social influences (Engel 1977, 1980). In doing so, it offers a complex and multivariate, but potentially more comprehensive, explanation of human experience of illness.

Behaviour and health

The dramatic increases in life expectancy witnessed in Western countries in the twentieth century, partially due to advances in medical technology and treatments, most notably the advent of antibiotics in the 1940s (although Fleming discovered penicillin in 1928, it was some years before it and other antibiotics were generally available), has led to a general belief, in Western cultures at least, in the efficacy of traditional medicine and its power to eradicate disease. Increased control of infectious disease through vaccination, improved sanitation and developments in pharmacological treatments are partial explanations of life expectancy at birth increasing from 47 years in 1900 to 74.6 years in 1980 (Whelan 1988); by the mid-1980s it ranged in different Western countries from 74.1 in Greece to 77.4 in Japan and 74.7 in the USA. However, it is worth noting that the fall in mortality preceded the major immunisation programmes and that wider social and environmental reasons, such as developments in education and agriculture, which led to changes in diet, or the development of sewerage and waste disposal systems, are hugely responsible for improved public health.

One hundred years ago, the ten leading causes of death were infectious diseases such as tuberculosis and pneumonia, with diseases such as diph-theria and tetanus highly common. If people living then had been asked what they thought being healthy meant, they may have replied 'avoiding infec-tions, drinking clean water, living into my 50s/60s'. Death was frequently a result of highly infectious disease becoming epidemic in communities unpro-tected by immunisation or adequate sanitary conditions. However, in the last century, at least in developed countries, there has been a downturn in deaths resulting from infectious disease, and the 'top ten killers' make no mention of TB, typhoid or measles but instead list cancer, lung disease and accidents (Table 1.1). These diseases have a behavioural component in that they have been linked to behaviour such as smoking, excessive alcohol consumption, increasingly sedentary lifestyles and poor diet. It has been estimated that approximately two-thirds (Doll and Peto 1981) to three-quarters (Peto and Lopez 1990) of cancer deaths are attributable, in part at least, to our behaviour (note that Peto increased this estimate over the nine years between

Table 1.1 Comparison of leading causes of death, 1900–2000 (England and Wales)

Rank	1900	1995	2000
1.	Influenza and pneumonia	Cancer	Cancer (all)
2.	Tuberculosis, all forms	Heart disease	Heart disease
3.	Gastroenteritis	Stroke	Pneumonia
4.	Heart disease	Pneumonia	Stroke
5.	Stroke	Chronic lung disease	Lung disease
6.	Kidney disease	Accidents	Accidents
7.	Accidents	Suicide	Suicide
8.	Cancer	Diabetes mellitus	Liver disease
9.	Diseases of infancy	Liver disease	Diabetes
10.	Diptheria		

- 1900 data from World Health Organization, www.who.int/countries/gbr
- 1995 and 2000 data from Department of Health, *The Nation's Health*, www.doh.gov.uk
- Only gender difference in 1995 is suicide 7th in males, liver disease 7th in females; in 2000 is reversal of diabetes and suicide ranking in women, i.e. diabetes is 7th.

---

the two publications cited). The nature of disease has thus changed dramatically even in this century. The upturn in cancer deaths over the last 100 years is in part because people are living longer with illnesses they previously would have died from; thus they are reaching ages where cancer **incidence** is greater. In the USA, cancer deaths have tripled since 1900 (Baum, Gatchel and Krantz 1997), and although such figures are not wholly attributable to the increase in smoking and other cancer-related behaviour, a person's own behaviour does increase such disease risk significantly.

Worldwide, the leading causes of death include heart disease, cancer, accidents and respiratory disorders, with AIDS predominating in many African and Asian countries and globally being the fourth leading cause of death. The World Health Organization (2002) has cited life expectancy at birth in sub-Saharan Africa as being 47 years but notes that this would be approximately 62 years if there were no AIDS.

The links between individual behaviour, health and illness, not least in relation to HIV infection and AIDS, provide a key reason as to why health psychology has grown rapidly given its focus on personal and social influences on health-related behaviour (see Chapters 3 and 4).

It might be expected, given the changes in what people are dying from, that views of what health is may also have changed over time. For example, in eighteenth-century Britain, health was considered an 'egalitarian ideal', aspired to by all and considered as potentially being under an individual's control. Doctors were available to the wealthy as 'aids' to keeping oneself well. However, by the mid-twentieth century this had changed, with new laws regarding sickness benefit and medical and technological advances in diagnostic and treatment procedures. Health became inextricably linked to 'fitness to work', and doctors were required to declare whether individuals were 'fit to work' or whether they could adopt the 'sick role' (see also Chapter 10). Many today continue to see illness in terms of its effects on their working lives, although some also look at work role and conditions and consider the effects it has on illness (see discussion of occupational stress in Chapter 11).

incidence

the number of new cases of disease occurring during a defined time interval – not to be confused with prevalence, which refers to the number of established cases of a disease in a population at any one time.

Another change witnessed over time is in the assumption that traditional medicine can, and will, cure us of all ills. This has been challenged in recent decades to the extent that many more people now explore the potential negative consequences of treatments, particularly pharmacological ones, and as a result the 'alternative medicine' industry has burgeoned.

Individual, cultural and lifespan perspectives on health

Lay theories of health and illness

If a fuller understanding of health and illness is to be attained, it is necessary to find out what people think health, and illness, are. The simplest way of doing this is to ask them. An early study by Bauman (1961) asked the question 'what does being healthy mean?' and found that people make three main types of response:

1. that health means a 'general sense of well-being';
2. that health is identified with 'the absence of symptoms of disease';
3. that health can be seen in 'the things that a person who is physically fit is able to do'.

She argued that these three types of response reveal health to be related to:

- feeling
- symptom orientation
- performance.

It is worth noting that respondents in Bauman's study did not answer in discrete categories: nearly half of the sample used two of the above categories, and 12 percent used all three types of definition, highlighting the fact that the way we think about health is often multifaceted. A word of caution is also needed before generalising from these findings. Bauman's sample consisted of patients with diagnoses of quite serious disease, and it is likely that healthy people will think about health in a different way.

It has been shown that factors such as current health status do influence subjective views of health and reports of what 'health is'. For example, Benyamini, Leventhal and Leventhal (2003) asked almost 500 elderly people to rate factors in order of importance to their subjective health judgements, and the most important factors were found to relate to physical functioning and vitality (being able to do what you need/want to do). However, the current health status of the sample (poor/fair; good; very good/excellent) influenced other judgements; for example, those in poor/fair health based their health assessment on recent symptoms or indicators of poor health, whereas those in good health considered more positive indicators (being able to exercise, being happy). Subjective health judgements were more tied to health behaviour in 'healthier' individuals. Krause and Jay (1994), when examining the frames of reference drawn on by people when asked to evaluate their own health status, found that older respondents were more likely to refer to

health behaviour
behaviour performed by an individual, regardless of their health status, as a means of protecting, promoting or maintaining health, e.g. diet.

health *problems* when making their appraisals, whereas younger respondents referred to **health *behaviour*.** This raises the issue of health being considered differently when it is no longer present. Health is considered to be good when nothing is wrong (perhaps more commonly thought in older people) and when a person is behaving in a health-protective manner (perhaps more commonly thought in younger people). It also highlights that other personal and social factors, such as age, influence health perceptions, as described in the next section.

■ Social representations of health

A well-cited study by Herzlich (1973) conducted unstructured interviews with a small ($n = 80$) sample of French adults in order to ascertain the 'social representations' of health and illness (see also Chapter 9) and found that although it was hard for some to disentangle health from an absence of illness, health seemed to be viewed as a state of equilibrium across various aspects of the person, encompassing physical, psychological, emotional and social wellbeing. Bennett (2000: 67) considers these representations of health to distinguish between health as 'being', i.e. if not ill, then healthy; 'having', i.e. health as a positive resource or reserve; and 'doing', i.e. health as represented by physical fitness or function (as found in Benyamini *et al.*'s study of the elderly referred to above). The similarities between Herzlich's and Bauman's study are noticeable, although Bauman's respondents appear to have focused more on the 'being' healthy and 'doing' aspects, which may be in part because 'having' health as a resource was not prominent in the minds of her patient sample.

A more representative picture of the health concept can be obtained from a large, questionnaire-based survey of 9,000 members of the general public, the *Health and Lifestyles* survey (Blaxter 1990). Her findings suggest that health concepts are perhaps even more complex than the earlier studies had proposed. This survey asked respondents to:

■ Think of someone you know who is very healthy.
■ Define who you are thinking of (friend/relative etc. – do not need specific name).
■ Note how old they are.
■ Consider what makes you call them healthy.
■ Consider what it is like when you are healthy.

About 15 percent could not think of *anyone* who was 'very healthy', and about 10 percent could not describe what it was like for them to 'feel healthy'. This inability to describe what it is like to feel healthy was particularly evident in young males, who believed health to be a norm, a background condition so taken for granted that they could not put it into words. By comparison, a smaller group of mostly older women could not answer for exactly the opposite reason – they had been in poor health for so long that either they could not remember what it was like to feel well or they were expressing a pessimism about their condition to the interviewer (Radley 1994: 39).

The categories of health identified from the survey findings were:

■ *Health as not ill*: i.e. no symptoms, no visits to doctor therefore I am healthy.

■ *Health as reserve*: i.e. come from strong family; recovered quickly from operation.

■ *Health as behaviour*: i.e. usually applied to others rather than self; e.g. they are healthy because they look after themselves, exercise, etc.

■ *Health as physical fitness and vitality*: used more often by younger respondents and often in reference to a male – male health concept more commonly tied to 'feeling fit', whereas females had a concept of 'feeling full of energy' and rooted health more in the social world in terms of being lively and having good relationships with others.

■ *Health as psychosocial wellbeing*: health defined in terms of a person's mental state; e.g. being in harmony, feeling proud, or more specifically, enjoying others.

■ *Health as function*: the idea of health as the ability to perform ones duties; i.e. being able to do what you want when you want without being handicapped in any way by ill health or physical limitation (relates to the World Health Organization's concept of handicap; i.e. an inability to fulfill ones normal social roles, usually resulting from some impairment or disability (WHO 1980)).

These categories therefore confirm the presence of health as something more than physical, i.e. as something encompassing psychosocial wellbeing, and seem to fit with Herzlich's 'being' and 'doing' categorisations (see Bennett 2000: 66) and Bauman's findings of clusters of beliefs in 'health as not ill'. Generally, we can conclude that these dimensions of health are fairly robust (at least in Western culture).

Another important finding is that subjective health evaluations are reached through comparison with others, and in a similar way one's concept of what health is, or is not, can be shaped. For example, Kaplan and Baron-Epel (2003) interviewed 383 Israeli residents and found that young people reporting sub-optimal health did not compare themselves with people of the same age, whereas many older people in sub-optimal health did. When in optimal health, more young people than old compared themselves with people their age. The authors interpret these findings as showing that people try to get the best out of their evaluations – a young person will be likely to perceive their peers to be generally healthy, so if they feel that they are not, they will be unwilling to draw this comparison. In contrast, older people when in poorer health are more likely to compare themselves with same-aged peers, who may generally be thought to have normatively poorer health, and therefore their own health status seems less unusual. Asking, as Bauman's study did, a person to consider what it is that they would consider as 'being healthy' inevitably will lead people into making these types of comparison. Health is a relative state of being.

World Health Organization definition of health

The dimensions of health described in the preceding paragraphs are reflected in the WHO (1947) definition of health as a 'state of complete physical, mental and social well-being and . . . not merely the absence of disease or infirmity'. This definition sees individuals as ideally deserving of a positive state, an overall feeling of wellbeing, fully functioning. In 1978, the WHO launched the Global Strategy for Health for All by the Year 2000, which had the aim of 'the attainment by all citizens of the world by the year 2000 of a level of health that will permit them to lead a socially and economically productive life' (WHO 1981). This led to the development of health policy documents in many countries, such as England's *The Health of the Nation* White Paper (DoH 1992) and the *Saving Lives: Our Healthier Nation* report (Department of Health 1999b), which set out targets for reduction in cancers, heart disease, strokes and AIDS. In England, the targets were to reduce cancers by a fifth or more in the under-75 age group, and reduce heart disease and strokes by two-fifths, by 2010. Although the WHO targets were not fully attained by 2000, some progress has been made, for example reduction in mortality from some forms of cancer.

Each of these policy documents assumes that there is a clear relationship between people's behaviour, lifestyle and health. However, what they often address less clearly, and what is also not explicitly addressed in the WHO definition of health given above, are the socio-economic and cultural influences on health, illness and health decisions. These important influences on health are addressed in the next chapter. The WHO definition also fails to make explicit mention of the role of the 'psyche', which as this text will show, plays a major role in the experience of health and illness.

Cross-cultural perspectives on health

What is considered to be 'normal' health varies across cultures and as a result of the economic, political and cultural climate of the era in which a person lives. Think of how pregnancy is treated in most Western civilisations (i.e. medicalised) as opposed to many Third World regions (naturalised). Even the way in which certain behaviour is viewed differs across time and between cultures. For example, alcohol dependence has shifted from being seen as a legal and moral problem with abusers as deviant to a disease treated in clinics, and smoking has shifted from being considered as glamorous and even desirable to being socially undesirable and indicative of a weak will. Perhaps reflecting this shift, the prevalence of smoking in those aged over 16 in England has dropped from 41 percent in 1976 to 28 percent in 1996 (*General Household Survey*: Thomas, Walker, Wilmot and Bennett 1998).

What is normal and what is defined as sick in a given culture can have all sorts of consequences. If a particular behaviour is labelled as a sickness, the consequences will differ greatly from those received if the behaviour is labelled as deviant; for example, societal responses to illicit drug use have ranged from prohibition through criminalisation to an illness requiring treatment.

There is growing evidence that Westernised views of health differ in various ways from conceptualisations of health in non-Westernised civilisations. Chalmers (1996) astutely notes that Westerners divide the mind, body and soul in terms of allocation of care between psychologists and psychiatrists, medical professions, and the clergy. She observes that this is not the case in some African cultures, where these three 'elements of human nature' are integrated in terms of how a person views them, and in how they are cared for. This holistic view considers the social as well as the biological, the spiritual as well as the interpersonal, and health as an integrated state consisting of all these elements. Until recently, with the development of quality of life research (see Chapter 14), spiritual wellbeing was rarely considered as contributing to a person's perception of health. Furthermore, attributing continued health to a satisfied ancestor would be likely to raise a few eyebrows if stated aloud in a conversation with peers. Spiritual explanations are present in Western reports, if uncommon; for example, supernatural forces such as faith, God's reward, may be perceived as supporting health. Negative supernatural forces such as 'hexes' or the 'evil eye' can also share the blame for illness, as evidenced by cross-cultural studies of illness attributions (e.g. Landrine and Klonoff 1992, 1994), and, as we described above, in earlier historical periods.

In addition to spiritual influences on health, studies of some African regions consider that the community or family work together for the wellbeing of all. This **collectivist** approach to staying healthy and avoiding illness is far different to our **individualistic** approach to health (consider how long the passive smoking evidence was ignored). For example, we found in a study of preventive behaviour to avoid endemic tropical disease in Malawians that the social actions to prevent infection (e.g. clearing reed beds) were adhered to more consistently than the personal preventive actions (e.g. bathing in piped water or taking one's dose of chloroquine) (Morrison, Ager and Willock 1999). Collectivist cultures emphasise group needs to a greater degree than individualistic ones, which emphasise the uniqueness of its members (Matsumoto *et al.* 1996, cited in Marks *et al.* 2000: 56). Obviously, health promotion efforts need to acknowledge that different underlying ethos exist if the promotion of health preventive practices are to be maximally effective (see Chapters 6 and 7).

In the Western worlds, there is a growing recognition of the value of non-traditional (medical) remedies for health maintenance or treatment of symptoms, and the alternative medicine and therapy industries have grown enormously. This mixture of Western and non-medical/traditional medicine has long been common in many regions of sub-Saharan Africa, where, for example in Malawi, a person may visit a faith healer or a herbalist as well as a local Western clinic for antibiotics. The biomedical view of some illnesses is acknowledged (e.g. malaria), and Western medicine is growing in acceptance as both its availability and the population's understanding of its methods and efficacy grows (Ager, Carr, Maclachlan *et al.* 1996). However, our understanding of the underlying cognitions regarding illness and health behaviour is still limited, and there is a need for further research in such cultures.

Several Eastern cultures (Japanese, Chinese) have shown a similar **holistic** and collectivist approach to health. For example, following a comparative study of Canadian and Japanese students, Heine and Lehman (1995) highlighted a need to 'distinguish between cultures that promote and validate "independent selfs", i.e. find meaning through uniqueness and autonomy, and cultures that promote and validate "interdependent selfs", i.e. find meaning through links with others and one's community' (Morrison, Ager and Willock 1999: 367). This relates back to the earlier distinction between 'collective' and 'individualistic' cultures and may also exert an influence on how one perceives health. Cultures that promote interdependent selfs are more likely to view health in terms of social functioning rather than simply personal functioning, fitness, etc. Several research studies by George Bishop and colleagues (e.g. Quah and Bishop 1996; Bishop and Teng 1992) have noted that Chinese Singaporean adults view health as a harmonious state

collectivist
a cultural philosophy that emphasises the individual as part of a wider unit and places emphasis on actions motivated by collective, rather than individual, needs and wants.

individualism
a cultural philosophy that places responsibility at the feet of the individual; thus behaviour is often driven by individual needs and wants rather than by community needs or wants.

holistic
root word 'wholeness', holistic approaches are concerned with the whole being and its wellbeing, rather than addressing the purely physical or observable.

where the internal and external systems are in balance, and on occasions where they become imbalanced, health is compromised. *Yin* – the positive energy – needs to be kept in balance with the *yang* – the negative energy (also considered to be female!). Eastern cultures hold spiritual beliefs about health and illness, with illness or misfortune commonly being attributed to predestination. As we will discuss in a later chapter (Chapter 9) the use of healthcare, either traditional or Western, will in part be determined by the strength to which an individual holds these cultural values and beliefs. Illness discourse will reflect the dominant conceptualisations of individual cultures, and it should become clear at various points throughout this text that how people think about health and illness shapes their expectations, health behaviour, and their use of health promotion and healthcare resources.

Lifespan, ageing and beliefs about health

Psychological wellbeing, social and emotional health are not only influenced by the ageing process, they are also affected by illness, disability and hospitalisation, all of which can be experienced at any age. It is not simply older people who experience longstanding illness, as evidenced by a survey of young people aged 2–24 (using parent proxy reports for those aged under 13), which found that approximately a quarter of the young people had a longstanding illness (predominantly respiratory conditions such as asthma) (statistics from the Health Survey for England, www.doh.gov.uk/stats/selfrep.htm).

However, there are developmental issues, of which, if health professionals are to be able to promote the physical, psychological, social and emotional wellbeing of their patient or client, they should be aware. While the subsequent section briefly considers lifespan issues in relation to health perceptions, it is recommended that interested readers also consult a health psychology text focusing specifically on such issues, e.g. Penny, Bennett and Herbert's edited collection (1994).

■ Developmental theories

The developmental process is a function of the interaction between three factors:

1. *Learning*: a relatively permanent change in knowledge, skill or ability as a result of experience.
2. *Experience*: what we do, see, hear, feel, think.
3. *Maturation*: thought, behaviour or physical growth, attributed to a genetically determined sequence of development and ageing rather than to experience.

Erik Erikson (Erikson 1959; Erikson, Erikson and Kivnick 1986) described eight major life stages (five related to childhood development, three related to adult development), which varied across different dimensions, including:

- cognitive and intellectual functioning;
- language and communication skills;
- the understanding of illness;
- healthcare and maintenance behaviour.

It is important that each of these dimensions be taken into consideration when examining health and illness perceptions or behaviour. Deficits or limitations in cognitive functioning (due to age, accident or illness) may, for example, influence the extent to which an individual can understand medical instructions, report their emotions or have their healthcare needs assessed. Communication deficits or limited language skills can impair a person's willingness to place themselves in social situations or impede their ability to express their pain or distress. The understanding that an individual has of their symptoms or their illness is crucial to healthcare-seeking behaviour and to adherence, and individual health behaviour influences one's perceived and/or actual risk of illness and varies hugely across the lifespan. All these aspects are covered in this textbook in the relevant chapters.

Piaget (1930, 1970) was largely responsible for developing a maturational framework for understanding cognitive development, which has also provided a good basis for understanding the developmental course of concepts regarding health, illness and health procedures. Piaget proposed a staged structure to which, he considered, all individuals follow in the sequence described below:

1. *Sensorimotor* (birth–2 years): an infant understands the world through sensations and movement, lacks symbolic thought. Moves from reflexive to voluntary action.
2. *Pre-operational* (2–7 years): symbolic thought develops by around age 2, thereafter simple logical thinking and language develop, generally egocentric.
3. *Concrete operational* (7–11 years): abstract thought and logic develop hugely, can perform mental operations (e.g. mental arithmetic) and manipulate objects.
4. *Formal operational* (age 12 to adulthood): abstract thought and imagination develop as does deductive reasoning. Not everyone may attain this level.

Piaget's work is influential in terms of providing an overarching structure within which to view cognitive development. For example, his work describes how an infant, from birth to 2 years, slowly acquires symbolic thinking and language and the ability to imitate the actions of others, but that it is only in the latter part of the second stage that children begin to develop logical thought (albeit generally very egocentric thought). Of more relevance to a health psychology text, however, is work that has more specifically addressed children's developing beliefs and understanding of health and illness constructs. The subsequent sections describe this work, using Piagetian stages as a broad framework.

■ Sensorimotor and pre-operational stage children

egocentric
self-centred, such as in the pre-operational stage (age 2–7) of children, when they see things only from their own perspective (cf. Piaget).

Little work with infants at the sensorimotor stage is possible in terms of identifying health and illness cognitions, as language is very limited until the end of this stage. At the pre-operational stage, children develop linguistically and cognitively, and symbolic thought means that young children develop awareness of how they can affect the external world through imitation and learning, although they remain very **egocentric**. Health and illness are considered in black and white, i.e. as two opposing states rather than as existing on a continuum. Children here are slow to see or adopt other people's viewpoints or perspectives. This ability is crucial if one is to empathise with others, and thus a pre-operational child is not very sympathetic to a family member being ill, not understanding why this means they can no longer expect the same amount of play, for example.

Illness concept

It is important that children learn over time some responsibility for maintaining their own health; however, few studies have examined children's conception of health, which would be likely to influence their behaviour. Research has instead focused more often on generating illness concepts. For example, Bibace and Walsh (1980) suggest, on the basis of asking children aged 3–13 questions about health and illness, that an illness concept develops gradually. The questions were about knowledge – 'what is a cold?'; experience – 'were you ever sick?'; attributions – 'how does someone get a cold'; and recovery – 'how does someone get better?' They revealed that there is a progression of understanding and attribution for causes of illness and described six developmentally ordered descriptions of how illness is defined, caused and treated.

Under-7's generally explain illness on a 'magical' level – explanations are based on association.

- *Incomprehension*: child gives irrelevant answers or evades question; e.g. sun causes heart attacks.

- *Phenomenonism*: illness is usually a sign or sound that the child has at some time associated with the illness, but with little grasp of cause and effect; e.g. a cold is when you sniff a lot.

- *Contagion*: illness is usually from a person or object that is close by, but not necessarily touching the child; or it can be attributed to an activity that occurred before the illness; e.g. 'you get measles from people'. If asked *how*? 'Just by walking near them'.

■ Concrete operational stage children

Children over 7 are described by Piaget as capable of thinking logically about objects and events, although they are still unable to distinguish between mind and body until around age 11, when adolescence begins.

Illness concept

Bibace and Walsh describe explanations of illness at around 8–11 years as being more concrete and based on a causal sequence:

- *Contamination*: i.e. children at this stage understand that illness can have multiple symptoms, and they recognise that germs, or even their own behaviour, can cause illness; e.g. 'you get a cold if you take your jacket off outside, and it gets into your body'.

- *Internalisation*: i.e. illness is within the body, but the process by which symptoms occur can be partially understood. The cause of a cold may come from outside germs that are inhaled or swallowed. These children *can* differentiate between body organs and function and can understand specific, simple information about their illness. They can also see the role of treatment and/or personal action as returning them to health.

In this concrete operational stage, medical staff are still seen as having absolute authority, but their actions might be criticised/avoided: e.g. reluctance to give blood, accusations of hurting unnecessarily, etc. Children can, like adults, be encouraged to take some personal control over their illness or treatment at this stage in development, and this can help the child to cope. They also need to be encouraged to express their fears. Parents need to strike a balance between monitoring a sick child's health and behaviour and being overprotective, as this can detrimentally affect a child's social, cognitive and personal development and may encourage feelings of dependency and disability (see Chapter 15 for further discussion of coping with illness in a family).

■ Adolescence and formal operational thought

Adolescence is a socially and culturally created concept only a few generations old. Many primitive societies today do not acknowledge adolescence, and children move from childhood to adulthood with a ritual performance, not the years of transition seen in our society as a distinct period in life. Puberty is a period of both physical and psychosocial change that can influence self-perception. Early adolescence, i.e. 11–13, is when people prepare for independence and peers take on more credence than parents, which offers a partial explanation for why much health-damaging behaviour starts here, e.g. smoking (see Chapter 3).

Illness concept
Bibace and Walsh describe illness concepts at this stage as those at an abstract level – explanations based on interactions between the person and their environment:

- *Physiological*: children from around 11 years reach a stage of physiological understanding, and most can now define illness in terms of specific bodily organs or functions, and with age begin to appreciate multiple physical causes, e.g. genes plus pollution plus behaviour.
- *Psychophysiological*: in later adolescence (from around 14 years) and adulthood many people grasp the idea that mind and body interact, and they understand or accept the role of stress, worry, etc. in the exacerbation and even the cause of illness. It is worth noting that many adults may not achieve this level of understanding about illness and may continue to use more cognitively simplistic explanations.

It should be noted that Bibace and Walsh's study focuses predominantly on the issue of illness causality. Other work has shown that children and young people are able to think about health and illness in terms of other dimensions, such as controllability and severity (e.g. Goldman, Whitney-Saltiel, Granger *et al.* 1991; see Chapter 9 for fuller discussion of illness perceptions).

Adolescents perceive themselves as having more control over the onset and cure of illness and are more aware that personal actions can influence outcomes. This means that advice and interventions are understood more and may be acted upon as they can understand complex remedial and therapeutic procedures: e.g. they understand that taking blood can help to monitor the progress of disease.

As we have shown, childhood is an important period for the development of health concepts, also for the development of attitudes and patterns of health behaviour that will impact on future health status (see Chapter 3). According to these staged theories, a child's ability to understand their condition and associated treatment is determined by the level of cognitive development attained. This level of understanding will subsequently determine how children communicate their symptom experience to parents and healthcare staff, their ability to act on health advice, and the level of personal responsibility for disease management that is feasible. These aspects should not be overlooked when care and educational programmes are developed. While cognitive development is important, such staged theories have not met with universal support (e.g. Dimigen and Ferguson 1993, in relation to concepts of cancer). Illness concepts are now thought to derive more from a range of influences, such as experience and knowledge, rather than from relatively fixed stages of cognitive development (see RESEARCH FOCUS).

RESEARCH FOCUS

Children's conceptions of health: how complex are they?

Normandeau, Kalnins, Jutras and Hanigan (1998). A description of 5- to 12-year-old children's conception of health within the context of their daily life, *Psychology and Health*, 13(5): 883–96.

Background

Studies based on stage theories of cognitive development suggest that children move from very concrete and rigid views of illness based on observables to more abstract concepts that understand causality, interior body and mental health. However, cognitive development is not the only influence – experience of health and illness plays a role, as does socialisation, thus it is suggested that studies of children's concepts of health (as well as other concepts) are best studied in relation to context and experience.

Aims

The study aimed to describe 5–12-year-old children's conceptions of health in the context of their daily lives by asking them to consider health in terms of their daily experiences and getting them to generate themselves the features of illness that they consider most important. A further aim was to examine the influence of demographic and socio-economic variables on illness concepts.

qualitative methodologies concerned with describing (qualifying) the experiences, beliefs and behaviours of a particular group of people.

quantitative methodologies concerned with counting (quantifying) the frequency or level of experiences, beliefs and behaviours of a large, ideally representative, group of people.

Methods

1,674 children (well balanced for gender – 828 boys, 846 girls) from four different urban areas and three different rural areas in the province of Quebec, Canada, were recruited using sampling methods that generated representative gender and socio-economic backgrounds. The cross-sectional study employed mixed **qualitative** and **quantitative methods**, using structured interviews as well as open-ended questioning. Qualitative data were coded, categorised and systematised using content analysis, and then categories of data were analysed according to gender, age group and social class. Children were assessed in terms of what is described as 'four complementary dimensions': (1) *criteria of good health* – 'Can you tell me the name of two or three friends who are healthy?', 'What do you see (*see note below) as signs of good health in your friends?'; (2) *behaviours necessary to maintain health* – 'Is it necessary to do particular things to be healthy?', if yes, 'Which things are necessary?'; (3) *consequences of being healthy* – 'What does being in good health allow you to do?'; and (4) *threats to health* – 'Can you tell me, in general, what is the most dangerous thing to children's health?' (*The use of 'see' as opposed to 'think' may lead the children to consider visible signs of health, which is perhaps leading).

Results
Only response categories mentioned by 100 or more children were considered for detailed analysis (thus losing data from those children who had unusual conceptions and beliefs).

Criteria of good health
The children generally identified three main criteria for good health:

1. being functional (practising sports, absence of disease)
2. mental health (wellbeing, looking healthy, feeling good about oneself, good relationships with others)
3. lifestyle health behaviour (healthy diet, good hygiene, sleeping well).

Components of these dimensions showed some age variation: e.g. functionality in older children was more associated with sports participation and physiological functioning, whereas in younger children it was more related to 'going outside'. Older children also considered 'not being sick' as more important; in terms of lifestyle behaviour, older children more often referred to good diet than did younger children; and in terms of mental health older children more often referred to self-concept, whereas younger children referred more to the quality of relationships with others. No effects were found in terms of gender or socio-economic background.

Perception of health behaviour
Lifestyle factors were considered as the key to good health by all ages, but older children were more concerned with good diet, engaging in physical activity and sleeping well, whereas younger children thought eating specific healthy foods or avoiding specific 'bad' foods was most important.

   Socio-economic status influenced the extent to which children thought it was necessary to have healthy behaviour, with those from urban upper middle-class areas emphasisng this aspect of health most. Age interacted with socio-economic environment. Gender did not influence conceptions regarding health behaviour.

Consequences of being healthy
Mainly children think that the consequence of health is being able to function by doing things one wants to do, and to a lesser extent having good mental health.

   Age effects existed in that older children were more likely to mention being functional and being able to do more things including leisure activities, and more often mentioned better physiological functioning to be a consequence of health (relates to Bibace and Walsh's findings in this age group). No effect of socio-economic environment or gender was found in terms of perceived health consequences.

continued

Threats to health

The major threats to health were perceived to be poor lifestyle behaviour such as smoking, doing drugs, drinking and eating unhealthily. Age effects showed that perceptions of threat change significantly with age, particularly between the 5–6 and 8–12 age groups. Taking drugs and smoking was most commonly reported in the 8–9 and 11–12 age groups, whereas eating bad foods was most common in the youngest children (5–6 years). Dangerous behaviour and road safety issues were of greater concern to the younger children. Socio-economic environment interacted with age to affect the extent to which unhealthy eating was an issue. No effects were found for gender in terms of what was perceived as health threats.

Discussion

What this study clearly shows is that children as young as 5 have multidimensional concepts of health that are more complex than simply a change from concrete to abstract thinking as described by Piaget or Bibace and Walsh. Very early on, children's conceptions include a mental health dimension, which is contrary to that found in early research, and perhaps this is due to the methodology of inviting children to talk about their concepts in relation to their own lives and experience. Age differences existed across each of the four domains studied and are perhaps particularly evident in terms of perceived threats to health (although this probably reflects greater experience of smoking, drinking and drug use among the older children). Evidence from this study offers support for widening models of children's health concepts to include the role of personal experience and socialisation. No evidence was found for a gender effect on any of the assessed domains, suggesting perhaps that gender differences either do not exist or possibly do not emerge until later in adolescence.

Strengths and limitations

This is a large study with good sampling that asks young children to express their own views and beliefs, and as such is relatively unique. However, the study does not address actual behavioural practices and therefore there is no check on whether children report conceptions that are inconsistent with their actual behaviour. Examining subgroups of children in terms of, for example, smoking behaviour or diet may well have been informative in terms of early rationalisations of risk behaviour.

■ **Adulthood 17/18+**

The ages 17–40 are often described as early adulthood and as the prime of life. All sorts of transitions occur in these years: for example, graduation, new careers, pregnancy, marriage, childbirth; many will divorce, some will lose a parent. Adults are less likely than adolescents to adopt new health-risk behaviour and are generally more likely to engage in protective behaviour: e.g. screening, exercise, etc. for health reasons (see Chapter 4). Transitions in adulthood do not affect all sectors of the adult population in the same way; for example, marriage has been found to benefit health in men: i.e. they have lower illness scores than men living alone, whereas for women being married carries no such protection (Blaxter 1987; Macintyre 1986) suggesting differential social support perhaps (see Chapter 12 for a discussion of stress moderators).

Adulthood tends to be divided between early (17–40), middle age (40–60) and elderly (60/65+). Early adulthood blends out of adolescence as the person forges their identity and assumes the roles and responsibility of adulthood – a time of consolidation. While Piaget did not describe further developments in cognitive processes during adulthood, new perspectives develop from experience, and what is/has been learned is applied with a view to achieving life goals. The shift from acquisition of learning to application of what has been learned means that health education should be more practical in orientation, emphasising application of information.

■ Ageing and health

epidemiology
the study of patterns of disease in various populations and the association with other factors such as lifestyle factors. Key concepts include mortality, morbidity, prevalence, incidence, absolute risk and relative risk. Type of question: Who gets this disease? How common is it?

self-concept
those conscious thoughts and beliefs about yourself that allow you to feel are distinct from others and that you exist as a separate person.

In the UK, as elsewhere in the world, the ageing population (accepting the cut-off age for 'older people' to be 65 or over; cf. Woods 1999) has burgeoned, but more particularly the numbers of persons living into their late 70s or 80s has increased (Office of National Statistics, *Social Trends* 1999). The implications for health and social care resources are obvious given the **epidemiology** of illness: i.e. the fact that the incidence of many diseases increases with longevity. Not all elderly people are ill or infirm, but even among the minority who go on without chronic health problems (physical and/or mental), episodes of acute illness are commonplace. The 2000 Health Survey for England (www.doh.gov.uk/public/healtholderpeople2000pres.htm) reports that of those aged 65 and above, 13 percent of those living at home (10 percent of those aged 65–79; 25 percent of those over 80) have a serious disability, compared with 69 percent of men and 79 percent of women living in residential homes. This figure suggests that there is a considerable extent of disability in the community. What does the process of ageing bring to a person in terms of how they think about themselves and their health?

Empirical research has shown that **self-concept** is relatively stable through ageing (e.g. Baltes and Baltes 1990) and that changes in self-concept are not an inevitable part of the ageing process. In fact, *ageing is not necessarily a negative experience* (although it may become so because of the ageist attitudes that exist in many industrialised countries). Growing older may present an individual with new challenges, but this should not be seen as implying that ageing is itself a problem (Coleman 1999).

Middle age has been identified as a period of uncertainty, anxiety and change among men aged between 37 and 41 (Levinson, Darrow, Klein *et al.* 1978; $n = 40$ only). Many men question their achievements, goals and values, realising perhaps what they have missed through devoting time and energy solely to careers. Women, in contrast, may experience uncertainty of roles if they have been a 'housewife' and face an empty home now that children have gone. The years between maturity and the beginning of old age may often be regarded as the 'prime of life', so if chronic illness or death occurs here it is also, as with young adults, seen as unexpected and cruel.

With increasing age, sensory and motor losses are most common, with a large proportion of our elderly being physically impaired in some way. In an ageing society disability is common; 85 percent may experience some chronic condition (Woods 1999). Elderly people often report expecting to have poor health, which can result in poor healthcare checks and maintenance as they regard it as pointless; they may think loss of mobility, poor foot health and poor digestion as an inevitable and unavoidable part of growing old, so they may not respond to symptoms as they should (e.g. Leventhal and Prohaska

Plate 1.2   Improved fitness is attainable at any age.

Source: Mike King/Action Plus

1986; Sarkisian, Liu, Ensrud *et al.* 2001). Exercise tends to decline in old age as it may be avoided in the belief that it will over-exert the joints, heart, etc., and they tend to underestimate their own physical capacities, yet we shall see in Chapter 4 that exercise is both possible and beneficial.

So far in this chapter we have described what is often meant by 'health': in focusing on health and not on illness, it is important to acknowledge that health is a continuum, not simply a dichotomy of sick versus healthy but as having varying degrees of health and wellbeing along a continuum with illness at one extreme and optimal wellness, which some might never have, at the other. 'Health refers to a state of being that is largely taken for granted' (Radley 1994: 5) and is often only appreciated when lost through illness. We return to perceptions of illness in Chapter 9.

The remainder of this chapter introduces what is broadly considered to be covered within the discipline of health psychology. The closing chapter of this book addresses careers in health psychology.

What is health psychology?

Psychology is a science that can be defined as the study of human and animal behaviour, which later became accepted as the scientific study of mental and behavioural functioning. Studying mental processes through behaviour is limited, however, in that not all behaviour is observable (for example, is thought not behaviour?) and thus for many aspects of human behaviour we have to rely on self-report, the problems of which are described elsewhere.

empiricism
arising from a school of thought that all knowledge can be obtained through experience.

Psychology aims to describe, explain, predict and where possible intervene to control or modify behavioural and mental processes, from language, memory, attention and perception to emotions, social behaviour and health behaviour, to name just a few. The key to scientific methods employed by psychologists is the basic principle that the world may be known through observation = **empiricism**. Empirical methods go beyond speculation, inference and reasoning to actual and systematic analysis of data. Scientific research starts with a theory, which can be defined as a general set of assumptions about how things operate in the world. Theories can be vague and poorly defined (e.g. I have a theory about why sports science students generally sit together at the back of lectures) to very specific (e.g. sports science students sit at the back of lectures because they feel like 'outsiders' when placed with the large numbers of psychology majors). Psychologists scientifically test the validity of their hypotheses and theories. On an academic level this can increase understanding about a particular phenomenon, and on an applied level it can provide knowledge useful to the development of interventions.

Psychologists use scientific methods to investigate all kinds of behaviour and mental processes, from the response activity of a single nerve cell to the role adjustments required in old age:

1. We observe.
2. We define a problem.
3. We collect data.
4. We analyse data.
5. We develop a theory.
6. We test the theory by returning to data collection.

Different kinds of psychologist will employ different methods, and this text highlights those that are most commonly employed by health psychologists: for example, the use of questionnaires, interviews and psychometric assessments (such as of personality).

What connects psychology to health?

As shown already in this chapter, people have beliefs about health, are often emotional about it and have a behavioural role to play in maintaining their health and coping with any illness. Psychological approaches can help to explain why some people react well emotionally to ill-health and others do not, or even why some people seem to get ill all the time and others appear to be permanently healthy.

Health psychology can address questions such as why some people behave in a healthy way and others do not. Is it all a matter of personality? Does a person who behaves in a healthy manner in one way, e.g. doesn't smoke, also behave healthily in other ways, e.g. attend dental screening? Are we rational and consistent beings? Does gender, age or socio-economic status affect health either directly or indirectly via their effects on other things? Health psychology integrates many cognitive, developmental and social theories and explanations, but it applies them solely to health, illness and healthcare (you may also want to pick up an introductory psychology text and look at the learning, motivation, social, developmental and cognitive sections in more detail).

The main goals of health psychology, derived from Matarazzo's definition (1982), are to develop our understanding of biopsychosocial factors involved in:

- the promotion and maintenance of health;
- improving healthcare systems and health policy;
- the prevention and treatment of illness;
- the causes of illness: e.g. vulnerability/risk factors.

Unlike some other domains of psychology (more basic science), health psychology can be considered as an applied science, although not all health psychology research is predictive. For example, some research aims only to *quantify* (e.g. what percentage of school pupils drink under age?) or *describe* (e.g. what are the basic characteristics of underage drinkers such as age, sex, socio-economic status). Descriptive research ideally provides the foundation for the generation of more causal questions: e.g. what is it about low socio-economic status that increases the incidence of risky behaviour? By simply measuring health beliefs and attitudes, we can begin to grapple with the issue of predictors (see Chapters 3–5).

■ Health psychology and other fields

Health psychology has grown out of many fields within the social sciences and has adopted and adapted models and theories originally found in social psychology, behaviourism, clinical psychology, cognitive psychology, etc. Health psychology in the UK and Europe today is, as in the USA, linked with other health and social sciences (e.g. health economics, behavioural medicine, medical sociology) and with medicine and allied therapeutic disciplines. Few academic or practitioner health psychologists work alone; most are involved in an array of inter- and multidisciplinary work (for a discussion of professional health psychology, see Chapter 18).

There are several contrasts with other popular disciplines, as highlighted below. Each model of thinking can in turn affect methods of assessment, research, treatment and intervention.

Medical psychology

This is based upon an essentially mechanistic medical model: i.e. an underlying impairment causes some symptom that requires treatment/cure in order to enable a return to 'normal' (however defined) health. Health psychologists do not dispute the biological basis of health and illness but have aided in the development of a more holistic model. Health psychologists still have to have an understanding of the various body systems (nervous system, endocrine system, immune system mainly), but also relevant to areas studied in the psychology of health are the respiratory and digestive systems (see Chapter 8).

Behavioural medicine

This is an interdisciplinary field drawing on a range of behavioural sciences, including psychology, sociology and health education, in relation to medical conditions (Schwartz and Weiss 1977). Behavioural medicine developed in the 1970s at around the same time as health psychology, and it also provided a challenge to the biomedical model dominant at the time. Behavioural medicine examines the development and integration of behavioural and

operant conditioning
attributed to Skinner, this theory is based on the assumption that behaviour is directly influenced by its consequences (e.g. rewards, punishments, avoidance of negative outcomes).

biomedical knowledge and techniques of relevance to health and illness. As its name suggests, behavioural principles are employed (i.e. that behaviour results from learning through classical or **operant conditioning**). This underlying principle is then applied to techniques of prevention and rehabilitation, and not solely to treatment. Behaviour also includes emotions such as fear and anxiety, although behavioural medicine is not concerned with mental health problems on their own. Behavioural medicine furthered the view that the mind had a direct link to the body (e.g. anxiety can raise blood pressure, fear can elevate heart rate), and some of the therapies proposed, such as biofeedback (see Chapter 13), work on the principle of operant conditioning and feedback.

What do YOU think?	Think of some health behaviours you think you might have learned and consider the circumstances under which you learned them. What factors influence your maintenance of these behaviours? Think of any health problem you have experienced and whether you consider a role for your behaviour in either avoiding that problem in the future or in helping recovery from it.

Psychosomatic medicine

This developed in the 1930s and initially was the domain of now well-known psychoanalysts, e.g. Alexander, Freud. Psychosomatic medicine offered an early challenge to biomedicine. 'Psychosomatic' refers to the fact that the mind and body are both involved in illness, and where an organic cause is not easily identified the mind may offer the trigger of a physical response that is detectable and measurable. In other words, mind and body act together, not just the mind. Illnesses with no physical evidence are known as psychogenic. Until the 1960s, psychosomatic research was predominantly psychoanalytical in nature, focusing on psychoanalytic interpretations of illness, such as asthma, ulcers or migraine being triggered by repressed emotions. Psychosomatic medicine today is more concerned with mixed psychological, social and biological/physiological explanations of illness, and illnesses addressed are often referred to as 'psychophysiological' (e.g. DSM-II) or as psychological factors affecting physical conditions (DSM-IIIR and DSM-IV). This change in the American Psychiatric Association's manuals of mental disorders acknowledges that psychological factors can affect any illness and not just those traditionally examined under the heading 'psychosomatic' (e.g. Stoudemire and Hales 1991).

Medical sociology

This reflects the close relationship between psychology and sociology. Medical sociology attempts to understand health and illness on the basis of various social factors that may influence individuals. It takes a wider (macro) approach to the individual: e.g. role of family, kinship, culture. While health psychology also considers external influences on health and illness, it is more focused on the individual's cognitions/beliefs and responses to the external world from a psychological rather than a sociological perspective. The advent of critical health psychology (see below) may make the boundaries between medical sociology and health psychology more blurred.

Health psychology

This operates in what has been described as a biopsychosocial model (Engel 1977, 1980) and thus considers biological, social and psychological factors involved in the aetiology, prevention or treatment of illness, as well as in the promotion and maintenance of health. However, health psychology has been criticised (e.g. Eiser 1996; Radley 1996) for being too individualistic in focus, too concerned with individual aspects at the expense of the social. This book hopes to address some of these concerns by addressing wider influences on health and illness such as culture, lifespan and socio-economic variables. Humans do not operate in a vacuum but are interacting social beings shaped, modelled and reinforced in their thoughts, behaviour and emotions by people close to them, by less known people, by politicians, by their culture, and even by the era in which they live. Consider, for example, women and work stress – this was not an issue in the 1900s, when society neither expected nor particularly supported women to work, whereas in the twenty-first century we have a whole new arena of women's health issues that in part may relate to the way women's roles have shifted in society.

Health psychology is changing as it grows and recently it has been suggested (Marks 2002: 3–7) that four approaches to health psychology are developing in parallel:

1. *clinical health psychology*, which merges clinical psychology's focus on assessment and treatment with a broader biopsychosocial approach to illness and healthcare issues and which is generally the domain of clinical psychologist practitioners (e.g. Johnston and Kennedy 1998);

2. *public health psychology*, with an emphasis on public health issues, e.g. immunisation programmes, epidemics, and resultant health education and promotion – this area draws from multidisciplinary sources (e.g. social science, economics, politics);

3. *community health psychology*, which employs the methods of action research and aims at the achievement of healthy groups and healthy communities; and

4. *critical health psychology*, which warrants a little more attention here.

Critical health psychology

This is an emerging domain of academic endeavour. Over-individualistic and insufficiently social is one criticism aimed at health psychology in the early twenty-first century, as is the criticism of being more about illness than about health (e.g. Marks *et al.* 2000: 22). There is a growing 'critical health psychology' voice currently, which is inevitable when a discipline has been evolving for only thirty or so years, and it will continue to evolve by attending to these and other voices. Such a critique of one's own discipline is important and beneficial in opening up debates and discussions so that the discipline and those within it do not become complacent. As potential health psychologists of the future, it is right that readers should be aware of the body of criticism and, where available, the empirical support behind it. This text aims to refer to critical issues, although the majority of space will provide the mainstream voice and cover mainstream topics, questions and methods.

Critical health psychologists argue that the biopsychosocial model needs clearer distinction from the biomedical model, particularly in relation to the development of the 'social' component. As Crossley (2000: 6) points out, the biopsychosocial model is more often treated in health psychology research as if the three components are simultaneous influences (but still separate) rather than fully integrated ones. The focus on individual thought, feeling and action, she claims, underplays the role played by society and politics in our human experience of health and illness. Contexts and cultures need more attention: for example, a greater acknowledgement of the rich and growing diversity of cultures in the UK and the rest of Europe. Unlike many undergraduate health psychology texts, we aim to provide you with an understanding of cultural influences on health and the responses to illness.

Central to the argument of critical health psychologists is that *understanding* human health and illness should be the central goal. This text will provide you with that crucial understanding.

Summary

This chapter has introduced key areas of interest to health psychologists, including:

- What is health?
  - Health appears to consist broadly of domains of 'having', 'doing' and 'being', where health is a reserve, an absence of illness, a state of psychological and physical wellbeing; is evident in the ability to perform physical acts, as fitness, and is generally something that is taken for granted until it is challenged by illness.

- How has health and illness been viewed over time?
  - Views of health have shifted from fairly holistic views, where mind and body interact, to more dualist views, where the mind and body are thought to act independently of one another. This is shifting back towards holism, with the medical model being challenged by a more biopsychosocial approach.

- What influence does culture have on how health is perceived?
  - Cultures can be grounded in collective or individualistic orientations, and these will influence explanations for health and illness as well as the behaviour of those within the culture.

- What influence might lifespan play on how health is perceived?
  - Children can explain illness in complex and multidimensional terms, and human expectations of health change over the lifespan as a function of background and experience as well as of cognitive development.

- What is health psychology?
  - Health psychology is the study of health, illness and healthcare practices (professional and personal).
  - Health psychology aims to understand, explain and ideally predict health and illness behaviour in order that effective interventions can be

developed to reduce the physical and emotional costs of risky behaviour and illness.

■ Health psychology offers a more holistic but fundamentally psychological approach to issues in health, illness and healthcare.

Further reading

Penny, G.N., Bennett, P. and Herbert, M. (eds) (1994) *Health Psychology: A Lifespan Perspective*. Switzerland: Harwood Academic.
In particular, Bibace and Walsh's chapter on children's perceptions of illness. The chapter on adolescent health behaviour by Nutbeam and Booth is interesting in terms of cognitive development, but the chapter on caring for the elderly is more relevant to Chapter 15 on caring, as sadly little is said about the health concept either in the elderly or in the middle-aged.

Radley, A. (1994) *Making Sense of Illness: The Social Psychology of Health and Illness*. London: Sage Publications.
This book is well worth a look in order to get a broader perspective than the predominantly psychological one offered here. It is also highly relevant to Chapter 2 in its discussion of social inequalities.

Breakwell, G.M., Hammond, S. and Fife-Shaw, C. (1995) *Research Methods in Psychology*. London: Sage Publications.

McQueen, R.A. and Knussen, C. (1999) *Research Methods in Psychology: A Practical Introduction*. Prentice Hall Europe. (A bit limited in terms of qualitative methods.)
Research methods simply cannot be avoided if you are studying for a degree in psychology. The above are both relatively easy-to-follow texts with specific tips for conducting research and analysis.

Crossley, M.L. (2000) *Rethinking Health Psychology*. Buckingham: Open University Press.
This book is best read when you have grasped the basics of mainstream health psychology.

CHAPTER 2

Health inequalities

Learning outcomes

By the end of this chapter, you should have an understanding of:

■ the impact of poverty on health

■ causes of variations in health between and within countries

■ the impact of social deprivation on health and theories of why this occurs

■ the health impact of having a minority status in society

■ the impact of gender on health

■ the relationship between work stress, unemployment and health

CHAPTER OUTLINE

This chapter considers differences in health status that arise not as a result of individual behaviour but from the social context in which we live. Among other things, it considers why better-off people tend to live longer than those who are less well-off, why women generally live longer than men, and why people from social and ethnic minorities are more likely to die earlier than those from majority populations. While some of the factors that influence these health outcomes are the result of individual behaviour, many of them are the result of social and psychological processes. The greatest killer in the world is poverty, which is associated with poor nutrition, unhealthy water supplies, poor healthcare, and other factors that directly influence health. Among people who do not experience such poverty, more subtle social and psychological factors influence health. Men's health, for example, may be influenced by a general reluctance to seek medical help following the onset of illness. People who are economically deprived may experience poorer health because of problems of accessing healthcare and greater levels of stress than the more economically well-off. This chapter examines how social and psychological processes differentially influence health as a result of **socio-economic status** (SES), ethnicity, gender and working environment.

socio-economic status
a measure of the social class of an individual. Different measures use different indicators, including income, job type or years of education. Higher status implies a higher salary or higher job status.

Health differentials

Where we live can impact on our risk for disease as much, if not more, than how we live. The biomedical model and even health psychology have typically focused on personal risk factors for disease such as personality, diet and levels of exercise when considering factors that moderate our risk for disease. We discussed some of these issues in Chapter 1. However, there is an emerging body of evidence that environmental and social factors may have an equal, if not greater, influence on our health than these individual risk factors. In Western societies, the better-off live, on average, five years longer than the poor. Similarly, people who occupy minority roles in society as a result of ethnic or other factors may experience more illness or die earlier than the majority population. Even findings that women live longer than men may be as much the result of social and psychological factors as biological ones. Evidence in support of these assertions has only emerged relatively recently, and because of its political implications it has, on occasion, been controversial. Attempts have even been made to suppress relevant data. This is perhaps best illustrated by publication of the Black Report (available as Whitehead, Townsend and Davidson 1992). This was one of the first British publications to identify poverty as a cause of ill-health. Commissioned by a Labour government in 1977, the committee reported in 1980, when a Conservative government was in power. Unable to prevent its publication, their immediate response was to 'bury' the report, publishing a limited number of copies on the August bank holiday, when it received minimal publicity. The only way for most people to access the report was to read the book version (Whitehead *et al.* 1992) published over a decade later.

This chapter considers how people in various groups in society may experience differing levels of health and longevity as a result of their SES, gender, working conditions and ethnicity. It considers each factor separately, although in reality each of them may be intimately intertwined. People in ethnic minorities, for example, still tend to be less well-off than the majority population and may suffer adverse health effects as a result of both their ethnicity and SES. Accordingly, although this chapter attempts to identify the specific health risks or gains associated with different social contexts, it should be remembered that many individuals face multiple disadvantages or advantages as a result of occupying several social contexts.

Evidence of health differentials

health differential
a term used to denote differences in health status and life expectancy across different groups.

There are clear **health differentials** across whole populations both within and between countries. With some important exceptions, the richer a country is, the longer its population lives. The World Health Organization (WHO: www.who.int/inf-pr-2000/en/pr2000-life.html) has recently developed a new system for measuring life expectancy. This focuses on the expected number of years to be lived in what it terms the 'equivalent of full health'. Perhaps not surprisingly, all the countries with the worst life expectancy at the turn of the century were in sub-Saharan Africa. The longest-lived populations were scattered around the world, although European countries predominated (see Table 2.1).

Of interest is that the richest country in the world, the USA, actually fared rather badly on this index, at only 24th place in the rankings. It had an average 'equivalent of good health' expectancy of 70.0 years. A number of explanations for this apparent anomaly include the following, some of which are considered in more depth later in the chapter:

Table 2.1 The average time of 'equivalent full health' in the top ten and bottom ten countries of the world

Top 10	Average years of 'full health'	Bottom 10	Average years of 'full health'
Japan	74.5	Sierra Leone	25.9
Australia	73.2	Niger	29.1
France	73.1	Zambia	30.3
Sweden	73.0	Botswana	32.2
Spain	72.7	Uganda	32.7
Greece	72.5	Rwanda	32.8
Switzerland	72.5	Zimbabwe	32.9
Monaco	72.4	Mali	33.1
Andorra	72.3	Ethiopia	33.5

Source: WHO (2000)

- Some social groups in the USA, such as Native Americans and the inner-city poor, have extremely poor health – more characteristic of poor developing countries than a rich industrialised one.

- The HIV epidemic caused a higher proportion of death and disability in young and middle-aged Americans than in most other advanced countries.

- The USA is one of the leading countries for cancers relating to tobacco, especially lung cancer and chronic lung disease.

- The USA has high levels of violence, especially of homicides, when compared with other industrial countries.

IN THE SPOTLIGHT

The registrar-general's social scale

Evidence of health differentials across the social scale can be based on a number of indices of wealth within a society. One way of measuring wealth is simply to identify people's income. As many people are reluctant to disclose their income, other measures have also been developed. One of the most frequently used measures is the type of work an individual has. This does not provide such an accurate measure of wealth but is generally acknowledged as providing a reasonable proxy for income. The ranking system developed for the UK registrar-general used the following broad bands of job type.

I   professional and self-employed
II   managerial and technical occupations
IIIN   skilled non-manual occupations
IIIM   skilled manual occupations
IV   partly skilled occupations
V   unskilled occupations
VI   armed forces

This scheme has now been replaced by a more detailed eight-rank system, but the data presented here are still based on this older scheme.

The richer people *within* countries are also likely to live longer than the less well-off. Evidence from the UK, for example, suggests that people of a higher SES, that is those in social groups I/II (see box), live longer and healthier lives than people in social groups IV/V. Similar data can be found in all industrialised countries (Wilkinson 1992). The gap between rich and poor also seems to be getting wider over time, even while overall rates of disease are falling. Data from Table 2.2, for example, indicate that between 1981 and 1985 women in social groups IV/V were 29 percent more likely to die within the age range 35–64 than women in social groups I/II. Between 1986 and 1992, this figure rose to a 55 percent additional risk.

These health differentials are clearly important and stem from a variety of causes. The next section of the chapter considers some of the explanations that have been proposed to explain them.

Table 2.2   UK mortality rates per 100,000 people aged between 35 and 64 by social class as a result of (a) all causes and (b) coronary heart disease

Social group	Women (35–64 years)		Men (35–64 years)	
	1981–5	1986–92	1981–5	1986–92
(a)				
I/II	344	270	539	455
IIIN	387	305	658	484
IIIM	396	356	691	624
IV/V	445	418	824	762
Ratio of IV/V to I/II	1.29	1.55	1.53	1.68
(b)				
I/II	45	29	185	160
IIIN	57	39	267	162
IIIM	67	59	269	231
IV/V	76	78	293	266
Ratio of IV/V to I/II	1.69	2.69	1.58	1.66

Source: adapted from Acheson (1998)

The haves versus the have-nots: the impact of poverty on health

Perhaps the most important social and economic influence on health is poverty. The comparisons of life expectancy across countries shown above indicate that those people who live in developing countries can expect to live significantly shorter lives than those that live in the more affluent developed countries. The majority of the world's population live in developing countries (approximately 4.4 billion of a total world population of 5.6 billion). Nearly one-third of deaths in the developing countries occur before the age of 5 (WHO 1995), while a further third of deaths occur before the age of 65. This contrasts with the average two-thirds of deaths that occur after the age of 65 among developed countries.

The factors that contribute to these statistics are economic, environmental and social. They include a lack of safe water, poor sanitation, inadequate diet and poor access to healthcare, which, even when accessed, is frequently rudimentary and lacking in resources. The WHO (1995) estimated that poverty caused 12 million deaths annually in children under the age of 5, with the most common causes of death being diarrhoea, dysentery and lower respiratory tract infections, all of which are relatively easily treated in countries where there are good medical facilities. Major killers among the adult population included tuberculosis and malaria. One particular problem now facing many developing countries in Africa is that of HIV infection and AIDS. Here, a lack of finances to treat HIV-infected individuals with **anti-retroviral drugs**, and an initial unwillingness to acknowledge the role of HIV in the development of AIDS in South Africa has contributed to a pandemic that is costing the lives of millions of people across the continent.

anti-retroviral drugs
drugs that prevent the reproduction of a type of virus known as a retrovirus. Most well known in the treatment of the HIV.

Plate 2.1 Poor nutrition and other associated factors will contribute to the long-term health of these children.

Source: Reuters/Corbis

Even the 'haves' experience health differentials

While the developed world may not have the profound levels of poverty found in the developing world, there are still gradients of wealth in these countries, and differentials in health that match them (see Table 2.2). Within the industrialised countries, the richer people tend to live longer and have less illness while alive than the economically less able. It is important to note that there is a *linear* relationship between income (however measured) and health (see Figure 2.1). This indicates more than that the very poor die earlier than the very rich. Instead, it indicates that quite moderate differences in wealth or social factors indicative of wealth impact on health throughout the social groups. This effect can be incredibly subtle. Marmot, Davey-Smith and Stansfeld (1991), for example, reported that middle-class executives who owned one car were more likely to die earlier than the equivalent earners who had two cars.

Explanations of socio-economic health inequalities

A number of explanations for these health inequalities have been proposed, some of which attribute responsibility to the individual as a result of their behaviour. Others suggest that something about occupying different social groups itself can directly impact on health. But the first question that has to be addressed is the causal direction between socio-economic status (SES) and health. Does SES influence health, or does health influence SES?

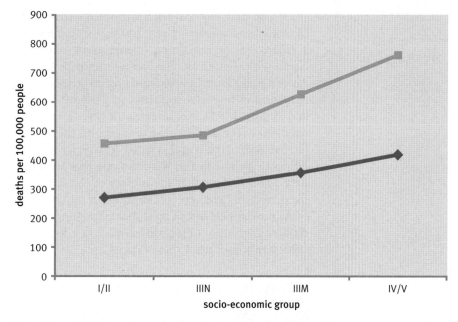

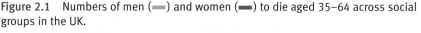

Figure 2.1   Numbers of men (▬) and women (▬) to die aged 35–64 across social groups in the UK.

Source: Acheson (1998)

■ Social causation versus social drift

The first explanation for health differentials pits a social explanation against a more individual one. The first, known as the social causation model, suggests that low SES 'causes' health problems: that is, there is something about occupying a low socio-economic group that negatively influences the health of individuals. The opposing view, known as the social drift model, suggests that when an individual develops a health problem, they may be unable to maintain a job or the levels of overtime required to maintain their standard of living. They therefore drift down the socio-economic scale: that is, health problems 'cause' low SES.

Longitudinal studies have provided evidence relevant to these hypotheses. These typically identify a representative population of several thousand healthy individuals, who are then followed over a number of years to see what diseases they develop and from what causes they die. Differences in measures taken at baseline between those who do and do not develop disease are considered to be risk factors for disease: people who die of cancer, for example, are more likely to have smoked at baseline than those who do not, suggesting that smoking contributes to risk for developing cancer. Each of the studies using this form of analysis has found that baseline measures of SES predict subsequent health status, while health status does not predict SES so strongly. Socio-economic status is therefore generally seen as a *cause* of differences in health status rather than a consequence (e.g. Marmot Davey-Smith and Stansfeld 1991).

Other data that support the social causation model show that as people move from employment to unemployment as a result of companies restructuring (i.e. not due to any personal factors) they experience higher levels of both emotional and physical health problems than while in employment. Ferrie, Martikainen, Shipley *et al.* (2001), for example, found that not obtaining a secure job or remaining unemployed following redundancy were associated with significant increases in minor psychiatric and health complaints. Accordingly, it seems that moving to a lower socio-economic group or a reduction in financial security can cause ill-health. Data from Davey-Smith and Philips (1991) are also relevant here. They considered the relative role of childhood versus adult environments on the health of adults. Their analyses indicated that the social context in which we live as an adult has a greater influence on our health than the one that we experienced as a child. These data again suggest that the impact of the environment on our health is not fixed, and that changes in SES throughout the lifespan will affect our health.

As the data clearly suggest that something about being in the lower socio-economic groups confers differential risk for disease, we must now turn to consideration of what these factors are.

■ Differential health behaviour

We identified in Chapter 1 how a range of behaviour influences our health. With this in mind, one obvious potential explanation for the higher levels of ill-health and premature mortality among people in the lower socio-economic groups is that they engage in more health-damaging and less health-promoting behaviour than those in the higher socio-economic groups. This does seem to be the case. People in the lower socio-economic groups do tend to smoke and drink more alcohol, eat a less healthy diet, and take less leisure exercise than the better-off (e.g. Health Promotion Authority for Wales 1996).

However, these differences do not provide the whole explanation for the health differentials. A number of studies have explored the relationship between traditional risk factors for disease, socio-economic circumstances and mortality. All have found that while differences in health-related behaviour may account for some of the socio-economic differences in health, they do not provide the full story. Marmot, Shipley and Rose (1984), for example, examined the impact of job level and health behaviour on health outcomes over a period of ten years. After taking account of levels of smoking, alcohol consumption, obesity, plasma cholesterol (indicative of dietary levels of fat intake) and blood pressure, Marmot and colleagues found that occupational status still remained independently predictive of health status. Men in the lowest work grade were three times more likely to die than those in the highest grade over this period, even after statistically partialling out the effects of individual behaviour.

While acknowledging that SES exerts an influence on health independently of health-risk behaviour, it is still important to note that many people in lower SES groups do engage in more health-damaging behaviour than people in higher SES groups. Accordingly, many people in low SES groups are potentially doubly disadvantaged because of both their social position and the frequency with which they engage in health-compromising behaviour – but see the findings of Hein, Suadicani and Gyntelberg (1992) discussed below. What is perhaps worth considering here is *why* people in the lower socio-economic groups engage in more health-compromising behaviour. It does not seem to be lack of knowledge. A number of surveys have shown that people in lower SES groups are as aware of the risks associated with health-compromising behaviour such as smoking as those in the higher SES groups, but they do not appear as willing to act on this information. One explanation for this may be that the lack of opportunities and the daily stress associated with economic deprivation may lead to high levels of risk behaviour that help the individual to get through the day – and inhibit a longer-term consideration of the health consequences. Work by Graham (1994), for example, who interviewed a number of working-class women smokers, revealed that they were well aware of the adverse health consequences of smoking but continued to do so as it helped them to cope with the day-to-day stresses of running a family with low economic resources. The type of health-behaviour choices we make, and in some cases the availability of such choices, may itself be constrained by the social context in which we live.

coronary heart disease
a narrowing of the blood vessels that supply blood and oxygen to the heart. Results from a build-up of fatty material and plaque (**atherosclerosis**). Can result in **angina** or **myocardial infarction**.

Of particular interest is that socio-economic factors may, on occasion, actually overwhelm the effects of individual behaviour. An example of this can be found in the work of Hein, Suadicani and Gyntelberg (1992), who reported the outcomes of a seventeen-year prospective study of **coronary heart disease** (CHD) in Danish men. As predicted, they found that smokers were, overall, three and half times more likely to develop CHD than non-smokers. However, they also found that white-collar smokers were six and half times more likely to develop CHD than the equivalent non-smokers, while blue-collar workers experienced no additional risk for CHD as a result of their smoking status. These data suggest that the health risks associated with smoking may be most influential among those people who were not placed at risk of disease as a result of their socio-economic position: among those in the lower socio-economic groups, the impact of smoking on health was almost lost: SES appeared to be a much more important determinant of health. This may come as some relief for the women smokers interviewed by Graham and has implications for the type of health policy and intervention that may influence the health of such individuals.

■ Environmental insult

A second, seemingly non-psychological, explanation for differences in health across social groups is that people in lower socio-economic groups are exposed to more health-damaging environments. People in lower socio-economic groups are more likely to be exposed to working in dangerous settings such as building sites and have more accidents than those in the higher socio-economic groups throughout their working lives (Acheson 1998) (differential exposure to toxic chemicals is relatively rare nowadays due to health and safety legislation). In addition, they may experience home conditions of low-quality housing, dampness and higher levels of air pollution than those in the higher socio-economic groups (Stokols 1992). However, environmental factors may also work through social and psychological pathways. One mechanism through which this may occur is the stress associated with overcrowding. There is clear evidence from both animal and human research that overcrowding is associated with high levels of stress hormones. Animal work has also shown overcrowding combined with a high-cholesterol diet to be associated with accelerated development of **atheroma** and the development of CHD (Baum, Garofalo and Yali 1999).

atheroma
fatty deposit in the intima (inner lining) of an artery.

More subtle processes may also be at work. One example of this can be found in the effect of the type of housing we occupy. In Britain, mortality rates are about 25 percent higher among tenants than owner-occupiers (Filakti and Fox 1995). Tenants also report higher rates of long-term illness than owner-occupiers (Lewis, Bebbington, Brugha *et al.* 1998). Woodward, Oliphant, Lowe *et al.* (2003), for example, found that after adjusting for age, male renters were 1.48 times more at risk of developing CHD than male owner-occupiers; women renters were 2.6 times more likely to develop CHD than their owner-occupier counterparts. There are a number of explanations for these differentials:

■ Renters may experience more damp, poor ventilation, overcrowding and so on.

■ Rented occupation may be further away from amenities, making access to leisure facilities or good-quality shops more difficult.

■ Renters earn less than people who own their house.

■ The psychological consequences of living in differing types of accommodation may directly impact on health.

Although the fourth pathway has received little attention, Macintyre and Ellaway (1998) found that a range of mental and physical health measures were significantly associated with housing tenure, even after controlling for the quality of housing and the age, sex, income and self-esteem of their occupiers. They interpreted these data to suggest that the type of tenure itself is directly associated with health. They suggested, for example, that the degree of control we have over our living environment may influence mood, levels of stress and perceived control over a wider set of health behaviours – all of which may contribute to ill-health.

■ Stress, strain and depression

The implication of the previous section is that poor housing leads to stress, which in turn leads to ill-health. This argument can be widened to suggest that differences in more general stress experienced across the social groups leads to differences in health across the social groups. This seems a reasonable hypothesis. There is consistent evidence that people in the lower socio-economic groups not only experience more stress than those in the higher socio-economic groups (Marmot, Ryff, Bumpass *et al.* 1997; McLeod and Kessler 1990), they frequently have fewer resources to help them to cope. As a result, they may be more vulnerable to stress than those in the higher economic groups. They may also have fewer uplifts that reduce stress than people in higher socio-economic groups. There is also significant evidence to suggest that stress can adversely impact on health. We consider the evidence for this, and the mechanisms that explain how stress can lead to disease, in Chapter 11.

Here we consider the first part of this linkage: the contention that people in lower socio-economic groups experience more stress than those in higher groups. Some of the stresses (and health-compromising behaviour and restrictions in life opportunities) that may be experienced more by people in lower socio-economic groups than the more economically better-off are summarised below (see Carroll, Davey-Smith and Bennett 1996):

■ *childhood*: family instability, overcrowding, poor diet, restricted educational opportunities;

- *adolescence*: family strife, exposure to smoking and own smoking, leaving school with poor qualifications, experiencing unemployment or low-paid and insecure jobs;
- *adulthood*: working in hazardous conditions, financial insecurity, periods of unemployment, low levels of control over work or home life, negative social interactions;
- *older age*: no or small occupational pension, inadequate heating, food, etc.

These types of data have been formalised in Hobfoll and Lilly's (1993) conservation of resources model, which proposed that mental and physical health are determined by the amount of resources available to the individual. These may be:

- economic (e.g. job, income)
- social (e.g. family support)
- structural (e.g. housing)
- psychological (e.g. coping skills, perceived control).

A high level of resources is health-protective. Low levels of resources place an individual at risk of health problems. Although the model has received general support (e.g. Hobfoll 2001), its relation to socio-economic factors has yet to be fully examined. The model is contrary to the individual appraisal models of stress discussed in Chapter 11 and suggests that some factors impact so markedly on our mental and physical health that they are not mediated by individual appraisals but affect us all in similar ways. As such, the model indicates the type of factors that will impact on the health of people across society, albeit without explaining how these factors actually do so.

A more specific emotion that is increasingly associated with disease, and in particular CHD, is depression. Just as in the case of stress, depression rates are not equally distributed through society. They are relatively high among the poor, ethnic minorities, and those with poor social or marital support. Accordingly, differences in the **prevalence** of depression across the social groups may also contribute to the differences in health. One final factor that may interact with SES to influence risk for disease is the social support available to the individual. A large number of positive social relationships and few conflictual ones may buffer individuals against the adverse effects of the stress associated with low economic resources. Conversely, low SES combined with a poor social support system may significantly increase risk for disease (Taylor and Seeman 1999). Sadly, the potentially protective effect of good social support may be less widely available than previously. In contrast to research conducted in the 1950s, those in the higher social groups now appear to have more social support than those in the lower social groups (e.g. Marmot, Davey-Smith and Stansfield 1991; Ruberman, Weinblatt, Goldberg *et al.* 1984).

prevalence
the number of established cases of a disease in a population at any one time.
Often described as a percentage of the overall population or cases per 100,000 people.

■ Access to healthcare

Access to healthcare is likely to differ according to both personal characteristics and the healthcare system with which the individual is attempting to interact. Perhaps the most studies of this phenomenon have been conducted in the USA, where different healthcare systems operate for those with and

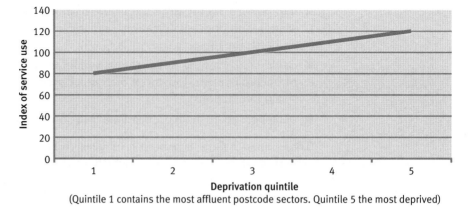

Figure 2.2   Health service use according to level of social deprivation in Scotland in 1999.

Source: Scottish Executive (1999)

mammography
a low-dose X-ray procedure that creates an image of the breast. The X-ray image can be used to identify early stages of tumours.

without health insurance. Here, the less well-off clearly receive poorer healthcare. Qureshi, Thacker, Litaker *et al.* (2000), for example, noted that while access to **mammography** screening in the USA did not vary according to ethnicity or education level, it was lower among those with 'healthcare access or insurance problems'. Even among those with some form of health insurance (Medicare), patients who live in poor neighbourhoods received worse healthcare than those from better-off areas, particularly in rural and non-teaching hospitals (Kahn, Pearson, Harrison *et al.* 1994).

By contrast, in the UK, where there is universal access to healthcare, people in the lower socio-economic groups do access healthcare systems more frequently than those in the higher SES groups (see Figure 2.2). At one level, it therefore appears that there are no problems in accessing healthcare. However, what these data do not address is whether the increased use of healthcare resources is sufficient to counter the additional levels of poor health linked to the lower SES groups.

What evidence there is suggests that this is not the case. In the Scottish Executive's (1999) report on health inequalities, for example, considerable differences were reported between the rates of some medical and surgical procedures between the poor and the more affluent across Scotland: rates of hip replacements, hernia repairs and varicose vein surgery were much higher per head of population among the better-off than those living in economically deprived areas. In addition, although a higher percentage of the most deprived sections of society received **coronary artery bypass grafts** for CHD than did those in the higher SES groups, the relative difference was not as great as the larger differences in the prevalence of CHD between the groups. Although more people received surgery, the poorer population remained relatively deprived of healthcare in comparison with those in the higher SES groups.

coronary artery bypass graft
surgical procedure in which veins or arteries from elsewhere in the patient's body are grafted from the aorta to the coronary arteries, bypassing blockages caused by atheroma in the cardiac arteries and improving the blood supply to the heart muscle.

These data suggest that the provision of healthcare differs according to where you live in the UK (see IN THE SPOTLIGHT). However, other factors associated with social and economic deprivation may also influence the uptake of healthcare, even when it is provided. Goyder, McNally and

Botha (2000), for example, reported that attenders at a routine diabetes clinic were more likely to be younger, to have access to a car and to have a white collar job than people who did not attend. People with low resources may be affected both by limited access to healthcare resources and by limited means to access them when they are provided.

IN THE SPOTLIGHT

Inequalities of health provision

Health provision involves both provider and user. The 'postcode lottery' suggests that providers are failing to provide equity of care across different parts of the UK, with those in the poorest areas generally receiving less care than those in better-off areas. We have shown how the Scottish Executive demonstrated that while more resources are available for the care of people in more deprived areas in Scotland, these are not sufficient to cope with the serious health needs of the population. Inequalities in the provision of service are not simply evident on a local scale. Whole regions may differ in their health provision. An audit of the prescription of a drug known as herceptin (see www.cancerbacup.org.uk/fund/press/RocheAudit.doc), which can be effective in the treatment of advanced breast cancer, found that 14 percent of women in the Midlands had access to it in 2003. This figure rose to 28 percent in the North and North-east, 33.5 percent in the South-east and East Anglia, and 61 percent in the South-west. These differences were found despite herceptin being recommended for the treatment of women with advanced breast cancer by the government's treatment advisory body (the National Institute for Clinical Excellence – NICE).

But it is not just at a geographical level that there are inequalities in health provision. We show later in this chapter that differential levels of care may be provided within hospitals to patients of different ethnic origins. African American patients, for example, may be offered less curative surgery for CHD than white patients in some hospitals in America. People who are poor may access healthcare less than the better-off. Finally, doctors may select patients to have different treatments as a result of their behaviour – some high-profile doctors have suggested, for example, that smokers should not be offered cardiac surgery as their smoking would prevent their gaining maximum benefit from it. As economic resources become or remain tight across all healthcare systems, inequalities in the provision of healthcare are likely to become more frequent, and perhaps more explicit. But they only make evident what has been the case for many years – albeit with much less publicity.

■ Socio-economic status as a *relative* issue

So far, the discussion has considered factors that differ across socio-economic groups that may affect health. Wilkinson (1992) suggested a further factor – that simply knowing you are less well-off than your neighbours may in itself contribute to ill-health. His analysis of levels of ill-health and premature mortality both within and between countries led him to suggest that it is not just *absolute* wealth that determines health: rather, it is *relative* wealth. He drew on evidence that shows only a weak relationship between the absolute wealth of a society and overall life expectancy. More important is the distribution

Plate 2.2   The health of these children will be affected both by factors within their immediate environment, and as a result of their environment being relatively deprived when compared to financially more secure children.

Source: Nathan Benn/Corbis

of wealth within a society. To illustrate his argument, Wilkinson (1990) compared data on income distribution and life expectancy across nine Western countries. He found that while the overall wealth of the country was not associated with life expectancy, the variation in income distribution across the various social groups (i.e. the size of the gap between the rich and poor) was. The correlation between the two variables was a remarkable 0.86: the higher the income disparity across the population, the worse its overall health.

Longitudinal data also contribute to the strength of his argument. Forwell (1993), for example, tracked average age of mortality and income distribution in Glasgow between 1981 and 1989, over the life of the Conservative government. During this time, there was a significant increase in the income distribution within the population: the income of the richer section of society increased significantly more than that of the people in the lower SES groups. As the differences between the income of people who lived in the poorer and better off areas of Glasgow increased over this period, so did rates of **premature mortality** among people occupying the lower socio-economic groups, despite their access to material goods, food, clothing and so on remaining relatively constant over time. These and similar data led Wilkinson (1992) to suggest that for the majority of people in Western countries, health is the result of relative rather than absolute living standards. One explanation of these data suggests that we engage in some form of comparison of our living conditions with others in society, and that knowledge of a relative deprivation in some way increases risk of disease, although the mechanisms through which this may influence health are far from understood.

premature mortality
death before the age it is normally expected. Usually set at deaths under the age of 75.

RESEARCH FOCUS

Ferrie, J.E., Shipley, M.J., Stansfeld, S.A. (2003). Future uncertainty and socioeconomic inequalities in health: the Whitehall II study. *Social Science and Medicine*, 57: 637–46.

Background

The Whitehall studies may appear an odd way of addressing the relationship between personal behaviour, social inequalities and health. The first study, Whitehall I, involved a cross-sectional study of people working in the British civil service headquarters in Whitehall. Whitehall II was a longitudinal study examining the long-term relationship between these factors. Among other things, the studies have examined the relationship between the type of job people held, their behaviour and their health. Its 'take home' message has been that after taking account of individual behaviour, the grade an individual holds within the civil service is strongly predictive of how long they will live – the higher the grade, the better the outcome.

But what does a study of London-based British civil servants have to tell us? The strength of the Whitehall study is the similarity of working and living conditions of the entire cohort of people studied. Other studies have examined the relationship between disease rates and socio-economic status in much more diverse populations. While this has some advantages, it also means that comparisons between people from different socio-economic groups inevitably involves comparisons of people in different types of job, as well as working and living environments. Accordingly, differences in mortality between these various groups may be the result of differential exposure to pollutants, accidents, and so on. In the civil service, no such differences exist – from cleaner to chief civil servant, all people work in the same environment. Similarly, virtually all the workers live in London and thus share the same levels of air pollution and other environmental factors. These similarities mean that any differences in health or mortality across the social spectrum cannot be accounted for by differences in working or living environment.

The Whitehall studies were seminal in identifying the risk of ill-health and premature mortality associated with low socio-economic status. They have now begun to explore some of the mechanisms through which these differences may arise. The paper by Ferrie *et al.* examined the relationship between job and financial insecurity and both mental and physical health.

Method

Participants

Participants in the Whitehall II study were all London-based civil servants. At baseline, the study population comprised 6,895 men and 3,413 women of all grades in the civil service.

Data collection

Baseline data were collected between 1985 and 1988. Follow-up measures were taken at various times since then. The present study reported the fifth follow-up assessment (phase 5), which occurred between 1997 and 1999. Participants received a clinical examination measuring blood pressure, cholesterol, weight, and so on. In addition, they completed a questionnaire that included lifestyle, work characteristics, social support, life events and chronic difficulties. Of particular relevance to this report were the following measures:

- *Health rating*: 'In general would you say your health is: excellent, very good, good, fair, poor?'
- *General health questionnaire* (Goldberg 1997): measuring depression and anxiety;
- *Job security*: 'How secure do you feel in your present job?'
- *Financial security*: 'Thinking of the next ten years, how financially secure do you feel?'

continued

Results

By the fifth phase of the study, 7,270 of the original participants had completed the full follow-up assessment. A further 560 participants completed a shorter assessment process by telephone, bringing the total number of people with relevant data to 7,630: 76 percent of the original sample. This is a good response rate, particularly as non-completers included people who had died over the intervening years or who had left the civil service and could not be found. The key results of the study were:

- Participants in higher-ranked jobs reported better physical and mental health, less long-standing illness, lower levels of obesity and lower blood pressure levels. However, they did not vary in their cholesterol levels.

- A similar association between *previous* job rank and measures of health was found among people unemployed at the time of phase 5 assessment.

- People in lower job grades reported higher levels of job insecurity than those in the higher job grades.

- People in lower grades, or who were unemployed at the time of the assessment and who had been in lower grades, reported more financial insecurity than those in the higher grades.

- Job insecurity was only marginally associated with any of the measures of health.

- By contrast, financial insecurity was associated with poorer self-rated health, long-term illness (in men but not women) and levels of depression among both employed and unemployed people.

Discussion

This is an interesting paper in many ways, but it also leaves a number of questions. An important finding was the association between job grade and health. People in higher grades did better on both objective and subjective measures of health. What was also evident was that these inequalities in health continue even when people leave the civil service and become unemployed.

Also of interest was that *financial* security but not job security was associated with health. It seems that we are less concerned about whether we can keep a particular job than whether we are likely to continue to earn sufficient money to maintain an established lifestyle.

Minority status and health

A second set of factors that discriminate between people in society is whether or not they occupy majority or minority status within the general population. This is usually considered in terms of the ethnic or cultural background of the individual, but it may also reflect other differences such as those associated with sexuality and religion.

Ethnic minorities

Perhaps the most obvious minority in any population are people who differ from the majority in terms of skin colour, religion and so on: often considered under the rubric of ethnic minorities. Nazroo (1998) pointed out that ethnicity encompasses a variety of issues: language, religion, experience of races and migration, culture, ancestry, and forms of identity. Each of these may individually or together contribute to differences between the health of different ethnic groups. He therefore warned about considering all people in all ethnic minority groups as one single entity and thereby failing to recognise the reality of their differing lives.

These cautions are perhaps reflected in findings that in the UK, while rates of ill-health and premature mortality among people from ethnic minorities are generally higher than those of the white population, people from the Caribbean experience better health (Wild and McKeigue 1997). Levels of disease also differ across ethnic groups. Rates of heart disease among British men from the Indian subcontinent, for example, are 36 percent higher than the national average. Among young people, these differences are even greater: young Indian men are nearly three times more likely to develop heart disease than their white counterparts. The Afro-Caribbean population has particularly high rates of **hypertension** and **strokes**, while levels of diabetes are high among Asians. By contrast, rates of lung cancer are relatively low in people of Caribbean or West African origin (Balarajan and Raleigh 1993).

In searching for explanations for the relatively poor health of people from ethnic minorities, a number of issues have to be borne in mind. Perhaps the most important is that a disproportionate number of people from ethnic minorities also occupy low socio-economic groups. Before suggesting that being in an ethnic minority *alone* influences health, the effects of these socio-economic factors need to be taken into account in any comparison between ethnic minorities and majority populations. This can be done by comparing disease rates between people in ethnic minorities and people from the majority population matched for income or other markers of SES, or by statistically partialling out the effects of SES in comparisons between majority and minority populations. Once these are done, any differences in mortality between the two groups lessen. Haan and Kaplan (1985), for example, found significantly higher rates of disease and premature mortality between American black and white populations (as large as a 30 percent difference), which disappeared after partialling out the effects of SES. Other studies (e.g. Sorlie, Backlund and Keller 1995) have found a reduction, but not negation, of health differentials after partialling out the effects of SES.

Socio-economic status certainly exerts an influence within ethnic minorities: just as for the majority population, people in the higher socio-economic groups generally live longer and have higher health ratings throughout the life course than those with fewer economic resources (Harding and Maxwell 1997; Davey-Smith *et al.* 1996). However, again highlighting the dangers of considering people in different ethnic minorities as one single group, there are some exceptions to this rule. In the UK, for example, there appears to be no SES-related differential risk for CHD among men born in the Caribbean or West or South Africa (e.g. Harding and Maxwell 1997). Despite these cautionary notes, there is a general consensus that ethnicity does impact on health, although different factors may affect different ethnic groups. A number of explanations for these differences have been proposed. These mirror, to some extent, those associated with SES: differences in health-related behaviour, stress and access to healthcare.

hypertension
chronically high blood pressure (considered to be high if systolic pressure exceeds 160 and diastolic exceeds 120).

stroke
involves damage to the brain as a result of either bleeding into the brain tissue or a blockage in an artery, which prevents oxygen and other nutrients reaching parts of the brain. More scientifically known as a cerebro-vascular accident (CVA).

■ Differential health behaviour

As with SES, the behavioural hypothesis suggests that variations in health outcomes may be explained by differences in behaviour across ethnic groups. In the UK, for example, many African-Caribbean men and Asian males of Punjabi origin consume high levels of alcohol and develop alcohol-related disorders: levels of consumption among Muslim people are minimal, with total abstinence being common. The British Asian population has a relatively high level of fat consumption and its associated illnesses such as CHD (Rudat 1994; Nazroo 1997). Smoking is more common among African-Caribbean and Bangladeshi men than in the white population (Nazroo 1997).

Fewer men and women aged 16–74 from minority ethnic groups than the majority population engage in levels of activity that would benefit their health. The Health Education Authority (1997), for example, reported that 67 percent of Indians, 72 percent of Pakistanis and 75 percent of Bangladeshis reported that they did not engage in enough physical activity to benefit their health. This contrasts with 59 percent of men in the general population. A similar pattern emerged among women. Different levels of such health behaviour may reflect social and cultural beliefs and behavioural norms that differ across ethnic groups.

■ The stress of occupying a minority status

A second explanation for the health disadvantages of people in minority groups focuses on the social impact of occupying minority status. Ethnic minorities may experience wider sources of stress than majority populations as a consequence of specific stressors such as discrimination, racial harassment, and the demands of maintaining or shifting culture.

One area where this has become evident is in the relatively high rates of CHD and hypertension among black American men (Onwuanyi, Clarke and Vanderbush 2003). A number of explanations have been proposed to account for this phenomenon. One that was frequently expounded in the 1970s was that black men's blood pressure rose more while they experienced stress and strong emotions such as anger than did that of their white counterparts, and that they experienced such emotions more frequently. This process was thought to gradually push up resting blood pressure until an affected individual would present with long-term hypertension (see also Chapter 8). In other words, this health problem was linked to genetically mediated biological differences between black and white populations. More recently, these differences have been ascribed to the different social contexts that people in these two groups may experience. Rises in blood pressure and the higher reactivity found among black men are now seen as a result of the increased stress to which they are exposed in comparison with their white counterparts.

Evidence to support this explanation can be found in the work of Harburg, Erfurt, Chape *et al.* (1973), who found no differences in blood pressure between black and white people living in low-stress areas. By contrast, the highest blood pressure readings they had were those of black people living in areas of low income and high crime. Similarly, James, LaCroix, Kleinbaum *et al.* (1984) found high blood pressure in black men to be associated with low job security, lack of job success and discrimination. An experimental study conducted by Clarke (2000) added to these population data. In this, Clarke found that among a sample of young African American women, the more they reported experiencing racism, the greater their rises in blood pressure during a task in which they talked about their views and feelings about animal rights. They took this to indicate that they had developed a stronger emotional and physiological reaction to general stress as a result of their long-term responses to racism. This, in turn, was contributing to the long-term development of hypertension (Brosschot and Thayer 1998). A related explanation is known as 'John Henryism'. This suggests that successful black men have had to push harder than their white equivalents to achieve such success, and their increases in blood pressure reflect the stress of such effort (Merritt, Bennett, Williams *et al.* 2004; see also IN THE SPOTLIGHT in Chapter 8).

■ Access to healthcare

A third explanation for the relatively poor health among ethnic minorities may be found in the problems some face in accessing healthcare. In addition, once within the hospital system, ethnic minority patients may be less likely to receive expensive treatments than the equivalent white patient. Mitchell, Ballard, Matchar *et al.* (2000), for example, found that, even after adjusting for demographic factors, the presence of other health conditions, and the ability of patients to pay, African American patients with **transient ischaemic attacks** were significantly less likely to receive specialist diagnostic tests or to have a specialist doctor than white patients. In addition, there is consistent evidence that in the USA blacks are less likely than whites to receive curative surgery for early-stage lung, colon or breast cancer (e.g. Brawley and Freeman 1999) and that these failures result in higher mortality rates among black people than among whites. Furthermore, blacks with chronic renal failure are less likely to be referred for transplantation and are less likely to undergo transplantation than are whites (Ayanian, Cleary, Weissman *et al.* 1999).

transient ischaemic attack
a short period of reduced blood flow to the brain, resulting in symptoms including short periods of confusion, weakness and other minor neurological symptoms.

In the UK, many of the inequities associated with healthcare appear to result more from economic than from ethnic disparities. Chinese people consult their GP less than whites and African Asians. However, all other groups consult more (Nazroo 1997). Unfortunately, poor communities that are most at risk of ill-health tend to experience the least access to the full range of prevention services: a phenomenon known as the 'inverse prevention law' (Acheson 1998). In addition, specific factors may affect some ethnic groups. Access to female GPs is lowest in areas with high concentrations of Asian residents (Birmingham Health Authority 1995): a factor that may inhibit Asian women's use of healthcare services, and, in particular, uptake of screening for cervical cancer (Naish, Brown and Denton 1994). Access to secondary (hospital) care may also affect some people from ethnic minorities. As mortality rates for CHD in South Asians is 40 percent higher than in the general population, rates of medical and surgical intervention should be higher for this population than the general norm. The evidence suggests the opposite is the case – even after adjusting for SES and geographical factors (Goddard and Smith 1998). However, there is no evidence of systematic inequities in access for many other hospital treatments (Gillam, Jarman, White and Law 1989).

Other minorities

Minority status may also result from differences in behaviour from the norm. Following the initial onset of HIV and AIDS, both infection and death rates were higher among gay men than in the rest of the sexually active population. As a result, it was initially considered to be a consequence of the 'gay lifestyle'; indeed, AIDS was called the 'gay plague' by many in the media (see Shilts 2000). Now, levels of HIV infection among the heterosexual population in most Western countries are similar to those in the gay community, and the most prevalent mode of transmission is through heterosexual sex. Accordingly, HIV infection can no longer be considered to affect minority groups in society. However, the isolation experienced as a consequence of sexual orientation may impact significantly on the development of AIDS following infection with the HIV. Cole, Kemeny, Taylor *et al.* (1996), for example, found that HIV-infected gay men who experienced social rejection as a result of their sexuality showed a significant acceleration towards a critically low CD4+ lymphocyte level (see Chapter 8) and time to diagnosis of AIDS in comparison with their counterparts who were more socially integrated. They also found that healthy gay men who hid their sexual identity were significantly more likely to develop cancer or infectious diseases than those men who felt able to express their sexuality, even in the absence of any underlying viral infection.

Gender and health

risk ratio
a way of comparing whether the probability of a certain event is the same for two groups. A risk ratio of 1 implies that the event is equally likely in both groups. A risk ratio greater than 1 implies that the event is more likely in the first group. A risk ratio of less than 1 implies that the event is less likely in the first group.

An average woman's life expectancy in the West is significantly greater than that of men in the same birth cohort. In the United Kingdom, for example, at the time of writing women were likely to live six years longer than men, with women dying on average at the age of 80 and men at 74, (WHO 2002: www.who.int; note that this differs from the WHO data reported earlier which is based on years lived with 'good health'). A large part of this difference is the result of the earlier onset of CHD in men than in women. Nearly three-quarters of those who die of an MI before the age of 65 are men (American Heart Association 1995). However, cancer rates for men and women of the same age also favour women (Reddy *et al.* 1992). Reddy, Fleming and Adesso (1992) identified the following **risk ratios** of dying prematurely from a variety of diseases for men versus women (Table 2.3).

These data indicate, for example, that men are nearly twice as likely to die before the age of 65 of heart disease than women – and also three times more likely to die from violence (legal intervention appears to be a US euphemism for the death penalty). Despite these differences in mortality, men report higher levels of self-rated health, contact medical services less frequently and experience less acute illness than women (Reddy *et al.* 1992). By contrast, women report higher levels of physical symptoms and longstanding illnesses than men (Lahelma, Martikainen, Rahkonen *et al.* 1999).

Table 2.3 Relative risk for men dying prematurely (before the age of 65) from various illness in comparison with women

Cause	Male/female ratio
Coronary heart disease	1.89
Cancer	1.47
Stroke	1.16
Accidents	2.04
Chronic lung disease	2.04
Pneumonia/flu	1.77
Diabetes	1.11
Suicide	3.90
Liver disease	2.32
Atherosclerosis	1.28
Renal disease	1.54
Homicide/legal intervention	3.22
Septicaemia	1.36

It is, perhaps, cautionary to note that while this pattern of mortality is common among industrialised countries, the pattern of health advantage is often different in industrialising countries. Here, differences in the life expectancy of men and women are smaller and in some cases are reversed. Women in many industrialising countries are more likely to experience higher rates of premature illness and mortality than men as a result of their more frequent experience of pregnancy and its associated health risks, as well as inadequate health services (Doyal 2001).

Biological differences

Perhaps the most obvious explanation for the health differences between men and women is that they are biologically different – being born female brings with it a natural biological advantage in terms of longevity. Some have suggested that these differences may be genetically mediated through differences in male and female immune systems – women, for example, appear to have greater resistance to infections than men across the lifespan. Other biological explanations implicate the role of our sex hormones. High levels of oestrogen in women appears to delay the onset of CHD by reducing the tendency of blood to clot and keeping blood cholesterol levels low. As oestrogen levels in women fall following the menopause, their risk for CHD rises, indicating a lessening of the protective effect of oestrogen. By contrast, high levels of testosterone in men increase the risk of blood clots, which contribute to the development of atheroma and can trigger a **myocardial infarction** (McGill and Stern 1979).

myocardial infarction death of the heart muscle due to a stoppage of the blood supply. More often known as a heart attack.

A second apparently biological cause of higher levels of disease in men results from their greater physiological response to stress than women. Men typically have greater increases in stress hormones, blood pressure and cholesterol in response to stressors than women – all responses that may make them at more risk for CHD (see Chapter 8). Whether these differences are the result of innate biological differences or contextual factors, however, is not always clear. Lundberg, de Chateau, Winberg et al. (1981) found that women in traditionally male occupations exhibited the same level of stress

hormones as did men in similar jobs. She also found that when women felt equally or more threatened by a laboratory stressor than men, their physiological response equalled those of men. It seems that it is not so much the gender of the individual that drives their physiological reactivity. Rather, it is the type of stress that the person is exposed to. Accordingly, any differences in stress reactivity may be more the result of long-term exposure to different stresses between the genders rather than biologically determined differences.

Behavioural differences

Further evidence that these gender differences in mortality are not purely biological stems from studies that show clear health-related behavioural differences between men and women. More men than women engaged in all but three of fourteen non-gender-specific types of health-risk behaviour examined by Powell-Griner, Anderson and Murphy (1997), including smoking, drinking alcohol, drink driving, not using safety belts and not attending health screening. Men may also encounter adverse working conditions more frequently than women. About 6–7 percent of men drink alcohol heavily – in comparison with 2 percent of women. In addition, women are more likely than men to eat wholemeal bread, fruit and vegetables at least once per day, and to drink semi-skimmed milk. In addition, although rates of smoking are higher among adolescent girls than among adolescent boys, this is only a short-term effect, and more men than women smoke in adulthood.

Not only do men engage in more health-risking behaviour, they are also less likely than women to seek medical help when necessary. Men visit their doctor less frequently than do women, even after excluding visits relating to children and 'reproductive care' (Verbrugge and Steiner 1985). Even when they are ill, men are less likely to consult a doctor than women. Socially disadvantaged women are twice as likely to consult a doctor than their male counterparts when they are ill. High-earning men are even less likely to consult a doctor when ill than their female counterparts (Department of Health and Human Resources 1998).

The reasons for these behavioural differences may be social in origin. Courtenay (2000), for example, contended that they arise from different meanings given to health-related behaviour by the different sexes. They reflect issues of masculinity, femininity and power. According to Courtenay, men show their masculinity and power by engaging in health-risking behaviour and not showing signs of weakness – even when ill. Societal norms endorse the beliefs that men are independent, self-reliant, strong and tough. Courtenay suggested, for example, that when men say 'I haven't been to a doctor in years', they are both reporting a health practice and making a statement about their masculinity. Similar processes are at work when men refuse to take sick leave from work or claim that their driving is better when they've had something to drink. By contrast, illness is threatening to masculinity. Jaffe (1997), for example, noted the advice given to a US senator not to 'go public' about his prostate cancer as some men might think his willingness to go public with his private struggle a sign of weakness. Charmaz (1994) also noted several examples of quite extreme behaviour in which men would engage in order to hide their disabilities. Examples included a wheelchair-bound diabetic man skipping lunch (and risking a coma) rather than embarrass

himself by asking for help in the dining area, and a middle-aged man with CHD declining offers of easier jobs to prove he was still capable of strenuous work. The one health behaviour that men consistently engage in more than women is leisure exercise (Reddy, Fleming and Adesso 1992). Interestingly, this may also act as a marker of masculinity and power and carry a social message as well as having implications for health.

Gender inequalities may also impact on other people's behaviour. Evidence from studies of young people's intentions whether or not to engage in safer sex practices suggests that young women are less empowered than men in the negotiation of sexual practices and are less able to follow their intentions to engage in safer sex practices than their male partners. Abbott (1988), for example, found that 40 percent of a sample of Australian women reported having had sexual intercourse on at least one occasion when they did not want to do so as a result of the pressure from their sexual partner.

Socio-economic differences

More women than men may be affected by socio-economic factors. In the UK, for example, nearly 30 percent of women are economically inactive and those in work are predominantly employed in clerical, personal and retail sectors in low-paid work. About two-thirds of adults in the poorest households in the UK are women, and women make up 60 percent of adults in households dependent on Income Support (a marker of a particularly low income) (see Acheson 1998). Social isolation is also more frequent among women than men: women are less likely to drive or to have access to a car than men, and older women are more likely than older men to be widowed and to live alone. These factors may also impact adversely on health.

Work and health

Some of the excess mortality among people in lower socio-economic groups may result from the different work environments experienced by people across the socio-economic groups. Part of this difference may reflect the physical risks associated with particular jobs. Although health and safety legislation has improved the working conditions of most workers, there are still environments, such as building sites, that carry a significant risk of injury or disability. Work factors may also influence levels of engagement in health-compromising behaviour. Ames and Janes (1987), for example, found that job alienation, job stress, inconsistent social controls and the evolution of a drinking culture were particularly associated with heavy drinking among blue-collar workers. Similarly, Westman, Eden and Shirom (1985) found that long work hours, lack of control over work and poor social support were each associated with high levels of smoking among blue-collar workers. Despite these differences across social groups, most psychological research has focused on theories that suggest there is something intrinsic to different work environments that impacts directly on health – work stress.

Work stress

One of the first, and certainly the most influential, models to systematically consider elements of the work environment that contributed to work stress and illness was the job strain model of Karasek and Theorell (1990). Their model identified three key factors that contribute to work stress:

1. the demands of the job;
2. the degree of freedom to make decisions about how best to cope with these demands (job autonomy); and
3. the degree of available social support.

These elements interact to predict stress and stress-related risk of disease. Karasek and Theorell's model differed markedly from previous models of work stress, which suggested that stress was simply an outcome of the demands placed on the person – a model that gave rise to the idea of the classic 'stressed executive'. Instead, it suggests that only when high levels of demand are combined with low levels of autonomy, and perhaps low levels of social support, will the individual feel stressed and be at risk for disease. This high demand–low autonomy combination is called high job strain by Karasek and colleagues. Where an individual experiences high levels of demand combined with high levels of autonomy (e.g. being able to choose when and how to tackle a problem) and good social support, they will experience less stress than in the high-strain segment. Measures of each dimension of this model suggest that those who are in the highest-strain jobs are often blue-collar workers or those in relatively low-level supervisory posts (see Figure 2.3).

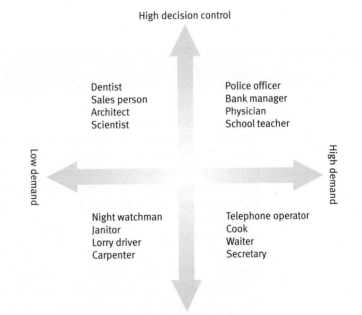

Figure 2.3 Some of the occupations that fit into the four quadrants of the Karasek and Theorell model.

The majority of studies exploring the health outcomes of differing combinations of these work elements support Karasek's model. Kristensen (1995), for example, reviewed sixteen studies measuring the association between job strain and mental and physical health outcomes. Fourteen reported significant associations between conditions of high job strain and an increased incidence of either CHD or poor mental health. More recently, Nordstrom, Dwyer, Merz *et al.* (2001) measured the degree of atheroma in the arteries of 467 working men and found that levels of atheroma were highest among men with the highest job strain scores. No such association was found among women. By contrast, there is no evidence that job strain is related to the development of cancer (e.g. Achat, Kawachi, Byrne *et al.* 2000).

An alternative model of work stress has been proposed by Siegrist, Peter, Junge *et al.* (1990). They suggested that work stress is the result of an imbalance between perceived efforts and rewards. High effort with high reward is seen as acceptable; high effort with low reward combine to result in emotional distress and adverse health effects. This theory has received less attention than that of Karasek, and most studies of this model (see de Lange *et al.* 2003) have focused on the impact of imbalance on wellbeing rather than physical health. Nevertheless, in a five-year longitudinal study tracking over 10,000 British civil servants (the Whitehall Study II, see RESEARCH FOCUS above; Stansfeld *et al.* 1998), both theories received some support: lack of autonomy, low levels of social support in work, and effort–reward imbalance each independently predicted poor physical health.

Gender differentials

Reflecting some of the previous discussion, there is consistent evidence that working environments have a differing effect on men and women. For men, the experience of work stress and its impact on health is generally a function of the working environment alone. For women, work stress frequently combines with other areas of demand in their lives to influence levels of stress and risk for disease. The term 'work–home spillover' has been used to describe this issue. Women still tend to carry more responsibilities in the home and outside work than men. As a consequence, once they have finished paid work, women are more likely than men to continue working in the home and experience strain. This argument is perhaps exemplified in the physiological findings of Lundberg, de Chateau, Winberg *et al.* (1981), who found that female managers' stress hormone levels remained raised following work, while those of male managers typically fell. This effect was particularly marked where the female managers had children. It seems that while the men they studied relaxed once they went home, the women continued their efforts – only the context changed.

This psychological and physiological strain also appears to influence risk for disease. Having a job appears to improve the health of both men and women – the so-called 'healthy worker effect'. This may be because of the social contact available at work as well as feelings of control, self-esteem and the financial security associated with work. However, there appears to be a stress threshold, which differs for men and women, related to work–home spillover, above which work may have a detrimental effect on health. Haynes and Feinleib (1980), for example, found that working women with three or more children were more likely to develop CHD than those with no children.

Adding to this issue, Alfredsson, Spetz and Theorell (1985) found important gender differences in the impact of working overtime. They found, as predicted by Karasek's model, that high levels of job strain were associated with high rates of CHD in both sexes. However, working overtime was associated with a *decreased* risk of CHD among men, while it was associated with an *increased* risk in women. For women, working ten hours or more of overtime per week was associated with a 30 percent increase in risk of CHD. It appears that men may have compensated for their increase in working hours by a decrease in demands elsewhere in life. Such compensation may not have been possible for the women they studied, and working overtime simply increased the total demands made on them and resulted in increased rates of stress and ill-health.

Unemployment

Not having a job appears to have negative effects on both mental and physical health, at least in the short to medium term (e.g. Bartley, Sacker and Clarke 2004). Many of the studies that have investigated the impact of unemployment on long-term health have been confounded by the fact that some of those made unemployed were already in poor health, which led to poor work performance and their unemployment (the social drift model: Dooley, Fielding and Levi 1996). In addition, those who are ill when they become unemployed or become ill in the short term are unlikely to gain further employment, meaning that unless these factors are taken into account in any analysis, explanation of any association between long-term unemployment and ill-health as causal may be spurious. This has led cautious commentators such as Weber and Lehnert (1997) to contend that the evidence of a direct causal link between long-term unemployment and poor health is, at present, unwarranted. Their concerns are further added to by findings that those who become unemployed increase their levels of smoking and alcohol consumption. While it is possible to argue that this makes unemployment a cause of ill-health within a chain of events (unemployment – increased smoking and alcohol consumption – poor health), it cannot be shown that unemployment is a direct cause of ill-health (Stronks, VandeMheen, VandenBos *et al.* 1997).

Despite this cautionary note, there is some evidence of short-term increases in ill-health among employees who are made redundant as the result of large-scale lay-offs not related to their own job performance that cannot be attributed to excessive smoking or drinking. Ferrie, Martikainen, Shipley *et al.* (2001; see RESEARCH FOCUS above), for example, found that not obtaining a secure job or remaining unemployed following redundancy were associated with significant increases in minor psychiatric and health complaints, the main cause of which appeared to be the financial insecurity that goes with unemployment rather than the loss of a job *per se*. Other studies (e.g. Janlert, Asplund and Weinehall 1992) have reported links between unemployment and increases in cholesterol levels or systolic/diastolic blood pressure, but the clinical relevance of such slight changes is not great.

What do YOU think?

If health is, at least in part, a result of the social and environmental contexts in which we live, then how can society go about reducing them? Most health promotion has focused on changing individual behaviour, such as smoking or lack of exercise. But is this just tinkering at the edge? Should society work towards changing the health inequalities associated with low SES? Or should we adopt the American model of 'opportunity' to become economically upwardly mobile, and those left behind fend for themselves? If society does take responsibility for reducing social inequalities, how can it set about doing so? And what about the health disadvantages of people in ethnic minorities and women with children at work? How much should society involve itself in improving the health of these groups?

Summary

Poverty is the main cause of ill-health throughout the world. However, psychosocial factors may also influence health where any relatively subtle effects of profound poverty are not found.

One broad social factor that has been found to account for significant variations in health across different social groups is the socio-economic status of different groups. This relationship appears to be the result of a number of factors, including:

- differential levels of behaviour, such as smoking and levels of exercise, across the social groups;
- differing levels of stress associated with differences in the living environment, levels of day-to-day stress, and the presence or absence of uplifts, which differ across social groups;
- differential access to healthcare and differential uptake of healthcare that is provided;
- a process of negative social comparison that results from relative inequalities.

A second factor that may influence health is being part of a social minority, whether defined by culture and skin colour or behaviour. In both cases, the experience of prejudice may contribute significantly to levels of stress and disease.

- As many people in minority ethnic groups may also occupy lower socio-economic groups, they may experience further stress as a result of this double inequity.
- Among individuals in potentially 'hidden' minorities, such as people who are gay or who have HIV infection, the strain of keeping their status hidden may in itself be detrimental to their health.

Gender may influence health, but not only because of biological differences between the sexes. Levels of hormones such as progesterone, for example, appear to protect women against CHD, a protection that disappears following the menopause. However, many apparent biological differences may result from the different psychosocial experiences of men and women:

■ The type of work setting appears to be a more important cause of physiological stress processes than the gender of the individual.

■ Men engage in more health-compromising behaviour than women.

■ Men are less likely to seek help following the onset of illness than women.

■ Many women are economically inactive or in lower-paid jobs than men. This makes them vulnerable to the problems associated with low socio-economic status.

The relationship between work and health is complex. Having a job is better for one's health than not having a job. However, if the strain of having a job is combined with significant demands away from the job, this can impact adversely on health. Many women, for example, appear to have high levels of work–home spillover, with its adverse effects on both mental and physical health.

■ Jobs with high levels of demand and low levels of autonomy appear to be more stressful and more related to ill-health than other types of job.

■ The financial uncertainties associated with unemployment also appear to have a negative impact on health.

Further reading

Adler, N.E., Boyce, T., Chesney, M.A. *et al.* (1994). Socioeconomic status and health. The challenge of the gradient. *American Psychologist*, 49: 15–24.
A widely cited and well-regarded American view of the socio-economic issues.

Carroll, D., Davey Smith, G. and Bennett, P. (1996). Social class and health: the widening gap. *Journal of Health Psychology*, 1: 23–39.
A European take on the same issues.

Nazroo, J.Y. (2003). The structuring of ethnic inequalities in health: economic position, racial discrimination, and racism. *American Journal of Public Health*, 93: 277–84.
A useful review by an acknowledged expert in the area.

Doyal, L. (2003). Sex and gender: the challenges for epidemiologists. *International Journal of Health Services*, 33: 569–79.
A recent review considering both biological and social factors relating to women's health.

Orth-Gomer, K. *et al.* (eds) (1997). *Women, Stress and Heart Disease*. Lawrence Erlbaum.
An interesting collection of papers addressing issues related to gender and heart disease.

Kuper, H. and Marmot, M. (2003). Job strain, job demands, decision latitude, and risk of coronary heart disease within the Whitehall II study. *Journal of Epidemiology and Community Health*, 57: 147–53.
A recent report from the Whitehall Study examining the relationship between job strain and CHD.

CHAPTER 3

Health-risk behaviour

Learning outcomes

By the end of this chapter, you should have an understanding of:

- how to define and describe health behaviour
- what health behaviour is associated with elevated disease risk
- the range and complexity of influences upon the uptake and maintenance of health-risk behaviour
- some of the challenges facing health behaviour research

Image: Rex Features/Jon Angerson

CHAPTER OUTLINE

Behaviour is linked to health. This has been shown over decades of painstaking research that has examined individual lifestyles and behaviour and attempted to identify relationships between these and the development of illness. For example, it has been estimated that up to three-quarters of cancer deaths are attributable to a person's behaviour. This chapter provides an overview of the evidence pertaining to an array of behaviour shown to increase an individual's risk of disease, such as an unhealthy diet, smoking, excessive alcohol consumption and unprotected sexual behaviour. Evidence regarding the negative health consequences of each type of behaviour is reviewed, and the prevalence of each behaviour considered in relation to health guidelines. Both the health-risk behaviour described here and the health-enhancing behaviour described in Chapter 4 provide the impetus for many educational and public health initiatives worldwide.

What is health behaviour?

Kasl and Cobb (1966a: 246) defined health behaviour as 'any activity undertaken by a person believing themselves to be healthy for the purposes of preventing disease or detecting it at an asymptomatic stage'. This definition was influenced by a medical perspective in that it assumes that healthy people engage in particular behaviour, such as exercise or seeking medical attention, purely to prevent their chance of disease onset. However, this very specific definition should be viewed with caution. Many people engage in a variety of apparently health-related behaviour, such as exercise, for reasons other than disease prevention, including weight control, appearance, as a means of gaining social contacts, and pleasure. Nevertheless, whether intentional or not, engaging in health behaviour may prevent disease and may also prevent the progression of disease once it is established. This perspective was acknowledged by Harris and Guten (1979), who defined health behaviour as 'behaviour performed by an individual, regardless of his/her perceived health status, with the purpose of protecting, promoting or maintaining his/her health'. According to this definition, health behaviour could include the behaviour of 'unhealthy' people. For example, an individual who has had a heart attack may change their diet to help to control their disease, just as a healthy person may change their diet in order to reduce their future risk of heart disease. Further elaboration of definitions of health behaviour was provided by Matarazzo (1984), who distinguished between what he termed 'behavioural pathogens' and 'behavioural immunogens'.

behavioural pathogen a behavioural practice thought to be damaging to health, e.g. smoking.

behavioural immunogen a behavioural practice considered to be health-protective, e.g. exercise.

In spite of such definitional differences, health behaviour research now generally adopts the view that health behaviour is that which is associated with an individual's health status, regardless of current health or motivations. In order to test such associations, longitudinal studies are necessary, and the Alameda County study is notable in this regard (e.g. Belloc and Breslow 1972; Breslow 1983). This study has, to date, followed 7,000 adults, all of whom were healthy at the beginning of the study, for over fifteen years. By comparing the differences on a variety of baseline measures between those people who developed disease and those who remained healthy, this study enabled the identification of key behavioural factors associated with health and longevity. These have been termed the 'Alameda seven':

■ sleeping seven–eight hours a night;
■ not smoking;
■ consuming no more than one–two alcoholic drinks per day;
■ getting regular exercise;
■ not eating between meals;
■ eating breakfast;
■ being no more than 10 percent overweight.

The benefits of engaging in these types of behaviour were cumulative – the more an individual engaged in, the longer they were likely to live. Fewer than 4 percent of both females and males who engaged in all seven types of behaviour had died at the fifteen-year follow-up, compared with 7–13 percent of females and males who reported performing fewer than four of these activities. Also of note was that the benefits of performing these activities were not simply additive but multiplicative: not smoking and moderate levels of drinking alcohol, for example, conferred more than twice the benefit of having only one of these 'immunogens'. The association between such behaviour and death was also found to increase with age, with marked effects found in those over the age of 65. That the effect of lifestyle continues into older age is important as it suggests that the longer we engage in a particular lifestyle, the more it affects our health; that is, the effects of lifestyle behaviour are not only multiplicative but cumulative.

From a health psychology perspective, understanding that behaviour is predictive of mortality is only part of the story. We also need to know what behaviour is associated with which diseases. If we are to prevent people from engaging in risky behaviour (which is the goal of health promotion – see Chapters 6 and 7), we also need to understand the psychological and social factors that contribute to the uptake of risk behaviour or the avoidance of preventive behaviour. Many epidemiological and clinical studies have examined the relationship between behaviour and the onset of major illnesses such as heart disease or cancer. The associations that have been identified are reviewed in the next section. Other studies, more often conducted by health and social psychologists, have examined how individual and social factors influence the uptake of health behaviour. These factors are alluded to in this and the subsequent chapter but are addressed more fully in Chapter 5.

Individual behaviour, where positively or negatively associated with health, can be a sensitive issue, with some people preferring to keep their practices and motivations to themselves. This can create many challenges for those interested in measuring health or risk behaviour with a view to developing understanding of it. While measurement issues are not confined to studies of health behaviour, they are particularly pertinent in this domain (see ISSUES below).

The challenge of measuring health behaviour

The research tradition assumes that the objects of study, e.g. health, illness, or in the context of this chapter, behaviour, remain as fixed entities in people's minds. However, without a researcher actually being present and observing the individual behaving over long periods of time, it is difficult to know whether the behaviour a person reports to the researcher (or clinician) accurately reflects their actual behaviour. Obtaining valid measures of behaviour is made increasingly difficult when one is interested in behaviour that is perhaps considered 'undesirable' (e.g. excessive alcohol or drug use), or when it is private behaviour (e.g. sexual behaviour). Even when considering 'positive' behaviour such as exercise, researchers face the challenge of knowing how best to define it, and it is only through appropriate definition that measurement becomes possible. For example, rather than defining exercise in terms of organised activity, it could be defined as any physical activity that requires the individual to expend energy, such as walking or doing housework. The definition adopted will influence the questions asked. Furthermore, it is also necessary to note not just the type of exercise but also the frequency, duration and intensity with which it is performed.

In relation to health behaviour, where direct observation and/or objective measurement (for example, taking blood or urine sample) are not possible, researchers have to rely on *self-report*. When studies are interested in the frequency with which certain behaviour is performed, it is commonplace to ask study participants to complete a diary record, for example of cigarettes/alcohol/foods consumed or activities undertaken. Such studies generally require participants to either record behaviour daily for a period of a week (obtaining longer diaries is placing high demand on study participants), or to reflect back on the previous week's activity (a retrospective diary – RD). The latter has obvious memory demands – could you accurately recall how many units of alcohol you drank seven days ago? While there is no evidence of a systematic trend towards overestimation or underestimation (Maisto and Connors 1992; Shakeshaft, Bowman and Sanson-Fisher 1999), some studies attempt to cross-validate behavioural self-reports by obtaining observer ratings or blood samples. However, observation is not always ethical, and biochemical tests are intrusive and costly. Other studies rely on asking participants about their 'typical or average' behaviour. In such studies, individuals, for example, report the typical amount of alcohol consumed (quantity), and the 'typical or average' number of days on which they consume alcohol (frequency) (e.g. Norman *et al.* 1998). However, this type of measure, known as a quantity/frequency index (QFI) may provide over-general information. For example, Shakeshaft and colleagues (1999) compared an RD method of collecting weekly alcohol consumption information, with a QFI, and found that the RD method elicited higher reported levels of consumption than did the QFI. In fact, neither way may be totally accurate.

One way of minimising inaccuracies in reporting is by using continuous *self-monitoring techniques*, such as smoking or food consumption diaries, with a much shorter recording period, e.g. hourly. Self-monitoring by means of diary keeping can be a useful method of establishing patterns of behaviour and the circumstances in which they occur (e.g. McCann, Retzlaff, Dowdy *et al.* 1990, dietary adherence; Morrison 1988, alcohol and illicit drug use). For example, smoking or food consumption diaries commonly instruct the person completing them to note not only the time at which each cigarette is smoked/meal or snack consumed but also the location, whether anyone else was present, whether any particular 'cue' existed and the reasons for consumption. Some will also invite the person to note whether they are currently experiencing positive or negative emotions. A potential limitation of self-monitoring is that it can be reactive; in other words, it acts as an intervention itself, with participants modifying their consumption on the basis of their increased awareness of their intake. Behaviour that is seen as undesirable is likely to decrease while being monitored, whereas desirable behaviour is likely to increase. This may be useful in a clinical context, where the intention of self-monitoring *is* behaviour change, but in a research context it may be obstructive; for example, it may prevent researchers from obtaining reliable baseline measurement of behaviour against which to evaluate the efficacy of an intervention programme. Reliance on self-monitoring data can also create problems clinically; for example, Warren and Hixenbaugh (1998) reviewed evidence that people with diabetes make up their self-monitored blood glucose levels and found that, in some studies, individuals did so in order to present a more positive clinical profile to their medical practitioner (i.e. self-presentation bias/**social desirability bias**). This behaviour could potentially disadvantage treatment efficacy or disease management and outcomes.

social desirability bias the tendency to answer questions about oneself or one's behaviour in a way that is thought likely to meet with social (or interviewer) approval.

Self-monitoring techniques are not the only data collection technique with the potential to elicit self-presentation bias. For some purposes, researchers choose to collect data via *face-to-face interviews*. These can enable a researcher to seek more explanation for a person's behaviour through the use of open-ended questions such as 'Think back to your first underage drink of alcohol. What would you say motivated it? How did you feel afterwards?' Interviews also facilitate the building of rapport with participants, which may be particularly important if the study requires participants to attend follow-up interviews or complete repeated assessments. Rapport may increase commitment to the study and improve retention rates. However, in spite of these advantages, the interview process, content and style may also influence participants' responses. For example, some people may not report their 'risk behaviour' practices (e.g. illicit drug use, unprotected sexual intercourse) or lack of preventive behaviour practices (e.g. toothbrushing, exercising) if they believe they will be judged to be 'deviant', in poor health, or simply as being careless with their health (e.g. Davies and Baker 1987). Impression management is common; i.e. people monitor and control (actively construct) what they say in order to give particular impressions of themselves (or to achieve certain effects) to particular audiences (Allport 1920 first noted this in the domain of social psychology). So is what is assessed a true representation of behaviour or simply the outcome of self-presentational processes? It is probably best to assume that they are a bit of both, and when reading statistics regarding the prevalence of particular behaviour, stop to consider the methods used in generating the data and ask yourself what biases, if any, may be present.

Health-risk behaviour

The message of the director-general of the World Health Organization (WHO), in the opening to the *World Health Report* (WHO 2002: 3) was stark, but clear. It stated:

> in many ways, the world is a safer place today. Safer from what were once deadly or incurable diseases. Safer from daily hazards of waterborne and food-related illnesses. Safer from dangerous consumer goods, from accidents at home, at work, or in hospitals. But in many other ways the world is becoming more dangerous. Too many of us are living dangerously – whether we are aware of that or not.

This report by the WHO followed massive worldwide research into health risks in developed, developing and underdeveloped countries. Although specific health risks may vary across the world (for example, under-consumption of food in many African nations versus over-consumption in most Western countries), there are many commonalities such as risk conferred by smoking tobacco.

The WHO lists the 'top ten' leading risk factors globally, which together account for more than a third of all deaths worldwide, as:

1. being underweight
2. unprotected sexual intercourse
3. high blood pressure
4. tobacco consumption
5. alcohol consumption
6. unsafe water, poor sanitation and hygiene
7. iron deficiency
8. indoor smoke from solid fuels
9. high cholesterol
10. obesity.

For reasons of length, it is impossible to address all ten of these in this chapter, even though the statistics attached to some are horrendous and thought-provoking. Over three million childhood deaths, for example, occur every year in developing countries as a result of being underweight. By contrast, about half a million people die each year in North America and Europe as a result of an obesity-related disease. Behaviour which is associated with high levels of **mortality** in developed countries such as the USA and Europe are highlighted below and discussed in more detail, as they tend also to be the behaviour that has attracted the greatest attention from health psychologists to date.

mortality
death. Generally presented as mortality statistics, i.e. the number of deaths in a given population and/or in a given year ascribed to a given condition (e.g. number of cancer deaths among women in 2000).

- *heart disease*: smoking tobacco, high-cholesterol diet, lack of exercise;
- *cancer*: smoking tobacco, alcohol, diet, sexual behaviour;
- *stroke*: smoking tobacco, high-cholesterol diet, alcohol;
- *pneumonia, influenza*: smoking tobacco, lack of vaccination;
- *HIV/AIDS*: unsafe/unprotected sexual intercourse.

With the exception of HIV/AIDS, these diseases are more common in middle age and beyond than in younger people. Given the worldwide increase in the proportion of the population aged 60 or above, the prevalence of such diseases in our communities will make increasing and significant demands on healthcare systems. To illustrate this point further, the proportion of individuals aged over 65 has doubled between 1940 and 2000; worldwide it is estimated that those over 60 years old will increase from the current one in ten, to one in five by 2050; and those over 80 years old is likely to increase from 11 to 19 percent in the same period (United Nations Secretariat 2002).

Unhealthy diet

What and how we eat plays an important role in our long-term health. Heart disease and some forms of cancer have been directly associated with diet. Our dietary intake and behaviour (e.g. snacking, bingeing) may also confer an indirect risk of disease through its effect on weight and obesity – something we turn to later in the chapter.

The degree of risk for cancer conferred by diet may be surprising. While many cancer deaths (approximately 30 percent: Doll and Peto 1981) are attributed to smoking cigarettes, it is perhaps a lesser-known fact that 35 percent of cancer deaths are attributable, in part, to poor diet. A diet involving significant intake of high-fat foods, high levels of salt and low levels of fibre appears to be particularly implicated (World Cancer Research Fund 1997).

Fat intake and cholesterol

Excessive fat intake has been found to be implicated in disease and death from several serious illnesses, including coronary heart disease and cancer (particularly breast cancer; e.g. Cohen 1987). Fatty foods, particularly foods high in saturated fats (such as animal products and some vegetable oils), contain substances known as low-density lipoproteins (LDL), which enter our bloodstreams. These LDLs carry cholesterol molecules around the bloodstream and can result in the formation of plaques in the arteries. Cholesterol carried by LDL's is often called 'bad cholesterol' whereas cholesterol carried by high density lipoproteins is called 'good cholesterol' as it appears to increase the processing and removal of LDLs by the liver. Cholesterol is a lipid (fat) which is present in our own bodily cells but these normal levels can be increased by a fatty diet (and by other factors such as age). Normal circulating cholesterol has a purpose in that it is synthesised to produce steroid hormones and is involved in the production of bile necessary for digestion, but high levels in our bloodstream can reflect high saturated fat intake which is damaging to our health. Some foods, such as polyunsaturated fats which can be more easily metabolised in the body, or foods such as oily fish which contain Omega-3 fatty acids and which have been found to raise HDL levels, are beneficial to one's health.

The health argument is that if fat molecules, a good store of energy in our bodies, are not metabolised during exercise or activity, then their circulating levels become high, and plaques (fatty layers) are laid down on the artery walls (**atherosclerosis**), causing them to thicken and restrict blood flow to the heart. An often related condition, **arteriosclerosis**, exists when increased blood pressure causes artery walls to lose elasticity and harden, with resulting effects on the ability of the cardiovascular system to adapt to increased blood flow (such as during exercise). These arterial diseases are together referred to as CAD (coronary artery disease) and form a major risk factor for angina pectoris (a painful sign of arterial obstruction restricting oxygen flow) and coronary heart disease (CHD). The 'bad' cholesterols (LDLs) are implicated in this process, although the actual strength of the link between fatty food intake and blood cholesterol levels is unclear.

Reduced fat intake is therefore a target of health interventions, not solely because of its effects on body weight and potentially obesity (see later) but because of the links with CHD. Evidence for this link has come from many studies, including the large prospective MRFIT (multiple risk factor intervention trial) study, which followed over 350,000 adults over six years and found a significant linear relationship between baseline cholesterol level and subsequent heart disease or stroke (Neaton, Blackburn, Jacobs *et al.* 1992). It has been shown that a 10 percent reduction in serum (blood) cholesterol is

atherosclerosis
formation of fatty plaque in the arteries.

arteriosclerosis
loss of elasticity and hardening of the arteries.

associated at five-year follow-up with a 54 percent reduction in the incidence of coronary heart disease at age 40, a 27 percent reduction at age 60 and a 19 percent reduction at age 80 (Law, Wald and Thompson 1994; Navas-Nacher, Colangelo, Beam *et al.* 2001). Additional evidence as to the role of fat intake in breast cancer incidence comes from multi-centre studies of diet and cancer deaths. Cohen (1987), for example, presented correlational evidence of higher breast cancer death rates in countries where high fat intake is common (e.g. the UK, the Netherlands, the USA) than in countries where dietary fat intake is lower (e.g. Japan, the Philippines). However, firm causal data is still required.

As a result of these and other data, governmental policy documents have been produced in many countries that provide guidelines for healthy eating and dietary targets. In the UK, for example, the Department of Health produced *The Health of the Nation* report (1992), which recommended that a maximum of 35 percent of food energy should be derived from fat intake, of which a maximum of only 11 percent should come from saturated fats. Despite these recommendations, average consumption figures appear to remain around 40 percent. It is worth noting that a systematic review (*Cochrane Review*) of evidence derived from four randomised controlled trials concluded that fat-restricted diets were no more effective than calorie-restricted diets in terms of long-term weight loss among overweight or obese individuals (Pirozzo, Summerbell, Cameron *et al.* 2003), suggesting that dietary change should not focus solely on fat intake, but on total intake.

Salt

systolic blood pressure
the maximum pressure of blood on the artery walls, which occurs at the end of the left ventricle output/contraction (measured in relation to **diastolic blood pressure**).

diastolic blood pressure
the minimum pressure of the blood on the walls of the arteries between heart beats (measured in relation to **systolic blood pressure**).

Salt intake is also a target of preventive health measures, with high salt (sodium chloride) intake being implicated in those with persistent high blood pressure, i.e. hypertension. The detrimental effects of high salt intake appear to persist even when levels of physical activity, obesity and other health behaviour are controlled for (Law, Frost and Walde 1991).

A recent systematic review and meta-analysis of intervention trials assessed the impact of lowering salt intake in adults who were either normotensive (i.e. 'normal' blood pressure), who had high blood pressure that was not being treated, or who had high blood pressure that was being treated using drug therapy (Hooper, Bartlett, Davey-Smith *et al.* 2002). Overall, the results of these trials were somewhat mixed in that salt reduction resulted in reduced **systolic** and **diastolic blood pressure**; however, the degree to which blood pressure fell was not related to the amount of salt reduction. In addition, the trials had no impact on the number of heart disease-related deaths over follow-ups lasting from seven months to seven years, with deaths found to be equally distributed across the intervention and control groups. The authors therefore concluded that interventions targeting salt intake provide only limited health benefits.

In spite of mixed findings such as these, guidelines exist as to recommended levels of salt intake. High salt intake is considered to be in excess of 6 g per day for adults and over 5 g per day for children aged 7 to 14 (British Medical Association 2003a). While it is perhaps difficult to establish the unique health benefits of a reduced-salt diet when examining individuals engaged in more general dietary change behaviour, the BMA guidelines raise awareness of the need to monitor salt intake from early childhood onwards.

Obesity

We address obesity in this chapter, in spite of it not being a behaviour, because of growing national and international concern about its increasing prevalence and because it is contributed to by a combination of poor diet and a lack of exercise, both of which are types of behaviour that health psychologists are seeking to understand.

How is obesity defined?

When exactly is a person considered clinically obese? Obesity is generally measured in terms of an individual's body mass index (BMI), which is calculated as a person's weight in kilograms divided by their height in metres squared (weight/height^2). An individual is considered to be

- 'normal' if their BMI is between 20 and 24.9;
- mildly obese (grade 1) if their BMI is between 25 and 29.9 (although these individuals are generally referred to simply as overweight);
- moderate or clinically obese (grade 2) if their BMI falls between 30 and 39.9;
- severely obese (grade 3) if their BMI is 40 or greater.

Negative health consequences of obesity

We noted at the outset of this chapter that while being underweight is the largest global cause of mortality, a growing number of people, predominantly in Western or developed countries, are at risk from the opposite problem – obesity. Obesity has been identified as a major risk factor in a range of physical illnesses, including hypertension, heart disease, type 2 diabetes, osteoarthritis and lower back pain, and it is also implicated in psychological ill-health such as low self-esteem and social isolation (British Medical Association 2003a). The relative risk of disease appears to increase proportionately in relation to the percentage overweight a person is, although evidence as to this linear relationship remains mixed.

In terms of mortality, the longitudinal Framingham heart study shows that the relationship between obesity and mortality is seen only in the long term (over two–three decades), with the risk of death within twenty-six years being increased by 1 percent per extra pound in weight in those aged between 30 and 42 and by 2 percent per extra pound in those aged 50 to 62. The J-shaped curve shown in Figure 3.1 also reminds us of the risk of being underweight, with the lowest mortality in those within the ideal weight range (body mass index 20–24.9).

Prevalence of obesity

The European Commission (1999) estimates that 31 percent of the EU adult population is overweight, with a further 10 percent reaching weights defined as clinically obese. Alarmingly, excess body weight has recently been identified as the most common child disorder in Europe (International

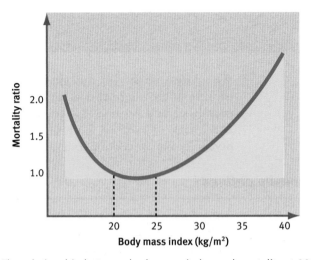

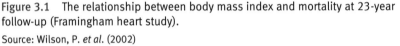

Figure 3.1   The relationship between body mass index and mortality at 23-year follow-up (Framingham heart study).

Source: Wilson, P. *et al.* (2002)

Obesity Taskforce and European Association for the Study of Obesity 2002). A 1997 survey of young people (16–24) combined interviews about health behaviour with an array of physical measurements, including lung function tests and blood samples. Six percent of young males and 8 percent of young females were classified as clinically obese; a further 23 percent and 19 percent, respectively, were overweight, and 17 percent of both genders were underweight (Department of Health 1998a). Unlike the findings from studies of mid–older adults (e.g. White, Nicolaas, Foster *et al.* 1993), social class was related to increased obesity for young females, but not for males. Obese children tend to grow up to be obese adults. Obesity also increases the childhood risk of metabolic diseases and psychological ill-health, exemplified by low self-esteem often made worse by feelings of being socially stigmatised (e.g. Strauss 2000; Stunkard and Wadden 1993).

What causes obesity?

A simple explanation of obesity is that it is a condition that results from an energy intake that grossly exceeds the energy output (Pinel 2003). However, there is also evidence from twin studies and studies of adopted children (e.g. Meyer and Stunkard 1993; Price and Gottesman 1991) that there is a genetic component to obesity. Genetic explanations are generally one of three types:

1. Suggestions that obese individuals are born with a greater number of fat cells. Evidence of this is limited. For example, the number of fat cells in a person of average weight and in many mildly obese individuals is typically 25–35 million, yet the number of cells is dramatically increased in a severely obese person, implying the formation of new fat cells.

2. Suggestions that obese persons inherit lower metabolic rates. However, obese people are not consistently found to have lower metabolic rates than comparable thin persons.

3. Explanations arising from studies that have sought to identify a hormone responsible for appetite control, or lack of control.

This latter explanation has received growing attention since the 1950s, when a scientific laboratory containing a mice colony identified a gene mutation in some of the mice that had become highly obese (Coleman 1979). Subsequent cloning of this mutated gene found that it was only expressed in fat cells and that it encoded a protein hormone called leptin (Zhang, Proenca, Maffie *et al.* 1994). Leptin levels are positively correlated with fat deposits in humans; low levels of injected leptin have been found to reduce eating behaviour and thus body fat in obese mice. This appears to happen due to leptin-signalling receptors in the hypothalamus, which controls functions such as eating (see Chapter 8). However, Pinel (2003) describes how research has not found similar genetic mutation in all obese humans and how injected leptin has not consistently reduced body fat in the obese. However, for the small number of individuals who have been found to hold the gene mutation, leptin therapy may have some potential (e.g. Farooqi, Jebb, Langmack *et al.* 1999). Another avenue of research has identified that serotonin, a neurotransmitter (see Chapter 8), is directly involved in producing satiety (the condition where hunger is no longer felt). Early animal experiments investigating the effects on hunger of administering a serotonin **agonist** have had their findings confirmed in humans, where the introduction of serotonin agonists into the body induced satiety, reduced the frequency and quantity of food intake, and body weight (Halford and Blundell 2000). This line of research holds promise for future intervention.

agonist
a drug that simulates the effects of neurotransmitters, such as the serotonin agonist fluoxetine, which induces satiety (reduces hunger).

However, the recent upsurge in obesity in developed Western countries is more plausibly attributed to environmental factors such as lifestyle and behaviour patterns than to any increase in genetic predisposition towards obesity. There is a growing tendency for people of all ages to pass their time indoors, for example with media and computing technology (Allied Dunbar National Fitness Survey 1992). Sedentary activities such as watching television can in fact reduce a person's metabolic rate, so that their bodies burn up existing calories more slowly. Lack of physical activity in combination with overeating, or eating the wrong food types (particularly fatty foods) are potent predictors of obesity, although the main (or primary) causal factor is unclear. Our energy intake has perhaps not risen as much as our energy output has declined (Prentice and Jebb 1995) but with epidemiologists predicting a threefold increase in obesity in the UK between 1980 and 2005 (Department of Health 1995), effective interventions are high on the public health agenda in the UK as elsewhere in Europe, and in the USA (see Chapters 6 and 7). These interventions have the aim of making our currently 'obesogenic' environments (BMA 2003a) and behaviour more healthy, and addressing healthy eating and, perhaps even more so, exercise behaviour (see Chapter 4).

■ A final thought on obesity

A word of caution is drawn from the BMA report (2003a) referred to previously: we as individuals, and as a society, must be careful not to over-focus on the weight of individual children – while obesity is on the increase, so too is extreme dietary behaviour and eating disorders. Several recent studies point to increasing body dissatisfaction among children and adolescents, particularly females (e.g. Ricciardelli and McCabe 2001; Schur, Sanders and Steiner 2000). Body dissatisfaction, if taken to extremes in terms of dietary restraint, can potentially have adverse physical and psychological consequences in terms of eating disorders (e.g. Patton, Johnson-Sabine, Wood *et al.* 1990).

Alcohol consumption

Many people drink alcohol (ethanol); it is an integral part of many cultures and a feature of many life events, such as weddings, birthdays and even funerals. Its social use is widespread, although only a small number of people will become dependent on it to the extent that alcohol will lead to damaging health or social consequences.

Negative health effects of excessive alcohol consumption

Alcohol is 'the second most widely used psychoactive substance in the world (after caffeine)' (Julien 1996: 101), and although it is commonly perceived as a stimulant it is in fact a central nervous system depressant. Low doses cause behavioural disinhibition, while high levels of intoxication lead to a 25-fold increase in the likelihood of an accident, and extremely high doses severely affect respiratory rate, which can cause coma and even death (see Figure 3.2).

It is not only alcohol dependence that causes health problems; so too can acute and prolonged episodes of heavy drinking. Heavy alcohol consumption is implicated in accidents (while driving or operating machinery for example);

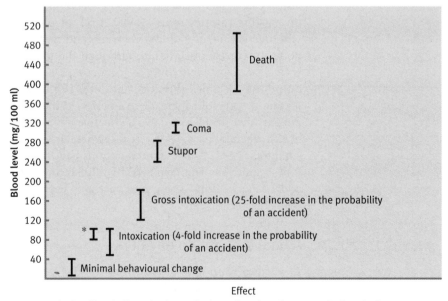

* The legal level of intoxication varies by region, thus the range of values is shown.

Figure 3.2   The particular consequences correlated with different levels of alcohol in a person's bloodstream.

Source: adapted from Julien (1996: 109)

in behavioural problems (aggression, suicide, marital disharmony, etc.), and in diseases such as liver cirrhosis, some forms of cancer, hypertension, heart disease and stroke (e.g. Doll and Peto 1981; Hart, Davey-Smith, Hole *et al.* 1999). For example, Hart *et al.* (1999) carried out a 21-year follow-up study among 5,766 Scottish men and found that those who consumed more than 35 units of alcohol a week were at twice the risk of death from stroke than men whose drinking was at light or moderate levels. Table 3.1 presents World Health Organization data relating to alcohol-related liver cirrhosis mortality reported across Europe (countries reported any year between 1987 and 1993), where it can be seen that incidence per 100,000 population ranged from a substantial 54.8 in Hungary to a much lower incidence of 2.9 in Ireland (contradicting many a myth about Irish drinkers!).

What is also worth noting in the data presented in Table 3.1 are the differences in the male–female ratio in different countries, with the United Kingdom and Ireland having almost the same rates of female cirrhosis as male. Culture and social policy are extremely important in predicting drinking behaviour. Consider, for example, Finland, where previously strict legislation on alcohol sales and consumption was liberalised in the mid-1970s and where cirrhosis deaths showed subsequent increases in figures reported in the 1980s and 1990s.

Table 3.1   Deaths in Europe from liver cirrhosis per 100,000 population, ranked highest to lowest with age standardisation

Country	Total	Standardised mortality		
		Males	Females	M/F ratio
Hungary	54.8	79.7	32.6	2.4
Romania	38.1	47.5	28.8	1.6
Germany, former Democratic Republic	33.7	47.9	19.4	2.5
Austria	28.2	41.2	16.4	2.5
Portugal	26.9	39.3	15.1	2.5
Italy	26.8	31.7	18.0	1.8
Czechoslovakia	25.1	38.1	13.4	2.8
Germany, Federal Republic	22.2	30.4	14.6	2.1
Spain	21.0	30.0	12.9	2.3
Luxembourg	18.7	21.9	15.4	1.4
Former Yugoslavia	18.4	27.7	10.2	2.7
France	17.0	23.3	10.6	2.2
Bulgaria	15.0	22.0	7.8	2.8
Poland	13.9	19.1	9.2	2.1
Belgium	11.9	14.4	9.5	1.5
Finland	10.7	15.3	4.2	3.6
Switzerland	9.5	12.9	6.1	2.1
Malta	9.0	14.0	3.9	3.6
Greece	8.9	12.1	5.8	2.1
Israel	8.7	10.3	7.0	2.5
Sweden	6.8	8.8	4.7	1.9
United Kingdom	6.1	6.9	5.3	1.3
Netherlands	5.1	6.3	3.9	1.6
Norway	4.4	5.4	3.3	1.6
Ireland	2.9	3.1	2.7	1.1

Source: Adapted from Edwards, G. *et al.* (1994)

Recommended levels of drinking

Different individuals respond differently to the same amount of alcohol intake, depending on factors such as body weight, food intake and metabolism, the social context in which the drinking occurs, and the individual's cognitions and expectations. It is therefore difficult to determine 'safe' levels of drinking alcohol. While the recommended guidelines on 'safe' levels of alcohol consumption vary from country to country, the UK government's recommended limit for weekly consumption has recently been raised from 21 units of alcohol to 28 units for males, and from 14 to 21 units of alcohol for females (where half a pint of normal-strength lager or a standard single measure of spirit ($\frac{1}{6}$ gill) or wine of average strength (11–12 percent alcohol) = 1 unit). The lower level of these guidelines had been in existence since 1986, and although the move to increase the guidelines to 28 and 21 units for males and females, respectively, came in 1995 (Royal College of Physicians 1995), many health advisors continue to use the 21/14 limits.

However, there is some confusion internationally as to what constitutes a 'standard' measure. Does it mean the 'strength' of the alcohol or the 'volume'? For example, a standard drink in Japan is defined by government guidelines as 19.75 g alcohol, whereas in the UK a standard drink would contain 8 g. There are many variations in between, as seen in Table 3.2.

Prevalence of drinking alcohol in the young

In *The Health of Young People 1995–1997* survey (Department of Health 1998a), it was found that drinking more than the recommended guidelines of 21 units for males and 14 units for females had remained fairly stable among 16–24-year-olds between 1993–4 and 1995–7. However, a survey of a sample of English 11–15-year-olds (2000 Survey DoH, National Centre for Social Research) showed a significant increase in the amount of alcohol consumed in this age group, from 5.3 units in 1990 to 10.4 units in 2000. The authors suggest that the growth in marketing and sale of alcopops (alcoholic drinks with sweetening and flavourings, marketed with a trendy appearance) played a role in the increased consumption pattern of these young people.

Table 3.2 International definitions of what comprises a 'standard' drink (alcohol in g)

Austria	6
Ireland and UK	8
Iceland	9.5
Netherlands	9.9
Italy, Australia, Spain	10
Finland	11
Denmark, France	12
Canada	13.5
Portugal, USA	14
Hungary	17
Japan	19.75

Source: International Center for Alcohol Policies (1998)

Twenty-four percent of this total sample of over 7,000 children had had an alcoholic drink in the previous week – 5 percent of 11-year-olds and 48 percent of 15-year-olds. Children in Wales (where both authors are based) top the European league for the numbers who drink weekly and get drunk (Paton 1999).

In other parts of Europe, too, there is concern about adolescent drinking. Sweden, a country with historically high government control over alcohol production and sale, actively campaigns for non-consumption of alcohol among teenagers. However, an impressive survey of nearly 13,000 16-years-olds found that about 80 percent had consumed alcohol, 25 percent of whom had drunk illegal, smuggled alcohol, and 40 percent had drunk home-distilled alcohol. Although levels of consumption are not clear, alcohol is clearly not outwith the grasp of these teenagers (Romelsjö and Branting 2000).

Are there positive effects of drinking alcohol?

It is generally accepted that there is a direct linear relationship between the amount of alcohol consumed over time and the accumulation of alcohol-related illness. However, there are a few question marks around the level of drinking that is damaging. For example, it has been suggested that moderate alcohol consumption may be health-protective, with evidence of a J-shaped relationship between alcohol consumption and CHD risk (e.g. Doll, Peto, Hall *et al.* 1994). Moderate drinkers seem to have less risk of heart disease than do heavy, light or even non-drinkers. This surprising finding has emerged from both cross-sectional and prospective studies. The consensus view is that moderate alcohol intake reduces circulating low-density lipoprotein (LDL) levels (high levels are a known risk factor for CHD) (e.g. Jackson, Scragg and Beaglehole 1991; Shaper, Wannamethee and Walker 1994; see IN THE SPOTLIGHT below). However, there are problems in concluding from this, and from studies of non-drinkers where risk of CHD was found to be higher than average, that not drinking confers increased risk. Non-drinkers may choose not to consume alcohol because they are already in poor health, or because they are members of particular religious or ethnic groups that forbid such use: these factors may hide some other 'cause' of CHD. It is safer to conclude only that heavy drinking has negative effects on health that increase in line with consumption; that moderate levels of drinking may not increase risk and may in fact be protective against CHD (although the protective effects are lost on people who smoke); and that the effects of not drinking at all need further exploration.

IN THE SPOTLIGHT

Is drinking red wine good for your health?

For some time, it has been known that fruit and vegetable consumption is associated with a reduced rate of some cancers, in particular cancer of the gastrointestinal tract (e.g. Potter, Slattery, Bostick and Gapstur 1993). This has been attributed to the presence of compounds

continued

known as 'polyphenols'. Red wine contains many different polyphenolic compounds, and red wine intake has been associated with reduced cardiovascular deaths (e.g. German and Walzem 2000; Wollin and Jones 2001). Early studies identified an association between alcohol ingestion and high-density lipoproteins (HDL – see section on unhealthy diet above) thought to be protective against CHD (e.g. Linn, Carroll, Johnson *et al.* 1993). More recently, it has been proposed that red wine polyphenols may also be beneficial in cancer prevention. It is thought that polyphenols inhibit the initiation of carcinogenesis due to their antioxidative or anti-inflammatory properties. Additionally, polyphenols may act as suppressing agents by inhibiting the growth of mutated cells or by inducing apoptosis, i.e. cell death. Recent laboratory and animal studies (e.g. Briviba, Pan and Rechkemmer 2002) have shown that polyphenols isolated from red wine did in fact inhibit the growth of different colon carcinoma cells, but not breast cancer cells.

Medical authorities and public health officials are wary of announcing health 'benefits' of behaviours usually portrayed as detrimental to health, and results of this nature need to be carefully checked and double-checked. Even the authors of one of the research studies, finding a positive effect of alcohol on HDL level, underplayed the implications of their findings (Linn, Carroll, Johnson *et al.* 1993: 811). It is unlikely that many individuals presenting to their GPs with health concerns around a family history of heart disease are told to increase their light alcohol consumption to moderate, and instead will most likely be advised to follow a low-fat diet, yet the protection offered is similar!

When the most recent findings relating to cancer reached the attention of the media, it resulted in the kind of headlines that would lead you to believe a cure for cancer had been found! However, there remains a need for further research among human samples, with tight controls over other contributory factors. It will be some years before the evidence as to the effects of red wine drinking on people already with cancer becomes clear. In relation to coronary heart disease, however, the evidence is of longer standing, and it would appear that moderate ingestion of alcohol, and not solely red wine, has health-protective effects (e.g. Nestle 1997).

Things to think about and research yourself

- Does red wine differ from white wine in terms of its potential effects on health, and if so, how?
- How might some people interpret these kinds of findings – what beliefs might be reinforced?

Why do some people develop drinking problems?

The reasons why young people start to drink alcohol are, as with most social behaviour, many and varied, with genetics and environment playing important roles. Two commonly cited reasons for having that first drink of alcohol are curiosity and sociability (e.g. Morrison and Plant 1991), but curiosity, unlike sociability, is unlikely to be cited as the reason for continued use. For most people, drinking does not become a problem. Much research effort has gone into trying to distinguish between individuals who maintain safe levels of drinking and those who develop problem drinking. The main aspects considered are:

- Genetics and family history of alcohol abuse: children of problem drinkers are more likely to develop problem drinking than children of non-problem drinkers (e.g. Heather and Robertson 1997). Evidence is inconclusive as

Plate 3.1 The importance of social context on behaviour can be seen in these clubbers, where music, company and, often, alcohol (and sometimes other substances) combine to disinhibit behaviour.
Source: Royalty-Free/Corbis

parent–child drinking tendencies could also be socialised (see below), although adoptee studies support evidence of heredity to an extent.

■ The pre-existence of certain psychopathology: mood disorders, anxious **predisposition**, sensation-seeking personality tendencies (e.g. Clark and Sayette 1993; Khantzian 2003; Zuckerman 1979, 1984), although evidence as to personality's role in drinking, or indeed in other substance-use behaviour, remains controversial (Morrison 2003).

■ The social learning experience: social learning theory considers alcohol abuse or dependence to be a socially acquired and learned behaviour that has received reinforcement (internal or external, physical, social or emotional rewards). Addiction may result from repeatedly seeking the pleasurable effects of the substance itself (e.g. Wise 1998).

predisposing factors
factors that increase the likelihood of a person engaging in a particular behaviour, such as genetic influences on alcohol consumption.

Among older people, evidence points to lower levels of alcohol consumption, and in elderly samples, problem drinking has been shown to be influenced by physical health, access to social opportunities and financial status, with the affluent elderly having higher rates of drinking problems (Livingston and Hinchliffe 1993). For some individuals, however, an increase in alcohol consumption can be attributed in part to loneliness, bereavement or physical symptomatology (e.g. Atkinson 1994).

■ Alcohol dependence

Alcohol problems and how those with such problems are viewed by society have changed over time, from being seen as the immoral behaviour of weak individuals unable to exert personal control over their consumption during the seventeenth–eighteenth centuries, to being the behaviour of passive victims of an evil and powerful substance in the nineteenth century. The earlier 'moral' view considered individuals as responsible for their behaviour and therefore the ethos of treatment was punishment. The latter view considered the individual to have less control over their behaviour, and as such the prohibition of alcohol sales in the USA was considered an appropriate societal response, and treatment was offered to those who 'succumbed'. The medical treatment of individuals with alcohol problems reflects the beginnings of a disease concept of addiction. By the early twentieth century, the model of alcoholism developed into one that placed responsibility back onto the individual. In 1960, Jellinek described alcoholism as a disease but considered both the nature of the substance and the pre-existing characteristics of the person who used it. While alcohol could be used by the majority without any resulting harm, a minority of individuals developed alcohol dependence, and for these individuals pre-existing genetic and psychological 'weaknesses' were acknowledged. Addiction was seen as an acquired, permanent state of being over which the individual could regain control only by means of abstinence, and treatment reflected this: for example, the self-help organisation, Alcoholics Anonymous, founded in 1935, had the primary goal of helping individuals to achieve lifelong abstinence.

However, in psychology during the early twentieth century, the growth of **behaviourism** brought with it new methods of treatment for those with drinking problems that drew from the principles of social learning theory and conditioning theory. These perspectives consider behaviour to result from learning and from the reinforcement that any behaviour receives. Excessive alcohol consumption, according to these theories, can be 'unlearned' by applying behavioural principles to treatment. Such treatment would aim to identify the cues for an individual's drinking behaviour and the type of reinforcement individuals receive for their behaviour (see Chapter 6). These approaches therefore consider the individual, their drinking behaviour and the social environment.

Nowadays, at least in the UK and elsewhere in Europe, abstinence is considered as one possible treatment outcome among others, such as controlled drinking. In controlled drinking, individuals are encouraged to restrict their consumption to certain occasions/settings/times of day, or to control the alcoholic content of drinks consumed by, for example, switching to low-alcohol alternatives (Heather and Robertson 1981).

Patterns of heavy drinking laid down in late childhood and early adulthood tend to set the pattern for heavy drinking in adulthood. Alcohol-related health problems tend to accumulate in middle age. Health promotion efforts therefore have two targets: primary prevention in terms of educating children about the risks of heavy drinking and about 'safe' levels of consumption; and secondary prevention in terms of changing the behaviour of those already engaged in heavy drinking. Examples of these types of intervention are described in Chapter 6 and 7.

behaviourism
the belief that psychology is the study of observables and therefore that behaviour, not mental processes, is central.

Smoking

After caffeine and alcohol, nicotine is the next most commonly used psychoactive drug in society today. While smoking behaviour receives a vast amount of negative publicity arising from the death toll attached to it, nicotine is a legal drug, with sale of nicotine-based substances (cigarettes, cigars) providing many tobacco companies and many governments (as a result of tobacco tax) with a vast income. A shift in how society views smoking is perhaps slowly taking shape, and tobacco advertising is becoming restricted in many countries, but in the meantime smoking prevalence remains high. Reducing smoking behaviour remains high on the public health agenda.

Negative health effects of smoking

A 1990 report estimated that approximately three million people worldwide die each year as a result of their use of tobacco cigarettes and, to a lesser degree, cigars (Peto and Lopez 1990). By 2000, smoking-attributable deaths had risen by over one million per year (estimated deaths of 4.9 million; World Health Organization 2002).

Tobacco products contain carcinogenic tars and carbon monoxide, which are thought to be responsible for approximately 30 percent of cases of coronary heart disease, 75 percent of cancers (90 percent of lung cancer) and 80 percent of cases of chronic obstructive airways disease. In addition, passive smoking is considered to account for 25 percent of lung cancer deaths among non-smokers.

Carbon monoxide reduces circulating oxygen in the blood, which effectively reduces the amount of oxygen feeding the heart muscles; nicotine makes the heart work harder by increasing blood pressure and heart rate; and together these substances cause narrowing of the arteries and increase the likelihood of thrombosis (clot formation). Tars impair the respiratory system by congesting the lungs, and this is a major contributor to the highly

Plate 3.2   The risks attached to passive smoking are well publicised, but some occupations present a greater risk to staff than others.

Source: Getty Images

prevalent chronic obstructive pulmonary disease (COPD; e.g. emphysema) (Julien 1996). Overall, the evidence as to the negative health effects of smoking tobacco is indisputable, and more recently the evidence as to the negative effects of passive smoking has been increasing (Department of Health 1998b).

Prevalence of smoking

As a result of growing awareness of the negative health consequences of smoking, changes in the prevalence and uptake of smoking have been reported from many Western societies. However, the reduced prevalence of smoking is not as evident in developing countries as it is in developed countries, which is thought to account in part for the WHO's report of increased smoking-related mortality by 2000. Some figures are encouraging; for example, approximately 80 percent of men and 40 percent of women smoked in the UK during the 1950s, whereas by 1998 these percentages had declined significantly, to approximately 39 percent of men and 33 percent of women (Peto, Darby, Deo *et al.* 2000). This reduction in the prevalence of smoking has been associated with a decrease in lung cancer rates, but the full benefits of more recent declines in smoking prevalence will only be seen in mortality figures of future decades. A less encouraging finding is that the downturn in the number of men smoking is not reflected among women, who show a slower rate of reduction, and among young girls, who show a greater increase in smoking initiation (Blenkinsop, Boreham and McManus 2003; Department of Health 2000, National Statistics Office 2001). The increased incidence of lung cancer among women over the last two decades is, in part, traceable to the increased prevalence of women smoking since the Second World War, but this worrying upturn is likely to continue if recent survey figures are considered.

Ethnic differences in smoking prevalence have also been reported (British Heart Foundation 2004, www.heartstats.org). Bangladeshi men have been found to be at greater risk of coronary heart disease than other groups due, for example, to their tendency to exercise less and smoke more than their white counterparts (Nazroo 1997; Health Education Authority 1997). To illustrate this further, Figure 3.3 presents data from a survey conducted in 1999, which found that 42 percent of Bangladeshi males smoked, in comparison with 27 percent of males across the general population. Also contributing to the higher levels of CHD in this group is the fact that these males also eat less fruit and vegetables and engage in low levels of physical activity in comparison with the general population of males. In contrast, the percentage of Bangladeshi, Indian and Pakistani women smoking is significantly below the general population norm.

Smoking remains at high levels among the elderly – a population that initiated smoking before the medical evidence as to the health-damaging effects of the behaviour was clear and publically available. Bratzler, Oehlert and Austelle (2002) review the impact of smoking on the elderly in terms of increased morbidity, disability and death and provide a strong argument for the continued need for health promotion efforts to target smoking cessation in order to enhance the quality of life and longevity of older individuals. Evidence of the health gains of smoking cessation have been demonstrated: the American Cancer Society cancer prevention study II, for example, reported

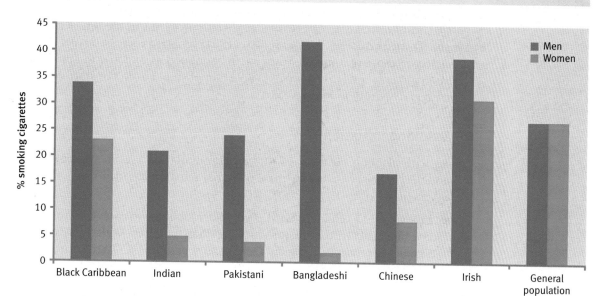

Figure 3.3 Cigarette smoking by gender and ethnic group, England, 1999.
Source: www.heartstats.org

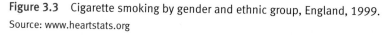

age-specific mortality
typically presented as
the number of deaths
per 100,000, per
annum, according to
certain age groups, for
example comparing
rates of death from
cancer in 2001 between
those aged 45–54 with
those aged 55–64.

a significant decrease in **age-specific mortality** rates for former smokers
compared with current smokers, with the benefit being present in those aged
over 60, and even in those who ceased smoking aged 70–74. Although elderly
groups may be hard to persuade to change, due to the consistent finding that
they attribute many health consequences of smoking to the general ageing
process, and that they are often highly dependent on the behaviour (psychologically and physically), interventions that combine age-relevant risk
information and support are likely to be as effective as similar interventions
in younger populations.

Smoking as an addiction

The addictive potential of smoking arises from the pharmacological substance, nicotine, which acts as a brain stimulant, releases our natural opiates,
beta-endorphins, and causes an increased metabolic rate (Julien 1996).
Physical dependence arises when an individual develops tolerance to the
effects of nicotine and smokes more to attain the same effects or to avoid
the withdrawal effects that follow a diminished bloodstream nicotine level
(e.g. cravings, insomnia, sweating, increased appetite; e.g. West 1992). In
this way, smoking can become self-reinforcing. Psychological symptoms
of withdrawal such as anxiety, restlessness and irritability are often so pro-
nounced that individuals may recommence smoking in a deliberate attempt
to eliminate these symptoms, which are distressing not only for them but also
for those around them! Resuming smoking provides reinforcement in terms
of the avoidance of any further withdrawal symptoms.

Why do people smoke?

Smoking behaviour is generally adopted in youth, and there are a significant
number of young people smoking and accumulating lung and airway damage

that will, for many, create significant health problems in the future (Walker and Townsend 1999). Doll and Peto (1981) reported increased risks of lung cancer in those that initiate smoking in childhood as opposed to adulthood, although only a relatively small proportion of smokers do not start smoking until early adulthood (19+ years).

■ Smoking initiation

As with alcohol, the reasons for smoking initiation are many and varied, and the list below covers the main ones that research has identified, although others may exist:

- Modelling: i.e. children with peers, elder siblings or parents who smoke are more likely to initiate smoking than children with non-smoking significant others (e.g. Biglan, Duncan, Ary *et al.* 1995; Warburton, Revell and Thompson 1991).

- Social pressure, social learning and reinforcement: i.e. if friends smoke a child/young person can develop shared positive attitudes towards smoking, or reduced perceptions of risk. Image is important during adolescence, and wanting to 'fit' with one's social group is considered crucial to social functioning (e.g. Aloise-Young, Hennigan and Graham 1996; Tyas and Pederson 1998).

- Weight control has been identified as a motive for smoking initiation and maintenance among young girls but not among young males (e.g. Camp, Klesges and Relyea 1993; Crisp, Sedgwick, Halek *et al.* 1999; French, Perry, Leon and Fulkerson 1994).

- Gender differences in attitudes towards smoking may emerge during adolescence. Michell and Amos (1997), for example, found that young males were more ambivalent than females about smoking, as they saw it as behaviour that conflicted with their desire for physical fitness. They suggest that among boys 'status' in the pecking order was conferred by fitness, whereas for girls high status was attached to appearing cool and sophisticated or rebellious, and this status, for some, may be achieved through smoking.

- Smoking as part of a larger array of 'risk-taking' or problem behaviour, such as truancy, petty theft or underage drinking (Jessor and Jessor 1977; Sutherland and Shepherd 2001).

- Health cognitions such as 'unrealistic optimism' regarding the potential of experiencing negative health outcomes: i.e. 'it won't happen to me as I smoke less than other people my age' – see Chapter 5.

These underlying differences in motivation for smoking are crucial to our understanding of why national statistics in many Western countries are showing reducing levels of smoking among boys but less so among girls. It would seem that the greater concern about body image and weight seen among girls needs to be addressed in parallel with perceptions of smoking if smoking behaviour is to be reduced.

Given existing evidence that stress is often cited as a smoking-maintaining factor among adults and adolescents, Byrne and Mazanov (2003) set out to examine whether stress was a factor in smoking initiation among Australian adolescents. Over 2,600 school pupils aged approximately 16 entered the study, and 64 percent of the sample completed a follow-up assessment twelve months later. Interestingly, pupils who failed to complete the follow-up assessment had initially reported a significantly higher number of friends who smoked than did those who took part in both phases of the study. More smokers also failed to complete the study. The hypothesis that stress levels would precede smoking onset was only weakly supported by the data of young males who were non-smokers at the first interview but who had become smokers by the time of follow-up. In contrast, there was a significant and strong relationship between stress and smoking initiation for girls. Those girls who commenced smoking between the two assessment periods reported higher total stress, school-specific stress, family conflict, parental control and perceived educational irrelevance than girls who remained non-smokers at both assessment points. Given the prevalence of smoking uptake in young girls, research such as this is particularly illuminating.

Family behaviour and family dynamics are important socialisation processes that inevitably shape the subsequent behaviour of children. For example, low family cohesion was associated with higher levels of smoking and drinking among adolescents and young adults aged 12 to 22 (Boureaudhuij 1997; Boureaudhuij and van Oost 1998), although these studies assessed adolescents and adults at one time point only, thus it is not possible to establish the direction of the effects reported. As noted earlier in the chapter, parents' own behaviour is also influential, with the children of parents who smoke being significantly more likely to smoke than the children of non-smoking parents. Some authors have suggested that smoking parents increase the 'preparedness' of their children towards smoking. That is, parental smoking results in the establishment of positive attitudes towards smoking, with the influence of smoking peers resulting in this preparedness turning into action (e.g. Jarvis 2004).

■ Smoking maintenance

Reasons for continuing to smoke are not exclusively the same as reasons given for initiation. In general, people who continue to smoke report:

■ pleasure or enjoyment of the behaviour, taste and effects reinforces positive attitudes towards smoking;

■ smoking out of habit (psychological and/or physical dependence);

■ smoking as a form of stress self-management/coping, anxiety control;

■ a lack of belief in their ability to stop smoking.

Psychological dependence is highly complex and depends greatly on the rewards and incentives, motivations and expectations that a person places on their smoking behaviour. For example, Cox and Klinger (2004) describe a motivational model of substance use based on consistent findings that people's decisions about substance use, including tobacco, are not necessarily rational but involve a range of motivational and emotional components. For example, a person considering their smoking behaviour may do so in relation to other aspects of their lives that they may or may not derive satisfaction from. Individuals without commitment to healthy life goals or the motivation to work towards attaining them are less likely to perceive their substance use as a problem and consider themselves as less able to change the behaviour.

■ Stopping smoking

Even people who stop smoking when aged between 50 and 60 can avoid most of their subsequent risk of developing lung cancer or other smoking-related disease or disability (Bratzler, Oehlert and Austelle 2002). Better still, stopping when aged 30 leads to more than 90 percent of lung cancer risk being avoided (Peto *et al.* 2000). Attempts to help people to stop smoking are viewed positively by the public, and in fact the majority of smokers wish to stop smoking. For example, two-thirds of smokers surveyed in 1996 as part of the UK General Household survey reported wanting to give up (Office for National Statistics 1998). It has been found that stopping smoking is more likely among individuals of a higher socio-economic status (dispelling expectations of significant downturns in smoking among those of lower socio-economic status caused by increases in cigarette prices). For example, in a 6.5-year follow-up study of over 1,300 smokers in the Netherlands, Droomers, Schrijvers and Mackenbach (2002) found that the higher the level of education the greater the success rates for smoking cessation. Whether this effect is directly attributable to higher levels of knowledge and under-standing about potential health consequences, or whether it is confounded by social class (perhaps quitters in higher social classes have fewer smoking acquaintances and friends than non-quitters), remains unclear. Various studies have shown that smoking networks are associated with quitting to a larger degree than health beliefs, whereby not being part of a smoking net-work facilitates cessation (e.g. Rose, Chassin, Presson and Sherman 1996).

Chapters 6 and 7 describe interventions aimed at promoting smoking cessation.

Unprotected sexual behaviour

Negative health consequences of unprotected sexual intercourse

Notwithstanding unwanted pregnancy, unprotected sexual intercourse carries with it several risks: infections such as chlamydia and HIV. Sexual behaviour as a risk factor for disease has received growing attention since the 'arrival' of the human immunodeficiency virus (HIV) in the early 1980s and the recognition that AIDS affects heterosexually active populations as well as homosexual populations and injecting drug users who share their injecting equipment. Unlike the other behaviour described in this chapter, sexual prac-tices are not inherently individual behaviour but behaviour that occurs in the context of an interaction between two individuals. Sex is fundamentally 'social' behaviour (although drinking behaviour may also be considered 'social', the actual physical act of drinking is down to the individual). As such, researchers studying sexual practices and the influences upon them, and health educators attempting to promote safer sexual practices such as condom use, face particular challenges.

CHAPTER 4

Health-enhancing behaviour

Learning outcomes

By the end of this chapter, you should have an understanding of:

- the behaviour found to have health-enhancing or health-protective effects
- the relevance of healthy diet, exercise and screening behaviour to health across the lifespan
- the range and complexity of influences upon the uptake and maintenance of health-enhancing behaviour

Image: Mike Hewitt/Action Plus

health status, regardless of whether or not health reasons lay behind their performance. The behaviours addressed in this chapter are sometimes referred to as 'behavioural pathogens' or health-damaging behaviour and includes smoking, heavy consumption of alcohol, unprotected sexual behaviour and an unhealthy diet. (Others are described as 'behavioural immunogens' or health-enhancing behaviour, such as exercise, a balanced diet, health screening and immunisation; see the next chapter.)

This chapter has described behaviour that has been found to have clear associations with prevalent illnesses, and as such this behaviour accounts for a vast amount of research enquiry in the field of health psychology. This chapter has also brought to the reader's attention some of the challenges to effective measurement of health behaviour, including, for example, potential distortions in self-reports of private behaviour caused by self-presentation bias, or problems in a person's recall of the frequency and volume of certain behaviour, such as alcohol consumption.

Within health psychology, a significant body of work has addressed the complexity of social, emotional and cognitive factors that contribute to health-damaging behaviour, and a range of theories and models of health behaviour have been developed and tested. These are the subject of Chapter 5.

Further reading

Pitts, M. (1996). *The Psychology of Preventative Health*. London: Routledge.
For a well-structured and researched overview of the key lifestyle factors associated with increased health risk, see Chapters 4 and 5.

Orford, J. (2001). *Excessive Appetites: A Psychological View of Addictions*, 2nd edn. Chichester: John Wiley.
For a thorough exploration of 'appetitive' behaviour including smoking, drinking, eating and sexual behaviour, this book is a classic read. Orford addresses both the changed societal views of health behaviour thought to be addictive and the psychological and physiological explanations of such behaviour.

For a useful overview of current Department of Health survey statistics pertaining to health behaviour and illness (UK):
www.doh.gov.uk/stats

For a copy of the recent UK survey of adolescent health and health behaviour, including recommendations for interventions:
www.bma/org.uk

CHAPTER OUTLINE

As shown in the previous chapter, behaviour is linked to health. However, not all our behaviour has potentially negative effects on our health; much behaviour has been found to be beneficial to health, and indeed protective against illness. These are sometimes called 'behavioural immunogens'. This chapter provides an overview of the evidence pertaining to an array of such health-protective behaviour, including healthy diet, exercise behaviour, health screening and immunisation. The evidence pertaining to the health benefits of each behaviour is considered, and the current guidelines are reviewed in relation to statistical evidence regarding the practice of each behaviour. A broad array of influences on the uptake or maintenance of specific health-enhancing behaviour is introduced to the reader here in order to provide a foundation for Chapter 5, where psychosocial theories of health behaviour are explored more fully.

The health-enhancing behaviour described in this chapter is a common target of educational and health promotion endeavours worldwide, many examples of which are described in Chapters 6 and 7.

It is important to acknowledge that individual behaviour can both undermine a person's health and can act to protect and maintain it. In a society where chronic disease is prevalent and where the population is ageing, it is becoming increasingly important to take positive steps towards healthy living and healthy ageing. Although media coverage and public health campaigns work towards increasing awareness of the beneficial or damaging effects of certain behaviour on our health, it is important to remember that people do not act solely out of a motivation to protect their health or to reduce their risk of illness. As health psychologists, it is important to develop an understanding not only of the consequences of certain behaviour for health but also of the many psychosocial factors that influence health behaviour. The dominant theories applied and tested in this field of health psychology research are described in Chapter 5, but first let us look at some of the behaviour.

Healthy diet

As described in the previous chapter, what we eat plays an important role in our long-term health and illness status. Diet has been found to have both direct and indirect links with illness; for example, fat intake is directly linked to various forms of heart disease by a range of physiological mechanisms, and indirectly related to disease by virtue of its effects on weight control and, in particular, obesity. Furthermore, given evidence that 35 percent of cancer deaths are attributable, in part, to poor diet, particularly diets involving significant intake of high-fat foods, high levels of salt and low levels of fibre (World Cancer Research Fund 1997), it is no surprise that government bodies and medical authorities are producing guidelines on how to eat healthily, and that health researchers are working towards identifying factors that facilitate the adoption of these guidelines in our daily lives.

The health benefits of fruit and vegetable consumption

antioxidant
oxidation of low-density lipoprotein (LDL or 'bad') cholesterol has been shown to be important in the development of fatty deposits in the arteries; antioxidants are chemical properties (polyphenols) of some substances (e.g. red wine) thought to inhibit the process of oxidation.

meta-analysis
a review and re-analysis of pre-existing quantitative datasets that combines the analysis so as to provide large samples and high statistical power from which to draw reliable conclusions about specific effects.

ischaemic heart disease
a heart disease caused by a restriction of blood flow to the heart.

Fruit and vegetables contain, among other things, vitamins, **antioxidants** and fibre, all of which are essential to a healthy body. They may also offer protection against diseases such as some forms of cancer (e.g. bowel). Block, Patterson and Subar (1992) collated 170 studies that investigated the association between fruit and vegetable consumption and all types of cancer. They concluded that a significant majority of studies (132) found that fruit and vegetables conferred significant protection against cancer. However, evidence to date does not suggest that vegetarianism is protective against all types of cancer or heart disease, although a large **meta-analysis** of data involving 76,000 men and women did find that vegetarianism reduced the risk of dying of **ischaemic heart disease** (Key, Fraser, Thorogood *et al.* 1998). However, in this study, vegetarians also reported lower rates of smoking and lower levels of alcohol consumption than non-vegetarians, and although these factors were controlled for in the analyses, other unidentified but important differences may also have existed between the two groups that may further explain the health differences. Overall, however, research evidence across individual studies is fairly consistent in finding positive benefits of fruit and vegetable intake, not just in relation to cancer but also for other diseases such as stroke (Cummings and Bingham 1998; Ness and Powles 1997). A large-scale systematic review (*Cochrane Review*) of all the evidence pointing to an association between fruit and vegetable intake and cardiovascular morbidity and mortality, as well as all-cause mortality, is currently underway (Ness, Hooper, Egger *et al.* 2003). The ISSUES box below raises the question of whether supplementing a person's diet with antioxidant vitamins (vitamins A, C and E; beta-carotene; folic acid) has benefits in terms of reducing disease risk.

ISSUES

Do vitamins protect us from disease?

Cancer and cardiovascular disease are major killers in our society. Research has suggested that a lack of vitamins A, C and E, beta-carotene and folic acid in a person's diet plays a role in blood vessel changes that potentially contribute to heart disease, and low beta-carotene has been linked with the development of cancer. Such associations are attributed to the antioxidant properties of these vitamins. Additionally, vitamins C and E have anti-inflammatory effects, and both inflammation and oxidation have been linked with cognitive decline and progression towards dementia.

Naturally, such findings stimulate media and public interest, and taking vitamin supplements as a means of protecting one's health has become commonplace, in the USA and more recently across Europe. Vitamin supplements are a growth industry.

However, what is the evidence base as to their effectiveness? To answer this question, the United States Preventive Services Task Force (USPSTF; an expert group formed to review research evidence in order to make informed health recommendations) conducted two large-scale reviews of studies of vitamin supplements published between 1966 and 2001. One reviewed the evidence regarding reduced risk of cardiovascular disease (USPSTF 2003); the other reviewed evidence in relation to reduced risk of breast, lung, colon and prostate cancer (Morris and Carson 2003). They concluded that even well-designed randomised controlled trials comparing vitamin supplements with an identical-looking placebo pill, in terms of sub-sequent development of disease, were inconclusive in their findings. Worryingly, they report 'compelling evidence' that beta-carotene supplements were associated with increased lung cancer risk, and subsequent death in smokers. The reviewers noted that it tended to be poorly designed studies that claimed to have found associations between vitamin supplementation and reduced disease risk. For example, observational studies reporting reduced breast cancer risk and vitamin A intake generally failed to control for other aspects of their sample's behavi-our, such as general diet or exercise behaviour. Other evidence, such as reduced risk of colon cancer among those taking folic acid supplements, was based on retrospective reports of those affected/not affected, rather than on long-term prospective follow-up studies of initially healthy individuals, and therefore such findings also need to be interpreted with caution.

In making recommendations for vitamin usage, the USPSTF concluded, with the exception of smokers not taking beta-carotene, there was little evidence of vitamins causing harm, but neither was there conclusive evidence as to their benefits in terms of reduced risk of heart disease or of many cancers, and that eating a healthy diet was the key factor rather than relying on supplements.

In terms of vitamin C and E supplements and the halting of cognitive decline, the evidence is more preliminary in that well-designed randomised controlled trials of those taking vitamins compared with those taking a placebo are still required (Haan 2003). However, what evidence there is has pointed to beneficial effects of vitamins C and E on the verbal fluency and verbal memory scores of healthy elderly women (both the loss of verbal fluency and short-term memory are implicated in the development of dementia). However, the benefits were found only when the vitamins were taken together, and not for either one taken separately (Grodstein, Chen and Willett 2003). These effects are encouraging, and certainly this is an area worthy of further study given that cognitive decline and dementias are likely to become more widespread in our society with its ageing population.

Overall, therefore, the jury remains out on whether vitamin supplements protect us from disease. Furthermore, and perhaps more importantly, evidence is emerging that some supple-ments may even be detrimental to the health of a specific subgroup (smokers), and we know little about dose–response effects: i.e. beyond what amount do effects become harmful?

■ Recommended fruit and vegetable intake

Current recommendations are to eat five or more portions of fruit and veg-etables a day; however, less than 20 percent of boys and 15 percent of girls aged 13 to 15 were found to be doing so recently (Department of Health 1998a; Bajekal, Primatesta and Prior 2003). There is also substantial evidence that adults are also not following these recommendations (e.g. Baker and Wardle 2003; Wardle and Steptoe 2003).

Why do people not eat sufficient fruit and vegetables?

In spite of growing public awareness of the link between eating and health, fruit and vegetables tend not to be the food of choice of many young people today. For example, the National Diet and Nutrition Survey (Food Standards Agency 2000) found that the foods most frequently consumed by British adolescents were white bread, savoury snacks (e.g. crisps), biscuits, potatoes and confectionery. Although the average vitamin intake was not deficient, intake of some minerals was low. These food preferences can in part be understood by the findings of another recent survey of British young people (Haste 2004), which found that children gave 'it tastes good' (67 percent) and 'it fills me up' (43 percent) as the top two reasons for their favourite food choice, above 'because it is healthy' (22 percent) and 'it gives me energy' (17 percent).

Unfortunately, tasting 'good' often appears to correlate with sugar and fat content rather than with healthy food, and preconceptions exist about healthy food that can work against a person making healthy food choices. For example, 37 percent of Haste's sample agreed with the statement 'healthy food usually doesn't taste as good as unhealthy food'. Where do these preferences and perceptions come from?

Food preferences

Parents play a major role in setting down patterns of eating, food choices and leisure activities in as much as they develop the rules and guidelines as to what is considered appropriate behaviour. For example, parental permissiveness was associated with less healthy eating behaviour among adolescents and young adults aged 12 to 22 (Boureaudhuij 1997; Boureaudhuij and van Oost 1998). Food preferences are generally learned through socialisation within the family, with the food provided by parents to their children often setting the child's future preferences for:

- *cooking methods*: e.g. home-cooked/fresh v. ready-made/processed;
- *products*: e.g. high-fat v. low-fat, organic v. non-organic;
- *tastes*: e.g. seasoned v. bland, sweet v. sour;
- *textures*: e.g. soft–crunchy, tender–chewy;
- *food components*: e.g. red/white meat, vegetables, fruit, grains, pulses and carbohydrates.

Various interventions have targeted the fruit and vegetable intake of young people, such as the Food Dudes programme in North Wales, which targets pre-school and primary school children (Tapper, Horne and Lowe 2003; Horne, Tapper, Lowe *et al.* 2004). This programme draws on established learning theory techniques of increased taste exposure to fruit and vegetables, modelling of healthy behaviour through cartoon youth characters, and reinforcement by means of child-friendly rewards (e.g. stickers, crayons) for eating the fruit and vegetables provided at snack and meal times (Lowe, Horne, Tapper *et al.* 2004). Long-term effectiveness of a peer-modelling and rewards-based intervention on the fruit and vegetable consumption of inner-city children was found, with particular gains among those children who ate less fruit and vegetables at the study outset (Horne *et al.* 2004). However, an exposure-only study, a randomised controlled trial of having fruit 'tuck shops' in primary schools, did not find an increase in fruit consumption (Moore, Paisly and Dennehy 2000; Moore 2001), suggesting that availability alone is insufficient to motivate change.

Plate 4.1   'We are what we eat?' The importance of providing positive norms for healthy eating in children.

Source: University of Wales Bangor, School of Psychology

Exercise

The physical health benefits of exercise

Exercise is generally considered as health-protective, reducing an individual's risk of developing diseases such as cardiovascular disease, type 2 diabetes mellitus and obesity, and with some forms of cancer, including colorectal and breast cancer (Kohl 2001; Knowler, Barrett-Connor, Fowler *et al*. 2002; World Health Organization 2002) . An early pointer towards the benefits of exercise came from a longitudinal study of the lifestyles of 17,000 former graduates of Harvard University. This study reported 1,413 deaths between 1962 and 1978 and noted that significantly more deaths had occurred among those who had reported leading a sedentary life. In particular, those who exercised the equivalent of 30–35 miles running/walking a week faced half the risk of premature death of those who exercised the equivalent of five miles or less per week. Moderate exercisers were defined as exercising the equivalent of 20 miles per week, and these individuals also showed health benefits in that on average they lived two years longer than the low-exercise group (<5 mile equivalent) (Paffenbarger, Hyde, Wing *et al*. 1986). A similar follow-up study of an elderly male sample (61–81 years) found that the twelve-year death rate was halved in those who walked more than two miles per day compared with those who walked less (Hakim, Petrovitch, Burchfield *et al.* 1998). Furthermore, these authors found that the incidence of cancer and heart disease was also lower among those who walked more, and that this effect remained even when other common risk factors such as alcohol consumption and blood pressure were controlled for. All individuals who participated in this study were non-smokers and smoking behaviour therefore did not need to be controlled for; however, this otherwise careful study did not control for an individual's dietary behaviour, which may in part be implicated in the findings.

A review of evidence from several prospective observational studies has suggested that regular physical activity can reduce the risk of coronary heart disease associated with excessive body weight (Blair and Brodney 1999). For example, one study found that overweight individuals – a body mass index (BMI, see Chapter 3) of 25.0 or more – who were active had a lower rate of heart attacks (1.3/1,000 man years) than non-active normal weight (BMI less than 24.9) individuals (heart attack rate 5.5/1,000 man years) (Morris, Clayton, Everitt *et al.* 1990). Being 'fat' does not inevitably mean being 'unfit'.

Exercise is also protective against the development of osteoporosis, a disease characterised by a reduction in bone density due to calcium loss, which leads to brittle bones, a loss of bone strength and an increased risk of fractures. It is estimated that, in the UK, someone experiences a bone fracture due to osteoporotic bones every three minutes, and that one in three women and one in twelve men over the age of 50 will have this condition. Regular exercise, particularly low-impact exercise or weight-bearing exercise such as walking and dancing, is not just important to bone development in the young but is also important to the maintenance of peak levels of bone density during adulthood. Additional benefits to muscle strength, coordination and balance can be gained from resistance-strengthening exercise, which in turn can benefit older individuals by reducing the risk of falls and subsequent bone fractures.

In general, therefore, regular exercise is an accepted means of reducing one's risk of developing a range of serious health conditions; furthermore, it is associated with a significant downturn in all-cause mortality among both men (Myers, Froelicher, Do *et al.* 2002) and women (Manson, Greenland, LaCroix *et al.* 2002).

Once a relationship between behaviour and a health outcome has been established, it is important to ask 'how' this relationship operates. In terms of exercise and reduced heart disease risk, it appears that regular performance of exercise strengthens the heart muscle and increases cardiac and respiratory efficiency; it also tends to reduce blood pressure, and people who exercise regularly have a lesser tendency to accumulate body fat (e.g. Pate, Pratt, Blair *et al.* 1995; UK Health Education Authority and UK Sports Council 1992). Exercise therefore helps to maintain the balance between energy intake and energy output and works to protect physical health in a variety of ways; it has also been shown to have benefits on psychological wellbeing.

The psychological benefits of exercise

Exercise has repeatedly been associated with psychological benefits in terms of elevated mood among clinical populations (e.g. those suffering from depression; Glenister 1996) and non-clinical populations (Plante and Rodin

1990). It is not simply that regular exercise brings about long-term benefits to mood as a result of improved body image or increased physical fitness. Limited-frequency aerobic exercise has been found to be associated with reduced anxiety (e.g. Petruzzello, Jones and Tate 1997), and Biddle's (1995) review of the effects of exercise on mood, self-esteem and **prosocial behaviour** reported the effects of intense periods of exercise on psychological wellbeing. These psychological benefits of exercise have been attributed to various biological mechanisms, including:

- exercise-induced release of the body's own natural opiates into the blood stream, which produce a 'natural high' and act as a painkiller;
- stimulation of the release of **catecholamines** such as **noradrenaline** and **adrenaline**, which counter any stress response and enhance mood (Chapters 8 and 12);
- by muscle relaxation, which reduces feelings of tension.

However, the relationship between exercise and positive mood states is perhaps not as simple as these biological routes suggest. For example, evidence exists of an inverse relationship between exercise intensity and adherence, whereby individuals are less likely to maintain intense exercise than moderate exercise, possibly because it is experienced as adversive (Brewer, Manos, McDevitt *et al.* 2000). This suggestion that, beyond a certain level, exercise may in fact be detrimental to mood has been explored further by Hall, Ekkekakis and Petruzzello (2002). They examined the affective response of thirty volunteers to increasing levels of exercise intensity and found that not only did intense exercise cause negative mood but also that the timing of mood assessments (pre- and post-exercise assessment, compared with repeated assessment during exercise) profoundly changed the nature of the relationship found between exercise and mood. Studies measuring mood before exercise and again after exercise has ended and the person has recovered generally report positive affective responses. However, Hall and colleagues' data clearly show considerable mood deterioration as exercise intensity increases, with mood rising to more positive levels only on exercise completion. These authors propose that remembering the negative affective response experienced during exercise is likely to impair an individual's future adherence, and that this may explain why some studies report poor exercise adherence rates. These interesting findings suggest that methodological factors play a role in whether or not exercise is associated with positive mood. Additionally, other factors such as cognitive distraction or actual physical removal from life's problems, or social support gained from exercising with friends, may further combine with biological factors to influence the affective experience reported.

Moderate regular exercise appears to offer various routes to wellbeing. For example, for some individuals, self-image and self-esteem may be enhanced as a result of exercise contributing to weight loss and control. Rightly or wrongly, we live in a society where trim figures are judged more positively (by others as well as by ourselves) than those that are considered to be overweight. Another potential route to wellbeing may be seen in those who use exercise as a means of coping with stress. Exercise for these individuals may act as a positive distraction from negative and stressful appraisals, or as time out from work or other demands. During exercise, a person may

---

prosocial behaviour
behavioural acts that are positively valued by society and that may elicit positive social consequences, e.g. offering sympathy, helping others.

catecholamines
these chemical substances are brain neurotransmitters and include adrenaline and **noradrenaline**.

noradrenaline
this **catecholamine** is a neurotransmitter found in the brain and in the **sympathetic nervous system**. Also known as norepinephrine.

adrenaline
a neurotransmitter and hormone secreted by the adrenal medulla that increases physiological activity in the body, including stimulation of heart action and an increase in blood pressure and metabolic rate. Also known as epinephrine.

focus on aspects of the physical exertion or on the heart-rate monitor, they may distract themselves by listening to music or planning a holiday, or they may use the time to think through current stressors or demands and plan their coping responses (see Chapter 12). Finally, exercise can have psychological benefits for those experiencing cognitive decline as a result of ageing or dementia. Cotman and Engesser-Cesar (2002) recently reported that physical activity was associated with delays in the age-related neuronal dysfunction and degeneration that underlies the types of cognitive decline often associated with Alzheimer's disease, such as memory lapses and not paying attention.

In summary, engaging in regular physical activity is considered to be beneficial for both physical and psychological health, and possibly even for survival, but as with much behaviour, it may be that moderation is required.

The negative consequences of exercise

Paradoxically, excessive reliance on exercise to the extent that exercise becomes a compulsion and produces dependence (evidenced by, for example, experience of withdrawal effects, guilt and irritability when an exercise period is missed) is also an area of investigation by health psychologists (e.g. Hausenblaus and Symons Downs 2002; Ogden, Veale and Summers 1997). Experimental studies have shown that depriving regular exercisers of exercise can lead to reductions in mood and to irritability (e.g. review by Biddle and Murtrie 1991), with mood restored when exercise is reinstated. The long-term physical consequences of excessive exercising relate to muscle wastage and weight loss rather than to any specific disease; however, these findings are a reminder that moderate levels of behaviour – even behaviour considered health-protective – are better than extreme levels. Furthermore, health advice is for a previously inactive individual to build up their exercise levels gradually, rather than making dramatic changes to both the frequency and intensity of exercise performance, and that where a pre-existing health complaint exists, plans to become more active should first be discussed with a medical professional.

Recommendations to exercise

Growing awareness of increases in sedentary lifestyles in the twenty and twenty-first century and the increasing incidence of obesity among children and adults alike has led to many bodies making specific recommendations regarding physical activity (e.g. US Department of Health and Human Services 1996; Health Education Authority 1998). The aim of any guidelines is to set activity targets in order to obtain the related benefits of reductions in blood pressure, diabetes, osteoporosis, coronary heart disease and obesity, as well as improving general wellbeing. Guidelines regarding the recommended levels of exercise are not intended to be set so high as to be outwith the reach of the average individual. For example, a large-scale study of almost 40,000 healthy females aged over 45 concluded that the minimum level of exercise required to reduce heart disease risk may be as little as 20–60 minutes of purposeful but gently paced walking per week (Lee, Rexrode, Cook *et al.* 2001).

Public health recommendations relevant to all ages do generally set higher targets than that, however, with suggested moderate physical activity for young people being one hour per day (beginning with half an hour if currently inactive), and for adults one hour per day three times a week (e.g. Health Education Authority 1998).

In spite of obvious health benefits and active campaigning on the part of many health authorities and the media to encourage people of all ages to become more active, exercise levels in some parts of Europe remain low.

■ Levels of exercise

Only about 45 percent of the British adult population do some form of exercise at least once a month, and Norman, Bennett, Smith *et al.* (1998) estimated that only about 25 percent of this population exercise with sufficient regularity to obtain any protective effects of exercise behaviour. This pattern is not only evident in Britain. For example, a survey conducted across twenty-one European countries found that approximately one-third of 18- to 30-year-olds did not engage in regular physical activity (Steptoe, Wardle, Fuller *et al.* 1997). Gender and age differences have also been reported, with women generally found to be more inactive than men, and older women being less active than younger women (e.g. Stephenson, Bauman, Armstrong *et al.* 2000). Further evidence of an age effect on participation in regular physical activity was reported by Skelton, Young, Walker *et al.* (1999), who found that while 18 percent of men and 20 percent of women aged 50–54 were participating in activity at least once a week, only 9 percent of men and 4 percent of women aged 80 or more were doing so. The proportions exercising to a level that would be likely to produce health benefits is significantly less again.

In terms of older adults and their exercise behaviour, many surveys simply compare people who are under 65 years of age and those over 65, thus data on the behaviour of the 'very old' (i.e. 85+) is limited. Exercise behaviour is likely to be influenced by factors such as current health status and physical functioning, access to facilities, and even personal safety concerns (in terms of walking alone). There is evidence that longevity is predicted by the extent to which a person is physically active. For example, Hakim and colleagues (Hakim *et al.* 1998) followed a cohort of 61–81-year-old men over a period of twelve years and monitored the amount of walking they did. Men who walked more than two miles a day lived significantly longer than those who walked less (21.5 percent died over the 12 years, compared with 43 percent).

The prevalence of such inactivity is also high in younger samples; for example:

■ The National Diet and Nutrition Survey (2000) estimated that 40 percent of boys and 60 percent of girls surveyed in the UK were not meeting the Health Education Authority (UK) recommendations (see above).

■ A large survey of English youth (Prescott-Clarke and Primatesta 1998) found that 71 percent of 15-year-old boys undertook 30 minutes of activity on most days, compared with only 36 percent of girls of this age.

■ A World Health Organization study of 162,000 young people aged 11, 13 and 15 in thirty-five countries across Europe and North America found that

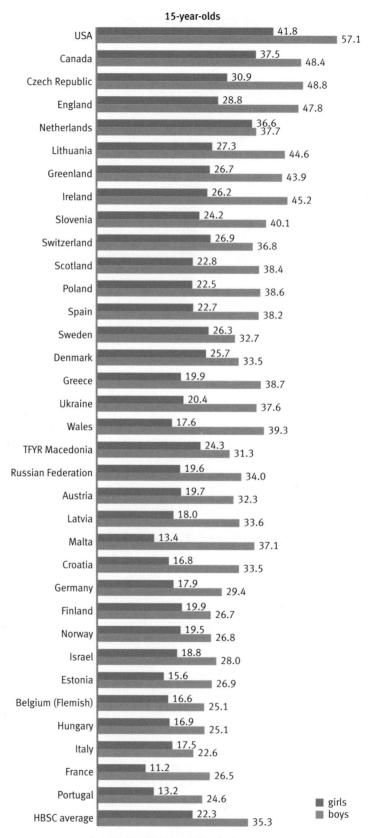

15-year-olds

	girls	boys
USA	41.8	57.1
Canada	37.5	48.4
Czech Republic	30.9	48.8
England	28.8	47.8
Netherlands	36.6	37.7
Lithuania	27.3	44.6
Greenland	26.7	43.9
Ireland	26.2	45.2
Slovenia	24.2	40.1
Switzerland	26.9	36.8
Scotland	22.8	38.4
Poland	22.5	38.6
Spain	22.7	38.2
Sweden	26.3	32.7
Denmark	25.7	33.5
Greece	19.9	38.7
Ukraine	20.4	37.6
Wales	17.6	39.3
TFYR Macedonia	24.3	31.3
Russian Federation	19.6	34.0
Austria	19.7	32.3
Latvia	18.0	33.6
Malta	13.4	37.1
Croatia	16.8	33.5
Germany	17.9	29.4
Finland	19.9	26.7
Norway	19.5	26.8
Israel	18.8	28.0
Estonia	15.6	26.9
Belgium (Flemish)	16.6	25.1
Hungary	16.9	25.1
Italy	17.5	22.6
France	11.2	26.5
Portugal	13.2	24.6
HBSC average	22.3	35.3

Figure 4.1 Proportion of 15-year-olds across a selection of thirty-five countries who engage in recommended exercise levels (at least one hour of moderate or higher-intensity activity on five or more days per week).

Source: WHO (2004); www.euro.who.int

only 35 percent of 15-year-old boys and only 22 percent of girls engage in at least one hour of moderate or heavier exercise five days a week, with huge geographical as well as gender differences (www.euro.who.int) (see Figure 4.1).

As illustrated above, many large-scale studies report a gender difference in exercise frequency, with boys generally found to be more active from an early age than girls, and with differences being maintained through adolescence. Cultural differences in the frequency of physical activity have also been reported. For example, the activity levels of Bangladeshi, Indian, Pakistani and Chinese men and women aged over 55 living in the UK was lower than levels reported by white respondents (Joint Health Surveys Unit 2001). Various studies have identified common clusters of reasons for choosing to exercise or not to exercise, although the extent to which this evidence is used to usefully inform intervention programmes has been questioned (e.g. Brunton, Harden, Rees *et al.* 2003).

Why do people exercise?

People who choose to exercise cite a variety of reasons for doing so, including, most commonly:

■ desire for physical fitness
■ desire to lose weight/change body shape and appearance
■ desire to maintain or enhance health status
■ desire to improve self-image and mood
■ as a means of stress reduction
■ as a social activity.

However, it is not to be inferred that choosing *not* to exercise reflects an absence of the types of desire and goals listed above. Many perceived barriers exist that contribute to people's reasons for not exercising, even when they simultaneously report, for example, a desire to lose weight. Barriers commonly mentioned include:

■ lack of time
■ cost
■ lack of access to appropriate facilities and equipment
■ embarrassment
■ lack of self-belief
■ lack of someone to go with/support.

Differences have been found in the beliefs and attitudes towards exercise held by those who are active and those who are not active. For example, individuals who exercise regularly are more likely to perceive positive outcomes of exercise than those who do not (Dzewaltowski 1989), perceive fewer barriers to exercising (Marcus, Rakowski and Rossi 1992) and believe that exercising is under their own control (Norman and Smith 1995). These individual health cognitions are discussed in more detail in Chapter 6.

Health-screening behaviour

There are two broad purposes of health screening:

1. to detect early asymptomatic signs of disease in order to treat;
2. identification of risk factors for illness to enable behaviour change.

What do YOU think?	What type of health screening behaviour do you engage in? Do you attend dental check-ups? Do you attend even when you have had six months without any symptoms of tooth decay? If not, consider your reasons for not doing so. If you receive a 'clean bill of health', how do you feel? Do you change the way you look after your teeth at all due to feeling reassured that they are 'healthy'?
	Do you engage in any form of self-examination (breasts, testes)? If so, what made you start doing this? What would influence whether or not you would go to your doctor if you found something atypical?

Screening for disease detection

Screening for the purpose of disease detection is based on a biomedical model, which states that by identifying abnormalities in cell or organ functioning, treatments can be implemented prior to the onset or advancement of disease symptoms. This is basically secondary prevention in that a specific screening test is offered to individuals identified as being at moderate to high risk of a certain condition on the basis of factors such as family history or age. The best-known examples of this form of screening are:

■ screening for breast cancer (mammography);
■ screening for cervical cancer (cervical smear or pap test);
■ antenatal screening, e.g. for Down's syndrome or spina bifida;
■ bone density screening.

Screening programmes for breast and cervical cancer are based on the fact that incidence of the former is high, and early treatment can reduce 40 percent of the associated mortality (Fletcher, Black, Harris *et al.* 1993), and although cervical cancer is less common (it is about the eighth most common form of cancer in women) the mortality rate associated with untreated cancer of the cervix is high. Cervical cancer is in fact the top-ranked cancer in females under the age of 35, with regular 'smear tests' (pap tests) being advocated from early adulthood. Most Western countries have a programme of routine invitation of adult women to cervical screening every five years, with older women (aged 60 or over) being invited every three years in some countries. Antenatal procedures such as amniocentesis also screen for disease by checking whether maternal serum alphafoetoprotein levels are indicative of spina bifida or Down's syndrome. In this instance, screening is routinely offered, at least in the UK, to pregnant women over the age of 30. If screening proves positive, there are no treatment options, but rather decisions to be made regarding continuation or termination of the pregnancy. Another example of screening for disease detection is most common among middle-aged women (and men) and consists of screening to check for signs of bone density deterioration and osteoporosis. In this case, an individual receiving a result indicating early signs of bone disease can take action in terms of increased calcium intake or increased weight-bearing exercise.

Screening for risk factors

The second broad purpose of screening, that of screening for risk factors in those individuals thought to be healthy, is based on the principle of susceptibility. This form of screening aims to identify an individual's personal level of risk for future illness (and in the case of genetic testing, also in their offspring) in order to offer advice and information as to how to minimise further health risk, or to plan further investigation and treatment. Examples of this form of screening include:

- screening for cardiovascular risk (cholesterol and blood pressure assessment and monitoring);
- eye tests to screen for diabetes, glaucoma or myopia;
- genetic testing for carrier status of the Huntington's disease gene, or for breast or colon cancer;
- prenatal genetic testing;
- antenatal screening.

Bearing testimony to the importance of primary prevention, some community or worksite-based programmes offer blood pressure and cholesterol testing, along with an assessment of lifestyle factors and family history of heart disease. These measures and assessments generate an index of general susceptibility, or personal 'risk score' related to potential morbidity. For example, if a person's risk of disease is thought to be moderate or high, preventive measures can be suggested, such as dietary change or smoking cessation. In order for screening to be of public health (societal) benefit as well as benefit to the individual, many of those identified as at risk of future disease would be required to change their behaviour. It will become evident in later chapters that predicting behaviour change is highly complex (Chapter 5), and thus interventions to change individuals' risk behaviour face many challenges (Chapters 6 and 7).

■ Genetic screening

One particular form of risk factor screening deserving of further mention is that of screening for genetic susceptibility. With advances in the diagnostic technology for carrier status of genes predisposing to a range of conditions, such as breast cancer (e.g. genes BRCA1 and BRCA2) or obesity (e.g. gene MC4R) brought about by programmes of scientific research such as the Human Genome Project, screening has perhaps become more controversial. Stone and Stewart (1996: 4) state: 'the benefits of large-scale genetic screening to individuals, families or society as a whole remain largely theoretical. There is scant evidence to support the view that the public at large perceives a need for carrier screening'.

In contrast, Braithwaite, Sutton and Steggles (2002) conclude from their review of studies pertaining to specific genetic testing for hereditary cancer that between 60 and 80 percent of the general population samples studied report high levels of interest in such tests. Family history of cancer generally takes interest levels to around 80 percent, and, as found with screening generally, interest is frequently found to be higher among more educated samples with greater income (e.g. Lerman, Marshall and Caminero 1996).

What do YOU think?	What does it mean when a person has been tested for carrier status of a particular gene? Do you know? It has been found that the general public commonly do not understand the issues of heritability, recessive genes or gene penetrance. There is an obvious and growing need for education and information about these very issues as more and more genes are identified that predispose us to various diseases.

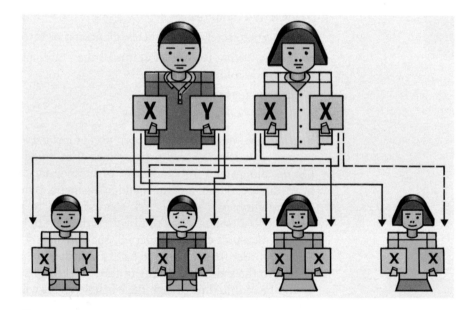

Figure 4.2 A genetic family tree.
Source: © Dorling Kindersley

The costs and benefits of screening

While screening programmes for both disease detection and risk factor status have proliferated, questions remain as to whether there are as many benefits to the individuals undergoing screening as there are to wider society. Furthermore, some findings call into question whether the benefits of screening – in terms of eliciting behaviour change that reduces disease risk to the individual, or in terms of enabling early disease symptoms to be treated and subsequently the threat of disease progression to be reduced or removed – justify the financial costs of implementing large-scale screening programmes.

In order to try to maximise the benefits of screening to both the individual and to society, some researchers have set out what they consider to be necessary criteria for effective screening programmes.

■ Criteria for establishing screening programmes

Austoker (1994: 315) describes several criteria on which the introduction of screening programmes aimed at early detection of prostrate, ovarian and testicular cancer should be based. These criteria can usefully be applied to all forms of screening for disease detection, and many also apply to genetic testing:

- The condition should be an important health problem: i.e. prevalent and/or serious.
- There should be a recognisable early stage to the condition.
- Treatment at an early stage should have clear benefits to the individual (e.g. reduced mortality) compared with treatment at a later stage.
- A suitable test with good **sensitivity** and **specificity** should be available.
- The test should be considered acceptable by the general population.
- Adequate facilities for diagnosis and treatment should be in place.
- Issues of screening frequency and follow-up should be agreed.
- The costs (individual and healthcare) should be considered in relation to the benefits (individual and public health).
- Any particular subgroups to target should be identified.

However, it is difficult to conclude whether some screening programmes meet the criteria of benefits outweighing costs, one of Austoker's listed criteria. For example, while public health, disease prevention and detection concerns are being addressed by screening, it is important not to lose sight of the individual. Marteau and Kinmouth (2002: 78) note that:

> a traditional public health approach to screening regards the population benefits of reduced morbidity and mortality as inherent, not to be appraised by individuals before they decide whether or not to participate. In keeping with this, the information accompanying the invitation (to screening) tends to be brief, emphasising the general health benefits of participation.

This suggests that informed choice procedures (where the individual is fully informed prior to making a decision) are not being fully implemented at present. These authors go on to note that providing opportunities for fully informed choice would require informing potential patients about the possible adverse outcomes of screening and the limited prognostic benefits of some treatments (if any are available) for some individuals. This may affect the uptake of screening by some of those who would in fact have benefited from early detection and treatment.

In the case of genetic testing, for example to identify whether an individual carries the gene that predisposes towards the development of Huntington's disease (an adult-onset disease), there is actually nothing that can be done to change the individual's risk, and therefore some question the value of screening other than preparing the individual for their future. In contrast, some individuals, when identified as carrying the BRCA1 or BRCA2 gene for

sensitivity
(of a test): the probability that a test is correctly positive or correctly negative; for example, a sensitive test may have 95 percent success in detecting a disease among patients known to have that disease, and 95 percent success in not detecting a disease among disease-free individuals.

specificity
(of a test): the likelihood that a test will produce a few false positive results and a few false negatives; i.e. does not produce a positive result for a negative case, and vice versa.

breast cancer, opt for prophylactic surgery (i.e. breast removal) in order that disease cannot manifest itself (Lerman, Hughes, Croyle *et al.* 2000).

It is obviously difficult to control where individuals receive health information from; for example, individuals considering any form of health screening, including genetic testing, will not approach solely health professionals for information. It has been reported, for example, that in the EU, an average of 23 percent of the population will use the Internet for health information, and in some countries, such as Denmark, that figure doubles (Jørgensen and Gøtzsche 2004). Jørgensen and Gøtzsche undertook a large-scale review of the nature of information about breast cancer screening mammography presented on the websites of international and national organisations. They found that in many cases the information was unbalanced and biased towards screening uptake, and it provided limited clear information as to the possibility of false positive and false negative results and as to the adverse effects of screening; such as over-diagnosis and over-treatment. Few websites informed readers of the limited evidence of a reduction in risk of mortality in those screened compared with unscreened individuals (which is in fact only about 0.1 percent reduction in relative risk of breast cancer over ten years). Overstating the benefits of screening, or understating potential risks or adverse consequences of screening, is not providing the individual with fully informed choice.

If any shift in policy towards shared decision making and fully informed patient choice takes place in the screening domain, it will be essential for the effects of this on the individual (in terms of emotional and behavioural consequences) to be fully evaluated.

Screening is therefore a growing part of preventive medicine across the industrialised world, with genetic testing becoming the 'hot issue' for the twenty-first century. Some forms of screening have been put forward as long-term goals of public health, such as mass screening for the gene for cystic fibrosis among couples during pregnancy (Stone and Stewart 1996). Screening, for whatever risk factor or disease, is not as yet compulsory, and therefore the generally low level of uptake of screening opportunities plays an important part in whether people go on to develop diseases that they may have been able to avoid or reduce their risk of developing.

As shown, health screening covers many conditions across the lifespan, and in relation to the procedures and conditions described above, generally involves an individual attending a screening appointment. However, other forms of health screening exist that rely on an individual performing the screening themselves.

Self-screening behaviour

Self-examination behaviour is most commonly advocated and studied in relation to early detection of breast cancer, although testicular self-examination and skin self-examination are now getting more attention. Among women, breast cancer is the most common cause of cancer death (although the incidence of lung cancer in women is growing), and despite increasing numbers of screening programmes available in healthcare settings, up to 90 percent of all breast cancers are first detected through self-examination. Among men, testicular cancer is the most frequently occurring form of cancer and the second leading cause of death among those aged 15 to 35. Surviving testicular cancer is possible in 95–100 percent of cases if the disease is detected early; however, over 50 percent of cases present to health professionals after the early, treatable, stage has passed. Likewise, skin cancer incidence is also increasing, particularly in those aged 20 to 40, yet early detection of skin lesions through self-examination can lead to high cure rates (McCarthy and Shaw 1989; Eiser, Eiser and Pauwels 1993).

While the majority of studies on skin self-examination and skin protection behaviour (use of sunscreen, avoidance of sunbeds) have originated in Australia, where the incidence of skin cancer is high, one British study of university students found that females, while more prepared to protect their skin, also placed higher value on sun-bathing behaviour (Eiser, Eiser and Pauwels 1993). Such a gender difference suggests the need for interventions to address the value placed on 'risk behaviour' by individuals, something that we referred to in the previous chapter when looking at reasons for smoking behaviour.

While health campaigns have attempted to promote self-examination behaviour such as that described above, there has in fact been some controversy over the efficacy of breast self-examination. One study contributing to this controversy is a large, ten-year study carried out in Shanghai, China (Thomas, Gao, Ray *et al.* 2002), which we describe further in RESEARCH FOCUS below.

RESEARCH FOCUS

Is self-examination an effective means of disease detection?

Thomas, D.B., Gao, D.L., Ray, R.M., Wang, W.W. *et al.* (2002). Randomized trial of breast self-examination in Shanghai – final results. *Journal of the National Cancer Institute*, 94: 1445–57.

Background
While breast self-examination (BSE) is acknowledged as increasing the detection of cancerous tissue in the breast at an early, treatable stage, the evidence as to subsequent increases in survival among those who have tumours detected and treated following BSE is mixed. Therefore the aim of this study was to conduct a randomised trial of an intervention where BSE was either taught or not taught, and examine whether reduced breast cancer mortality could be found in those instructed in, and practising, BSE.

Methods

Participants
289,392 women born between 1925 and 1958 working in textile factories across Shanghai were recruited in 1988 (i.e. aged 30 and over). Over 22,000 were subsequently excluded due to changes in their circumstances, mental or physical illness, refusal, death, omitted baseline questionnaire, or due to having a history of breast cancer (1,336 individuals). The final sample was therefore 266,064.

Design
Factories were randomised to being recruiting centres for either the intervention group (IG) or the control group (CG); in this way, 132,979 participants were allocated to the IG and 133,085 to the CG.

continued

Measures
Proficiency in performing BSE was assessed in a random sample of over 2,400 women in the IG and CG, where the women had to demonstrate breast cancer examination techniques on silicone breast models that had a varying number of lumps to detect. Women also reported the frequency of their own BSE practice.

Procedure
Members of the IG were instructed in when and how best to perform breast self-examination in groups of ten individuals taught by specially trained medical workers. Techniques were demonstrated, practised and discussed. Reinforcement sessions took place after one and three years; actual BSE practice was conducted under medical supervision every three months in Year 1 and then every six months in Years 2–5; and participants received regular reminders at work and at home. In stark contrast, the CG participants received no instruction or information on BSE, but concurrent with the IG's second reinforcement session they received an education session on the prevention of lower back pain (to provide a health focus for these participants that may enhance continued participation).

Follow-up procedures were rigorous, using factory medical workers who collated reports of breast lump detection and referred women with confirmed lumps to hospital surgeons for evaluation. The medical decisions (regarding biopsy, further referrals, diagnosis and treatment) were all recorded. Hospital staff were unaware of which arm of the trial women were in (i.e. blind). The medical records of women with confirmed breast tumours – both benign and malignant – were examined by trained medical staff. Details of the size and spread of malignant tumours, and whether the lymph nodes were implicated (which indicates potential for spread), were recorded.

Deaths up to the end of 2000 were identified from clinical records and regional death registers, and where this failed to provide an up-to-date status, women's homes were visited. Death from breast cancer was defined as one that would not have occurred at the time it did in the absence of the breast cancer.

Results
Analysis took baseline demographic (e.g. age, alcohol and tobacco consumption) and breast cancer risk factors (e.g. number and age of pregnancies, age of menopause, family history of breast cancer) into account and found no differences between those women in the IG and those in the CG. Furthermore, unlike in many other countries, Chinese factory workers are constrained in their choice of hospital – each factory provides primary medical care and refers on, where necessary, to a specific hospital under contract with that factory. There were no effects of hospital in terms of the baseline risk factors of the women in the IG or the CG, and the groups shared affiliations with the same hospitals, thus diagnostic and treatment facilities available to each group were comparable.

Women in the IG had good levels of competence in performing BSE, although it did decline over time. The IG women also found a higher proportion of breast lumps than those in the CG, although the numbers of cancers diagnosed were similar in both groups for each year of the trial after the first year. However, the IG women who detected lumps subsequently found to be malignant did not detect them at a sufficiently less advanced stage to confer an advantage in terms of treatments likely to enhance survival. The study did not find any significant effects of BSE on survival over a 10–11-year period, and an identical percentage of women developed breast cancer and died in each group (0.10 percent).

Discussion
While the authors report greater detection of lumps in the breast by women in the BSE IG, a higher number of these lumps were found to be benign. The finding of more lumps, which

resulted in an increased number of biopsies (many for lumps subsequently found to be benign), has extensive cost implications.

The authors conclude that BSE is unlikely to reduce breast cancer mortality, and as a result of these and similar earlier findings, breast self-examination recommendations have generally been minimised, although some authorities still promote the practice (e.g. the American Cancer Society).

Conclusion

This is a well-conducted, large-scale study that gives ample consideration to factors that may have influenced the results by means of rigorous examination of clinical and contextual data and by impressive follow-up procedures. However, one limitation is that the data pertaining to the frequency of BSE practice is limited and lacking in specificity (most simply reported 'monthly' BSE) and it is therefore unclear just how frequently the IG were in fact performing BSE outwith the actual supervised sessions. Therefore the conclusion is more that the *teaching* of BSE had no survival benefits, and that further study is needed where frequency is more rigorously assessed. For other researchers to obtain such a sample size and such commitment to long term follow-up as Thomas and colleagues report will be quite a challenge.

Uptake of screening behaviour

Psychology, particularly health and social psychology, has a large part to play in helping to identify predictors of the uptake of screening programmes, such as individual attitudes and beliefs about illness, about screening, and about preventive behaviour. While the increasing availability of screening programmes for many diseases and disease risk factors seems to have increased uptake, generally uptake remains at a lower level than is considered optimal in terms of disease reduction at a societal level.

■ Factors associated with screening behaviour

A range of factors have been found to be associated with the non-uptake of screening opportunities or self-examination behaviour, including:

- lower levels of education and income;
- age (e.g. younger women tend not to attend risk-factor screening);
- lack of knowledge about the condition;
- lack of knowledge about the purpose of screening;
- lack of knowledge about potential outcomes of screening;
- embarrassment regarding the procedures involved;
- fear that 'something bad' will be detected;
- fear of pain or discomfort during the procedure;
- lack of self-belief (self-efficacy, see Chapter 5) in terms of being able to practise self-examination correctly.

In terms of self-screening behaviour, knowledge of testicular cancer and the practice of self-examination have generally been found to be at a low level. Studies of breast self-examination have found that even among women who do perform it, many do not do so correctly (i.e. it should ideally be carried out mid-menstrual cycle, in an upright position as well as when lying down, and should include examination of all tissue in the breast, nipple and under-arm areas). Worryingly, a recent study (Steadman and Quine 2004) confirmed low levels of knowledge among young adult males about testicular cancer and also found low levels of knowledge regarding the potential benefits of self-examination. This study went on to demonstrate that a simple inter-vention, which required half of the participants to write down and visualise when, where and how they would self-examine their testes over the forth-coming three weeks, led to a significantly higher proportion of them self-examining than that found in the control group, who did not form such plans. This study demonstrates the relative ease with which behaviour can be changed, although a longer-term follow-up would be beneficial to check whether self-examination practices were maintained beyond the study period. This intervention focused specifically on making an individualised plan for action, referred to in health psychology as forming an 'implementation inten-tion'. This construct, and further research supporting its practical utility in developing interventions, is described in the next chapter.

Immunisation behaviour

The purpose of immunisation

antigen
unique protein found on the surface of a pathogen that enables the immune system to recognise that pathogen as a foreign substance and therefore produce antibodies to fight it. Vaccinations introduce specially prepared viruses or bacteria into a body, and these have antigens.

Vaccination is the oldest form of immunisation, in which immunity is pro-vided to an individual by introducing a small amount of an **antigen** into their body (either orally, intramuscularly or intradermally (injecting into the skin)), which triggers off the development of antibodies to that specific anti-gen. Some vaccinations, such as orally administered polio vaccine, measles, mumps and rubella, use live components, while others, such as hepatitis B, use inactivated components. Vaccinations against infectious disease have been credited with the virtual eradication of diseases that in previous centuries caused widespread morbidity and mortality, such as smallpox, diptheria and polio (e.g. Woolf 1996). Public health specialists consider vaccines both safe and successful and at least in developed countries, the incidence of many common, predominantly childhood diseases, such as measles, is low. However, infectious diseases still account for approximately seventeen mil-lion deaths in developing countries and half a million deaths in industrialised countries (BMA 2003a). Although immunisation is offered to various sub-groups in the population, such as influenza vaccination to the elderly or to those with pre-existing conditions that increase their vulnerability to infec-tion (e.g. asthma), the main emphasis of immunisation is on the prevention of childhood disease. It is policy in the UK to advise parents to immunise their child, as shown in Table 4.1.

Public health policy is to provide vaccinations that provide long-lasting pro-tection against specific disease without adverse consequences to the individual,

Table 4.1   Immunisation policy in the United Kingdom

Age	Vaccine	Means of administration
2–4 months	polio	by mouth
	diptheria, tetanus, pertussis (whooping cough) and Hib (haemophilus influenza type b)	combined injection
	meningitis C	injection
12–15 months	measles, mumps and rubella (MMR)	combined injection
3–5 years	polio	by mouth
	diptheria, tetanus and acellular pertussis	combined injection
	measles, mumps and rubella	combined injection
10–14 years	rubella (girls)	injection
	BCG (tuberculosis)	injection
15–18 years	tetanus booster	injection
	polio booster	injection

Plate 4.2   Immunisation behaviour is crucial to public health, yet is influenced by many cultural, social, emotional and cognitive factors. Here, a queue of mothers take up the first opportunity of vaccination for their child against measles to be offered in their village.

Source: Jacob Silberberg/Getty

and with the costs of providing the vaccination being outweighed by the costs of having to treat the disease if no vaccination were to be provided. However, immunisation coverage varies in different parts of the world, and even in different regions within countries, and there is growing concern that some diseases, such as whooping cough and measles, may re-emerge as uptake has not reached saturation level.

Costs and benefits of immunisation

Over the last century, the widescale benefits of childhood vaccination programmes have become apparent. It is now rare for a child living in the

Western world, and increasingly in developing countries where vaccination programmes are being promoted, to die from measles, diphtheria or polio. The World Health Organization had set a target for almost universal vaccination by 2000, and in 1997 there were high hopes of achieving population immunity against measles, at least in Britain, with uptake a reported 97 percent (Bellaby 2003).

However, widespread publicity following a 1998 study that reported adverse effects of the combined MMR vaccination has largely been 'credited' with the downturn in immunisation uptake, caused by a lack of public confidence. The public debate about vaccine safety has spread generally but has been at its most vociferous in relation to the MMR vaccine, originally introduced in 1988. This is addressed below, IN THE SPOTLIGHT.

While socio-economic variables such as low educational attainment have been found to influence the uptake of vaccination (e.g. New and Senior 1991; and see Chapter 2) so too do emotional and cognitive variables. For example, Bennett and Smith (1992) studied the vaccination status of 300 children aged 2 to 2½ in Wales and found that those parents who did not have their child vaccinated exhibited anxiety about the risks of vaccination as well as low perceptions of the potential benefits of vaccination. Beliefs such as these and the research evidence as to their utility in explaining health behaviour are examined in Chapter 5.

IN THE SPOTLIGHT

Immunisation debate and the MMR vaccination

In order to achieve population immunity, the required uptake of a measles vaccine is between 92 and 95 percent (BMA 2003b). The figure for 2001 uptake of the MMR (measles, mumps and rubella combined vaccine) in the UK was below 90 percent, which signifies a drop of several percent. In Scotland, MMR coverage dropped from 93.2 percent in 2000 to 88.5 percent in 2001, whereas the level of MenC (meningitis C) uptake was 93.7 percent. Why is one immunisation being taken up less commonly than another? It is likely that this is in part due to differing perceptions of the illnesses concerned (meningitis is almost universally feared, whereas measles may be considered a less serious illness); in part due to the manner in which health professionals advocate the different vaccines (e.g. New and Senior 1991) and in part due to the nature of publicity attracted by the different diseases/vaccines.

Concerns about immunisation and vaccination are not new, but over recent years debate has raged in relation to the suggested link between the measles, mumps and rubella (MMR) vaccine and autism, and to a lesser degree (at least in terms of publicity) inflammatory bowel disease (IBD). Media concerns have a tendency to become public and parental concerns, and as a result a significant decline in the percentage of children immunised against these diseases has been witnessed.

What stimulated the media debate?
Wakefield, Murch, Anthony *et al.* (1998) published a paper in the highly respected medical journal, *The Lancet*, which speculated that there may be a link between MMR vaccine and autism and/or IBD on the basis of their finding that among twelve children referred for gastroenterological investigation, nine manifested varying degrees of behavioural problems that

had received autistic spectrum diagnoses. In eight cases, parents attributed the onset of behavioural symptoms to a time following the MMR vaccine. However, this study was seriously limited by its small sample size, and the link was only speculative, but the media did not address these weaknesses. Many other larger-scale studies have followed Wakefield *et al.*'s, such as Peltola, Patja, Leinikkii *et al.*'s (1998) study, which found no evidence of a link between MMR, autism and inflammatory bowel disease in spite of conducting a fourteen-year prospective study; or Taylor, Miller, Farrington *et al.*'s (1999) study, which reviewed 500 children with autism born between 1979 and 1994 and found no sudden increase in autism cases associated with the introduction of the MMR vaccine in 1988 and no difference in the age of autism diagnosis between those who had been immunised and those who had not (Taylor *et al.* 1999). Taylor and colleagues more recently confirmed these findings in a population study conducted in five health districts in England (Taylor, Miller, Lingam *et al.* 2002).

In spite of ongoing media debate, there is therefore little current evidence to support a link. The current stance of the World Health Organization and thus the medical authorities elsewhere is that there is no link between MMR and autism or IBD as evidenced by methodologically valid studies.

However, parental fears remain, along with some cynicism about the medical profession's statements on the matter. One option proposed to address concerns that the combined vaccine was problematic, was to provide measles, mumps and rubella vaccines singly. However, the World Health Organization advised against this on the grounds that the extended period of time necessary to provide three separate injections increases overall levels of non-adherence to the vaccination programme, which then exposes children to infection and increases the likelihood of epidemics occurring. Concerned parents point to the fact that some countries, such as France, provide the vaccines singly to babies aged 9–12 months (although it is usually given in combined MMR form subsequently) and use this as support for the argument that the MMR vaccine is unsafe.

Things to think about and research yourself

Do you think that you would provide your child(ren) in the future with vaccination protection? Would you consider all vaccines as equally important or would you weigh up the pros and cons for each one independently? Where can people find reliable evidence of the pros and cons of immunisation?

How do you think health professionals could better convince the public as to the benefits of immunisation? Where do policy makers and public health speakers go 'wrong' in communicating the need for immunisation?

Summary

This chapter has provided an overview of a range of behaviour often described as 'behavioural immunogens': behaviour that acts in ways that protect or enhance an individual's health status. A lack or low level of 'immunogens' is also detrimental to health, as is reflected in the rising obesity figures (see Chapter 3) attributed in large part to low levels of physical activity. Given the convincing evidence of a behaviour–disease association reviewed in this chapter and in Chapter 3, we could perhaps be forgiven for expecting that the majority of people would behave in a manner that protects their health. However, this is not borne out by statistics, and it is increasingly evident that there is a complexity of influences on health behaviour practices. Chapter 5 goes on to describe the key psychosocial theories and models of health behaviour that dominate current thinking in health psychology research.

Further reading

Pitts, M. (1996). *The Psychology of Preventative Health*. London: Routledge
For a well-structured and researched overview of the key preventive health behaviour, including vaccination and screening, see chapters 2 and 3.

Hopwood, P. (1997). Psychological issues in cancer genetics: current issues and future priorities. *Patient Education and Counselling*, 32: 19–31.
This paper offers a clear review of important issues in relation to cancer genetic testing, such as for the BRCA1/2 genes.

CHAPTER 5

Predicting health behaviour

Learning outcomes

By the end of this chapter, you should understand and be able to describe:

■ how social and cognitive factors influence uptake of health or risk behaviour

■ the components of several key psychosocial models of health behaviour

■ how 'continuum' or 'static' models differ from 'stage' models in terms of how they consider behaviour change processes

■ the research evidence that supports the social and cognitive factors found to be predictive of health behaviour and health behaviour change

CHAPTER OUTLINE

The previous two chapters have described behaviour that is associated with health and illness. This chapter aims to describe the key theoretical models that have been proposed and tested in terms of their ability to explain and predict why people engage in health-risk or health-enhancing behaviour. Personality, beliefs and attitudes play an important role in motivating behaviour, as do our goals and intentions, social circumstances, and social norms. The key psychological models and their components are described and critiqued, drawing on evidence from studies of an array of health behaviours. While our understanding of health behaviour remains incomplete due to the complexity of influences upon human behaviour generally, the empirical studies described have identified many significant and modifiable influences upon health and health behaviour that offer potential targets for future health promotion and health education.

Influences on health behaviour

One way of considering the factors predictive of health behaviour is to view some influences as 'distal', such as socio-economic status, age, ethnicity, gender and personality, and others as 'proximal' in their influence, such as specific beliefs and attitudes towards health-compromising and -enhancing behaviour. This division is somewhat arbitrary but is intended to reflect the fact that some influences operate on behaviour by means of their effects on other factors, such as a person's attitudes, beliefs or goals. For example, there is reasonably consistent evidence that people in the lower socio-economic groups drink more, smoke more, exercise less and eat less healthy diets than those in the higher socio-economic groups, in both the UK and elsewhere in the European Union (e.g. Cavelaars, Kunst and Mackenbach 1997; Health Promotion Authority for Wales 1996), but this finding does not fully explain 'why' this is the case (see Chapter 2 for a full discussion of socio-economic inequalities in health). Further explanation can be offered through studies that have found (as described in Chapter 1) that social class affects perceptions of health. These perceptions could be considered 'closer' to the behaviour (more proximal) and would also offer a potentially more changeable target for intervention than would an intervention aimed at altering a person's social class. Beliefs may therefore **mediate** the effects of more distal influences, and this hypothesis can be tested statistically.

In terms of age, the health behaviour that receives the majority of attention from educational, medical and public health specialists (i.e. smoking, alcohol consumption, unprotected sexual activity, exercise and diet) are patterns of behaviour set down in childhood or early adulthood. For example, according to the 1996 General Household Survey in the UK, 82 percent of smokers took up the habit as teenagers (Thomas, Walker, Wilmot and Bennett 1998). However, attitudes also change at this time. Adolescents generally begin to seek autonomy (independence), which may include making health-related decisions for themselves: for example, whether or not to

mediate/mediator
some variables may mediate the effects of others upon an outcome, for example, individual beliefs may mediate the effects of gender upon behaviour, thus gender effects would be said to be indirect, rather than direct, and beliefs would be mediator variables.

start smoking, whether or not to brush their teeth before bed. Influences on decisional processes, attitudes and behaviour change during these years, with more credence being given to the attitudes, beliefs, values and behaviour of one's peers than to the advice or attitudes of parents or teachers (e.g. Chassin, Presson, Rose and Sherman 1996; Hendry and Kloep 2002). While establishing a sense of identity among one's peer group, it is perhaps not surprising that, for some adolescents, this will include the initiation of 'risk' behaviour as part of rebelling against authority or because the behaviour is considered to be 'cool' or sophisticated and grown-up (Camp, Klesges and Relyea 1993; Michell and Amos 1997).

Many models of health behaviour have been proposed and tested in terms of their ability to explain and predict the practice, or non-practice, of health-risk and health-enhancing behaviour, through the examination of individual attitudes and health beliefs. The attitudinal, social and cognitive components of these models are the main focus of this chapter; however, first we provide an outline of some broad influences on behaviour.

Personality

Personality is, generally speaking, what makes individuals different from one another, in that each of us thinks and behaves in a characteristic manner, showing traits that are particularly enduring regardless of situation. Different scientists have proposed different numbers of key traits or dimensions of personality; two of the major examples are presented here.

Eysenck's three-factor model

1. *extroversion* (outgoing social nature): dimensionally opposite to *introversion* (shy, solitary nature);
2. *neuroticism* (anxious, worried, guilt-ridden nature): dimensionally opposite to *emotional stability* (relaxed, contented nature);
3. *psychoticism* (egocentric, aggressive, antisocial nature): dimensionally opposite to *self-control* (kind, considerate, obedient nature).

According to Eysenck (1970, 1991), individual personality is reflected in an individual's scores along these three dimensions; for example, one individual may score positively and high on neuroticism and extroversion but negatively on psychoticism, whereas another may score positively and high on neuroticism, and negatively and high on extroversion and psychoticism. These three factors have received a lot of support from research studies and are considered to be valid and robust personality factors (Kline 1993). However, another model exists, often referred to as the 'big five' (McCrae and Costa 1987, 1990), which identifies five primary dimensions of personality.

McCrae and Costa's five-factor model

1. neuroticism
2. extroversion
3. openness (to experience)
4. agreeableness
5. conscientiousness.

The big five have subsequently been validated in different cultures (with the exception of conscientiousness) and at different points in the lifespan from age 14 to 50+ (McCrae, Costa, Ostendorf *et al.* 2000). The big five traits are therefore relatively stable and enduring.

Although the trait approach to personality is limited in its acknowledge-ment of situational and cognitive factors that also affect personality and behaviour (as acknowledged by Bandura's social learning/social cognitive theory, see Chapter 3), studies have shown that these relatively stable per-sonality factors are associated with health behaviour. For example, Goldberg and Strycker (2002) carried out a large-scale community survey of the associ-ations between personality and dietary behaviour and found openness to predict a range of dietary behaviour, including healthy practices, low meat fat consumption and high fibre intake. This is consistent with the findings of Steptoe, Pollard and Wardle (1995), where openness was associated with a willingness to try novel situations, including new food tastes and types. Con-scientiousness is generally associated with positive health behaviour, whereas neuroticism is associated with negative health behaviour (Goldberg and Strycker 2002; Booth-Kewley and Vickers 1994). Neuroticism is further associ-ated with 'pickiness' (fussiness) and **neophobia** among a sample of 451 Scottish children aged between 11 and 15 (MacNicol, Murray and Austin 2003).

In seeming contradiction to this negative influence of neuroticism, it has also been associated with high levels of healthcare use. This is attributed to the tendency of highly neurotic individuals to report greater attention to bodily sensations and to label them as 'symptoms' of disease more than people lower in neuroticism (Jerram and Coleman 1999; and see Chapter 9). However, Friedman (2003) concluded that there is no consistent evidence that people scoring high on neuroticism engage in a greater range or frequency of health-enhancing behaviour or in less damaging health behaviour than those people with low neuroticism, and that 'healthy neurotics' may exist as well as 'unhealthy neurotics'. This suggests therefore that personality traits such as neuroticism offer insufficient explanation for health or risk behaviour.

Another commonly investigated aspect of personality is generalised **locus of control** (LoC) beliefs (Rotter 1966). Rotter originally considered individuals to have either an internal LoC orientation (i.e. they place responsibility for outcomes on themselves and consider that their actions affect outcomes) or an external orientation, which suggests that they place responsibility for out-comes at the door of external factors such as luck. Subsequent to Rotter's internal–external control scale, Kenneth Wallston and colleagues (Wallston, Wallston and deVellis 1978) developed an LoC scale specific to health beliefs, the MHLC (multidimensional **health locus of control**) scale, which identified three statistically independent dimensions:

1. *Internal*: strong internal beliefs consider the individual themselves as the prime determinant of their health state. Internal beliefs are theoretically associated with high levels of health-protective behaviour and with Bandura's self-efficacy construct (see below).

2. *External/chance*: strong external beliefs consider that external forces such as luck, fate or chance determine an individual's health state, rather than their own behaviour.

neophobia
a persistent and chronic fear of anything new (places, events, people, objects).

locus of control
a personality trait thought to distinguish between those who attribute responsibility for events to themselves (i.e. internal LoC) or to external factors (external LoC).

health locus of control
the perception that one's health is under personal control; controlled by powerful others such as health professionals; or under the control of external factors such as fate or luck.

3. *Powerful others*: strong beliefs on this scale consider health state to be determined by the actions of powerful others such as health and medical professionals.

Wallston argued that these dimensions become relevant only if an individual values their health. This reflects the theoretical underpinning to locus of control, that of social learning or social cognitive theory (Bandura 1986), whereby an individual acts on the expectancy of certain valued outcomes. If individuals do not value their health, it is thought that they are unlikely to engage in health-protective behaviour (even if they feel they have control over their health), because health is not a high priority (e.g. Wallston and Smith 1994). Individuals with an internal HLC or a powerful others HLC who also value their health are therefore more likely to behave in a health-protective manner, whether that be, in the case of internal LoC, commencing an exercise programme, or in the case of a powerful others HLC, going to a local health clinic for dietary advice. Powerful others beliefs may detract from an individual taking active responsibility for the relevant behaviour, with such individuals being over-reliant on medical 'cures'.

Despite Wallston's refinements to the Rotter internal–external scale, generalised LoC dimensions have proved to be only a modest predictor of behaviour. Norman and Bennett (1996), for example, reviewed studies that investigated the associations between Wallston's three subscales and the protective health behaviour of healthy people and concluded that the relationship was a weak one. This weak association was subsequently confirmed in a large-scale survey of over 13,000 healthy individuals. Positive health behaviour was weakly correlated with higher internal control, and even more weakly associated with lower external and powerful others control beliefs (Norman, Bennett, Smith *et al.* 1998). Such findings suggest that a generalised health LoC (such as assessed by the MHLC) has only a modest influence on specific health behaviour, and research attention has in many cases turned to examining more behaviourally proximal constructs, such as **perceived behavioural control** (see theory of planned behaviour below) and **self-efficacy** (see below and also discussion of the health action process approach model). However, Armitage (2003) found that generalised internal control beliefs independently predicted the relationship between perceived behavioural control and intention (in other words, the ability of more specific perceived behavioural control beliefs to explain intention was strongest among those individuals with high internal LoC). Armitage therefore proposed that research needs to examine further the influence of dispositional control beliefs on proximal control. Although this debate is relatively new, it suggests that interventions aiming to enhance specific perceived behavioural control beliefs may be most effective if targeted at those with an internal locus of control.

perceived behavioural control
one's belief in personal control over a certain specific action or behaviour.

self-efficacy
the belief that one can perform particular behaviour in a given set of circumstances.

Social norms, family and friends

Humans are fundamentally social beings. Our behaviour is a result of many influences: the general culture and environment into which we are born; the day-to-day culture in which we live and work; the groups, subgroups and individuals with whom we interact; and our own personal emotions, beliefs, values and attitudes, all of which are influenced by these wider factors. We learn from our own positive and negative experience, but we also learn 'vicariously' through exposure to, and observation of, other people's behaviour and experiences. The behaviour of people around us creates a perceived 'social norm', which suggests implicit (or explicit) approval for certain behaviour. For example, a four-year follow-up study of nearly 10,000 American high school students found that 37 percent of non-smokers at high school had started smoking by college follow-up; 25 percent of original 'experimental' smokers had increased their smoking behaviour; and the remaining students had stayed the same (either non-smokers, experimenting with smoking (none in last month), current smokers or ex-smokers) (Choi, Harris, Okuyemi *et al.* 2003). Clear differences were found in the factors that explained initiation to smoking from non-smoking (i.e. white, rebellious students who did not like school) and progression from experimental (irregular, social, short-term) smoking to current smoker. Those who progressed in their smoking behaviour perceived peer approval for their smoking and perceived experimental smoking as safe. Additionally, perceived parental approval was a more important influence on starting smoking than on progression.

In relation to health-risk behaviour, there are many sources of information that a person is exposed to: for example, televised advertisements graphically illustrating the negative consequences of smoking; an older sibling or parent appearing to be healthy in spite of regular binge drinking episodes; a classroom workshop on how to 'just say no' to the first offer of a cigarette or other drug; a friend who smokes telling you that smoking is cool. There is

Plate 5.1 Social norms have been found to be important predictors of whether or not a person initiates specific health behaviours, in this instance smoking.

Source: © copyright royalty-free/Corbis

consistent evidence to show that the credibility, similarity to self and even the attractiveness of the source of information influences whether or not attitudinal change or behaviour change occurs as a consequence (e.g. Petty and Cacioppo 1986, 1996; see Chapter 7 for further discussion of influences on the effectiveness of health promotion).

Attitudes

Attitudes are thought to be the common-sense representations that individuals hold in relation to objects, people and events (Eagly and Chaiken 1993). Some theorists have described attitudes as a single component based on affective evaluation of an object/event (i.e. you either like something/someone or you do not; e.g. Thurstone 1928); others have presented a two-component model, where attitude is defined as an unobservable and stable predisposition or state of mental readiness that influences evaluative judgements (e.g. Allport 1935). From the 1960s onwards, there has been growing acceptance of a three-component model of attitude, whereby attitudes are considered as relatively enduring and generalisable and made up of three related parts – thought (cognition), feeling and behaviour:

1. *Cognitive*: beliefs about the attitude-object; e.g. cigarette smoking is a good way to relieve stress; cigarette smoking is a sign of weakness.

2. *Emotional*: feelings towards the attitude-object; e.g. cigarette smoking is disgusting/pleasurable.

3. *Behavioural* (or intentional): intended action towards the attitude-object; e.g. I am not going to smoke.

Early attitudinal theorists considered the three components to be generally consistent with each other and likely to predict behaviour; however, the empirical evidence to support this direct association between attitudes and behaviour has proved difficult to find (Eagly and Chaiken 1993). An individual may hold several different, sometimes conflicting, attitudes towards a particular attitude-object, depending on context and many other factors. I may, for example, enjoy the taste of a cream cake but be worried about the negative health implications of high fat/high calorie intake. Such contradictory thoughts can produce what is known as 'dissonance', which many people will attempt to resolve by bringing their thoughts into line with one another. However, some individuals maintain a dissociation between attitudes and behaviour, for example so-called dissonant smokers, who continue to smoke despite holding a number of negative attitudes towards smoking. This conflict is sometimes referred to as **ambivalence**, where a person's motivation to change could potentially be undermined by the holding of ambivalent attitudes, such as believing low-fat food to be a healthy option while not wanting to appear obsessive about their diet (e.g. Sparks, Conner, James *et al.* 2001).

ambivalence
the simultaneous existence of both positive and negative evaluations of an attitude object, which could be both cognitive and emotional.

Risk perceptions and unrealistic optimism

People often engage in risky or unhealthy behaviour because they do not consider themselves to be at risk, or at least do not do so accurately, believing for example that 'I do not smoke as much as "person X" and therefore won't be at risk of cancer compared with them'. Weinstein (1984) found this type of biased risk perception to be common and named it 'unrealistic optimism' – 'unrealistic' because quite obviously not everyone can be at low risk. He noted that individuals engage in forms of social comparison that reflect best on themselves (comparative optimism/optimistic bias) (Weinstein and Klein 1996; Weinstein 2003); for example, in relation to HIV risk: 'I may sometimes forget to use a condom, but at least I use them more than my friends do'. He found that the negative behaviour of peers is focused on more when making these judgements than is the same peers' positive health behaviour. Selective attention in this way leads to unrealistically positive appraisals regarding personal risk.

Weinstein (1987) identified four factors that are associated with unrealistic optimism:

1. a lack of personal experience with the behaviour or problem concerned;

2. a belief that their individual actions can prevent the problem;

3. the belief that if the problem has not emerged already it is unlikely to do so in the future; e.g. 'I have smoked for years and my health is fine, so why would it change now?';

4. the belief that the problem is rare; e.g. 'cancer is quite rare compared with how common smoking is, so it is pretty unlikely I'll develop it'.

There is some evidence that unrealistic optimism is associated with greater belief in control over events (e.g. 'I am at less risk than others because I know when to stop drinking') and that such beliefs are associated with risk-reducing behaviour (Hoorens and Buunk 1993; Weinstein 1987). However, others, for example Schwarzer (1994), refer to unrealistic optimism as 'defensive optimism' and suggest instead that the relationship between such optimism and behaviour is likely to be negative because individuals underestimate their risk and thus do not take precautions against the risk occurrence. There remains a need to explore further the actual relationship between these constructs and health behaviour.

Goals and motivation for behaviour

outcome expectancies
the outcome that is expected to result from behaviour, e.g. exercise will make me fitter.

self-regulation
the process by which individuals monitor and adjust their behaviour, thoughts and emotions in order to maintain a balance or a sense of normal function.

Social cognition theory assumes that behaviour is motivated by **outcome expectancies** and goals (both short- and long-term goals) and related to this is the process of **self-regulation**, which is defined as the cognitive and behavioural process by which individuals act in a way that brings about desired outcomes or reduces undesired outcomes; such behaviour is viewed as being goal-directed (e.g. Fiske and Taylor 1991). Goals focus our attention and direct our efforts, with more valued goals leading to greater and more persistent effort (Locke and Latham 2002).

Ingledew and McDonagh (1998) have shown that health behaviour serves coping functions (which may be considered as short-term goals of the behaviour); for example, for some individuals smoking may serve the function of coping with stress. Using data obtained from a newly developed questionnaire, these authors identified five coping functions: problem solving, feeling better, avoidance, time out and prevention – attached to health behaviour. For example, exercise behaviour loaded onto a prevention with problem-solving function, but also onto a time out with problem-solving function. This finding highlights the often neglected fact that there are many reasons for why individuals behave in the way that they do; in this case, individuals exercised as a means of preventive health behaviour but also as a means of time out or relaxation. The implication of this is that interventions designed to reduce 'unhealthy' behaviour need to take account of the coping functions or goals that individual behaviour serves for each individual (see Chapter 6).

What do YOU think?	What is important to you in your current life? Think of three aspects of your life that you currently value highly. Why do you value them? What function do they serve? What goals do you hope to achieve over the next ten years? If you engage in any specific health or risk behaviour, how does it 'fit' with your current values and goals? Now, project your mind ahead to when you reach middle age (or if you have already reached this, think of your post-retirement years). What do you think will be important to you then? Will the areas of importance change, and why do you think this? Do you think your behaviour will change, and if so, in what way and why?

Self-efficacy

The construct of self-efficacy is defined as 'the *belief* in one's capabilities to organize and execute the sources of action required to manage *prospective* situations' (Bandura 1986). For example, believing that a future action (for example, weight loss) is within your capabilities is likely to generate other cognitive and emotional activity, such as the setting of high personal goals (losing a stone rather than half a stone), positive outcome expectancies and reduced anxiety. These cognitions and emotions in turn affect actions, such as dietary change and exercise, in order to achieve the goal. As Bandura (1997: 24) states: 'It is because people see outcomes as contingent on the adequacy of their performance, and care about those outcomes, that they rely on efficacy beliefs in deciding which course of action to pursue and how long to pursue it'. Success in attaining a goal also feeds back in a self-regulatory manner to further a person's sense of self-efficacy (Bandura 1997). In situations where competence of one's own performance is unrelated or less closely tied to outcome (for example, the outcome of physical recovery following a head injury will depend to a large degree on the extent of neurological damage), self-efficacy will be less predictive of outcome.

In relation to the outcomes of individual health behaviour change and maintenance of change, personal performance is important and therefore efficacy has unsurprisingly been found to be predictive. Self-efficacy is also important in terms of recovery from setbacks; for example, in a study of newly unemployed men (Mittag and Schwarzer 1993) low perceived self-efficacy regarding re-employment and dealing with the challenges of unemployment was associated with heavy drinking behaviour, where high self-efficacy was not.

Humans are inconsistent

People can be very inconsistent in their practice of health behaviour; for example, many individuals who are keen exercisers also smoke. Not only do individuals differ from one another in terms of justifications or motivations for behaviour, but their own motivations are likely to change over time. Inconsistencies can perhaps be explained by the findings that:

■ Different health behaviour is controlled by different external factors: e.g. smoking may be socially frowned upon, while exercise may be socially supported; however, cigarettes are readily available, but access to exercise facilities or time may be limited.

■ Attitudes towards health behaviour vary within and between individuals.

■ In the same individual, health behaviour may be motivated by different expectations: e.g. they may smoke to relax, exercise to improve appearance and consume alcohol to socialise.

■ Individuals differ in their goals and motivations: e.g. a teenager may diet for fashion reasons, while a middle-aged man may diet to avoid a second heart attack.

■ Motivating factors may change over time: e.g. drinking alcohol when under age may be a form of rebellion but may later be considered essential to social interaction.

■ Triggers and barriers to behaviour are influenced by context: e.g. smoking may be banned in the workplace, and alcohol consumption may be restricted in front of parents or colleagues in comparison with peers.

The next part of the chapter addresses a range of theories and models that have been developed in an attempt to explain and thereby predict health behaviour.

Models of health behaviour

First, it is important to remind the reader that by adopting healthy habits we are only reducing the statistical risks of ill-health, not guaranteeing that we will lead a long, healthy life. Furthermore, we should not expect that by examining human behaviour and the motives for it, we shall ever be able to fully explain the huge variations in people's health. Behaviour is not the only factor that causes disease. We can, at best, offer a partial (social, cognitive and behavioural) explanation of illness, and an evidence-based conclusion as to how to intervene to prevent or reduce the likelihood of illness in some individuals.

Behaviour change

Early theories as to why we changed our behaviour were based on the simplistic assumption that:

information → attitude change → behaviour change

These were found to be naïve. Simply providing information, for example about the benefits of stopping smoking or the value of a low-cholesterol diet, may or may not change a person's attitudes towards this behaviour, and even if attitudes do become more negative, it is not inevitable that this will influence behaviour change (e.g. Eagly and Chaiken 1993). Although many past, and sometimes current, health education campaigns still draw upon this simplistic premise, several models have been proposed as explanations for health behaviour and behaviour change. These are described in the following sections.

Continuum models of behaviour change

The health belief model

One of the first and best-known models is the health belief model (HBM) (Rosenstock 1974; Becker 1974; Strecher, Champion and Rosenstock 1997). The HBM proposes that the likelihood that a person will engage in particular health behaviour depends on demographic factors: e.g. social class, gender, age and a range of beliefs that may arise following a particular internal or external cue to action (see Figure 5.1). These beliefs encompass perceptions of threat and evaluation of the behaviour in question, with cues to action and health motivation added at a later date.

In terms of how the various components fit together, this can best be illustrated through specific examples:

- Perception of threat:
  - I believe that coronary heart disease (CHD) is a serious illness contributed to by being overweight: *perceived severity*.
  - I believe that I am overweight: *perceived susceptibility*.

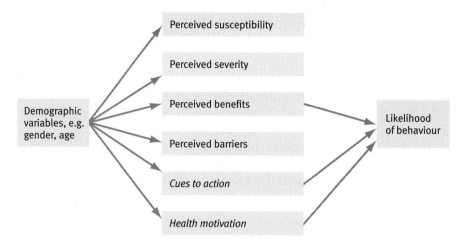

Figure 5.1   The health belief model (original, plus additions in italics).

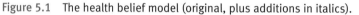

- Behavioural evaluation:
    - If I lose weight my health will improve: *perceived benefits* (of change).
    - Changing my cooking and dietary habits when I also have a family to feed will be difficult, and possibly more expensive: *perceived barriers* (to change).
- Cues to action (added in 1975; Becker and Maiman):
    - That recent television programme on the health risks of obesity worried me (*external*).
    - I am regularly feeling breathless on exertion, so maybe I should really think about dieting (*internal*).
- Health motivation (added in 1977; Becker, Haefner and Maiman):
    - It is important to me to maintain my health.

The HBM has been applied to a wide range of behaviour over many years, as illustrated below.

The HBM and preventive behaviour

The consensus finding in the breast self-examination (BSE) literature is that many people do not practise it at all, that adherence rates are low and that practise decreases with age, even though the incidence of breast cancer increases with age. The health belief model has been widely used for predicting BSE. Perceiving benefits of self-examination and few barriers to its performance have shown the most consistent and highest correlations with self-examination behaviour (e.g. Champion 1990). Being motivated towards health (e.g. seeking health information and generally engaging in health-promoting activity) distinguished between low, medium and high BSE performers, and in a later prospective study (Champion and Miller 1992) health motivation predicted BSE one year later. This supports the need to assess health motivation rather than assume that all people value health or are motivated to pursue it in the same way.

Studies have shown that different components of the HBM are more or less salient, depending on the behaviour under study. For example, in a review of thirteen studies using the HBM components, Curry and Emmons

(1994) found evidence of uptake of breast cancer screening being explained by perceived susceptibility beliefs, low perceived barriers, and cues to action. In contrast, Pakenham, Pruss and Clutton (2000) did not find susceptibility beliefs to be predictive of mammography uptake. In relation to another preventive behaviour, that of exercise, it appears that perceived benefits are important predictors (e.g. Saunders, Pate, Felton *et al.* 1997).

In terms of adherence to medication or treatment regimes, it appears that perceived barriers and benefits are stronger predictors of adherence than are perceptions of susceptibility to, or the severity of, a health threat. For example, Koikkalainen, Lappalainen and Mykkanen (1996) found that levels of dietary adherence were lower among cardiac patients who perceived barriers to following the dietary recommendations; and Letherman, Blackburn and Davidhizar (1990) found that women's uptake of antenatal care was influenced not only by having financial barriers, but by low perceived benefits of attendance.

■ The HBM and reducing risk behaviour

In relation to safer sex practices, Abraham, Sheeran, Abrams and Spears (1996) found that HBM variables were not significantly predictive of consistent condom use among sexually active adolescents once a measure of previous condom use had been taken into consideration. This suggests that one of the best predictors of what we do in the future is what we have done in the past. More recent theoretical developments and research studies have acknowledged this by including measures of previous behaviour in their design and analyses (e.g. Yzer, Siero and Buunk's 2001 study of condom use with new sexual partners).

Abraham, Krahé, Dominic and Fritsche (2002) have also concluded, from a review of the evidence prior to conducting a subsequent study of condom use behaviour, that 'threat perceptions are weaker correlates of condom use than action-specific cognitions, such as attitudes towards condom use, perceived self-efficacy in relation to condom use, the social acceptability of condom use and condom use intentions' (p. 228). These factors are not addressed in the HBM.

■ Limitations of HBM

Problems with this model lie in how it has been applied and in its basic content. For example, in terms of application there have been several versions of this model, with different authors employing different versions, not all of which include cues to action and health motivation (see Sheeran and Abraham 1996). Further limitations include:

- Rosenstock (1966), in outlining the model, did not specify the manner in which the different variables interact with one another or combine to influence behaviour. He implied that the components operate independently and could usefully be added to each other. Many studies have examined components independently (e.g. Abraham *et al.* 1996).

- Becker *et al.* (1977) suggested that perceived benefits were weighted against perceived barriers, although no guidance was given as to how the combined score was to be calculated (i.e. do you subtract the number of barriers from the number of benefits reported, or vice versa? Can all benefits and barriers carry equal weight to an individual?)

- Strecher and Rosenstock (1997) suggested that adding or multiplying susceptibility scores with severity scores to get an overall 'perceived threat' score may enable greater prediction than using each independently; that cues to action and perceived benefits and barriers may better predict behaviour in situations where perceived threat is high; and that the model may be better tested against intention than actual behaviour. Few of these hypotheses have been tested empirically.

- The HBM is a static model, suggesting that various beliefs occur simultaneously in a 'one-off' assessment. This does not allow for a staged or dynamic process of change in beliefs, as later models show is crucial.

- The HBM assumes that human beings are rational decision makers, which is not necessarily the case.

- The HBM may overestimate the role of 'threat'. Perceived susceptibility has not consistently been found to be a significant predictor of health behaviour change.

- Even if perceived susceptibility is shown to be predictive (in some studies), it is important that health promotion messages do not overuse fear arousal. Fear arousal has been shown to be counter-productive to behaviour change by provoking denial (e.g. van der Pligt, Otten, Richard et al. 1993).

- The HBM takes limited account of social influences on behaviour. For example, while young children, who take their cues about health and health behaviour from important adults in their lives, show generally good adherence to medication, adolescent adherence is poorer, reflecting a shift in influence and beliefs about health maintenance (e.g. Bryon 1998).

- The HBM fails to consider whether the individual feels able to initiate the behaviour (or behaviour change) required. Two constructs relate to this: perceived behavioural control and self-efficacy, as exemplified in two of the models discussed next (the theory of planned behaviour and the HAPA).

Given these limitations, it is perhaps not surprising that studies employing the HBM have found that its components account for only a small proportion of variance in behaviour change. By initially failing to consider the interactions between its components, the role of social norms and influences, and the factors that can turn beliefs into more proximal (close-up) determinants of behaviour (such as efficacy in carrying out the required behaviour), it provided only a limited account of human action, and more extensive models were developed and adopted.

The theory of reasoned action and the theory of planned behaviour

While the HBM is predominantly a cognitive model of health behaviour derived from subjective expected utility theory (i.e. individuals are active and generally rational decision makers who are influenced by the perceived utility (usefulness to them) of certain actions or behaviour (cf. Edwards 1954), the theory of reasoned action (TRA) and, subsequently, the theory of planned behaviour (TPB) are known as social cognition models (Figure 5.2). These

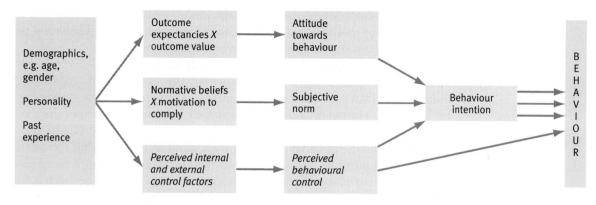

Figure 5.2 The theory of reasoned action and the theory of planned behaviour (TPB additions in italics).

models assume that social behaviour is determined by a person's beliefs about behaviour in given social contexts and by their social perceptions and expectations (cf. social learning theory: Bandura 1986) and not simply by their cognitions or attitudes.

■ The theory of reasoned action

This model (Ajzen and Fishbein 1970; Fishbein 1967) assumes that individuals behave in a goal-directed manner and that the implications of their actions (outcome expectations) are weighed up in a rational manner before the decision is taken whether to engage in the behaviour or not. The model aims to explore and develop the psychological processes involved in making a link between attitude and behaviour by incorporating wider social influences and the necessity of intention formation.

Behaviour is thought to be proximally determined by intention, which in turn is influenced by a person's attitude towards the object behaviour (*outcome expectancy beliefs*, e.g. positive outcome expectancy: if I stop smoking, exercising will become easier for me; negative outcome expectancy: if I stop smoking, I will perhaps gain weight; and *outcome value*, e.g. it is important for me to be healthier) and their perception of social pressure regarding the behaviour (e.g. my friends and parents really want me to stop smoking) (known as a **subjective norm**). The extent to which they wish to comply or fall into line with the preferences or norms of others is known as motivation to comply (I would like to please my parents and friends). The model states that the importance of the person's attitudes towards the behaviour is weighted against the subjective norm beliefs, whereby a person holding a negative attitude towards behaviour change (I don't really like dieting) may still develop a positive intention to change in situations where their subjective norm promotes dieting and they wish to comply with their significant others (e.g. all my friends eat more healthily than I do, and I would like to be more like them).

Intention is considered to be the proximal determinant of behaviour, and it reflects both the individual's motivation to behave in a certain manner and how hard they are prepared to try to carry out that behaviour (Ajzen 1991:

subjective norm
a person's beliefs regarding whether important others (referents) would think that they should or should not carry out a particular action. An index of social pressure, weighted generally by the individual's motivation to comply with the wishes of others (see theory of planned behaviour).

199). This compares favourably with the HBM, which simply stated that a combination of motivational beliefs predicted greater or lesser likelihood of action, without a statement of intent ever having been formed.

Few studies today use this model (because it has been extended and developed into the more powerful TPB); however, the vast array of studies that did use the TRA (see review and a meta-analysis of eighty-seven studies by Sheppard, Hartwick and Warshaw 1988) confirmed the importance of attitudes and subjective norms in explaining intention, and of intention in predicting subsequent behaviour. This meta-analysis reported that the mean correlation of attitudes and social norms with intentions was approximately 0.67, and the correlation between intention and behaviour was between 0.53 and 0.62. This therefore improves significantly on the prediction afforded by the HBM components; however, the model still has limitations. Note also that research evidence supporting a link between intention and subsequent behaviour has been limited by an over-reliance on cross-sectional studies.

Limitations of the TRA

volition
action or doing (the post-intentional stage highlighted in the HAPA model of health behaviour change).

- The TRA was initially developed for application to **volitional** behaviour (that under the person's control) and as such does not examine a person's belief in their ability to perform the behaviour in question. However, much behaviour is not completely volitional (for example, addictive behaviours such as smoking, or the negotiation of condom use during sexual encounters).

- The TRA does not acknowledge the potential transaction between the predictor variables (attitudes and subjective norms) and the outcomes of intention or behaviour. Behaviour itself may shape attitudes. This highlights the need for prospective longitudinal studies that examine the changing relationships between variables over time and make more possible the disentangling of cause–effect relationships (note that this criticism can also be applied to the TPB – see below).

■ The theory of planned behaviour

In order to improve the model's ability to address non-volitional behaviour, the TRA was extended to include the concept of perceived behavioural control, becoming known as the theory of planned behaviour (Ajzen 1985, 1991; see Figure 5.2).

Perceived behavioural control (PBC) is defined as a person's belief that they have control over their own behaviour in certain situations, even when facing particular barriers (e.g. I believe it will be easy for me not to smoke even if I go to the pub in the evening). The model also proposed that PBC would directly influence intention and thus, indirectly, behaviour. A direct relationship between PBC and behaviour was also considered possible if perceptions of control were accurate, meaning that if a person believes that they have control over their diet, they may well intend to change it and subsequently do so, but if the preparation of food is in fact under someone else's control, behavioural change is less likely even if a positive intention had been formed) (Rutter and Quine 2002: 12). PBC beliefs themselves are influenced by many factors, including past behaviour and past successes or failures in relation to the behaviour in question, and in this way the PBC construct is very similar to that of self-efficacy. For example, a person who has never tried to stop smoking before may have lower PBC beliefs than a person who has succeeded in stopping previously and who therefore may believe that it will be relatively easy to do so again.

Generally, the TPB has had more success in predicting behavioural change than its predecessor (Sheeran and Orbell 1998). With Ajzen (1991) reporting a mean correlation between PBC and intention of 0.71, it is clear that this construct has been an important addition, although intention remains a stronger predictor of subsequent behaviour than PBC is directly. It has been suggested that PBC may be most powerful when it is considered in inter-action with the other components of the model, such as attitudes and motivations (Eagly and Chaiken 1993) and even more dispositional measures of locus of control (e.g. Armitage 2003). In a large-scale meta-analysis of studies employing the TPB, its variables accounted for between 40 and 50 per-cent of variance in *intention* and between 19 and 38 percent of the variance in *behaviour* (Sutton 1998). The TPB has been tested extensively in relation to health behaviour, or behavioural intention, and interested readers are referred to Sutton's (*ibid.*) review of studies, as we can provide only a few examples here.

The TPB and preventive behaviour

Hagger, Chatzisarantis, Biddle and Orbell (2001) used the TPB to examine children's physical activity intentions and behaviour and found that atti-tudes, perceived behavioural control and intention were significant influences on exercise behaviour at a one-week follow-up. Perceived behavioural control and attitude both predicted intention, whereas, surprisingly, subjective norm did not. This is in contrast to an earlier study by Godin and Shephard (1986) in exactly the same age group, where subjective norm was predictive. How-ever, various differences exist between the two studies, including for example the fact that Godin's sample was American, where the benefits of exercise – or the risks of obesity – have possibly become more known over the last twenty-five years, hypothetically strengthening the role of personal attitudes and beliefs over social norms.

The uptake of screening opportunities for cervical cancer and breast cancer has been extensively explored. For example, Rutter (2000) found that intention to attend screening was predicted by attitude, perceived behavioural control and subjective norm, although only attitude and sub-jective norm were predictive of actual uptake of screening. Studies of self-screening, in terms of breast or testicular self-examination, report similar differences in predictors of intention compared with predictors of actual behaviour, but more longitudinal studies are crucial if a causal relationship is to be confirmed.

Armitage and Connor (2002) found that the intention to eat or not eat a low-fat diet could be distinguished on the basis of more positive attitudes towards a low-fat diet (higher outcome expectancies and value), although it should be noted that the subsequent intervention targeting attitudes had a limited effect on actual dietary behaviour.

Hunter, Grunfeld and Ramirez (2003) examined the predictors of inten-tion to seek help from a GP for breast cancer symptoms among a general population sample of women. Attitudes towards help seeking (e.g. 'making an appointment to see my doctor for a symptom that might be cancer would be good/bad, beneficial/harmful, pleasant/unpleasant, wise/foolish, necessary/unnecessary) and perceived behavioural control (e.g. 'there is nothing I could do to make sure I got help for a breast cancer symptom': agree–disagree (seven-point scale)) explained a small but significant amount of variance in intention (7.1 percent). Subjective norms were not predictive of intention to seek help for such symptoms. It is important to note that the authors also examined participants' perceptions of cancer (**illness representations**; see Chapter 9) and entered these variables into the regression analysis before the TPB variables. Illness representations explained 22 percent of the variance in intention, and the TPB variables added a further 7.1 percent thereafter. This highlights the importance of considering individuals' perceptions of the illness that the behaviour in question is related to. For example, when examining smoking behaviour, perhaps perceptions of cancer or COPD should be more fully addressed.

illness representations
beliefs about a particular illness and state of ill health – commonly ascribed to the five domains described by Leventhal: identity, timeline, cause, consequences and control/cure.

Cross-sectional studies of TPB variables and intention to attend breast screening found subjective norm and perceived behavioural control to be significantly predictive of mammography intention, and attitudes and PBC predictive of intention to undergo a clinical breast examination (Godin, Gagné, Maziade *et al.* 2001). A prospective longitudinal study of predictors of mammography uptake is presented in RESEARCH FOCUS.

RESEARCH FOCUS

Belief salience and theory of planned behaviour variables predict breast screening attendance

Steadman, Rutter and Field (2002). *British Journal of Health Psychology*, 7: 317–31.

Background
This study draws upon findings from earlier studies using the theory of planned behaviour, where subjective norm (SN) beliefs have been found to be partial explanations of intention to act (in addition to attitude and perceived behavioural control) but less often predictors of behaviour. In these studies, subjective norm is generally assessed by asking individuals to state what they believe the norms and expectancies of a range of listed other people are in relation to the behaviour in question. In this method of questioning, an individual is prompted to think of many people or many influences and a 'modal' belief is what is analysed. The same applies to calculations of attitudes, as totals are used rather than examining the strength and **salience** of individual attitudes therein. Steadman and colleagues argue that in modal beliefs there may be one or more highly salient beliefs that hold high importance to the individual and that prediction of outcomes may be improved if such salient beliefs are analysed rather than modal beliefs.

salience
strength and importance.

Aims of study
To establish both the modal subjective norm beliefs and the individually salient beliefs held by a sample of women who had been invited for breast cancer screening mammography, either as a result of being aged between 50 and 53 and newly eligible for mammography

screening, or as older women (54–64) being re-screened as part of the National Health Service breast screening programme. It was hypothesised that individually generated subjective norm beliefs would have a stronger relationship with intention, and with subsequent uptake of screening, than would modal subjective norm beliefs.

Methods

1,000 women were randomly assigned to either a condition receiving a questionnaire composed of items assessing TPB constructs, which included a section assessing modal SN beliefs, or to a condition receiving the same core questionnaire but with a section enabling participants to generate individual SN beliefs. The first condition responded to items that asked whether 'My husband or partner/daughter/friends/GP/sister/friends from my religion/experts from the media . . . think that I should have my breasts screened if invited', followed by a further question for each influence acknowledged: 'Generally speaking I want to do what (the specific normative influence e.g. husband) . . . thinks I should do' (motivation to comply). The scores on each item are then added. In the second condition, women were first invited to name one person 'in particular' who would want them to attend screening, and if they could do this they also identified who it was, and then scored their motivation to comply with this person's wishes. If they could not identify one person in particular (the most salient), they were invited to think of up to six people and score the motivation to comply item for each of these individuals.

Results

64 percent of the initial sample completed the study. 15 percent of women in the individual condition were unable to elicit a normative influence, and 9 percent of those in the modal condition ticked 'not relevant' to each of the listed potential normative influences. Data from these women were not used further.

The mean number of normative influences elicited in the individual condition was significantly lower than the mean number of influences in the modal condition (mean 2.11, s.d. 1.04) compared with mean 4.17 (s.d. 1.72), but their overall subjective norm rating score was significantly higher (mean 18.12, s.d. 4.14) compared with mean 13.97 (s.d. 5.33). Partners were the most commonly mentioned normative influence in the individual group (74 percent), whereas in the modal group GPs were the most frequent (88 percent). No between-group differences were found on the other TPB items, i.e. attitude, perceived behavioural control or intention.

Contrary to the hypothesis, there was not a stronger association between individual SNs and intention than there was between modal SN beliefs and intention. (In both groups, attitudes and pbc also correlated with intention.) However, there was a significant relationship between individual SNs and subsequent attendance (attitude and intention also correlated with attendance), whereas modal SNs were not associated with attendance (and neither were attitude or PBC, although intention was).

These correlations were then tested prospectively. For the condition assessing modal SN beliefs, the TPB model was supported (attitude, SN and PBC predicted 30 percent variance in intention – but not behaviour), and intention predicted 7 percent variance in behaviour. In contrast, the condition assessing individual SN beliefs found direct links between attitude, SN, PBC and intention (24 percent variance explained), but, in addition, SN had a direct effect on actual attendance, adding to the prediction offered by intention (13 percent variance explained). While these findings suggest better prediction of attendance by assessing individually salient SNs, the difference between the two conditions (modal versus individual SN beliefs) was not actually significant.

continued

Additional analysis examining only the first two normative influences endorsed by those in the individual condition found that these data explained as much as the total SN data, suggesting that the first-named normative influences are the most salient. Similarly, when the normative influences in the modal condition were examined individually, only those pertaining to husband/partner had a significant relationship with intention and behaviour.

Discussion

The results only partially confirmed the authors' hypotheses. There was not a stronger association between individual beliefs and intention or attendance behaviour than between modal beliefs and intention or attendance. However, there was evidence of individual beliefs adding to the prediction of attendance, a result not found in terms of modal SN beliefs. Previous studies have not reported an effect of SN on mammography uptake behaviour, and this may be, as the authors conclude, because 'an individually generated subjective norm is a more sensitive and accurate estimate of the true effect of normative pressure' (p. 327). The hypothesis that the first-mentioned individual influences would be the most salient predictors was confirmed. The finding that, in the modal group, while total SN had no relationship with attendance behaviour, the husband/partner items *did*, is highly important. Such a finding may explain why few studies have previously reported effects of SN on behaviour; i.e. they have been relying on grouped SN data and not considering that different normative influences may be more salient. The implications of this finding alone for how future studies assess TPB components are significant.

It is worth noting that while the removal of data for those who could not identify a normative influence on their behaviour was necessary for this study, this group of women are an interesting group in that their decisions about screening uptake are likely to be made on a very individual basis.

The TPB and risk-reducing behaviour

Two very different examples of a 'risk' behaviour will be illustrated briefly here: smoking, which is fundamentally an individual behaviour requiring one person only for its performance (although there are undisputed social influences and consequences) and which is generally considered 'addictive'; and, second, unprotected sexual intercourse, a behaviour that (generally) involves two people. Sexual behaviour involves a social encounter or interaction and is likely to be more situationally influenced. Unlike smoking, few would argue that sex was addictive for the majority of those engaged in it (although sexual addiction may exist for some people; see Orford 2001). There are sufficient differences between these two types of behaviour to perhaps expect that the predictors of each may differ.

In relation to smoking, Godin, Valoise, Lepage *et al.* (1992) reported that the frequency of smoking behaviour over a six-month period among a general population sample could be explained primarily by low perceived behavioural control beliefs. Norman, Conner and Bell (1999) applied the TPB to smoking cessation and found that the best predictor of intention to quit was perceived behavioural control, but also beliefs in one's susceptibility to the negative health consequences of continued smoking. Few studies have actually applied the TPB to smoking cessation, acknowledging that addictive behaviour is subject to other controlling and contributing factors than is behaviour of a more volitional nature. In saying that, however, beliefs in control over the behaviour, and in particular self-efficacy beliefs (as defined in a later model, the HAPA), have been found to be salient.

Sutton, McVey and Glanz (1999) compared the TRA and the TPB in predicting the use of condoms and did not find that perceived behavioural control added significantly to the TRA components' explanation of this behaviour. This is in spite of the fact that PBC has been cited as an issue for women regarding the use of condoms in sexual encounters (e.g. Abraham, Sheeran, Abrams *et al.* 1996; Bury, Morrison and MacLachlan 1992; Chan and Fishbein 1993; Yzer, Fisher, Bakker *et al.* 1998). Factors associated with condom use include previous use of condoms, a positive attitude towards use, subjective norms of use by others, self-efficacy in relation to both the purchase and use of condoms, and intentions (see Sheeran, Abraham and Orbell (1999) for a meta-analysis of studies). However, many studies have been conducted in educated young adult populations (e.g. students) rather than in more 'chaotic' populations such as injecting drug users, who are at above average risk of HIV infection (e.g. Morrison 1991a) and for whom behaviour change is crucial. It is also important to address whether sexual partners are long-term or casual, as this will also affect real and possibly perceived risk, as well as potentially attitudes towards the need for, and importance of, 'safe sex'. These factors are likely to influence whether or not the issue of using condoms is raised with a potential partner. It has been suggested that for some individuals the non-use of condoms (or the use of condoms) is less governed by intention (and by implication the cognitive processes that the TPB claims precede intention) than by habit, and as such interventions should be targeted very early in a sexual career so as to facilitate the development of 'safer sex' habits (cf. Yzer, Siero and Buunk 2001).

Limitations of the TPB

The prediction of behaviour from the TPB variables is significantly lower than the prediction of intention (e.g. Godin and Kok 1996), providing strong evidence for the need to identify further variables that move an individual from intention to action. While the model claims to be 'sufficient', i.e. that other variables *not* in the model would not account for additional prediction of intention or behaviour, several authors have challenged this and pointed to other factors that have in fact added additional explained variance in intention, and in subsequent behaviour. These include variables that are either affective (emotional) in nature or that relate to planning processes that are involved in the initiation of action following intention formation:

- *'Moral norms'*: rather than a behaviour being influenced only by subjective social norms as in the TPB, it has been recognised that some intentions and behaviour may be partially motivated by moral norms, particularly behaviour that directly involve others such as condom use or drink-driving (e.g. Evans and Norman 2002; Armitage and Conner 1998; Manstead 2000).

- *Anticipatory regret* (Triandis 1977; Bell 1982): it has been shown that anticipating that regret would result if a certain behavioural decision was made influences both future behavioural intentions and behaviour. For example, anticipatory regret regarding unprotected sexual intercourse increased an individual's intention to use condoms (e.g. Richard, van der Pligt and de Vries 1996; van der Pligt and de Vries 1998), although in relation to a single occasion of heavy drinking, anticipating negative affect was not associated with changes in drinking intentions or behaviour (Murgraff, McDermott, White and Phillips 1999). The nature of the behaviour and how it is perceived (e.g. risky unprotected sex/less risky drinking occasion) may therefore moderate the effect of anticipatory regret, and further research is needed to explore this. Perugini and Bagozzi (2001) propose that anticipatory emotions (including regret) arise from a person's consideration of the likelihood of attaining or not attaining the desirable outcomes or goals of the behaviour.

- *Self-identity*: how one perceives and labels oneself may influence intention above and beyond the effect of core TPB variables. For example, self-identifying as a 'green consumer' increased intention to eat organic vegetables (Sparks and Shepherd 1992), suggesting that we behave in a manner that is consistent with our self-image.

- *Implementation intention* (II): forming an II is thought to be part of the process involved in turning an intention into action, i.e. filling the intention–behaviour gap highlighted by limitations in behavioural prediction by TPB studies (see below).

- Armitage, Conner, Loach and Willetts (1999) compared the predictive utility of *self-efficacy beliefs* with *perceived behavioural control beliefs* in relation to the use of legal and illegal drugs and found that self-efficacy beliefs were more strongly associated with behaviour than were perceived behavioural control beliefs.

Of these possible additions to theories of behaviour change, self-efficacy, anticipatory regret and implementation intentions are currently receiving the most research attention and the most empirical support in terms of adding to the explanation of behaviour.

Implementation intentions

One of the reasons why people may not always translate their intentions into action is that they have not made adequate plans as to how, when and where they will implement their intention. Gollwitzer suggests that individuals need to shift from a mindset typical of the motivation (pre-doing) phase towards an implementational mindset, which is found in the volition (doing) phase (Gollwitzer 1993, 1999; Gollwitzer and Oettingen 1998; Gollwitzer and Schaal 1998). Individuals need to make a specific 'when, where and how' plan that commits them to a certain time and place and to using a particular method of action. For example, rather than stating, as is typical in the TPB measures, how strongly I intend to stop smoking, an implementation intention would require me to state that I intend to stop smoking first thing next Sunday morning, at home, using a nicotine replacement patch. Although Ogden (2003) argues that this method of questioning is manipulative rather than descriptive and serves a different purpose to that of simply asking questions about one's attitudes or beliefs (i.e. it has the purpose of intervention and not description), many studies now include a measure of II.

Goal intentions can be distinguished from implementation intentions; e.g.:

- goal intention: 'I intend to go on a diet' (motivational, part of TPB);

- implementation intention: 'I intend to go on a diet on Monday after my party weekend' (planning, not part of TPB).

Implementation intentions have been shown to increase a person's commitment to their decision and the likelihood of their attaining a specified goal by carrying out the intended action. For example, Orbell, Hodgkins and Sheeran (1997) assessed the attitudes, social norms and intentions of women to perform breast self-examination and then instructed half of the sample to form an II as to when and where they would carry it out. This half of the sample showed a significantly higher rate of subsequent self-examination than the sample that had not formed an II.

Commonly reported barriers to attaining goals or implementing intended behaviour, such as forgetting or being distracted from it, can be overcome by committing the individual to a specific course of action when the environmental conditions specified in their II are encountered (Rutter and Quine 2002: 15). Illustrating this, Gollwitzer and Brandstätter (1997) describe how an II creates a mental link between the specified situation (e.g. next Monday) and the behaviour (e.g. starting a diet). It seems likely that IIs obtain their effects by making action more automatic, i.e. in response to a situational stimuli set down in the II, and in this way enable the person to overcome the 'when will I do this?' type of procrastination that stops many intentions being put into action.

Gollwitzer (1999) also notes that while forming proximal (more immediate) goals leads to better goal attainment than forming distal (long-term) goals, IIs do show persistence over time. For example, forming an II to take vitamin pills persisted over a three-week period in Sheeran and Orbell's (1999) study. This kind of finding could have implications for a range of groups; for example, hospitalised patients could be encouraged to form IIs about their home-based rehabilitation in order to improve exercise adherence and recovery post-discharge. While some people spontaneously form IIs when they form the motivational intention ('I intend to exercise'), many others do not and therefore the encouragement of the formation of IIs offers a fruitful avenue for health education and intervention (see Chapter 6).

Generally, goal attainment is influenced by the value placed on the likely outcome; by the belief that the goal is attainable through the person's actions, i.e. self-efficacy; and by the receipt of feedback on progress made (particularly important where long-term goals, such as weight loss, are involved) (Locke and Latham 2002). It is becoming clear that models of health behaviour change need to address personal goals more effectively.

ISSUES

How the method of measurement may influence the data obtained

It has been suggested that studies reporting evidence of unrealistic optimism (UO) in a sample may actually be witnessing a measurement artefact; i.e. UO may be appearing as a result of the manner in which the questions are asked (Harris and Middleton 1994). Weinstein originally asked one simple question in an attempt to establish the presence of UO: 'compared with others of my sex/age . . . my chances of developing "disease *x*" are . . . (great/average/low)'. In other studies, however, two questions have been asked: the first

continued

generating a rating for personal risk, the second generating a rating for the risk of similar others (see, for example, Perloff and Fetzer 1986; van der Velde, Hooykaas and van der Pligt 1992), and UO is considered to be present when the second rating is higher than the first. Hoorens and Buunk (1993) manipulated the ordering of these two questions and also the comparison group that their sample of adolescents were required to think of when making their risk judgements. They found significant effects of ordering whereby those rating personal risk first, and then comparative others' risk, exhibited lower levels of UO than those receiving the questions in the opposite order.

To illustrate ordering effects further, Budd (1987) carried out an experiment where the order of theory of reasoned action items was muddled across different versions of a questionnaire. He found that muddling significantly altered the intercorrelations between perceptions of threat, attitude, normative beliefs and intention to either smoke, brush teeth three times per day, or exercise for twenty minutes. Sheeran and Orbell (1996) tried to replicate this using *protection motivation theory* components (see later in the chapter) in relation to different behaviour – that of condom use and dental flossing. While fewer effects of ordering were found, correlation strengths between some key cognitive variables did change. These authors also report that scores on a social desirability scale, along with the perceived salience (relevance and importance to the individual) of the behaviour being addressed, had small but reliable effects on the associations between the health beliefs assessed in the PMT. These types of study highlight the need for researchers to take possible demand effects and questionnaire design factors into consideration when interpreting their findings.

Ogden (2003) further highlights these issues in a review of forty-seven empirical papers that tested the social cognition models outlined in this chapter. She concludes that while social cognition models offered useful tools to guide research, and that research had provided evidence of many of the model components explaining and predicting health behaviour, many findings did not in fact support the theoretically predicted associations. She suggests that part of the 'problem' is that the components of such models are generally assessed using self-completed questionnaires, which may in themselves create beliefs about the behaviour concerned. For example, a questionnaire with items addressing perceived susceptibility to a particular illness may increase awareness of an issue or may cause the individual to reflect upon their own behaviour and change their belief structure. Potentially, these changed beliefs may alter subsequent behaviour. For example, a recent research study examining beliefs and intentions about future, hypothetical genetic testing uptake for breast cancer (e.g. Morrison *et al.* 2005, in revision) asked participants to rate their attitudes towards genetic testing, their outcome expectancies, perceived benefits of or barriers to testing, and their intention to undertake testing were it to become available. For some individuals, this type of questioning probably caused them to think about something they may not have done previously. The questions provide information to the participant about the behaviour: e.g. 'To what extent do you think that genetic testing will: reduce uncertainty about my long-term risk of breast cancer; enable me to make positive decisions about my future', and this information could potentially change beliefs and attitudes. Some of health psychology's commonly employed methods of measurement, intended to describe beliefs or behaviour, may actually and unwittingly be operating as cognitive intervention! The direction of change could be manipulated by changing the wording of the questions, in the same way as other studies attempt to change beliefs by manipulating the nature of information provided (e.g. Morrison *et al.* 2005). While this may be desirable in certain circumstances, this issue of questions as interventions requires greater attention in research designs and greater acknowledgement in the discussion of findings.

Stage models of behaviour change

So far in this chapter we have reviewed static or continuum models, which describe additive components whereby perceptions or beliefs (or sets of them) are used in combination to try to predict where an individual will lie on an outcome continuum such as an intention or behaviour. Stage models, on the other hand, consider individuals as being at 'discrete ordered stages', each one denoting a greater inclination to change outcome than the previous stage (Rutter and Quine 2002: 16). The models described in this final section are stage models.

According to Weinstein (Weinstein, Rothman and Sutton 1998; Weinstein and Sandman 2002) a stage theory has four properties:

1. *A classification system to define stages*: it is accepted that the stage classifications are theoretical constructs, and although a prototype is defined for each stage, few people will perfectly match this ideal.

2. *Ordering of stages*: people must pass through all the stages to reach the end-point of action or maintenance, but progression to the end-point is neither inevitable nor irreversible. For example, a person may decide to quit smoking but not do so; or may quit smoking but lapse back into the habit sometime thereafter.

3. *Common barriers to change facing people within the same stage*: this idea would be helpful in encouraging progression through the stages if people at one stage have to address similar issues, for example if low self-efficacy acted as a common barrier to the initiation of dietary change.

4. *Different barriers to change facing people in different stages*: if the factors producing movement to the next stage were the same regardless of stage (e.g. self-efficacy), the same intervention could be used for all, and the stages would be redundant. Ample evidence exists that barriers are different in the different stages (see below).

The transtheoretical model (TTM)

This model was developed by Prochaska and di Clemente (1984) to address intentional behavioural change and was initially applied mostly to smoking cessation (e.g. di Clemente, Prochaska, Fairhurst *et al.* 1991) although much behaviour has now been examined by these authors in their work to validate the existence of 'stages of change' (e.g. smoking cessation, cocaine use cessation, taking up exercise, consistent condom use, sunscreen use, weight control, radon testing, reduction of dietary fat intake, mammography screening, and even the modification of delinquent behaviour; Prochaska 1994; Prochaska, Velicer, Rossi *et al.* 1994).

The model makes two broad assumptions: that people move through stages of change; and that the processes involved at each stage differ. As such, this model meets several of the requirements outlined by Weinstein above.

■ Stages of change

The stages of change proposed by the TTM are stages of motivational readiness and are outlined below, using dietary behaviour as an illustration:

- *Pre-contemplation*: a person is not currently thinking of dieting, no intention to change dietary intake in next six months, may not consider that they have a weight problem.

- *Contemplation*: e.g. 'I think I need to lose a bit of weight, but not quite yet' reflects awareness of a need to lose weight and consideration of doing so. Generally assessed as planning to change within next six months.

- *Preparation*: a person is ready to change and sets goals such as planning a start date for the diet (within three months). Stage includes thoughts and action, and people make specific plans about change.

- *Action*: for example, a person starts eating fruit instead of biscuits, overt behaviour change.

- *Maintenance*: keeps up with the dietary change, resists temptation.

While the above stages are the five most commonly referred to, there are also:

- *Termination*: where behaviour change has been maintained for adequate time for the person to feel no temptation to lapse and who believe in their total self-efficacy to maintain the change.

- *Relapse*: di Clemente and Velicer (1997) acknowledged that relapse (where a person lapses into their former behaviour pattern and returns to a previous stage) is common and can occur at any stage. This is therefore not an additional stage found at the end of the cycle as an alternative to termination.

People do not necessarily move smoothly from one stage to another. For example, some individuals may go from preparation back to contemplation and stay there for some time, even months or years before re-entering the preparation phase and successfully moving on to action. For others action can fail, maintenance may never be achieved, and relapse is common. The model therefore allows for 'recycling' from one stage to another and is sometimes referred to as a 'spiral' modal (e.g. Prochaska, Norcross, Fowler *et al.* 1992). The first two stages are generally considered to be defined by intention or motivation, the preparation stage combines intentional and behavioural (volitional) criteria, whereas the action and maintenance stages are purely behavioural (Prochaska and Marcus 1994).

To help to understand factors that influence progression through the stages, the model outlines the psychological processes that are considered to be at play in the different stages (with some being important in more than one stage). These processes include the covert or overt activities that people engage in to help them to progress, for example seeking social support and avoiding settings that 'trigger' the behaviour, as well as more 'experiential' processes that individuals may go through emotionally and cognitively, such as self-re-evaluation or consciousness raising.

These and other processes are the targets of intervention efforts to 'move' individuals through the stages towards effective and maintained behaviour change: for example, motivation-enhancing interventions or self-efficacy training (see Chapter 6).

- In the pre-contemplation stage, individuals are more likely to be using denial and/or may report lower self-efficacy (to change) beliefs and more barriers to change.

- In the contemplation stage, people are more likely to seek information and may report reduced barriers to change and increased benefits, although they may still underestimate their susceptibility to the health threat concerned.

- In the preparation stage, people start to set their goals and priorities, and some will make concrete plans (similar to implementation intentions as described in an earlier section) and small changes in behaviour (e.g. joining a gym). Some may be setting unrealistic goals for success, or underestimating their own ability to succeed. Motivation and self-efficacy are crucial if action is to be elicited.

- In the action stage, realistic goal setting is crucial if action is to be maintained. The use of social support is important in order to receive reinforcement that will help to maintain the lifestyle change.

- Many individuals, for example up to 80 percent of smokers who quit (Oldenburg, Glanz and French 1999), will not succeed in maintaining behavioural change and will relapse or 'recycle' back to contemplating a future attempt to change. Maintenance can be enhanced by self-monitoring and reinforcement.

The perception of barriers and benefits, or 'pros and cons' are also found to differ between the stages; for example, an individual in the contemplation stage is likely to focus on both benefits of change and barriers to change, but barriers may be weighted more heavily (e.g. 'even if I get healthier in the long term I am probably going to gain weight if I stop smoking'), whereas someone in the preparation stage is likely to focus more on the benefits of change (e.g. 'even if I gain weight in the short term it will be worth it to start feeling healthier'). The relative weight between pros and cons is referred to as **decisional balance**.

decisional balance
where the costs of behaviour are weighed up against the benefits of that behaviour.

- ## The TTM and preventive behaviour

Several interventions aimed at increasing exercise behaviour in middle-aged samples have been based upon the TTM. For example, Cox, Gorely, Puddey *et al.* (2003) conducted a longitudinal trial of an exercise behaviour change programme among sedentary Australian women aged 40–65. The intervention was either exercise centre or home-based and promoted either 'moderate' or 'intense' exercise levels. The study assessed participants' 'stage of change' regarding exercising and also explored the role of self-efficacy and decisional balance in relation to changes in exercise behaviour observed over time. Eighteen months following the intervention the women were reassessed. An increase in the activity levels of those who had received either intervention was found, almost independently of the stage of readiness that women had been in following the intervention. Additionally, the intervention produced increases in self-efficacy in line with the 'stage of change' achieved (i.e. self-efficacy increased as the stage progressed towards action) and appeared to be critical, whereas decisional balance findings were inconclusive. This reflects the findings of Marcus and colleagues (Marcus, Selby, Niaura *et al.* 1992), where regular exercisers (in either the action or maintenance stage) had significantly higher self-efficacy scores than participants in the earlier stages.

- ## The TTM and risk-reducing behaviour

In general, the notion of stages of change has received support; however, several studies have questioned whether the change processes outlined by

Prochaska and colleagues are in fact useful predictors of change. For example, Segan, Borland and Greenwood (2002) examined the changes in specific behavioural and experiential processes, self-efficacy and decisional balance among a sample of 193 individuals who were preparing to stop smoking and making the transition to the action stage. Results suggested that some changes in TTM components resulted *from* the transition to action, rather than preceded it; for example, increases in situational confidence and counter-conditioning (where positive behaviour is substituted for smoking). The main findings for the effect of behavioural and experiential processes were not reported, even though the TTM claims that these act as 'catalysts' for change. Furthermore, although self-efficacy was associated with making a quit attempt, it did not predict the success or failure of that attempt. Decisional balance was not predictive of any behaviour change, from quitting to remaining quit or relapsing.

Although a relatively small study, these findings have further questioned the validity of the TTM as a model of change, and they further reinforce the central role of self-efficacy, which is addressed fully in our discussion of a further model, the HAPA, below.

■ Limitations of the TTM

- Prochaska and di Clemente made suggestions for a timeframe within which they distinguish contemplaters from preparers (i.e. thinking of changing but not in the next six months versus thinking of changing within the next three months), but there is little empirical evidence that these are qualitatively different or differ in terms of the attitudes or intentions of stage members (e.g. Godin, Lambert, Owen *et al.* 2004; Kraft, Sutton and McCreath-Reynolds 1999).

- Past behaviour has subsequently been found to be a powerful predictor of future behaviour change efforts. This has questioned the usefulness of stages, where readiness or intentions to change are assumed to be key (Sutton 1996). For example, Godin *et al.* (2004) present findings of a model whereby recent past behaviour is combined with future intentions to produce four 'clusters' of individuals with different attributes in terms of current behaviour and future intention to exercise. These authors find that attitudes and perceived behavioural control in relation to readiness for exercise associate more strongly with membership of these staged clusters than with membership of the five stages of change that do not consider past behaviour. Such findings, if replicated longitudinally, would suggest that studies and interventions should be assessing both intentions and current or recent behaviour.

- Some authors have questioned the validity of five independent stages of 'readiness to change' on the basis of data that did not succeed in allocating all participants to one specific stage (e.g. Budd and Rollnick 1996). Such findings suggest that a continuous variable of 'readiness' may be a better description of this construct than one considered in discrete stages (Sutton 2000).

- The model may not sufficiently address the social aspects of much health behaviour, such as alcohol consumption (Marks, Murray, Evans and Willig 2000).

Table 5.1 Stages in the transtheoretical model and the precaution adoption process model

Stage	Transtheoretical model	Precaution adoption process model
1	pre-contemplation	unaware of issue
2	contemplation	unengaged
3	preparation	considering whether to act
4	action	deciding not to act (exit the model)
5	maintenance	deciding to act (proceed to next stage(s))
6		action
7		maintenance

The precaution adoption process model (PAPM)

This stage model (Weinstein 1988; Weinstein and Sandman 1992) was developed as a framework for understanding deliberate actions taken to reduce health risks and was intended to meet the criteria for a stage theory described by Weinstein himself (see above). Weinstein wanted to identify factors that distinguished stages of change in order that interventions could target the factors most likely to induce movement to the subsequent stage. Weinstein's model has seven stages, and it highlights important omissions in the TTM (and indeed omissions in other models) (Table 5.1). However, this model has not been widely utilised, and this is reflected in the time we devote to it here.

The PAPM asserts that people pass through stages in sequences, but as with the TTM there is no time limit within which to reach the action stage. The major difference between this model and the TTM is that the PAPM has a more sophisticated consideration of those in pre-action stages.

- *Stage 1*: a person is basically 'unaware' of the threat to health posed by a certain behaviour; they have no knowledge and therefore are not aware of a risk. This is likely when a rare or new illness is being considered (such as in the early days of HIV/AIDS or BSE (bovine spongiform encephalopathy)), or when the risk concerned is not subject to publicity, such as that initially attached to mobile phone use.

- *Stage 2*: termed 'unengaged', here a person has become aware of the risks attached to a certain behaviour but believes that the levels at which they engage in it is insufficient to pose a threat to their own health (I know smoking can cause various diseases, but I don't smoke enough for them to be a threat). This is seen as an 'optimistic bias' and led to Weinstein's development of the construct of **unrealistic optimism** (see earlier).

- *Stage 3*: a 'consideration' stage, akin to pre-contemplation. Individuals are deciding about acting on something they have considered. So many things compete for our limited time and attention that you can know a fair amount about a hazard but have only just begun to consider whether you need to do anything about it.

- *Stage 4*: this stage is important as it acknowledges that although perceived threat and susceptibility may be high, some people may actively 'decide not to act', which is different from intending to act but then not doing so.

unrealistic optimism also known as 'optimistic bias', whereby a person considers themselves as being less likely than comparable others to develop an illness or experience a negative event.

- *Stage 5*: a 'decide to act' stage, similar to intention/preparation. There are important differences between people with a definite stance who have decided to act and those who are undecided (stage 3). Individuals in stage 3 may be more open to information and persuasion than those with a definite stance (decided not to act as in stage 4 or deciding to act as in stage 5). As noted previously, stating an intention to act does not inevitably imply that a person will act. Perceived susceptibility beliefs are considered necessary here to motivate progression to action. Moving from stage 5 to stage 6 relates to moving from motivation to volition.

- *Stage 6*: the action stage, when a person has initiated what is necessary to reduce their risk.

- *Stage 7*: This final stage is not always required. This stage is about maintenance and unlike with smoking cessation, some health behaviour processess are not long-lasting, for example deciding whether or not to have a vaccination or a mammogram.

Weinstein has applied the PAPM to studies of home testing for radon, an invisible odourless radioactive gas produced by the decay of naturally occurring uranium in soil in some geographical areas. It enters homes through cracks in foundations, and although little heard of, it is the second leading cause of lung cancer after smoking (Weinstein and Sandman 2002). Perceived susceptibility (or vulnerability) was found to be crucial in the transition between stage 3 (trying to decide) and stage 5 (deciding to act). However, a stage-matched intervention, as with those based on the TTM, was not as successful in moving 'decided to act' stage 5 participants into action (buying a home radon-testing kit), as it was in shifting the undecided participants into making a decision to act (but not action necessarily).

More research using this model is needed to more clearly identify the processes that occur within and between stages in order to provide greater justification for stage-matched interventions, which to date have had limited effectiveness and are more costly than 'one size fits all' interventions (see Chapters 6 and 7 for examples).

The health action process approach (HAPA)

The HAPA is a model that has really taken on board the issue of stages and attempts to fill the 'intention–behaviour gap', crucially by highlighting the role of self-efficacy and action plans (Schwarzer 1992).

The HAPA model was developed to apply to all health-compromising and health-enhancing behaviour. It is particularly influential because it suggests that the adoption, initiation and maintenance of health behaviour must be explicitly viewed as a process that consists of at least a pre-intentional motivation phase and a post-intentional volition phase (Figure 5.3).

■ Motivation phase

As we have seen in earlier models such as the TPB, individuals form an intention to either adopt a precautionary measure (e.g. use a condom during sexual intercourse) or change risk behaviour (e.g. stop smoking) as a result of various attitudes, cognitions and social factors. The HAPA proposes that self-efficacy and outcome expectancies are important predictors of goal intention (as found in studies with the TPB and perceived behavioural control).

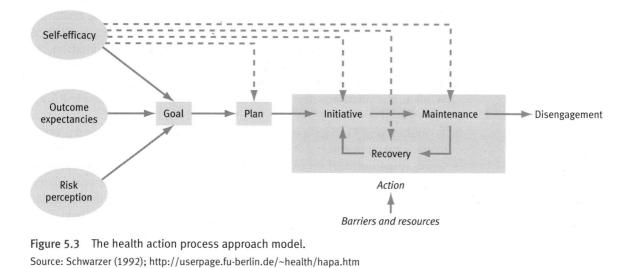

Figure 5.3 The health action process approach model.

Source: Schwarzer (1992); http://userpage.fu-berlin.de/~health/hapa.htm

Perceptions of threat severity and personal susceptibility (perceived risk) are considered a distal influence on actual behaviour, playing a role only in the motivation phase. In terms of 'ordering' of self-efficacy and outcome expectancies, the latter may precede the former (e.g. an individual probably thinks of the consequences of their action before working out if they can do what is required). Under conditions where individuals have no previous experience with the behaviour they are contemplating, the authors suggest that outcome expectancies may have a stronger influence on behaviour than efficacy beliefs.

Intention in the motivation phases is considered as a goal intention: e.g. I intend to stop smoking to become healthier. Schwarzer also proposes phase-specific self-efficacy beliefs, with self-efficacy in the motivational stage being referred to as 'task/pre-action self-efficacy': e.g. 'I can succeed in eating a healthy diet even if I have to change my lifestyle a bit'. At this stage, it is important for an individual to imagine successful outcomes and be confident in their ability to achieve them.

■ Volition phase

Once an intention has been formed, the HAPA proposes that in order to turn intention into action, planning has to take place. Here the model incorporates Gollwitzer's (1999; Gollwitzer and Oettingen 2000) concept of implementation intentions, described previously. These when, where and how plans turn the goal intention into a specific plan of action. Schwarzer proposes that at this stage a different kind of self-efficacy is involved, that of *initiative* self-efficacy, whereby an individual believes that they are able to take the initiative when the planned circumstances arise (for example, the morning of the planned smoking cessation arrives and the individual needs to believe that they can then implement their plan).

Once the action has been initiated, the individual then needs to try to maintain the new, healthier behaviour, and at this stage *coping* (or *maintenance*) self-efficacy is considered important to success (e.g. I need to keep going with this diet even if it is hard at first). This form of self-efficacy describes a belief in one's ability to overcome barriers and temptations (such as being faced with a birthday celebration) and is likely to enhance resilience, positive coping (such as drawing upon social support) and greater persistence. If, as many do, the individual suffers a setback and gives in to temptation, the model proposes that *recovery* self-efficacy is necessary to get the individual back on track (Renner and Schwarzer 2003).

While it is a relatively new model, early findings based on the HAPA are encouraging. For example, in a longitudinal study of breast self-examination behaviour among 418 German women, pre-actional self-efficacy and positive outcome expectancies (and not risk perception) were significant predictors of (goal) intention. Self-efficacy beliefs also predicted planning. In terms of actual BSE behaviour by the time of follow-up (twelve–fifteen weeks later) planning was, as hypothesised, highly predictive, with maintenance and recovery self-efficacy also predicting greater frequency of the behaviour (Luszczynska and Schwarzer 2003). This work offers strong support for the HAPA's development of phase-specific self-efficacy beliefs and a possible focus for future intervention studies. Although it is perhaps surprising that

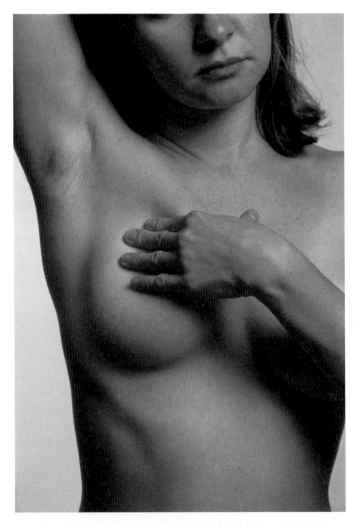

Plate 5.2 Breast self-examination can detect early breast abnormalities, which may be indicative of cancer. Early detection increases the chance of successful treatment.

Source: Alain Dex, Publiphoto diffusion/Science Photo Library

risk perception was not predictive (given findings of studies using both the HBM and the TPB), it may well be that risk perceptions influenced participants *before* they were actually assessed for the study and therefore effects on the HAPA variables had passed. It is always hard in research to establish an absolute 'baseline' for measurement, and such results should not be taken as proof that risk perceptions are not important – the body of evidence would prove otherwise.

ISSUES

Are models of health behaviour globally useful?

Health models such as those described in this chapter have brought our understanding of behaviour a long way. However, we are still far from being able to predict all behaviour (perhaps thankfully), and we are further still from successfully developing and implementing interventions that will maximise the adoption or maintenance of healthy lifestyles. While research employing these models has been plentiful, much of it, particularly in relation to the TPB, has been conducted among young healthy populations. The prolific use of student samples, for example, enables theories to be tested and built, and interesting questions to be addressed (such as what influences students' drinking behaviour and given its normative function can it be changed? Or what factors influence non-regular use of condoms, and does drinking alcohol interfere with even the best of intentions?). However, the findings of studies such as these may not translate across to prediction of behaviour among less educated individuals, or to those leading less structured lives, such as the homeless drinker or drug user; or even to those who are attempting to change behaviour as a response to a life-threatening condition, such as dietary change or smoking cessation following a heart attack. Other social, environmental, cognitive and emotional factors are likely to play a role in these diverse populations.

It is often thought that the models described here and used in a great deal of health psychology research focus more on individual cognitions than perhaps is required. Behaviour is influenced hugely by context, by socio-economic resources, by culture and by laws and sanctions. Presented below are some of the criticisms of research based on such models that should be considered if you are planning some research of your own:

- Different factors may be salient in relation to some behaviour but not others (for example, subjective norm may be more important to smoking cessation than to vitamin intake).

- The salience of certain factors may vary by age (attitude may predict intention to adhere to medication in adults, but not in children, where adherence may be influenced more by parental behaviour and beliefs).

- Culture and religion may significantly influence one's beliefs about health and preventive health, thus making the model components hugely diverse and hard to measure in a reliable and valid manner. For example, condom use is considered to be a sin against some religions and therefore health promotion efforts targeting increased susceptibility beliefs about HIV or STDs will face added barriers. Among those of certain faiths, drinking alcohol is banned, thus an individual who is drinking heavily faces very different emotional and normative pressures.

It is important therefore at all times for research to remember the context of behaviour and address such social and cultural factors. Health promotion efforts are likely to have limited success if the health behaviour is treated as though it exists independently of other aspects of human functioning.

Summary

Many proximal and distal factors influence our behaviour, and our health behaviour, such as our age, gender, attitudes, beliefs and goals. Continuum models like the HBM and the TPB have demonstrated the importance of social and cognitive factors in predicting both intention to act and action, although the static nature of these models leaves a need for better understanding of the processes of change.

Stage models like the TTM, the PAPM and the HAPA address processes of change and have gone some way towards filling the gap between intention and behaviour, and in particular the basic distinction between motivational and volitional processes is useful and important.

Perceived susceptibility and self-efficacy have been identified as important and consistent predictors of change. As such, they carry intervention potential, but tailored interventions for different stages are more costly than a 'one size fits all' approach, and evidence is mixed as to their success.

Further reading

Conner, M. and Norman, P. (eds) (1996). *Predicting Health Behaviours*. Buckingham: Open University Press.
An excellent text that provides comprehensive coverage of social cognition theory and all the models described in this chapter (with the exception of the HAPA). A useful resource for sourcing measurement items for components of the models if you are designing a questionnaire.

Conner, M. and Norman, P. (eds) (1998). Special issue: social cognition models in health psychology. *Psychology and Health*, 13: 179–85.
An excellent volume of this respected journal that presents research findings from many studies of health behaviour change.

Strecher, V.J. and Rosenstock, I.M. (1997). The health belief model. In A. Baum, S. Newman, J. Weinman, R. West and C. McManus (eds), *Cambridge Handbook of Psychology, Health and Medicine* (pp. 113–17). Cambridge: Cambridge University Press.
A useful brief review of research utilising the HBM, which raises the need for more complex examination of the interaction between, and weighting of, the various components.

Rutter, D. and Quine, L. (2002). *Changing Health Behaviour*. Buckingham: Open University Press.
An extremely useful text, which updates the empirical story told by Conner and Norman in 1996. The key social cognition models are now reviewed in terms of how the theoretical models have been usefully applied to changing a range of health risk behaviour, from wearing cycle helmets or speeding to practising safer sex or participating in colorectal cancer screening.

CHAPTER 6

Reducing risk of disease – individual approaches

Learning outcomes

By the end of this chapter, you should have an understanding of:

■ the costs and benefits of screening programmes for the early detection of risk of disease or disease itself

■ the use (and theoretical limitations) of the stages of change model in determining interventions likely to be most effective following detection of risk behaviour

■ the process and outcomes of the motivational interview

■ the impact of information provision on health-related behaviour following screening for disease risk

■ the nature and use of problem-solving approaches to behavioural change

■ how modelling and practice may increase the likelihood of behavioural change

■ the use of cognitive techniques to facilitate risk factor change

CHAPTER OUTLINE

This chapter considers strategies used to encourage individuals with no evidence of disease to adopt health-enhancing behaviour or stop health-damaging activities. It starts by considering the simplest approach to this issue – looking at the costs and benefits of screening people for risk of disease as a consequence of either their genetic make-up or their behaviour. The chapter goes on to consider whether screening for health-compromising behaviour, such as smoking or eating a high-cholesterol diet, by health professionals and offering advice to change is sufficient to motivate changes in risk behaviour.

The chapter then considers a number of more complex ways of motivating and maintaining behavioural change based on the degree of motivation an individual may have to achieve change. The first approach we examine is known as motivational interviewing. At its name implies, this has been used particularly with people with low levels of motivation to change their behaviour. The chapter then considers how effective educational programmes are in facilitating change before examining approaches based on problem-solving techniques, those involving learning from modelling and rehearsing new behaviour, and, finally, approaches targeting cognitive change. The principles of each approach are outlined, and evidence of their effectiveness is considered.

Promoting individual health

How we live our lives has important implications for how long we live, and the degree of physical wellbeing we enjoy while alive (see Chapters 1 and 2). Awareness of these issues, and also the potential financial consequences of an increasingly elderly and potentially unhealthy population, has led governments across the world to invest significant resources in programmes designed to prevent illness and promote higher levels of fitness and health among the population as a whole.

In the 1960s and 1970s, when health promotion became a serious issue for governments and healthcare programmes, most programmes targeted behaviour known to increase our risk for disease. Fortuitously, perhaps, one of the most widely prevalent diseases, CHD, is also the one most strongly linked to factors such as smoking or a sedentary lifestyle. These behaviours therefore formed a significant target for those involved in public health and health promotion. The emerging role of this behaviour in the development of some cancers (see Chapter 3) has reinforced the need to promote healthy lifestyles, and this remains at the heart of most health promotion programmes to this day.

The one significant exception to this generalisation is the increasing emphasis on encouraging safer sex behaviour in the light of the development of HIV infection and AIDS. Biomedical advances have also contributed to the type of preventive services that are now provided by many healthcare services. The ability to identify people at risk of breast, ovarian and bowel cancer due to their genetic make-up has led to programmes designed to identify whether individuals carry the genes that result in increased risk

of these diseases, although how that risk is managed once identified is perhaps less clear.

Two broad approaches to facilitating risk factor change can be identified. The first assumes that if we could inform people of their risk for certain diseases this will result in them engaging in long-term preventive behaviour. This model has resulted in screening programmes for risk factors for diseases such as CHD being established throughout the world. More recently, more complex technologies have been used to facilitate behavioural change. The rest of this chapter considers the impact of screening programmes on our physical and psychological health before considering some of these more complex strategies that have been used to facilitate individual behavioural change.

Screening programmes

A number of types of screening programme now exist (see Table 6.1). These include testing for genetic risk for breast and ovarian cancer, screening for the early detection of breast disease through regular mammography, and screening for the behavioural risk for disease in the case of CHD. Each carries significant implications for those involved and brings particular benefits and challenges:

- Women and men identified as carrying the genes for breast cancer may choose to take preventive action such as breast removal before the onset of disease and will have to live with the knowledge of their risk for many years.

- People identified as hypertensive may be placed on drugs for the rest of their lives.

- Those found to have behavioural risk factors for disease may choose to make lifestyle changes that have implications for both them and their family.

Table 6.1   Some of the common types of screening programme

Type of screening	Example of detection	Outcome of screening
Genetic risk for disease	BRCA1, BRCA2 genes for risk of breast and ovarian cancer	Screening for early detection of disease Preventive surgical procedures
Early detection of disease or its precursors	Cervical screening Hypertension Early breast cancer lumps	Medical or surgical treatment of any abnormalities found
Behavioural risk for disease	Smoking Sedentary lifestyle Poor diet	Behavioural change

Genetic screening

We have now identified the genes linked to a number of significant diseases. Here, we focus on the implications of screening for just one of them – the gene mutations that increase risk of breast and ovarian cancer, known as BRCA1 and BRCA2. The BRCA1 and BRCA2 gene mutations are responsible for breast and ovarian cancer in approximately 45 and 40 percent, respectively, of individuals with an inherited susceptibility to the disease (Hodgson and Maher 1999). However, while the risk of cancer associated with the BRCA1 and BRCA2 genes is high, they are relatively rare within the population, and only 4–5 percent of cases of breast cancer may be due to this mutation.

The Welsh Cancer Genetic Service (WCGS) provides an example of how a programme for detecting the level of risk an individual has of developing breast cancer and BRCA gene mutations can work. In this programme, both men and women thought to be potentially at genetic risk for breast cancer (and women at risk for ovarian cancer) are referred to the service by their general practitioner. Referral is followed by a letter to the patient from the service explaining the nature of the service and asking them to complete and return a family history questionnaire, which gives detailed information about their family history of cancer. Once returned, this is scored by medical geneticists, who assign a level of risk that an individual is at for developing cancer: population, moderate or high. Patients are informed of their risk level for developing cancer by letter and through telephone contact.

- Women at high level of risk are invited for further counselling and formal genetic testing involving taking blood and looking for the BRCA gene mutation, and they are offered annual mammography to detect breast lumps that may be tumours, or preventive removal of the breasts (mastectomy).
- Women in the moderate risk level are offered annual mammography.
- Women in the population risk group are discharged from the service.

Knowledge of risk can therefore have significant impact on the individual – and their children, who may also be at genetic risk. With these profound implications, one may expect participation in the testing process to be stressful. It is for some people, although most people seem to cope with no great anxieties. Brain, Gray, Norman et al. (2000) reported that 25 percent of women in the initial stages of assessment by the WCGS had clinical levels of anxiety and high levels of intrusive thoughts about the potential negative consequences of testing. Similarly, Watson, Lloyd, Davidson et al. (1999) reported that 28 percent of their sample of women undergoing genetic testing said they worried about their risk of getting cancer frequently or constantly, while 18 percent reported that worry about their genetic risk was a severe or definite problem. These levels remained relatively constant both before and after testing. Of particular concern is that this may not be a short-term phenomenon. Brain et al. found that while concerns about cancer typically fell in the period after participants were told their risk level, they rose again over the following months and by the one-year follow-up were at the same level as when the women entered the testing programme. In addition, being assigned a population risk level does not necessarily prevent anxiety. Lerman and Croyle (1994) and others have found high levels of distress even among those given apparently good news. It appears that once some people are alerted to their potential risk for cancer, this becomes a longer-term

health worry. We are not sure why this is the case. Perhaps these people find it more difficult to tolerate the idea of *any* level of risk than those who find such information reassuring and who stop worrying about their health. Despite this focus on negative emotions in response to risk assessment, most people do benefit emotionally from the testing process – something we consider below, see IN THE SPOTLIGHT.

People other than patients may also experience significant anxiety in the context of the testing process. Lodder, Frets, Trijsburg *et al.* (2001) interviewed both women undergoing testing for BRCA gene mutations and their partners before and after receiving a test result. They found that 20 percent of the women who were found to carry the mutation and 35 percent of their partners reported high anxiety levels after being told their risk level. Levels of anxiety were lower but still significant among the couples in which the woman was found not to carry the genetic mutation: 11 percent of these women and 13 percent of their partners were clinically anxious.

IN THE SPOTLIGHT

A different viewpoint on emotional reactions to health screening

Most studies of the emotional effects of cancer genetic screening have focused on measures of anxiety and depression. Studies with these *outcome* measures include those of Brain *et al.* (2000) described in the main text. An alternative model of anxiety or worry as a *motivator* to engage in testing is exemplified by studies such as Glanz, Grove, Lerman *et al.* (1999), who sent a questionnaire to first-degree relatives of patients diagnosed with colorectal cancer, assessing their willingness or intentions to attend counselling for risk of colorectal cancer. While 45 percent indicated an interest in taking it up, 26 percent said they definitely would when testing was available. Strength of intentions was predicted by the degree of cancer worry and perceived risk of cancer.

Despite these and similar studies, the wider emotional responses to cancer genetic screening have been largely ignored. One may go even further to suggest that screening programmes are viewed through a psychopathological perspective – asking what harm we do to people who go through them rather than what benefits people gain. This is clearly a very important issue, but such data present only a partial picture of the emotional response to cancer genetic testing, which may be more positive. Women are unlikely to take part in the testing process unless they have some positive expectation of benefit – evident perhaps through emotional states such as hope or optimism. Similarly, they may feel relief if the testing shows them to be at population risk.

What evidence there is suggests that many individuals with a family history of cancer seek to clarify their genetic risk partly to *reduce* anxiety (Hopwood 1997). Many enter the process with high levels of optimism and hope. In one of the few studies to examine these positive emotional responses to screening, one of the authors (PB) followed a cohort of women going through genetic testing in the WCGS, measuring their emotions at the beginning of the process and following risk information provision. The overall picture for these women was that although they felt anxious about their test results, they also felt optimistic about the testing process. After being told their risk level all the women, regardless of the genetic risk assigned, were more relieved, calm and hopeful and less anxious and sad when they thought about the testing process and their risk for cancer than when they entered the testing process.

Disease detection – the example of mammography

ultrasound
the use of ultra high-frequency sound waves to create images of organs and systems in the body.

fine needle aspiration
entails placing a very thin needle into a mass within the breast and extracting cells for microscopic evaluation. It takes seconds, and the discomfort is comparable with that of a blood test.

biopsy
the removal of a small piece of tissue for microscopic examination and/or culture, usually to help to make a diagnosis.

false positive result
a situation in which an individual is told that they may have a disease or are at risk of disease, but subsequent tests show that they are not at risk or do not have the disease.

Breast cancer is the most common cancer in women and the second leading cause of death in women. Mammography provides a means of detecting early cancers before they become obvious to the woman involved. Regular mammography screening among women aged 50 and older has resulted in reductions in breast cancer by as much as 30 percent within this age group (Fletcher, Black, Harris *et al.* 1993). The benefits of screening younger women are significantly lower, partly because of the lower frequency of tumours in this population, and partly because the higher density of breast tissue in younger women makes it difficult to identify small lumps within it.

Despite its benefits, mammography brings a number of concerns and anxieties, particularly for women who consider themselves to be at high risk for breast cancer. Such women frequently report high levels of anxiety both before and after testing – even when their mammogram is found to be normal (Absetz, Aro and Sutton 2003). Recalls for further testing may add to this anxiety. Mammography is not an exact science, and women may be called back for a second mammogram or an **ultrasound** scan, which provides a more accurate view of the breast if the results of the initial mammogram are not clear. Where lumps in the breast *are* found, some women may also have a small operation involving a **fine needle aspiration** or a **biopsy** to identify whether they are malignant or benign. Following this procedure, women may be told that the lump is benign (known as a **false positive**) or that it is cancerous and requires some form of medical or surgical intervention (a true positive).

This process is clearly stressful. Unfortunately, while some women may be reassured following these various procedures, others maintain high levels of anxiety for a long time. Austoker and colleagues (e.g. Brett and Austoker 2001), for example, followed a cohort of women who had experienced a false positive result. These women reported higher levels of anxiety than a group of women with an initially clear result for up to a year after their initial assessment. Although their anxiety levels then fell, they rose again in the month before their next routine breast screening was due – presumably as they began to worry about its implications. This anxiety prevents many women attending subsequent mammography screening (McCann, Stockton and Godward 2002) – an outcome that may result in increased levels of undetected early cancers in this group.

Given this potentially adverse outcome, a number of studies have tried to find out how best to reduce the stress associated with this type of testing. One approach has involved compressing all the testing procedures into one day rather than over a period of days or even weeks – a process known as one-stop testing. This approach has had mixed results – and the psychological outcomes may depend on the medical outcome. Harcourt, Ambler, Rumsey and Cawthorn (1998), for example, found that women found to have no problems (about 90 percent of those referred) appeared to benefit from it emotionally. By contrast, women found to have breast abnormalities did less well than those who took part in a testing and reporting process that took several days. Why this should be the case is unclear. Perhaps a longer time period allowed the affected women to adjust to the possibility of there being problems more than a relatively rushed process that occurred in one day. It may also have given them more confidence that the testing was accurate.

A different type of intervention targeted at women who were given false positive results was assessed by Bowland, Cockburn, Cawson *et al.* (2003). They randomly allocated women who had been called back for further investigations and then found to be free of disease into one of three conditions: face-to-face counselling, telephone counselling and usual care. In the counselling sessions, they were encouraged to express their distress, given relevant information and helped to develop solutions to any problems they had. The session took up to one hour. When the outcome data were analysed for all the people to be offered each intervention, there were no differences between the conditions. However, when the analysis was restricted to just those people who actually took part in the counselling process, those who were counselled scored better on measures of psychological and physical functioning than those who received the usual care. These results reflect the need to provide counselling not to everybody, just those who need or want it.

■ Increasing uptake

Despite the potential health benefits of mammography, uptake levels remain lower than optimal. In the USA, for example, the percentage of women aged 40 or more to take part in mammography screening rose from 14 to 19 percent between 1987 and 1992 (Martin, Calle, Wingo, *et al.* 1996), but over 80 percent of eligible women still did not take part in any screening programme. Many programmes are advertised through television advertisements, leaflets in general practitioner surgeries and so on. More complex interventions to try to increase uptake have also been used. One of the more impressive interventions was reported by Allen, Stoddard, Mays *et al.* (2001), who recruited a number of volunteers from the workforces of thirteen US worksites. These women talked about their own positive experiences of screening, gave breast and cancer information to their co-workers and provided social support for women thinking of or going to mammography. In addition, they each led a number of small-group discussion sessions, which provided information about screening, how to talk to healthcare professionals and how to set goals for health. They also ran two high-profile educational campaigns. Participants in control worksites had no such interventions. Despite these efforts, the percentage of women to report having had a recent mammogram increased only marginally in the worksites that ran the intervention over the course of the programme – from 5.6 to 7.2 percent: a non-significant difference. It seems that there remains a significant reluctance to attend for mammography.

Risk behaviour change

Screening programmes targeted at changing health behaviour have generally focused on risk behaviour for coronary heart disease (CHD): smoking, high-cholesterol diet, low levels of exercise, and so on. Some of the best programmes were established in the UK in the 1990s. Perhaps the most widely used approach was developed by the OXCHECK group (OXCHECK Study Group 1994). In this, all adults in participating general practices around Oxford who went to their doctor for any reason were invited to attend a health check conducted by a nurse. This involved an interview to identify risk behaviour for CHD as well as measurement of blood pressure and cholesterol

levels. Where appropriate, participants were advised to stop smoking, eat a low-cholesterol diet and increase their exercise levels as well as given medical treatment for hypertension and high cholesterol levels. Unfortunately, the outcome of this procedure was only measured some time after the intervention – at the one- and three-year follow-ups – and we therefore cannot be sure about the short-term effects of the intervention. Nevertheless, at both times there was evidence that some people had benefited from the screening programme. At the one-year follow-up, participants blood pressure levels were lower than those of people who did not take part in the screening programme, as were the cholesterol levels of women, but not men. There were no differences between the groups on measures of smoking or **body mass index**. By the three-year follow-up (OXCHECK Study Group 1995), cholesterol levels, systolic blood pressure and body mass index of both men and women who took part in the programme were lower than those of the controls. Smoking levels remained the same in both groups. It is difficult to disentangle from their results how much any changes in blood pressure and cholesterol were the result of behavioural change, and how much they resulted from the use of medication. However, the lack of change in smoking levels and, to a lesser extent, body mass index suggests that long-term behavioural changes were difficult to achieve. Indeed, the authors concluded that although the programme proved of benefit, changing difficult-to-change behaviour such as smoking may require a more intensive and specialised intervention.

Such an approach was reported by the Family Heart Study Group (1994). They evaluated the impact of a screening procedure similar to that of the OXCHECK intervention but added further counselling at between two- and six-monthly intervals over the following year. By this time, participants had greater reductions in weight, blood pressure and levels of cigarette smoking than people who did not receive the intervention. Their cholesterol levels did not differ. It seems that screening programmes may usefully be enhanced by the addition of counselling or other more complex interventions.

body mass index
a measurement of the relative percentages of fat and muscle mass in the human body, in which weight in kilograms is divided by height in metres and the result used as an index of obesity.

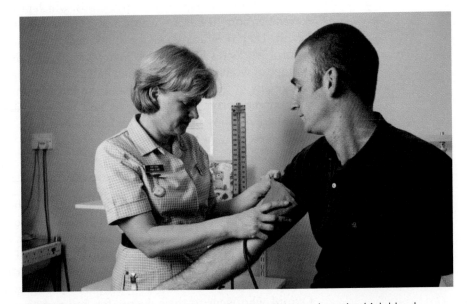

Plate 6.1 The simple process of measuring, identifying and treating high blood pressure can save thousands of lives a year.

Source: Alamy/ Medical-on-line

More limited interventions have targeted individual risk behaviour such as smoking. A classic study of the impact of the effects of simple advice on smoking levels was reported by Russell, Wilson and Baker (1979). In it, general practitioners either gave verbal advice to attenders at their surgeries to stop smoking or combined this with a leaflet giving advice on how to stop smoking. One year after the intervention, 3 percent of those in the verbal advice and 5 percent in the advice plus leaflet condition had stopped smoking. Only 0.3 percent of a comparison group who received no intervention had stopped smoking. Although these quit rates are relatively modest, given the simplicity of both interventions and the number of people attending general practitioners, these were impressive results.

These data were gathered nearly thirty years ago, when levels of smoking were higher and the health messages related to smoking were perhaps less well understood than at the present. It is questionable whether this level of intervention would have a significant effect now. As a consequence, many screening programmes now incorporate follow-up sessions in an attempt to encourage behavioural change. Lang, Nicaud, Slama *et al.* (2000), for example, reported on the outcomes of a screening programme conducted in a workplace setting. In this, doctors who identified smokers during routine annual health checks either advised them to stop smoking or developed a contract with the smoker with an agreed quit date followed by a telephone call made one week later to reinforce or encourage them to act on their decision. A second visit to the doctor was arranged between one and two months later. Information, brochures and educational tools were provided to both groups by worksite nurses. One year later, 13.5 percent of the advice only and 18.4 percent of the advice plus active intervention reported having stopped smoking – a small but significant difference.

One final issue should be addressed in the context of CHD-risk screening. Stoate (1989) found that a percentage of men who went through screening for high levels of blood cholesterol reported high levels of anxiety even when they were told their cholesterol levels did not place them at additional risk for CHD. It seems that some individuals may be vulnerable to similar health anxieties following screening for risk factors for disease as have been associated with other types of screening programme.

What do YOU think?

Combining genetic counselling and attempts at coronary risk factor change, Audrain, Boyd, Roth *et al.* (1997) fed back participants their level of genetic risk for developing lung cancer in an attempt to motivate smoking cessation. They randomly allocated smokers to either a counselling intervention or counselling combined with level of genetic risk. The risk factor information seemed to increase the motivation of some smokers to change, with almost a doubling of initial cessation rates in this group in comparison with the no risk information condition. By the one-month follow-up, however, any between-condition differences had dissipated, and there were no longer any differences in cessation rates between the groups. The authors noted that those who received the risk information were initially more depressed than those who did not, but these differences also dissipated over time.

Given that high levels of fear typically do not lead to long-term behavioural change (see Chapter 7) and may result in depression and learned helplessness (and may also result in long-term health anxieties), is it fair or ethical to use genetic risk factor information to motivate a difficult behaviour change?

Strategies for changing risk behaviour

The evidence reviewed above suggests that while some people will strive to change their behaviour once they are aware of being at risk for an illness such as CHD, many will not try to change their behaviour or will not be able to sustain any changes that they make over time. It has become increasingly obvious that making people aware of their risk status may not be enough to foster behavioural change (see Bennett and Murphy 1997). As a consequence, more sophisticated interventions have been developed to achieve these goals, some of which are considered in this section.

Historically, most one-to-one psychological interventions have been targeted at people who are relatively motivated to change their behaviour. Clinics are held in hospitals, out-patient departments or primary care centres, and the people who take the trouble to attend them are usually motivated to take an active part in any programme of change. However, this is not always the case. The introduction of screening programmes in primary care, for example, has resulted in the identification of many people who are not particularly motivated to change their behaviour. In response to this, efforts have been made to develop interventions that take into account people's differing levels of motivation to consider or engage in change rather than a 'one intervention fits all' approach. This targeted approach has generally been based on a stage model of change developed by Prochaska and di Clemente (1986). Their trans-theoretical, or **stages of change, model** identified a series of five stages through which they considered an individual passed when considering change:

stages of change model developed by Prochaska and di Clemente, this identifies five stages through which an individual passes when considering behavioural change: pre-contemplation, contemplation, preparation, change and maintenance/relapse.

1. *pre-contemplation*: they are not considering change;
2. *contemplation*: they are considering change but have not thought through its exact nature or how it can be achieved;
3. *preparation*: they are planning how to achieve change;
4. *change*: they are actively engaged in change;
5. *maintenance or relapse*: they are maintaining change (for longer than six months) or relapsing.

The model is thought to be applicable to virtually any decision relating to change, from giving up cigarettes to buying a new car. Prochaska and di Clemente noted that the factors that may shift an individual from one stage to another – and they can move back and forth along the change continuum or even skip stages – can differ enormously. As a consequence, the model does not attempt to specify what these factors are – merely that they occur and shift the individual from stage to stage. Accordingly, a smoker may shift from pre-contemplation to contemplation as a result of developing a chest infection, move to preparation and action after seeing a book on giving up smoking in the local library, and relapse after being tempted to smoke while out for a beer with friends.

Other stage models of change have also been developed. Heckhausen (1991), for example, identified four stages of change, each with a different cognitive content:

1. *pre-decisional phase*: thoughts about the desirability and feasibility of change predominate;

2. *decisional phase*: includes consideration of plans about how to change;

3. *change phase*: thoughts about how to initiate and maintain initial change predominate;

4. *evaluative phase*: consideration of how well any outcomes achieved compare with initial goals – leads to regulation of behaviour, maintenance or relapse.

Some studies have found differences in cognitive content in different stages of change. In an examination of incentives and barriers to physical activity for working women, for example, Jaffe, Lutter, Rex *et al.* (1999) found that while pre-contemplators had few positive expectations regarding exercise, contemplators had positive expectations but reported a higher number of perceived barriers. Despite this, stage theories of change have been criticised on both theoretical and empirical grounds.

Empirical studies have struggled to find a sequential process of change or to be able to consistently place any individual into one stage of change at any one time. Budd and Rollnick (1996), for example, reported that a readiness-to-change questionnaire was able to categorise only 40 percent of their sample of heavy drinkers as being in one single stage. Many of their responses to the questionnaire suggested that they were in several stages of change – a finding at odds with the idea of differing and exclusive states (or stages) of change. The model has also been found to have mixed predictive utility. While di Clemente, Prochaska, Fairhurst *et al.* (1991) found that the stage of change in which smokers began attending a smoking cessation programme to be predictive of subsequent levels of smoking, Carlson, Taenzer, Koopmans *et al.* (2003) found that participants' stage of change at baseline was not predictive of smoking status following a cognitive-behavioural smoking cessation group. Of course, in neither case do we know what influence taking part in the intervention had on participants' stages of change. Nevertheless, these data add little to support the stage of change model. These and other data have led critics of the model (e.g. Weinstein, Rothman and Sutton 1998) to suggest that motivation to change may best be thought of as a continuum, possibly measured as a strength of intention to change, rather than a series of steps from one cognitive and behavioural state to a differing one.

Despite these criticisms of the model, the stages of change approach has been useful from an intervention perspective in that it has focused consideration on what is the best type of intervention to conduct at each stage of change (or level of motivation to change if it is conceptualised in this way). The most obvious implication of the model is that there is little point in trying to show people *how* to achieve change if they are in the pre-contemplation or possibly the contemplation stage. Such individuals are unlikely to be sufficiently motivated to try to change a behaviour they feel no great need to change. By contrast, an individual in the planning or action stage may be more motivated to address issues of how they achieve change, as this is a pertinent issue for them at this time.

Motivational interviewing

The intervention generally considered most likely to be effective for people who are reluctant to engage in change is known as **motivational interviewing**

motivational interview
developed by Miller
and Rollnick, a set of
procedures designed
to increase motivation
to change behaviour.

(Miller and Rollnick 2002). Its goal is to increase an individual's motivation to consider change – not to show them how to change. If the interview succeeds in motivating change, only then can any intervention proceed to considering ways of achieving that change.

Motivational interviewing developed from work with people with problems of addiction but is now used in a variety of settings. It is designed to help people to explore and resolve any ambivalence they may have about changing their behaviour (Miller and Rollnick 2002). The approach assumes that when an individual is facing the need to change, they may have beliefs and attitudes that both support and counter change. Prior to the interview, thoughts that counter change probably predominate – or else the person would be actively seeking help to achieve change. Nevertheless, the goal of the interview is to elicit both sets of beliefs and attitudes and to bring them into sharp focus ('I know smoking does damage my health', 'I enjoy smoking', and so on). This is thought to place the individual in a state of **cognitive dissonance** (Festinger 1957), which is resolved by rejecting one set of beliefs in favour of the other. These may (or may not) favour behavioural change. If an individual decides to change their behaviour, the intervention will then focus on consideration of how to achieve change. If the individual still rejects the possibility of change, they would typically not continue in any programme of behavioural change.

cognitive dissonance
a state in which
conflicting or
inconsistent cognitions
produce a state of
tension or discomfort
(dissonance). People are
motivated to reduce the
dissonance, often by
rejecting one set of
beliefs in favour of
the other.

The motivational interview is deliberately non-confrontational. Miller and Rollnick consider the process of motivational interviewing to be a philosophy of supporting individual change and not attempting to persuade an individual to go against their own wishes rather than a set of specific techniques. Nevertheless, a few key strategies can be identified. Perhaps the key questions in the interview are:

- What are some of the good things about your present behaviour?
- What are the not so good things about your present behaviour?

The first question is important as it acknowledges that the individual is gaining something from their present behaviour and should reduce the potential for resistance. Once the individual has considered each issue (both for and against change), they are summarised by the counsellor in a way that highlights the dissonance between the two sets of issues: 'So, smoking helps you cope with stress, but it causes trouble at work because the rest of your office are non-smokers'. Once this has been fed back to the individual, they are invited to consider how this information makes them feel. In addition, Miller and Rollnick suggested that patients may be encouraged to consider more actively the benefits of change, and how things may be different were change to be achieved. Only if they express some interest in change should the interview then go on to consider how to change. Other key elements and strategies include:

- expressing empathy by the use of reflective listening (see the section on problem-focused counselling below);
- avoiding arguments by assuming that the individual is responsible for the decision to change;
- rolling with resistance rather than confronting or opposing it;
- supporting self-efficacy and optimism for change.

Given that the goal of motivational interviewing is to motivate people to consider change and to engage in any therapeutic intervention, it is perhaps surprising that most outcome studies have not examined this issue at all. Instead, they have focused largely on whether it can alter behaviour in the mid to long term. However, those studies that have examined levels of **motivation** have found it to be at least as good if not better at encouraging participation than more direct attempts at persuasion. Carroll, Libby, Sheehan *et al.* (2001) found that individuals referred to a treatment programme for **drug abuse** were more likely to continue to attend after an initial session that involved a motivational interview than if it did not do so: 59 percent of referrals attended at least one further session following a motivational interview, compared with 29 percent following a standard first session. By contrast, Schneider, Casey and Kohn (2000) compared the effectiveness of confrontational or motivational interviewing in persuading substance users to enter treatment for their drug use. At three and nine months into the treatment, an equal percentage of both groups had completed their initial treatment programme – and had made similar gains in terms of reduced drug use. However, the motivational interview was more acceptable and less stressful for both counsellors and clients than the confrontational approach – suggesting that it should be the approach of choice.

Initially, motivational interview techniques were used to help people who presented with substance misuse problems, a context in which it has proved effective. Hulse and Tait (2002), for example, found a motivational interview to be more effective than an information package in the treatment of early problem drinkers. More recently, the approach has been used with an increasing range of other behaviour. Rescinow, Jackson, Wang *et al.* (2001), for example, examined the impact of the 'Eat for Life' programme conducted among African Americans who attended black churches. They compared the effect of two interventions in trying to increase fruit and vegetable intake in the target group. The interventions involved either a self-help intervention with a telephone call to encourage use of the programme, or this approach combined with three telephone calls using motivational interviewing techniques. At the one-year follow-up, participants in the second group were eating more fruit and vegetables than those in the self-help only group, who in turn were eating more than a no treatment control group. Whether this was due to the increased attention given to the combined intervention group or the motivational elements is not clear. Harland, White, Drinkwater *et al.* (1999) reported an attempt to increase physical activity in a primary care setting using motivational interviewing. They conducted up to six motivational interviews over a period of six weeks designed to increase exercise levels, comparing them with a simple 'advice to exercise' control intervention. The programme showed some short-term gains, with more participants in the motivational intervention reporting increased exercise over the twelve weeks following the intervention than controls (38 versus 16 percent). Longer-term measures found no differences between the two interventions, however, suggesting that while motivational strategies may encourage initiation of a behaviour, differing strategies may be necessary to maintain behavioural change, particularly where this is a complex and demanding change as in the case of exercise.

motivation
memories, thoughts, experiences, needs and preferences that act together to influence (drive) the type, strength and persistence of our actions.

drug abuse
involves use of a drug that results in significant social or work-related problems.

Information provision

The OXCHECK programme described above provides a good example of a programme based on information provision. Such programmes have frequently been based on the assumption that people will make necessary changes if they are informed of the need to change and the nature of the changes they need to make. Many small-scale health education programmes are still premised on this assumption – screening programmes in many British general practitioners, for example, test for high levels of cholesterol and provide risk information and alternative dietary suggestions that a person found to have high levels may use. However, the relatively low impact of such interventions, as well as an increasing awareness and use of psychological theory (see below), has led to a recognition that any information provision about *what* to change may be significantly enhanced by information about *how* to change. A good example of this transition can be found in leaflets on smoking cessation available in the UK, the emphasis of which has shifted from a major emphasis on disease and damaged lungs to consideration of planning and implementing strategies of change. Booklets explaining the need to stop smoking have been added to by step-by-step programmes showing the individual *how* to stop and teaching any skills that may benefit them: e.g. cut down till you smoke about twelve cigarettes a day, choose a quit day, work out strategies to cope with habit cigarettes such as not carrying them with you, and so on. We consider a number of approaches that can enhance the effectiveness of simple information provision in the next few sections.

Problem-solving approaches

problem-focused counselling
a counselling approach developed by Gerard Egan that attempts to foster a collaborative and structured approach between counsellor and client to solving life problems.

Problem-focused interventions provide one form of strategy for considering how, rather than what, to change. They are best used for people who are willing to consider changing their behaviour and need help working out how to do this. Perhaps the most clearly described **problem-focused counselling** approach was developed by Egan (e.g. 2001). His form of problem-focused counselling is complex in parts but has an elegantly simple basic framework. It emphasises that the importance of appropriate analysis of the problem the individual is facing is a critical element of the counselling process. Only when this has been achieved can an appropriate solution to the problem be identified. A further element of Egan's approach is that the job of the counsellor is not to act as an expert solving the person's problems once they have been identified. Instead, their role is to mobilise the individual's own resources both to identify problems accurately and to arrive at strategies of solution. Counselling is problem-oriented. It is focused specifically on the issues at hand and in the 'here and now', and it has three distinct phases:

1. problem exploration and clarification
2. goal setting
3. facilitating action.

Some people may not need to work through each stage of the counselling process. Others may be able to work through all the phases in one session. Still others may require several counselling sessions. However, it is important to deal

with each stage sequentially and thoroughly. Flitting from stage to stage serves only to confuse both the counsellor and the individual being counselled.

■ Problem exploration and clarification

The goal of the first stage of counselling is to help the person to identify the problems he or she is facing (or may face) in achieving change. Various ways of finding out the information necessary to work out the nature of the problem an individual is facing include:

- direct questions
- prompts
- empathic feedback.

The most obvious way of eliciting information is to ask direct questions. These should be open-ended, in order to discourage one-word answers. Questions such as 'What does your family eat on a typical weekend?' are likely to elicit much more information than 'How often does your family eat green vegetables?' A second approach similar to direct questioning is known as prompting. Here, requests for information take the form of prompts and probes requesting information: 'Tell me about . . .', 'Describe . . .'. A further method of encouraging problem exploration is through the use of empathic feedback. Reflecting back to people an understanding of their situation or feelings through a simple comment ('So, it can be quite difficult to please all the family when you cook healthily') can encourage problem exploration as much if not more than direct questioning. Such feedback also shows the individual that the person counselling them has some understanding of the problems they are facing.

■ Goal setting

Once particular problems have been identified, some people may feel they have the resources to deal with them and need no further help in making appropriate changes. However, others may need further support in determining what they want to change and how to change it. The first stage in this process is to help the individual to decide the goals they wish to achieve and to frame them in specific rather than general terms (e.g. 'I will go to the gym on Tuesday and Thursday evenings' versus 'I must do more exercise'). If the final goal seems too difficult to achieve in one step, consideration of sub-goals working towards the final goal should be encouraged. Short-term success in achieving modest, short-term goals is more likely to motivate further change than pursuing difficult-to-attain, long-term goals. It is easier to lose two pounds of weight per week than to strive for a three-stone weight loss over an ill-defined time period. Goals must pay heed to an individual's personal resources, and their social and environmental circumstances. Even a short walk lasting ten minutes two or three times a week may be a sufficient initial goal for someone who has not exercised for some time.

Some goals may be apparent following the problem exploration phase. However, should this not be the case, Egan identified a series of strategies designed to help an individual to identify and set goals. A good summary of the problems an individual has identified can provide a concise and

structured means of focusing on the changes required. Challenge involves inviting the person to explore new perspectives. It is particularly useful when the person appears locked into old ways of thinking or feels that little can be done. These should be conducted with care. Direct challenges, however well phrased ('Well, why don't you try to lose two pounds of weight a week?'), are likely to result in resistance to change or feelings of defeat (see above). Accordingly, challenge in this context involves inviting the individual to explore new solutions, using phrases such as 'Perhaps it would be useful to look at some different ways of solving this problem'.

■ Facilitating action

Once goals have been established in the second phase of counselling, some individuals may feel they need no further support in achieving them. Others,

---

CASE STUDY

An example of problem-focused counselling at work

Mrs T took part in a regular screening clinic held at her local GP's surgery, where she was found to be obese and to have a raised serum cholesterol level. Following standard dietary advice, Mrs T agreed to a goal of losing two pounds a week over the following months. She was given a leaflet providing information about the fat and calorific content of a variety of foods and a leaflet describing a number of 'healthy' recipes.

On her follow-up visits, her cholesterol level and weight remained unchanged – so she saw a counsellor to provide her with more help. The counsellor used the problem-focused approach of Egan. In the first session, she explored why Mrs T had not made use of the advice she had previously been given. Mrs T explained that she already knew which were 'healthy' and 'unhealthy' foods. Indeed, she had been on many diets before – without much success. Together, she and the counsellor began to explore why this was the case. At this point, a number of problems became apparent. One important factor was that she was not receiving support from her family, and in particular her two grown-up sons. Mrs T was the family cook, in a family that often demanded 'fry-ups'. She accepted this role but had difficulty in not nibbling the food as she cooked it. Although she actually ate quite small (and low-fat) meals, her nibbling while cooking significantly increased her calorie and cholesterol intake.

Mrs T's husband supported her attempts to lose weight and was prepared to change his diet to help her. However, her sons often demanded meals when they got back from the pub, late at night and often the worse for drink. The upshot of this was that Mrs T often started to cook late at night at the end of what may have been a successful day of dieting. She then nibbled high-calorie food while cooking. This had two outcomes. First, she increased her calorie input at a time when she did not need calories. Second, she sometimes catastrophised ('I've eaten so much, I may as well abandon my diet for today') and ate a full meal at this time. It also reduced her motivation to follow her diet the following day.

Once this specific problem had been identified, Mrs T set a goal of not cooking late night fry-ups for her sons. She decided that, in future if her sons wanted this, they could cook it themselves. Once the goal was established, Mrs T felt a little concerned about how her sons would react to her no longer cooking for them, so she and the counsellor explored ways in which she could set about telling them – and sticking to her resolution. She finally decided she would tell them in the coming week, explaining why she felt she could no longer cook for them at that time of night. She even rehearsed how she would say it. This she did, with some effect, as she did start to lose weight.

who by this stage may have a good idea of what they want to achieve, can remain unsure of *how* to achieve them. This third phase of the Egan model therefore involves consideration of how to achieve any desired changes. Discussion between the counsellor and the person may still be necessary. One useful strategy at this stage is to brainstorm. This involves thinking through as many possibilities as possible. Once a list has been generated, these possibilities can then be sifted and the best strategies to resolve the particular problem developed.

Despite the generally acknowledged effectiveness of the problem-focused counselling approach, there has been surprisingly little empirical examination of its effectiveness. In one of the few studies conducted in a health promotion context, Gomel, Oldenburg, Simpson *et al.* (1993) screened hundreds of factory workers for risk factors for coronary heart disease (CHD), assigning them to one of three groups if at least one risk factor was found:

1. risk factor education
2. problem-focused counselling
3. no intervention control.

Participants in the educational programme received standard advice on the lifestyle changes needed to reduce their risk of CHD (following an information provision model) and some videos showing how to modify these risk factors. Participants in the problem-solving programme first went through an exercise based on motivational interviewing techniques. Following this they identified a number of high-risk situations in which they were likely to engage in CHD-risk behaviour (such as smoking or eating high-fat meals) or that could interfere with new more healthy behaviour (such as lack of planning leaving no time for exercise) and thought through how they could minimise their effect. This more complex intervention proved the most effective. Participants in this condition had greater reductions in blood pressure, body mass index and smoking than those in either the education-only intervention or no intervention control.

In a study targeted more specifically at reducing blood pressure, Elmer, Grimm, Laing *et al.* (1995) also reported on the effects of a programme that incorporated an element of problem solving. Participants were taught to recognise environmental or psychological cues that led to overeating and to plan how to change or cope with them as well as considering how to begin and maintain an exercise programme. They also worked with their partners to develop a joint strategy to support any lifestyle changes they made. One year after the programme started, the intervention appeared to be a success. By this time, 70 percent of the participants had significantly reduced their alcohol intake and increased their exercise levels. As a consequence, they had achieved significant weight loss over the year, and their blood pressure had fallen significantly.

■ Smoking cessation as a form of problem solving

Although they may not explicitly state it, many other behavioural change programmes have within them an element of problem identification and resolution. The example of smoking cessation can illustrate this point. Smoking is driven by two processes:

1. a conditioned response to a variety of cues in the environment – picking up the telephone, having a cup of coffee, and so on – the so-called habit cigarette;

2. a physiological need for nicotine – to top up levels of nicotine and prevent the onset of withdrawal symptoms.

acetylcholine
a white crystalline derivative of choline that is released at the ends of nerve fibres in the parasympathetic nervous system and is involved in the transmission of nerve impulses in the body.

Nicotine is an extremely powerful drug. It acts on the **acetylcholine** system, which, in part, mediates levels of attention and activation in the brain and muscle activity in the body. Its activity is bi-phasic: that is, short, sharp inhalations result in increased activity in this system as the nicotine bonds with the acetylcholine receptors and activates the neurons – resulting in increased alertness. Long inhalations, by contrast, result in the nicotine remaining in the post-synaptic acetylcholine receptors, preventing further uptake of nicotine or acetylcholine by the receptors – resulting in feelings of relaxation. Accordingly, when an individual stops smoking, they may have to deal with:

■ the loss of a powerful means of altering mood and level of attention;

■ withdrawal symptoms as a consequence of a biological dependence on nicotine;

■ the urge to smoke triggered by environmental cues.

The best smoking cessation programmes address each of these issues. Following a 'quit day' most call for complete cessation of smoking, following which the individual may have to cope with varying degrees of cravings to smoke as a result of withdrawal symptoms or encountering cues that previously were associated with smoking. Any withdrawal symptoms may take up to two or three weeks to subside, and be at their worst in the first two to three days following cessation. Accordingly, there is an acute period of high risk for relapse following cessation that may be driven by the immediate psychological and physiological discomfort associated with quitting.

Many programmes prepare ex-smokers to cope with these problems. Each set of strategies involves a degree of problem solving, as the smoker has to identify both the particular problems they may face and individual solutions to those problems (see Table 6.2). The strategies may involve:

nicotine replacement therapy (NRT)
replacement of nicotine to minimise withdrawal symptoms following the cessation of smoking. Delivered in a variety of ways, including a transdermal patch placed against the skin, which produces a measured dose of nicotine over time.

■ how to cope with cues to smoking – this may involve avoiding them completely or working out ways of coping with temptation triggered by smoking cues;

■ how to reduce the possibility of giving in to cravings should they occur;

■ how to cope with any withdrawal symptoms.

One strategy for coping with any withdrawal symptoms involves the use of **nicotine replacement therapy** (NRT), either as a gum or, more recently, as a **transdermal patch**. The development of NRT was initially seen as a major breakthrough that would prevent the need for any psychological intervention to help people to stop smoking. This has not proved to be the case. Indeed, most manufacturers of nicotine replacement products now recommend using a number of problem-solving strategies along with the NRT – a recommendation clearly supported by the outcome of clinical trials of their use. Studies that have examined the use of transdermal nicotine patches, for example, have shown high levels of cessation during their use but high levels of relapse

transdermal patch
a method of delivering a drug in a slow release form. The drug is impregnated into a patch, which is stuck to the skin and gradually absorbed into the body.

Table 6.2 Some strategies that smokers may use to help them to cope in the period immediately following cessation

Avoidant strategies	Coping strategies
Sit with non-smoking friends at coffee breaks	If you feel the urge to smoke, focus attention on things happening around you – *not* on your desire for a cigarette
Drink something different at coffee breaks – to break your routine and not light up automatically	Think distracting thoughts – count backwards in sevens from 100
Go for a walk instead of smoking	Remember your reasons for stopping smoking – carry them on flashcards and look at them if this helps
Chew sugar-free gum or sweets at times you would normally smoke	
Move ashtrays out of sight	
Try to keep busy, so you won't have time to think of cigarettes	
Make it difficult to smoke	**Cognitive re-labelling**
Don't carry money – so you can't buy cigarettes	These horrible symptoms are signs of recovery
Avoid passing the tobacconist where you usually buy your cigarettes	

when their use has stopped – or in some cases inappropriately long periods of use of the patches themselves (see Seidman and Covey 1999). Now most interventions use a combination of nicotine replacement therapy and problem-solving approaches.

Measuring the effectiveness of this approach, Molyneux, Lewis, Leivers *et al.* (2003), compared the effectiveness of usual care (no advice) versus a problem-solving approach alone or in combination with NRT in 274 hospital patients. The percentage of people who stopped smoking was higher in the combined NRT plus problem-solving group than in the counselling alone or usual care groups. The difference between the groups was significant when the patients were discharged from hospital: 55 percent, 43 percent and 37 percent of each group, respectively, had stopped smoking. By the twelve-month follow-up, the equivalent figures were 17, 6 and 8 percent. Similarly, Richmond, Kehoe and de Almeida Neto (1997) compared a problem-solving programme combined with either an active transdermal nicotine patch or a placebo patch. By the twelve-month follow-up, 28 percent of those in the problem-solving group plus active transdermal patch were not smoking at the time of assessment; 12 percent of those in the problem-solving plus placebo were not smoking.

So far, comparisons between intervention types have largely ignored the type of smoker in the trial. However, one interesting study took regard of the type of smoker who entered their programme. Hall, Tunstall, Rugg *et al.* (1985) identified smokers as being primarily nicotine-dependent or primarily habit smokers and assigned half of each type of smoker to either a problem-focused programme, which should be of maximum benefit for habitual smokers, nicotine gum aimed at nicotine-dependent participants, and a combination of both approaches. Each group did indeed fare better from the intervention targeted at their particular problem, although only the nicotine-dependent group benefited from the combined intervention. By the one-year follow-up, 50 percent of the nicotine-dependent smokers who received the combined programme were still not smoking, compared with 32 percent who only received the NRT and eleven percent of those who received the problem-focused intervention. Among the habitual smokers, the equivalent rates were 42, 38 and 47 percent.

RESEARCH FOCUS

Steptoe, A., Doherty, S., Rink, E., Kerry, S., Kendrick, T. and Hilton, S. (1999). Behavioural counselling in general practice for the promotion of healthy behaviour among adults at increased risk of coronary heart disease: randomised trial. *British Medical Journal*, 319: 943–8.

The authors note that while the Family heart study and OXCHECK trials only achieved modest improvements in the health of people going through screening programmes, their effectiveness could be improved first by only targeting people at high risk for CHD, and second by providing more behavioural and motivational interventions than the traditional educational methods used in these studies.

Their screening intervention was based on the stages of change model (see main text), with differing types of advice and behavioural interventions given to patients at different stages of readiness to change their behaviour. The intervention was carried out by practice nurses in patients at high risk for CHD. They reasoned that this more targeted approach on people at significant risk for CHD would result in more change than that achieved by the OXCHECK and Family heart study trials.

Participants and methods
Twenty general practices were allocated either to provide the intervention or to act as controls. The practices were matched for the level of social deprivation in the areas they served. Patients entered the trial at each practice if they were identified as having one or more modifiable risk factors for CHD:

- smoking more than one cigarette per day;
- high serum cholesterol;
- being overweight combined with low levels of exercise (fewer than twelve episodes of vigorous or moderate exercise for at least 20 minutes in the previous month).

Patients were excluded if they were receiving drugs related to heart disease or high blood pressure, or already had CHD. They received either behavioural counselling or a minimal treatment control intervention.

Behavioural counselling
One practice nurse from each of the ten intervention practices was trained in behavioural counselling. They were trained to assess patients' readiness to change and to use motivational techniques, goal setting and specific behavioural advice to enable change. The various goals and intervention approaches they used were:

- *smoking*: complete cessation – behavioural counselling + nicotine replacement therapy (see main text);
- *high cholesterol*: advised to increase fruit and vegetable consumption in the context of a balanced diet;
- *overweight/low exercise*: counselled to increase (their) activity levels to twelve sessions of moderate or vigorous activity a month.

Patients were invited for up to three 20-minute sessions with the nurse if they had two or more risk factors and for two sessions if they had one. These contacts were augmented by telephone calls as agreed by patients and nurses.

Measures
Outcome measures included:

- *Blood cholesterol levels* were measured before entry to the study, at four months (for those with high cholesterol only) and one year following screening.
- *Smoking* was measured using a questionnaire of the number of cigarettes per day at four months and one-year follow-up. Smokers who claimed to have quit smoking were asked to provide a saliva sample (taken as a swab using an instrument similar to a cotton bud). This allowed a measure of cotinine (a metabolite of nicotine) levels and provided a biological measure of whether or not people were smoking.
- *Dietary fat* was measured from a questionnaire measuring the frequency of various food-stuffs eaten.
- *Exercise levels* were measured from self-report of the number of episodes of moderate or vigorous episodes of exercise taken in the previous month, and at four-month and 12-month follow-up.

Results
A total of 316 intervention and 567 control patients were recruited. There were no differences on measures of age (average = 46.7 years), gender (406 men; 477 women) or marital and educational status between the intervention and control groups. At baseline, 404 participants (46 percent) smoked cigarettes, 365 (42 percent) had high cholesterol levels, and 699 (79 percent) were overweight and exercised infrequently. Of those invited to attend counselling, 90 percent attended at least one counselling session, 73 percent attended two, and 58 percent attended three.

Drop-out from the study
Overall, 71 percent of those people who entered the study completed the four-month assessment, and 59 percent completed the 11-month assessment. Those who dropped out were more likely to have been younger, to smoke, and less likely to have high cholesterol levels than those who completed questionnaires at each phase of the study.

Key outcomes
At four-month and 12-month follow-ups, participants in the intervention group achieved significantly greater percentage changes on a number of outcomes than those in the control group:

- greater reductions in dietary fat;
- greater reductions in reported number of cigarettes smoked per day;
- a higher percentage of people to quit smoking;

continued

- greater increases in physical activity;
- greater reductions in systolic blood pressure;
- there were no between-group differences on measures of cholesterol, weight relative to height, and diastolic blood pressure.

By 12-month follow-up, these between-group differences had been sustained.

Discussion

The authors note that the study had difficulty in recruiting and keeping people in the programme. Young smokers were particularly difficult to recruit and keep in the programme. This means that although the intervention appears to have changed behaviour, it did so in only a limited percentage of people at risk for CHD. Also of note was that the primarily self-report measures were not reflected in changes on biological measures such as cholesterol or weight – although the levels of smoking were verified biologically and of significance in reducing risk for CHD. Thus, the impact on long-term health may be quite limited. We note in this and the next chapter that changes in CHD-related behaviour have become increasingly difficult to achieve in time-limited interventions such as this, due to the wide availability of information about CHD. The impact of such screening programmes therefore still remains in question.

Modelling change

vicarious learning
learning from observation of others.

social learning theory
a theory that has at its core the belief that a combination of outcome expectancy and outcome value will shape subsequent behaviour. Reinforcement is an important predictor of future behaviour.

Problem-focused interventions can help individuals to develop strategies of change. However, achieving change can still be difficult, particularly where an individual lacks the skills or confidence in their ability to cope with the demands of change. Egan himself noted that it may be necessary to teach people the skills to achieve any goals they have set.

One way that these deficits can be remedied is by learning skills from observation of others performing them – a process known as **vicarious learning**. Bandura's (1977) **social learning theory** (see Chapter 5) suggested that both skills and confidence in the ability to change (self-efficacy) can be increased through a number of simple procedures, including observation of others performing relevant tasks (vicarious learning), practice of tasks in a graded programme of skills development, and active persuasion. The effectiveness of learning from observation of others can be influenced by a number of factors. However, the optimal learning and increases in self-efficacy can generally be achieved through observation of people similar to the learner succeeding in relevant tasks. This may be further enhanced by the use of what Bandura called coping models, in which those being observed demonstrate a skill or other behaviour in a way that does not leave the observer feeling de-skilled and not capable of gaining the skills. Where complex skills are being taught, behaviour may be shaped by observation of the progressive learning of skills by the models.

One way that this approach can work is through the use of video – an approach that has proved particularly effective in modifying sexual behaviour. O'Donnell, O'Donnell, San Doval *et al.* (1998), for example, monitored over 2,000 people who attended sexually transmitted disease (STD) clinics who were randomly allocated to either a control or an intervention group used to encourage them to use safer sex techniques – in particular to use a condom during sex. The intervention involved them watching a video that provided information about STDs and their prevention, portrayed positive attitudes about condom use and modelled appropriate strategies for negotiating condom use in different sexual relationships. The latter was an important element of the package: most sexually active people know how to use a condom, but many lack the skills of negotiating their use with a new sexual partner. Attendance at further clinics for both groups was tracked for an average of seventeen months following the intervention. By this time, the rate of new infection was significantly lower among those given the video-based prevention education than among controls (23 percent compared with 27 percent). Among a sub-group of individuals with a relatively high number of sexual partners, infection rates were 32 percent among controls and 25 percent among those who saw the video.

More direct measures of behavioural change also support the use of videos in this context. Zimmers, Privette, Lowe *et al.* (1999) found that reported use of a female condom among women who saw a video about its use at an HIV clinic was twice that of controls who did not see it. Mathews, Guttmacher, Coetzee *et al.* (2002) reported a different, and important, use of video in the context of HIV infection. They used it to teach attenders at an STD clinic in Kwazulu Natal in South Africa how to tell their sexual partners, who they may have infected with HIV, about the need to check their sexual health status. This is important as it would allow these individuals to be treated and to prevent further spread of HIV. As a consequence of the intervention, attenders' confidence in their ability to notify their sexual partners rose, as did the rate of sexual contacts who subsequently attended the clinic.

The effectiveness of video intervention may be enhanced by adding other behavioural change techniques. O'Donnell, San Doval, Duran *et al.* (1995), for example, compared the effectiveness of either a video condition alone or combined with a problem-solving skill-building session, with a no-treatment control in an intervention attempting to promote safer sexual behaviour among attenders at an STD clinic. Both active interventions proved better than no intervention, with the combined intervention proving most effective. One way of directly assessing the impact of their intervention was to provide all of the study participants with a voucher that they could exchange at a local pharmacy for free condoms; 40 percent of the people who took part in the combined intervention made use of this service, compared with 28 percent of those in the video condition alone and 21 percent of the no-intervention control group. It seems that while learning how to do things from a video can be effective, it can still be enhanced by encouraging people to think through how change can be achieved in their own context.

How long the effects of any gains of combining interventions may last is not clear. Kalichman, Cherry and Browne-Sperling (1999), for example,

Plate 6.2   Both watching others, and practice, increases the chances of people purchasing and using a condom.

Source: Royalty-Free/Corbis

compared the effects of a video and education group lasting for six hours with a group intervention using the same video combined with a programme designed to enhance motivation and skills as part of a programme to reduce HIV risk behaviour. At a three-month follow-up, participants in the motivation-skills intervention reported lower rates of unprotected sex than those in the video/education group. By the six-month follow-up, the gains in the combined programme had dissipated. These short-term benefits were similar to those reported by Jenkins, Jenkins, Nannis *et al.* (2000), who found that watching an interactive video increased their participants' intentions to abstain from sex and to change risky partner behaviour in the short term, but that these changes were no longer evident at follow-up. They concluded that risky sexual behaviour was particularly resistant to change but that the single-session intervention had some impact, which could be viewed as a 'priming' effect that could enhance multi-session interventions.

Behavioural practice

A further addition or alternative to problem-solving strategies involves the actual practice of new behaviour. Here, solutions to problems as well as skills needed to achieve change can be taught in an educational programme – increasing both skills and self-efficacy. In one study of this approach, again in the context of sexual behaviour, Kelly, Murphy, Washington *et al.* (1994) reported on the effectiveness of an intervention to reduce risky sexual behaviour among women at high risk of HIV infection who had attended an STD clinic. The programme included risk education, training in condom use and practising sexual assertiveness skills such as negotiating the use of a condom. This was compared with a standard education-based programme. The complex intervention proved the most effective. While the women in both groups did not reduce their number of sexual partners, those in the complex intervention reported that more of their partners used condoms on more occasions over the three months following the intervention. Evidence showing the benefits of including even a simple behavioural element in an intervention was reported by Weisse, Turbiasz and Whitney (1995). As part of an AIDS workshop run for young adults, they considered how to reduce the embarrassment of purchasing and using condoms. During the workshop, half the participants were asked to buy a condom from a local shop. Following the workshop, while all participants knew more about HIV infection prevention, only those who took part in the behavioural exercise reported less embarrassment than before while purchasing condoms.

Cognitive strategies

The interventions so far considered can be thought of as behavioural interventions, in that they attempt to directly influence behaviour. They may also result in cognitive change – increasing an individual's confidence in their ability to make and maintain any lifestyle changes, and so on – but this is an indirect effect. By contrast, cognitive strategies attempt to change cognitions directly – in particular, those that drive an individual to engage in behaviour that may be harmful to their health or prevent them making appropriate changes (see also the discussion of the principles of stress management in Chapter 13).

The central principle of cognitive therapy is that our thoughts are central to the regulation of behaviour. They influence our feelings, motivations and actions. Beliefs that encourage substance use or abuse, for example, may include 'I cannot cope with going to a party without a hit' or 'Drinking makes me a more sociable person'. The nature of such beliefs may change over time. At the beginning of a history of drug use, positive beliefs such as 'It will be fun to get high' may predominate. As the individual begins to rely on the drug to counteract feelings of distress, relief-oriented thoughts may predominate: 'I need a shot to get me through the day'. Cognitive interventions may be of benefit where such thoughts interfere with any behavioural change.

Key to any intervention is that the beliefs we hold about events that have happened or will happen in the future are *hypothetical*. Some of these guesses may be correct; some may be wrong. In some cases, because maladaptive beliefs ('I need a shot of whisky to get through this') come readily to mind, they are taken as facts and alternative thoughts ('Well, I might be able to cope without') are not considered. The role of cognitive therapy is to teach the individual to treat their beliefs as hypotheses and not facts, to try out alternative ways of looking at the situation and to have different responses to it based on these new ways of thinking ('Well, I've coped in this situation before without having a drink. Perhaps I can do the same this time'). This cognitive change can be brought about through a variety of processes. In therapy, the therapist may engage the person in what Beck (1976) termed a **Socratic dialogue** or guided discovery, in which their beliefs about particular issues are identified and questioned by the therapist. This is used to help the individual to identify distorted patterns of thinking that are contributing to their problems. It encourages them to consider and evaluate different sources of information that provide evidence of the reality or unreality of the beliefs they hold. Once they can do this in the therapy session, they can be taught to identify and challenge these automatic thoughts in the real world and to replace thoughts that drive inappropriate behaviour with those that support more appropriate behaviour. An example of their use is provided by this extract from a session adapted from Beck, Wight, Newman *et al.* (1993) using a technique known as the downward arrow technique designed to question the very core of an individual's beliefs – in this case about their drinking:

Socratic dialogue exploration of an individual's beliefs, encouraging them to question their validity.

Therapist:	You feel quite strongly that you need to be 'relaxed' by alcohol when you go to a party. What is your concern about being sober?
John:	I wouldn't enjoy myself and I wouldn't be much fun to be with.
Therapist:	What would be the implications of that?
John:	Well, people wouldn't talk to me.
Therapist:	And what would be the consequence of that?
John:	I need to have people like me. My job depends on it. If I can't entertain people at a party, them I'm no good at my job.
Therapist:	So, what happens if that is the case?
John:	Well, I guess I lose my job!
Therapist:	So, you lose your job because you didn't get drunk at a party?
John:	Well, put like that, perhaps I was exaggerating things in my head.

Here, the downward arrow technique has been used both to identify some of the client's core beliefs and to get them to reconsider the accuracy of those beliefs.

A second strategy is to set up homework tasks that directly challenge any inappropriate cognitive beliefs that individuals may hold. An example of this may be if a person believes that they cannot go to a party without drinking, they may be set the homework task of trying to do so. Clearly, such challenges should be realistic. If a person tries a task too hard and fails to achieve it, this may maintain or even strengthen the pre-existing beliefs. Accordingly, they have to be chosen with care and mutually agreed by both the individual concerned and the therapist. However, success in these tasks can bring about long-term cognitive and behavioural changes.

The complexities of cognitive therapy mean that it is used only infrequently in the context of prevention, although it is the dominant psychological approach for many mental health disorders (see Bennett 2003) and is more frequently used in people who have already developed health problems (see Chapter 17). However, it can be a useful form of therapy with people who have difficult-to-change behaviour such as addiction to alcohol or other drugs that may have harmful health consequences. In such cases, it has proved to be an effective intervention, although whether it is more effective than some alternatives is not clear. Balldin, Berglund, Borg *et al.* (2003) found it to be superior to supportive therapy. However, it may not be more effective than other active interventions. This is perhaps best exemplified by the results of Project MATCH (Project MATCH Research Group 1998). This large study compared three treatment approaches in over 1,500 American problem drinkers:

Alcoholics Anonymous
a worldwide self-help organisation for people with alcohol-related problems. Based on the belief that alcoholism is a physical, psychological and spiritual illness and can be controlled by abstinence. The twelve steps provide a framework for achieving this.

relapse prevention
a set of skills taught to people needing to achieve long-term behavioural change that prepare them to resist temptation and how to minimise the impact of any relapse should it occur. Often used with people taking addictive drugs.

- twelve-step facilitation (based around **Alcoholics Anonymous** and involving total abstinence);
- a combination of cognitive and behavioural techniques;
- motivational enhancement therapy (similar to but not the same as motivational interviewing).

By the end of treatment, 41 percent of people who received the cognitive behaviour therapy and the same percentage of those in the twelve-step programme were abstinent or drank moderately, while 28 percent of the motivational enhancement group achieved the same criteria. However, by one- and three-year follow-up, there were few differences between the three groups.

Other programmes have focused on teaching interpersonal and assertive skills to help participants to cope more effectively with stressful situations, refuse drinks, and so on. In **relapse prevention** programmes, high-risk situations are identified, and the individual develops and rehearses specific strategies to help them to cope with them should they arise. These may include specific strategies to challenge addictive beliefs and to cope with cravings to drink. Relapse is frequently associated with marital problems and prevented by strong marital cohesion. For this reason, some programmes involve the problem drinker's partner where this is possible. O'Farrell and Fals-Stewart (2000), for example, described an intervention intended to increase the communication and problem-solving skills of couples rather than just the individual. Both the problem drinker and their partner learned strategies to reduce consumption, including the partner changing behaviour that may trigger alcohol use, finding new ways to discuss drinking and situations involved with it, and new responses to their partner's drinking (see Longabough and Morgenstern 1999).

Summary

This chapter has reviewed two broad sets of issues. First, it examined the implications of programmes that set out to identify risk factors for disease or, in the case of mammography, to identify diseases at a sufficiently early stage that they can be treated before they became life-threatening. Second, it considered a number of methods by which people found at risk of disease can be encouraged and helped to change any health-compromising behaviour.

The first section considered three kinds of screening programme:

1. screening for genetic risk of disease;
2. screening for the early detection of disease or its precursors;
3. screening for behaviour that places an individual at risk of disease.

Each approach can be particularly stressful, although most people who go through these screening programmes benefit emotionally from them.

One of the outcomes of screening is that an individual may be asked to change any health behaviour that places them at particular risk of disease. A number of approaches to behavioural change in which the healthcare professional can work on a one-to-one basis were considered, each of which is likely to be optimally effective in people with differing levels of motivation or ability to change. The approaches considered were:

■ *Motivational interviewing*: a process of increasing motivation when people are not thinking of change or are not strongly motivated to consider change.

■ *Problem-focused counselling*: a structured approach to identifying causes of problems or elements that are preventing change, identifying new goals, and developing strategies through which to achieve those goals. This works best in people who are motivated to address particular issues.

■ *Modelling and rehearsal of change*: these can both increase the belief that an individual has in their ability to achieve change (self-efficacy) and provide them with the skills needed to achieve change if they do not have them.

■ *Cognitive behavioural approaches*: these address cognitions that may be preventing an individual from working on change, and they provide a structured approach to achieving change.

Each of these various approaches can be used either jointly or singly depending on the nature and magnitude of the problems an individual faces.

Further reading

Broadstock, M., Michie, S. and Marteau, T. (2000). Psychological consequences of predictive genetic testing: a systematic review. *European Journal of Human Genetics*, 8: 731–8.
A qualitative review of the psychological consequences of screening for genetic problems.

Egan, G. (2001). *The Skilled Helper: A Problem-Management and Opportunity-Development Approach to Helping*. Wadsworth.
One of the bibles of problem-focused counselling.

Miller, W. and Rollnick, S. (2002). *Motivational Interviewing: Preparing People to Change Addictive Behaviour*. New York: Guilford Press.
A guide to motivational interviewing from its originators.

Weinstein, N.D., Rothman, A.J. and Sutton, S.R. (1998). Stage theories of health behavior: conceptual and methodological issues. *Health Psychology*, 17: 290–9.
A good critique of the stage theories of change by some of their main opponents.

CHAPTER 7

Population approaches to public health

Learning outcomes

By the end of this chapter, you should have an understanding of:

- the benefits and limitations of using the mass media
- the elaboration likelihood model and its use in media campaigns
- how new ideas – including those related to health – may be transmitted through the general population
- how the environment may be used to influence health-related behaviours
- the outcomes of interventions targeting whole populations' heart and sexual health
- the nature and effectiveness of interventions targeted at more specific populations: worksite and school health promotion initiatives

CHAPTER OUTLINE

In the last chapter, we considered how we can influence health-related behaviour through individually based interventions. While these may be effective, no government or body involved in public health has the resources to intervene at a one-to-one level with the entire population – nor would people in the population want to be involved in any attempt to do so. So attempts to influence the health-related behaviour of large groups of people or entire populations necessarily involve other approaches. Perhaps the most obvious means through which health promoters attempt to influence our behaviour is through media campaigns. However, there are a number of other potential routes through which our behaviour can be influenced, including economic and environmental influences. This chapter considers the strengths and limits of the use of mass media approaches to health promotion before considering some of the other approaches that have been used. We look at the effectiveness of influencing behaviour through the use of environmental factors in the workplace and school, and the use of peer education. Theories relating to each approach are considered as well as the effectiveness of interventions based on them.

Promoting population health

In the previous chapter, we considered a number of one-to-one or small group interventions that have been used to change health-related behaviour. These have generally proved reasonably effective, so from the viewpoint of their absolute effectiveness, they could generally be considered 'a good thing'. However, they are expensive to provide and achieve change in relatively few individuals. Accordingly, from a cost-effectiveness perspective, they are perhaps less impressive. They are also impractical to provide on a large-scale basis. As a result of this, a parallel set of theories and studies have considered how to change the behaviour of large groups of individuals. Approaches that target whole populations are likely to be less effective in achieving change in any one individual than one-to-one interventions. Nevertheless, because of the large number of individuals who may be reached through this type of intervention, they may still achieve significant change over an entire population. A one-to-one intervention that achieved change in, say, 1 percent of those who took part would be considered highly ineffective. A large-scale intervention that targeted hundreds of thousands if not millions of individuals and achieved a similar success rate could be considered highly effective at least in terms of the resources and costs necessary to achieve any changes. That is, such interventions have the potential to be highly cost-effective.

Using the mass media

Perhaps the most obvious contribution of psychology to public health initiatives can be found in the design and implementation of mass media campaigns. The earliest media campaigns adopted a 'hypodermic' model of behavioural change, which assumed a relatively stable link between knowledge, attitudes and behaviour (something we now know to be somewhat optimistic: see Chapter 5). The approach assumed that if we could 'inject' appropriate information into the recipients, this would change their attitudes and in turn directly influence their behaviour. This approach, led by people such as McGuire (e.g. 1985), suggested that the key to success was to make the information persuasive and for it to come from appropriate sources. Defining each of these elements is not easy. What is persuasive for one person may not be for another. Good sources of information may be an 'expert', 'someone like you', a neutral individual or someone clearly linked to the issue such as a doctor providing health information. Seeing someone affected by a particular condition or who has achieved significant behavioural change can be a much more potent source of information than a neutral person or even an expert. It is much more powerful to see a 34-year-old man explain how smoking caused his lung cancer, for example, than to have the risks of developing lung cancer explained by a doctor who has not been personally affected by the condition. Similarly, Scollay, Doucett, Perry *et al.* (1992) reported that a lecture about the risks of unsafe sex by someone known to be HIV-positive resulted in greater increases in knowledge, less risky attitudes and safer behavioural intentions than a neutral source following a presentation to a school audience.

Despite the popularity of media campaigns, a key issue is whether they result in any behavioural change. This cannot be taken for granted – nor can the fact that the target audience even notices the campaign. There is surprisingly little evidence that isolated mass media campaigns have a significant impact on health-related behaviour. There is no evidence, for example, that any of the HIV/AIDS or smoking media campaigns sponsored by the UK government had any influence on health-related behaviour (e.g. Sherr 1987), although this may be because the approach used in them was less than optimal (see below). As an example of an isolated health campaign, focusing on attempting to increase levels of exercise in the community, Wimbush, MacGregor and Fraser (1998) assessed the effect of a mass media campaign in Scotland designed to promote walking. Although 70 percent of those asked about the campaign were aware of its existence, it had no impact on behaviour. Such limited outcomes have led some to argue that media campaigns are best used to raise awareness of health issues rather than as attempts to engender significant behavioural change (Stead, Hastings and Eadie 2002).

More positively, the cumulative effects of repeated media campaigns may influence attitudes and behaviour. Although individual 'drink-drive' media campaigns do not appear to have influenced attitudes, for example, there is a general assumption among those involved in public health that they have contributed to the development of negative attitudes towards drink-driving among younger people – although a significant minority continue to drink alcohol and drive, and they have been less successful in changing attitudes in a generation that was already used to doing so (Stevenson, Palamara, Rooke *et al.* 2001). This, combined with higher-profile policing, may have resulted in reduced rates of drink-driving over the past decade (Shinar, Schechtman and Compton 1999). A similar argument could be proposed for a range of behaviour, such as smoking cigarettes and eating healthy diets.

Despite the limited effect of single media campaigns, they remain an attractive and frequently used means of influence because they can reach large numbers of people with relative ease. Those adopting this approach have used a number of methods to maximise its effectiveness, including:

- refining communication to maximise their influence on attitudes
- the use of fear messages
- more specific targeting of interventions.

Refining communication

We noted above that different people may be influenced by different types of information or sources of information – they may also be more or less motivated to consider any information that they receive. We considered this issue in relation to working with individuals in our discussion of the stages of change model (Prochaska and di Clemente 1984) in the previous chapter. Media campaigns can also adopt different arguments depending on the stage of change of people in its target audience. They can provide motivating messages, show how to achieve change and even encourage people to plan change. An alternative method of refining communication for those more or less motivated to consider change is provided by a theoretical model known as the elaboration likelihood model (ELM) developed by Petty and Cacioppo (1986; see Figure 7.1). This suggests that attempts to influence people who are not interested in a particular issue by rational argument will not work (nor will they succeed if the arguments for change are weak). Only those with a pre-existing interest in the issue are likely to attend to such information

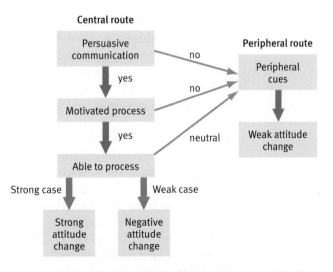

Figure 7.1 The elaboration likelihood model of persuasive communication.

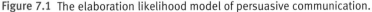

and, perhaps, act on it. In their jargon, individuals are more likely to 'centrally process' messages if they are 'motivated to receive an argument' when:

- it is congruent with their pre-existing beliefs
- it has personal relevance to them
- recipients have the intellectual capacity to understand the message.

Such processing involves evaluation of arguments, assessment of conclusions and their integration into existing belief structures. According to the ELM, any attitude change resulting from such deliberative processes is likely to be enduring and predictive of behaviour. However, given that health promotion is often targeted at individuals who are not interested in an issue and who are not motivated to process messages, how then do we attempt to influence them? According to the ELM, influence here is less reliable but still possible. The model suggests that this can be achieved through what it terms 'peripheral processing'. This is likely to occur when individuals:

- are not motivated to receive an argument
- have low issue involvement
- hold incongruent beliefs.

Peripheral processing involves maximising the credibility and attractiveness of the source or the message using indirect cues and information. Attempts, for example, to influence middle-aged women to take part in exercise may involve a technical message about health gains that can be achieved following exercise (the central route) but also include images associated with exercise that appeal to the target audience, such as making friends while engaging in gentle exercise and wearing attractive clothes in the gym (the peripheral route). Similarly, the importance of a message can be emphasised by a senior person such as a medical professor presenting information. According to the ELM, any attitude change fostered by this processing route is likely to be transient and not predictive of behaviour.

A good example of combining the central and peripheral routes with a credible source can be found in a series of UK television advertisements targeted at smokers. These involved real people who had serious smoking-related illnesses – we were told that one person died soon after filming – talking about the adverse outcomes of their smoking. The film was black and white, and the images involved the people sitting in a chair with a very sparse background. The message was that smoking kills, and the peripheral cues associated with the image were downbeat and gloomy. It did not encourage the viewer to take up smoking! Of course, one danger of this negative portrayal is that viewers may find it too depressing and simply disengage from the adverts – either mentally by thinking about something else, or physically by switching the television to another channel. To avoid such an outcome, and in order to find the maximally persuasive approach, it is necessary to develop media campaigns based on sound psychological theory and also to include a testing process, discussing them with their target population – perhaps through the use of focus groups – to fine-tune the finished product.

The ELM has been subject to a number of experimental tests, most of which (e.g. Agostinelli and Grube 2002) suggest that information containing carefully chosen peripheral cues can facilitate attitudinal change in people who are relatively unmotivated to consider particular issues or that combining central processing with peripheral cues can enhance the effectiveness of some interventions. Kirby, Ureda, Rose *et al.* (1998), for example, showed African American women two health messages about mammography involving both central and peripheral cues. They systematically varied the number of each type of cue over four messages embedded as advertisements in a television talk show. They found that women who reported a high involvement in the issue reported stronger intentions to seek mammography than low-involvement women regardless of the presence of central arguments or peripheral cues. By contrast, women with a low involvement in the issue were more likely to report strong intentions to seek mammography if they had been exposed to high levels of favourable peripheral cues than if they had not. However, whether these attitudinal changes result in behavioural change is less clear. Drossaert, Boer and Seydel (1996) found this not to be the case. Again, in the context of attempts to increase attendance at mammography, they made two versions of a leaflet designed to increase such attendance. The main arguments were the same in each leaflet, but one leaflet had low levels of peripheral cues and the other had high levels. Attendance rates of women exposed to the differing leaflets sent out with the invitation to attend did not differ, suggesting that there was little or no benefit from adding peripheral cues to their leaflets. Perhaps this is the real limitation of the ELM and other models of attitude change. They can suggest means of maximising attitudinal change, but many other factors will influence whether any attitudinal change or even behavioural intentions are translated into action (see Chapter 5 for a discussion of the relationship between attitudes and behaviour).

The use of fear

A second potential approach to increasing the influence of mass media communication is through the use of fear messages. This has proved popular among both health promoters and politicians who fund their activities, perhaps because it conforms to lay beliefs about their influence on behaviour (Rhodes and Wolitski 1990). Despite this popularity, though, high levels of threat have proved relatively ineffective in engendering behavioural change. The problems with this approach can be demonstrated in both the UK and Australian governments' early attempts to change sexual practices in response to the development of HIV/AIDS. Both countries used high-fear messages, including visual images of the chipping of a gravestone with the words AIDS (in the UK) and a celestial bowling alley in which a 'grim reaper' representing HIV bowled down families and children (in Australia). These were associated with portentous messages declaring the need to avoid HIV infection and to use safer sex practices. Both increased HIV-related anxiety in audiences that saw them, but they did not result in an increase in knowledge about HIV/AIDS or any appropriate behavioural change (Rigby, Brown, Anganostou *et al.* 1989; Sherr 1987).

One explanation of this effect may be found in protection motivation theory (Rogers 1983; see Chapter 5). This suggests that individuals will respond to information either in an adaptive or maladaptive manner depending on their appraisal of both threat *and* their own ability to minimise that threat (their self-efficacy judgements). The theory suggests that an individual is most likely to behave in an adaptive manner in response to a fear-arousing health message if they have evidence that both engaging in certain behaviour will reduce any threat and that they are capable of engaging in it. Rogers argued that the most persuasive messages are therefore those that:

- arouse fear – unsafe sex increases your risk of getting HIV;
- increase the sense of severity if no change is made – HIV is a serious condition;
- emphasise the ability of the individual to prevent the feared outcome (efficacy) – here's how you engage in safer sex practices.

If this third step is not taken, any fear messages may actually inhibit behavioural change. Such messages may increase resistance to the message (Franzkowiak 1987), denial that it applies to the individual (Soames-Job 1988), and even increased engagement in the targeted risk behaviour. Louria (1988), for example, found that fear messages actually increased drug use, while Malfetti (1985) reported that they were counterproductive in a programme designed to reduce drink-driving. Despite these cautionary results, health messages frequently emphasis vulnerability and severity and neglect efficacy. This is illustrated by a content analysis of leaflets encouraging breast self-examination reported by Kline and Mattson (2000), who found that they typically contained many more threat than efficacy arguments.

A more positive slant to health messages is to consider the benefits that may occur should an individual change their behaviour – with the implied threat that this will not occur should the behaviour continue without change. This approach is known as 'framing' the message. Health messages can be framed in either positive (stressing positive outcomes associated with prevention) or negative terms (emphasising negative outcomes associated with failure to act). While some have argued that negative frames are more memorable (Newhagen and Reeves 1987), others have suggested that positive messages enhance information processing. This may particularly be the case when time is short and individuals are not highly motivated to receive a message (Isen 1987). The effectiveness of positive framing is illustrated by a study reported by Detweiler, Bedell, Salovey et al. (1999), who examined the relative effectiveness of factual information that either emphasised the positive outcomes of using sunscreen or the negative consequences of not using it. Measures of attitudes and intentions were collected before and after the intervention, and behaviour was assessed via a redeemable voucher for sunscreen. Results showed that compared with messages that emphasised the losses that may follow not using sunscreen, those that emphasised the gains in doing so resulted in significantly higher numbers of requests for sunscreen, stronger intentions to reapply sunscreen at the beach and the use of higher-factor sunscreen than negatively framed threat messages. By contrast, Banks, Salovey, Greener et al. (1995) attempted to persuade women to attend mammography screening using either benefit-oriented information or information that emphasised the costs of not obtaining mammography. Over a one-year period, women who viewed the loss-framed message were more likely to have a mammogram than those in the positively framed condition. Finally, Finney and Iannotti (2003) found no effect of type of framing on attendance at screening. Overall, these data suggest that we can make no strong *a priori* judgements about what type of framing will affect particular populations – again emphasising the need to test out any intervention as a pilot before it is finally aired in public.

Audience targeting

Early attempts to influence behaviour via the mass media frequently targeted whole populations. This meant that the messages received by those in the population were more or less relevant, and the message had to be so broad that it had some potential relevance to all those who received it. As a consequence, health messages were frequently so diluted that they had little relevance to those who received them. Media attempts to influence sexual behaviour illustrate the point. Early media approaches promoting safer sex, as noted above, were based on fear messages, and the same messages were received by all, whether they were elderly, non-sexually active widows and widowers or young sexually active gay men enjoying multiple partners. The outcome of such an approach was the raising of unnecessary fears among a group of people for whom HIV/AIDS had little immediate relevance while not speaking the language of, or giving relevant advice to, the groups to whom it was most relevant. One way in which any media messages can be made more effective is through more effective targeting of its audience. Now, media messages on sexual behaviour are more carefully targeted and use the language of their differing target audiences, making them much more effective (e.g. Dearing, Rogers, Meyer *et al.* 1996).

Audience targeting can be based on a number of factors, including behaviour, age, gender and socio-economic status. The Terrence Higgins Trust leaflet in Plate 7.1, for example, would be considered outrageous by many, but it fits the profile of its target audience – young, sexually active, gay men – well.

Plate 7.1 An example of a health promotion leaflet targeted at gay men – with a sense of humour – encouraging them to have three vaccinations against hepatitis, produced by the Terrence Higgins Trust.
Source: Terrence Higgins Trust

Audiences may also be segmented along more psychological factors such as their motivation to consider change. An evaluation of a worksite exercise programme reported by Peterson and Aldana (1999), for example, involved attempts to increase levels of participation in exercise among 527 corporate employees who either received written messages tailored to their reported stage of change or general information about exercise. Six weeks after the material was received, participants in the group receiving the tailored, staged-based messages increased their activity by 13 percent and were more likely to shift towards contemplating change (as well as actual change) than those receiving general information.

IN THE SPOTLIGHT

Who uses research?

One of the key issues in health psychology is how to link theory to practice. This is a particularly salient issue as relatively few health psychologists work directly in health promotion. Furthermore, much of the research reported by health psychologists is in the journals they read. How much these journals are read by others, such as health promotion practitioners – and how much what they read is translated into actual practice – is questionable.

This issue was highlighted in a paper published by Abraham, Krahé, Dominic et al. (2002), who performed a content analysis on safer sex promotion leaflets used in the UK and Germany. They first identified the types of information that we know from theory and/or empirical data are likely to influence behaviour. They then examined the frequency with which these types of information were presented in their sample of safer sex leaflets. Of the twenty categories of information they identified as influencing behaviour, only one-quarter of the leaflets used text that referred to more than ten. Two-thirds of the leaflets used two or less of these information categories.

These data highlight a key issue facing health psychology – how to influence people involved in the healthcare system, whether in prevention or treatment of illness. Without this influence, our research is of little benefit to health professionals and those they seek to care for. So what can health psychologists do to influence healthcare practitioners, health promoters, and so on? Should we simply carry on as we are now? Or should we look at other ways of influencing these important people?

Diffusion of innovations

Many people adopt new ideas and behaviour as an indirect result of media advertising – from observation of others who have adopted the innovation (in the case of public health, stopping smoking, dietary change, and so on) and their reaction to it. Rogers (E. Rogers 1983) suggested that any new idea or behaviour that proves successful is sequentially adopted by different groups of individuals in society:

1. *Innovators*: this small group of individuals are usually of high status with an interest in new ideas. They seek out and gain ideas from a wide range

of sources and are willing and able to test out new ideas gained from such sources. This group is relatively isolated from the 'mainstream'. However, they bring the innovation to a second group of people – early adopters.

2. *Early adopters*: this larger group of people has a wider sphere of influence than the innovators. They are often described as opinion leaders. Potential adopters look to this group for information about an innovation, and they serve as role models for the wider population. Adoption of an innovation by this group is critical to its uptake in the general population.

3. *Early majority*: this group adopts ideas reasonably quickly but does not have the power to influence of the early adopters.

4. *Late majority*: these people adopt the innovation fairly quickly after the early majority. They are a fairly cautious group and are only likely to adopt an innovation after it has been well tested by the previous groups.

5. *Laggards*: the last group of people to adopt an innovation. This group tends to be suspicious of change, and to adopt it late – or not at all.

Innovation factors that influence uptake include:

- Its advantage over previous behaviour – the bigger the advantage, the more likely the new behaviour is to be taken up by the population.

- Its compatibility with the values and norms of the social system it is trying to influence – if the innovation is too radical, it will be rejected.

- Ease of uptake – if the innovation is difficult to understand and do, it is less likely to be taken up than if it is simple and easy.

- Evidence of effectiveness – the more its effectiveness can be seen, the more it is likely to be adopted. Advertising short-term benefits such as weight loss may make a stronger case than advertising longer-term pay-offs such as a longer and healthier life.

The model of diffusion has a number of implications for people involved in public health promotion. It suggests a number of ways in which any innovation can be marketed. It also suggests that any health promotion programme may either target or utilise the influence of opinion leaders (something we return to later in the chapter).

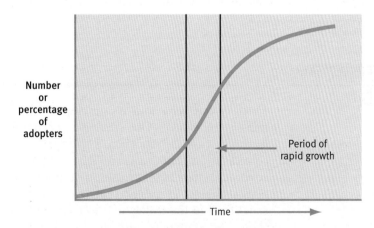

Figure 7.2 The S curve of diffusion, showing the rate of adoption of innovations over time.

Environmental influences on health behaviour

Behaviour and behaviour change do not occur in isolation from the environment in which they occur. The environment may contribute directly to risk of disease (see Chapter 2). It can also indirectly influence health by influencing the ease with which health-promoting or health-damaging behaviour can be conducted. However keen young single mothers may be to exercise, not having someone to look after their child while they are doing so may prevent them from exercising; asking people to eat healthily at work may not be possible unless they are offered healthy choices in the work canteen; and so on. The health belief model (Becker, Haefner and Maiman 1977; see Chapter 5) provides a simple guide to key environmental factors that can be influenced in order to encourage behavioural change. In particular, the model suggests that an environment that encourages healthy behaviour should:

- provide cues to action – or remove cues to unhealthy behaviour;
- enable healthy behaviour by minimising the costs and barriers associated with it;
- increase the costs of engaging in health-damaging behaviour.

What do YOU think?

This next section concerns environmental and social issues that can facilitate or inhibit our health-related behaviour. Before considering this in a relatively theoretical way, consider for a moment your own behaviour. What parts of your life increase the possibility of you behaving in a health-enhancing way? What factors prevent this? Do you have easy access to sports or leisure facilities? If you wanted to, would you feel safe cycling or walking around the area where you live? Does your locality offer easy access to good-quality shops, or does accessing them easily require a car or bus ride? Does this restrict your (or other people's) access to healthy foodstuffs? What about people with fewer resources than you – or with higher demands on their time – single mothers with limited income, for example. How does the environment influence their health choices?

Cues to action

Much of our behaviour is routine, based on habit. Accordingly, we rarely think about change. One strategy to encourage change may therefore simply be to interrupt the sequence of habitual behaviour, allowing or even forcing consideration of new ways to behave. Hunt and Martin (1988), for example, advocated changing the location of more or less healthy foodstuffs on supermarket shelves in order to interrupt routine patterns involving placing the usual food in the trolley and to encourage active consideration of the food choice. Supermarkets already do this to encourage purchasing of special offers and so on – Hunt and Martin suggested that similar tactics could be used to encourage healthy eating.

Cues to action, things that remind us to behave healthily or to change our unhealthy behaviour, can also remind people of the need to change their behaviour. Two key areas where this has been used involve health warnings on cigarettes and nutritional information on food. These approaches may be of some benefit, although the evidence suggests that they reinforce existing behaviour rather than prompt consideration of behavioural change. Part of this lack of effect may be due to poor understanding of the issues raised and/or the low visibility of such cues. Both Glanz, Lankenau, Foerster *et al.* (1995) and Levy, Patterson, Kristal *et al.* (2000), for example, found that many people in the general public, and particularly those on low incomes, did not understand the nutritional information on food packaging. Health warnings on cigarettes have also been found to be ineffective in changing existing smokers' behaviour, although they may prevent smoking initiation (Richards, Fisher and Conner 1989).

Interestingly, the design of advertising may actually discourage looking at health warnings on tobacco advertisements: the clear delineation between the picture that grabs attention and the warning that is not integrated into it may inhibit reading the warning. Increasing the salience of such cues may therefore increase their effectiveness. Borland (1997) evaluated the effect of the introduction of larger and clearer health warnings on cigarette packets in Australia by comparing self-reported responses to health warnings in two surveys between which the new warnings were introduced. Before the changes were initiated, 37 percent of respondents reported noticing the health warning. Following increases in its size, 66 percent reported noticing the warning. The equivalent figures for refraining from smoking as a result of the warning rose from 7 to 14 percent.

Environmental cues can not only act as prompts for healthy behaviour, they can also act as reminders to behave in unhealthy ways. Accordingly, those involved in public health frequently strive to limit and legislate against such things as tobacco and alcohol advertising and the depiction of unhealthy behaviour in the media. These efforts may have been of benefit. Smee, Parsonage, Anderson *et al.* (1992), for example, reported that smoking levels fell by between 4 and 16 percent across a number of countries following bans on advertising tobacco. With these data in mind, the UK government banned television advertising in 1965 and totally banned the advertising of tobacco from 2003.

However, advertising is not the only media influence on attitudes about health-related behaviour. MacFadyen, Amos, Hastings *et al.* (2002), for example, found that UK students considered images in magazines that depicted smoking to represent smokers as attractive, reassuring and sociable. These associations affirmed and reinforced the positive aspects of smoking among smokers who saw them. Similarly, Smith, Roberts and Pendleton (1988) found that 80 percent of popular television programmes made verbal or visual references to alcohol and portrayed its use as an acceptable personal coping strategy. Clearly, the state should not control the content of media images or television programmes. Nevertheless, the potential influence of such images has led some health promoters to work with the producers of television programmes to reduce the overly positive portrayal of alcohol consumption given in some US soap operas (DeFoe and Breed 1989).

Minimising the costs of healthy behaviour

The environment in which we live can either facilitate or inhibit our level of engagement in health-related behaviour. Poor street lighting, busy roads and high levels of pollution may inhibit some inner-city dwellers from taking exercise such as jogging or cycling, shops that sell healthy foods but that are a long way from housing estates may result in more use of local shops that sell less healthy foodstuffs, and so on. Making the environment safe and supportive of healthy activity presents a challenge to town planners and governments. Such an environment should promote safety, provide opportunities for social integration and give the population control over key aspects of their lives.

A number of projects, under the rubric of the 'Healthy Cities movement' (World Health Organization 1988), have attempted to design city environments in ways that promote the mental and physical health of their inhabitants. To be a member of the movement, cities had to develop a city health profile and involve citizen and community groups. Priorities for action included attempts to reduce health inequalities as a result of socio-economic factors (see Chapter 2), traffic control, tobacco control, and care of the elderly and those with mental health problems (Kickbusch 2003). Unfortunately, this rather broad set of strategies has proved difficult to translate into measurable and concrete action. Nevertheless, where the principles of the healthy cities movement have been enacted, this does seem to influence health behaviour. Sharpe, Granner, Hutto *et al.* (2004), for example, found that levels of moderate or vigorous exercise were greater in the general population when there was good street lighting, safe areas for jogging or walking, well-maintained pavements, and easy access to exercise facilities than where these did not exist.

More specific studies have shown that environmental manipulations aimed at minimising the costs of engaging in exercise may result in significant change. Linegar, Chesson and Nice (1991), for example, took advantage of the closed community of a naval base to manipulate both its physical and organisational environment. They established cycle paths, provided exercise equipment, and organised exercise clubs and competitions within the base. In addition, they gave workers 'release time' from other duties while they participated in exercise. Not surprisingly, perhaps, this combination of interventions resulted in significant increases in exercise, even among people who did not previously exercise. This combination of approaches is rarely possible, but the results indicate what is possible when one has the freedom to manipulate a wide range of environmental factors. A more 'doable' pro-gramme, intended to increase levels of exercise among women in a suburb of Sydney, was reported by Wen, Thomas, Jones et al. (2002). They targeted women aged between 20 and 50 through a marketing campaign and increas-ing opportunities for participation in exercise. Their marketing included establishing community walking events, the initiation of walking groups and community physical activity classes, and the promotion of the pro-gramme through the media. Campaign ephemera included fridge maps and tee-shirts combined with newsletters and walking maps to advertise the programme. At a political level, local council members were invited onto the project group to raise the profile of the project with council members and to ensure that the project fitted within the council's social and environ-mental plans. Pre- and post-project telephone surveys indicated a 6.4 percent reduction in the proportion of sedentary women in the local population, as well as an increased commitment to promoting physical activity by the local council.

Another area where the costs of healthy behaviour have been particularly considered is that of needle-exchange schemes to prevent the transmission of HIV and hepatitis among needle-injecting drug users. These minimise the costs of using clean needles by making them freely available and avoiding risk of detection, which has resulted in many injecting drug users sharing needles, often with many people on many occasions. Needle-exchange schemes exchange old for new needles and prevent the need for sharing, reducing the risk of cross-infection of various blood-borne viruses, including HIV and hepatitis. Longitudinal studies generally suggest that where syringes cannot legally be obtained elsewhere, needle-exchange programmes are effective in reducing the use of shared needles (Gibson, Flynn and Perales 2001). That said, one important study published since Gibson and colleagues' review (Taylor, Goldberg, Hutchinson et al. 2001) showed a reduction in the use of shared needles between 1990 and 1992 in Scotland following the introduc-tion of needle-exchange schemes, but then a gradual increase in sharing in the following years despite their continued provision. These changes mirror some of the changes in risk behaviour in other populations at risk for HIV, where initial changes towards safer behaviour have dwindled, and riskier behaviour has returned over time (e.g. Dodds, Mercey, Parry et al. 2004). The reasons for this are unclear but may relate to the relatively low profile given to HIV/AIDS awareness in the UK and increasing (inappropriate) beliefs that AIDS can be 'cured'.

Increasing the costs of unhealthy behaviour

Making unhealthy behaviour difficult in some way (often through pricing) can act as a barrier to unhealthy behaviour and a facilitator of healthy behaviour. Economic measures related to public health have been largely confined to taxation on tobacco and alcohol. The price of alcohol impacts on levels of consumption (UK Central Statistics Office 1980), particularly for wines and spirits: beer consumption may be less sensitive to price (Godfrey 1990). These effects may hold not just for 'sensible' drinkers but also for those who have alcohol-related problems (Sales *et al.* 1989). Increases in tobacco taxation may also be the most effective measure in reducing levels of cigarette smoking, with an estimated reduction in consumption of 4 percent for every 10 percent price rise (Brownson, Koffman, Novotny *et al.* 1995).

To show the magnitude of this effect, Hu, Sung and Keeler (1995) compared the relative likely effectiveness of taxation and media campaigns on tobacco consumption in California. They estimated that a 25 percent tax increase would result in a reduction in sales of 819 million cigarette packs, compared with 232 million packs due to media influences. Taxation seems to be a particularly effective deterrent among young people, who are three times more likely to be affected by price rises than older adults (Lewit, Coates and Grossman 1981). However, these findings must now be interpreted against attempts to avoid these costs. In the UK, for example, increasing levels of bootleg tobacco and alcohol from the continent (where tax levels are much lower) compete against increased prices in formal outlets.

While prohibition may be seen as a necessary barrier by some, others have called for more modest barriers to availability. Godfrey (1990), for example, has suggested restricting the number of outlets for drugs such as alcohol. This would result in increasing transaction 'costs' as people will have to travel further and make more effort to purchase their alcohol, and in reduced cues to consumption from advertising in shop windows and other signs.

A more direct form of control over smoking has been the introduction of smoke-free work and social areas. These clearly reduce smoking in public places – although whether they stop people smoking or they just transfer their smoking to specified areas is unclear. Heloma and Jaakalo (2003), for example, found that secondary smoke inhalation levels fell among non-smokers, while smoking prevalence rates at work only fell from 30 percent to 25 percent following a national smoke-free workplace law. Restaurants and bars have expressed some concern that smoking bans will reduce their profits. Countering this claim, the Centers for Disease Control and Prevention (2004) reported the outcome of a ban on smoking in all public work and social outlets, including restaurants and bars, in El Paso, Texas. Breaking the ban would result in a $5,000 fine. There was no reported fall in profits or consumption in any bar or restaurant. However, many countries, including the UK, are not implementing such an approach despite their medical authorities advocating it (Gulland 2002), and the European Union stated in 2004 that it had no intention of introducing a ban on tobacco in the workplace (Houston 2004).

Health promotion programmes

So far, we have looked at some broad approaches to behavioural change in large populations, and some of the underlying principles that underpin them. The next sections of this chapter consider how these, and some other, approaches have been used in health promotion programmes targeted at whole populations and more specific target groups. Most of these programmes have targeted behaviour related to coronary heart disease (CHD), HIV infection, and the causes of cancer such as smoking or poor nutrition. In the following section, we consider a number of differing target populations, the approaches that have been used to change their behaviour, the theoretical models that have guided the interventions, and their effectiveness.

Plate 7.2   For some, changing the environment is far from complex. Here we see Indian people receiving fresh water from a tanker, without which they would be exposed to a variety of pathogens in dirty water.

Source: Khandel Light

Targeting coronary heart disease

Some of the first health promotion programmes targeted at the adult populations of whole towns aimed to reduce the prevalence of key risk factors for CHD – smoking, low levels of exercise, high fat consumption and high blood pressure – across the entire adult population. The first of these, known as the Stanford Three Towns project (Farquhar, Maccoby and Wood 1977), provided three towns in California with three levels of intervention.

The first town received no intervention. The second received a year-long media campaign targeting CHD-related behaviour. Although the media programme preceded the stages of change model (Prochaska and di Clemente 1984; see Chapter 6) by some years, it followed a programme very similar to that suggested by that model. It started by alerting people of the need to change their behaviour (itself a relatively novel message in the early 1970s). This was followed by a series of programmes showing people *how* to change their behaviour – for example by broadcasting film of people attending a smoking cessation group and showing cooking skills. This was followed by further slots reminding people to maintain any behavioural changes they had made and showing images of people enjoying the benefits of behavioural change such as a family enjoying a healthy picnic. The latter two phases were based on social learning theory (Bandura 1977; see Chapter 6) and were aimed at teaching skills and increasing recipients' confidence in their ability to change and maintain change of their own behaviour. In the third town, a group of individuals at particularly high levels of risk for CHD and their partners received one-to-one education on risk behaviour change and were asked to disseminate their knowledge through their social networks. This strategy was used to provide another channel for disseminating information – through the use of people given the role of opinion leaders – and increasing motivation in both high-risk people and the general public.

Accordingly, there were three levels of intervention, each of which was expected to result in a decremental increase in effectiveness (see Table 7.1). The expected outcomes were found. By the end of the one-year programme, scores on a measure of CHD risk status based on factors including blood pressure, smoking and cholesterol level indicated that average risk scores among the general population actually rose in the control town, while they fell significantly among the general population who received the media campaign alone and to an even greater extent among those who lived in the town that received the combined intervention. After a further year, risk scores in the intervention towns were still significantly lower than those of the control town, although because scores in the media-only town had continued to improve there was no difference between the two intervention towns (Farquhar, Fortmann, Flora *et al.* 1990a).

The European equivalent of this programme was established in North Karelia in Finland (Puska, Tuomilehto, Nissinen *et al.* 1985). This five-year programme differed slightly from the Stanford approach in that in addition to a media approach, it also changed environmental factors, encouraging

Table 7.1 The three levels of intervention in the Stanford Three Towns project

Approach	What it involved	Expected effect
Ongoing health promotion activity	A minimal intervention 'comparison' town	+/–
Year-long media campaign	Phase 1: alerting people to the need to change Phase 2: modelling change Phase 3: modelling continued change	+
Media campaign + high-risk intervention	Media as influence combined with dissemination of knowledge from lay experts	++

local meat manufacturers and butchers to promote low-fat products, encouraging 'no smoking' restaurants, and so on. It was generally considered to be a success, with reductions in a number of risk factors including blood pressure, cholesterol levels, and smoking among men. However, its final summary paper showed that these reductions in risk factors were not consistently better than those in a control area, which received no intervention, against which the impact of the intervention was assessed.

Unfortunately, this apparent lack of success has been repeated in a number of subsequent large-scale interventions. A second study conducted around Stanford, called the Five City project (Farquhar, Fortman, Flora *et al.* 1990b), for example, combined its previous media approach with an increased emphasis on community-initiated education and environmental interventions such as encouraging local shops and restaurants to provide healthy foodstuffs. In a cohort followed for the duration of the intervention, the general population in the intervention area showed improvements in cholesterol levels, fitness and rates of obesity in the early stages of the intervention. However, by its end, the only differences between a comparison area that did not receive the intervention and intervention areas was on measures of blood pressure and smoking (the latter being perhaps the most important risk behaviour due to its links with so many other diseases). Accordingly, the intervention could be considered a modest success. Unfortunately, on a series of cross-sectional studies comparing control and intervention areas over time, smoking and risk levels for CHD did not differ at any time during the course of the programme – questioning the success of the intervention.

A final US intervention to be considered here used virtually all the approaches so far considered in this and the previous chapter. The Minnesota Heart Health program (Jacobs, Luepker, Mittelmark *et al.* 1986) used the mass media to promote awareness and to reinforce other educational approaches. In addition, the programme established large-scale screening programmes in primary care settings, as well as a number of other interventions including telephone support, classes in the community and worksite, self-help materials, and home correspondence programmes. Environmental interventions included healthy food labelling (low fat, high fibre, etc.), establishing healthy menus in restaurants, smoke-free areas in public and work areas, and increased physical recreation facilities. Despite this complex and sophisticated approach, the programme had surprisingly little impact on health and health behaviour. Levels of smoking in the intervention areas, for example, differed little from those in the control areas, while the average adult weight in both control and intervention areas rose over the course of the study by seven pounds. Similar findings were found for another intervention known as the Community Intervention Trial for Smoking Cessation (COMMIT Research Group 1995), which did not change heavy smokers' behaviour and had only a marginal effect on light smokers.

At first glance, these data appear disappointing. Indeed, they provide little encouragement to suggest that the approaches they used should be continued. However, before they are dismissed it is important to contextualise their findings. First, apart from the original Stanford study, they occurred at a time when there were significant changes in health behaviour and disease throughout the countries in which the studies were conducted. Rates of CHD have fallen by 20 percent over the past decade (Lefkowitz and Willerson 2001), and there has been a general increase in health-promoting behaviour and a concomitant fall in health-damaging behaviour such as smoking over the past few decades (*ibid.*). Why have these changes occurred, and what implications do they have for interpretation of the results of the large-scale programmes considered above?

Perhaps the experiences of the five-year Heartbeat Wales programme (Tudor-Smith, Nutbeam, Moore *et al.* 1998) sum up those of all the programmes so far considered. This programme combined health education via the media with health screening and environmental changes designed to promote behavioural change. These included some of the first food labelling (low fat, low sugar, etc.) in the UK, establishing exercise trails in local parks, no-smoking areas in restaurants, the promotion of low-alcohol beers in bars, and so on. It also used doctors and nurses as opinion leaders within their own communities to argue the case for adopting healthy lifestyles. Remember that the interventions in each programme were compared with 'control' areas – areas that did not receive the intervention. However, these were not true 'control' areas in the sense that they received no intervention at all. They received whatever local health education programmes were being conducted at the time. In addition, any innovations conducted by these major research programmes could not be guaranteed to remain only in the intervention area. In the case of Heartbeat Wales, for example, its 'control' area was in the northeast of England, which itself was subject to large-scale heart health programmes conducted in England at the same time as Heartbeat Wales. It was certainly not a 'no intervention' control. In addition, innovations such as food labelling, originally conducted just in Wales, spread through to England via supermarkets such as Tesco over the course of the programme. It is perhaps not surprising, therefore, that although levels of risk factors for CHD fell in Wales over the five-year period of Heartbeat Wales, they did not fall any further than levels in the control area. The research programme essentially compared the effectiveness of two fairly similar interventions. In addition, the majority of health promotion affecting the population with regard to CHD is now probably provided by the mass media as part of its general reporting – through reporting and discussion of healthy diets, issues such as men's health, and so on. It is therefore increasingly difficult for any health promotion programme to add further to this information and result in a meaningful reduction in risk for CHD.

Reducing risk of HIV infection

In contrast to interventions targeted at CHD, those targeted at sexual behaviour in relation to HIV and AIDS appear to have been more successful (Merzel and D'Afflitti 2003). Summing up some of the key data, the Centers for Disease Control and Prevention (1996) reported significant increases in rates of condom use with main or casual partners in areas that received interventions in comparison with control areas that had not. In addition, they reported significant increases in the rates of carrying condoms both among those at whom the intervention was targeted and among community members as a whole. In the intervention areas, a 74 percent increase in condom carrying was reported. In addition, among injecting drug users, although both intervention and control communities reported a similar rise in the use of bleach to clean their needles and other equipment, those who lived in the intervention area who were not using bleach were more likely to be considering its use.

These positive outcomes have often been achieved using an approach called peer education. In this, opinion leaders and others from specific communities are involved in projects and form a key part of the programme. The approach draws upon social learning theory as these individuals provide particularly strong role models of change and diffusion of innovations, as opinion leaders within specific communities are used as agents of change. Using people known and respected within a particular community makes their message salient and shows that appropriate change can be achieved. In one study using this approach, Kelly, St Lawrence, Stevenson *et al.* (1992) tried to increase levels of safer sexual behaviour among patrons of gay bars in three small southern US cities. They identified and recruited opinion leaders in these bars and trained them to talk to patrons on issues of risk behaviour change and to distribute relevant health education literature. Following this intervention, levels of high-risk sexual behaviour fell by between 15 and 29 percent. In a larger community trial conducted by the same team in eight US cities (Kelly, Murphy, Sikkema *et al.* 1997), levels of unprotected anal intercourse fell from 32 to 20 percent among men frequenting gay bars in the intervention group – a contrast to a 2 percent rise among those in the control cities. The RESEARCH FOCUS below reports in some detail on an attempt to replicate this type of intervention in gay bars in the Scottish city of Glasgow.

RESEARCH FOCUS

Williamson, L.M., Hart, G.J., Flowers, P., Frankis, J.S. and Der, G.J. (2001). The Gay Men's Task Force: the impact of peer education on the sexual behaviour of homosexual men in Glasgow. *Sexually Transmitted Infections*, 77: 427–32.

Background

A number of American studies – some of which are described in the main text – have found peer-led interventions to both increase awareness of risky sexual behaviour and to reduce its prevalence. The present study attempted to replicate this approach in Scotland. It aimed to find out whether this type of approach could work in the context of a different culture than that of the USA. It also tried to increase use of hospital sexual clinics. In particular, it encouraged uptake of vaccination against the hepatitis B virus. This virus can be sexually transmitted and can cause lifelong infection, cirrhosis (scarring) of the liver, liver cancer, liver failure, and death. The study compared the attitudes, risk behaviour and use of sexual clinics between people who had been exposed and who had not been exposed to a peer-led campaign conducted in five 'gay bars' in Glasgow.

Method

The intervention

The Gay Men's Task Force (GMTF) initiative involved training forty-two peer educators to work in gay bars in the city of Glasgow. The peer educators wore distinctive clothing: T-shirt, jacket and bags. They distributed GMTF leaflets on sexual health and 'behavioural issues'

continued

and approached men to discuss these and other issues as well as advocating the use of local hospital sexual clinics. The intervention operated for a nine-month period. A 'contact' involved a conversation between a peer educator and a customer at the bar. In them, issues raised by both people could be discussed. The discussions covered a wide range of health topics, including hepatitis B vaccination, HIV testing, and the use of condoms and lubricants.

The research programme

Evaluation of the programme involved research staff returning to the bars seven months after the end of the programme. They asked men to complete a short questionnaire. This included basic demographics (age, job, etc.) as well as the following outcome measures:

- level of contact with the programme;
- self-report 'consideration of sexual behaviour';
- self-report changes to sexual behaviour as a result of contact with the programme;
- levels of hepatitis B vaccination;
- levels of HIV antibody testing;
- number of sexually transmitted diseases (STDs) in the previous year;
- sexual behaviour: frequency of unprotected intercourse with casual partner.

Results

Questionnaires were completed by 1,442 men – 75 percent of those asked. Half the sample was between the ages of 26 and 36 (overall mean age = 32.1 years), and 54 percent of the sample came from social groups I and II. About 97 percent of the sample reported being sexually active. One-third of the sample reported having had unprotected sex in the previous year – of these, one-third reported that on some occasions this had been with casual partners. And 29 percent of respondents had attended a sexual health clinic in the previous year – the majority of whom had attended a 'gay-specific' clinic.

- 42 percent of the sample recognised the GMTF logo;
- 36 percent of the sample knew what the logo stood for;
- 32 percent reported speaking to a peer educator. Of these:
  - 53 percent had spoken on one occasion only; 47 percent had spoken more than once;
  - 49 percent reported having thought about their sexual behaviour;
  - 26 percent reported having changed their sexual behaviour 'to some extent' as a result of these discussions.

Analyses of the differences in behaviour between those who did and did not have contact with the programme were reported using odds ratios (OR). Here, an OR is the relative odds of an individual in an intervention group engaging in particular behaviour in comparison with those in the no-contact group. An OR of 2, for example, means that people were twice as likely to engage in the particular behaviour, an OR of 1.5 means they were one and half times as likely to do so, an OR of 0.5 means they were half as likely to do so, and so on.

Table A reports the ORs for key behavioural outcomes comparing no contact with minimal, intermediate and maximum contact groups. The ORs suggest that people with some degree of contact with the GMTF were more likely to engage in protective behaviour such as hepatitis B vaccination and HIV antibody testing, but there were no differences between these groups in terms of the likelihood of having unprotected sex with a casual partner – the key risk behaviour.

Table A   Odds ratios for key behavioural outcomes comparing people with varying levels of contact with the GMTF and those with none

	Recognise logo	Understand logo	Talk to peer
Hepatitis B vaccination	1.49***	1.43***	1.66***
HIV antibody test	1.42**	1.35**	1.32**
No. of STDs	1.68*	1.46	1.69*
Unprotected sex with casual partner	0.97	0.82	0.76
Sexual clinic use	2.91***	2.83***	2.25***

*** $p < 0.001$
** $p < 0.01$
* $p < 0.05$

Their next set of analyses examined whether higher levels of peer contact were associated with a greater probability of behavioural change. These analyses compared the same outcomes among people who were not sure they had talked to a peer educator, those who had talked once, and those who had talked more than once. These data suggested a benefit of the additional contacts. Those who had talked more than once were more likely than the 'not sures' to have had a hepatitis B vaccination or an HIV antibody test, to have had less unprotected sex, and to have attended a sexual health clinic. But, note, they were also likely to report having had more sexually transmitted diseases than those in the 'not sure' group. Those who had spoken once only also achieved some gains (see Table B), but not as many.

Table B   Odds ratios for key behavioural outcomes comparing people having had varying levels of contact with peer educators with those who were not sure whether they had had contact

	One contact	More than one contact
Hepatitis B vaccination	1.61**	1.73***
HIV antibody test	1.08	1.65**
No. of STDs	1.50	1.90
Unprotected sex with casual partner	1.08	0.44
Sexual clinic use	1.94***	3.99***

*** $p < 0.001$
** $p < 0.01$
* $p < 0.05$

Discussion

The data suggest that the intervention was reasonably effective in encouraging people to engage in some health protective behaviour but did not change the frequency with which they had unprotected sex. This may reflect, in part, reports of the peer educators, who found it easier to talk about sexual health than safer sex. The key issue in engendering change appears to have been direct contact with a peer educator – and the more contact was made, the more likely people were to make meaningful changes to their behaviour. However, these results are difficult to interpret. Did people who had more contact change more because they had more contact – or did they have more contact because they were more interested and willing to consider change?

continued

This study represents one of the common dilemmas of health promotion research. The data are difficult to interpret for a number of reasons. First, they asked people about contact with the programme and their behaviour seven months following an intervention. This may mean that the research failed to capture any short-term behavioural or attitudinal changes that may have occurred. The comparison between people who were aware of the programme and those who were not may have resulted in a number of methodological biases. A more rigorous approach to this study (but a lot less practical one) would be to randomly assign bars to either receive the intervention or act as no-treatment controls, then to identify baseline behaviour of a representative group of people in each group of bars and to follow them for a period of, say, a year with assessments of attitudes related to behaviour change and actual behaviour change taken three, six and twelve months after the intervention. This would give a more accurate picture of who had been exposed to the programme and what changes they had made. The practical problems of conducting such a study are immense – and participation rates are likely to have been low, so the compromise method used by Williamson and colleagues may provide the best data we can realistically gather.

Merzel and D'Afflitti (2003) noted that the HIV/AIDS prevention programmes have been markedly more successful that those targeted at CHD. Why this should be the case is unclear. Perhaps the most obvious difference between the approaches used was the use of peers by those involved in HIV prevention – working with specific groups of people rather than trying to impose change from without. This may have been a crucial factor. Janz, Zimmerman, Wren *et al.* (1996), for example, conducted a process evaluation of thirty-seven AIDS prevention programmes and concluded that the use of trained community peers whose life circumstances closely resembled those of the target population was one of the most important factors influencing acceptance of health messages. Similarly, Kelly, Murphy, Sikkema *et al.* (1993) suggested that the use of peers and role models was an important means of delivering health messages.

Merzel and D'Afflitti speculated that a second reason for these differences may lie in the natural history of the diseases that each programme was trying to influence. Coronary heart disease develops over time, and there is no marked increase in risk as a result of particular behaviour – 'one bar of chocolate won't do me any harm'. It is therefore relatively easy to minimise risk and put off behaviour change. By contrast, the risks associated with unsafe sex are highly salient. It can take relatively few unsafe sexual encounters to contract HIV – thus the imperatives of change are much more salient than in CHD.

While the above studies allow comparison of interventions within the same culture, it should not be forgotten that AIDS is a global issue. Given the devastating impact of HIV/AIDS in Africa, interventions here and in other parts of the developing world are of paramount importance. Galavotti, Pappas-DeLuca and Lansky (2001) described a model known as the Modeling and Reinforcement to Combat HIV (MARCH), which has been developed for use in developing countries. The intervention model has two main components:

1. use of the media
2. local influences of change.

It used the media to provide role models in 'entertainment that educates'. Interventions include testimonials from people living with HIV/AIDS and peer education similar to that used in the USA and UK. These provide information on how to change and model steps to change in sexual behaviour. Serial dramas on television were also used to educate, because they involve the viewer emotionally with the action on the screen, increase its salience and encourage viewing. Interpersonal support involves the creation of small media materials such as flyers depicting role models progressing through stages of behaviour change for key risk behaviour, mobilisation of members of the affected community to distribute media materials and to reinforce prevention messages, and the increased availability of condoms and bleacher kits for injecting drug users. In one study of effectiveness of the media elements of this approach (Vaughan, Rogers, Singhal *et al.* 2000), Radio Tanzania aired a radio soap opera called *Twende Na Wakati* ('Let's go with the times'). This soap played twice weekly for two years with the intention of promoting reproductive health and family planning, and preventing HIV infection. In comparison with one area of Tanzania that did not receive national radio at the time of the study, people who lived in areas where the radio programme was received reported greater commitment to family planning and higher uptake of safer sex practices. In addition, attendance at family planning clinics increased more in the intervention than control area.

Worksite health promotion

One response to the problems encountered by the large-scale population interventions has been to target smaller, more easily accessible target groups. One such group is people at work, and the past few decades have seen the development of many impressive health promotion programmes in the workplace. The majority of these have been conducted in the USA, perhaps because enhancing the health of the workforce reduces the cost of workers' health insurance – often paid by the employer – and therefore benefits the company as well as the individuals in it. Worksite programmes have targeted a range of health-related behaviour, including diet, exercise, smoking and stress (generally focusing on risk factors for CHD and cancer). Because the worksite offers a wide possibility of interventions, these have utilised a variety of formats, some extremely innovative. Approaches include:

■ screening for risk factors for disease;

■ providing health education;

■ provision of healthy options, such as healthy food in eating areas;

■ providing economic incentives for risk behaviour change;

■ manipulating social support to facilitate individual risk behaviour change;

■ provision of no-smoking areas (and more recently smoking rooms) in the work environment.

The effectiveness of screening programmes in the worksite does not differ from that offered in other contexts and was discussed in the previous chapter.

Other programmes have met with mixed success. The Treatwell program (Sorensen, Morris, Hunt *et al.* 1992), for example, set up classes and food demonstrations open to factory workers to teach them about healthy eating and provided healthy options and food labelling in their worksite eating areas. The programme lasted fifteen months and achieved modest reductions in dietary fat consumption but no changes in the consumption of dietary fibre. The Well Works programme reported by Sorensen, Stoddard, Hunt *et al.* (1998) also recorded modest improvements in fat and fruit and vegetable consumption following a programme in which they combined health education programmes and providing health food options. Smoking levels, a second target of the intervention, did not change. Similarly, the Health Works for Women programme (Campbell, Tessaro, DeVellis *et al.* 2002) targeted blue-collar women employed in small to medium-sized workplaces. They provided information on healthy lifestyle behaviour and suggestions on how to change to it, tailored to what each participant reported in a questionnaire completed before the intervention. The programme also worked at developing peer support for behavioural change from social networks among the workforce. Despite these complex interventions, they found no long-term changes in fat intake, smoking or physical activity levels among the intervention group. Their only gain was modest increases in self-reported fruit and vegetable intake. In a review of ten worksite programmes involving similar approaches, Glanz, Lankenau, Foerster *et al.* (1996) found little evidence of any sustained behavioural change. The reasons that this type of intervention may have met with only limited success may be similar to those described for the community-based interventions: a backdrop of significant health education and behavioural change within the general population.

The worksite provides more than an opportunity for the provision of health education and health food options. It gives the opportunity to exert more influence over behaviour than can be achieved elsewhere. One way that employers can influence their workforce is to provide financial incentives for change – to provide an external reward system for appropriate behavioural change rather than relying on employees' personal motivation to change. These have proved quite successful. Glasgow, Hollis, Ary *et al.* (1993) offered monthly lottery prizes to people in a factory workforce who quit and maintained their no-smoking status for up to one year: 19 percent of smokers in the workforce took part in the intervention, 20 percent of whom remained abstinent by the end of the programme. The study provided no control group, but a 20 percent abstinence level compares favourably with many more complex interventions (see Chapter 6). By contrast, Jeffery *et al.* (1993) deducted money from participants' pay (on a voluntary basis) and refunded this money for weight loss and smoking cessation – meaning that participants who were unsuccessful lost money. This programme also proved successful for those who took part in it – but participation rates were, perhaps understandably, low.

The worksite can also provide strong social support for those involved in behavioural change. Koffman, Lee, Hopp *et al.* (1998), for example, compared a multi-component smoking cessation programme similar to that described in the last chapter with a combination of this programme and financial incentives for abstinence and a team competition in which groups supported each other in the weeks and months following cessation. Six

months after the initiation of the programme, 23 percent of those in the multi-component group were abstinent, in comparison with 41 percent of those who also received the incentive programme and competition programme. By the one-year follow-up, the equivalent figures were 30 and 37 percent, respectively.

The impact of restrictive policies on smoking levels is complex. They certainly reduce levels of secondary exposure to cigarette smoke among non-smokers. In addition, the discomfort associated with smoking outside buildings may provide a disincentive for many smokers. This may impact on smoking levels. Longo, Johnson, Kruse *et al.* (2001), for example, studied the smoking habits of employees in hospitals that became smoke-free and those that continued to permit smoking over a period of three years. They found that the percentage of smokers who quit smoking was over twice as high in the non-smoking hospitals than in those that continued to allow smoking. Similar effects were found in an uncontrolled study of the impact of a smoking ban in one hospital, where levels of smoking fell from 22 to 14 percent following introduction of a no-smoking policy (Hudzinski and Frohlich 1990; see also the previous discussion in this chapter).

Most worksite interventions have followed a 'traditional' route in attempting to influence the behaviour of employees. A more innovative, and difficult to implement, approach is to change the whole nature of the working environment directly. One of the few studies to report this approach – in relation to stress at work – was by Maes, Kittel, Scholten *et al.* (1993), who combined a health education programme aimed at facilitating CHD risk behaviour change with a series of modifications to the working environment, each of which was intended to reduce the inherent stresses and boredom of assembly work in a large factory. The research team ran analyses of the various work patterns held by workers and changed the job design to avoid short repetitive tasks and provide workers with additional control over the organisation of work tasks, and facilitated social contact within the working environment. They also trained managers in communication and leadership skills and taught them to recognise and reduce stress in the workforce. Evaluation of the impact of this intervention was limited, with no direct measures of stress taken. However, levels of absenteeism fell and quality of production rose following its implementation. These are often seen as indicators of the quality of work life and suggest some benefit to the workforce.

School-based interventions

A second closed community is that of school pupils. Over the past decade, there has been a significant development of what has been termed 'the health-promoting school'. These schools prioritise the health of their pupils and develop an integrated approach to enhancing health, preventing uptake of unhealthy behaviour and educating pupils about health-promoting activities. This removes health education from simply being a taught part of the curriculum to something central to the aims of the school, around which the school activities and infrastructure are based. The framework around which schools involved in this sort of programme base themselves was established by the World Health Organization (1996) and now includes:

- school health policies – developing policies for school behaviour, such as a 'no helmet, no bike at school' policy for cycle safety or an Australian 'no hat, no play' policy (to avoid sunburn), as well as more traditional policies such as no smoking on school premises and no tolerance of bullying;
- establishing a safe, healthy physical and social environment;
- teaching health-related skills;
- providing adequate health services within the school;
- providing healthy food;
- school site health promotion programmes for staff;
- availability of school counselling or psychology programmes;
- a school physical education programme.

These provide much the same approach to health promotion as has been adopted in the adult population: teach appropriate skills and provide an environment in which use of the skills is supported. St Leger (1999) summarised the health outcomes of this integrated approach as being generally successful when significant efforts are placed on its successful implementation but having minimal or no effect if only partially implemented. As the concept of the healthy school is relatively new, only a few studies have examined the impact of these policies – with mixed results. One such study focused on traditional health targets. Kuntzleman (1985) examined the effects of a fitness and nutrition programme provided via school lessons and activities, and school events such as sports and games. Following the intervention, they found improvements in knowledge, attitudes and fitness among all participants. Interestingly, boys showed more improvements on biological measures such as reduced body fat and cholesterol levels than girls, although more girls than boys increased their physical activity. In the Kids in Action program, Kalnins, Ballantyne, Quartaro et al. (1994) gave children a choice over a local health problem they wished to address. They were involved in identifying the problem, planning and implementing approaches to address the problem, and reviewing the effectiveness of the intervention – using a similar set of strategies to the problem-focused counselling discussed in the previous chapter. The problem they chose to tackle was that of drug distribution near the school. As a result of the programme, the children gained skills in community development and knowledge of community action strategies and advocacy. Interestingly, the issue addressed was not one considered by the school – and it raised issues of the safety of the children at the same time as it tried to empower them to change the situation. Once the target of an intervention is taken out of the control of those in power, the outcome may be far from what is intended!

Out-of-school activities

One alternative to school-based programmes is provided by a programme known as Smokebusters. This is a community – deliberately not school-based – intervention aimed at preventing young people smoking. It involves a series of clubs throughout Europe, each of which emphasises the positive aspects of non-smoking rather than the negative aspects of smoking. They are 'fun clubs', where non-smoking is portrayed as the norm and smokers as

the minority. The intention is to develop strong social peer groups of non-smokers, intended to assist in self-empowerment and development of rejection skills. Events established by the clubs include discos and outdoor events, and they often provide discount schemes for local shops. Being a non-smoker is often rewarded by free membership of the club. The programme is considered to be more attractive to many smokers, who may reject the authoritarian context of school-based programmes. Bruce and van Teijlingen (1999) summarised the reports of thirty-six Smokebuster clubs throughout the UK. As community-based programmes with no particular research remit, only three had attempted to measure long-term effects of the club on knowledge, attitudes and smoking behaviour. One such study evaluated the effects of a North Yorkshire-based programme. They measured smoking levels, knowledge and attitudes in 866 primary and secondary schoolchildren – only half of whom had subsequent access to the club – before and one year after a local Smokebusters club had been established. Over this time, levels of regular smoking rose in both groups, but less so in the group of young people who had access to the club: an 11 percent versus 3 percent rise in smoking prevalence. Similar gains were reported by the two other studies to report smoking prevalence levels (Bruce and van Teijlingen 1999). More disappointingly, intentions to smoke in the future did not differ consistently across the studies – the intervention may have delayed rather than prevented smoking – although some have argued that this is a significant benefit.

Peer education

One final approach to health education in schools involves a process known as peer education. This typically involves training influential pupils in a school about a particular health issue such as smoking, alcohol consumption or HIV education and encouraging them to educate their peers about the issues, hopefully in a way that encourages healthy behaviour. The methods used vary considerably. They may involve teaching whole classes, informal tutoring in unstructured settings, or one-to-one discussion and counselling. In some contexts, peer educators have set up theatre stalls or exhibitions (see Turner and Shepherd 1999). One of the authors (PB) has been involved in the evaluation of a peer education programme among schools in South Wales. This adopted an informal approach to peer education and involved a number of stages. In the first, pupils in Year 8 were asked to identify particularly influential people within their social group. From this, the intervention team identified a group of people who were particularly influential among the target population – some of whom may not have been the choice of their form teachers! Volunteers from this group were then taken to a hotel for two days, where they were taught about the nature, costs and benefits of excess alcohol consumption. These away days also involved a number of group exercises to increase support and confidence among the peer education group. Following their training days, these peer educators were then asked to talk to their friends and anyone else they felt appropriate about sensible drinking, sharing information and advice. This model of uncontrolled dissemination contrasts strongly with some of the more formal methods adopted by other programmes.

The strengths of peer education programmes are thought to be a result of peers providing a more credible source of information than standard educational programmes provided by teachers. They may also make health education more acceptable to school pupils than when it is provided by teachers. Peer education also provides an opportunity to empower those involved and for them to act as positive role models. Whether these claims are accurate is not always clear. Pupils may find it hard to teach their peers and adopt the role of teacher either formally or informally. It is also possible that using pupils as channels of legitimised health information actually removes them as a source of genuine influence, or it may result in them pulling back from providing information or advice so as not to appear outside their established peer group and its norms. Even if one accepts the positive principles supporting peer education, evidence of its effectiveness is inconclusive. Most studies have not compared the effectiveness of teacher versus peer education. Among those that have, some (e.g. Perry and Grant 1988) have found peers to be more effective than teachers in school health education programmes; others have not found this effect (see Greenwood, Carta and Kamps 1990).

Summary

This chapter has examined a number of issues related to interventions targeted at improving the health of whole populations. The key targets examined have been those aiming to change incremental risk of disease, in this case CHD, and behaviour that may result in diseases after being enacted on one occasion – those related to safer sex and HIV infection.

The prime method of influence has been use of the media. Three methods of optimising its use were considered:

1. refining communication to maximise their influence on attitudes through the use of differing channels depending on recipients' motivation to consider the information presented;
2. the use of fear messages – and how these may be optimised not only by raising health anxiety but also by providing an easy way of reducing it;
3. more specific targeting of interventions – targeting at groups within society, categorised by such indices as behaviour, social class and prevailing attitudes.

The diffusion of innovation model also provides important guides concerning the nature of any innovation that may be attempted and the groups to target in its marketing. Innovations need to:

■ have obvious advantages over present behaviour;
■ be compatible with prevailing norms;
■ by relatively easy to engage in;
■ show obvious benefit.

Key target groups when trying to influence whole populations are early adopters (opinion leaders), who have access to innovations, and the power to influence their uptake among people in their social group

The environment may also be manipulated to make health behaviour more salient, to make it easier to engage in and to reward those who engage in it. In particular, environmental manipulations can:

- provide cues to action – or remove cues to unhealthy behaviour;
- enable health behaviour by minimising the costs and barriers associated with it;
- increase the costs of engaging in health-damaging behaviour.

Interventions using these various principles (and some considered in the previous chapter) have proved reasonably successful at changing behaviour in large and more defined populations such as those in worksites or schools.

Early interventions targeted at changing CHD-related behaviour proved successful, although their very success may have reduced the apparent intervention-specific success of subsequent interventions. By contrast, interventions targeted at safer sex behaviour appear to have been particularly successful.

Interventions in the worksite have had mixed success, although the ability of the worksite to offer financial rewards and to establish peer support makes it a useful arena for influencing public health. Innovative attempts to change working practice may also reduce stress in the workforce.

Finally, schools appear to be the key to establishing health behaviour. 'Healthy schools' appear to benefit the health of children – if their implementation is not half-hearted. Peer education may also have some benefits, although many children may find it difficult to act as health educators, reducing the effectiveness of the approach.

Further reading

Acheson, D. (1998). *Independent Inquiry into Inequalities in Health. Report.* London: HMSO.
Looks at some alternative approaches to health promotion, particularly in relation to economic inequalities.

Bennett, P. and Murphy, S. (1997). *Psychology and Health Promotion.* Buckingham: Open University Press.
It may be getting old now, but it's still a good one!

Merzel, C. and D'Afflitti, J. (2003). Reconsidering community-based health promotion: promise, performance, and potential. *American Journal of Public Health*, 93: 557–74.
An excellent, readable account of the pros and cons of community-based interventions.

Naidoo, J. and Wills, J. (2000). *Health Promotion: Foundations for Practice.* London: Bailliere Tindall.
A good review from theoretical and practitioner perspective.

White, J. and Bero, L.A. (2004). Public health under attack: the American Stop Smoking Intervention Study (ASSIST) and the tobacco industry. *American Journal of Public Health*, 94: 240–50.
A reminder that the health promotion agenda is not adopted by all.

PART 2

Becoming ill

CHAPTER 8

The body in health and illness

Learning outcomes

By the end of this chapter, you should have an understanding of:

- the basic anatomy and function of:
    - specific parts of the brain
    - the autonomic nervous system
    - the immune system and key disorders that can result from immune dysfunction
- the basic anatomy, physiology and disorders of:
    - the digestive system
    - the cardiovascular system
    - the respiratory system

CHAPTER OUTLINE

This chapter provides an introduction to the basic anatomy and physiology of key organ systems within the body. Each section considers the basic anatomy and physiology of each system, and describes some of the disease processes that may occur within them. These may be diseases that are associated with particular risk behaviours or other psychological processes – usually stress. Others include diseases that present individuals with particular challenges. Later chapters consider how people can prevent or cope with these diseases, and in some cases the psychological interventions that may help them do this.

We start by examining two systems that influence the whole body:

1. the brain and autonomic nervous system
2. the immune system.

We then go on to examine three other organ systems:

1. the digestive system
2. the cardiovascular system
3. the respiratory system.

The behavioural anatomy of the brain

The brain is an intricately patterned complex of nerve cell bodies. It is divided into four anatomical areas (see Figures 8.1 and 8.2):

1. *Hindbrain*: contains the parts of the brain necessary for life – the medulla oblongata, which controls blood pressure, heart rate and respiration; the reticular formation, which controls alertness and wakefulness; and the pons and cerebellum, which integrate muscular and positional information.

2. *Midbrain*: contains part of the reticular system and both sensory and motor correlation centres, which integrate reflex and automatic responses involving the visual and auditory systems and are involved in the integration of muscle movements.

3. *Forebrain*: contains key structures that influence mood and behaviour, including:

   ■ *Thalamus*: links the basic functions of the hindbrain and midbrain with the higher centres of processing, the cerebral cortex. Regulates attention and contributes to memory functions. The portion that enters the limbic system (see below) is involved in the experience of emotions.

   ■ *Hypothalamus*: regulates appetite, sexual arousal and thirst. Also appears to have some control over emotions.

   ■ *Limbic system*: (Figure 8.3) a series of structures including a linked group of brain areas known as the Circuit of Papez (the hippocampus–fornix –mammillary bodies–thalamus–cingulate cortex–hippocampus). The hippocampus–fornix–mammillary bodies circuit is involved in memory. The hippocampus is one site of interaction between the perceptual and

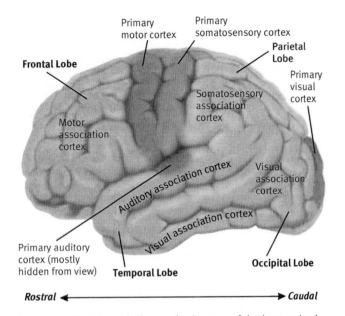

Figure 8.1   A cross-section through the cerebral cortex of the human brain.

Source: Carlson, N. (2003). Published by Allyn and Bacon, Boston, MA. Copyright © 2004 by Pearson Education. Reprinted by permission of the publisher.

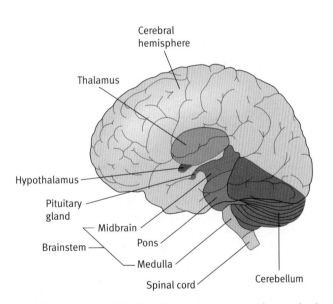

Figure 8.2   A lateral view of the left side of a semi-transparent human brain with the brainstem 'ghosted' in.

Source: Carlson, N. (2003). Published by Allyn and Bacon, Boston, MA. Copyright © 2004 by Pearson Education. Reprinted by permission of the publisher.

memory systems. A further part of the system, known as the amygdala, links sensory information to emotionally relevant behaviour, particularly responses to fear and anger. It has been called the 'emotional computer' because of its role in coordinating the process that begins with the evaluation of sensory information for significance (i.e. threat) and then controls the resulting behavioural and autonomic responses (see below).

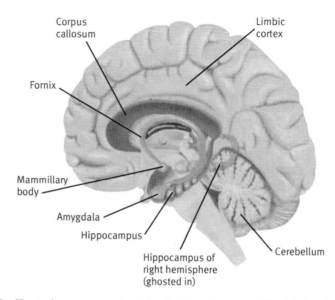

Corpus callosum

Limbic cortex

Fornix

Mammillary body

Amygdala

Hippocampus

Hippocampus of right hemisphere (ghosted in)

Cerebellum

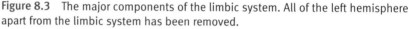

Figure 8.3 The major components of the limbic system. All of the left hemisphere apart from the limbic system has been removed.

Source: Carlson, N. (2003). Published by Allyn and Bacon, Boston, MA. Copyright © 2004 by Pearson Education. Reprinted by permission of the publisher.

4. *Cerebrum*: the most recently evolved part of the brain includes:

- *Basal ganglia*: responsible for complex motor coordination.
- *Cortex*: the convoluted outer layer of grey matter comprising nerve cell bodies and their synaptic connections. It is divided into two functional hemispheres linked by the corpus callosum, a series of interconnecting neural fibres, at its base and is divided into four lobes: frontal, temporal, occipital and parietal:
  - The frontal lobe has an 'executive' function, as it coordinates a number of complex processes, including speech, motor coordination and behavioural planning. The frontal lobes also influence motivation. The pre-frontal lobes are connected to the limbic system via the thalamus and motor system within the cortex. Links between the pre-frontal cortex and the limbic system are activated during rewarding behaviour.
  - The temporal lobes have a number of functions. In right-handed people, the main language centre is located in the right hemisphere, and visuo-spatial processing is located in the left hemisphere. In left-handed individuals, there is less localisation within hemispheres. The temporal lobes are also involved in the sense systems of smell and hearing. They integrate the visual experience with those of the other senses to make meaningful wholes. The temporal lobes have an important role in memory and contain systems that preserve the record of conscious experience. Finally, they connect to the limbic system and link emotions to events and memories.
  - The occipital and parietal lobes are primarily involved in the integration of sensory information. The occipital lobe is primarily involved in visual perception. Links to the cortex permit interpretation of visual stimuli.

The autonomic nervous system

The autonomic nervous system is responsible for control over levels of activity in key organs and organ systems in the body. Many organs have some degree of control over their functioning. The heart, for example, has a basic rhythm of 110 beats per minute. However, these intrinsic levels of activity may not be appropriate at all times. The heart may have to beat more at times of exercise, less at times of rest. The autonomic nervous system overrides local control to provide this higher level of coordinated control across most of the bodily systems in response to the varying demands being placed on the body. Its activity is controlled by a number of brain areas, the most important of which is the hypothalamus. The hypothalamus receives information about the demands being placed on the body from a variety of sources, including:

- information about skin temperature from the reticular formation in the brainstem;
- information about light and darkness from the optic nerves;
- receptors in the hypothalamus provide information about the ion balance and temperature of the blood.

The hypothalamus also has links to the cortex and limbic systems of the brain, which are involved in the processing of cognitive and emotional demands. This allows the autonomic system to respond to psychological factors as well as physical demands being placed on the body. Accordingly, the autonomic nervous system can initiate sweating in high temperatures, increase blood pressure and heart rate during exercise, and also make us physiologically responsive at times of stress, distress or excitement (we discuss these responses further in Chapters 11 and 13).

The autonomic nervous system controls these varying levels of activity through two opposing networks of nerves (see Figure 8.4):

1. the sympathetic nervous system: involved in activation and arousal – the fight–flight response;
2. the **parasympathetic nervous system**: involved in relaxation – the rest–recover response.

Both sets of nerves arise in an area in the brainstem known as the medulla oblongata (which is linked to the hypothalamus). From this, they pass down the spinal cord to various **synapses**, where they link to a second series of nerves that are linked to all the key body organs, including the heart, arteries and muscles (Figure 8.4). For the sympathetic arm, the **neurotransmitter** involved at the synapse between the spinal cord nerves and the nerve to the target organ is acetylcholine. Activity at the synapse between this second nerve and the end organ mainly involves a neurotransmitter known as noradrenaline (known alternatively as norepinephrine) and to a lesser extent adrenaline (epinephrine). The parasympathetic system uses acetylcholine at both synapses. The activity in each of the organs depends on the relative activity in the sympathetic and parasympathetic nervous systems. When

parasympathetic nervous system
arm of the autonomic nervous system that is responsible for rest and recuperation.

synapse
junction between two neurons or between a neuron and target organ. Nerve impulses cross a synapse through the action of neurotransmitters.

neurotransmitter
a chemical messenger (e.g. adrenaline, acetylcholine) used to communicate between neurons and other neurons and other types of cell.

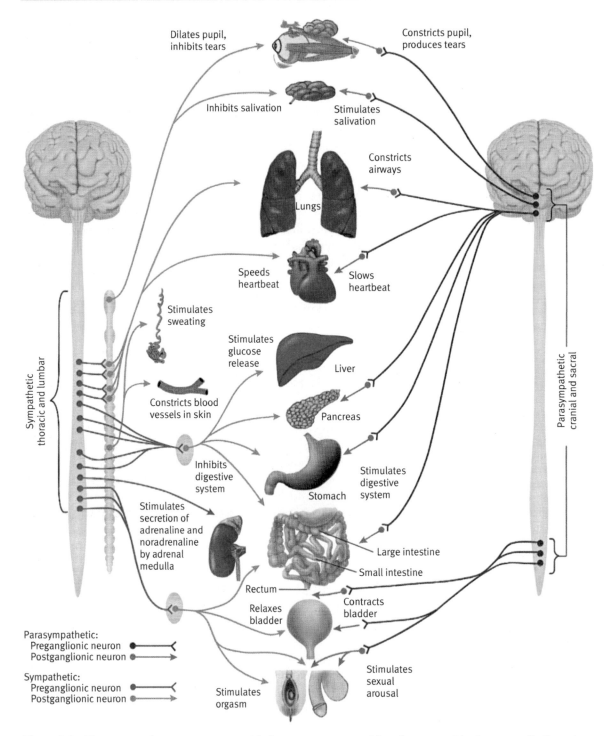

Figure 8.4   The autonomic nervous system, with the target organs and functions served by the sympathetic and parasympathetic branches.

Source: Carlson, N. (2003). Published by Allyn and Bacon, Boston, MA. Copyright © 2004 by Pearson Education. Reprinted by permission of the publisher.

activity in the sympathetic system predominates, the body is activated: when the parasympathetic system is dominant the body is resting and relatively inactive, allowing basic functions such as digestion and the production of urine to occur more easily (see Table 8.1).

Table 8.1 Summary of responses of the autonomic nervous system to sympathetic and parasympathetic activity

Structure	Sympathetic stimulation	Parasympathetic stimulation
Iris (eye muscle)	Pupil dilation	Pupil constriction
Salivary glands	Saliva production reduced	Saliva production increased
Heart	Heart rate and force increased	Heart rate and force decreased
Lung	Bronchial muscle relaxed	Bronchial muscle contracted
Stomach	Peristalsis reduced	Gastric juice secreted; motility increased
Small intestine	Motility reduced	Digestion increased
Large intestine	Motility reduced	Secretions and motility increased
Liver	Increased conversion of glycogen to glucose	
Kidney	Decreased urine secretion	Increased urine secretion
Bladder	Wall relaxed Sphincter closed	Wall contracted Sphincter relaxed

Endocrine processes

endocrine glands
glands that produce and secrete hormones into the blood or lymph systems. Includes the pituitary and adrenal glands, and the islets of Langerhans in the pancreas. These hormones may affect one organ or tissue, or the entire body.

adrenal glands
endocrine glands, located above each kidney. Comprises the cortex, which secretes several steroid hormones, and the medulla, which secretes noradrenaline.

corticosteroids
potent anti-inflammatory hormones (including cortisol) made naturally in the body or synthetically for use as drugs.

cortisol
a stress hormone that increases the availability of energy stores and fats to fuel periods of high physiological activity. It also inhibits inflammation of damaged tissue.

The activity initiated by the sympathetic nervous system is short-lived. A second system is therefore used to provide longer-term arousal. This system uses **endocrine glands,** which communicate with their target organs by releasing hormones into the bloodstream. The endocrine glands that extend the activity of the sympathetic nervous system are the **adrenal glands,** which are situated above the kidneys. These have two functional areas, each of which is activated in different ways:

- the centre or adrenal medulla;
- the surrounding tissues, known as the adrenal cortex.

The adrenal medulla is innervated by the sympathetic nervous system. Activity in this system stimulates the adrenal medulla to release the hormonal equivalent of the neurotransmitter noradrenaline into the bloodstream, in which it is transported to the organs in the body. Receptors in the target organs respond to the hormone and maintain their activation. Because the hormone can be released for a longer period than the neurotransmitter, this can enhance and extend the period of arousal.

A second activating system involves the pituitary gland, the activity of which is also controlled by the hypothalamus. This lies immediately under the brain (see Figure 8.2), and when stimulated by the hypothalamus, it releases a number of hormones into the bloodstream, the most important of which is adrenocorticotrophic hormone (ACTH). When the ACTH reaches the adrenal cortex, it causes it to release hormones known as **corticosteroids,** the most important of which is **cortisol** – also known as hydrocortisone. Cortisol increases the availability of energy stores and fats to fuel periods of high physiological activity. It also inhibits inflammation of damaged tissue.

The immune system

Components of the immune system

pathogen
a collective name for a variety of challenges to our health and immune system, including bacteria and viruses.

antigen
unique protein found on the surface of a pathogen that enables the immune system to recognise that pathogen as a foreign substance and therefore produce antibodies to fight it. Vaccinations introduce specially prepared viruses or bacteria into a body, and these have antigens.

antibodies
immunoglobulins produced in response to an antigen.

lymphocyte
a type of white blood cell. Lymphocytes have a number of roles in the immune system, including the production of antibodies and other substances that fight infection and disease. Includes T and B cells.

phagocyte
an immune system cell that can surround and kill micro-organisms and remove dead cells. Phagocytes include macrophages.

The immune system is very sophisticated and complex and is designed to help the body to resist disease. It provides a variety of protective mechanisms that respond to attacks from bacteria, viruses, infectious diseases and other sources from outside the body – collectively known as **pathogens** or **antigens**. In this section, we first identify and briefly describe the role of different elements of the immune system. We then go on to look at the links between them and how they combine to combat invading antigens and the development of cancers.

A number of organs and chemicals form the front line of the system. These include:

- *Physical barriers*: provided by the skin.
- *Mechanical barriers*: cilia (small hairs in the lining of the lungs) propel pathogens out of the lungs and respiratory tract – coughs and sneezes achieve the same goal more dramatically. Tears, saliva and urine also push pathogens out of the body.
- *Chemical barriers*: acid from the stomach provides an obvious chemical barrier against pathogens. Sebum, which coats body hairs, inhibits the growth of bacteria and fungi on the skin. Saliva, tears, sweat and nasal secretions contain lysozyme, which destroys bacteria. Saliva and the walls of the gastrointestinal tract also contain an **antibody** known as immunoglobulin A (IgA).
- *'Harmless pathogens'*: a variety of bacteria live within the body and have no harmful effects on us. However, they defend their territory and can destroy other bacteria that invade it.
- *Lymph nodes*: secondary organs at or near possible points of entry for pathogens. This system includes the tonsils, Peyer's patches in the intestines, and the appendix. They have high levels of **lymphocytes** (see below), ready to attack any invading pathogens.

As well as these relatively static defences against attack, there are a number of cells that circulate around the body. This can be through the circulatory system (see below) or a parallel system known as the lymphatic system. This carries a fluid called lymph and transports cells important to the destruction of antigens to the sites of cellular damage and the waste products of this destruction away from them.

Two groups of cells in the circulatory and lymphatic systems provide protection against a variety of pathogens. **Phagocytes** (sometimes called white blood cells) circulate within the circulatory system. They are created in the bone marrow and attract, adhere to and then engulf and destroy antigens – a process known as phagocytosis. The immune system has a number of phagocytes, including:

- *Neutrophils* have a short life of a few hours to days. They provide the major defence against bacteria and the initial fight against infection by engulfing and digesting them. They are followed by macrophages about three to four hours later.

■ *Macrophages* are long-lived and are best at attacking dead cells and pathogens capable of living within cells. Once a macrophage destroys a cell, it places some of its own proteins on its surface. This allows other immune cells to identify cells as invaders and to attack them.

A second group of cells known as lymphocytes circulate in the blood (where they are also known as white blood cells) and lymph system. These include **T cells** and **B cells**:

■ *Cytotoxic T cells* bind onto antigens, including virus-infected cells and tumour cells. They form pores in the target cell's plasma membrane, allowing ions and water to flow into the target cell, making it expand then collapse and die.

■ *Helper T cells* trigger or increase an immune response. They identify and bind to antigens, then release chemicals that stimulate the proliferation of cytotoxic T and plasma B cells (see below). Helper T cells are also known as **CD4+ cells** because of their chemical structure.

■ *Plasma B cells* destroy antigens by binding to them and making them easier targets for phagocytes. They attack antigens in the blood system before they enter body cells.

■ *Memory B cells* live indefinitely in the blood and lymphatic systems. They result from an initial attack by a novel antigen. In their initial response to such attacks, memory B cells 'learn' the chemical nature of such antigens and are able to deal with them more effectively should they encounter them again.

A third group of attacking cells are **natural killer (NK) cells**, which move in the blood and attack cancer cells and virus-infected body cells.

■ Central nervous system links with the immune system

The immune system is intimately linked to the central nervous system. The influence of these two interacting systems affects the development and activity of the phagocytes, and the B, T and NK cells. Lymphocytes also have adrenal and cortisol receptors, which are affected by hormones from both the adrenal cortex and medulla (see above). The influence of these neuro-transmitters and hormones is complex. Increases of adrenaline in response to short-term stress can stimulate the spleen to release phagocytes into the bloodstream and increase NK cell counts, but decrease the number of T cells. Cortisol release decreases the production of helper T cells and ingestion of cells by macrophages. These issues are complex and differ over the time course of stress and the nature of the stressor. However, it is generally recognised that chronic stress significantly impairs the effectiveness of the immune system, leaving us less able to ward off infection.

T cell
a cell that recognises antigens on the surface of a virus-infected cell, binds to that cell and destroys it.

B cell
a form of lymphocyte involved in destruction of antigens. Memory B cells provide long-term immunity against previously encountered pathogens.

CD4+ cells
otherwise known as helper T cells, these are involved in the proliferation of cytotoxic T cells as part of the immune response. HIV infection impairs their ability to provide this function.

natural killer (NK) cells
cells move in the blood and attack cancer cells and virus-infected body cells.

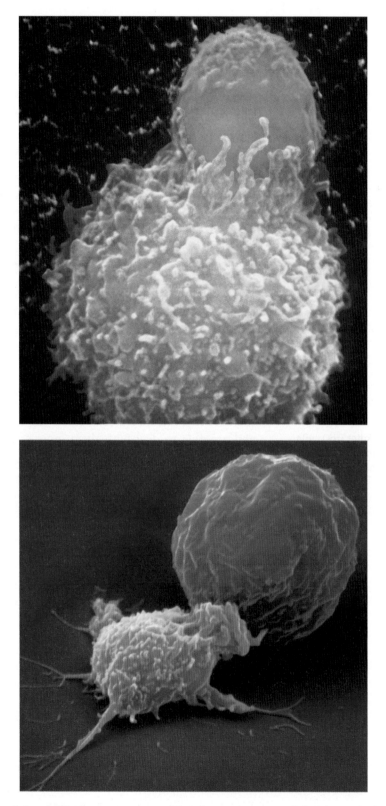

Plates 8.1 and 8.2 Here we see two cells, a virus and cancer cell, being attacked and either engulfed by B cells (8.1) or rendered inert by NK cells (8.2).

Source: Dr Andrejs Liepins/Science Photo Library (8.1) and Eye of Science/Science Photo Library (8.2)

Immune dysfunction

■ Human immunodeficiency virus infection

The human immunodeficiency virus (HIV) is the cause of a potentially fatal condition known as acquired immunodeficiency syndrome (AIDS). The virus belongs to a subgroup of viruses known as 'slow viruses'. These typically have a long interval between the initial infection and the onset of serious symptoms – potentially up to ten years and beyond. The virus affects the helper T cells (CD4+) cells, and as they replicate it too replicates. Unfortunately, these compromised cells are unable to respond effectively to viruses, some bacteria and other threats to health (although the first-line parts of the immune system can provide some protection), and they do not activate their target B and T cells, reducing the immune system's response to such threats. In addition, the virus can cause the helper T cells to stick together and render them unusable. Finally, the immune system may recognise these virus-laden cells as invasive and begin to attack its own helper T cells. Each of these various processes gradually impairs the efficiency of the B and T cell systems until they are overwhelmed and the onset of serious illnesses can occur.

Because helper T cells are so key to the body's response to a variety of antigens, repeated exposure to antigens that provoke helper T cells to proliferate can increase the speed of development of the HIV infection and its progression to AIDS. When the helper T cell count in the blood falls below $500/mm^3$, approximately half of the immune system reserve has been destroyed. At this point, minor infections such as cold sores and fungal infections begin to appear. Once the helper T cell count falls below $200/mm^3$, life-threatening opportunistic infections and cancers typically occur. AIDS, the end-point of HIV disease, occurs when the helper T cell count is less than $200/mm^3$ or with the presence of potentially life-threatening infections such as pneumonia or a cancer such as **Kaposi's sarcoma**.

Kaposi's sarcoma
a malignant tumour of the connective tissue, often associated with AIDS. The tumours consist of bluish-red or purple lesions on the skin. They often appear first on the feet or ankles, thighs, arms, hands and face.

autoimmune condition
a group of diseases, including type 1 diabetes, Crohn's disease and rheumatoid arthritis, characterised by abnormal functioning of the immune system in which it produces antibodies against its own tissues – it treats 'self' as 'non-self'.

Autoimmune diseases

diabetes (type 1 and 2)
a lifelong disease marked by high levels of sugar in the blood and a failure to transfer this to organs that need it. It can be caused by too little insulin (type 1) resistance to insulin (type 2), or both.

pancreas
gland in which the islets of Langerhans produce insulin. Also produces and secretes digestive enzymes. Located behind the stomach.

The immune system is able to identify cells that are part of the body ('self') and those that are 'non-self': antigens, developing cancers, and so on. On occasion, this process breaks down and the immune system treats cells in the body as non-self and begins to attack them. This can result in a number of so-called **autoimmune conditions**, including diabetes, rheumatoid arthritis and multiple sclerosis.

■ Diabetes

Two types of **diabetes** have been identified. In type 1 diabetes, the body does not produce sufficient insulin in the islets of Langerhans in the **pancreas**. Its onset is frequently triggered by an infection, often by one of the Coxsackie virus family. This virus expresses a protein similar in structure to an enzyme involved in the production of insulin, and the immune response to this virus can also destroy the insulin-producing cells in the pancreas.

Insulin normally attaches itself to glucose molecules in the circulatory system, permitting them to be taken up by the various body organs that require glucose to provide them with energy. Without insulin, these glucose molecules cannot be absorbed, leading to high levels of glucose in the blood, which the body cannot use. Both the high levels of circulating glucose and the lack of sugar to vital organs can result in significant problems for people with diabetes. Symptoms are usually sudden in onset and include increased thirst and urination, constant hunger, weight loss, blurred vision, and extreme fatigue. If not diagnosed and treated with insulin, a person with type 1 diabetes can lapse into a life-threatening diabetic coma, also known as diabetic ketoacidosis. In the longer term, diabetes increases the risk of a variety of health problems, including impaired circulation, peripheral nerve damage and coronary heart disease.

A second form of the condition is known as type 2 diabetes. In this condition, the body produces sufficient insulin (or close to sufficient), but the cells that take up the glucose–insulin molecules become 'resistant' to them and no longer absorb them. Type 2 diabetes often develops later in life and is associated with obesity – a person's chances of developing type 2 diabetes increases by 4 percent for every pound of excess weight. The symptoms of type 2 diabetes develop gradually; their onset is not as sudden as in type 1 diabetes, and they may include fatigue or nausea, frequent urination, unusual thirst, weight loss, blurred vision, frequent infections, and slow healing of wounds or sores. Some people have no symptoms.

■ Rheumatoid arthritis

rheumatoid arthritis
a chronic autoimmune disease with inflammation of the joints and marked deformities. Something (possibly a virus) triggers an attack of the synovium in the joint by the immune system, which stimulates an inflammatory reaction that can lead to destruction of the joint.

Rheumatoid arthritis is an autoimmune condition that may be triggered by viruses in individuals with a genetic tendency for the disease. It is a systemic disease that affects the entire body and is characterised by inflammation of the membrane lining of the joints – known as the synovium. It is a chronic condition, characterised by flare-ups and periods of remission. During flare-ups, people with the condition experience significant pain, stiffness, warmth, redness and swelling. Other features include rheumatoid nodules that form under the skin in areas that experience external pressure, such as the elbows. It may also be associated with fatigue, loss of appetite, fever and loss of energy. The inflamed synovium can invade and damage bone and cartilage. Inflammatory cells release enzymes that may digest bone and cartilage. This may result in the joint losing its shape and alignment, causing pain and restricted movement within the joint.

■ Multiple sclerosis

multiple sclerosis
a disorder of the brain and spinal cord caused by progressive damage to the myelin sheath covering of nerve cells. This results in decreased nerve functioning, which can lead to a variety of symptoms, including weakness, paralysis, tremor, pain, tingling, numbness and decreased coordination.

myelin sheath
a substance that contains both protein and fat (lipid) and surrounds all nerves outside the brain. It acts as a nerve insulator and helps in the transmission of nerve signals.

Multiple sclerosis (MS) is a neurological condition involving repeated episodes of inflammation of nervous tissue in any area of the central nervous system (brain and spinal cord). These episodes occur when the body's own immune cells attack the nervous system. The location of the inflamed areas varies from person to person and from episode to episode. The inflammation destroys the covering of the nerve cells (**myelin sheath**) in that area, leaving multiple areas of scar tissue (sclerosis). This results in slowing or blocking of the transmission of nerve impulses in that area, leading to the symptoms of

MS. As this may occur in any part of the brain or spinal cord, the symptoms they cause differ markedly across individuals and include loss of limb function, loss of bowel and/or bladder control, blindness due to inflammation of the optic nerve, and cognitive impairment. Muscular spasticity is a common feature, particularly in the upper limbs, and 95 percent of people with MS experience debilitating fatigue, which prevents any sustained physical activity in about 40 percent of people. Between 30 and 50 percent of people with the condition require walking aids or a wheelchair for mobility.

The course of MS differs across individuals. Onset before the age of 15 is rare, and 20 percent of those who have MS have a benign form of the disease in which symptoms show little or no progression after the initial attack. A few people experience malignant MS, resulting in a swift and relentless decline and significant disability or even death shortly after disease onset. Onset of this type of MS is usually after the age of 40. The majority of people have an episodic condition, with acute flare-ups followed by periods of remission. Each flare-up is usually followed by a failure to recover to previous levels of function, resulting in a slowly deteriorating condition. Death is usually due to complications of MS, including choking, pneumonia and renal failure.

The digestive tract

The digestive tract is the system of organs responsible for the ingestion of food, absorption of nutrients from that food, and finally the expulsion of waste products from the body. It comprises the following components:

- mouth
- pharynx
- oesophagus
- stomach
- small intestine, divided into three parts:
  - duodenum
  - jejunum
  - ileum
- large intestine, also divided into three parts:
  - caecum, to which the appendix is attached
  - colon
  - rectum, terminating in the anus.

Each organ in the system has a different role:

- *Mouth*: here, food is masticated by chewing, causing the release of enzymes in the saliva and beginning the process of digestion.
- *Oesophagus*: this transports food from the mouth to the stomach, compressing it in the process.
- *Stomach*: here, food is churned and mixed with acid to decompose it chemically.
- *Small intestine*: this is responsible for mixing the bowel contents with chemicals to break it into its constituent parts and then absorb them

bile
a digestive juice, made in the liver and stored in the gallbladder. Involved in the digestion of fats in the small intestine.

gallbladder
a structure on the underside of the liver on the right side of the abdomen. It stores the bile that is produced in the liver before it is secreted into the intestines. This helps the body to digest fats.

into the bloodstream for transportation to other organs. Key chemicals involved in this process include **bile**, which is made by the liver and stored in the **gallbladder** and digests fats, and enzyme-rich juices released from the pancreas.

■ *The large bowel* (colon): this is largely responsible for reabsorption of water from the bowel contents and expulsion of the unused bowel contents. Movement between and along these various organs is controlled by a process known as peristalsis. This involves smooth muscle within the walls of the organs narrowing and the narrow sections moving slowly along the length of the organ in a series of waves, pushing the bowel contents forward with each wave.

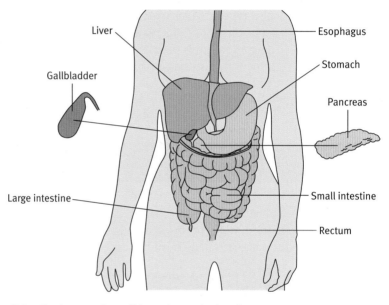

Figure 8.5   The large and small intestine and related organs.

Controlling digestion

Each of these digestion processes is controlled by both hormone and nerve regulators.

■ ## Hormone regulators

Hormones are produced and released by cells in the mucosa (lining) of the stomach and small intestine at key stages in the digestive process. Among other roles:

■ Gastrin causes the stomach to produce its acid.

■ Secretin causes the pancreas to produce a fluid that is rich in bicarbonate and enzymes to break down food into its constituent proteins, sugars, and so on. The bicarbonate is alkaline and prevents the bowel wall from being damaged as the highly acidic stomach contents are released into the small intestine. Secretin also stimulates the liver to produce bile, the acid that aids fat digestion.

- Cholesystokinin triggers the gallbladder to discharge its bile into the small intestine.

Nerve regulators

Activity in the digestive system is also controlled by a complex local nervous system known as the enteric nervous system, in which:

- Sensory neurons receive information from receptors in the mucosa and muscle. Chemoreceptors monitor levels of acid, glucose and amino acids. Sensory receptors respond to stretch and tension within the wall of the gut.
- Motor neurons, whose key role is to control gastrointestinal motility (including peristalsis and stomach motility) and secretion, control the action on smooth muscle in the wall of the gut.

Key neurotransmitters involved in the activity of the enteric nervous system are noradrenaline and acetylcholine: the former provides an activating role, the second an inhibitory role. The enteric nervous system works independently of the central nervous system. However, the gut also has links to the central nervous system, providing sensory information (such as fullness) to the hypothalamus and also allowing the gut to respond to the various excitatory or inhibitory processes of the autonomic nervous system. In general, sympathetic stimulation inhibits digestive activities, inhibiting gastrointestinal secretion and motor activity, and contracting gastrointestinal sphincters and blood vessels. The latter may be experienced as feelings of 'butterflies in the stomach' that we may experience at times of anxiety – and also some other, perhaps even more obvious, symptoms! Conversely, parasympathetic activity typically stimulates digestive activities.

Disorders of the digestive system

Gastric ulcer

Gastric ulcers are ulceration of the lining of the stomach (mucosa), which can result in a number of symptoms. Their most common symptom is abdominal discomfort or pain. The characteristics of this discomfort are that it:

- comes and goes for several days or weeks;
- occurs two to three hours after eating;
- is relieved by eating;
- may be at its worst during the night – when the stomach is empty following a meal.

Other symptoms include poor appetite, weight loss, bloating, nausea and vomiting. If the disease process is not treated, the ulcer may erode through the entire stomach wall, resulting in the potentially fatal outflow of its contents into the abdomen. Until relatively recently, gastric ulcers were thought to be the result of stress, which was thought to increase acid secretion in the stomach.

inflammatory bowel disease

a group of inflammatory conditions of the large intestine and, in some cases, the small intestine. The main forms of IBD are Crohn's disease and ulcerative colitis.

More recently, this psychological explanation has been replaced by a simpler biological model. This suggests that a bacterium known as *Helicobacter pylori* is responsible for the disorder. *H. pylori* infection is thought to weaken the protective mucous coating of the stomach and duodenum, which allows acid to get through to the sensitive lining beneath. Both the acid and the bacteria irritate the lining and cause the ulcer. Overall, *H. pylori* infection appears to be the most frequent cause of peptic ulceration, and its treatment the most effective way of curing the condition. However, stress may still be implicated in its development and maintenance either as an independent factor, one that influences other risk behaviour such as smoking or alcohol consumption, or by influencing levels of *H. pylori* in the gut (Bennett 2005a).

■ Inflammatory bowel disease

Crohn's disease

autoimmune disease that can affect any part of the gastrointestinal tract but most commonly occurs in the ileum (the area where the small and large intestine meet).

ulcerative colitis

a chronic inflammatory disease of the large intestine, characterised by recurrent episodes of abdominal pain, fever and severe diarrhoea.

colostomy

a surgical procedure that creates an opening (stoma) in the abdomen for the drainage of stool from the large intestine (colon). It may be temporary or permanent.

irritable bowel syndrome

a disorder of the lower intestinal tract. Symptoms include pain combined with altered bowel habits resulting in diarrhoea, constipation, or both. It has no obvious physiological abnormalities, so diagnosis is by the presence and pattern of symptoms.

Inflammatory bowel disease (IBD) is a group of inflammatory conditions of the large intestine and, in some cases, the small intestine. The main forms of IBD are:

- Crohn's disease
- ulcerative colitis.

Crohn's disease

Crohn's disease can involve any part of the gastrointestinal tract. It is an autoimmune and inflammatory condition, involving episodes of severe symptoms followed by periods of remission. Its key symptoms are chronic diarrhoea and disrupted digestion. At times of acute symptoms, this can present significant problems of dehydration and a failure to digest food and absorb necessary nutrients, resulting in the need for significant medical care. Over time, the inflammation process can result in a thickening of the bowel wall. As a result of this, the diameter of the bowel may become so constricted that food cannot pass through these damaged sections, which may need to be cut out using surgery. Unfortunately, as the disease tends to recur at these sites, this constriction may also recur and require further surgery within a few years. For this reason, surgery is often considered the treatment 'of last resort'. There is some evidence that the condition may be exacerbated by stress (Searle and Bennett 2001).

Ulcerative colitis

Ulcerative colitis is an inflammatory disease of the bowel that usually affects the terminal part of the large intestine and rectum. It is similar to Crohn's disease and may develop into cancer after a decade of disease. For this reason, patients may have regular checks for the beginnings of the cancer or even preventive removal of segments of the bowel. This may result in the affected individual needing a **colostomy**. As with Crohn's disease, the condition may be exacerbated by stress (Searle and Bennett 2001).

■ Irritable bowel syndrome

Irritable bowel syndrome (IBS) is a condition of the bowel involving a period of three months abdominal discomfort or pain, having at least two of the following features:

- pain is relieved by defaecation;
- pain is associated with a change in the frequency of bowel movements;
- or with a change in the form of the stool (loose, watery, or pellet-like).

Also central to a diagnosis of IBS is that these symptoms occur in the absence of any obvious physical pathology. Because of this lack of physical pathology, IBS was at one time considered to be the archetypal psychosomatic disorder. Indeed, Latimer (1981) went as far as to suggest that anxiety and IBS were the same condition, with IBS symptoms reported by people who were unwilling or unable to attribute their symptoms to psychological factors. However, evidence of this link to stress is not as strong as was previously thought, although in some cases it may be a key factor (see Bennett 2005b), and as we will see in Chapter 17, teaching people to manage their stress may result in reductions in IBS symptoms. However, other factors are now also associated with IBS. These include food hypersensitivities and the presence of bacteria such as *Blastocystis hominis* and *Helicobacter pylori* (see Singh, Pandy and Singh 2003).

IN THE SPOTLIGHT

Cancer

Hundreds of genes play a role in the growth and division of cells. Three classes of gene control this process and may contribute to the uncontrolled proliferation of cells, which is cancer:

1. *Oncogenes* control the sequence of events by which a cell enlarges, replicates its DNA, divides and passes a complete set of genes to each daughter cell. When mutated, they can drive excessive proliferation by producing too much of – or an overactive form of – a growth-stimulating protein.

2. *Tumour suppressor genes* inhibit growth. Loss or inactivation of this gene may produce inappropriate growth by losing this inhibitory control.

3. *Checkpoint genes* monitor and repair DNA, which is often damaged prior to reproduction and needs to be repaired before cell division. Without these checking mechanisms, a damaged gene will become replicated as a permanent mutation. One of the most notable checkpoint proteins is known as p53, which prevents replication of damaged DNA in the normal cell and promotes **cell suicide** in cells with abnormal DNA. Faulty p53 allows cells carrying damaged DNA to replicate and survive and has been found to be defective in most human cancers.

cell suicide
a type of cell death in which the cell uses specialised cellular machinery to kill itself.

Other factors are also important in tumour development. Growing tumours are dependent on a good blood supply. To promote this, local tissues may be transformed into blood vessel cells, allowing the tumour to establish its own blood supply. Some modern treatments of cancer attack this blood supply as well as the tumour mass itself. Tumours also acquire the ability to migrate and invade other tissues, forming tumour masses at different sites in the body. This process is known as metastasis – and in some cases these secondary tumours may be more deadly than the original tumour.

■ **Colorectal cancer**

Colorectal cancer is the third most common cancer in men and women. As with breast cancer, risk for the condition is increased by both biological and behavioural factors, including genetic factors, pre-existing inflammatory conditions, including ulcerative colitis, and a diet high in fat and low in fibre. As with many cancers, the condition can be described in terms of its stages, with the higher stage being more difficult to treat and having a poorer **prognosis**:

prognosis
the predicted outcome
of a disease.

- *Stage 1*: the cancer is limited to the inside of the bowel.

- *Stage 2*: the cancer penetrates through the wall of the bowel to the outside layers.

- *Stage 3*: the cancer involves the lymph glands in the abdomen.

- *Stage 4*: the cancer has metastasised to other organs.

The cardiovascular system

The main function of the cardiovascular system is to transport nutrients, immune cells and oxygen to the body's organs and to remove waste products from them. It also moves hormones from their point of production within the body to their site of action. The transport medium used in this process is the blood: the pumping system that pushes the blood around the body involves the heart and various types of blood vessel:

- *Arteries*: transport blood away from the heart. These vessels have a muscular sheath that allows them to contract or expand slightly. This activity is controlled by the autonomic nervous system.

- *Arterioles*: these are small arteries, linking the large arteries to the organs of the body.

- *Veins*: these transport blood back to the heart once the oxygen and nutrients have been absorbed from it and replaced by carbon dioxide and a variety of waste products. They are thinner than arteries, and because they are so far from the heart have much lower pressures than the arteries. Blood is pushed along them partly by the pressure of the pulse of blood from the heart (see below), partly through the action of the moving muscles. As large muscle groups contract during everyday activities, they also push blood through the veins. To prevent back flow of blood at times when the muscles are not providing positive pressure to the veins, they have a series of valves, which allow the blood to flow in only one direction. When the body is inactive, this process no longer operates, so blood may no longer flow freely in the veins and may even stagnate and begin to clot – the so-called deep vein thrombosis that may occur after long-haul flights or other periods of inactivity in some susceptible individuals.

Blood

exogenous
relating to things
outside the body.

erythrocyte
a mature blood cell that
contains haemoglobin to
carry oxygen to the
bodily tissues.

platelets
tiny bits of protoplasm
found in the blood that
are essential for blood
clotting. These cells bind
together to form a clot
and prevent bleeding at
the site of injury.

The body usually contains about 5 litres of blood. Its constituents include a fluid known as plasma and a variety of cells. As well as the various **exogenous** cells carried in the blood (nutrients, oxygen, etc.), it produces its own cells. These are manufactured by stem cells in the bone marrow. Three different types of cell are produced:

1. **Erythrocytes** (or red blood cells) transport oxygen around the body. In them, oxygen combines with haemoglobin in the lungs and is transported to cells in need of oxygen, where it is released, allowing cell respiration.

2. Phagocytes and lymphocytes (or white blood cells; see above) include the immune system's B cells and T cells described earlier in the chapter.

3. **Platelets** are cells that respond to damage to the circulatory system. They aggregate (form a clot) around the site of any damage and prevent loss of blood from the system. They are also involved in repair to damage within the arteries themselves and contribute to the development of atheroma. We consider this process later in the chapter.

The heart

The heart has two separate pumps operating in parallel. The right side of the heart is involved in the transportation of blood to the lungs; the left side pumps blood to the rest of the body (Figure 8.6). Each side of the heart has two chambers (Figure 8.7), known as atria and ventricles. The right atrium

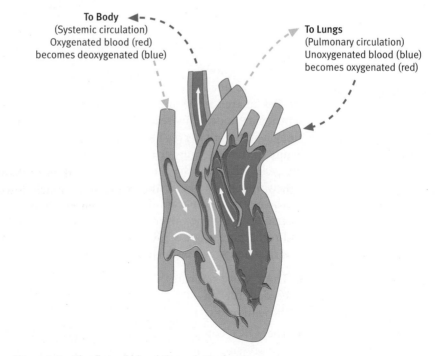

To Body
(Systemic circulation)
Oxygenated blood (red)
becomes deoxygenated (blue)

To Lungs
(Pulmonary circulation)
Unoxygenated blood (blue)
becomes oxygenated (red)

Figure 8.6   The flow of blood through the heart.

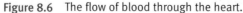

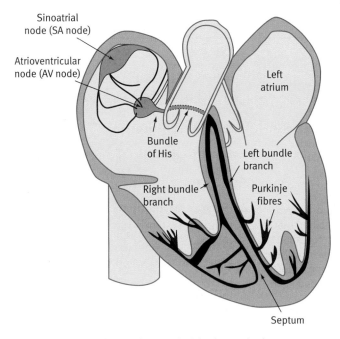

Figure 8.7 Electrical conduction and control of the heart rhythm.

takes deoxygenated blood from veins known as the superior and inferior vena cava and pumps it into the right ventricle. Blood is then pumped into the pulmonary artery, taking it to the lungs, where it picks up oxygen in its haemoglobin cells. Oxygen-laden blood then returns to the heart, entering through the left atrium. It is then pumped into the left ventricle, and then into the main artery, known as the **aorta**, which carries blood to the rest of the body.

aorta
the main trunk of the systemic arteries, carrying blood from the left side of the heart to the arteries of all limbs and organs except the lungs.

The rhythm of the heart is controlled by an electrical system. This is initiated by an electrical impulse generated in a region of the right atrium called the sinoatrial node. This impulse causes the muscles of both atria to contract. As the wave of electricity progresses through the heart muscle and nerves, it reaches an area at the junction of the atria and ventricles known as the atrioventricular node. This second node then fires a further electrical discharge along a system of nerves including the bundle of His and Purkinje fibres (see Figure 8.7), triggering the muscles of both ventricles to contract, completing the cycle. Although the sinoatrial node has an intrinsic rhythm, its activity is largely influenced by the autonomic nervous system.

The electrocardiogram (ECG) is used to measure the activity of the heart. Electrodes are placed over the heart and can detect each of the nodes firing and recharging. Figure 8.8 shows an ECG of a normal heart, indicating the electrical activity at each stage of the heart's cycle.

■ The P wave indicates the electrical activity of the atria firing – the time needed for an electrical impulse from the sinoatrial node to spread throughout the atrial musculature.

■ The QRS complex represents the electrical activity of the ventricles compressing.

■ The T wave represents the repolarization of the ventricles.

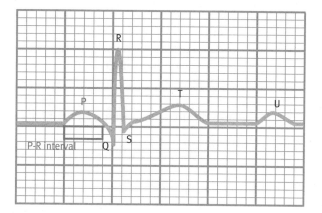

Figure 8.8 An electrocardiograph of the electrical activity of the heart (see text for explanation).

defibrillator
a machine that uses an electric current to stop any irregular and dangerous activity of the heart's muscles. It can be used when the heart has stopped (cardiac arrest) or when it is beating in a highly irregular (and ineffective) manner.

When the heart stops beating or its electrical rhythm is completely irregular and no blood is being pushed around the body, doctors may use a **defibrillator** to stimulate a normal (sinusoidal) rhythm.

Blood pressure

Blood pressure has two components:

1. the degree of pressure imposed on the blood as a result of its constriction within the arteries and veins – known as the diastolic blood pressure (DBP);

2. an additional pressure as the wave of blood pushed out from the heart forms flows through the system (our pulse) – known as the systolic blood pressure (SBP).

This pressure is measured in millimetres of mercury (mmHg), representing the height of a tube of mercury in millilitres that the pressure can push up (using a now old-fashioned sphygmomanometer). This varies around the body, being at its highest close to the heart and at its lowest as the blood re-enters the heart. To standardise the measurement of blood pressure, it is usually measured at the top of the arm. Healthy levels of blood pressure are an SBP below 130–140 mmHg and a DBP below 90 mmHg (written as 130/90 mmHg: see also the discussion of hypertension later in the chapter).

baroreceptors
sensory nerve endings that are stimulated by changes in pressure. Located in the walls of blood vessels such as the carotid sinus.

carotid artery
the main artery that takes blood from the heart via the neck to the brain.

A number of physiological processes are involved in controlling blood pressure. Those of particular interest to psychologists involve the autonomic nervous system. The brainstem (and the hypothalamus) receives continuous information from pressure-sensitive nerve endings called **baroreceptors** situated in the **carotid arteries** and aorta. This information is relayed to a centre in the brainstem known as the vasomotor centre. Reductions in blood pressure or physical demands such as exercise that require increased blood pressure causes activation of the sympathetic nervous system. Sympathetic activation results in increases in the strength and frequency of heart contractions (via the activity of the sinoatrial and atrioventricular nodes) and a contraction of the smooth muscle in the arteries. Together, these actions result in an increase in blood pressure, and allow sustained flow of blood to organs such as the muscles at times of high activity. Parasympathetic activity results in an opposing reaction.

What do YOU think?	**How do caffeine, smoking and drinking alcohol influence blood pressure?**

How do caffeine, smoking and drinking alcohol influence blood pressure?

People who drink significant amounts of alcohol have a one and a half to two times greater risk of developing hypertension than those who do not drink. The association between alcohol and high blood pressure is particularly noticeable when the alcohol intake exceeds five drinks per day. In addition, the connection is a dose-related phenomenon. In other words, the more alcohol that is consumed, the stronger is the link with hypertension (e.g. Saremi, Hanson, Tulloch-Reid *et al.* 2004).

Smoking also increases the risk of heart disease and stroke in people who already have hypertension, although it is not strongly associated with the development of hypertension. Nevertheless, smoking a cigarette can produce an immediate, temporary rise in the blood pressure of 5 to 10 mmHg. However, steady smokers may actually may have a lower blood pressure than non-smokers. This is because the nicotine in the cigarettes causes a decrease in appetite, which leads to weight loss. This, in turn, lowers the blood pressure. Stopping smoking can lead to increased food consumption and increased weight (e.g. Janzon, Heblad, Berglund *et al.* 2004).

Finally, there is extensive evidence that normal levels of caffeine can increase blood pressure. Overall, the impact of dietary caffeine on population BP levels is likely to be modest – probably about 4 mmHg of diastolic blood pressure and 2 mmHg of systolic blood pressure. Despite this relatively modest increase in blood pressure, James (2004) estimated that they could contribute to 14 percent of premature deaths resulting from coronary heart disease and 20 percent of those from a stroke.

Are the risks associated with these types of behaviour something that those involved in public health should act upon? Should we place health warnings on coffee, tea, alcohol? Should advertising warn that coffee – and other caffeine-containing drinks – can do you harm? What are the limits to health promotion and how the state advises our consumption of potentially harmful substances – tea, coffee, caffeine supplements, alcohol, cigarettes, marijuana? After all, any limit is going to be arbitrary, and something we should all consider.

Diseases of the cardiovascular system

■ Hypertension

Hypertension is a condition in which resting blood pressure is significantly above normal levels (see Table 8.2).

Two broad causes of hypertension have been identified:

1. *Secondary hypertension*: here, hypertension is the result of a disease process, usually involving the kidneys, adrenal glands or aorta. This type of hypertension accounts for about 5 percent of cases.

Table 8.2 Typical blood pressure readings in normal and hypertensive individuals

	Diastolic (mmHg)	Systolic (mmHg)
Normal	<90	<140
Mild hypertension	90–99	140–159
Hypertension	>100	>160

2. *Essential (primary) hypertension*: in the majority of cases, there is no known disease process that causes the problem. It seems to be the 'normal' consequence of a number of risk factors, such as obesity, lack of exercise and a high salt intake. It is a progressive condition, and people with the condition usually experience a gradual rise in blood pressure over a period of years.

Psychological stress may also contribute to the development of essential hypertension (e.g. Ming, Adler, Kessler *et al.* 2004). At times of stress, sympathetic activity increases muscle tone in the arteries and the strength of the heart's contractions – both of which contribute to short-term increases in blood pressure, which then falls as parasympathetic activity follows a period of stress. If the stress is sustained or frequent, however, the activity of the sympathetic nervous system begins to dominate and gradually pushes blood pressure up for longer periods until the individual develops chronically raised blood pressure.

Hypertension may be present and remain unnoticed for many years, or even decades. It is usually considered to be a syndrome with few if any symptoms, and many cases of hypertension are detected during routine screening (see Chapter 6). If high blood pressure has no symptoms, why bother treating it? At low levels of high blood pressure – mild hypertension – some have argued that medical treatment may actually be of little benefit, and that the side-effects of treatment may outweigh its benefits (although this position is now being challenged as new drugs are used to treat the condition: see Weber and Julius 1998). However, as blood pressure rises, so too does the amount of damage it can do. High blood pressure increases the risk of a heart attack (myocardial infarction; MI – see below), stroke, kidney failure, eye damage and **heart failure**. It also contributes to the development of atheroma, described below.

heart failure
a state in which the heart muscle is damaged or weakened and is unable to generate a cardiac output sufficient to meet the demands of the body.

IN THE SPOTLIGHT

The life and (heroic) death of John Henry

John Henry was born a slave in the USA in the 1840s or 1850s. So what has he got to do with modern-day psychology? Well, legend has it that he was a giant of a man, who rose to any challenge he faced – a characteristic that eventually resulted in his death. He died while working as a labourer on the railroad tunnelling through a mountain in West Virginia. One of his jobs was to pound holes into rock, which were then filled with explosives and used to blast

continued

through tunnels. When the railroad owners brought in steam drills to do the same job more quickly and cheaply, he challenged the steam drill to a contest. He won the contest but died of exhaustion soon after. His name has now become synonymous with a process, initially at least, thought to drive hypertension in black males – John Henryism.

Hypertension is particularly prevalent in African Americans. Black people in the USA are up to four times more likely than whites to develop hypertension by the age of 50 (Roberts and Rowland 1981). One of the reasons for this is thought to be that black people are more frequently placed in situations of high effort coping with difficult psychological stressors – poverty, racism, and so on – than their white counterparts. This chronic high effort coping results in chronic and sustained increases in heart rate and blood pressure. This, in turn, overcomes the body's homeostatic processes and pushes the resting blood pressure increasingly up until they develop long-term hypertension. Although initially viewed as an issue for black men, the process is increasingly being seen as the outcome of the stresses associated with low socio-economic position – and may account for some of the health inequalities considered in Chapter 2.

■ Coronary heart disease

low-density lipoprotein (LDL)
the main function of LDLs seems to be to carry cholesterol to various tissues throughout the body. LDLs are sometimes referred to as 'bad' cholesterol because elevated levels of LDL correlate most directly with coronary heart disease.

high-density lipoprotein (HDL)
lipoproteins are fat protein complexes in the blood that transport cholesterol, triglycerides and other lipids to various tissues. The main function of HDL appears to be to carry excess cholesterol to the liver for 're-packaging' or excretion in the bile. Higher levels of HDL seem to be protective against CHD, so HDL is sometimes referred to as 'good' cholesterol.

Like hypertension, coronary heart disease (CHD) is often a silent disease in that it may develop over many years before becoming evident. Indeed, people may have quite significant CHD and never be aware of their condition. The long-term, and silent, element of CHD is the development of atheroma in the blood vessels. This may result in more obvious manifestations of CHD, including an MI and angina (see below).

Atheroma
Atheroma is now understood to be the result of the process of damage and repair of artery walls and inflammatory processes involving the immune system. One of the key constituents of atheroma is cholesterol. This is a waxy substance that is present in blood plasma and in all animal tissues. It is also a key chemical in the body. Without it, cells throughout the body could not maintain the integrity of their walls, and we would become seriously ill or die. Too much cholesterol, on the other hand, may be harmful.

To get to body cell walls in order to repair and maintain them, cholesterol must be transported through the body – via the bloodstream. However, it is insoluble in the blood. To allow such transport, it is therefore attached to groups of proteins called lipoproteins. **Low-density lipoproteins** (LDLs) transport cholesterol to the various tissues and body cells, where it is separated from the lipoprotein and is used by the cell. It can also be absorbed into atheroma on the inner surface of the blood vessels. **High-density lipoproteins** (HDLs) transport excess or unused cholesterol from the tissues back to the liver, where it is broken down to bile acids and is then excreted. LDLs are therefore characterised as 'harmful' cholesterol: HDLs are considered to be health-protective. Although some cholesterol is absorbed from our food through the gut, about 80 percent of cholesterol in our bodies is produced by the liver.

The development of atherosclerosis:

1. *Early atherosclerosis*: fatty streaks are laid down in artery walls. These usually occur at sites of disturbed blood flow, such as bifurcations of arteries. They occur as part of a repair process to damage of the artery wall caused by the disturbed blood flow and increases in pressure associated with high blood pressure linked to sympathetic activation. In this process, inflammatory monocytes, which are precursors to macrophages (see the section on the immune system earlier in the chapter), absorb LDL cholesterol from the circulating blood to become what are known as foam cells. These form a coat over the lining of the damaged artery. As the foam cells die, they lose their contents of LDL, resulting in pools of cholesterol forming between the foam cells and the artery wall. The presence of foam cells may trigger the growth of smooth muscle cells from the artery wall to cover them. In this way, the walls of the artery are lined with lipids, foam cells and finally a wall of smooth muscle. This process results in a gradual reduction of the diameter of the artery.

2. *Later atherosclerosis*: the progress of atherosclerosis is determined by the relative influence of the inflammatory monocytes and development of smooth muscle. Monocytes and their subsequent foam cells add to the development of atherosclerosis; the building of smooth muscle repairs the artery and provides a smooth artery wall – albeit of decreasing diameter. At times, clots of cholesterol and foam cells may be pulled out of the artery wall, resulting in two potential outcomes:

   ■ A clot blocks an artery in a key organ such as the heart, resulting in a myocardial infarction (MI) (see below).

   ■ The damage to the artery wall initiates acute repair processes, including the deposition of platelets around the damage site, before more smooth muscle cells build over the damage – dramatically increasing the degree of occlusion of the artery.

The distribution of atheroma within the circulatory system is not uniform throughout the body. It may be most developed around the junctions of arteries because disturbances in blood flow at such points can facilitate these processes, but the heart arteries are also one of the areas most likely to be affected.

■ ## Acute manifestations of CHD

Myocardial infarction

As we noted earlier in the chapter, an important end-point of CHD is when a clot is pulled off an artery wall and enters the circulating blood. This may prove a harmless event, with no health implications for the individual. However, if the circulating clot has a greater diameter than the blood vessels it is passing through, it will inevitably block such blood vessels and prevent the flow of blood beyond them. This blockage (occlusion) may result in significant health problems if it occurs in the arteries supplying oxygen and nutrients to the heart. Unless rapidly treated, the cells of the heart muscle no longer receive their nutrients and oxygen will die – a process known as an MI. The severity of damage that will occur as a consequence of this is determined by how large a blood vessel is affected (larger is worse) and which parts of the heart are damaged.

The classic symptoms of an MI include what is often called a 'crushing chest pain'. The affected individual may feel like their chest is trapped in a vice. Other symptoms include shortness of breath, coughing, pain radiating down the left arm, dizziness and or collapse, nausea or vomiting, and sweating. An MI may also be much less dramatic. Indeed, many people delay seeking help for an MI as their symptoms are vague, may be confused with heartburn or indigestion, and the affected individual hopes that the symptoms will go away without treatment. Perhaps the strangest symptom that can rarely be indicative of an MI is toothache – although we would not recommend you visit your local hospital complaining of a heart attack should you be unfortunate enough to develop this problem! Approximately 45 percent of people will die of their MI immediately or in the week or so following the event. The majority of people go on to make a good recovery. This may be aided by treatment with drugs known as '**clot busters**'. These drugs dissolve the clot causing the blocked artery and, if given within an hour or so of the infarction, can prevent the permanent muscle damage that will occur if they are not given.

clot busters
drugs which dissolve clots associated with myocardial infarction and can prevent damage to the heart following such an event. Are best used within one hour of the infarction.

IN THE SPOTLIGHT

According to the Royal College of Physicians, giving clot-busting drugs saves about thirty lives per 1,000 patients treated. They estimate that this proportion could be increased, perhaps up to sixty-five per 1,000, if treatment is started within the first hour after onset of symptoms. The problem is that only about 55 percent of patients with an MI are admitted into hospital – where they can receive medical treatment – within one hour of its onset, rendering such drugs of little benefit.

We know that one of the most important reasons for delay is because patients are not sure their symptoms are serious – and that they are more likely to seek medical help if there is someone with them at the time of their onset. Most of us are aware of the acute and dramatic symptoms that may signal a myocardial infarction. However, we may be less aware of the potentially rather vague symptoms that may accompany one. Of course, over-responding to such symptoms may result in health services being overwhelmed by the 'worried well'. So the health services have a clear dilemma: educate the public that a myocardial infarction may be associated with vague symptoms, including feeling nauseous, weak, vague discomfort in the chest, and there is the potential for overuse of health services. Don't warn the public, and many people may delay seeking treatment until it is too late. Appropriate education of the public is not easy.

However, there is another way in which treatment speed can be increased. Delay can be broken into two components. Patient delay in contacting the health service, and the delay between the ambulance call and them actually receiving treatment – usually in hospital. An alternative and potentially more attractive way of minimising the delay between onset and this specific treatment is to allow emergency ambulance personnel to treat patients using clot busters. While it has its obvious benefits, and this issue is now being considered within the emergency services, this also has a number of problems. In particular, treatment requires ambulance personnel to make a diagnosis, and to give a drug with potentially negative side-effects. These responsibilities usually lie with medical staff, who cannot go to all emergencies. Whether they will eventually come within the remit of ambulance personnel – and potentially save lives – is a topic of hot debate.

Angina

angina
severe pain in the chest associated with a temporary insufficient supply of blood to the heart.

The key symptom of **angina** is similar to that of an MI. It is a central chest pain that may radiate to the left shoulder, jaw, arm or other areas of the chest. Some patients may confuse arm or shoulder pain with arthritis or indigestion pain. It is a temporary condition, which occurs when the heart muscle needs more oxygen than can be provided by the heart arteries. It is frequently precipitated by exertion or stress. It may result from three underlying causes:

1. atheromatous lesions of the coronary arteries, reducing their diameter and limiting the blood flow through them;

2. **vasospasm** of the coronary arteries, resulting in a temporary reduction in their diameter;

3. a combination of 1. and 2.

vasospasm
a situation in which the muscles of artery walls in the heart contract and relax rapidly, resulting in a reduction of the flow of blood through the artery.

Classic angina is associated with high levels of atheroma in the coronary arteries and occurs when blood flow does not meet the needs of the heart muscle. Physical exertion, emotional stress and exposure to cold are among the triggers for this type of angina. A second type of angina, known as variant angina, results from the coronary arteries going into spasm. This results in significant reductions in the diameter of the arteries and reduced blood flow through them. This effect may be exacerbated by the reductions in the normal diameter of the arteries as a result of atheroma. Unlike classic angina, variant angina typically occurs during rest and may occur at night. What causes the coronary arteries to go into spasm is not fully understood. It may involve sympathetic nervous system activity or problems in the calcium processes involved in the firing of neurons.

The respiratory system

The respiratory system delivers oxygen to and removes carbon dioxide from the blood. The exchange of oxygen and carbon dioxide occurs in the lungs. The system comprises:

- the *upper respiratory tract*, including the nose, mouth, larynx and trachea;
- the *lower respiratory tract*, including the lungs, bronchi, bronchioles and alveoli. Each lung is divided into upper and lower lobes – the upper lobe of the right lung contains a third subdivision known as the right middle lobe.

The bronchi carry air from the mouth to the lungs. As they enter the lungs, they divide into smaller bronchi, then into smaller tubes called bronchioles (see Figure 8.9). The bronchioles contain minute hairs called cilia, which beat rhythmically to sweep debris out of the lungs towards the pharynx for expulsion and thus form part of the mechanical element of the immune system – see earlier in the chapter. Bronchioles end in air sacs called alveoli – small, thin-walled 'balloons', which are surrounded by tiny blood capillaries. As we breathe in, the concentration of oxygen is greater in the alveoli than in the

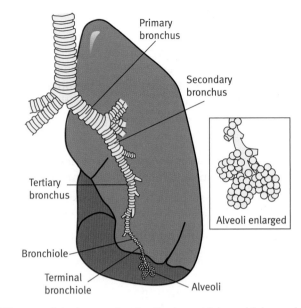

Figure 8.9 Diagram of the lungs, showing the bronchi, bronchioles and alveoli.

haemoglobin in the blood travelling through the capillaries. As a result, oxygen diffuses across the alveolar walls into the haemoglobin. As we breathe out, carbon dioxide concentration in the blood is greater than that in the alveoli, so it passes from the blood into the alveoli and is then exhaled.

Respiration is the act of breathing:

■ *Inspiration*: two sets of muscles are involved in inhalation. The main muscle involved is the diaphragm. This is a sheet of muscle that divides the abdomen and is found immediately below the lungs. Contraction of this muscle pulls the lungs down and sucks air into them. The second set of muscles is known as the intercostal muscles. These are found between the ribs and can expand the chest – again pulling air into the lungs.

■ *Expiration*: relaxation of the diaphragm and intercostal muscles allows the lungs to contract, decreases lung volume, and pushes air out of them. The air then passively flows out.

The rate of breathing is controlled by respiratory centres in the brainstem. These respond to:

■ the concentration of carbon dioxide in the blood (high carbon dioxide concentrations initiate deeper, more rapid breathing);

■ air pressure in lung tissue. Expansion of the lungs stimulates nerve receptors to signal the brain to 'turn off' inspiration. When the lungs collapse, the receptors give the 'turn on' signal, known as the Hering-Breuer inspiratory reflex.

Other automatic regulators include increases in blood pressure, which slows down respiration, a fall in blood acidity, which stimulates respiration, and a sudden drop in blood pressure, which increases the rate and depth of respiration.

RESEARCH FOCUS

Matthews, K.A., Katholi, C.R., McCreath, H., Whoolry, M.A., Williamson, D.R., Zhu, S. and Markovitz, J.H. (2004). Blood pressure reactivity to psychological stress predicts hypertension in the CARDIA study. *Circulation*, 110: 74–8.

This paper considered whether blood pressure reactivity predicted long-term hypertension. The team used a longitudinal method, measuring blood pressure reactivity at one point in time and hypertension up to 13 years later to see whether these initial measures were predictive of later levels of blood pressure. They hypothesised that high levels of blood pressure increases in response to psychological stress measured at baseline would be predictive of resting blood pressure when measured later.

Method
The CARDIA study is a longitudinal study, initially, of 5,115 black and white men and women recruited in various parts of the USA. They were aged between 18 and 30 at baseline. Two years into the study, their blood pressure reactivity was measured by comparing blood pressure at rest and during 'stressful' tasks. At this time, 4,624 participants were still in the study. Of these, 422 participants did not take part in the reactivity study. Accordingly, the study sample comprised 4,202 people, all of whom had normal blood pressures at baseline.

Subsequent measures of blood pressure were taken three, five, eight and thirteen years following these initial measures. The study investigated whether levels of blood pressure and the development of hypertension over the period of the study could be predicted by the level of blood pressure reactivity at baseline.

Data collection
Resting blood pressure on each occasion was measured using a mercury sphygmomanometer. Three measurements were taken at one-minute intervals, and the last two were averaged to form the reported resting blood pressure.

At baseline, this measure was added to by blood pressure readings during three stress tests. The testing period involved an eight-minute baseline period during which the participants sat quietly, followed by three tasks:

1. a three-minute video game (Atari's Breakout – a state-of-the-art game when the baseline data were gathered);
2. a three-minute star-tracing task – participants had to trace the image of a star while looking at their drawing through a mirror;
3. a cold pressor task – involved placing a hand in cold water for 45 seconds.

The tasks appeared in a random order. Blood pressure was measured using an automated blood pressure machine at one-minute intervals during the baseline period and the first two tasks and was measured once during the cold pressor task (the paper does not specify when).

Blood pressure reactivity was calculated by subtracting the average of the final three baseline readings from the average pressure during each task.

Results
Participants averaged 27 years of age at the time of testing. The results were considered in terms of ethnic group and gender:

■ Blacks had greater increases in DBP during the video game and cold pressor tasks than whites.
■ Men had greater increases in DBP than women during the cold pressor and star-tracing task and larger increases in SBP during the video game and star-tracing task.

continued

- When risk for hypertension over time was assessed, the main predictors were being older at the time of testing, being less well educated, having a higher body mass index and higher resting SBP or DBP. However, greater changes in SBP and DBP during all tasks added significantly to the regression equations used to predict whether or not participants were hypertensive at each subsequent assessment time.

- The relationship between reactivity and subsequent measures of blood pressure differed according to race, gender and task.

- Reactivity to the cold pressor tasks predicted earlier raised SBP most strongly in white women.

- Reactivity to the video game predicted earlier raised DBP in both black and white men, but not women.

Discussion

These data suggest that blood pressure reactivity during a stressful task increases risk for the development of hypertension. However, the authors note that the mechanism through which this process occurs is not understood. It should also be noted that the effects were quite small and specific. The effect of blood pressure reactivity on subsequent levels of blood pressure may be significant, but among all the other potential influences on blood pressure such as smoking and salt intake, it cannot be considered a strong effect.

Diseases of the respiratory system

■ Chronic obstructive airways disease

chronic obstructive airways disease
a persistent airway obstruction associated with combinations of chronic bronchitis, small airways disease, asthma and emphysema.

emphysema
a late effect of chronic infection or irritation of the bronchial tubes. When the bronchi become irritated, some of the airways may be obstructed or the walls of the tiny air spaces may tear, trapping air in the lung beyond them. As a result, the lungs may become enlarged, at the same time becoming less efficient in exchanging oxygen for carbon dioxide.

Chronic obstructive airways disease (COAD) is a group of lung diseases characterised by limited airflow through the airways resulting from damage to the alveoli. Its most common manifestations are **emphysema** and **chronic bronchitis**. The leading cause of both conditions is smoking. Prolonged tobacco use causes lung inflammation and variable degrees of destruction of the alveloli. Chronic bronchitis results from inflammation and a consequent narrowing of the airways. Emphysema results from the destruction of the alveoli, resulting in reduced lung elasticity and reductions in the surface area on which the exchange of oxygen and carbon dioxide can occur. Both result in significant and long-term shortness of breath, an unproductive cough (which produces no phlegm), and a marked reduction in exercise capacity. Severe cases of each condition may require the affected individual to be on a constant supply of oxygen.

The conditions result from exposing the alveoli to irritants, whether as a result of direct or passive smoking or living or working in a polluted environment. About 15 percent of long-term smokers will develop COAD (Mannino 2003). More rarely, an enzyme deficiency called alpha-1 anti-trypsin deficiency can cause emphysema in non-smokers.

■ Lung cancer

Lung cancer is the second most common cancer affecting both sexes. As women have taken up smoking following the Second World War, rates of

chronic bronchitis
an inflammation of the bronchi, the main air passages in the lungs, which persists for a long period or repeatedly recurs. Characterised by excessive bronchial mucus and a cough that produces sputum for three months or more in at least two consecutive years.

lung cancer among this group have risen, while those among men have fallen (Tyczynski, Bray, Aareleid et al. 2004). Key risk factors for lung cancer include:

- smoking
- exposure to carcinogens, including asbestos and radon.

Two different types of lung cancer have been identified:

1. Small cell cancer. The main treatment is chemotherapy. The overall survival depends on the stage of the disease. For limited-stage small cell cancer, cure rates may be as high as 25 percent, while cure rates for extensive-stage disease are less than 5 percent.

2. Non-small cell cancer (between 70 and 80 percent of cases). The main treatment for this type of cancer involves removal of the cancer through surgery. Where the tumour is small and has not spread, up to 50 percent of people with the condition may survive. The prognosis is worse the larger the tumour. Where the tumour has spread and lymph nodes are involved, the disease is almost never cured, and the goals of therapy are to extend life and improve quality of life (Beadsmoore and Screaton 2003).

IN THE SPOTLIGHT

Snoring – a health warning

Forty-five percent of normal adults snore at least occasionally, and 25 percent are habitual snorers. It is more frequent in males and people who are overweight. It usually grows worse with age. Snoring is the result of an obstruction to the free flow of air through the passages at the back of the mouth and nose. This area is the collapsible part of the airway, where the tongue and upper throat meet the soft palate and uvula. Snoring occurs when these structures strike each other and vibrate during breathing.

Snoring presents the sufferer and any companion during sleep with a number of short-term problems. But it may also be a risk factor for CHD. In a large longitudinal study, Hu, Willett, Manson *et al.* (2000) followed a cohort of 71,779 female nurses for a period of eight years. Women who reported snoring occasionally at baseline were 20 percent more likely to have either a myocardial infarction or a stroke over this time. Regular snorers were 33 percent more likely to do so. Both groups were also more at risk of stroke than their non-snoring colleagues. These risks were independent of age, smoking, BMI and other cardiovascular risk factors – suggesting that snoring independently adds to the risk of developing coronary heart disease in women. Snoring may also add to the risk of developing hypertension (Ohayon, Guilleminault, Priest *et al.* 2000), although the process involved in either condition is not yet understood.

Snoring may also be associated with a more serious condition in which breathing is totally obstructed, known as obstructive sleep apnoea. Episodes can last more than ten seconds and may occur hundreds of times a night. Each episode can reduce blood oxygen levels, causing the heart to pump harder than usual during sleep. In addition, the snorer needs to sleep lightly and keep his or her muscles tense in order to maintain airflow to their lungs. This may make them tired during the day. In the longer term, the chronic strain placed on the heart may result in elevated blood pressure and heart enlargement.

Summary

This chapter reviewed some of the anatomy and physiology relevant to health psychology and other chapters of this book. In the first section, it briefly described key functions of the brain and their situation within it. Key functional areas include:

- the medulla oblongata, which controls respiration, blood pressure and heartbeat;
- the hypothalamus, which controls appetite, sexual arousal and thirst. It also exerts some control over our emotions;
- the amygdala, which links situations of threat and relevant emotions such as fear or anxiety, and controls the autonomic nervous system response to such threats.

One of the key systems controlled by the brain is the autonomic nervous system. This comprises two parallel sets of nerves:

1. The sympathetic nervous system is responsible for activation of many organs of the body.
2. The parasympathetic nervous system is responsible for rest and recuperation.

The highest level of control of the autonomic nervous system within the brain is the hypothalamus, which coordinates reflexive changes in response to a variety of physical changes, including movement, temperature and blood pressure. It also responds to emotional and cognitive demands, providing a link between physiological systems and psychological stress.

Activation of the sympathetic nervous system involves two neurotransmitters – adrenaline and noradrenaline – which stimulate organs via the sympathetic nerves themselves. Sustained activation is maintained by their hormonal equivalents, released from the adrenal medulla. A second system, controlled by the hypothalamus and pituitary gland, triggers the release of corticosteroids from the adrenal cortex. These increase the energy available to sustain physiological activation and inhibit inflammation of damaged tissue.

The immune system provides a barrier to infection by viruses and other biological threats to our health. Key elements of the system include phagocytes, such as macrophages and neutrophils, which engulf and destroy invading pathogens. A second group of cells, known as lymphocytes, including cytotoxic T cells and B cells, respond particularly to attacks by viruses and developing tumour cells. Both groups of cells can collaborate in the destruction of pathogens through a complex series of chemical reactions.

Slow viruses, including HIV, attack the immune system – by infecting CD4+ cells – and prevent the T and B cell systems from responding effectively. This leaves the body open to attack from viruses and cancers, either of which may result in life-threatening conditions.

The immune system may, itself, cause problems by treating its own cells as external invading agents. This can result in diseases such as multiple sclerosis, rheumatoid arthritis, and type 1 diabetes.

The digestive tract is responsible for the ingestion, absorption and expulsion of food. Activity within it is controlled by the enteric nervous system, which is linked to the autonomic nervous system. Activity in the system is therefore responsive to stress and other psychological states. That said, some conditions thought to be the result of stress are now thought to be the result of physical as well as psychological factors. Gastric ulcers are thought to result from infection by *Helicobacter pylori*, while irritable bowel syndrome is no longer seen as entirely the result of stress but has a multi-factor aetiology of which stress is but one strand.

The cardiovascular system is responsible for carrying oxygen, nutrients and various other materials around the body. Its activity is influenced by the autonomic nervous system. Two long-term 'silent' conditions that may lead to acute illnesses such as myocardial infarction or stroke are hypertension and atheroma. Both involve long-term processes. One way in which hypertension may develop is by blood pressure being pushed up through the action of the autonomic nervous system in response to stress. Atheroma develops as a result of repair processes to the artery wall. Two obvious outcomes of this process are myocardial infarction, in which an artery supplying the heart muscle is blocked and dies. Angina presents with similar symptoms but is the result of spasm of the arteries and is reversible.

Finally, the respiratory system is responsible for inspiring and carrying oxygen around the body, and the expulsion of carbon dioxide. It is prone to a number of disease processes, including chronic obstructive airways disease and lung cancer, which are significantly exacerbated by cigarette smoking.

Further reading

Lovallo, W.R. (1997). *Stress and Health. Biological and Psychological Interactions*. Thousand Oaks, Calif.: Sage.
A relatively easy introduction to the autonomic and immune systems, as well as how stress can influence their activity.

Kumar, P.J. and Clark, K.L. (2002). *Clinical Medicine*. W.B. Saunders.
At 1,464 pages, this is not a textbook you may want to buy. But if you want to know more about the development of various diseases, this is an excellent starting point.

Vedhara, K. and Irwin, M. (eds) (2005). *Human Psychoneuroimmunology*. Oxford University Press.
A readable guide to psychoneuroimmunology, written for those people who do not want to plough through £250, 400-page tomes (or so say the editors).

CHAPTER 9

Symptom perception, interpretation and response

Learning outcomes

By the end of this chapter, you should have an understanding of:

- contextual, cultural and individual influences upon symptom perception
- the core dimensions upon which illness can be represented
- key theoretical models of symptom perception, interpretation and response
- a broad range of influences upon symptom interpretation
- factors that influence delay in seeking healthcare advice for symptoms

CHAPTER OUTLINE

How do we know if we are getting ill? Do we all react in the same way to symptoms? What influences how we perceive and interpret symptoms of illness? Do beliefs about illness differ across the lifespan? Do illness perceptions and their interpretation influence healthcare seeking? These types of question are important to our understanding of how people cope with illness and of differentials in healthcare-seeking behaviour. They are questions that you need to ask yourself when thinking about the study of health and illness, whether as a future health psychologist or healthcare practitioner.

How do we become aware of the sensations of illness?

Illness generates changes in bodily sensations and functions that a person may perceive themself or perhaps have pointed out to them by another person, who says for example, 'You look pale'. The kind of sign that is likely to be noticed by the individual themselves includes changes in bodily functions (e.g. increased frequency of urination, heartbeat irregularities), emissions (such as blood in one's urine), sensations (e.g. numbness, loss of vision) and unpleasant sensations (e.g. fever, pain, nausea). Other people may not notice these changes but would perhaps notice changes in bodily appearance (weight loss, skin pallor) or function (e.g. paralysis, limping, tremor). Radley (1994) distinguishes between '*bodily signs*' and '*symptoms of illness*'. The former can be objectively recognised, but the latter requires interpretation; for example, a person has to decide whether a raised temperature (a bodily sign) is symptomatic of illness (e.g. influenza) or simply a sign of physical exertion.

While some diseases have visible symptoms, others do not and instead involve a subjectively sensed component of bodily responses, e.g. feeling sick, feeling tired, being in pain, which cannot be seen *per se*. Many people regularly experience symptoms, but there is huge variability between individuals when it comes to attending to, or reporting, symptoms. Although 70 to 90 percent of us have, at some time, a condition that could be diagnosed and treated by a health professional, only about one-third will actually seek medical attention. Health psychologists are interested in why this is the case.

As described in Chapter 1, people's views about health are shaped by both their prior experience of illness and their understanding of medical knowledge, whether expert or lay. People therefore learn about health in the same way as they learn about everything else – through experience, either their own or of other people's. People 'fall ill against a background of beliefs about good and poor health' (Radley 1994: 61). Furthermore, Radley notes, people's lives are 'grounded in *activity*', i.e. on the everyday activities or behaviour that depends upon the body, whether they be instrumental activities such as being able to run for a bus or expressive activities like being able to look attractive. Illness can therefore challenge a person at a fundamental level.

Illness or disease?

Cassell (1976) used the word 'illness' to stand for 'what the patient feels when he goes to the doctor', i.e. the experience of not feeling quite right as compared with one's normal state; and 'disease' to stand for 'what he has on the way home from the doctor's office'. Disease, then, is considered as being something of the organ, cell or tissue that denotes a physical disorder or underlying pathology, whereas illness is what the person experiences. People can feel ill without having an identifiable disease, and furthermore, people can have a disease and not feel ill (think of well-controlled asthma or diabetes, or early HIV infection for example). A routine visit to a doctor may lead to a person who considered themselves healthy on arrival finding out that they are 'officially' ill as indicated by the result of some routine test. By providing a diagnosis, doctors therefore mark the entry of a person into the healthcare system.

How does a person know if they are getting ill? This chapter will attempt to answer this by describing the processes underlying three stages of response:

1. perceiving symptoms;
2. interpreting symptoms as illness;
3. planning and taking action.

| **What do YOU think?** | How many of the symptoms below have you experienced in the last two weeks? Of those that you have experienced, how many have you seen a health professional about? Think of the reasons why you did, or did not, seek professional advice about the symptoms you have experienced. |

- fever
- nausea
- headache
- tremor
- joint stiffness
- excessive fatigue
- back pain
- dizziness
- stomach pains
- visual disturbance
- chesty cough
- sore throat
- breathlessness
- chest pain.

Perceiving symptoms

Many different stimuli compete for our attention at any given moment, so why do certain sensations become more salient than others do? Why do we

Plate 9.1 Sometimes we do not know all the possible symptoms of an illness, even though we think we might.

Source: Meningitis Research Foundation

seek medical attention for some symptoms when we perceive them and not for others? While an early study of American college students found that they had experienced an average of seventeen different symptoms per month (Pennebaker and Skelton 1981), few will have sought medical attention. This is partly because most symptoms are transient and pass before we think too much about them, but also because people are not necessarily the best judges of whether their own perceived symptoms are in fact signs of illness.

There are several models of symptom perception. The attentional model of Pennebaker (1982) addresses the competition for attention between multiple internal or external cues or stimuli and notes how the same physical sign or physiological change may go unnoticed in some contexts and not in others. The cognitive–perceptual model of Cioffi (1991) focuses more on the processes of interpretation of physical signs and their attribution as symptoms and acknowledges also the role of selective attention (Cioffi 1991). Overall, research has highlighted an array of biological, psychological and contextual influences upon symptom perception (see Figure 9.1), with bottom-up influences upon perception arising from the physical properties of a bodily sensation, and top-down influences being seen in the influence of attentional processes or mood.

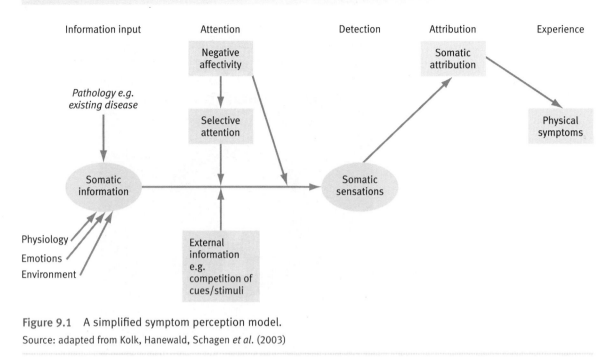

Figure 9.1 A simplified symptom perception model.
Source: adapted from Kolk, Hanewald, Schagen *et al.* (2003)

Characteristics of bodily signs that increase likelihood of symptom perception

Bodily signs are physical sensations that may or may not be symptoms of illness; for example, sweating is a bodily sign, but it may not indicate fever if the person has simply been exerting themselves. Signs can be detected and identified; for example, blood pressure is a sign, whereas symptoms are what is experienced and as such are more **subjective**. Symptoms generally result from physiological changes with physical (somatic) properties, but only some will be detected by the individual. Those receiving attention and interpretation as a symptom are likely to be:

subjective
personal, i.e. what a person thinks and reports (e.g excitement) as opposed to what is **objective**. Subjective is generally related to internal interpretations of events rather than observable features.

- *Painful or disruptive*: if a bodily sign has consequences for the person, e.g. they cannot sit comfortably, vision is impaired, or they can no longer perform a routine activity, then the person is more motivated to perceive this as a symptom (Cacioppo *et al.* 1986, 1989).

- *Novel*: subjective estimates of prevalence have been shown to significantly influence (1) the perceived severity of a symptom and (2) whether the person will seek medical attention (e.g. Ditto and Jemmott 1989; Jemmott, Croyle and Ditto 1988). Experiencing a 'novel' symptom (either for oneself or considered not to have been experienced by others) is more likely to be considered indicative of something rare and serious, whereas experiencing a symptom thought to be common leads to assumptions of lower severity and a reduced likelihood to seek out health information or care. For example, tiredness among students may be normalised and interpreted as a sign of late nights studying or partying.

- *Persistent*: a bodily sign is more likely to be perceived as a symptom if it persists for longer than is considered usual or if it persists in spite of self-medication.

■ *Pre-existing chronic disease*: having a chronic disease increases the number of other symptoms perceived and reported. Past or current illness experience has a strong influence upon somatisation (i.e. attention to bodily states) (e.g. Epstein, Quill and McWhinney 1999; Kolk, Hanewald, Schagen *et al.* 2003).

There are many trivial symptoms that do not really require medical attention but could be self-managed successfully without the costs associated with attendance at a doctor (e.g. most flu episodes), but there are also some illnesses that have few initial symptoms, such as HIV infection. This has led some authors to conclude that symptoms alone are 'unreliable indicators of the need for medical attention' (Martin, Rothrock, Leventhal *et al.* 2003: 203.)

Attentional states and symptom perception

attention
generally refers to the selection of some stimuli over others for internal processing.

Individual differences exist in the amount of **attention** people give to their internal state and external states (Pennebaker and Skelton 1981; Pennebaker 1982, 1992). Pennebaker discovered that somatic sensations are less likely to be noticed when a person's attention is engaged externally than when they are not otherwise distracted. Think, for example, of an athlete going on to win a race in spite of having sustained a leg injury. On the other hand, individuals are more likely to notice tickling sensations in their throats and start coughing towards the end of lectures as attention begins to wane than at the beginning of the lecture or during highly interesting sections. Individuals are limited in their attentional capacity, so internal and external stimuli have to compete for attention; a bodily sign that may be noticed immediately in some contexts may remain undetected in others. (This also points to findings that manipulating attentional focus, through cognitive or behavioural distraction, can be a useful form of symptom management; see Chapter 13.)

A high degree of attention increases a person's sensitivity to new, or different, bodily signs. Consider the effects of outbreaks of well-publicised illnesses or infections on symptom perception, for example outbreaks of Legionnaire's disease such as that in Cumbria in England 2002, *E. coli* outbreaks, toxin leaks or the identification of SARS in 2003. Attendance at doctors increases on a huge scale at such times, with panic and anxiety about proximity to the publicised 'victims', however tenuous the link, heightening a person's attention to their own bodily signs and producing the often false belief that they too have contracted the illness. Many people who seek medical attention at these times will find that there is no organic cause of their symptoms. At the extreme, this can lead to what is termed '*mass psychogenic illness*', which illustrates the powerful effect of anxiety and suggestion on our perceptions and behaviour. Another example of external stimuli altering attention to bodily signs can be seen in the effect of increased knowledge about disease-specific symptoms upon the self-reported experience of exactly these symptoms among medical students. The resulting selective attention and increased processing of somatic information led to what was termed '*medical students disease*' in over two-thirds of the students studied (Mechanic 1962).

Social influences on symptom perception

It has been shown that people hold stereotypical notions about 'who gets' certain diseases and that this can interfere with perception and response to initial symptoms. For example, Martin, Rothrock, Leventhal *et al.* (2003) describe studies showing that the general public associate males with vulnerability to heart disease and not females, and that among heart attack patients females less often recognised initial bodily signs as symptoms of heart disease. The implications for healthcare-seeking behaviour are obvious.

Cacioppo, Andersen, Turnquist *et al.* (1989) pointed to the notion of 'salience' and suggested that our motivation to attend to and detect signs or symptoms of illness will depend on the context at the time the symptom presents itself. As referred to above, people tend not to notice internal sensations when their environment is exciting or absorbing, but a lack of alternative distraction may increase perception of symptoms. Furthermore, situations bring with them varying expectations of physical involvement, as illustrated in Figure 9.2.

Bodily signs, for example muscle spasms, when playing sport or giving birth are expected and thus would not generally be taken as symptomatic of illness. These two situations also differ in the extent to which they would expect a person to contain the pain caused by the spasms. In contrast, few bodily signs are expected when sitting in lectures or watching TV, and unless the bodily sign (e.g. stiffness) can be attributed to something like posture, then it may be interpreted as a symptom of illness. In terms of containment or expression, the home and the lecture setting also differ significantly, with suppression of physical discomfort by means of motivated distraction being more likely in the lecture setting (e.g. listening to the lecturer) than pain expression.

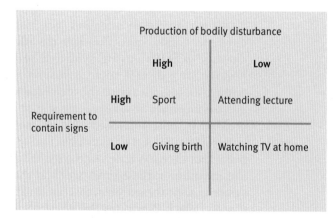

Figure 9.2   Situational differences in the production and containment of physical symptoms.

Source: adapted from Radley (1994: 69)

Individual differences affecting symptom perception

The same bodily sign may, or may not, be perceived as a symptom on the basis of individual difference variables such as gender, emotional state or personality traits, and the effect such factors have on attentional states. Research has tried to identify factors that distinguish between those who frequently seek healthcare even for trivial symptoms and those who do not seek healthcare even when faced with potentially serious symptoms.

■ ### Gender

pain threshold
the minimum amount of pain intensity that is required before it is detected (individual variation).

socialisation
the process by which a person learns – from family, teachers, peers – the rules, norms and moral codes of behaviour that are expected of them.

It has been suggested that women are socialised into a greater readiness to attend to and perceive bodily signs and symptoms, perhaps as a result of menstruation; however, the evidence is mixed and appears to vary according to the symptom (Baum and Grunberg 1991; Macintyre 1993). It may be that physiological differences influence **pain thresholds** in the first place, or that the evidence that women attend healthcare more is not so much reflecting a gender difference in symptom perception but one in reporting behaviour. Whatever the case, it is generally acknowledged that gender **socialisation** exists in the extent to which males and females are 'allowed' to respond to bodily signs.

■ ### Emotions

Generally, mood is crucial. People who are in a positive mood have been found to rate themselves as more healthy and indicate fewer symptoms, whereas people in negative moods report more symptoms, are more pessimistic about their ability to act to relieve their symptoms and believe themselves to be more susceptible to illness (Leventhal, Hansell, Diefenbach *et al.* 1996). Negative emotional states, particularly anxiety or depression, may increase symptom perception by means of its effect on attention, as well as by increasing the recall of prior negative health events, which makes it more likely that new bodily signs will be viewed as symptoms of further illness (Cohen, Doyle, Skoner *et al.* 1995; Watson and Pennebaker 1989; see pain, Chapter 16).

neuroticism
a personality trait reflected in the tendency to be anxious, feel guilty and experience generally negative thought patterns.

negative affectivity
a dispositional tendency to experience persistent and pervasive negative or low mood and self concept (related to **neuroticism**).

Neuroticism can be described as a trait-like tendency to experience negative emotional states and is related to the broader construct '**negative affectivity**' (NA). NA can manifest itself either as a state (situation-specific) or a trait (generalised). While state NA can incorporate a range of emotions, including anger, sadness and fear, trait NA, like neuroticism, has been found to affect the perception, interpretation and reporting of symptoms. In terms of perceptual style, neurotics and those high in trait NA are more introspective and attend more negatively to somatic symptomatology and thus they report more frequent and serious symptomatology (Bennett, Smith and Gallacher 1996; Deary, Clyde and Frier 1997; Watson and Pennebaker 1989, 1991). However, heightened perception does not equate with greater objective illness experience (Costa and McCrae 1987), suggesting that neurotic or trait NA individuals over-attend to and exaggerate the meaning and implications of perceived symptoms. They are more likely to make negative

type A behaviour (TAB)
a constellation of characteristics, mannerisms and behaviour including competititiveness, time urgency, impatience, easily aroused hostility, rapid and vigorous speech patterns and expressive behaviour. Extensively studied in relation to the aetiology of coronary heart disease, where hostility seems central.

repression
a defensive coping style that serves to protect the person from negative memories or anxiety-producing thoughts by preventing their gaining access to consciousness.

comparative optimism
initially termed 'unrealistic optimism', this term refers to an individual's estimate of their risk of experiencing a negative event compared with similar others (Weinstein and Klein 1996).

monitors
a generalised coping style that involves attending to the source of stress or threat and trying to deal with it directly, e.g. through information gathering/attending to threat-relevant information (as opposed to **blunters**).

interpretations of symptoms than individuals low in these traits, and it is these interpretations that lead them to seek healthcare.

It is worth noting that while such traits appear associated with retrospectively reported symptom experience, the support for longitudinal effects of negative affectivity on symptom perception is mixed. For example, trait NA did not predict symptom complaints over time among an elderly sample (e.g. Diefenbach, Leventhal, Leventhal *et al.* 1996; Leventhal *et al.* 1996).

Another emotion associated with symptom perception is that of *fear*, specifically fear of pain and fear of recurrence, which can increase a person's attention and responsiveness to bodily signs. For example, heart attack survivors report becoming increasingly vigilant of their internal states in the hope of detecting, at an early stage, signs of possible recurrence.

■ ## Cognitions and coping style

How people characteristically think and respond to external or internal events has also been shown to influence symptom perception. For example, there is some evidence that individuals characterised by time urgency, impatience, hostility and competitive drive (i.e. **type A behaviour**: Friedman and Rosenman 1959; Rosenman 1978) are less likely to perceive symptoms. This is possibly because they are highly focused on the task in hand (Larsen and Kasimatis 1991) or because they avoid paying attention to signs of self-weakness. Their desire for control on the other hand is associated with prompt healthcare-seeking behaviour once a severe health threat is acknowledged (Matthews, Siegel, Kuller *et al.* 1983). It has also been shown that people who cope with aversive events by using the cognitive defence mechanism of **repression** are less likely to experience symptoms than non-repressors (Ward, Leventhal and Love 1988; Myers 1998), with repression being associated with higher levels of **comparative optimism** regarding controllable health threats such as tooth decay and skin cancer (Myers and Reynolds 2000). Both repressive coping and comparative optimism have previously been related to poor physical health (Weinstein and Klein 1996).

A further distinction has been drawn between monitoring and blunting coping styles (Miller, Brody and Summerton 1987). **Monitors** deal with threat by monitoring their situation for threat-relevant information, whereas **blunters** ignore or minimise external and internal stimuli. Where one stands on this dimension will influence symptom perception as well as determine how quickly a person uses health services (see below).

Lifespan influences on symptom perception

blunters
a general coping style that involves minimising or avoiding the source of threat or stress i.e. avoiding threat-relevant information (as opposed to **monitors**).

With age comes experience and increasing awareness of one's internal organs and their functions and sensations; and just as there are age differentials in perceptions of health and illness (Chapter 1), age differences exist in whether or not bodily signs are perceived as symptoms of illness. Such differences may contribute to identified differentials in healthcare-seeking behaviour (Grunfeld, Hunter, Ramirez *et al.* 2003; Ramirez, Westcombe, Burgess *et al.* 1999; see Chapter 2). Ageing populations certainly bear the burden of many chronic and life-threatening diseases, such as heart disease, stroke, arthritis and breast cancer, but do they, because of this, pay less attention to their bodily states and perceive fewer symptoms? There is little evidence of this. However, it does appear that older adults *interpret* and respond differently to perceived symptoms (see later section).

Children develop a conceptual understanding of illness during the course of their cognitive development and socialisation, but whether children perceive specific symptoms differently to adults is less known. Limited language development in young children makes the study of symptom perceptions difficult. Crying, rubbing or other behaviour is relied upon by adults as indicators of symptom experience in the very young, with pain, for example, being exhibited rather than reported. It is likely that symptom perception is influenced by similar attentional, contextual, individual and emotional influences as reported from studies of adults, but that age or developmental stage may have a greater effect upon symptom interpretation and response.

Perceiving illness

Once a symptom has been perceived, people do not generally consider it in isolation but generally relate it to other aspects of their experience and to their wider concepts of illness.

Illness representations and the 'common-sense model' of illness

Illness representations are organised conceptions of individual illnesses acquired through the media, through personal experience and from family and friends. They can be vague, inaccurate, extensive or detailed, but whatever they are, they influence preventive behaviour and also coping responses among those facing symptoms or illness. Illness representations are thought to exist in memory from previous illness experience (generally common illnesses such as colds or flu), and as a result the perception of a new symptom may be matched to a pre-existing model or 'prototype' of illness that the person holds. These disease prototypes (sometimes referred to as cognitive 'schemata') shape how a person perceives and responds to bodily signs and influence whether bodily signs are perceived to be symptomatic of illness or not. Obviously, 'matching' chest pain erroneously to previously experienced indigestion could be dangerous if it is in fact a heart attack!

Many different terms are employed, sometimes interchangeably, by authors discussing illness models: for example, cognitive schemata (Pennebaker 1982); **illness cognition** (Croyle and Ditto 1990); common-sense models of illness and illness representations (Lau and Hartman 1983; Lau, Bernard and Hartman 1989; Leventhal, Meyer and Nerenz 1980; Leventhal, Nerenz and Steele 1984); and illness perceptions (Weinman, Petrie, Moss-Morris *et al.* 1996). One well-known model is the self-regulatory model of illness and illness behaviour proposed by Howard Leventhal and colleagues (see Figure 9.3). In this model, illness cognitions are defined as 'a patient's own implicit common-sense beliefs about their illness' (e.g. Leventhal, Meyer and Nerenz 1980; Leventhal, Diefenbach and Leventhal 1992). This 'common-sense

illness cognition
the cognitive processes involved in a person's perception or interpretation of symptoms or illness and how they represent it to themselves (or to others) (cf. Croyle and Ditto 1990).

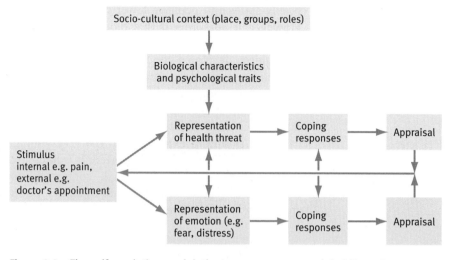

Figure 9.3 The self-regulation model: the 'common-sense model of illness'.
Source: Leventhal, Diefenbach and Leventhal (1992: 147)

model' states that mental representations provide a framework for coping with illness and understanding illness, and they help a person to recognise what to look out for when ill. What Leventhal and his colleagues proposed is a dual-processing model, which considers in parallel the objective components of the stimuli: e.g. the symptom is painful (cognitive), and the subjective response to that stimulus, e.g. anxiety (emotional). This model suggests that people actively process this information, which then elicits a coping response thought to be appropriate. Coping efforts, if subsequently appraised as being unsuccessful, can be amended, or alternatively the initial representation of the stimuli/health threat can be revisited and amended. For example, if a person experiences a headache that they believe is a hangover, they are unlikely to be too worried about it and may simply self-medicate and wait for the symptoms to pass. If the symptoms persist, however, they may rethink their coping response (e.g. go to bed), or rethink their initial perception (e.g. maybe this isn't a hangover) and thus alter their coping response (e.g. go to the doctors). The existence of feedback loops from coping to representations and back again contributes to the model being called 'self-regulatory'. Feedback loops enable responsiveness to changes in situations, appraisals or coping responses and thus maximise the likelihood of coping in a way that facilitates a return to a state of 'normality' (for that individual).

Illness representations (IRs) emerge as soon as a person experiences a symptom or receives a diagnostic label as they start a memory search to try to make sense of the current situation by retrieving pre-existing illness schemata with which they can compare (Petrie and Weinman 2003). Early work leading to this model asked open-ended questions of people suffering from a range of common conditions, including the common cold (Lau *et al.* 1989), cancer or diabetes (Leventhal *et al.* 1980) and found five consistent themes in the content of IRs reported. These were:

1. *Identity*: variables that identify the presence or absence of the illness. Illnesses are identified by label, concrete signs and concrete symptoms. For example, 'I feel shivery and my joints ache, I think I have flu'.

2. *Consequences*: the perceived effect of illness on life: physical, emotional, social, economic impact or a combination of factors. May be short-term or long-term. For example, 'Because of my illness I won't be able to go to the gym today' or 'Because of my illness I will have to take early retirement'.

3. *Cause*: the perceived cause(s) of illness. May be biological (e.g. germs), emotional (e.g. stress, depression), psychological (e.g. mental attitude, personality), genetic or environmental (e.g. pollution), or as a result of an individual's own behaviour (e.g. overwork, smoking). Some of these causes may overlap, e.g. stress and smoking behaviour, and may overlap with **attributions** of cause made after the onset of illness (e.g. French, Senior, Weinman *et al.* 2001; French, Marteau, Senior *et al.* 2002).

4. *Timeline*: the perceived timeframe for the development and duration of the illness. Can be acute (or short-term, with no long-term consequences), chronic (or long-term) or episodic (or cyclical). For example, 'I think my flu will last only three or four days' or 'My pain comes and goes'.

5. *Curability or controllability*: Lau and Hartmann (1983) added questions to assess the extent to which individuals perceive they, or others, can control, treat or limit progression of their illness. For example, 'If I take this medicine it will help to reduce my symptoms' or 'The doctor will be able to cure this'. As early work was primarily conducted on those with acute, manageable conditions, this fifth dimension may be particularly relevant for those facing chronic disease.

attributions
a person's perceptions of what causes beliefs, feelings, behaviour and actions (based on attribution theory).

These dimensions were captured in a quantitative scale developed by John Weinman and colleagues (Weinman *et al.* 1996), the illness perception questionnaire, which has been validated across a range of illnesses in a wealth of studies. The IPQ has been revised to include two further IR dimensions – emotional representations and illness coherence – and also distinguishes between beliefs about personal control over illness and beliefs about treatment control (Moss-Morris, Weinman, Petrie *et al.* 2002; Moss-Morris and Chalder 2003; see ISSUES below). The content and organisation of IRs can vary between individuals and even within the same individual over time, and can be attributed to underlying beliefs about disease. Illness beliefs also exist in childhood; for example, healthy pre-school children, when asked open-ended questions about common illnesses such as the common cold, elicited all five of Leventhal's IR components (Goldman, Whitney-Saltiel, Granger *et al.* 1991).

■ Illness representations and outcomes

There are logical interrelationships between component IRs; for example, strongly believing that an illness can be controlled or cured is likely to be associated with fewer perceived serious consequences of the illness and a short expected duration (Weinman and Petrie 1997). While thought to affect illness outcome via effects on coping, illness representations have also been shown to have more direct effects on a wide range of outcomes, including, for example:

■ seeking and using medical treatment (Leventhal, Diefenbach and Leventhal 1992);

■ emotional reactions to symptoms (Prohaska *et al.* 1987);

■ engagement in self-care behaviour or treatment adherence (Hampson, Glasgow and Zeiss 1994; Horne and Weinman 2002);

■ illness-related disability and return to work (Lacroix, Martin, Avendano *et al.* 1991; Petrie, Weinman, Sharpe *et al.* 1996).

The association between illness representations, coping behaviour and a range of illness outcomes was reviewed in a meta-analysis of forty-five empirical studies (Hagger and Orbell 2003) and is discussed further in Chapter 12. This meta-analysis provided support for the IR domains of consequences, cure/control, identity and timeline but did not consider 'cause' representations because the multitude of overlapping causal attributions made meta-analysis problematic. The authors propose that measurement of this cause dimension requires refinement (see ISSUES below). Other authors, for example Turk, Rudy and Salovey (1986), present findings that do not support the five IR dimensions, instead reporting factors labelled 'seriousness', 'personal responsibility', 'controllability' and 'changeableness'. However, these results emerged when asking participants to *compare* two diseases, suggesting perhaps that their dimensions are more what discriminates *between* illnesses, rather than domains like Leventhal's, which relate to perceptions of individual illnesses.

Addressing the question of whether different illnesses elicit different domains of illness representations, Monique Heijmans and Denise de Ridder in the Netherlands (Heijmans and de Ridder 1998), compared the IRs of patients with either chronic fatigue syndrome (CFS) or Addison's disease (AD), both chronic illnesses with common symptoms of fatigue and weakness. AD is associated with gastrointestinal complaint and responds to medication, whereas CFS is generally very limiting and has no well-established treatment. Results showed that illness perceptions associated with each other similarly in the two disease groups: identity (both frequency and seriousness of symptoms) was positively associated with timeline and consequences, and negatively with control/cure (i.e. those reporting a high number of symptoms perceived more consequences and a longer timeline, and less control over their illness). A chronic timeline was also associated with low perceptions of control or cure and more serious consequences. However, when looking at differences between illness groups, CFS patients viewed their illness more negatively than AD patients, reporting more frequent and serious consequences and less positive future expectation of control or cure. The majority of both CFS and AD patients perceived the cause of their illness to be biological, but many also reported psychological and other causes. This study shows that although IR components are robust across these illnesses in terms of how they relate to each other, illnesses differ in the specific strengths of each component. These kinds of difference should be considered when planning interventions with specific populations or when communicating with patients about their illness.

Eliciting illness representations

Opinions vary about how best to elicit and assess individuals' privately held illness perceptions and beliefs. The use of open-ended interviews as a method of eliciting illness representations (as used in Leventhal and colleagues' early work) has led to some suggesting that questions such as 'To what extent when thinking about your illness do you think about its consequences' may well be leading. Furthermore, interviews are very time-consuming and generally restrict sample size, although some studies have managed to successfully employ open-ended questioning (using prompts where necessary) (e.g. Hampson, Glasgow and Toobert 1990; Hampson, Glasgow and Zeiss 1994).

While Leventhal's model provides a useful framework on which to base studies of illness perceptions, a recent review found that few studies attempted to examine all five constructs (Scharloo and Kaptein 1997). Many studies instead assess specific component beliefs, for example perceived control over illness (e.g. multidimensional health locus of control scale, Wallston, Wallston and deVellis 1978; beliefs about pain control questionnaire (see Chapter 16), e.g. Skevington 1990).

Addressing these limitations, a team of UK- and New Zealand-based researchers led by Rona Moss-Morris, Keith Petrie and John Weinman developed a quantitative measure known as the illness perception questionnaire (IPQ; Weinman *et al.* 1996). This measure has been used in an impressive range of health conditions across varying time spans, and a recent meta-analysis (Hagger and Orbell 2003) found it to have both construct and predictive validity (although the latter requires further confirmation through more longitudinal studies). The IPQ has undoubtedly been an extremely useful measurement tool and has recently been revised (IPQ-R) to address some concerns over the internal reliability of the cure/control and timeline subscales, and the role of emotions (clearly part of Leventhal's self-regulatory model but not well addressed in the earlier IPQ). The IPQ-R separates personal control over illness from outcome expectancies and from perceived treatment control; strengthens the timeline component by adding items regarding cyclical illnesses as well as acute/chronic timeline items; adds items that address emotional representations (emotional responses to illness such as fear and anxiety); and finally examines the extent to which a person feels they understand their condition, defined as illness coherence (Moss-Morris, Weinman, Petrie *et al.* 2002).

Leventhal's framework, although dominant in the field, is not the only model of illness perceptions, and indeed other measures of illness perceptions exist, for example the implicit models of illness questionnaire (IMIQ; Turk, Rudy and Salovey 1986) and the personal models of illness framework (Hampson *et al.* 1990). The former of these, the IMIQ, when administered to three groups (diabetic patients, diabetic educators, college students), found four slightly different dimensions to those described by Leventhal: seriousness, personal responsibility, controllability and changeability. When the IMIQ was employed in 1995 by Schiaffino and Cea, slightly different factors emerged again: serious consequences, personal responsibility, curability and symptom variability. This study employed those with a range of conditions and led to the suggestion that it may be impossible to have a model to fit all illnesses; for example, the potential for cure or treatment simply does not exist for all illnesses.

The use of quantitative measures such as described above should not be taken as implying that open-ended interview methods are neither necessary nor useful. For example, understanding the sources of beliefs and perceptions, and the reasons behind the salience attached to certain beliefs over others, could be crucial to the development of targeted interventions, and therefore the 'ideal' research study would perhaps use combined methods.

Symptom interpretation

As shown already, symptoms are more than labels for the various changes that happen to the body; they not only derive from medical classifications of disease, they can influence how we think, feel and behave. Culture will influence the meanings that individuals ascribe to symptoms, as will past experience, illness beliefs and representations. When a physical sensation is perceived as a 'symptom', what is it that leads a person to believe they are sick? This arises when the symptoms a person is experiencing 'fit' a model of illness retrieved from their memory. One might expect that the recognition that one has symptoms would be a sufficient condition for deciding that one is sick, but Radley (1994: 71) suggests that one must question that assumption. Think of your own experience – symptoms do not necessarily precede sickness – sometimes being deemed to be sick is an important element in appearing symptomatic, and perhaps adopting what is termed **sick role behaviour** (Parsons 1951; Kasl and Cobb 1966b).

sick role behaviour
the activities undertaken by a person diagnosed as sick in order to try to get well.

Cultural influences on symptom interpretation

Cultural differences have been shown to exist in the extent to which members of specific cultures believe in supernatural causes of illness, e.g. evil spirits, divine punishment (Landrine and Klonoff 1992). These causal beliefs influence the coping response that follows, for example in terms of seeking medical attention or complying with treatment.

Westernised cultures have been found to promote an independent sense of responsibility, i.e. the individual has supreme importance, whereas African cultures (e.g. Chalmers 1996; Morrison, Ager and Willock 1999), and Chinese and Japanese cultures (e.g. Heine and Lehman 1995; Tan and Bishop 1996) have been shown to perceive health and illness more collectively and interdependently, in terms of the effects of health and illness on group function. As a result, different cultures may exhibit broadly different belief systems and different attitudes towards, and responses to, illness. To illustrate this, Bishop and Teng's (1992) study of Singaporean Chinese students found that while severity and contagiousness were commonly used dimensions of illness perception (as found among Western students), an additional dimension existed whereby illness was tied to behaviour and to blocked *qi* – the source of life and energy. These beliefs were associated with the use of traditional and Western healthcare, where it appeared that when dual healthcare systems operate in parallel in a society they are used differentially depending on the specific illness and illness perceptions (Heine and Lehman 1995; Quah and Bishop 1996; Lim and Bishop 2000). African studies (Chalmers 1996) have shown that the use of traditional medicine such as faith healers remains strong even as Westernised healthcare availability increases.

Aside from the use of healthcare, it has also been shown that cultural variation exists in the extent to which individuals react to physical illness. For example, Sanders, Brena, Spier *et al.* (1992) compared the behavioural and emotional functioning of individuals with long-term back pain and found that Americans reported the greatest impairment, then Italians and New Zealanders, followed by Japanese, Colombian and Mexican patients.

Further differences in the readiness to respond to perceived physical symptoms have also been found among male American pain patients of either Jewish, Italian, Irish or 'old' American origin. While Jewish and Italian American men expressed pain readily, the two groups differed in the aim of their pain expression; Italian Americans complained about pain discomfort, while Jewish Americans typically expressed worries about what the pain might mean in terms of their underlying and future health. These differences in pain expression and interpretation were associated with group differences in the willingness to accept treatment, with Italian American men more likely to trust the doctor and accept pain medication and Jewish American men more cynical as to the benefits of analgesics. A further difference was found in terms of willingness to complain about pain at home: Italian Americans felt that they lacked the freedom to complain about their pain at home as they wanted to project the image of being the strong 'head of the family', whereas Jewish American men did not see pain expression at home as a sign of weakness. The 'old' Americans differed from both these other groups in that they did not complain or display their feelings but instead reported in a factual way. These men saw emotional expression as pointless in a context where they thought that the doctor's knowledge, skill and efficiency would be effective and would be aided by uncomplaining compliance. At home, the 'old' American men withdrew from other people if their pain got too severe, and even their wives reacted with either embarrassment or grave concern if they saw their husbands express emotional responses to their pain. Irish Americans were found to stoically accept or deny the pain, again reflecting a socialised gender phenomenon. Zborowski (1952) states that such cultural variations are learned during socialisation, where people's ideas about what is acceptable pain to bear and express is shaped. The lengthy illustration above shows that not only do pain perception and expression differ, but that they have a social function in terms of influencing treatment expectations or even the reactions of others (see also Chapter 16).

Individual differences and symptom interpretation

individual differences
aspects of an individual that distinguish them from other individuals or groups (e.g. age, personality).

Some individuals can maintain their everyday activities when experiencing what would be perceived as debilitating symptoms of illness by another person. Why? This is because of **individual differences** in how symptoms are interpreted. Prior experience affects interpretation of and response to symptoms in that having a history of particular symptoms or vicarious experience (e.g. experience of illness in others) leads to assumptions about the meaning and implications of some symptoms. A symptom considered to be rare in either a person's own experience, or in that of others consulted, is more likely to be interpreted as potentially serious than a symptom previously experienced or known to be widespread (Croyle and Ditto 1990). Believing some symptoms to be 'just a bug that's going round' can mean that people sometimes ignore potentially dangerous 'warning signals'.

A knowledge of which bodily signs are associated with particular behaviour or illnesses (e.g. sweats and flu, sweats and exercise) will enable interpretation and attachment of a meaning to the symptom. These reserves of knowledge are known as 'disease prototypes' and were referred to earlier when describing illness perception.

■ Disease prototypes

People have disease prototypes that help them to organise and evaluate information about physical sensations that might not otherwise be interpretable (Table 9.1). Symptoms are placed in the context of a person's past knowledge and experience, which has led to the development of protypical expectations of certain illnesses. Matching or not matching symptoms to a disease prototype will influence whether or not that symptom is perceived as a symptom and then how it is interpreted and responded to. Illnesses that have clear sign-sets (symptoms) associated with them are more likely to be easily recognised in self-diagnosis; for example, a person experiencing serious abdominal pains may quickly consider appendicitis, and another person experiencing mild chest pain may quickly consider indigestion. It would be easy to assume therefore that a lump found in the breast would, generally, prompt concerns that it may signify cancer and result in healthcare seeking, and this is generally the case (see Chapter 4 for a discussion of influences on breast-screening behaviour). However, there are other symptoms of breast cancer, such as breast pain or skin scaling around the nipple, that may not be in a person's 'prototype', and thus such symptoms may go unidentified. This inability to correctly identify various potential breast cancer symptoms predicted help-seeking delay among a general population sample of 546 women (Grunfeld, Hunter, Ramirez *et al.* 2003). In a similar vein, Theisen, MacNeill, Lumley *et al.* (1995) compared forty patients who sought treatment for a heart attack (myocardial infarction, MI) with thirty patients who were found on routine electrocardiogram to have had an MI for which they had not sought medical care. The authors concluded that prototypes and expectations of what a heart attack would feel like had impeded perception and recognition of symptoms. Such delay in responding to symptoms had impeded the effective treatment of the heart attack. Supporting this, Perry, Petrie, Ellis *et al.* (2001) reported that when heart attack symptoms do not 'match' the existing illness prototype in their severity, delay in seeking medical attention is greatest.

Table 9.1   Disease prototypes

	Influenza	AIDS
Identity	runny nose, fever, shivery, sneezing, aching limbs	weight loss, swollen glands, fever, skin lesions, pneumonia
Cause	virus	virus
Consequences	rarely long-term or serious (except if new 'strain')	long-term ill-health, death, uncertainty
Timeline	24 hours to a week	Months to years
Cure	time and self-medication	none, multiple treatments to delay progression
Type of person	Anybody	High-risk groups of injecting drug users, increasingly anyone via unprotected sexual intercourse

■ The influence of 'self' and identity on illness perception and interpretation

It has been suggested that the medical sociological tradition of assessing lay models of health and illness (e.g. Blaxter's study – see Chapter 1), which takes a broader view of illness beliefs shaped by social factors, and the health psychological model of individual cognitions, should be merged. Levine and Reicher (1996) proposed an account of symptom evaluation based on self-categorisation theory (e.g. Turner, Hogg, Oakes *et al.* 1987), which highlights the importance of **social identity**. Most people have several social identities depending on context (e.g. student/partner/daughter), and it is proposed that the interpretation of symptoms differs depending on a person's current salient social identity. For example, they found that female teacher training students specialising in PE (physical education) evaluated illness and injury scenarios differently depending on whether they were in a condition that identified them by gender or as a PE student. The extent to which the illness scenario details were perceived as threatening their salient gender identity was important. These findings were explored in two further studies, one involving female secretaries and the other involving rugby-playing males. In the secretary sample, different scenarios (based around threat to attractiveness, occupation or emotionality) elicited different responses depending on whether the women were in the 'gender-identity' group or the 'secretary-identity' group. Perceived illness severity was highest when the scenario posed an attractiveness threat to the gender-identity group, or an occupational performance threat (e.g. hand injury) to the secretary-identity group. The study of male rugby players introduced two hypothetical comparison groups, telling the men that their results would be compared with either females or 'new men'. This allowed the research team to explore the effect of context on symptom representations and self-identity. Scenarios presented threatened either physical attractiveness, emotionality or physicality. Attractiveness threat led to greater illness severity perceptions when the comparator group was females, and the threat to emotionality led to less serious perceptions of the illness when compared with 'new men'. There was no difference in the perceived severity of illness when the threat was to physicality.

social identity
a person's sense of who they are at a group, rather than personal and individual, level (e.g. you are a student, possibly a female).

What this shows is that social identity may alter illness and injury perceptions. This suggests that models of illness representation commonly applied in health psychology research should perhaps expand to consider self and social identity influence. Although participants in Levine's series of studies were dealing with hypothetical illness and injuries in an artificial experimental setting, the reality is that most people fulfil a variety of social roles, and therefore it is logical to suppose that salient identity may differ in different contexts with potential effects upon symptom perception and interpretation.

RESEARCH FOCUS

Do perceptions of cancer differ according to own health status?

Buick, D. and Petrie, K. (2002). 'I know just how you feel': The validity of healthy women's perceptions of breast cancer patients receiving treatment. *Journal of Applied Social Psychology*, 32: 110–23.

Background
It is a sad fact that most people will encounter cancer at some point in their lives, either personally or through a family member or friend. Buick and Petrie note that cancer is generally a feared disease that can still elicit stigma in the response of others. Previous studies had shown that healthy women differed in the perceived causes of cancer from women with cancer, and that healthy women often had misperceptions about treatments. It was thought that such misperceptions could potentially interfere with preventive behaviour or a person's interactions with those diagnosed with cancer. Understanding how and whether the illness perceptions of healthy individuals influence their emotional and behavioural response to that illness in others leads us to consider the wider impact of illness representations. This study therefore aimed to identify and compare cancer perceptions of patients with those of a healthy sample drawn from the community of Auckland, New Zealand.

Method

Participants
Representations about post-surgical treatment of breast cancer were assessed in two groups: seventy-eight post-surgical (partial mastectomy or lumpectomy) breast cancer out-patients receiving either radiation or chemotherapy, and seventy-eight healthy women drawn from the community and matched with patients on age, marital status and level of education. The reason for matching on these criteria is that age may influence perceptions and responses to cancer, level of education may affect knowledge about cancer and its treatment, and marital status may influence social support factors and exposure to others' cancer perceptions. Matching on these variables removes their potential confounding effects. None of the healthy sample had a prior cancer diagnosis, they ranged from 27 to 78 years old (mean 51 years, s.d. 10.55), 71–72 percent were married, 90 percent were of European ethnicity, about three-quarters had high school qualifications or above, and slightly over half were in employment. Patients had completed either 50 percent or 95 percent of their treatment, and were either receiving adjuvant chemotherapy ($n = 26$) or localised radiation ($n = 52$).

Design
The study employed a questionnaire that was administered once, i.e. a cross-sectional study.

Measures

Illness perceptions were assessed using the IPQ (Weinman *et al.* 1996), which is based on Leventhal's five dimensions: identity (participants indicate which of fifteen listed symptoms they feel are part of breast cancer and indicate the frequency with which they are experienced); timeline (e.g. my illness will last a short time); cause (e.g. my breast cancer was caused by stress); consequences (e.g. my illness is a serious condition); and cure–control (e.g. my treatment will be effective in curing my cancer). With the exception of identity, participants rated how much they agreed or disagreed with the statements. Healthy participants responded on the basis of what they thought was true of breast cancer, whereas patients responded from their own experience. The scales components performed well in the study, attaining reliability coefficients (Cronbach's alpha) of between 0.75 and 0.87 (with 1.0 being total consistency). *Emotional distress levels* were assessed using the profile of mood states (POMS; McNair *et al.* 1971). Participants indicated the intensity to which they experienced each of sixty-five adjectives (0 = not at all, 4 = extremely), reflecting moods of tension–anxiety; anger–hostility, vigour–activity, depression–dejection and confusion–bewilderment. Reliability coefficients were good (between 0.84 and 0.95). All participants were asked to rate the adjectives in accordance with emotions they thought/felt were associated with post-surgical breast cancer treatment. *Coping* (or for healthy participants, imagined coping) was measured using the sixty item coping orientation to problems experienced scale (COPE; Carver, Scheier and Weintraub 1989). This measure consists of fifteen distinct scales: mental disengagement; behavioural disengagement; seek instrumental support; seek emotional support; vent emotions; use alcohol or drugs; suppress competing activities; denial; use religion; acceptance; active coping; planning; restraint coping; use humour; positive reinterpretation and growth. Healthy women rated their perception of a 'typical' response of women receiving post-surgical treatment for breast cancer (scored as 0: didn't use at all; 4: used a little; 8: used a medium amount; 12: used a lot). Reliability of subscales was good (0.66 to 0.95), and the intercorrelations between subscales were not strong, which supports the fifteen subscales being treated as conceptually different. Finally, participants rated the perceived health status of breast cancer patients on a single item that asked them to compare their own (or a breast cancer patient's, in the case of the healthy sample) current health status with that of a person in 'excellent health' (between 1 and 7, where 1 is terrible, 4 is fair, and 7 is excellent).

Procedure

Patients were recruited on the basis of a physician referral. Healthy women were recruited using a three-stage process: first, a seminar to organisations broadly described the research (but did not mention cancer); second, fliers called for participants for a study investigating 'attitudes to illness' were placed in worksites and social venues. Those interested were invited to contact the researchers, and if they could be matched to a patient on the criteria listed above, an interview was arranged. Of ninety-seven women initially contacted, seventy-eight took part, which is a highly satisfactory 80 percent response rate.

Analysis

Between-group differences were examined in terms of mean scores and variances (standard deviations) on key variables, and in terms of their effect sizes (Wilks lambda produces a coefficient between 0 and 1, where values closer to 0 highlights that means differ between groups, and values closer to 1 do not).

Results

In terms of *perceptions of breast cancer*, healthy women differed significantly from patients. Healthy women rated patient health as poorer, consequences of breast cancer as

continued

worse, treatment as offering less of a cure or control over illness, and the illness as having a longer timeline. Healthy women also overestimated the number, severity and frequency of patient symptoms (identity component) and believed more strongly in chance, patient-related, genetic and environmental causes for breast cancer. *Perceptions of coping* also differed, with healthy women thinking that breast cancer patients would focus on the illness and vent emotion, mentally and behaviourally disengage from treatment, plan and suppress competing activities, and use denial, alcohol and drugs, religion and restraint coping to a higher degree than patients themselves reported. Furthermore, healthy women thought that patients were less likely to use positive reappraisal and acceptance than other strategies, yet in reality these were the two most common strategies reported by patients (who also did not report using alcohol or drugs)! The two groups shared perceptions of the use of support seeking (emotional and instrumental), humour and active coping. Given these differences, it was not surprising that healthy women also overestimated the *emotional impact of breast cancer treatment*, rating patient depression, tension, anger, confusion, inertia and, surprisingly, vigour higher than patients did themselves.

Discussion
This study revealed significant discrepancies in the illness/treatment perceptions and responses between healthy women and those undergoing post-surgical treatment for breast cancer. Healthy women imagine breast cancer and its treatment to be significantly worse along many dimensions and, furthermore, believe that patients cope using strategies generally considered to be avoidant in nature. They also attribute cause more internally than do patients, as well as rating environmental and genetic causes highly. A crucial finding is that healthy women misperceive how patients cope with breast cancer and its treatment and differ in terms of where they attribute cause to. If someone believes that an internal controllable cause is behind a person's cancer (e.g. poor diet, smoking), then this may limit their expression of sympathy or concern for that person. Furthermore, if a social perception of cancer is that patients cope by denial, then healthy members of society may perceive attempts to discuss the illness with patients as being unhelpful. These mismatched perceptions have obvious implications in terms of social support and care provision for patients, but they also hold implications for healthy individuals. For example, if social perception is that treatments offer little hope of cure, this may influence preventive health practices such as screening behaviour. If social perception is that breast cancer has severe consequences, this may contribute to fear of receiving a diagnosis, which is a further barrier to the uptake of screening.

Limitations
Some methodological weaknesses are evident, only some of which are noted by the authors. For example, the study is limited to patients who have already experienced surgery, and their perceptions of their illness and treatment may be shaped by this experience. Furthermore, the fact that some had completed 50 percent of treatment and others 95 percent was not considered in the analysis. It is also impossible to establish whether there was selection bias during either doctor referral or in recruitment as no detail is provided of the number of patients approached in order to get the seventy-eight patient participants. Treatment type also differed (chemotherapy versus radiation therapy) but was not examined in terms of effects on perceptions and coping. Furthermore, chemotherapy patients were significantly younger than women receiving radiation. The form of surgery also varied, with radiation patients most likely to have had a lumpectomy and chemotherapy patients a partial mastectomy. Such differences within the patient sample in terms of what they had experienced may have influenced results: women who have had a lumpectomy (lump removed from breast but

conserving the breast) may differ in terms of perceived cure/control and treatment consequences, for example, from those who have had a partial mastectomy (losing some actual breast tissue). While these differences are not central to the aim of the current study, between-patient differences may have obscured the real extent of differences between patients and healthy women.

The method of assessing perceptions of a specific illness from healthy individuals is possibly a bit messy ('Imagine how a breast cancer patient would cope', for example, is asking a person to put themselves into another's shoes – some people are more able to do this than others, depending on their natural qualities of empathy and imagination). The authors suggest that it may be better in future studies to use detailed case scenarios for the healthy participants to rate. However, it has to be said that there is no easy improvement on the methodology used – proxy or hypothetical views are always going to be just that. It is reasonable that researchers wanting to highlight social perceptions of an issue or illness use methods such as those used here. Many currently healthy people will be patients or carers in the future, and it is important that perceptions that may elicit negative attitudes or negative helping behaviour are identified and addressed.

■ Causal attributions of illness and attribution theory

Attributional models are all about where a person locates the 'cause' of an event, and they thus underpin one of Leventhal's five identified illness representations. The majority of research on attributions in health psychology has addressed 'ill populations' such as those who have suffered a heart attack (myocardial infarction) (e.g. Affleck, Tennen, Croog *et al.* 1987; Gudmunsdsdottir, Johnston, Johnston *et al.* 2001), or those with cancer (Lavery and Clarke 1996; Timko and Janoff-Bulmann 1985). The study featured in RESEARCH FOCUS above provided evidence of differences in attributions of cause between healthy individuals and breast cancer patients and produced results with implications for the way individuals respond to illness in others. Attributions of cause also influence how a person responds to their own illness. A recent review of studies of attributions for heart disease among heart disease patients and healthy individuals concluded that lifestyle factors and stress were the most common attributions made, with the latter more likely to come from heart attack patients than non-patients, suggesting a form of self-preservation bias (French, Senior, Weinman *et al.* 2001). The same main attributions of cause for heart attack were found in another study, where stress, it being in the family, smoking, eating fatty foods and work were recorded regardless of whether attributions were *spontaneous* (asked to describe what they think about their illness), *elicited* (asked directly about their ideas of what may have caused their heart attack) or *cued* (asked to respond 'yes', 'no' or 'might have' to a list of thirty-four causes) (Gudmundsdottir *et al.* 2001).

When attributions were examined at an earlier stage in illness experience, i.e. at the time of symptom perception, Swartzman and Lees (1996) found that the attributional dimensions of controllability, locus (internal/external) and stability consistently reported in studies of illness attribution were only partially supported. Symptoms addressed were primarily those reflecting

physical discomfort and were found to be attributed to either a physical (e.g. age, exertion)–non-physical (e.g. stress, mood) dimension; a high–low personal controllability dimension; and a dimension thought to reflect controllability by health professional/treatable versus stability/not treatable, although this dimension was less clear. Attributions of causes of symptoms (rather than attributions of cause of a confirmed illness) may be an area worth further exploration. Perceiving a cause of discomfort as being non-physical, under high personal control and stable/not treatable may lead to very different interpretation, response and healthcare-seeking behaviour than a cause of discomfort with physical, low personal control and treatable attribution.

Attributions of cause can be wrong, and this has implications for illness behaviour such as seeking medical help; e.g. a middle-aged man may attribute chest pain to indigestion rather than the first signs of heart trouble/angina; or persistent headaches may be put down to stress, whereas they may indicate an underlying tumour.

■ Lifespan influences

Young people with diabetes, both pre-adolescents and adolescents, have been described as having 'a basic understanding of the nature, cause and timeline of their illness and treatment recommended' (Standiford, Turner, Allen *et al.* 1997, cited in Griva, Myers and Newman 2002). However, it is likely that young children are distinct from adolescents in their cognitive awareness of illness and its implications simply by virtue of the stage of cognitive development attained (Bibace and Walsh 1980; see Chapter 1) and life experience or knowledge accumulated (Bird and Podmore 1990; Eiser 1985; Goldman *et al.* 1991). Limited research has been conducted with very young and ill children and their illness perceptions, interpretation and response, for a variety of reasons, including ethical issues in assessing sick children and the demands of face-to-face interviews, methodological issues such as the limited availability of child-validated assessment tools, or the challenges of limited linguistic and cognitive skills. However, some studies have been carried out. For example, when healthy children were compared with children with diabetes, little difference was found in terms of knowledge of illnesses other than diabetes itself (Eiser, Paterson and Tripp 1984). Where several early studies of healthy children focused on attributions of cause, later research has acknowledged the multidimensionality of illness perceptions. One useful example is a study of French 5–12-year-olds (Normandeau, Kalnins, Jutras *et al.* 1998), where a multidimensional conception of health was found, albeit with some differences according to age group (this study was described in Chapter 1). Of course, the responsibility for acting on illness perceptions or symptom interpretation and subsequently seeking healthcare (or not) often lies with the parent or guardian rather than with the child themselves, and therefore some studies seek to elicit the illness perceptions of parents as well as the child. In a pilot study with nine asthmatic children (aged 12–15) and eleven of their parents (Morrison, Hutchinson and McCarthy 2000), while no significant differences emerged in the perceived severity of the illness, use of the IPQ elicited higher perceptions of control over the child's asthma in parents than the children reported themselves. Fuller exploration is needed as to whether these differences influence health outcomes such as adherence.

Planning and taking action: responding to symptoms

illness behaviour
behaviour that characterises a person who is sick and who seeks a remedy, e.g. taking medication. Usually precedes formal diagnosis, when behaviour is described as **sick role behaviour**.

lay referral system
an informal network of individuals (e.g. friends, family, colleagues) turned to for advice or information about symptoms and other health-related matters. Often but not solely used prior to seeking a formal medical opinion.

As this chapter has described, the first step towards seeking medical care begins with a person recognising that they have symptoms of an illness, and it may take some time for this step to occur. In many cases, people choose to treat an illness themselves by self-medicating with either pharmaceutical products, or herbal or non-proprietary drugs, and others will rest or go to bed and wait to see whether they recover naturally. A number of surveys have suggested that less than one-quarter of illnesses are seen by a doctor.

Kasl and Cobb (1966a) refer to the behaviour of those who are experiencing symptoms but who have not yet sought medical advice and received a diagnosis as **illness behaviour**. Illness behaviour includes lying down and resting, self-medication, and seeking sympathy, support and informal advice in an attempt to determine one's health status. Many people are reluctant to go to the doctor on the initial experience of a symptom and instead first seek advice from a **lay referral system**, generally including friends, relatives or colleagues (Croyle and Barger 1993). Symptoms are therefore not always sufficient to motivate a visit to the doctor.

Once people recognise a set of symptoms, label them and realise that they could indicate a medical problem, they therefore have the option of:

- ignoring the symptoms and hoping they recede;
- seeking advice from others;
- presenting themselves to a health professional.

Some people will do all three over time.

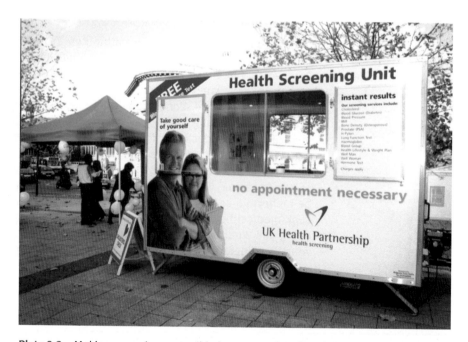

Plate 9.2   Making screening accessible by means of such mobile screening units outside workplaces or supermarkets may increase the likelihood of screening uptake.
Source: © Health Screening (UK) Ltd

Our response even to serious symptoms may still involve some delay to see whether things improve or whether attempts at self-care will improve the situation. A dramatic example of this was reported by Kentsch, Rodenmerk, Muller-Esch *et al.* (2002), who found that over 40 percent of patients who thought they were having a heart attack, *and who considered this to be potentially fatal*, waited over one hour before calling for medical help. This delay would have had a significant impact on the outcome of their illness. Treatment with 'clot-busting' drugs, which dissolve the clot that causes an MI and minimise damage to the heart, are at their most effective when given within an hour of the onset of problems. An example of delay in a more chronic but equally serious condition was reported by Prohaska, Funch and Blesch (1990), who found that the first response of over 80 percent of their sample of patients with colorectal cancer was the use of over-the-counter medication. Patients waited an average of seven months before seeking medical help. Cockburn, Paul, Tzelepis *et al.* (2003) also found significant evidence of our ability to ignore important symptoms. In a survey of over 1,000 adults, they found that 23 percent of their sample reported having had blood in their stools (a potential symptom of bowel cancer) – but only one-third had ever reported these symptoms to a doctor. Perhaps more encouraging was the reporting of breast lumps by women in a study by Meechan, Collins and Petrie (2002). They found that of their sample of women who identified breast lumps following breast self-examination, 40 percent had seen their doctor within seven days, 52 percent within fourteen days, 69 percent within thirty days, and only 14 percent had waited over ninety days. However, it should be noted that even among this group of health-aware women, who took active steps to identify and prevent disease, a significant proportion still delayed significantly in reporting their symptoms to their doctor.

What do YOU think?	Health is one of our most precious attributes. Yet many people who fear they have an illness – in some cases one they think may be fatal – delay in seeking medical help. Interestingly, people who are in the presence of someone else they know when their symptoms occur are more likely to call for help than people who are alone at the time they experience their symptoms. It seems that by talking with this person they are given 'permission' to call for medical aid. Most doctors will have stories of people who have delayed seeking medical help even in the face of clear signs that 'something is wrong'. Why should this be the case? Are people frightened that their fears, perhaps of having cancer, will be justified, or that the treatment they may receive will be ineffective or too difficult to cope with? What sort of people are likely to seek medical help at the onset of symptoms? What sort are likely to avoid doing so? What would be their motives for delay in seeking help? Think of your own illness experience and that of those close to you.

Delay behaviour

Delay behaviour in this instance refers to an individual's delay in seeking health advice as opposed to delays inherent in the healthcare system itself. Studies of cancer patients have shown that delay in presenting symptoms for

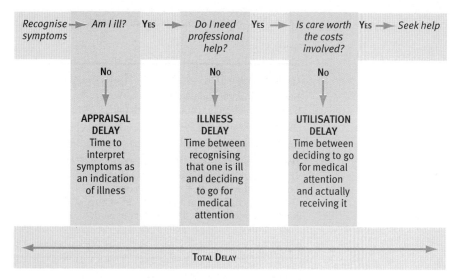

Figure 9.4   The delay behaviour model.

Source: adapted from Safer, Thorps, Jackson and Leventhal (1979)

morbidity

costs associated with illness such as disability, injury.

medical attention is highly related to outcomes of **morbidity** and mortality (e.g. Andersen, Cacioppo and Roberts 1995; Richards, Westcombe, Love *et al.* 1999), and thus it is important to gain an understanding of the factors that influence delay behaviour.

Safer, Tharps, Jackson *et al.* (1979) developed a model of delay behaviour, defined as the time between recognising a symptom and seeking help for it. They described three decision-making stages (see Figure 9.4) and point out that a person will enter treatment only after all three stages have been gone through and the questions in each stage have been answered positively.

In the first stage, a person infers that they are ill on the basis of perceiving a symptom or symptoms – the delay in reaching this decision is termed 'appraisal delay'. Next, the person considers whether or not they need medical attention, and the time taken to decide this is termed 'illness delay'. The final stage covers the time taken between deciding one needs medical attention and actually acting on that decision and making an appointment or presenting to a hospital. This is termed 'utilisation delay'.

To illustrate these three stages, let us imagine that on Sunday you wake up with a sore throat (recognise symptoms); by Tuesday you decide you are sick (appraisal delay); on Wednesday you decide to see your doctor (illness delay); on Friday you actually see the doctor (utilisation delay). The latter delay may not be under the individual's control if it includes time to the actual appointment (referred to as a 'scheduling delay'), as opposed to the time taken to *make* the appointment. The length of each delay period is likely to vary for different symptoms and illnesses, with, for example, appraisal delays being long for embarrassing personal symptoms such as rectal bleeding but scheduling delays likely to be short. It becomes obvious therefore that appraisals are crucial in getting the help-seeking process moving along, particularly when symptoms are potentially lethal.

Table 9.2 Reasons for seeking or not seeking a medical consultation

Reason	N	%
Consulters (N = 109)		
Seek information about symptoms	46	42
Seek explanation for causes of symptoms	37	34
Seek advice to cure symptoms	26	24
Non-consulters (N = 106)		
Do not have time	29	27
Think the symptoms will disappear very soon	27	25
Do not want to take sick leave from work	21	20
Think the symptoms are a normal part of busy city life	10	10
Have uncomfortable feelings about hospitals	9	8
Think it is OK or not a problem	6	6
Other	4	4

Source: Cheng, C. (2000) *Psychosomatic Medicine*, 62: 844–52

Why then do so many people delay in seeking help? There are many reasons for delaying seeking treatment, including social class and educational level (the lower one's level of education and income, the greater the delay; see Chapter 2), age, gender, ignorance of the meaning of the symptoms, getting used to the symptoms, feeling invulnerable (cf. unrealistic optimism), believing that nothing can be done (relates to treatment perceptions, see below) and, commonly, fear. The earlier sections on influences on symptom perception and interpretation are also relevant here. Table 9.2 presents a summary of reasons that distinguished between seeking and not seeking medical consultation among a sample of 215 Chinese adults suffering from functional dyspepsia – a condition manifested by upper gastrointestinal tract pain and excessive belching, which has no underlying structural or biochemical reason (Cheng 2000). This table highlights many of the reasons for and against healthcare seeking that we address in this section.

■ Symptom type, location and perceived prevalence

Symptoms that are visible, painful, disruptive, frequent and persistent generally lead to action (Mechanic 1978). If a symptom is easily visible to oneself and others, for example a rash, then one will delay less in seeking treatment. When people come to believe that their symptoms are serious (this perceived severity may or may not be confirmed by the doctor), unusual (e.g. no one else seems to have had them) and that they can be controlled or treated through medical intervention, they take action. The effects or consequences of symptoms are also important. When symptoms threaten normal relations with friends and family, or when they disrupt regular patterns of activity or interaction, people usually seek help (Prohaska *et al.* 1987; Peay and Peay 1998). However, Grunfeld and colleagues (2003) found that even when a potential symptom of breast cancer has been self-identified, a significant number of women aged 35–54 reported that seeking help would itself be disruptive to their lifestyle and thus delayed seeking healthcare.

The location of the symptom has been shown to influence use of a lay referral system and/or going to a doctor. For example, persistent headaches may well be discussed with friends and family before seeking medical help, but a persistent itch, or detection of a lump in the genital region, may not. Certain parts of the body are more open to discussion than others. The attributes associated with some diseases may also make them more or less easy to report. De Nooijer, Lechner and de Vries (2001), for example, noted that shame or embarrassment contributed significantly to delayed reporting of symptoms subsequently found to be associated with cancer. This is one of the reasons that many testicular cancers are diagnosed late, with potentially serious consequences for successful treatment (for further discussion of related issues of cancer screening, see Chapter 4).

Furthermore, it has been shown that people make judgements about the prevalence of symptoms and disease that influence their interpretation and whether medical attention is sought (e.g. Ditto and Jemmott 1989). Diseases that a person has experience of have been found to be judged as more prevalent by both students *and* by physicians, and diseases considered prevalent tend to be viewed as less serious or life-threatening (Jemmott, Croyle and Ditto 1988). This potential normalisation of some health threats could have dangerous consequences. Also worrying is evidence of biased views of the epidemiology of conditions among practitioners/physicians depending on their own experience of it – this could potentially bias diagnosis towards conditions perceived as very common rather than towards those considered so rare as to be unlikely.

Financial reasons for delay

For some, seeking refuge in the sick role following a formal diagnosis might be an attractive option as it can allow a person time out from normal duties and responsibilities. However, some people do not want to be declared sick because of the implications it may have for them socially (If I am sick how can I attend that party? If I am sick who will look after the children?); occupationally (If I am sick my workload will be double when I return. If I am off sick will someone else get my job?); or financially (I cannot afford to lose wages or overtime payments by being sick. I cannot afford to pay for tests or medicines). In the USA, some people delay seeking medical care when money for the anticipated treatment is limited; these people are generally among the 16 percent of American citizens (predominantly Hispanic and black people) who do not have health insurance (USBC 1999). Luckily, other countries have healthcare systems that make personal finance less of a barrier to treatment, for example the National Health Service in the UK.

Cultural influences on delay behaviour

Pachter (1994) suggests that delays in seeking professional medical help may be particularly extended among members of cultures who have beliefs about illness causation that do not 'fit' biomedical views of illness and treatment. Many of those with traditional cultural views of illness causation, such as are described previously in this chapter, will seek culturally relevant cures, including for example herbal or animal-based treatments, acupuncture, faith healing, and so on. In some cases, this may be associated with a parallel seeking of medical help – in others, seeking Westernised medical treatment may be considered only if the condition fails to respond to the more traditional remedies (Chalmers 1996; Heine and Lehman 1995; Lim and Bishop 2000; Quah and Bishop 1996).

■ Age and delay behaviour

The young and the elderly use health services more often than other age groups (see Chapter 2). Acute onset of severe symptoms tends to result in quicker seeking of medical attention, particularly among the middle-aged, whereas elderly people are generally found to present to their doctors more quickly regardless of symptom severity, and in spite of the fact that many symptoms are commonly attributed initially to ageing (Prohaska *et al.* 1987). The quicker presentation of older individuals to healthcare professionals has been interpreted as a need to remove uncertainty among the elderly, whereas middle-aged individuals may attempt to minimise their problems until they worsen or fail to disappear naturally (Leventhal and Diefenbach 1991). In terms of seeking medical help for a symptomatic child, the decision is generally taken by a parent or guardian/carer, although this changes somewhat in late adolescence, when these young people can become reluctant to seek medical attention, particularly if their symptoms are something they wish to conceal from their parents (Cheng, Savageau, Sattler *et al.* 1993). Adolescents may also delay in seeking healthcare out of a sense of invulnerability and a resulting optimism about susceptibility to health problems (see Chapter 3).

■ Gender and delay behaviour

As stated previously, women generally use health services more than men. This may reflect greater attention being paid to internal states and bodily signals (see symptom perception section), gender socialisation or women making better use of their social support and lay referral networks, which promote healthcare-seeking behaviour (Berkman 1984; Krantz and Orth 2000). Any explanation is likely to be multifaceted. A recent French study (Melchior, Berkman, Niedhammer *et al.* 2003) found that occupational status, and not gender, influenced social support usage, with those with low social status reporting better support. This contradicts American and British findings (Marmot *et al.* 1998; Stansfeld *et al.* 1998), where low socio-economic status was associated with less social support. The interaction between gender, socio-economic status, social support and healthcare use is not yet fully understood (see Chapter 2).

Gender differences in seeking medical help may occur as a result of different meanings given to health-related behaviour by the two sexes (Courtenay 2000). The differences, they propose, reflect issues of masculinity, femininity and power. Men show their masculinity and power by engaging in health-risking behaviour and not showing signs of weakness – even when ill. Women, conversely, experience no such issues and are more willing to seek medical help as they feel appropriate. Following a similar line of argument, Verbrugge and Steiner (1985) suggested that women typically have more knowledge of the signs and symptoms of disease than men, are more concerned about their health and are more willing to confront the implications of any symptoms than men. In the context of testicular, bowel and prostrate cancer, for example, women are often highly influential in encouraging their male partners to attend for doctor consultations.

Finally, parenthood (motherhood has been studied more extensively to date than fatherhood) may also influence seeking help. Perhaps surprisingly, it has been shown that self-help or medical aid may be sought more willingly for symptoms perceived as minor than for those perceived as serious, perhaps suggesting avoidance of diagnoses that may interfere with the parenting role (Timko and Janoff-Bulman 1985).

■ Influence of others on delay behaviour

Seeking healthcare does not inevitably lead a person into the sick role, as effective treatment may be provided that rids them of their symptoms and enables them to carry on as usual. However, people often take action only when they are encouraged to do so by others in their lay referral network or when they realise that others with the same problem sought help in the past. It appears that many people look for 'permission' to call for help from their friends or family members – and are more reluctant to call for help in its absence (Finnegan, Meischke, Zapka *et al.* 2000; Kentsch *et al.* 2002). Related to this are delays as a result of 'not wanting to bother anybody'.

Discussing symptoms with others can be helpful. For example, Turk, Litt, Salovey *et al.* (1985) found that discovering the presence of a family history of the symptoms currently being experienced led to healthcare contact being made. Such disclosures of family history or of others' illness experiences are a likely outcome of conversations within a lay referral network. However, not all social networks are helpful: some people consulted may distrust doctors after negative experiences of their own; others may believe in alternative treatment or therapies rather than traditional medical routes. The use of lay referral networks can therefore work for or against delays in the seeking of healthcare.

■ Treatment beliefs and delay behaviour

Horne and Weinman (Horne 1999; Horne and Weinman 1999) suggest an extension to Leventhal's self-regulation model (described earlier in the chapter) whereby, in addition to illness perceptions predicting illness responses, the perceived benefits that an individual foresees of any treatments they may obtain as a result of seeking medical help are also predictive. For example, believing that one has a serious illness but that it can be cured with treatment is more likely to result in seeking medical help than the opposite cluster of beliefs. The identification of treatment representations (Horne and Weinman 1999) highlights perceptions of medicines as restorative, as symptom relievers, or as disruptive, harmful or addictive. Representations of medication and knowledge about treatment rationale have been associated with treatment adherence among adult populations (e.g. McElnay and McCallion 1998; Horne and Weinman 1999, 2002), and this is a growing area of research. A further effect of beliefs about treatment might be an effect on decisions to seek or not seek health professional advice for a symptom.

Perhaps due to growing concerns about some traditional medical treatments (e.g. antibiotics, steroids, HRT – hormone replacement therapy), an increasing number of individuals are utilising what are known as complementary therapies involving both physical and non-traditional pharmaceutical interventions, such as acupuncture, chiropractice, homeopathy and traditional Chinese herbal medicine. Interestingly, those who use such treatments tend to be among the more highly educated and more economically well-off groups in society (Astin 1998).

■ Fear, denial and delay behaviour

Fear and anxiety have been inconsistently associated with delay in seeking healthcare. O'Carroll, Smith, Grubb *et al.* (2001), for example, found that people who had relatively high scores on a measure of dispositional anxiety were more likely to seek help quickly following the onset of symptoms than their less anxious counterparts. While fear of doctors, treatment procedures or medical environments can delay healthcare seeking, and trait anxiety, neuroticism and negative affectivity generally increase healthcare utilisation, illness-specific anxiety appears to be less influential. For example, Keinan, Carmil and Rieck (1991) found that delay in seeking medical care among women discovering a lump in their breast was not significantly associated with anxiety. This non-relationship has also been reported among those with head and neck cancer (Tromp, Brouha, DeLeeuw *et al.* 2004).

Emotion itself may be insufficient to determine the healthcare-seeking behaviour, given the previously described importance of illness prototypes, symptom perception and interpretations and treatment beliefs, all of which act together to shape a person's response to a health threat. For example, a person who is highly anxious about a symptom and believes it signifies a terminal illness for which there is no treatment is less likely to seek medical attention quickly than someone who is equally anxious but believes that the symptom may be an early warning sign of a condition for which preventive or curative treatment is available.

One further response to health threats is that of denial. It has been shown that people who engage in denial generally show reduced symptom perception and report, and greater delay in seeking help (Jones 1990; Zervas, Augustine and Fricchione 1993). Unrealistically optimistic beliefs about health status or illness outcomes were thought to reduce symptom report and preventive health behaviour by means of increasing the presence of denial. However, neither of these relationships was upheld in a recent study of symptom report among those with either multiple sclerosis or insulin-dependent diabetes (de Ridder, Fournier and Bensing 2004). However, Aspinwall and Brunhart (1996) have pointed out that optimism is not necessarily unrealistic and maladaptive, but that optimistic beliefs may actually benefit symptom report by enabling people to attend to symptoms without perceiving them as a threat. Tromp *et al.* (2004) offer support for this from a study of predictors of delay among patients with head and neck cancer, where delay was found to be greater (>3 months) in those scoring low on optimism, as well as low on active coping, the use of social support and low **health hardiness**.

Finally, following diagnosis, Kasl and Cobb describe how people engage in sick role behaviour, as the symptoms have been validated (and may increase once a label has been attached to them; Kasl and Cobb 1966b).

health hardiness
the extent to which a person is committed to and involved in health-relevant activities, perceives control over their health and responds to health stressors as challenges or opportunities for growth.

People are then working towards getting better or preserving health such as avoiding activity or further injury. How people communicate with health professionals and engage in their treatment is discussed in the following chapter.

Summary

This chapter has described the various processes that people go through before deciding that they might be getting ill. We have described how people may or may not become aware of certain bodily signs depending upon the context in which they are experienced or upon individual characteristics such as neuroticism. Both internal and external factors influence the extent to which a person attends to their bodily states, and how they subsequently interpret bodily signs as symptoms. We have described how, upon interpreting bodily signs as symptoms of some underlying illness, a person compares them with pre-existing illness prototypes derived from their personal experience or from external sources of information. People's beliefs about illness have commonly been found to cluster around five domains: perceived identity (label), timeline, consequences, cure–control and cause. These ways of thinking about illness are relatively stable across various patient groups, but specific beliefs can differ in the eyes of a healthy person. Finally we have described a range of personal, social and emotional factors that influence whether a person responds to their symptoms by seeking the advice of a healthcare professional. The journey from a bodily sign perceived as a symptom to the doctor's door is often a long one, and delay in seeking healthcare can itself be damaging to one's health. Health psychology therefore has an important role to play in identifying the factors that contribute to this journey in order to maximise the likelihood of positive health outcomes for patients.

Further reading

Buick, D. and Petrie, K. (2002). 'I know just how you feel': The validity of healthy women's perceptions of breast cancer patients receiving treatment. *Journal of Applied Social Psychology* 32: 110–23.
This paper highlights the fact that personal experience shapes one's perceptions of a particular illness in terms of its causes, consequences and treatment outcomes. Discrepant perceptions between lay and 'patient' populations has implications for societal and carer responses.

Leventhal, H., Nerenz, D.R. and Steele, D.J. (1984). Illness representations and coping with health threats. In A. Baum, S.E. Taylor and J.E. Singer (eds) *Handbook of Psychology and Health: Social Psychological Aspects of Health*, Vol. 4. (pp. 219–52). Hillsdale, NJ: Lawrence Erlbaum.

This chapter describes Leventhal's model of self-regulation of illness and outlines empirical evidence highlighting the implications of illness representations or cognition for coping with illness events.

Martin, R., Rothrock, N., Leventhal, H. and Leventhal, E. (2003). Common sense models of illness: implications for symptom perception and health-related behaviours. In J. Suls and K.A. Wallston (eds), *Social Psychological Foundations of Health and Illness* (pp. 199–225). Oxford: Blackwell.

This chapter, contained in an excellent and well-resourced text, provides a clear and comprehensive overview of common-sense models of how ordinary people interpret and act upon symptoms (addresses the role of attention, cognition and illness representations, mood, social context and culture).

CHAPTER 10

The consultation and beyond

Learning outcomes

By the end of the chapter, you should have an understanding of:

- the process of the medical consultation
- the movement towards 'shared decision making' and the issues it creates
- factors that contribute to effective and ineffective consultations with health professionals
- issues related to 'breaking bad news'
- issues in medical decision making
- factors that influence adherence to medical treatments
- interventions to improve adherence in patients and health professionals

CHAPTER OUTLINE

Whether in hospital or in the community, conversations between healthcare providers and patients are one of the most important means through which both groups give and receive information relevant to medical decisions, treatment and self-care. As such, the consultation remains one of the most important aspects of medical care. Good communication enhances the effectiveness of care; poor communication can lead doctors to make poor diagnoses and treatment decisions and leave patients feeling dissatisfied and unwilling or unable to engage appropriately in their own treatment. This chapter considers a number of factors that contribute to the quality of the consultation, and how doctors and patients act on information gained from it. It starts by examining the process of the consultation – what makes a 'good' or a 'bad' consultation. It then considers how doctors utilise the information given in the consultation to inform their diagnostic decisions. Finally, the chapter considers how factors in the consultation and beyond influence whether and how much patients follow medical treatments recommended in it.

The medical consultation

The nature of the encounter

Consultations are a critical time for both doctors and other health professionals to gain information to inform their diagnostic and treatment decisions. They can monitor progress and change their treatment accordingly. They also provide a time for the patient to discuss relevant issues and gain information about their condition and its treatment. As Ong, de Haes, Hoos *et al.* (1995) noted, the key goals of the consultation are:

■ developing a good relationship between healthcare provider and patient;
■ exchanging relevant information;
■ making relevant decisions.

The process through which these goals are achieved has been mapped by a number of researchers. One of the first such analyses was conducted by Byrne and Long (1976), who identified five phases in the typical medical consultation:

1. The doctor establishes a relationship with the patient.
2. The doctor attempts to discover the reason for the patient's attendance.
3. The doctor conducts a verbal or physical examination, or both.
4. The doctor, or the doctor and the patient, or the patient (in that order of probability) consider the condition.
5. The health professional, and occasionally the patient, consider further treatment or further investigation.

These phases appear to hold for most consultations, although as we shall see later, what happens within each 'stage' can vary significantly. Another way of addressing this issue is to consider the key elements that make for a successful interview. With this in mind, Ford, Schofield and Hope (2003) identified six key dimensions that were seen as important to a 'good' medical consultation by a variety of informants, including general practitioners, hospital doctors, practice nurses, academics and lay people:

1. the health professional has a good knowledge of research or medical information and is able to communicate this to the patient;
2. achieving a good relationship with the patient;
3. establishing the nature of the patient's medical problem;
4. gaining an understanding of the patient's understanding of their problem and its ramifications;
5. engaging the patient in any decision-making process: for example, treatment choices not simply being chosen by the health professional but being discussed with the patient;
6. managing time so that the consultation does not appear rushed.

Who has the power?

The consultation involves both patient and health professional. Both can contribute to the process of communication and decision making. However, the nature of the meeting means that the health professional usually has more power over the consultation than the patient. This power differential can be exacerbated by the patient's behaviour and expectations in the consultation. They may often defer to the professional and be reluctant to ask clarifying questions or to challenge any conclusions the professional may make. Such behaviour is more likely to occur in medical consultations than with other health professionals, such as nurses. Nevertheless, all health professionals have significant responsibility in determining the style and outcome of the consultation. This can result in approaches differing from 'doctor knows best', the professional-centred approach identified by Byrne and Long (1976), to a more patient-centred approach advocated by people such as Pendleton (1983).

Characteristics of the professional-centred approach include:

■ The health professional keeps control over the interview.
■ They ask questions in order to gain information. These are direct, closed (allow yes/no answers), and refer to medical (or other relevant) facts.
■ The health professional makes the decision.
■ The patient passively accepts this decision.

Characteristics of the patient-centred approach include:

■ The professional identifies and works with the patient's agenda as well as their own.
■ The health professional actively listens to the patient and responds appropriately.
■ The communication is characterised by the professional encouraging engagement and seeking the patient's ideas of what is wrong and how it may be treated.
■ The patient is an active participant in the process.

Over the past decade, there has been a gradual shift from the professional-centred model to the patient-centred approach. Increasingly, both health professional and patient are seen as collaborators in decisions concerning patient healthcare. This is perhaps expressed in a movement among health professionals towards what is often referred to as 'shared decision making' (Elwyn, Edwards, Kinnersley *et al.* 2000), in which the patient and health professional have an equal share (and responsibility) in any treatment decision. This may only truly occur where there is no dominant choice of treatment – the health professional's knowledge of the relative effectiveness of the various treatment possibilities may truly mean that 'doctor does indeed know best' under some conditions. This may occur in very important areas – such as a woman with breast cancer deciding whether or not to conserve a breast with a **lumpectomy** or to have more radical surgery and remove the whole affected breast. Here, there is little clear empirical evidence to support either option (a state known as equipoise), and the choice may be determined more by the patient's concerns over their appearance, wishes to eradicate the risk of recurrence, and so on. Although the health professional may provide information to inform the patient choice, or even offer an opinion about that choice, the final decision should be reached jointly. Where equipoise does not exist, for example in the case of a request for antibiotics for the treatment of a viral condition (where they will be of no benefit), the health professional may educate the patient to accept their choice of treatment and so arrive at a 'joint decision', but not a truly shared decision. Accordingly, the key features of shared decision making are:

lumpectomy
a surgical procedure in which only the tumour and a small area of surrounding tissue are removed. Contrasts with mastectomy, in which the whole breast is removed.

- A shared decision involves at least two (often more) participants – the healthcare professional(s) and the patient(s).
- Both parties take steps to participate in the process of treatment decision making.
- Information sharing is a prerequisite to shared decision making.
- A treatment decision is made and both parties agree with the decision.

This approach to the consultation is being advocated by the British National Health Service (NHS), which calls for 'active partnerships' between health professionals and patients (NHS Executive 1996). Despite this enthusiasm, a number of concerns about high levels of patient involvement in the decision-making process have been made. First, there are often power differentials between high-status health professionals (particularly doctors) and patients in the consultation. Accordingly, while the idea that the health professional should provide or disclose information to the patient at one level suggests equality in the decision-making process, it also implicitly accepts that the health professional has more relevant knowledge than the patient. The appearance of equality can therefore be an illusion and not reality, and both health professionals and patients can find it difficult to move away from this implicit power structure (Silverman 1987). Indeed, many patients want this asymmetry and reject moves to 'force' them into a decision-making role. Patients may be distressed and worried if a healthcare professional admits that there is no clear evidence about the best choice of intervention, or that the evidence is mixed or premised on poor methodology. By contrast, Van der Geest and Whyte (1989) argued that being prescribed a particular treatment by an expert health professional confers a certainty and reassurance in the treatment of disease that cannot be found when the patient is asked to make choices about a number of uncertain treatment options.

Empirical research confirms some of these cautions. Savage and Armstrong (1990) compared the effects of 'directive' or 'sharing' consultation styles on measures of patient satisfaction. They found that patients with both short-term problems and chronic conditions preferred the directive approach. Those people who received a prescription were also more satisfied than those who did not. In a much larger study, Lee, Back, Block *et al.* (2002) asked over 1,000 patients with either breast cancer or who were receiving **stem cell transplants** to identify their preferred consultation style. Only a minority of individuals opted for the shared decision-making approach:

stem cell transplant
stem cells are given to the person after chemotherapy to help the bone marrow to recover and continue producing healthy blood cells.

- physician makes treatment decisions: 10 percent
- physician makes decisions following discussion with patient: 21 percent
- shared decision making: 42 percent
- patient makes decision following discussion with doctor: 22 percent
- patient makes decision: 5 percent

Similar findings were reported by Beaver, Luker, Owens *et al.* (1996), who gave women newly diagnosed with breast cancer a role-preference card sort in which they were presented with five cards, each with a written statement and a cartoon portraying differing levels of patient involvement in treatment choices. They then asked them to indicate their preferred style of consultation: 20 percent of the women wanted an active role in deciding their treatment, 28 percent wanted a joint decision, while 52 percent wanted their surgeon to make their treatment choice for them. By contrast, many more women with **benign** disease wanted to be involved in the decision-making process. In a subsequent study, the same research team (Beaver, Bogg and Luker 1999) found that 78 percent of a group of patients with colorectal cancer preferred a passive role in decision making. Why people with more severe illness were less likely to want to be involved in decisions over their treatment is unclear, although two motives seem possible. First, they may have wanted to maximise the chances of making the correct decision by leaving this to an expert. Second, they may have wanted to avoid the risk of regret and guilt in the long term should their decision about treatment choice seem to be the wrong one.

benign (tumour)
tumour that cannot spread by invasion or metastasis. It does not carry the risk to health that a malignant tumour carries.

Other relevant issues were identified by Arora and McHorney (2000), who reported a four-year observational study of 2,197 patients with a number of chronic diseases, including heart failure, MI and diabetes. Sixty-nine percent of those who took part preferred to leave their medical decisions to the physicians. Women, older people, those with an active coping style and people with more education were most likely to want to be engaged in the decision-making process. Those with mild hypertension and heart disease were least likely to want to be involved in their treatment choice. Interestingly, participants who placed the lowest value on their health were more likely to want to be engaged in the decision-making process than those who placed a higher value on their health, perhaps because those who placed a high value on their health considered this to be such an important issue that they did not want to question the expert opinion of the doctor.

A related issue is how doctors deal with uncertainty about diagnoses and treatments. Ogden, Fuks, Gardner *et al.* (2002) noted that many doctors typically hide any uncertainty they may have in order to maintain confidence among their patients. Shared decision making moves from this approach and encourages doctors to share any uncertainty they may feel in order to be more open in the consultation and optimise the doctor–patient relationship. Ogden and colleagues set out to determine whether this approach would increase or decrease patients' confidence in the doctor and any outcomes of the consultation. In fact, their results suggested that it was not the expression of uncertainty that influenced patients' confidence – more important was the way that doctors attempted to resolve the uncertainty. Where doctors seemed passive (for example when they used expressions such as 'Let's see what happens' or 'I'm not sure about this'), patients' confidence fell. By contrast, active attempts to resolve uncertainty, such as using a book or computer to find out about a drug or asking another doctor for advice, actually increased confidence. The only behavioural act that decreased confidence was when doctors asked a nurse for advice – presumably because patients considered nurses to be less expert than doctors.

These issues are taken into account in Elwyn, Edwards, Kinnersley *et al.*'s (2000) patient-centred approach involving shared decision making, which involves the following steps:

1. Explore the patient's ideas about the nature of the problem and potential treatments.
2. Identify how much information the patient would prefer and tailor information to meet these needs.
3. Check the patient's understanding of ideas, fears and expectations of potential treatment options.
4. Assess patient's decision-making preference and adopt their preferred mode.
5. Make, discuss or defer decisions.
6. Arrange follow-up.

Despite these cautions, increased involvement in decision making can increase many people's satisfaction with the process of care and result in improved outcomes. There is evidence, for example, that consultations that involve patients in decision making can result in increased patient satisfaction, greater confidence in healthcare recommendations, improvements in self-care wellbeing and, on occasion, fewer drug prescriptions and less demand for inappropriate surgical treatments (see Ford, Schofield and Hope 2003). While increasing patient satisfaction, however, the medical outcomes may be less than optimal. Kinmonth, Woodcock, Griffin *et al.* (1998), for example, found that patients who were given a patient-centred approach to their treatment of non-insulin-dependent diabetes expressed higher levels of satisfaction with their communication with health professionals, greater treatment satisfaction and greater wellbeing than patients who received a standard health professional-led consultation. However, they were less careful in sticking to the calorie-controlled diet necessary to maximise control over their condition than those in the standard consultation condition. This may not be a bad outcome, of course. Rather, it implies that patients have knowingly opted to have a higher day-to-day quality of life rather than one constrained by medical 'necessities'. Ultimately, it is their life, and fully informed decisions such as this need to be supported.

Factors that influence the process of consultation

Health professional factors

A variety of factors may influence the behaviour of health professionals. Some may have strong beliefs in the type of consultation they wish to have with their patients and behave accordingly. But more subtle factors may also influence their behaviour. Gerbert (1984), for example, found that health professionals give more information to patients that they liked than those they disliked. Encounters may also be influenced by the time available and the type of problem being dealt with. Patients and health professionals may also hold different agendas and expectations of the consultation. Patients are frequently concerned about issues such as pain and how the illness may interfere with their everyday lives. Health professionals are frequently more concerned with understanding the severity of the patient's condition and developing their treatment plan. These differing agendas may mean that health professionals and patients fail to appreciate important aspects of information given and received and may not remember any relevant information very well.

They may also impact on the outcome of the consultation. The findings of Zachariae, Pederson, Jensen *et al.* (2003) typify the outcomes frequently found in studies of this phenomenon. They examined the relationship between the quality of a doctor's interaction with patients who had cancer and their satisfaction with the consultation and confidence in their ability to cope with their condition. They rated various aspects of the doctor's communication style, including:

- whether the doctor attempted to gain an understanding of the patient's viewpoint;
- how well patients considered the physician understood their feelings during the consultation;
- their satisfaction with the doctor's ability to handle medical aspects of their care;
- the quality of their personal contact with the doctor.

Their results indicated that higher scores on all measures were associated with higher levels of satisfaction with the interview, higher levels of confidence in coping with their illness and lower levels of emotional distress following the interview. Of note also was that doctors who evidenced poor communication skills were least aware of the patient's responses and level of satisfaction with the interview.

The type of health professional

As well as these subtle differences in skills and personal characteristics, broader factors may also influence the style of the encounter. It is often suggested that the style of interaction with different health professions itself will differ. Nurses, for example, are generally seen as more nurturing, easier to talk to and better listeners than doctors. Their role often involves exploring psychosocial issues more than, say, doctors. These different roles were high-lighted by Nichols (1993), who suggested that in some cases doctors may find it difficult to become emotionally involved or know their patients as people when they are involved in life and death decisions or actions such as surgery. With this in mind, he suggested that nurses should provide the main 'caring' role and be more involved in holistic care of the individual. For this reason, it may not be surprising that nurses typically do address more psychosocial concerns than doctors (e.g. Campbell, Mauksch, Neikirk *et al.* 1990).

Gender of the health professional

The gender of the health professional may also influence the nature of the consultation. Hall and Roter (2002), for example, concluded from their meta-analysis of seven relevant studies that patients spoke to female physicians more than male physicians, reported more medical and personal information, and made more positive statements. Patients also appeared more assertive and interrupted more when being interviewed by female doctors than by their male counterparts. Interestingly, perhaps, the gender of the doctor did not influence the degree to which emotional issues, such as concern, worries and personal feelings, were discussed. These findings may represent differences in expectations and gender differences that would have been found in other contexts. However, some of the differences may be a consequence of the doctor's behaviour: female physicians tend to ask more questions and make more active efforts to build a relationship between them and the patient – both factors that would lead to higher levels of disclosure than would otherwise occur.

The way information is given

The way information is given in consultations is also important. When information is given with a positive spin, for example, patients may be more likely to engage in risky healthcare options than when it is given in a more negative manner. Health professionals may also not be immune to such spin. McNeil, Pauker, Sox *et al.* (1982), for example, found that when given various probabilities for the outcome of treatment of a hypothetical case of lung cancer, patients, medical students and even surgeons were more likely to opt for surgery when the same risks for surgery were framed in terms of the probability of the individual surviving rather than dying. That is, they were more likely to choose surgery if the risk was presented as a 40 percent likeli-hood of survival than if presented as a 60 percent risk of dying. Similarly, Marteau (1989) reported that medical students were more likely to recom-mend surgery to hypothetical patients (fellow medical students) if they had previously been provided with information on survival rates following surgery described in terms of likelihood of survival rather than risk of dying.

The patient's contribution

Patient factors will also significantly influence the consultation. High levels of anxiety or distress during the interview, a lack of familiarity with the information discussed, a failure to actively engage with the interview and not having considered issues to be discussed in the consultation may minimise the patient's level of engagement. Patients may not think through what information they want, or they realise only after the interview what they could have asked. They may also be reluctant to ask questions of doctors and other health professionals, who are still frequently seen as of a higher status than the patient. Perhaps for these reasons, people who are well educated and with high socio-economic status tend to gain more information and to have longer consultations than people with low levels of education and less economic status (Stirling, Wilson and McConnachie 2001).

RESEARCH FOCUS

Grant, Nicholas, Moore and Salisbury (2002). An observational study comparing quality of care in walk-in centres with general practice and NHS Direct using standardised patients. *British Medical Journal*, 323: 1556–61.

General Practitioners in the UK are overwhelmed by the number of patients they have to see. Patients can often wait a week or more for an appointment with their doctor. As a consequence, treatment of minor illness may be delayed, and patients may lack appropriate advice on how to manage any illness themselves. One of the ways that the UK government has responded to this problem is to establish two alternative pathways to medical care. The first involves walk-in centres, which are located in city and town centres and provide immediate access mainly to nurses who can provide health advice, or NHS Direct, which can provide advice over the telephone.

The care provided by each approach can be summarised as:

- *Walk-in centres*: advice on minor illnesses and injuries. Most consultations are with nurses, who follow standardised protocols and clinical assessment software to guide their decision-making process. Average consultation length is 14 minutes.

- *General practice*: most consultations are with doctors, who do not use standardised protocols. Average consultation length is 9 minutes.

- *NHS Direct*: a telephone consultation with a nurse using similar protocols to those used in walk-in centres. Average consultation time is 14 minutes.

According to Grant and colleagues, previous evaluation of walk-in centres has found the quality of care to be 'disappointing' and even 'positively dangerous' on occasion. However, this research has been flawed. They therefore set out to compare the effectiveness of walk-in centres with NHS Direct and general practice consultations. The latter may be seen as the standard that these alternatives should be aiming for. The method they used to evaluate this involved the use of standardised patients. These are actors who play the part of patients – in this case unknown to the practitioners who saw them. By playing the same 'patient' with the same personality and presenting problems in each of the three settings, direct comparisons can be made of the type of response and quality of care in each setting.

Method

Sites for the study
A number of sites of each type were approached and asked to take part in the study. Twenty of twenty-five (80 percent) walk-in centres agreed to participate, as did eleven out of twelve

continued

NHS Direct sites (92 percent) and twenty-four out of sixty-two GP practices (39 percent) in Birmingham, Bristol and London.

Clinical scenarios
The standard patients were asked to role play five common clinical scenarios that were representative of the types of problem with which people present at walk-in centres:

1. a 23-year-old woman requesting 'day after' contraception;

2. a 30-year-old man with musculo-skeletal chest pain (e.g. not an MI or potentially fatal cardiac problem);

3. a 35-year-old woman with sinusitis due to a bacterial infection;

4. a 27-year-old man with a tension headache and underlying depression;

5. a 30-year-old man with worsening asthma caused by taking an anti-inflammatory drug (ibuprofen) purchased at a chemist without a prescription.

Each was selected because they required specific skills in managing – excluding potentially fatal illnesses, exploring psychosocial factors, awareness of side-effects of drugs, and so on.

Assessment of the clinical consultation
The practitioners were assessed on checklists of between eight and seventeen items depending on the condition, measuring the quality of their history taking, examination, diagnosis, advice and treatment. These were completed by the standard patients following the consultation.

Training of the standard patients
Fifteen standard patients were taught the role they had to perform and how to assess the consultation in a training day prior to their visits to the different healthcare settings. Each actor played one scenario in each of the sites in their local area. The reliability of their acting and assessments were measured at this time. Accuracy of presenting symptoms was assessed by observation of the final role play of the training day by two observers. Across all scenarios, 89 percent of clinical features were assessed correctly. Reliability of assessment involved comparing actors' assessments with those of general practitioners who saw videotapes of the assessed interviews (assessing the validity of the ratings), and by two actors rating the same tape independently (measuring inter-rater reliability). Reliability statistics (kappa) for each type of comparison were high (0.8 and 0.9, respectively).

Procedure
In each area, standard patients attended all the participating walk-in and GP surgeries in their area on one occasion, and they made contact with NHS Direct up to three times. Overall, 297 contacts were made over a 13-week period. All contacts were anonymous and not known to the practitioners. Participating health professionals were asked to contact the research team if they suspected they had seen a standardised patient. Of the twenty-three calls they received, five accurately reported having seen a standardised patient; the other eighteen calls related to consultations with real patients.

Results
Mean scores on the assessment criteria were calculated and between-group differences assessed. Statistical analyses compared walk-in centres with GP consultations and NHS Direct. Overall, walk-in centres fared well, generally either scoring better or not significantly different to both alternative approaches, depending on the outcome measure. The one exception to this was in the care of sinusitis, where NHS Direct scored significantly better than either walk-in centres or GPs.

Although no statistical comparisons are reported between GP and NHS Direct consultations, both appear to have strengths and weaknesses. NHS Direct, for example, appears to have had better scores for the care of headache and sinusitis, while GPs fared better with the issue of contraception and asthma.

	Walk-in centres	General practices	NHS Direct
All scenarios	67.3[1,2]	59.2	56.5
Contraception	76.9[1,2]	58.1	37.5
Chest pain	66.4	69.4	60.2
Sinusitis	64.2[2]	55.8	73.6
Headache	60.4	55.8	62.6
Asthma	68.3[1,2]	56.7	51.2

[1] = significantly different to general practice
[2] = significantly different to NHS Direct

NHS Direct and walk-in centres were much more likely than GPs to refer people on to an accident and emergency (A and E) department in their local hospital. No GP referred patients to A and E. By contrast, 5 percent of consultations in walk-in centres and 13 percent of consultations with NHS Direct resulted in advice to go to an A and E department, while 26 percent of walk-in cases and 82 percent of NHS Direct cases were advised to go to their GP.

Discussion

The authors' main conclusion was that walk-in centres provide 'adequate, safe, clinical care' to a range of patients compared with GPs and NHS Direct. Although they may be more cautious than GPs, they provide appropriate and safe care. By contrast, NHS Direct appears to fare less well – despite using similar diagnostic and decision-making software. Indeed, the frequency of advice to patients to attend either their GP or an A and E department made by NHS Direct staff suggests that the nurses have little confidence in their decisions and that the service may not provide a significant alternative to GP practices. Why these differences emerged is not clear. It is possible that having sight of a patient and being able to judge how well 'they are looking' may play an important role in decision making. It may be that patients are more able to describe their conditions in face-to-face contexts, and healthcare professionals can better read their non-verbal behaviour. More research into this important issue is clearly needed.

Breaking bad news

One type of consultation for which the necessary skills have received particular attention is called the 'bad news' interview. As its name implies, these interactions are typically those in which patients and/or their partners are told that they have a serious illness or that they may die of their illness. Clearly, such interviews are stressful for both patients and healthcare professionals. Historically, information about the likelihood of dying has frequently been withheld from patients – although their relatives were frequently told, placing a significant burden of knowledge on these people.

However, this is no longer considered ethical – patients are now considered to have the right to be told their prognosis.

There is increasing evidence that how such information is given will impact on patient wellbeing (Schofield, Butow, Thompson *et al.* 2003). Accordingly, increasing attention is being given to the best way of conducting the bad news interview. However, there remains little detailed empirical evidence about the best methods of doing so, and most guidelines are based on opinion (Farber, Urban, Collier *et al.* 2002) and basic principles of good communication. Buckman (1992), who has been both a doctor and a patient diagnosed with a terminal illness (which later proved non-fatal), suggested a six-step protocol for the process:

1. Give the news in person, in private, with enough time and without interruptions.
2. Find out what the patient knows about their diagnosis.
3. Find out what the patient wants to know.
4. Share the information: start with a 'warning shot' and then a small amount of information in simple language at a pace the patient can cope with.
5. Respond to the patient's feelings, including acknowledging and validating their emotional reaction to the news.
6. Plan and follow through: includes planning next steps, summarising what has been said, identifying sources of support and making an early follow-up appointment.

When these or similar guidelines are followed, patients appear to benefit. Schofield, Butow, Thompson *et al.* (2003), for example, asked patients to recall a bad news interview in which they received information about a 'life-threatening' **melanoma**. They were asked questions about how their diagnosis was given, whether they received as much information as they wanted about their diagnosis, its treatment options and its prognosis, and how the interview was conducted. They examined the relationship between their responses and levels of anxiety and depression at the time of diagnosis, and four and thirteen months later. Factors associated with low levels of anxiety included the health professional preparing the patient for their diagnosis, giving as much information as required by the patient, providing written information, talking about the patient's feelings, being reassuring, and the presence of other (supportive) people while being given the diagnosis. Practices associated with low levels of depression included encouraging the patient to be involved in treatment-related decisions, and discussing the severity of the diagnosis and how it may affect other aspects of their life.

The importance of non-specific issues in the interview was highlighted by the findings of Roberts, Cox, Reintgen *et al.* (1994), who found that the physician's caring attitude was more important than the information given during the interview in determining psychological adjustment to a diagnosis of breast cancer. In a similar study, Beeney, Bakry and Dunn (1996) asked people with diabetes about their experiences when being told of their diagnosis, and how this experience could be improved: 60 percent of their sample reported that being told their diagnosis was distressing, and nearly a quarter stated that they would have benefited from more emotional support at the time. As a consequence of their findings, they recommended that patients be asked about their emotional and informational needs and that health professionals respond to these various needs as appropriate.

melanoma
a form of skin cancer that arises in melanocytes, the cells that produce pigment. Usually begins in a mole.

| What do YOU think? | Many doctors considered it a kindness not to tell patients when they were dying – a belief that also obviated *their* need to go through this painful process (see below). Indeed, so common was this practice that a rule of thirds was often cited as relevant to this situation. That is, two-thirds of patients were assumed to wish to know their prognosis – and two-thirds of doctors did not want to tell them. It is now considered a patient's right to know they are dying, and the practice of telling the relatives and not the patient is no longer acceptable – and many patients know they are dying without being told.

Patients may be upset, or even distraught, when given such information. However, knowledge of a poor prognosis can allow patients to prepare for death – from the most prosaic preparation such as making sure bills are paid to dealing with relationship issues and other important aspects of their lives. When death is not immediate, patients may prepare life goals that they wish to achieve before they die, and so on. So there are both positive and negative issues to be considered. Do the benefits outweigh the costs? Perhaps this decision can only be made on an individual basis. But on what grounds? Or perhaps all patients should be told whatever their circumstances? |

Having identified 'best practice', a number of studies have examined how well physicians actually give bad news. Ford, Fallowfield and Lewis (1996), for example, used audiotapes of consultations to analyse cancer specialists' bad news interviews with their patients and found that the majority of the interviews was spent in giving biomedical information with relatively little emphasis on empathic responses or acknowledgement of distress. In addition, the doctors exerted significant levels of control over the interview, moving away from the patient-led interview that the guidelines indicate as being optimal. Another observational study by the same group (Fallowfield, Hall, Maguire *et al.* 1990) found that surgeons did not detect 70 percent of instances of emotional distress in women being diagnosed with breast cancer. Doctors' reports contrast with these observational findings. Farber, Urban, Collier *et al.* (2002) examined how many doctors reported following such guidelines in the USA. They found that over half their sample of junior doctors reported always or frequently performing ten of eleven emotionally supportive items (e.g. inquire as to patients' worries, fears and concerns when giving bad news) and six of the nine environmental support items (e.g. ensure that the patient has a support person present when giving bad news). The contrast with the observational findings of Fallowfield suggests that these optimistic figures should be considered with some caution. More positively, they also found that while only 25 percent of respondents reported having been trained in giving bad news, those who had were likely to endorse a higher number of emotionally supportive items than those who had not received any training. These findings indicate the need for further training in breaking bad news – a process that may result in significant improvements in this skill. Fallowfield, Jenkins, Farewell *et al.* (2002), for example, found evidence that a programme of skills building resulted in greater use of empathy, using fewer leading questions and making more appropriate responses to patients' emotional cues.

Plate 10.1 Being a friendly face and expressing empathy can help patients cope with bad news. Here a doctor talks to someone with AIDS in a completely informal and 'non-medical' manner.

Source: John Cole/Science Photo Library

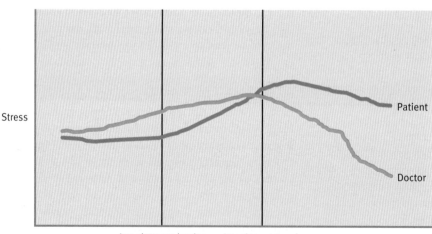

Figure 10.1 The timescale of stress experienced by healthcare professionals and patients in relation to the bad news interview.

Source: adapted from Ptacek and Eberhardt (1996)

Before ending this section, it should be acknowledged that the bad news interview is stressful for both patients and health professionals. Many health professionals also experience intense emotions themselves while breaking bad news. Ptacek and Eberhardt (1996) mapped out patient and doctor stress in relation to the interview (see Figure 10.1), which suggested that doctors experience significant anticipatory stress before the consultation, peaking during the 'clinical encounter', while patients' levels of stress typically peak following the interview. However, even for physicians the stress associated with giving bad news can last as long as three days or more (Ptacek, Ptacek and Ellison 2001).

Moving beyond the consultation

A key goal of the consultation is for healthcare professionals and patients to receive and provide information relevant to medical decision making and treatment. The next part of the chapter considers two outcomes of this process: one involving the healthcare professional, and one involving the patient.

Medical decision making

Healthcare decisions do not happen in a neutral setting, and they may be influenced by issues outside the consultation. They may be biased by healthcare professionals' expectations of their patients, their fellow professionals and the sheer pressure of making decisions in a short-time – often without all the information necessary to make a fully informed decision. Biases in healthcare may be the direct result of healthcare providers' own beliefs about the nature of the healthcare they provide. Some doctors, for example, state that they are only willing to treat patients who are also willing to be actively involved in their own health. Such doctors may, for example, refuse to provide expensive curative treatment for smoking-related diseases in patients who are unwilling to give up smoking. Other biases may be less conscious, or may be motivated by non-health-related issues. Mitchell, Ballard, Matchar *et al.* (2000), for example, found that, even after adjusting for demographic factors, the presence of other serious diseases and ability to pay, African American patients with transient ischaemic attacks were significantly less likely to receive specialist diagnostic tests or to have a specialist doctor than white patients. There is evidence that in the USA blacks are less likely than whites to receive curative surgery for early-stage lung, colon or breast cancer (e.g. Brawley and Freeman 1999) and that these differentials translate into higher mortality rates among black people. Gender differences may also influence the care people receive in hospital. Nurses are more likely to offer pain medication to women than men, at least in casualty departments (Raftery, Smith-Coggins and Chen 1995). By contrast, more men than women are likely to be offered a place on cardiac rehabilitation programmes following an MI (Allen, Scott, Stewart *et al.* 2004; Halm, Penque, Doll *et al.* 1999).

A key area of medical decision making involves diagnosing the illness with which a patient presents. Without an accurate diagnosis, patients will not receive a correct prognosis. Given the importance of medical decisions, it is also important to determine how they are arrived at. Elstein and Schwarz (2002) identified a number of ways that doctors arrive at a diagnosis:

- *Hypothesis testing*: the so-called 'gold star' level of decision making. This involves a logical sequencing of establishing and testing hypotheses about the nature of the diagnosis. Hypotheses are established, tested and when they fail are replaced by further hypotheses until a final 'correct' hypothesis is established.

- *Pattern recognition*: compared patterns of symptoms with disease prototypes. Perhaps a good way of reaching easy diagnoses, with the hypothesis-testing approach being utilised for more complex decisions.

- *Opinion revision*, or 'heuristics and biases': perhaps the least reliable approach to making diagnoses; involves making decisions based on partial evidence as a result of using rules of thumb or heuristics.

Clearly, most of the diagnoses assigned by doctors are accurate. However, their decision making may be prone to error, particularly when the third of these approaches is used. This may sometimes be inevitable in the context of medical decision making, which often occurs in the context of a need for rapid decisions using less than optimal information. Such situations may push doctors towards the use of diagnostic short-cuts. Tversky and Kahneman (1981) suggested that because we can handle only limited amounts of information when making decisions, we often take short-cuts known as heuristics or 'rules of thumb'. Those that are most useful for medicine may be 'fast and frugal' (Elstein and Schwarz 2002): that is, they aid quick decision making on the basis of minimal information. They allow doctors to make decisions at times of uncertainty and when information is lacking, but they may lead to errors because they are based on assumptions that may or may not be relevant to particular situations. André, Borgquist and Molstad (2002) identified two different types of heuristic frequently used by doctors in primary care. One doctor stated, for example, that he/she was so used to 40-year-olds presenting with chest pain having had an MI that he/she no longer tested for alternative diagnoses (as is recommended practice). Another doctor stated that if he/she thought a condition was psychosomatic, 'I begin to try to tie down the idea right away. I won't start with physical examination before talking about the possibility that it could be something emotional' – a process that may miss a physical disease process.

A key problem with the use of heuristics is that they limit thinking through the full diagnostic possibilities and may be biased by a number of factors (Elstein and Schwarz 2002). These include:

- *Availability*: diseases that receive considerable media attention are frequently thought to be more common than they actually are – even by doctors. Assuming a high probability of finding a condition may lead to it being diagnosed in error. A similar factor may be in play if the diagnosing doctor has knowledge of previous diagnoses given by colleagues.

- *Representativeness*: here, errors can occur because a set of symptoms is compared with a prototype set of symptoms and matched to one of two conditions without taking into account the likelihood of each of the two conditions being present. If these vary in prevalence within the population, the likelihood is that the condition being diagnosed will be the more prevalent disease. Heuristics that do not take this aspect into account may result in the physician not challenging their initial diagnosis through strict hypothesis testing.

- *The potential 'pay-off' of differing diagnoses*: if a diagnosis is unclear, the diagnosis assigned may be the one that carries the least cost and most benefit for the individual. When doctors are presented with a young child complaining of abdominal pain of no obvious origin, for example, a diagnosis of appendicitis and treatment of appendicectomy may be made, as treating the appendicitis successfully may be considered as outweighing the risks of an unnecessary operation.

In essence, heuristics reduce the cognitive load involved in making decisions at the cost of fully exploring all the potential issues that could be considered. These processes perhaps link to the findings of Ely, Levinson, Elder *et al.* (1995), who asked fifty-three family doctors to describe their most memorable errors and their perceived causes. The errors they described were generally very serious: 47 percent led to a patient death, and in only 26 percent of cases was there no adverse outcome. Only 10 percent of those who were asked to take part could not remember making any such errors. The key factors identified included a number related to the use of inappropriate heuristics in medical practice:

- *physician stressors*: including being hurried or distracted;
- *process-of-care factors*: including premature closure of the diagnostic process;
- *patient factors*: including misleading normal findings;
- *physician factors*: including lack of knowledge.

Interestingly, the study did not identify fatigue as a factor that may affect their decision-making processes. Empirical studies of this issue have typically involved doctors taking part in a variety of psychological tasks before and after times of naturally occurring sleep deprivation – usually working on call over one or two nights as well as working through the day. The evidence of

Plate 10.2   Some working contexts support appropriate decision making. Others, such as the presence of an overpowering and 'difficult' consultant, can increase anxiety and interfere with good decision making.

Source: From *Doctor at Large*. Ronald Grant Archives

such studies is relatively consistent. Samkoff and Jacques (1991) summarised the evidence as indicating that performance on tasks involving low levels of concentration and prolonged vigilance deteriorated with sleep deprivation. By contrast, brief tasks such as those measuring manual dexterity, reaction times and short-term memory recall show little reduction. They concluded that sleep-deprived doctors can cope well with acute short-term emergencies but will perform less well on routine or repetitive tasks that require sustained vigilance. This may be reassuring in one way – but as much of the workload of doctors is low-key and routine, these data actually suggest that fatigue is likely to result in errors in the routine work of doctors. Fatigue-related errors certainly happen. Gander, Merry, Millar *et al.* (2000), for example, reported on a survey of New Zealand anaesthetists in which 71 percent of trainees and 58 percent of trained anaesthetists said that they exceed what they considered their own limits of fatigue sufficient to affect patient safety; 86 percent of anaesthetists reported making fatigue-related errors at some time, while 32 percent recalled making one in the past six months.

IN THE SPOTLIGHT

More heads make worse decisions

Decisions may be affected by a number of factors beyond the consultation. Christensen, Larson, Abbott *et al.* (2000) examined the effect of group diagnostic decision making involving small teams of junior doctors and medical students. Information given to the groups was manipulated by asking the physicians to individually watch videos of actors acting as patients offering the same information to all those in the group, and some information unique to each viewer, including one viewer who was given information crucial to making a correct diagnosis.

Their results were interesting in that, once convened, the groups discussed the information common to all those involved more than they discussed the unique information held by each group member. As a result, they actually made more diagnostic errors than a control group of individual doctors given the same information. These data are particularly pertinent to making difficult diagnoses that may involve discussion by several doctors with information gleaned from a variety of different consultations or some medical specialties (particularly those involved in mental health), where information from many sources may be used to arrive at a diagnosis.

Following medical advice

Effective treatment of many medical conditions frequently requires the person with an illness to take an active role in any treatment programme. The most frequent requirement is that of taking prescribed medication at times and in sufficient quantities to provide a therapeutic dose. This may not be a simple task. Adherence to anti-retroviral HIV medication known as HAART (highly active anti-retroviral therapy), for example, is an extremely important and complex issue. Its basic form is as a combination of one protease inhibitor and two nucleoside reverse transcriptase inhibitors, which lead to reductions in viral load, greater immune system function and less likelihood of clinical immune deficiency. To achieve these benefits, people taking this medication not only have to take their medication on a daily basis, but they also have to take it within very tight time limits during the day. HAART medication may require different dosing schedules – some at twelve-, eight-, six-, or four-hour intervals. Some tablets need to be taken with food, some with fatty foods, some with non-fatty foods, and some on an empty stomach. Many result in serious side-effects that require taking further medication, and other medication may be required to treat opportunistic secondary infections. Not only is the required regimen for taking HAART complex, it may also take place in the absence of symptoms – indeed, it may cause more short-term symptoms than it appears to prevent. However, failure to stick to this regime can result in the virus mutating – with serious implications for both the individual involved and any person they may pass the mutated virus to. Patterson, Carlo, Kaplan *et al.* (1999) found that 81 percent of HIV-positive individuals with 95 or more percent adherence showed complete viral suppression, whereas only 64 percent of those with 90–95 percent adherence did so, and only 50 percent of those with 80–90 percent adherence. Only 30 percent of those with 80 percent adherence showed viral suppression. Despite these dire health consequences, many people prescribed this type of medication do not follow the drug regimen sufficiently closely for it to be effective. Malow, Baker, Klimas *et al.* (1998), for example, found that only 17 percent of their sample of inner-city living HIV-positive men fully adhered to their anti-retroviral medication.

The complexity of taking the anti-HIV regimen perhaps makes this a special case. However, adherence to much simpler drug regimens in serious illness is still mixed and may have significant implications for the individuals involved. About 10 percent of admissions to hospital are due to a failure to adhere to a recommended drug regimen (Schlenk, Dunbar-Jacob and Engberg 2004). Studies reveal relatively low levels of adherence to treatment recommendations across health states, treatments and ages (Dunbar-Jacob, Burke and Pucznski 1995). Indeed, as many as 60 percent of people with chronic disorders are poorly adherent to treatment. On average, it has been estimated that only half of those who are prescribed pharmacological therapies take enough doses of the medication to experience a therapeutic effect (e.g. Haynes, McKibbon and Kanani 1996). Looking at more specific disorders, Cramer (2004) reported adherence to **oral hypoglycaemic agents** of between 36 and 93 percent among patients prescribed the treatment for between six and twenty-four months. Between 50 and 70 percent of people are thought to adhere to treatments for hypertension (Caro, Speckman, Salas *et al.* 1999), although long-term adherence may be less good. Mallion, Baguet, Siche *et al.* (1998) noted a typical 50 percent reduction in adherence to anti-hypertensive medication over a one-year period. Adherence among people with asthma has been shown to be between 30 and 70 percent (Rand and Wise 1994).

Given the importance of taking these medications, one may wonder why people fail to take them. One simple explanation is that many people simply forget to take their medication or find their treatment regimen too complicated to cope with effectively. This may be particularly pertinent in the complex medical regimen associated with the treatment of HIV. Maggiolo, Ripamonti, Arici *et al.* (2002) found that 60 percent of failures of adherence

oral hypoglycaemic agents
various drug types, all of which reduce circulating blood sugar.

were associated with forgetfulness, 50 percent with being away from home, and 38 percent with problems with the drug schedule. Ley (1997) provided a simple rule of thumb in predicting adherence. Summarising the data, he suggested that non-adherence across all medications as a result of patient error alone is about 15 percent when one treatment is prescribed, 25 percent when two or more are prescribed, and 35 percent if five or more are prescribed. However, these data can be much more extreme. Kiernan and Isaacs (1981) reported that 75 percent of elderly patients were unable to recall accurately the recommended dosage of three tablets they were prescribed.

Other reasons for non-adherence may be more considered. One background factor that may determine much of our behaviour is that many people are inherently cautious about taking medication. Echabe *et al.* (1992) found that only 12 percent of a representative sample of nearly 1,000 people had a strong positive orientation towards medication, while 70 percent held what they termed an 'against medicine' orientation. A wide range of other factors have also been found to predict poor adherence to medication (e.g. Chesney 2003; O'Brien, Petrie and Raeburn 1992), including:

■ *social factors*: including low levels of education, unemployment and concomitant drug use, low levels of social support;

■ *psychological factors*: including high levels of anxiety and depression, use of emotion-focused coping strategies such as denial, a belief that continued use of a drug will reduce its effectiveness, taking drug holidays to prevent 'harm' as a consequence of long-term drug use;

■ *treatment factors*: including misunderstandings regarding treatment, complexity of the treatment regimen, high numbers of side-effects, little obvious benefit from taking medication, poor relationship between patient and healthcare provider, poor health professional–patient communication.

Another contextual factor that may affect adherence to medical regimens, particularly but not exclusively in children, are family systems. Tubiana Rufi *et al.* (1998), for example, found that children from families characterised as rigid, with low levels of cooperation and communication between family members, were more than six times less likely than children from families with more positive dynamics to adhere to insulin regimens to control their diabetes. Similar family dynamics have been associated with poor adherence to medication and dietary requirements associated with renal failure (Boyer, Friend, Chlouverakis *et al.* 1990). A further explanation why some people fail to follow medical advice is a denial of an illness or the expectation that things will get better without the need for medical intervention (Sherbourne, Hays, Ordway *et al.* 1992). Some people have argued that older people are less adherent to recommended treatment regimens than younger people. However, any age issues may be more apparent than real (Edelmann 1999). As older people tend to have more chronic diseases than younger people, any differences in adherence may reflect the problems of taking multiple prescriptions outlined by Ley above rather than being an age-related phenomenon.

A more theoretical perspective on adherence to medication can be provided by an extension of the health belief model (see Chapter 5). Horne (1997) has developed a model of adherence based on the health belief model used in combination with the illness representations model (Leventhal *et al.* 1992; see Chapter 9) to explain adherence). According to Horne's model,

adherence to medication is based on a combination of patients' beliefs about the nature of their illness and the treatment they are being given for it. Illness beliefs include understandings of the nature of the illness, its severity, cause, timeframe, likely prognosis and 'treatability'. Illnesses that are seen as minor, short-term and likely to self-remit may result in less use of active treatments than conditions that are seen as long-term and likely to benefit from treatment.

These issues form part of a cost-effectiveness equation that the patient considers when deciding whether or not to take any medication. The second arm of this deliberation involves an evaluation of the costs and benefits of taking any medication. These include consideration of how likely the treatment is to cure the condition and how 'costly' this is likely to be. Cost here usually involves, but is not limited to, consideration of the likely side-effects of the medication. Applying this model to a condition such as hypertension may explain why adherence to anti-hypertensive medication is frequently so low (Mallion, Baguet, Siche *et al.* 1998). Many people believe hypertension to be a short-term condition. It is symptom-free, so it is not clear to the patient that it is present for much of the time. Accordingly, people prescribed such medication may not see the need to take any medication over a long period of time. Add in a number of side-effects associated with this type of medication, such as dizziness or lightheadedness, dry mouth, constipation, drowsiness, headache and impotence, and the result is a scenario that involves patients taking medication for a condition they are not aware of having, which provides no obvious benefit, and which brings with it some unpleasant side-effects. Little wonder that adherence to such medication can be so low. Even in severe conditions such as HIV infection, these issues also hold. Siegel, Scrimshaw and Dean (1999) found that HIV-positive men and women stopped taking their anti-retroviral medication if they either considered it to make them sicker than their condition itself or if they considered it carried greater risks than benefits.

These assumptions may also interface with other factors – sometimes resulting in seemingly contradictory results. When a medical condition is severe, patients may in some cases actually welcome a treatment that brings high levels of side-effects – based on the belief that the treatment of severe illness needs to be sufficiently powerful that serious side-effects should be expected. Leventhal, Easterling, Coons *et al.* (1986), for example, found that some women who received chemotherapy for the treatment of breast cancer found the absence of side-effects distressing: their expectation was that treatment of serious illnesses involved serious side-effects, and the lack of them implied that the drug used was not sufficiently potent to cure their condition.

Improving adherence

■ Consultation factors

Most of the studies reviewed in the previous section have considered the issue of 'adherence' to medical recommendations or prescriptions. The implications of this label is that they have been prescribed by health professionals – patients have been told what to take and when to take it. They have not been the outcome of a negotiated agreement between health professional and

patient. Although data are lacking as yet, perhaps the best way to achieve high levels of adherence to prescribed medication is to establish a medication regimen about which the patient is fully informed and has been involved in its prescription.

In the absence of relevant data, we focus here on some key strategies that have been empirically validated and that remain relevant within a shared decision-making/patient-centred consultation framework. Ley (1988) suggested three strategies in the consultation that can increase knowledge about a condition and adherence to any recommended treatment:

1. maximise satisfaction with the process of treatment;
2. maximise understanding of the condition and its treatment;
3. maximise memory for information given.

Maximising satisfaction

Many of the communication skills noted in the discussion of the medical consultation and breaking bad news sections earlier in the chapter contribute to patient satisfaction and will not be reiterated here. Other factors that contribute to satisfaction include having sufficient time in the consultation to fully discuss relevant issues, seeing the same health professional on repeat visits, and good accessibility to health professionals. As noted above, patients report relatively low levels of satisfaction with health professionals who adopt a strong biomedical stance in the consultation and pay little regard for the social and emotional concerns that patients may bring to the consultation than with those that engage the individual and explore relevant social and psychological issues (Pendelton *et al.* 1984). Such a consultation style may relate to patient preferences for health professionals who work at building a relationship with the patient, and give more positive non-verbal behaviour and more positive talk (Hall, Roter and Katz 1988).

Maximising understanding

Many people leave a consultation without the information they want. This may be for a variety of reasons. Health professionals may lead the interview and, perhaps without realising it, inhibit the patient from asking questions. Alternatively, patients may not think through what information they want, or realise only after the interview what they could have asked. They may also be reluctant to ask questions of doctors who are still frequently seen as of a higher status than the patient. To avoid such lapses, a number of studies have examined whether preparing patients before a consultation can help them to ask questions to elicit information they want in the consultation. One study of this approach was reported by Jones, Pearson, McGregor *et al.* (2002), who evaluated the use of written lists of questions. They gave patients who were receiving radiotherapy for various cancers a sheet of paper with a single prompt inviting them to write questions they may wish to ask their doctor at their next appointment, some three weeks later. Forty-six percent of patients attended with a written list of questions. Their doctors considered 91 percent of the questions asked to be appropriate and to have led to a useful discussion; unfortunately, no such data were collected from the patients. In a similar study, Bruera, Sweeney, Willey *et al.* (2003) compared the effectiveness of giving a 'prompt sheet' providing suggested questions with a general information sheet given to women with breast cancer attending their first

out-patient consultation with a consultant. The prompt sheet was rated as more helpful than the information sheet by the women involved, but the women in this condition asked no more questions than those in the information-only condition. Nevertheless, these and other data suggest that encouraging patients to be actively involved in the consultation by prompting them to voice opinions or to ask clarifying questions will result in them achieving a greater understanding of their health problems and how these may best be treated. Advice given to people by the University of Michigan to maximise the effectiveness of their consultations with their medical services (www.mcare.org/healthathome/doctorpa.cfm) summarises the key issues well:

- Plan what you will say to the health professional about your problem ahead of time.

- Repeat in your own words what the health professional has told you. Use simple phrases like 'Do I hear you say that . . . ?' or 'My understanding of the problem is . . .'.

- Take notes on what is wrong and what you need to do.

- If you are confused by medical terms, ask for simple definitions. There is no need to be embarrassed by this. When a medication is prescribed, ask about its possible side-effects, its effectiveness and how long it must be taken. If your health professional discusses surgery, ask about alternatives, risks and a second opinion.

- Be frank with the health professional if any part of the office visit is annoying, such as lengthy waiting time or discourteous staff. Be tactful but honest.

- Don't be afraid to voice your fears about what you've heard. The health professional may be able to clarify any misconceptions.

- Discuss anything you've done that has relieved symptoms or that has made them worse.

- Find out the best time to call your health professional if you have any questions after you leave the office.

Maximising memory

Memory for information given in consultations is surprisingly poor. Ley (1997) summarised the relevant data, which suggested that half the information given in a consultation is almost immediately forgotten. In time, patients may even forget their own actions. Montgomery, Lydon, Lloyd *et al.* (1999), for example, reported that nearly a quarter of patients undergoing radiotherapy for the treatment of cancer could not recall having signed a consent form to permit the treatment, despite there being clear evidence that they had. Of those who did remember providing consent, a quarter could not remember being told about the side-effects of the treatment, while half could not remember being told that its most frequent side-effect is feelings of exhaustion.

The more information that is given in a consultation, the less it is likely to be remembered. Ley (1997) developed a simple 'rule of thumb', suggesting that 75 percent of information given in four statements is likely to be retained, but only 50 percent of information given in ten statements will be. However, a number of ways of providing information may enhance memory. Ley (1998), for example, suggested that information is best provided in a

structured form: 'I am going to tell you about three things . . . a, b and c', and using language and terms the patient can understand. The most important information should be given early or late in the flow of information to maximise primacy and recency effects, and its importance should be emphasised. Further strategies include repetition and the use of specific rather than general statements. To paraphrase part of his advice: 'Tell 'em what you're going to tell 'em, tell 'em, and tell 'em what you've told 'em'.

A second factor that may influence memory for information is the type of language used by the health professional. The use of technical language is particularly problematic. Lobb, Butow, Kenny *et al.* (1999), for example, found significant misunderstandings of information on prognosis and survival given to women diagnosed with breast cancer: not surprisingly, 73 percent of their sample did not understand the term 'median survival'; nor did the term 'good prognosis' carry a clear meaning. Even much simpler terms may not be understood by many patients. Words such as arthritis, jaundice, anti-emetic, dilated and haemorrhoids are not understood by nearly half the population (Ley 1997). Use of jargon may even result in significant anxiety. Abramsky and Fletcher (2002), for example, found that use of the words rare, abnormal, syndrome, disorder, anomaly and high risk in the context of genetic screening were particularly worrying to patients. They also found that risk for developing a disorder expressed as '1 in x' evoked more worry than when the same information was expressed as a percentage. These subtle uses of language show how careful healthcare professionals need to be in talking to patients.

A second way of maximising memory is through the provision of more permanent material, usually in the form of written information. This can have significant benefits over verbal information, the most obvious being that it provides an opportunity to give carefully prepared information presented in a way designed to be maximally effective. It provides a record that can be consulted to remind patients of salient information. Ideally, the potential content of any written information should be based on preparatory research with the patient group involved. This will increase the chances of any information being relevant and appropriate to its intended readership. An example of this is afforded by Glenton (2002), who conducted interviews with back pain sufferers in order to develop an information pack for people with back pain. Participants wanted to know about the causes of pain, information about diagnoses, diagnostic procedures and alternative treatment as well as information about the social and emotional costs of long-term pain, how to cope with everyday life, other people's experiences, and welfare rights.

The use of written information should take into account the same issues as those that relate to spoken information – it needs to be clear, jargon-free and at a level of complexity that is not so high as to make it unintelligible to the general population. With this in mind, the findings of Ley (1997) that about a quarter of published medical leaflets would be understood by only 20 to 30 percent of the adult population are of particular concern. In a similar study, Alexander (2000) reviewed American dental educational leaflets and found that 42 percent of them were written at a more complex level than could be understood by the majority of patients – many required a university-level education to understand them.

Permanent information need not necessarily be pre-prepared. Tattersall, Butow, Griffin *et al.* (1994), for example, compared the impact of an audiotape

of a consultation with that of individualised summary letters sent to patients after their first consultation with a cancer specialist. Patients listened to the tape an average of 2.3 times and read the letter 2.8 times over the following month. Ninety percent shared the contents of the tape or letter with a friend, relative or health professional. Both methods impacted equally on measures of recall, anxiety and depression. However, the audiotape proved the more popular method: when asked to rank six communication options, 46 percent of patients gave the highest rank to the tape and 21 percent to the letter.

Beyond the consultation

Whatever transpires in the consultation, patients have to be motivated and remember to take their medication or follow other advice in the hurly burly of their everyday life. Any intervention designed to maximise adherence has to take these contextual issues into account. McDonald, Garg and Haynes (2002) examined the effectiveness of thirty-nine interventions that did so and were designed to enhance adherence to medication in a variety of chronic health problems, including CHD, hypertension, asthma, chronic obstructive airways disease, HIV infection, rheumatoid arthritis and epilepsy. They concluded that the most effective interventions were generally complex and involved combinations of:

- convenient timing of drug taking;
- relevant information;
- reminders to take medications;
- self-monitoring (i.e. noting down when and where medication is taken);
- reinforcement of appropriate use of medication;
- family therapy.

They also noted that even the most effective interventions had 'modest' effects.

Perhaps the simplest approaches to increasing adherence are those targeted at what are assumed to be lapses in memory. One way that this can be addressed is through the use of reminders, although the outcome of such an approach is generally modest, particularly where the reminder does not occur at the time any medication is required to be taken. Guthrie (2001), for example, compared the effectiveness of postal or telephone reminders to take pravastatin, a drug used to reduce cholesterol levels. Patients who had had a myocardial infarction received either telephone or postal reminders to take their medication during the first two months of treatment. Adherence rates did not differ between patients receiving these interventions and a no-treatment control. Reminders that are closer to the time of taking the medication may be more effective, particularly where non-adherence is due to memory failure. Simple memory aids have been shown to reduce memory failures in elderly people (Cramer 1998). These include prescription of a simple dosage regimen, helping patients to select contextual cues to help them to remember to take medication (take with food or other daily routines), even alarms that go off at times to take medication. To simplify the process of taking medication, medication can be transferred to plastic medication boxes with compartments that are filled with the tablets to be taken at each time during the week. These can be filled by healthcare professionals or family members. Providing charts and organisers to remind people when to take their medication may also be of benefit (Park, Morrell, Frieske *et al.* 1992). One more high-tech approach has been to include microelectronic devices that measure whether a medication container is moved or opened. Failure to do so within certain time limits can result in electronic notification of healthcare providers, who then contact the patient to remind them of the need to take their medication (Cramer 1998). Providing a simple, easy-to-remember and action regimen can also be of benefit. Orrell, Bangsberg, Badri *et al.* (2003), for example, found that South African HIV-positive patients given a relatively simple anti-retroviral drug regimen, involving three daily doses, were three times more likely to be fully adherent than those on a more complex schedule.

A second group of interventions involves self-management programmes such as those discussed in Chapter 17. Here we consider self-management programmes specifically developed to increase adherence to medication regimens, focusing on one of the more complex regimens, that of using HAART medication. Safren, Otto, Worth *et al.* (2001) compared two different interventions in this context. The first intervention involved self-monitoring and use of a pill diary to record when each tablet was taken combined with visits to the clinic to provide feedback on medication use. A more active intervention, known as Life Steps, involved a single-session intervention involving an educational video, a motivational interview (see Chapter 6), training in planning medication schedules, cues to pill taking, and the use of guided imagery of successful adherence in response to daily cues. This may seem an overly complex process. However, it should be remembered that taking HAART medication can involve planning different types of meals and being in particular places at set times. Patients may even be taught skills to take pills surreptitiously so that no one knows they are taking them. With this in mind, this sort of training programme may not seem so excessive. Adherence was measured at two and twelve weeks following the intervention. They also examined a number of personal and social predictors of adherence. Both interventions led to improvements in adherence. However, among people with low levels of adherence, the Life Steps programme achieved these more quickly than the self-monitoring condition. It also appeared to improve adherence more than the self-monitoring programme in those people who were depressed – a particularly important finding, as depression was the one personal factor they found to be independently associated with non-adherence.

By contrast, a warning that some people can be particularly difficult to influence was provided by Martin, Sabugal, Rubio *et al.* (2001), who conducted a study comparing the effect of an educational intervention plus counselling with counselling alone to enhance adherence to HAART therapy. Seventy-four percent of those approached (many of whom were injecting drug users) refused to take part in the programme; 59 percent of those who refused to take part did so for 'personal reasons', while 33 percent did so because of trouble in their jobs. Those who were poor adherers to their HAART were most likely not to want to take part in the programme.

Increasing health professionals' adherence

It is not only patients who may benefit from following advice on what medication to take and when to take it. Health professionals are increasingly being asked to follow specific guidelines in the treatment of a variety of medical conditions. These are based on investigations of best practice and are intended to standardise treatment regimens wherever people are treated. Despite their empirical validity, many doctors do not adhere to them. As a consequence, a number of researchers have now begun to consider how best to get health professionals to adhere to their treatment guidelines. Ansari, Shlipak, Heidenreich *et al.* (2003), for example, compared two interventions to increase doctors' prescription of **β-blocker medication** in cases of heart failure. The first intervention involved educating doctors on the use of β-blockers in patients with heart failure combined with e-mailed information guidelines on the initiation and titration of the drug. A second group of doctors were sent a list of their patients who may benefit from β-blocker therapy, and computer alerts appeared when the doctor accessed these patients' electronic records for their next two visits. In addition, these doctors' patients were sent a letter informing them that they may be candidates for this therapy and that they should discuss this with their doctor at their next hospital visit. Interestingly, the first intervention proved the more effective: 67 percent of appropriate patients were placed and maintained on β-blockers in this condition, in comparison with 27 percent of those in the alerting condition and 16 percent in a control group who received no specific intervention. Perhaps doctors respond badly to interventions that are too direct and appear overly controlling.

β-blocker medication
a form of medication that acts to slow down and strengthen the heart contractions. Acts on the adrenergic receptors within the heart muscle.

Summary

The chapter has reviewed a number of issues related to how health professionals interact with patients and how this can influence the outcome of any treatment they may recommend. In the first section, we considered the shift from the paternal 'doctor knows best' type of consultation to more patient-centred approaches, and the ultimate outcome of this shift – shared decision making. It was noted that while the latter has many benefits, many patients are cautious in adopting it as it raises concerns over the apparent expertise of health professionals and may place a responsibility on patients for their treatment that they are unwilling to carry.

We went on to consider some other elements of the consultation that may influence its outcome, including:

■ the gender of the health professional – women appear more empathic and caring, factors usually associated with greater satisfaction with the interview;

■ the 'spin' given to information;

■ the input of the patient: people who ask more questions tend to gain more information from the consultation.

Breaking bad news involves telling patients that they have a serious illness, and that they may die from it. It is a stressful process for both patient and health professional. Key factors in optimising this process include:

■ Give the news in person, in private, with enough time and without interruptions.

- Find out what the patient knows about their diagnosis.
- Find out what the patient wants to know.
- Share the information, starting with a 'warning shot'.
- Respond to the patient's feelings.
- Plan and follow through.

Medical decision making can be influenced by a number of factors. Doctors often employ heuristics to help them to arrive at a diagnosis. This can speed the process up, but it increases the risk of diagnostic errors. Typical errors are those of:

- availability
- representativeness
- differing pay-offs of different diagnoses.

Adherence to recommended medical treatments is influenced by a number of factors, including:

- social factors
- psychological factors
- treatment factors
- family dynamics
- beliefs about the nature of the illness and its treatment regimen.

Adherence may be enhanced by:

- the use of patient-centred approaches and shared decision making;
- maximising satisfaction with the process of treatment;
- maximising understanding of the condition and its treatment;
- maximising memory for information given.

Beyond the consultation, these factors may be added to by a number of strategies, including:

- convenient timing of drug taking;
- relevant information;
- reminders to take medication;
- self-monitoring (i.e. noting down when and where medication is taken);
- reinforcement of appropriate use of medication.

Finally, consideration has to be given to the use of strategies to increase health professionals' adherence to professional issues, including the use of standardised medical treatment protocols. Just like their patients, some health professionals' behaviour may prove difficult to influence.

Further reading

Chesney, M. (2003). Adherence to HAART regimens. *AIDS Patient Care and STDs*, 17: 169–77.
An excellent review of issues related to adherence in the context of one of the most demanding and complex drug regimens – HAART therapy for the treatment of HIV infection.

Elwyn, G., Edwards, A., Kinnersley, P. and Grol, R. (2000). Shared decision making and the concept of equipoise: the competences of involving patients in healthcare choices. *British Journal of General Practice*, 50: 892–9.
A paper on the process of shared decision making by the leading UK research group.

Elstein, A.S. and Schwarz, A. (2002). Clinical problem solving and diagnostic decision making: selective review of the cognitive literature. *British Medical Journal*, 324: 729–32.
A useful insight into medical decision making.

Teutsch, C. (2003). Patient–doctor communication. *Medical Clinics of North America*, 87: 1115–45.
A substantial review of a variety of issues relating to communication with patients.

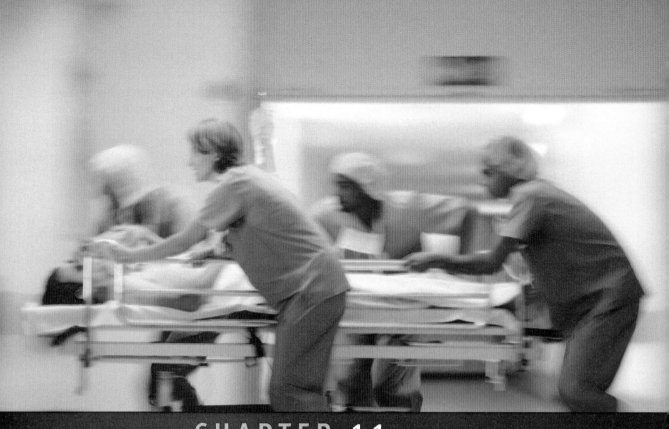

CHAPTER 11

Stress, health and illness: theory

Learning outcomes

By the end of this chapter, you should have an understanding of:

- stress as a stimulus (stressors)
- stress as a result of an interaction between an event and an individual
- the critical role of cognitive appraisal
- the nature of acute and chronic stress
- physiological processes invoked by the stress experience
- how stress manifests itself in various diseases

CHAPTER OUTLINE

The beginning of this chapter outlines the main thinking about stress in terms of nature and definition and highlights three main ways in which stress is studied: as a stimulus, as a transaction between a stimulus event and an individual's appraisal of it, and as a biological and physiological response. The psychological model of stress proposed by Richard Lazarus and his colleagues is described in detail to illustrate the central role of cognitive appraisal. This is done by examining how stress impacts upon us all in our living and working lives, and by examining acute and chronic stressors. The final part of the chapter provides evidence as to the physiological processes by which stress and our responses to it exert an influence on physical health, focusing particularly on cancer, CHD and HIV, although other illnesses are also covered. By the end of the chapter, the nature of stress and the processes by which it may impact on illness should be clear.

Concepts of stress

The term 'stress' is used very widely and with several meanings: everyone probably thinks they know what the term means, but few people define it in exactly the same way.

What do YOU think?

What does stress mean to you? What causes you to feel stressed? How do you respond?

Think of some recent events that you have experienced as stressful. Why was this? Reflect on your answers to these questions as the chapter progresses.

Stress has generally been examined in one of three ways: as a stimulus or event external to the individual; as a psychological transaction between the stimulus event and the cognitive and emotional characteristics of the individual; or as a physical or biological reaction. Each of these perspectives and their accompanying methodologies have their own strengths and weaknesses, which are outlined in the forthcoming sections.

Stress as a stimulus

In thinking of stress as a stimulus, researchers focus on stressful events themselves and on the external environment; i.e. a person will attribute their tension to an event or events such as moving house or getting married. The event and its properties are considered amenable to objective definition and measurement; for example, the event can be labelled (e.g. wedding) and aspects of it such as its proximity (e.g. next week, next year) can be assessed. Researchers taking this approach have studied the impact of a wide variety of stressors on individuals or groups, including *catastrophic events* such as earthquakes, floods or plane crashes, and more commonly, *major life events* such as losing one's job or starting a new job, getting married or divorced, giving birth, being bereaved, or going on holiday. Life events such as these are considered to require significant adjustment on the part of the person experiencing them, and they could include both positive and negative events (e.g. Pearlin 1983).

■ Life events theory

life events

a term used to describe occurrences in a person's life which may be viewed positively or negatively but which inherently require some adjustment on the part of the person (e.g. marriage, loss of job). Such events are implicated in the experience of stress.

The major proponents of this approach were Holmes and Rahe, who in 1967 proposed their **life events** theory. They proposed that naturally occurring life events did not simply have unitary consequences for a person but cumulative effects; in other words, the more life events one experienced, for example within the past year, the greater the likelihood of physical health problems. Furthermore, they claimed that specific kinds of event could be weighted against each other. To make these claims, Holmes and Rahe had carried out a series of interesting studies. First, they invited over 5,000 participants to generate a list of events that they found most stressful. Following this, Holmes and Rahe generated a representative list of forty-three commonly mentioned events, including positive, negative, frequent and rare events. They then asked a new sample of almost 400 people to rank the listed events in order of the degree of disruption the event, if experienced, had caused them. Furthermore, they asked participants to rate each event against marriage, which had arbitrarily been given a value of 500 by the researchers. For example, if divorce was considered by a respondent as requiring twice as much adjustment as marriage, it was given a value of 1,000. By averaging the ratings received for each event item and then ranking them, Holmes and Rahe were able to produce a scale known as the social readjustment rating scale (SRRS; Holmes and Rahe 1967; see Table 11.1), with values scaled out of 100 (maximum of 100 assigned to death of a spouse, which averaged out as the event requiring greatest adjustment). The values were called life change units (LCU). Social readjustment was defined as 'the intensity and length of time necessary to accommodate to a life event, *regardless of the desirability of this event*' (Holmes and Masuda 1974: 49), highlighting the fact that both positive events (e.g. marriage) and negative events (e.g. redundancy) would require some adjustment on the part of the individual. A subsequent study of eighty-eight physicians (Rahe 1974) found that the greater the LCU score the higher the risk of ill-health. Of the ninety-six major health changes reported by the participants, eighty-nine took place in individuals scoring over 150 LCUs; and when scores were greater than 300, over 70 percent of the physicians reported subsequent ill-health. Those individuals scoring less than 150 LCUs tended to report good health. Holmes and Masuda (1974) defined a *mild life crisis* as scoring between 150 and 199 LCUs, a *moderate life crisis* as scoring between 200 and 299 and a *major life crisis* as scoring over 300; they drew not only on their own work but also on that of other researchers of the time to support their hypothesis that life change could cause ill-health.

Limitations of life events measurement

The evidence of the associations between LCUs and ill-health (physical and/or mental) has been questioned (e.g. Dohrenwend and Dohrenwend 1982). Many of Holmes and colleagues' own studies, for example, relied on retrospective assessment, with participants who were already ill being asked to

Table 11.1 Representative life event items from the social readjustment rating scale and their LCUs

Event	LCU rating (1–100)
Death of a spouse	100
Divorce	75
Death of a close family member	63
Personal injury or illness	53
Marriage	50
Being fired from work	47
Retirement	45
Sex difficulties	39
Death of a close friend	37
Change to a different job	36
Foreclosure of mortgage or loan	30
Son or daughter leaving home	29
Outstanding personal achievement	28
Begin or end school	26
Trouble with boss	23
Change in residence	20
Change in social activities	18
Vacation	13
Christmas	12

Source: Holmes and Rahe (1967)

report whether or not they had experienced any life events prior to the onset of illness. In those studies employing prospective designs, the relationships found between life events and illness events were much weaker or non-existent. Other weaknesses exist in terms of the items included in the scale. For example, depending on your age, many of the listed events may not be applicable (divorce, childbirth, etc.). Some of the listed events may simply not occur with sufficient frequency to enable many individuals to report them or for their effects on health to be experienced (e.g. moving house, going to jail), and others may be intertwined and may cancel out, or enhance the effects of one another (for example, marriage requiring positive adjustments but co-inciding with a negatively perceived house move). Other events listed are vague and ambiguous; for example, reporting a 'change in social activities' could mean many things. Finally, allocating LCUs to events assumes that all people rank events in a similar way. However, think of divorce. For some people this will be a positive event reflecting the end of an unsatisfactory relationship, while for others it will be a devastating and possibly unexpected blow. The life events approach to stress therefore fails to systematically address the many factors (internal and external) that may moderate the relationship between stressful events and illness events. Chapter 12 describes many of these factors in depth.

In spite of many limitations, this body of work highlighted the fact that major life events can be stressful, and many prospective longitudinal studies continue to assess the life event experience of those studied on the basis that it may influence other variables of interest to their studies: for example, adjustment to an illness may be undermined by the occurrence of major life changes.

Life hassles

In addition to major and often rare life events, research has highlighted the stressful nature of daily *hassles*. Kanner, Coyne, Schaefer *et al.* (1981: 3) defined hassles as 'irritating, frustrating, distressing demands that to some degree characterize everyday transactions with the environment' and measured such things as not having enough money for food or clothing, losing things, being overloaded with responsibilities, making silly practical mistakes, or having a row with a partner. Unlike major life events, hassles do not generally require major adjustment on the part of the person experiencing them. Their impact was thought to be particularly evident if they were frequent, chronic or repeated over a particular period of time. To test this proposal, Kanner and colleagues developed a tool to assess daily hassles and found that they strongly associated with negative mental and physical outcomes even when major life events were controlled for. Positively rated events, described as 'uplifts' (e.g. getting away with something, completing a task, getting or giving a present or compliment, having a laugh) were acknowledged more thoroughly in this theory than in life events theory. Kanner studied three groups of people – middle-aged, professionals and students – and found that these groups differed in the importance they attached to particular events, in particular the importance they attached to economic concerns, work and time pressures, and social hassles. In terms of uplifts, the groups differed in their weighting of having good health, spending time with family, and hedonistic items such as socialising and having fun. This raises the important question of *how* events are perceived and appraised, and the influence that life stage or role can have upon perceptions of potential stressors. This approach is therefore moving away from considering stress simply in terms of the stimulus.

Kanner also reports a curious gender difference whereby women experienced psychological symptoms following uplifts as well as hassles, whereas men were unaffected by uplifts, suggesting perhaps that women are affected by 'change' in either a positive or negative direction. These findings highlight the need to acknowledge the individual variation in response to events. Two people could experience the same number of events and weight them equally but experience very different health outcomes. Why could this be? It has also been suggested that only negatively rated hassles lead to adverse outcomes and that positive uplifts may 'moderate' the impact of negative events (e.g. Cohen and Hoberman 1983), but the evidence for this is not conclusive. This is an issue we return to in Chapter 12.

If health outcomes are indeed affected by such events, what are the processes (psychophysiological or behavioural) by which this occurs? The stress-as-a-stimulus approach has proved attractive to many epidemiologists, who aim to identify significant stressful events and to calculate their effect on adverse health outcomes, for example studies of the effects of unemployment on morbidity and mortality (e.g. House *et al.* 1982, 1987). However, such studies do not tell us *how* unemployment affects illness or even death rates, or *why* it may in some people but not others (Marmot and Madge 1987). To answer the 'how' question leads us to consider physiological theories of stress (stress manifest in biological responses), whereas to answer the 'why' question requires consideration of psychological theories of stress (involving cognitive appraisal and emotion). One interesting study pointing to the physiological correlates of stress is provided by Burns, Carroll, Drayson *et al.*

(2003). These authors studied the effects of minor and major life events on the antibody response to influenza vaccination among a sample of undergraduate students followed up for five months. They found that participants with low antibody levels at five months after vaccination had reported significantly more life events in the intervening period. Although a relatively small-scale study, this points to important physiological pathways by which life event stress may operate its effects on health outcomes, and in this case, if replicated in larger studies, would have implications for the long-term success of vaccination programmes. Further research identifying physiological pathways involved in the stress process are discussed fully in a later section, but first we turn to the psychological explanations.

Stress as a transaction

According to psychological theory, stress is a subjective experience, an internal state of being that may or may not be considered by an outside observer as being appropriate to the situation that evoked the response. As John Milton (1608–74) put it when he wrote *Paradise Lost*: 'The mind is its own place, and in itself can make a heaven of hell, a hell of heaven'. This points to what has become the central tenet of psychological theories of stress: that appraisal is central to whether or not an event is deemed to be a stressor or not. The key figure in this domain is Richard Lazarus, who with colleagues (e.g. Lazarus and Launier 1987; Lazarus and Folkman 1984) proposed what is called a cognitive transactional model of stress. Evidence of the importance of psychological processes was drawn from early experimental studies of Lazarus and colleagues (e.g. Speisman *et al.* 1964), which quite simply exposed student participants to stressful films while monitoring self-reported stress levels and physiological arousal (i.e. heart rate and skin conductance). One example included a gruesome video about tribal initiation rites that included genital surgery. Before the film, participants were divided into four experimental conditions, each of which received different introductions and soundtracks. One group heard an intellectual description of the rites from a cultural perspective (to mimic a **distancing response**); another heard a lecture that de-emphasised the pain the 'willing' initiates were experiencing and emphasised the excitement they were feeling (to mimic a **denial response**); another heard a narrative that emphasised the pain and trauma the initiates were undergoing (to emphasise the perceived threat); and a control group received no information or soundtrack. Results showed quite clearly that the introductions influenced the way in which the film was seen, reflected in both self-reported stress and skin conductance, with the first and second groups (distancing and denial) showing significantly less stress than group 3. While these studies were initially intended to address the idea of 'ego defences' (i.e. what people do to protect themselves from threat), Lazarus realised that appraisal processes were mediating stress responses, and hence his subsequent work developed a theory of stress that is today one of the most influential in health psychology.

According to Lazarus, stress is a result of an interaction between an individual's characteristics and appraisals, the external or internal event (stressor) environment, and the internal or external resources a person has available to them. Motivational and cognitive variables are considered

distancing response
taking a detached view, often a scientific view, of an event or stimulus in order to reduce emotional activation.

denial response
taking a view that denies any negative implications of an event or stimulus. If subconscious, it is considered a defence mechanism.

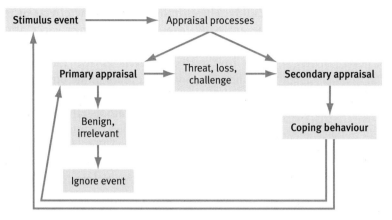

Figure 11.1 Lazarus's early transactional model of stress.
Source: adapted from Lovallo (1997: 77)

appraisals
interpretations of situations, events or behaviour that a person makes.

central. Lazarus's initial model maintained that when individuals confront a new or changing environment they engage in a process of **appraisal**, which is of two types: primary and secondary.

■ Primary appraisal processes

In primary appraisal, a person considers the quality and nature of the stimulus event. Lazarus distinguished three kinds of possible stressor: those that pose harm, those that threaten and those that set a challenge. Harm is considered as damage that has already been done, i.e. a loss or failure; threat is the expectation of future harm; and challenge results from demands that are appraised as opportunities for personal growth or opportunities that a person is confident about dealing with. Events that are not appraised as either harm, threat or challenge are considered to be benign events that require no further action. The questions asked of oneself are along the lines of 'Is this event something I have to deal with?', 'Is it relevant to me?' 'If so, what is at stake?' 'Is it a positive, negative or neutral event? If potentially or actually negative, then is it posing me harm/threat or challenge?' Simultaneously to making these appraisals, emotions may arise that elicit various physiological responses, as we shall describe later.

■ Secondary appraisal processes

At the same time as carrying out primary appraisals, Lazarus proposed that secondary appraisals are initiated whereby one assesses one's resources and abilities to cope with the stressor (coping potential). The questions asked of oneself at this stage are of the type: 'How am I going to deal with this?' 'What can I use or call upon to help me?' Resources can be either internal (e.g. strength, determination) or external (e.g. social support, money).

Using forthcoming exams as an example, various appraisal judgements may be made; for example:

■ There is no way I can possibly deal with this. I simply know I will fail (threat + no resources = stress).

- This will be really hard. I just am not as clever as the other students (threat + limited internal resources = stress).
- Maybe I can manage this if I revise really hard (challenge + possible internal resources = stress).
- I could perhaps do it if I get some help from my friends (challenge + external resources = less stress).
- This isn't a problem. I know the material really well (benign).
- I managed to pass the last time, I'll be okay this time (benign).

Lazarus's early work maintained that stress would be experienced when perceived harm or threat was high but perceived coping ability was low, whereas when perceived coping ability was appraised to be high (i.e. resources were considered to be available to deal with the threat) then stress was likely to be minimal. In other words, stress arose from a mismatch between perceived demands and resources, both of which could change over time. It is important that stress is viewed as a dynamic process.

■ Developments in Lazarus's framework

In the 1990s, Lazarus increasingly considered the stress process as part of the wider domain of emotions and modified his cognitive appraisal theory of stress accordingly (Lazarus 1991a). He also collaborated with an eminent colleague at this time (Smith and Lazarus 1993), although the two academics differed slightly in the components of appraisal proposed. Smith proposed that primary appraisal consists of two sequential assessments: one of *motivational relevance*, i.e. the extent to which the event is considered relevant to one's current goals or commitments; the other of *motivational congruence*, i.e. the extent to which the situation is perceived to be congruent with current goals. Stress was likely in situations where relevance was high and congruence was low. This is illustrated below:

APPRAISAL	
motivational relevance	motivational congruence
'The proposed class test is important to my studies'	*'I would prefer to party'*
high relevance	low congruence

Lazarus also included in primary appraisal an appraisal of *ego involvement*, whereby appraisals of threat to one's sense of self or social esteem would elicit anger, events violating one's moral codes would result in guilt, and any existential threat would create anxiety.

Removing threat/challenge and harm/loss appraisals from the core cognitive definition of primary appraisal and instead attaching them to emotion types is important to how we think about stress. Prior to this, it had often been overlooked that appraisals associate with emotions, yet it makes intuitive sense. For example, appraising an event as a threat is likely to precede the emotion of fear, whereas a loss appraisal is likely to precede the emotion of sadness (Smith and Lazarus 1993). Less well articulated are the appraisals associated with positive emotions, but positive appraisals such as that of benefit, gain or challenge may precede emotions such as joy or hope. An

Plate 11.1   Both negatively and positively perceived events may trigger physiological arousal suggestive of a stress response. Here we see a young woman engaging in a high-risk activity that could be considered as positive stress, or 'eustress'.

Source: Alamy/Aflo Foto

Table 11.2   Appraisal-related emotions (Lazarus 1993)

- *Loss/harm*: sadness, depression, despair, hopelessness
- *Threat*: anxiety, fear, anger, jealousy
- *Challenge*: worry, hope, confidence

early stress researcher, Hans Selye (1974), generally known for his work on physiological responses to stressful stimuli (see later section), had distinguished between good and bad stress; between 'eustress', i.e. good stress associated with positive feelings or healthy states, and 'distress', i.e. the bad kind of stress associated with negative feelings and disturbed bodily states. Although he did not detail how these two types of stress differed in terms of physiological response, their distinction remains an important one, and research attempts such as those examining the emotions attached to different forms of stress appraisal go some way towards addressing this distinction.

Also in working with Smith, secondary appraisal became more complex, consisting of four assessments (Smith) or three (Lazarus):

1. *Internal/external accountability* (*'blame/credit'*, *Lazarus*): concerned with attributing responsibility for the event. Is seen to distinguish between emotions of anger (other-blame) and guilt (self-blame). Credit is less studied than blame but may associate with emotions such as pride.

2. *Problem-focused coping potential*: considers the extent to which the situation is perceived as changeable by instrumental (practical, problem-focused) coping options. If not perceived as changeable, the emotions of fear and anxiety will be elicited.

3. *Emotion-focused coping potential*: concerned with perceiving an ability to cope emotionally with the situation. Perceptions of not being able to cope are associated with fear, anxiety or sadness.

4. *Future expectancy concerning situational change*: refers to perceived possibilities of the situation being changeable. Sadness is associated with perceptions of unchangeability.

Lazarus merged 2. and 3., referring simply to 'coping potential'.

The important factor to hold on to from these developments in Lazarus's theory is that the role of emotions is being addressed as well as the cognitions, with both aspects interlinked in an ongoing and dynamic transaction. Furthermore, this theory proposes that emotional impressions of events are stored in memory and will influence how we appraise the same event in any future encounters.

■ Criticism of Lazarus's framework

There appear to be many advantages of the transactional approach and its cognitive appraisal theory; it is compatible with both biological and social models, acknowledging as it does the role of the stimulus, of emotional and behavioural responses, of individual differences, and of the external environment. Certainly, in the psychological literature there is a large body of supporting empirical evidence, and few studies of coping with stress or illness are conducted without acknowledging the central role of individual difference variables and appraisals. This will become quite evident in the subsequent chapter. However, no model or theory escapes without criticism, as this is one way in which academic understanding is advanced. Some have criticised Lazarus's framework for its circularity. For example, limited research has attempted to examine the nature of interaction between primary and secondary appraisals, i.e. between perceived demands and perceived coping resources. Demand and coping capacity are not defined separately, leading to claims of the model being tautological (Hobfoll 1989) – put simply, this means that whether an event is demanding or not depends on perceived coping capacity, and whether coping capacity is perceived as adequate or not is dependent on perceived demand. Furthermore, it is unclear whether both primary and secondary appraisal are necessary; for example, Zohar and Dayan (1999) found positive mood outcomes in their sample to be affected mainly by coping potential variables and not by primary appraisal variables. Additionally, they found that stress arose and increased as the stakes or motivational relevance of an event increased, even in situations where coping potential was not restricted. They noted that any slight uncertainty about coping potential modified the effect of 'stakes' (primary appraisal) on stress. Imagine, for example, a situation where a person believes that their forthcoming mid-term examination is a 'mock' and does not count towards their final grade, but on turning up to the exam they are told that it is not a 'mock' but a 'real' exam. In spite of having revised the exam subject seriously and having no major concerns about the topic and their ability to answer the questions, this new situation is likely to be appraised differently because its value has changed (raised stakes), and the stress experience will therefore also change (increase), even though their resources (secondary appraisals of coping potential) have not. Such findings point to a need for further research

investigating the interaction between primary and secondary appraisals, and whether the assumption that demands need to outweigh resources in order for stress to be experienced can be upheld.

■ What factors influence appraisal?

Although Chapter 12 will deal with the personal and interpersonal influences on appraisals and stress responses, there are many aspects of the stimulus event itself that can influence the appraisals a person makes.

■ events that are *imminent* (e.g. test results due the next day; driving test tomorrow rather than next month);

■ events that occur at an *unexpected time* in life (e.g. being widowed in one's 30s compared with when in one's 70s; the death of a child);

■ events that are *unpredictable* in nature (e.g. being made redundant);

■ events that are *ambiguous* in terms of

■ personal role (e.g. starting a new job);

■ potential risk or harm involved (e.g. undergoing surgery or taking a new medication);

■ events that are *undesirable* (e.g. having to move house because of job loss and not through choice);

■ events over which the individual perceives *no control* (behavioural or cognitive);

■ events that elicit high amounts of *life change* (e.g. childbirth, relocation).

The nature of potential stressors therefore varies hugely, from, for example, receiving a final demand for an unpaid bill to being a victim of a natural disaster, from having a head cold to receiving a diagnosis of a life-threatening illness. As illustrated above, certain features of events have been found to increase the likelihood of their being appraised as stressful. Further distinction has been drawn (e.g. Sapolsky 1994: 5) between acute physical stressors, which demand immediate physiological adaptation (e.g. being attacked); chronic physical stressors (e.g. being ill or surviving in a hostile environment); long-term physiological demands that we are not so good at dealing with, such as pain; and psychosocial stressors, which involve our cognitions, emotions and behavioural responses as well as the physiological arousal that will be triggered. Many psychologists would argue that all three types described above are in fact psychosocial as they involve more than simply the event or stimulus.

Types of stress

Stress and resource loss

Hobfoll (1989) proposed a 'conservation of resources' model of stress whereby individuals are assumed to work to conserve or protect their valued resources (e.g. objects, roles, personal characteristics such as self-esteem, energy, time, money, skills). Hobfoll suggests that stress will result when there is actual or threatened loss of resources or a lack of gain after investing

resources. Resources are thought to be quantifiable and 'real' and therefore 'mean' the same to all people when they are lost. This therefore de-emphasises the role of individual appraisal, central to Lazarus's model. Hobfoll states that the more resources are lost, the more difficult it becomes to replace them, and the resulting stress will be greater. This quantification of resources fits with the kind of evidence discussed in Chapter 2, i.e. that of socio-economic deprivation, unemployment and poverty, all of which are found to associate with illness, independent of the individual's appraisals. By focusing on loss of quantifiable entities rather than appraisals, this model avoids any difficulties in distinguishing appraisals from responses. However, Marks, Murray, Evans *et al.* (2000) point out that the loss and resource constructs are not particularly well defined or easy to measure, and that many questions remain unanswered by this model. For example, how permanent must loss be for a person to experience stress? Does the speed and extent of resource loss matter? Is resource gain never stressful? (Some lottery winners would perhaps challenge this.)

Hobfoll (1991) found that rapid and extensive depletion of valued resources, such as that experienced following a natural disaster, was associated with traumatic stress responses. Natural disasters are generally acute-onset stressors, but many may have long-term consequences. Examples of other acute stressors are given below.

Acute stress

Studies of acute-onset stress generally distinguish between stimulus events that are rare but cataclysmic and more common acute stressors, such as exams.

■ Cataclysmic events

Earthquakes, hurricanes and air disasters are rare events that allow a person little or no preparation time. Natural catastrophes, such as the Asian tsunami in 2004, and technological disasters such as the nuclear meltdown at Chernobyl in 1986, produce intense physical and psychosocial suffering for victims and for the 'worried well', i.e. those not actually in the disaster but affected by it in that it raises issues for them about their own personal safety and future. Environmental stress theory (Fisher, Bell and Baum 1984; Baum 1990) considers stress to be a combined psychological and physiological response to demands, and support for this can be found in the many psychological and physical symptoms reported in survivors of a natural calamity. These include:

- initial panic
- anxiety
- phobic fear
- vulnerability
- guilt (survivor guilt)
- isolation
- withdrawal (including some suicide attempts)
- anger and frustration
- interpersonal and marital problems
- disorientation
- lack of attachment

Plate 11.2   Environmental events, such as the Asian tsunami, have devastating short-term effects, as shown above, but also have serious long-term effects for survivors, some of whom will experience post-traumatic stress disorder (PTSD).

Source: Rex Features/Cameron Laird

- loss of sense of security
- sleep disturbances
- eating disturbances.

The severity and duration of these effects seem to depend on the magnitude of the loss. In addition to this long list of possible outcomes, some people continuously relive the event in distressing dreams and/or suffer from 'flashbacks'. Such symptoms may lead to the individual being diagnosed as suffering from post-traumatic stress disorder (PTSD; see Chapter 13).

Hobfoll's 'conservation of resources' model of stress was applied in a study of lost resources or 'losses' among 135 individuals assessed following Hurricane Andrew in the United States (Benight, Ironson, Klebe *et al.* 1999). This study also investigated the extent to which **coping self-efficacy** (cf. Bandura 1986) determined stress responses and the ability of individuals to recover from their losses by employing their remaining coping resources. Coping self-efficacy was specific to the ability to meet needs following the hurricane, and losses were focused on loss of material resources rather than psychological resources, although both were assessed. Overall, the results confirmed a positive association between loss of resource, coping self-efficacy and subsequent distress. Resource loss was positively associated with long-term distress, with active coping efforts mediating this relationship and reducing the distress experienced.

This study highlights that quantifiable resource loss is in itself distressing, but that appraisals related to coping ability also play a significant role. Such findings highlight that acute-onset stressors can have chronic effects on a person's psychological wellbeing. Interventions to minimise distress therefore need to be targeted appropriately, with, for example, in the case of Hurricane Andrew survivors, interventions having best effect if they target both the restoration of lost resources (e.g. housing, water, clothing) and the self-

coping self-efficacy
the belief that one can carry out a particular coping response in a given set of circumstances.

efficacy beliefs of the victims. Stress management and coping-based interventions are discussed fully in Chapter 13.

■ Exam stress

Cohen, Evans, Stokols *et al.* (1986) found that high levels of stress can impair people's memory and attention during cognitive activities. For example, many students report the experience of having the answer to questions on the tip of their tongue, and even memories of revising it the night before, but being unable to remember it once in the exam setting. Others will misread and misinterpret clearly written questions. It has been found that there is an optimum level of arousal necessary to maintain attention and memory, but that too little arousal, or too much, can be detrimental to one's performance. This is known as the Yerkes–Dodson law, first described in 1908 (see Figure 11.2). An exam, the result of which is desired and valued, will generally elicit more arousal than an exam that is not; but the key to good performance lies in not becoming over-aroused so that all the learning goes to waste and the mind empties in the exam room.

Exams have been found to influence healthy and unhealthy behaviour such as smoking, snacking, alcohol consumption and exercise (e.g. Ogden and Mtandabari 1997), and stress arising from both educational factors and family factors predicted smoking among adolescent girls only (Byrne and Mazanov 2003). This association between stress and behaviour is an indirect route by which stress can be considered to influence illness status. Exam stress has also been found to affect bodily responses, such as blood pressure, which was found to increase among medical students on the day of their exams (Sausen *et al.* 1992). This kind of study is required to continuously assess physical indices of **stress reactivity** (such as blood pressure) in order to achieve multiple baselines against which to assess increases and decreases in blood pressure over time and during different activities. To obtain such data, Sausen and colleagues employed ambulatory monitoring techniques whereby devices attached to individual participants activated at set and regular intervals to read blood pressure.

stress reactivity
the physiological arousal, such as increased heart rate or blood pressure, experienced during a potentially stressful encounter.

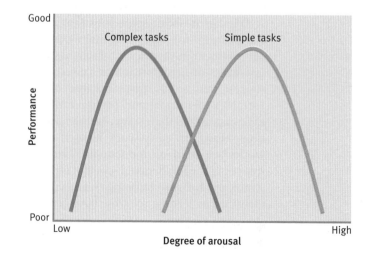

Figure 11.2 The Yerkes–Dodson law
Source: Rice (1992: 5)

A link between acute stressors such as exams and actual illness (rather than focusing on physiological reactivity, which is generally short-lived and poses no danger to the individual) has been proposed following findings that students exhibit increased prevalence of infections at exam periods compared with during non-assessment periods. These studies often include blood sampling and have examined immunological markers of the type discussed in a later section (e.g. Glaser, Rice, Sheridan *et al.* 1987). Exams appear to be, for many, sufficiently stressful to increase susceptibility to illness, via immunosuppressant effects.

Chronic stress

▪ Occupational stress

The workplace is a good environment in which to study the chronic effects of stress, although many other environmental situations have been studied, for example traffic jams and road rage, noise pollution, and overcrowding on public transport (Fisher, Bell and Baum 1984; Topf 1989). Loss of control in these situations appears to play a crucial role in the stress experienced (for discussion of this construct see Chapter 12). Most working individuals will experience workplace stress at some point, and while for many the stress is short-lived or manageable, for others it is chronic and damaging, being accompanied, for example, by changes in eating or sleep patterns, fatigue, or strain on personal relationships. Occupational stress has also been associated with 'burn-out' (Maslach 1982, 1997). Burn-out is considered to be the outcome of chronic long-lasting job stress and is seen as similar to the final stage of Selye's general adaptation syndrome: i.e. exhaustion, both mental and physical. Maslach defined burn-out as a three-part syndrome of emotional exhaustion, depersonalisation and reduced personal accomplishment that occurs among individuals who work with people in some capacity, and which can be associated with both physical and mental ill-health (Maslach 1997). Related to burn-out is the concept of carer strain or carer burden, commonly studied among those individuals that care for relatives with a chronic illness or condition such as Alzheimer's disease. This condition is discussed in Chapter 15, where we explore the impact of illness on family and friends.

What is it about some jobs that makes them so stressful? One possible explanation for stress in the work environment is offered by person–environment fit theories (cf. French, Caplan and Van Harrison 1982), or the 'goodness-of-fit' approach described by Lazarus (1991b). Such approaches suggest that stress arises because of a mismatch between environmental variables (demands) and person variables (resources). 'Fit' is considered as dynamic rather than static, in that demands and resources can change over time. However, early work focused more on environmental features of the workplace than on individual difference variables, a primary example of this being the job demand–control (JDC) model of occupational stress, or job strain, put forward by Karasek and colleagues (1979, 1981). The job features identified as leading to stress have been identified as:

- ▪ demand
- ▪ controllability
- ▪ predictability
- ▪ ambiguity.

Table 11.3 Examples of items to assess work-related stress

	Never	Rarely	Sometimes	Often	Most times
Demand					
■ My workload is never-ending					
■ Job deadlines are constant					
■ My job is very exciting					
Control					
■ I have autonomy in carrying out my duties					
■ There are too many bosses					
Predictability					
■ My job consists of responding to emergencies					
■ I am never sure what will be expected of me					
Ambiguity					
■ My job is not very well defined					
■ I am not sure about what is expected of me					

Source: adapted from Rice (1992: 188–2).

Each of these broad features can be assessed with specific questions, as illustrated in Table 11.3. Chronic ongoing stressors such as permanently excessive workload demands are thought to create stress in employees, as are sudden, unexpected requests or interruptions, being pushed to make a decision, or being unclear as to what is expected of one.

Karasek's model proposed that a combination of demand and control would determine whether or not the employee experienced stress (high demand and low control contributing to higher stress–strain than would situations of high demand and high control) (Karasek and Theorell 1990). While it was initially thought that perceived or actual control acted as a moderator of demand (in other words, that control 'buffered' the negative effects of demands), reviews of studies using the JDC model between 1979 and 1997 (van der Doef and Maes 1998, 1999) found only minimal evidence that either control or social support moderated the negative impact of high work demands upon wellbeing, or upon burn-out (Rafferty, Friend and Landsbergis 2001). It appears that demand and control have independent and direct effects on stress outcomes.

Attempts to challenge or resolve issues of overload, underload or ambiguity of role are not always easy or feasible in many workplaces, and coping behaviour, for example among police officers, has been found to include damaging health behaviour (e.g. excessive alcohol consumption) and absenteeism (e.g. Alexander and Walker 1994). These responses carry huge costs for employers in terms of loss of productivity, staffing shortages and accidents in the workplace (Cooper and Payne 1988). Interestingly, underload, as well as overload, has been found stressful with frustration and boredom proving as stressful for some employees as overload (French, Caplan and Van Harrison 1982).

Some models of occupational stress have succeeded in integrating what the individual brings to the workplace in terms of personal characteristics, cognitions and support resources with the environmental features (see RESEARCH FOCUS).

Demand–control–support models of occupational stress

Morrison, V., Cottrell, L., Dawson, J., Jere, C., Jones, V. and Waddon, A. (2005, in prep)
Stress, efficacy and support use amongst police staff.

Background

Karasek's demand–control/decision latitude model of occupational stress (job demand–control model, JDC) has been tested and has proved useful in many studies. However Johnson, Hall and Theorell (1989) proposed that control needs to be specified better and that social support, or lack of it, needed to be added to the model (see Searle *et al.* 2001; Van der Doef and Maes 1999 for reviews). The resulting model is known as the job demand–control–support model (JDCS). Over 100 studies have been carried out using the expanded model and as a result increasing attention is being paid to aspects of the individual that are potentially more amenable to intervention, such as skills, self-belief or the use of social support. Several studies of occupational stress have been carried out among police force staff in a range of countries (e.g. Germany: Kirkcaldy and Cooper 1992; Britain: Brown, Cooper and Kirkcaldy 1996; Wales: Morrison *et al.* 2002; New Zealand: Stephens *et al.* 1997; Scotland: Biggam *et al.* 1997; the Netherlands: Kop *et al.* 1999), an occupation considered to be inherently stressful due to operational, bureaucratic and interpersonal demands.

Aims

Morrison *et al.*, in a study of 699 police officers and 230 support personnel, investigated the personal and occupational sources of stress and set out to identify whether personal resource variables such as self-efficacy and home- and workplace-based support moderated perceived stress and emotional distress.

Methods used

A semi-structured questionnaire was employed that gathered information on position and length of employment in the police force, open-ended comments on a recent occupational and a recent interpersonal stressor, assessed optimism (LOT, Scheier and Carver 1985), self-efficacy (GSES, Jerusalem and Schwarzer 1992), perceived social support at home and in the workplace, perceived stress (single item), and distress (GHQ-12, Goldberg 1992).

Results

Perceived stress and emotional distress were significantly associated with low levels of dispositional optimism, low self-efficacy (a perceived control construct), and low levels of social support at home and in the workplace. Levels of stress and distress were high in both support staff and police officers. Significant differences emerged in the levels of stress reported by rank, with those employed in mid-high ranks, such as sergeants and above, reporting higher stress than junior-ranked constables. Rank was also significantly correlated with levels of support used in the workplace, with higher ranks reporting lower levels of access to, and use of, workplace support. Home support was associated with lower stress among support staff, whereas work-based and home support were important to reduced stress among police staff. The personal resources of self-efficacy and optimism were found to moderate stress levels, with females benefiting particularly from high self-efficacy (although as a group females had lower self-efficacy than male colleagues). Support staff generally had lower levels of self-efficacy beliefs than police staff. Occupational stressors were generally identified as being bureaucracy-associated (increased paperwork, poor communication with managers) among mid-low ranked staff and additionally job overload related in terms of increasing levels of unpaid overtime and the need to take work home among higher-ranked personnel.

Conclusions

Interventions to reduce workplace stress may need to address different factors dependent on rank and gender. For female staff, interventions may benefit from targeting self-efficacy beliefs and for higher ranks there is a need for enhanced provision of workplace support resources. Furthermore, findings point to differences in the use and benefits of different sources of social support dependent on rank, with higher ranks being more likely to use external sources than workplace-based sources.

We have thus far established that stress responses arise from events and from appraisals of these events, but we have not yet described what happens following these cognitive or emotional processes. Lazarus's transactional model of stress posits that appraisals and their attached emotions lead to cognitive and behavioural coping efforts, and in Chapter 12 coping theory and the role of coping in moderating stress outcomes is discussed fully. However, in addition to psychological stress responses there are also biological and physiological responses, and it is to this growing area of research that we now turn our attention.

Stress as a physiological response

Thinking of stress as a response takes us into the domain of seeking biological or physiological explanations of how stress affects the body and potentially illness; the assumption here is that stressors place demands on the person that are manifested in some response; in physics, this response would be termed 'strain'. Proponents of the 'response' model of stress describe how individuals react to danger or potentially harmful situations or even pleasant demands with a coordinated physiological and behavioural response (e.g. Cassel 1974, cited in Leventhal and Tomarken 1987). Initially, an event has to be appraised, and this involves the **central nervous system** (CNS). The sensory information and the appraisal of the event combine to initiate autonomic and endocrine responses, which feed back to the cortex and limbic system, which in turn links with the hypothalamus and brainstem. It has been found that, for example, appraising an event as *unpredictable* in nature affects various aspects of physiological activation (Zakowski 1995).

central nervous system that part of the nervous system consisting of the brain and spinal cord.

These processes are summarized below, although Chapter 8 provides greater physiological definition and detail.

Early work on the stress response

An early researcher, Walter Cannon (1932), outlined the role of catecholamines (adrenaline and noradrenaline), which, when released from the adrenal glands of the **sympathetic nervous system** as hormones, heighten arousal in order to facilitate the 'fight or flight' response. When faced with

sympathetic nervous system

the part of the autonomic nervous system involved in mobilising energy to activate and maintain arousal (e.g. increased heart rate).

imminent danger or a high level of threat (such as when being charged at by an angry dog), the typical response is one of physical arousal – dry mouth, increased heart rate, rapid breathing. It is this arousal that signifies the release of adrenaline, a hormone that enlarges the autonomic responses and facilitates the release of stored fuels for energy, which enables the rapid response of either running away or fighting the threat. This 'fight or flight syndrome', Cannon reasoned, was *adaptive* because it enabled quick responses to threat but also *harmful* because it disrupted emotional and physiological functioning and if prolonged could contribute to many medical problems (early animal work confirmed this, with dogs and monkeys exposed to prolonged periods of stress producing excessive hydrochloric acid in the stomach, contributory to ulcer formation). In other words, in situations of chronic or ongoing stress, this fight–flight response would not be adaptive.

Subsequent to Cannon another physiologist, Hans Selye (1956), discovered (quite accidentally while conducting animal research into the sex hormones), that a triad of responses commonly followed the unpleasant injecting procedures used – the adrenal glands enlarged, the thymus gland shrank, and ulcers developed in the digestive tract. He followed up his early findings with over forty years of research using different aversive stimuli (injections, heat, cold, exercise), and came to the conclusion that there were universal and non-specific responses to stress: i.e. the same physiological responses followed a range of stimuli, whether pleasant or unpleasant, and that the 'fight–flight' response was only the first stage of response to stress (e.g. Selye 1974). Selye's model of stress is known as the **general adaptation syndrome**. The response to stress was seen to be an innate drive of living organisms to maintain internal balance, i.e. homeostasis, and he proposed that it did so in a three-stage process:

general adaptation syndrome

a sequence of physiological responses to prolonged stress, from the alarm stage through the resistance stage to exhaustion.

1. *Alarm reaction*: the awareness of a stressor is the initial response that can cause a downturn in bodily defences, and blood pressure and heart rate may initially decrease before rising to higher than normal levels. Selye stated that this arousal could not be maintained for long periods. He attributed his stress response to activation of the anterior–pituitary–adrenal cortex system, although exact physiological processes only became clear some years later (Pinel 2003; Selye 1991; and see later section).

2. *Stage of resistance*: the next stage is where the body tries to adapt to a stressor that has not subsided in spite of resistance efforts made during the acute/alarm stage. Arousal decreases from that seen in the alarm stage but is still higher than normal, and Selye noted that this stage of mobilisation of bodily defences could not last indefinitely without the organism becoming vulnerable to illness.

3. *Stage of exhaustion*: exhaustion would occur if the resistance stage lasts too long, resulting in a depletion of bodily resources and energy. At this stage, the ability to resist the stress declines, and Selye proposed the increased likelihood of 'diseases of adaptation' such as cardiovascular disease, arthritis and asthma.

Later work on stress responses

Cannon's and Selye's work stimulated a huge amount of research into the physiology of stress. Much of it has not confirmed Selye's proposed 'non-specific response', as different physiological responses have been found to be associated with different kinds of stressor. Evidence for this comes from consistent findings of experimental studies carried out in the 1980s; for example, an experimental study that exposed participants to different types of challenge (mental or physical) and took continuous blood samples during exposure found that blood levels of adrenaline were increased during mental stress, whereas noradrenaline increased during physical stress (Ward, Mefford, Parker *et al.* 1983, cited in Rice 1992).

However, there is a large and growing body of evidence that shows that adverse events (and positive events) produce physiological changes. Typical stress responses (e.g. rapid and deeper breathing, increased heart rate, sweating or shaking) result not just from activation of the anterior pituitary adrenal cortex system as Selye thought but also from increased activity of the sympathetic branch of the autonomic nervous system (ANS). The ANS can be divided into two connected systems – the sympathetic nervous system (SNS) and the parasympathetic nervous system (PNS) – which 'exist in a state of dynamic but antagonistic tension' (Rice 1992: 126). The SNS is involved in arousal and expenditure of energy (such as during a 'fight–flight' response), whereas the PNS is involved in reducing arousal and in restoring and conserving the body's energy stores (such as during rest) (see Chapter 8). Both systems control the actions of many internal organs, such as the heart and skeletal muscles, with their activity initially mediated by the neurotransmitter acetylcholine. Acetylcholine links the neurons of the spinal synapse to the brainstem, where the nerves then act on their target organs. Mediation in the sympathetic branch is provided by noradrenaline (adrenergic fibres) and, to a lesser degree, adrenaline; whereas in the parasympathetic branch acetylcholine (cholinergic fibres) makes this final link.

The stress response is maintained following short-lived sympathetic arousal by neuroendocrine responses resulting from activation of the sympathetic–adrenomedullary system (SAM) and release of the catecholamines adrenaline (epinephrine) and noradrenaline (norepinephrine), those in brackets being the US terms), from the adrenal glands. This activation of the adrenal medullary system, in conjunction with the more crucial action of the hypothalamus in activating the pituitary–adrenal cortex (the hypothalamic–pituitary–adrenocortical (HPA) system), enables our bodily organs to alter their usual function to facilitate an adaptive stress response even in situations of prolonged stress.

The HPA system originates in the hypothalamus, which releases its own hormone, corticotrophin-releasing factor (CRF), which controls the anterior pituitary gland in its secreting of ACTH (adrenocorticotrophic hormone). ACTH then travels to the adrenal gland, where the hormones adrenaline and noradrenaline are released, as well as stimulating glucocorticoid secretion from the adrenal cortex, in particular the hormone cortisol. While Cannon's early model described the role of adrenaline, Selye was more interested in adrenocortical responses. We now know that circulating glucocorticoids provide energy for the 'alarm phase' as the release of glucocorticoids into the bloodstream regulates the levels of glucose in the blood from which energy can be drawn. Almost every cell in the human body contains glucocorticoid receptors, and hormones such as cortisol affect every major organ system in the body. For example, cortisol inhibits glucose and fat uptake by tissue cells so that more can be drawn on for immediate energy, it increases blood flow, it suppresses immune function by inhibiting the action of phagocytes and lymphocytes, and it inhibits inflammation of any damaged tissue (e.g. Antoni 1987; Dantzner and Kelly 1989). The suppression of the immune system caused by increased blood-circulating cortisol (serum or s-cortisol) can make a person vulnerable to infection. However, it has been noted following a review of evidence relating to endocrine responses in stressful situations, that cortisol activity undergoes extinction when exposed to chronic stress or to repeated acute stressors (Rose 1980, cited in Kasl 1996; Nicolson and van Diest 2000).

HPA activation also elevates the production of growth hormones and pro-lactin, beta endorphins and encephalin, which are also found in the brain in response to stress and are thought to play a role in immune-related disease and in problems such as depression. Beta endorphins have a useful analgesic (pain-killing) function and as such may explain why people can endure high levels of pain until they succeed in escaping stressful situations or completing demanding tasks: for example, soldiers with extreme injuries have been known to crawl long distances to receive help, and athletes can complete races in spite of damaged muscles (e.g. Wall 1979).

These responses within the autonomic nervous system and the endocrine (hormonal) system work together to prepare our bodies to meet the demands of our environment. Our autonomic nervous system may work 'behind the scenes', but its functions are essential to basic human responses. The duration of some of the stress responses, such as the release of cortisol, influences whether the responses are beneficial to the organism or not. For example, cortisol production over long periods of time can actually damage immunity. Animal research (Antoni 1987; Sapolsky 1986; Sapolsky 1996) has suggested that long-term exposure to such glucocorticoids can actually damage neurons in the hippocampal formation (see Chapter 8), an area of the brain crucial to learning and memory, with a link being proposed with ageing (Sapolsky, Krey and McEwen 1986), although human research is required to address this further. Prolonged release of adrenaline and noradrenaline is also known to have negative effects, including suppressed cellular immune function, increases in heart rate and blood pressure, heartbeat irregularities (arrhythmia) and, potentially, hypertension and heart disease (Fredrickson and Matthews 1990).

The need for combined psychological and physiological understanding of stress can be drawn from Fisher, Bell and Baum (1984), who proposed an *environmental stress theory* that combined physiological responses to stress (based on Selye's GAS) with the type of psychological processes described by Lazarus. Using this model, Baum (1990) examined survivors of various catastrophes, including the Three Mile Island nuclear testing incident (1979), and confirmed that cognitive stress processes coexisted with physiological arousal. Environmental events were found to have elicited threat appraisals, which triggered an 'alarm reaction' with associated autonomic arousal. Following the initial stage of horror, shock and alarm came a stage in which coping strategies were activated, such as those of flight, attack or compromise (stage of resistance), and emotions such as fear or anger accompanied these coping strategies. If the strategies were unsuccessful, a stage of exhaustion was reached, or if successful, adaptation to the stressor resulted. The model also identified 'costs' to the process of lowered resistance to stress in terms of deterioration in physical performance, psychosomatic disorders and lowered frustration tolerance. Some of these effects can be attributed to changes in immune responses.

Stress and immune function dysregulation

Declines or alterations in immune function have frequently been associated with the experience of stressful life events (e.g. Ader 2001; Dantzer and Kelley 1989; Salovey *et al.* 2000). The immune system, as described in Chapter 8, is the body's defence against disease. It operates by producing certain types of cell that operate against foreign organisms (e.g. bacteria, poisons, viruses, parasites) and abnormal cells (e.g. cancer cells) in the blood and lymphatic systems. These potential threats to the body are known as antigens. Immune cells are white blood cells of two major types, lymphocytes and phagocytes, which can be found in the lymphatic system, in the spleen and in the blood circulation. Phagocytes are attracted to sites of infection due to tissue releasing chemical messengers, and when they reach their destination they destroy abnormal cells or antigens by engulfing and consuming them. Lymphocyte action is triggered by the phagocytes (by a subtype known as a macrophage). Lymphocytes consist of T cells (CD4+ T cells or helper T cells, and CD8+ cells or cytoxic T cells), B cells (memory and plasma cells) and natural killer (NK) cells. B cells label invading antigens in order to identify them for destruction and also 'remember' the antigen to enable early detection of future attacks. Their plasma produces antibodies, which remain in the blood circulation until the germ or disease is no longer present.

NK cells slow down the growth of abnormal cells (in cancer, for example) so that other immune responses can form an attack. The role of the phagocytes and NK cells is often referred to as providing non-specific immunity in that they provide a general first line of defence against a wide variety of antigens, whereas specific immunity is provided by B and T cells to specific antigens that they have been sensitized to (see Table 11.4 for a summary of T and B cell roles).

Each type of cell, NK, B and T, interact and help one another in the fight against infection or the growth of abnormal cells. Chapter 8 details the more specific action of each of these cell types. The immune system is also affected by the workings of the sympathetic nervous system and the endocrine responses described earlier; for example, the HPA system causes the release of hormones such as cortisol from the adrenal glands, and these hormones are thought to stimulate the immune system. Unfortunately, cortisol appears to damage T and B cells and increase a person's susceptibility

Table 11.4 Specific immunity and cell types	
Humoral immunity: B cells	**Cell-mediated immunity: T cells**
Operate in the bloodstream	Operate at level of the cell
Work by releasing antibodies, which then destroy the antigen	Include memory, killer, helper (CD4+) and suppressor T cells
Include memory cells	Mature in the thymus and not the bone marrow as other white blood cells do

to infection, not decrease it (Antoni 1987). Generally, it is now accepted that there is communication both within and between the neuroendocrine and immune systems, with the brain providing an immuno-regulatory role (e.g. Blalock 1994).

What is important to health psychologists is that studies have found a link between the proliferation of B, T and NK cells and the subjective experience of stress; in other words, they have shown that psychological stress interferes with the workings of our body. One early study by Kiecolt-Glaser, Garner, Speicher *et al.* (1984) found a significant reduction in NK cell activity among students prior to important end-of-term exams compared with those tested in mid term. In addition, those students who reported feelings of loneliness plus a high number of recent stressful life events showed significantly less NK cell activity at both times than those students who were low in life events and low in loneliness.

This evidence was simultaneously being confirmed elsewhere, but it took a long time for the findings of such experimental studies to be accepted, because these findings necessitated a paradigm shift from where the body was thought to operate independently of the mind to acceptance of the fact that psychological factors could influence immuno-competence (i.e. the degree to which our immune system functions effectively). Since the late 1970s, work in this new area of psychoneuroimmunology (the study of how psychosocial factors interact with the nervous system and immune system) has gone from strength to strength (see Herbert and Cohen 1993; Cohen and Herbert 1996 for reviews). Such research provides scientists with the opportunity to assess 'objective' indices of the stress response alongside, and in relation to, subjective stress reports.

It should have become clear during the course of this chapter that stress is not a unitary physiological process but a highly complex one. The experience of stress is, to varying degrees, dependent on stimulus events (acute or chronic, physical or psychological), on internal representations of events, including a person's appraisals and emotional responses, and on the nature and extent of physiological and behavioural activation that follows. Stress indisputably has a strong psychological component, and furthermore stress responses change over time as a person adjusts (or not) to their situation. With all these features, it is hardly surprising that measuring stress is also complex, and some of the issues in stress measurement are presented in the ISSUES below.

ISSUES

Can stress be measured?

As with any concept, the manner in which it is defined will influence how it is measured or assessed. We have described three broad ways of thinking about stress – as a stimulus, as the result of cognitive appraisal and as a physiological response – and each of these views leads to different forms of assessment.

Measuring stress as a stimulus is problematic, given what was described earlier as weaknesses in the life events approach to stress – if many of the life events are irrelevant to the responder because of their age or life stage, does this mean that they are less stressed because their potential total scores are reduced? Additionally, people generally search for explanations for how they feel or for events that have happened to them – it is common, for example, for people to report many life events in the lead up to a heart attack – so measuring retrospective accounts of life events may in this instance lead to inflated estimates of the role that stress plays in illness.

Stress is based upon appraisal, which involves stimulus, cognition and emotion, and therefore it is necessary to measure people's appraisals of the stimulus event, their emotions, their perceived resources and their perceived coping potential. Stress appraisals tend to be assessed by simply asking people how they feel or getting them to complete a standardised psychometric assessment. One commonly employed example is the perceived stress scale, which assesses the degree to which life situations are appraised as stressful (Cohen, Kamarck and Mermelstein 1983). Examples include 'In the last month, how often have you been upset because of something that happened unexpectedly?' and 'In the last month, how often have you found that you could not cope with all the things you had to do?' (scored as 0 = never; 1 = almost never; 2 = sometimes; 3 = fairly often; 4 = very often). Higher scores are indicative of greater perceived stress.

In terms of assessing individual responses considered to be indicative of stress, many studies will include a measure of distress or more specific mood states (e.g. anger, depression or anxiety). One commonly used instrument is the general health questionnaire (GHQ; Goldberg and Williams 1988). There are various GHQs, which vary in the number of items included. The twenty-eight item version measures a combination of emotional states (anxiety, insomnia, social dysfunction, severe depression and somatic symptoms), whereas the commonly employed twelve-item version does not distinguish between each of these, although it has still proved a sensitive measure of psychiatric disorder. Respondents indicate whether they have experienced a particular symptom or behaviour 'less than usual', 'no more than usual', 'rather more than usual' or 'much more than usual', and example items include 'have you recently . . . been able to concentrate on whatever you're doing? . . . been feeling unhappy and depressed? . . . felt constantly under strain? The scale is most commonly used as an outcome measure.

In order to assess secondary appraisal processes central to Lazarus's model, research studies also commonly employ measures of personal resource, such as self-efficacy or perceived social support. Regardless of the number of assessment tools used, however, there are inherent limitations in assessing an experience as subjective as stress. For example, distress is likely to bias the answers one gives to questions regarding the nature of the stressor, or regarding the number of recent life events experienced. Being anxious or depressed is likely to influence the resources one considers to have available. Obviously, such aspects of the stress experience interact, and it is necessary for research studies to disentangle precursors of a stress response from the stress response itself.

Stress as a response can be measured using physiological and physical indices such as heart rate, blood pressure, galvanic skin response, levels of adrenaline, noradrenaline and cortisol levels in the blood or saliva, or other indicators of increased cortisol levels such as reflected decreases in salivary secretory immunoglobulins (Sig-A). However, even the 'objective' measures of stress such as heart rate are open to question, as some people are quite simply more 'stress-responsive' than others (Felsten 2004). For example, the level of heart rate increase caused by a physical threat is not universal (Sherwood and Turner 1992), and such differences may be related to variations in central nervous system activity (Lovallo 1997) as well as to other individual differences such as personality (e.g. neuroticism, Costa and McCrae 1992a) appraisals and past experience (Lazarus 1999).

continued

In spite of challenges of measurement, a vast amount of research is conducted in this field that acknowledges that since stress is a subjective experience, measuring it cannot expect to be an exact science. As Kasl (1996: 21) states: 'What we have, at best, are indirect and partial indicators of the stress process, and these indicators tend to measure both too much and not enough'. As an illustration of this he refers to the perceived stress scale, which measures 'too much' in that it correlates significantly with depression and measures 'not enough' in that it does not assess secondary appraisal processes, emotions or indicators of physiological reactivity. As this chapter has hopefully indicated, stress is by its very essence complex, and you will discover through your wider reading that many empirical research studies have acknowledged this by adopting multiple methods of assessment.

The final challenge in the domain of stress research is that of establishing causality between stressful events and illness. The concluding section of this chapter therefore describes some of the evidence that stress is associated with the development of illness.

The stress and illness link

In Chapter 8, the physiological and immunological systems were described in some detail. This final section describes the role of stress in activating these systems with resulting implications for the development of illness. First, however, it is worth knowing that there are different ways of viewing the relationship between stress and illness.

The direct route

As described above, stress can produce physiological changes in endocrine and immune system function that may lead to the development of illness, particularly in instances where the stress is chronic rather than brief (Cacioppo, Poehlmann, Kiecolt-Glaser *et al.* 1998). However, there is so much individual variation in responding to stressors that the direct route is complex (e.g. Cohen and Williamson 1991; Esterling, Kiecolt-Glaser and Glaser 1996; Vedhara, Cox, Wilcock *et al.* 1999). The mixed evidence for direct effects of stress on specific diseases are reviewed in this chapter.

The indirect routes

■ People, by virtue of their behavioural responses to stress such as smoking, eating habits and drinking, predispose themselves to disease. Such behaviour may serve coping functions (see Chapter 5).

■ People, by virtue of certain personality traits, predispose themselves to disease by the manner in which they respond to stress (see Chapter 12).

■ People experiencing stress are more likely to use health services than people who are not under stress. Stress can produce symptoms such as anxiety, fatigue, insomnia and shakiness, which people seek treatment for but which are not in themselves illnesses (see Chapter 12).

However, we should bear in mind a quote of Sapolsky's throughout the reading of the next sections: 'everything bad in human health now is not caused by stress, nor is it in our power to cure ourselves of our worst medical nightmares merely by reducing stress and thinking healthy thoughts full of courage and spirit and love. Would it were so. And shame on those who sell this view' (1994).

There is a moderate relationship between stress and illness. This can be best illustrated by selectively reviewing the evidence in relation to some of the many illnesses that have been found to have an association with stress. We do not address in the subsequent sections the many findings relating to psychosocial influences upon, or moderators of, the stress response. Discussion of such factors is contained in Chapter 12.

Stress and carer health

The nature, intensity, duration and frequency of stressor events have been found to influence the nature and extent of immune change in a dynamic manner in part dependent on the state of the immune system at the time the stressor event occurs (Dantzer and Kelley 1989). One population that has been relatively frequently studied in this regard is carers of those with chronic disease, for example those caring for elderly relatives with Alzheimer's disease. Ongoing mental, physical and social demands of caring have been found to cause stress among many elderly carers, stress that has been found to manifest itself immunologically, for example in terms of reduced wound healing (Kiecolt-Glaser *et al.* 1995; see also IN THE SPOTLIGHT), increased illness episodes compared with healthy controls (Kiecolt-Glaser *et al.* 1991) and reduced antibody build-up following vaccination (Kiecolt-Glaser *et al.* 1996), although studies of younger carers have not consistently supported such findings (e.g. Vedhara *et al.* 2002). For a fuller discussion of the effects of caring, see Chapter 15. Most research into the physical outcomes of carer stress have examined the increased vulnerability to disease resulting from immune changes rather than actual disease development.

IN THE SPOTLIGHT

Can stress prevent your wounds healing?

Janice Kiecolt-Glaser and Ronald Glaser have spent many years researching the mind–body relationship, in particular the relationship between the experience of stress and immune function. While this chapter has presented evidence of the physiological pathways underlying stress responses, you may not have stopped to consider how stress might affect you, not just in terms of potentially increasing your risk of diseases such as heart disease but in terms of more day-to-day health challenges, such as wounds received while participating in sporting activities. The Glasers (1985) have shown in studies of elderly carers of people with Alzheimer's disease that healing of experimentally induced tissue wounds took significantly longer among carers than among healthy age-matched control participants. However, this may in part be due to

continued

coexisting ageing processes, so further studies have explored whether similar effects can be found in younger samples. Vedhara and colleagues in Bristol (2003) examined the healing rates of foot ulcers among sixty adults with type II diabetes. They found that healing was reduced in those who had shown high anxiety, depression or stress. Importantly, similar effects of stress have been found on the healing rates of otherwise healthy students who are given a small experimental skin wound at two different times, one during the summer holiday, the other prior to sitting exams. The wound inflicted before exams took on average three days longer to heal, and this was reflected by decreases in immunological status (Marucha, Kiecolt-Glaser and Favgehi 1998). Broadbent, Petrie, Alley *et al.* (2003) have confirmed the impairing effects of high stress and worry levels on wound healing where wounds were not experimental but real, i.e. participants were recovering from hernia surgery.

Why do all these findings matter? Think of your own stress levels; think of your likelihood of becoming wounded in sport or other activity; or of the potential to be facing surgery in the future. Think of current concern about MRSA (methicillin-resistant *Staphylococcus aureus*) infections in hospitals and in the community. Effectively dealing with your own stress is important, not only in keeping you healthy but also in helping you to heal and recover when and if you become ill or injured or require surgery.

Stress and the common cold

Cohen and his colleagues (Cohen, Tyrell and Smith 1993a, 1993b; Cohen *et al.* 1998) have conducted a series of experiments where volunteers submitted themselves to exposure to respiratory rhinoviruses of the common cold (using nasal drops mainly). Participants then remained in a controlled environment for varying lengths of time while researchers waited to see whether colds or infections develop more often among those who received viral drops than among the control subjects, who received saline drops. Volunteers who had reported more chronic negative life events, perceived stress, negative affect and poor coping responses prior to the experiment were more likely to develop signs of respiratory infection and subsequent colds than both control subjects and experimental subjects with low-level life stress. Perceived stress and negative affect predicted infection rates, whereas negative life events did not predict infection itself but predicted the probability of illness among those who became infected. These associations persisted when health behaviour such as smoking and alcohol consumption or personality variable such as self-esteem and introversion–extroversion were controlled for. Similarly, Stone, Bovbjerg, Neale *et al.* (1993) found a similar dose–response relationship between the number of stressful life events experienced prior to the introduction of a rhinovirus and the subsequent presentation of cold symptoms.

Although the results relating to stress and susceptibility to influenza have been inconsistent, the work of Cohen's research group, summarised in their 1998 paper, provides convincing evidence of a relationship between chronic stress (as opposed to severity) and the common cold. They controlled for other potential influences such as mood and smoking behaviour and hoped to identify a physiological or immunological pathway that mediated the stress–colds relationship, but they failed to find one despite taking many careful neuroendocrine and immune function measures (Leventhal, Patrick-Miller and Leventhal 1998). The failure to identify such a pathway, and the fact that such studies are conducted in laboratory environments, means that there is still some way to go before full understanding of how stress operates and, in particular, how it operates in real-life environments can be achieved.

Prospective studies with clinical populations facing 'natural' stressors improve our understanding of the stress–immune function–illness link to a degree. While there is some evidence that stress-mediated physiological changes play a role in the initial onset of disease among healthy individuals (such as coronary heart disease), there is more evidence that stress experienced by 'ill' individuals can affect further progression of their symptoms or disease. We review some of this evidence below.

Stress and coronary heart disease

cardiovascular
pertaining to the heart and blood vessels.

Coronary heart disease (CHD) is a disease of the **cardiovascular** system that develops over time in response to a range of factors, such as family history and lifestyle factors (e.g. smoking and diet; see Chapter 3). As described in Chapter 8, the cause of CHD is a gradual narrowing of blood vessels that supply the heart. In situations of acute stress, activation of the sympathetic nervous system causes increased cardiac output and the blood vessels to constrict, thus restricting blood flow, so blood pressure increases. This can cause damage to the artery walls, a process that is contributed to further by stress-induced adrenaline and noradrenaline output (Rice 1992). If blood pressure remains raised for prolonged periods of time, a person is said to have hypertension, a contributory factor in CHD.

Stress also activates the sympathetic nervous system's release of fatty acids into the bloodstream, which, if not utilised for energy expenditure, are metabolised by the liver into cholesterol. A build-up of cholesterol is highly implicated in the 'furring up' of arteries or atheroma (the laying down of fatty plaques on artery walls), and a key feature of heart disease is this atherosclerosis. Furthermore, the release of catecholamines during the stress process also increases the stickiness of blood platelets (thrombocytes), which elevates the risk of a clot forming or thrombosis as they adhere to the artery walls with the fatty plaques, thus making the 'passageway' narrower for blood to flow through. If reduced blood flow causes a clot to form, it could then travel through a person's arteries until it becomes so big as to form a blockage (occlusion) and depending on whether it blocks an artery to the brain or to the heart, this will lead to either a stroke or a heart attack – both major causes of mortality worldwide.

Speculation as to the role of stress in the development of CHD has abounded. Rosch (1994), in an editorial in the journal *Stress Medicine*, pointed to the importance of distinguishing between causal factors and contributing factors when considering disease, arguing that the 'true cause' of any disease is biomedical and that behavioural or social factors such as smoking or stress are not 'true' causes but contributors. In terms of CHD, however, stress does appear to contribute to various related conditions, such as hypertension, elevated serum lipids (fats in the blood) and smoking behaviour, an acknowledged risk factor (e.g. Jousilahti, Vartiainen, Tuomilehto *et al*. 1995). Cardiovascular reactivity during stress (i.e. the extent to which a stressor produces cardiac arousal such as increased heart rate or blood pressure) has been implicated in various disease processes, such as the extent and progression of carotid artery atherosclerosis, and the emergence of coronary heart disease itself (Smith, Gallo and Ruiz 2003). Experimental studies of reactivity in response to aversive or rewarding stimuli have speculated that the individuals who responded to stressful tasks with sizeable heart rate and blood pressure increases (high reactives) but who showed no difference from controls in subjective ratings of the tasks had greater activation of the hypothalamic system and neuroendocrine responses such as those described earlier. High-reactive participants had larger noradrenaline increases in response to both types of task than low-reactive participants and larger cortisol increases to the aversive task but not to the reward task (Lovallo, Pincomb, Brackett and Wilson 1990).

Stress and cancer

Cancer, like heart disease, develops slowly and begins with mutation of cells and the development of generally undetectable neoplasms, which eventually develop into spreadable tumours (i.e. the cells metastasise). Forms of cancer vary hugely in terms of rates of growth, spread and prognosis, in terms of their sensitivity to neuroendocrine or immune system changes (Greer 1999), and in terms of available treatment options. Accordingly, it is perhaps unwise to expect stress to exert uniform if any effects on different forms of cancer. There has also been caution in adopting a biopsychosocial (see Chapter 1) perspective on this group of diseases because of the dominance of biomedical thinking and concerns about overstating the role of the individual and their cognitions, emotions and stress or coping responses in cancer progression (Spiegel 1992). Stress may affect tumour cell mutation by slowing down the cell repair process, possibly by virtue of its effects on hormonal activation and the release of glucocorticoids, or by influences on the immune system's production of lymphocytes (see Rosch 1996 for a review of both animal and human research).

A meta-analysis of forty-six studies investigating the association between psychosocial factors, including life event stress, and the development of breast cancer concluded that breast cancer could not be explained by life events, but it could by a combination of risk factors and psychosocial factors (McKenna *et al.* 1999). This is consistent with findings from another meta-analysis specifically examining the predictive role of life events (Petticrew, Fraser and Regan 1999), and the general consensus is that there is no clear link in terms of cancer aetiology, although there is mixed evidence in terms of stress and cancer recurrence. For example, Kiecolt-Glaser and Glaser (1999) have presented data from women with breast cancer tumours showing that those who experienced stressful life events had reduced NK cell activity, suggesting that the immune response had been down-regulated. However, a five-year prospective study of women diagnosed with breast cancer at a London clinic found that recurrence was not increased in those who had experienced one or more extremely stressful events in the year prior to diagnosis or in the five years subsequently (Graham, Ramirez, Love, Richards and Burgess 2002). This contradicts some single case-control studies where stressful events have been related to relapse (e.g. Ramirez, Craig,

Watson *et al.* 1989), but Graham and colleagues report a more robust finding given that their study is prospective in nature, it controls for biological prognostic indicators such as tumour size and the extent to which the cancer involved the lymph nodes, and it involves a good-sized sample of women.

However, there is a reasonable body of evidence suggesting that coping style (particularly one that is passive and indicative of helplessness and hopelessness) and mood may affect cancer outcome (progression, recurrence, death) (Walker, Heys and Eremin 1999; and see Spiegel 2001 for a brief discussion of the literature). These issues are addressed more fully in Chapter 12.

Stress and bowel disease

Two diseases of the bowel have been investigated in terms of their association with the experience of stress. In both, stress is examined as an exacerbating factor rather than one involved in the aetiology of the condition. First, *irritable bowel syndrome* is a disorder of the large intestine characterised by abdominal pain and prolonged periods of either diarrhoea or constipation, although no organic disease is identifiable. Naliboff *et al.* (1998) note that during stressful episodes, the reactivity of the gut is greater and symptoms such as bloatedness, pain or diarrhoea increase. A second bowel disease is *inflammatory bowel disease* (IBD), which can be subdivided into Crohn's disease (CD) and ulcerative colitis (UC). These diseases are both typified by pain and diarrhoea, which worsens and improves in an alternating and disruptive manner. UC is typified by inflammation of the lower colon (see Chapter 8), whereas CD can occur anywhere in the gastrointestinal tract and is seen as inflammation of the outer intestinal wall. Both diseases, as with IBS, were originally thought to be psychosomatic; however, evidence that stress plays a role in their aetiology is limited.

The existence of stress-responsive/reactive and non-responsive/reactive individuals has been found in many studies, including for example Dancey, Taghavi and Fox's (1998) study of thirty-one IBS patients. Using repeated measures of daily stress and daily symptomatology, they examined the associations over time and found that in half of the sample stress was associated with onset or exacerbation of symptoms, but it was not in the remaining patients. Stress reactivity is influenced further by personal characteristics of somatisation and attention to internal organs, often features associated with neuroticism (Pennebaker 1992; see Chapter 9 for a discussion of neuroticism and symptom perception).

There is also some evidence of a role for stress in symptom exacerbation in IBD. Duffy, Zielezny, Marshall *et al.* (1991), for example, examined exposure to stressful events among 124 individuals and found that over a period of six months, those exposed to stress showed a two- to fourfold increase in clinical disease episodes compared with those participants who did not report stressful incidents. When the authors distinguished between disease-related and disease-unrelated events (on the basis of patient report), the relationship between stress and illness was clearest when the reported events were health-related but not necessarily IBD-specific. When the authors examined the issue of time lag between event and disease activity (i.e. a stressful event preceding disease activity), they found instead that concurrent relationships were strongest. Furthermore, their results showed that disease activity was predictive of subsequent levels of stress. Such bidirectional relationships between variables makes the disentangling of issues of cause and effect difficult.

Stress and HIV/AIDS

Over the past twenty years, AIDS has spread throughout the world to become a major cause of death in Africa and a leading cause of death elsewhere (see Chapter 3). AIDS (acquired immune deficiency syndrome) is a syndrome characterised by opportunistic infections and other malignant diseases, and until the HIV (human immunodeficiency virus) was identified in 1984, the cause of such immunosuppression was unclear. As described in Chapter 8, the HIV virus is a retrovirus, which means that it contains RNA (ribonucleic acid, part of our genetic makeup) and is a slow-acting virus, referred to as a lentivirus. How the virus infiltrates the body is described in Chapter 8, but crucially, in terms of potential stress for the sufferer, it can be many years before an HIV-infected individual develops AIDS. As well as being life-threatening, the disease is itself often perceived to be psychologically stressful due to the continued social stigma attached to the disease (given its early associations with homosexuality, drug abuse and sexual promiscuity). Petrak, Doyle, Smith *et al.* (2001) found that self-disclosure of HIV status to family (53 percent of sample had told their family) and to friends (79 percent had told close friends) was significantly influenced by wanting to protect others from distress and out of fear of discrimination. Living with this illness is inherently stressful, and although there is only limited suggestion that stress influences the likelihood of infection when exposed to the virus (Marks, Murray, Evans and Willig 2000), there is evidence that stress plays an influential role in the progression of disease. Evidence is particularly strong when moderating variables such as depression, social support and coping responses are taken into consideration. For example, a meta-analysis (Zorrilla 1996) suggested that depressive symptoms, but not stress experience, were associated with increased speed of symptom onset in HIV-positive individuals, and that stress, but not depressive symptoms, was associated with reduced NK cell count. Other studies have also reported associations between baseline depression and a CD4+ cell decline (Burack *et al.* 1993) and in the same sample nine years later, faster progression to AIDS (Page-Shafer *et al.* 1996).

Progression to AIDS has been found to be quicker in those experiencing a build-up of stressful life events, depressive symptoms and low social support (Leserman *et al.* 1999). Within this disease group, a sad reality is that many individuals will face the loss of a partner through AIDS, which itself has been found to impact upon disease progression over subsequent years (Kemeny *et al.* 1994). Social support, or lack or loss of it, is discussed in Chapter 12.

Summary

This chapter set out to provide a definition of stress and has shown that there is no such thing as a simple definition of this phenomenon. Stress is generally examined in one of three ways: as a stimulus that focuses on the external event (stressors); as a transaction between the external event and the individual experiencing it; and as an array of physiological responses that are manifested when an individual faces demanding events. The transactional psychological model of stress highlighted the crucial role of appraisal and points to the importance of considering the individual in the stress experience. Many different events may be appraised as stressful, and stressor events can be acute or chronic in their manifestation and in the responses they require. Examples of these were presented, with particular emphasis on occupational stress, something that most of us will experience at some time. The neuroendocrine and autonomic pathways by which stress has been shown to affect health status were examined, and these processes were explored further in relation to evidence (or not) of their direct role in diseases such as coronary heart disease and cancer. While some evidence of a direct effect of stress on the development of illness exists, it will have become clear that such evidence is somewhat limited. Many of stress's effects are either indirect, for example via an influence on behaviour, or are more evident during the illness experience, when individual differences in personality, cognitions and social resources become important to outcome. These moderating variables are the focus of the next chapter.

Further reading

Rice, P.L. (1992). *Stress and Health*. California: Brooks/Cole.
For clearly written and well resourced coverage of the stress process, from theory to intervention, including biological, cognitive and social explanations.

Sapolsky, R.M. (1994). *Why Zebras Don't Get Ulcers*. New York: Freeman.
Another well-written and engaging book on the subject of stress with excellent coverage of both physiological and psychological theories.

Lazarus, R.S. (1993). From psychological stress to the emotions: a history of changing outlooks. *Annual Review of Psychology*, 44: 1–21.
This article provides a useful account of the transactional model of stress and the developments in thinking about appraisal in terms of relations with emotions.

CHAPTER 12

Stress and illness moderators

Learning outcomes

By the end of this chapter, you should have an understanding of:

- coping theory and the distinction between coping styles and coping strategies
- how coping responses influence the manner in which stress may affect health outcomes
- aspects of personality, such as neuroticism, hostility and optimism, which influence stress appraisal, coping response and illness outcomes
- aspects of individual cognitions, such as personal control and efficacy, which influence stress appraisal, coping response and illness outcomes
- aspects of emotion, such as depression and emotional expression, which influence stress appraisal, coping response and illness outcomes
- how the external resource of social support influences stress appraisal and illness outcomes

CHAPTER OUTLINE

The preceding chapter established that stress can be considered as both an objective and subjective experience, and evidence was provided as to physiological and immunological pathways by which stress may influence health and illness status. However, not all people will become ill when exposed to stressful events, and this raises questions of great fascination to health psychologists. What aspects of the individual, their stress responses, or their stress-coping resources moderate or influence the negative impact of stress on health? This chapter will present evidence showing that psychosocial factors are crucial to stress appraisals, responses and outcomes. Individual differences in personality, cognitions and emotions have direct and indirect effects on stress outcomes. Indirectly, such factors affect outcome via their influence upon appraisals and upon cognitive and behavioural responses to stressful demands placed on us – these efforts are known as coping. In addition, aspects of social relationships and social support act as external resource variables, which directly and indirectly influence the negative impact of stress. Evidence as to the direct and/or moderating role of such variables will be presented and their importance examined. By the end of the chapter, the complexities of the relationship between stress, health and illness should be clear.

In Chapter 11 we described stress theories and acute and chronic stressors and examined the broad theoretical links between stress and disease. We also presented evidence relating to the direct pathways by which physiological and immune processes affect the stress–disease relationship. Much of the evidence of direct effects of stress on disease has been conflicting, in large part due to there being so much individual variation in responding to stressors. This leads to a need to examine the indirect routes introduced in Chapter 11, i.e. how different personalities, beliefs and emotions influence stress–illness relationships, either directly or via an effect on behavioural and cognitive coping responses.

Lazarus's transactional model of stress and coping (Lazarus 1966; Lazarus and Folkman 1984) was introduced in the previous chapter, where we outlined the crucial role of appraisal (of events). Individual differences in the appraisal of events influence the cognitive, emotional and behavioural response to them. Some factors may operate directly to affect outcomes, but most operate indirectly via their effects on coping responses (and also via physiological responses described in Chapter 11). So what exactly do we mean by coping?

Stress and coping

It is unlikely that anyone can avoid stress, and certainly, as indicated in the previous chapter, some stress is good for us (eustress); but negative appraisals and negative emotions generally elicit a desire to reduce such thoughts and feelings in order to restore a sense of harmony or balance in our lives.

Although over thirty definitions of coping exist, Lazarus's transactional model (see Figure 11.1) has had the most profound impact on the conceptualisation of coping (cf. Lazarus 1993a, 1993b; Lazarus and Folkman 1984). According to this model, psychological stress results from an unfavourable person–environment fit, in other words when there is a perceived mismatch between demands and resources as perceived by an individual in a specific situation (Lazarus and Folkman 1984; Lazarus 1993a). Individuals are required to alter either the stressor or how it is interpreted in order to make it appear more favourable. This effort is called coping.

Coping is viewed as a dynamic process involving a constellation of cognitions and behaviour that arise from the primary and secondary appraisals of events, and the emotions attached to them (as described in Chapter 11). Coping is *anything* a person does to reduce the impact of a perceived or actual stressor, and because appraisals elicit emotions, coping can operate to either alter or reduce the negative emotions, or it can directly target the 'objective' stressor. Coping does not inevitably succeed in eliminating the stressor, but it may manage the stressor by various means, for example through mastering new skills to deal with it, tolerating it, reappraising it or minimising it. Coping is concerned therefore with trying to achieve adaptation. For example, if the stressor event is starting a new job and this is eliciting anxiety, coping can either deal with the 'job' (thinking about the benefits of the new post, making contacts with new colleagues, researching the company and its products), or it can deal with the anxiety (talking with a friend, getting drunk). As this example illustrates, coping can be cognitive or behavioural, active or passive. In fact, many different, often overlapping, terms are used in the coping literature, with two of the main groups of broad distinction being summarised in Table 12.1.

Within the broad dimensions described in Table 12.1 are a variety of coping subscales, which combine to make up the broader dimensions. The subscales of coping identified by different research groups have generally been derived from factor analysis of a large number of coping items in an attempt to identify statistically meaningful 'clusters' of items that can then be used in a new measurement scale. Folkman and Lazarus (1988), in the popular ways of coping scale, distinguish eight coping subscales that address the two broad dimensions of problem-focused and emotion-focused coping: confrontive coping, distancing, self-controlling, seeking social support, accepting responsibility, escape–avoidance, planned problem solving, and positive reappraisal. Carver and colleagues (1989) distinguish thirteen, and latterly fifteen, subscales: planning, active coping, suppressing competing activities, acceptance, turning to religion, venting emotions, seeking instrumental support, seeking emotional support, humour, positive reinterpretation, restraint coping, denial, mental disengagement, behavioural disengagement, alcohol or drug use. In contrast, Endler and colleagues (Endler and Parker 1993; Endler *et al.* 1998) assess across three dimensions: task-oriented coping, emotion-oriented coping and avoidance-oriented coping.

What is adaptive coping?

Cohen and Lazarus (1979) described five main coping tasks, each of which contribute to successful adaptation to a stressor:

Table 12.1 Commonly employed coping categories

1. **Problem-focused coping (problem-solving function)** i.e. instrumental coping efforts (cognitive and/or behavioural) directed at the stressor in order to either reduce the demands of it or increase one's resources. Strategies include planning how to change the stressor or how to behave in order to control it; suppressing competing activities in order to focus on ways of dealing with the stressor; seeking practical or informational support in order to alter the stressor; confronting the source of stress.

versus

Emotion-focused coping (emotion-regulating function) i.e. mainly, but not solely, cognitive coping efforts directed at managing the emotional response to the stressor; for example, positively reappraising the stressor in order to see it in a more positive light; seeking emotional support; venting anger; praying. (Lazarus and Folkman 1984, Folkman and Lazarus 1988: ways of coping questionnaire; Carver, Scheier and Weintraub 1989: COPE scale).

Related to this distinction, Endler, Parker, Summerfeldt (1998) split coping into *emotion-oriented* (person-oriented strategies such as daydreaming, emotional response or self-preoccupation); *task-oriented* (strategies to solve, minimise or reconceptualise the problem) and *avoidance-oriented* (includes distraction or social diversion (CISS scale)).

2. **Attentional/approach, monitoring, vigilant, active,** i.e. concerned with attending to the source of stress and trying to deal with the problem by, for example, seeking information about it, or making active cognitive or behavioural efforts to manage the stressor (see also coping styles).

versus

Avoidant, blunting, passive, i.e. concerned with avoiding or minimising the threat of the stressor; sometimes emotion-focused, sometimes involves avoiding the actual situation; for example, distraction by thinking of pleasant thoughts or distraction by engaging in other activities to keep one's mind off the stressor.

Krohne (1993) described vigilance and cognitive avoidance as two coping 'superstrategies', which he considered were orthogonal dimensions of attention orientation and likely to reflect underlying personality (coping styles: see later section).

1. reducing harmful external conditions;

2. tolerating or adjusting to negative events;

3. maintaining a positive self-image;

4. maintaining emotional equilibrium and decreasing emotional stress;

5. maintaining a satisfactory relationship with the environment or with others.

Coping responses may succeed in one or more of these tasks, but adaptation may not necessarily be long-lived, depending upon the context and the nature of the stressor (e.g. is it stable or does it fluctuate or worsen?). For example, it is unlikely that any person would cope with flu in the same way as they would a diagnosis of cancer, or would cope with failing a driving test the second time in the same way as they coped with failing the first time. Furthermore, it should not be assumed from the earlier example of starting a new job that coping that addresses the problem directly (researching the new role) is inherently more adaptive than coping that does not (getting drunk); there are some situations where emotion-focused coping, or even avoidant coping, is adaptive. Coping is highly contextual – to be effective it has to be amenable to change (see Figure 11.1, where there are arrows feeding back from coping to (re)appraisal as well as to the stimulus event, and Figure 12.1). Lazarus's model of coping suggests that it is hard to predict which coping

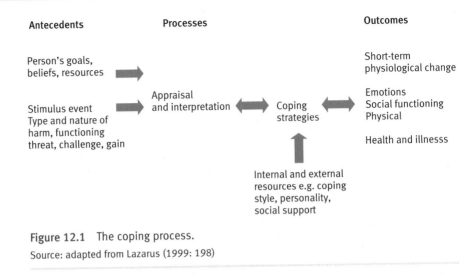

Figure 12.1 The coping process.

Source: adapted from Lazarus (1999: 198)

strategies will be effective in which situations, as both problem-focused and emotion-focused strategies are interdependent and work together to create the overall coping response in any situation (Lazarus 1993b). Tennen, Affleck, Armeli *et al.* (2000) confirmed this in an impressive longitudinal study of pain patients where daily measures of coping were taken. They found that emotion-focused coping strategies were 4.4 times more likely to be used on a day when problem-focused strategies were also used than on days where problem-focused strategies were not used. They also report that day-to-day pain symptomatology influenced the coping strategies used on a daily basis; for example, 'an increase in pain over yesterday's pain increased the likelihood that problem-focused coping yesterday would be followed by emotion-focused coping today' (p. 632). This highlights the role of appraisal and reappraisal of coping efforts: modifications are made depending on whether previous coping efforts are thought to have been successful or not.

Generally, it is considered that problem-focused coping is more likely to be adaptive when there is something that can be done to alter or control the stressor event. For example, using one or more cognitive or behavioural strategy such as focusing one's thoughts on aspects of the situation and planning how to deal with each, or seeking helpful information about the event. On the other hand, emotion-focused coping is more likely to be adaptive where the individual has little control over the event or if their resources to deal with it are low. Cognitive emotion-focused coping would be reflected in a person exhibiting denial or attending to other thoughts as a means of distraction, whereas behavioural examples of this form of coping could include venting and displaying emotion, or seeking emotional support.

Individuals who are typically problem-focused in their coping with stress may find that in some circumstances this is counter productive; for example, on receipt of a diagnosis of a life-threatening illness, emotion-focused coping may lead to better adjustment. For example, denial has been shown to be an effective coping response among women with breast cancer (Carver, Pozo, Harris *et al.* 1993; Greer, Morris, Pettingale *et al.* 1990). While early denial was associated with positive adjustment among Greer's sample, ongoing denial was associated with poorer fifteen-year survival outcomes, as were coping responses reflecting stoic acceptance, anxious preoccupation with the illness and helplessness/hopelessness.

One psychological coping response known as 'fighting spirit' (e.g. I am determined to beat this disease') has been associated with improved outcomes and long-term survival among breast cancer patients (Greer, Morris and Pettingale 1979; Greer *et al.* 1990). Fighting spirit reflects a kind of realistic optimism and determination, with people high in fighting spirit tending to face the illness head on rather than avoid it (Spiegel 2001). In contrast, feelings of hopelessness and helplessness (e.g. I feel there is nothing I can do to help myself) have been associated with poorer survival among breast cancer patients (Watson, Haviland, Greer *et al.* 1999) and stroke patients (Lewis, Dennis, O'Rourke *et al.* 2001). These coping responses of fighting spirit and helplessness differentially associate with either active, problem-focused or passive, avoidant coping behaviour. Findings such as these elicit hope for interventions that could enhance disease outcomes by targeting such attitudes and coping responses, for example increasing fighting spirit while decreasing feelings of helplessness. However, a recent review of twenty-six studies investigating the coping styles of fighting spirit or hopelessness/helplessness and cancer survival or recurrence concluded that the predictive associations between such variables can be questioned on the basis of limitations in the sample sizes or methodological quality of many studies that had reported relationships (Petticrew, Bell and Hunter 2002).

Finally, in relation to coping and adaptation, Stanton, Kirk, Cameron *et al.* (2000) have pointed out that emotions can have adaptive coping functions rather than disruptive functions as implied in the emotion-focused coping distinction. In a series of studies, they examined 'emotional-approach coping' and distinguished between 'emotional processing' (active attempts to understand the emotions experienced) and 'emotional expression'. Both forms of coping associated with indicators of positive psychological adjustment (see later section on emotional expression).

Coping styles or strategies

Coping style is the general tendency shown by individuals to respond to events in a particular way such as by avoidance versus attending to the stressor. Another distinction is that of monitors versus blunters. Monitoring reflects an approach style of coping, where threat-relevant information is sought out and processed, for example asking about treatments and side-effects, or seeking information about forthcoming exam content. Blunting reflects a tendency to avoid or distract oneself from threat-relevant information (e.g. Miller 1987; Miller, Brody and Summerton 1987), such as by sleeping or daydreaming, or engaging in other activities. Van Zuuren and Dooper (1999) examined the relationship between monitoring and blunting coping styles and engagement in disease detection (e.g. attending a doctor if frequently feeling tired, having blood pressure checked) and preventive behaviour (e.g. eating low-fat diet, exercising regularly). Monitoring was modestly, but significantly, associated with both detection and preventive behaviour, and individuals with a dominant blunting style were less likely to engage in protective behaviour than those where blunting was less dominant.

In contrast, however, monitoring was found to be associated with greater feelings of vulnerability and elevated distress among women with cancer, and the authors propose that this tendency to scan for and amplify threatening cues can be counterproductive (Miller, Fang, Manne *et al.* 1999). The conflicting outcomes of a monitoring style of coping shown by these two studies highlights the importance of context – the coping response made may not 'fit' the situation and as a result may be counter-adaptive.

Coping research in the field of health psychology has generally assessed coping in relation to context-specific strategies rather than in terms of styles; however, the two approaches can be addressed simultaneously in studies adopting repeated assessment periods to examine the nature and consistency of coping strategies over time (e.g. Tennen *et al.* 2000). To a certain extent, coping styles are considered as unrelated to the context or to the stressor stimulus; instead, they are general forms of coping that people have a tendency to adopt – for example, if you think about your own behaviour you will probably know whether you tend to duck and avoid difficult situations or whether you face them head on. In contrast, coping strategies derive from an approach that considers stress and coping as a dynamic process that varies according to context, event and the person's personal resources, mood, and so on, and coping at any one time might include a range of seemingly oppositional strategies. Lowe, Norman and Bennett (2000), for example, found that in the months following a heart attack, people used both passive coping (e.g. acceptance, positive reappraisal) and active, problem-focused coping simultaneously. In a similar vein, Macrodimitris and Endler (2001) found that a combination of instrumental and distraction coping strategies were employed by people with chronic illness. It is also important to consider coping intentions or goals (Laux and Weber 1991), as these are likely to influence the coping strategies employed in any given situation.

Coping goals

Why do people choose to cope in the way that they do? The reason for selecting one (or more) strategy to deal with a perceived stressor is related to past experience with that coping response, but more importantly it is related to the anticipated outcomes of that coping response, i.e. coping is a purposeful or motivational process (Lazarus 1993b). The general purpose of coping, i.e. to manage a situation so as to make it less distressing, brings with it an inherent need to maintain one's self-esteem and self-image, and to maintain good relations with others. To illustrate this, a study of arguments between married couples (Laux and Weber 1991) found that anger and attack coping responses arose when one or other party felt that their self-esteem was under threat and their coping goal was therefore one of self-defence. In contrast, when couples were in a situation where there was a shared anxiety about some external event, anger was more often suppressed and supportive forms of coping used instead, as the goal in such instances was that of resolving shared concerns.

Zeidner and Saklofske (1996: 506) note that 'Coping is more than simple adjustment; it is the pursuit of human growth, mastery and differentiation allowing us to evolve in an ever-changing world'.

What do YOU think?	Everyone experiences stress at some point in their lives. Think of a recent stressful experience you have faced. How did you cope with it? Think of any different strategies you adopted in order to deal with this event. What were the goals or aims of these strategies? Did different strategies have different goals or purposes for you? Which were effective, and which were not?

In revisiting that experience, can you think of anything in your personal background, your character or outlook on life that influenced how you responded to that event? There are many influences on how we appraise events and how we respond to them. Keep the experience you have just been thinking about in mind as you read the next sections of this chapter and consider whether any of the influences on stress and coping that we describe are relevant to how you deal with stress.

Stress, personality and illness

What is personality? Personality can be defined as the 'dynamic organization within the individual of those psychophysical systems that determine his characteristic behavior and thought' (Allport 1961: 28). This definition reflects a trait approach to personality, which considers a person's personality profile in terms of stable and enduring dimensions such as sensitivity, conscientiousness or neuroticism. Trait views dominated research until the late 1960s, but when traits failed to explain observed behaviour sufficiently well, attention turned to the role of external or situational variables and the existence of state-like characteristics (e.g. anxiety specific to a situation). Personality traits are constructs that provide a helpful means for us to typify behaviour patterns, with clusters of traits often providing 'typologies'; for example, an extroverted 'type' of person will generally exhibit sociable, adventurous and impulsive traits, while a psychotic 'type' will exhibit egocentric, aggressive, cold and impulsive characteristics (Eysenck 1982). Note that impulsivity features in both 'types', yet overall the two types differ in terms of clustered traits.

There are various possible models of association between personality variables and health and illness:

- Personality is in some cases predictive of disease onset (e.g. Friedman and Booth-Kewley 1987). This is the underpinning view of the psychosomatic tradition, whereby certain illnesses have been associated with certain personality traits (e.g. type A behaviour pattern and heart disease, see later section). The route by which this operates is likely to be physiological via trait-induced reactivity (see Chapter 11).

- Personality may be seen to change as a result of an illness, for example depression in chronic disease (see Chapter 15). This is a psychosomatic link, i.e. from body to mind.

- Personality may promote unhealthy behaviour predictive of disease, such as smoking; therefore personality has an indirect effect on disease risk (see also Chapter 3).

■ Personality may play a role in illness progression or outcome because it influences the manner in which an individual copes with symptom or illness events; e.g. hostile individuals may not use social support effectively.

The 'Big Five' personality dimensions

One current and popular way of conceptualising and assessing personality uses five dimensions (Costa and McCrae, 1992a, 1992b):

1. agreeableness, i.e. cooperative
2. conscientiousness, i.e. responsible
3. extroversion, i.e. sociable
4. neuroticism, i.e. tense, anxious
5. openness, i.e. imaginative, open to new experiences.

Each of these factors has been considered as an adaptive set of traits that enable both individuals and groups to adapt to demands of life. Studies employing five-factor models have found that each has differential associations with health behaviour (e.g. Booth-Kewley and Vickers 1994; Friedman, Tucker, Schwartz *et al.* 1995), symptom perception (Feldman, Cohen, Doyle *et al.* 1999), coping (e.g. David and Suls 1996) and illness behaviour (e.g. Korotkov and Hannah 2004), with this latter study finding that the personality factors related more to subjective health ratings than to objective indicators of disease.

Type A behaviour and personality

Coronary heart disease (CHD), and its outcomes (heart attack, angina, cardiac death) have been studied extensively in relation to personality variables and to emotion (see later section). The search for a coronary-prone personality led to the discovery of a constellation of behaviour labelled Type A behaviour (TAB) (Friedman and Rosenman 1959, 1974; Rosenman 1978). TAB is a multidimensional concept combining action and emotion and is manifest in individuals showing the following:

■ competitiveness
■ time-urgent behaviour (trying to do too much in too little time)
■ easily annoyed/aroused hostility and anger
■ impatience
■ achievement-oriented behaviour
■ a vigorous speech pattern.

In the 1960s and 1970s, TAB was found to modestly but consistently increase the risk of CHD and MI (heart attack) mortality when compared with persons showing a Type B behaviour pattern (the converse of Type A, i.e. relaxed with little aggressive drive) (e.g. the Western Collaborative Group study (WCGS) – Rosenman, Brand, Sholtz *et al.* 1976; and the Framingham heart study – Haynes, Feinleib and Kannel 1980). Yet most susbsequent research, including longer-term (twenty-two years) follow-up of the WCGS participants, failed to confirm these early associations (e.g. Hollis, Connett, Stevens *et al.* 1990; OrthGomer and Unden 1990; Ragland and Brand 1988; see Booth-Kewley and Friedman 1987 for review). In fact, some of these

studies found very different results to what was expected, for example, Ragland and Brand's twenty-two year follow-up of the WCGS cohort found that Type B's with prior CHD experienced a second heart attack sooner than Type A's with prior CHD, and healthy Type A's were no more likely than healthy Type B's to have experienced a fatal heart attack. Some of these contradictory findings may be explained by differences in the methods of assessment of TAB (for example, structured face-to-face interviews versus self-completed questionnaires), differences in the heart disease outcome assessed (e.g. heart attack event, heart attack death, angina, arterial disease) or in sampling differences. For example, some studies used healthy samples, others used heart attack survivors or those with other risk factors, such as smoking (see Miller, Turner, Tindale *et al.* 1991 for a review of explanations for contradictory findings from Type A behaviour research).

While evidence of a TAB–coronary illness link may be controversial, there is some evidence suggesting that Type A's respond more quickly and in a stronger emotional manner to stress, and that they exhibit a greater need for control than non-Type A individuals (Furnham 1990). These features of Type A may actually increase the person's likelihood of encountering stress, as they are likely to influence their interactions with others (Smith 1994) and result in the individual experiencing a more 'stressful' environment. Type A's also show greater physiological reactivity than Type B's, although this appears to be task-dependent and evident when tasks are competitive or challenging rather than in tasks that are irrelevant to the TAB character, such as simple perceptuo-motor tasks (e.g. Krantz, Glass, Shaeffer *et al.* 1982). Cardiovascular reactivity during stress has been implicated in various disease processes, such as the extent and progression of carotid artery atherosclerosis and the emergence of coronary heart disease (Smith, Gallo and Ruiz 2003), and therefore it is this reactivity that may provide the mechanism by which personality or Type A characteristics influence disease. Evidence exists that TAB can be altered through intervention, with resulting health gains (Friedman, Thoresen, Gill *et al.* 1986) supports the view that Type A is a behavioural response to provocative situations that is only in part the result of a stable personality trait. The core component appears to be antagonistic or hostile attitudes and behaviour, considered to be a trait.

■ **Hostility and anger**

Hostility is defined as a trait made up of emotional, cognitive and behavioural components. Trait anger is thought to be a central emotional component that is both experienced by the individual and manifested in aggressive or antagonistic actions or expressions. Cognitive components of hostility include having a cynical view of the world, a negative general attitude and negative expectations (cynicism, mistrust and denigration) about the motives of others (Miller, Smith, Turner *et al.* 1996). Behaviourally, hostile individuals may appear overtly aggressive or angry. The literature examining psychosocial factors in blood pressure and hypertension has consistently identified associations with both inhibited anger (anger-in) and anger expression (anger-out), although anger expression appears most implicated in coronary heart disease (Rosenman 1996; Suls, Wan and Costa 1995; Williams *et al.* 2000) and anger inhibition or suppression more so in hypertension risk (Vogele and Steptoe 1993; Vogele *et al.* 1997).

Hostility emerged as an important predictor of illness from various large-scale studies (e.g. the MRFIT study – Houston, Chesney, Black *et al.* 1992; the Western Collaborative Group study – Dembrowski, MacDougall, Costa *et al.* 1989; Barefoot, Dahlstrom and Williams 1983). While links were being established, so too were investigations of the pathways through which hostility affected health status, and several possibilities have been explored.

First, hostile individuals have been found to engage in health-risk behaviour which may itself be risk factors for illnesses such as heart disease, for example excessive smoking or alcohol intake (e.g. Lipkus, Barefoot, Williams *et al.* 1994; Scherwitz, Perkins, Chesney *et al.* 1992). Vögele (1998) also found that anger was associated with increased intake of alcohol and cigarettes (see Figure 12.2). It is therefore essential that studies investigating the hostility–disease link control for such risk factors, otherwise the actual extent to which hostility independently contributes to disease outcomes will be unclear.

Second, hostile individuals have been found to have a lower capacity to benefit from psychosocial resources or interpersonal support and thus they

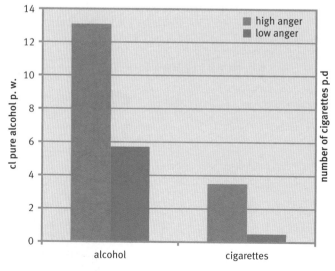

Figure 12.2 Anger and health behaviour.

Source: Vögele (1998)

are less 'buffered' against the negative effects of stressful or challenging events (Miller, Smith, Turner *et al.* 1996). This has been termed a 'psycho-social vulnerability hypothesis', whereby hostility is considered to be a moderator of the relationship between stressful environmental characteristics and health problems (Kivimäki *et al.* 2003). Their large-scale study of Finnish adults found that, for men only, hostility influenced the relationship between unemployment and ill-health, with hostile men having a high prevalence of health problems regardless of employment status, whereas non-hostile men had better health if employed.

Third, experimental studies have shown that hostile individuals are generally more stress-reactive than non-hostile individuals. Reduced 'buffers' plus a tendency to greater stress reactivity among hostile individuals makes them vulnerable to coronary heart disease. For example, in a series of experimental studies, Suarez and colleagues (e.g. Suarez and Williams 1989; Suarez, Kuhn, Schanberg *et al.* 1998) found that persons scoring high in cynical hostility on the Cook–Medley hostility scale produced larger blood pressure responses and greater neuroendocrine responses (e.g. raised cortisol levels) than non-hostile participants did when performing a task either during or immediately after an encounter with a rude and harassing laboratory assistant. Similar evidence from Everson, McKey and Lovallo (1995) showed that individuals scoring high in hostility had increased cardiovascular activation during a task performed after a staged interruption, and that furthermore hostile individuals differed in their evaluations of the experiment and the person who interrupted them than did low-hostility participants (e.g. they manifest more irritation and anger, and feelings of being personally insulted). As described in Chapter 11, prolonged or repeated episodes of elevated blood pressure may cause damage to the walls of vessels carrying blood to the heart (the coronary arteries).

Enough evidence has been amassed from systematic reviews and meta-analyses to conclude that hostility is a 'possible' risk factor for development of CHD (Hemingway and Marmot 1999), with several authors suggesting that the association is most evident in younger samples (aged 60 or under) (Kop and Krantz 1997; Miller *et al.* 1996; Smith, Gallo and Ruiz 2003). Some authors suggest that risk 'characteristics' such as hostility (and anger) may be created by certain social contexts that undermine an individual's ability to attain goals or financial security, and that hostility may be less of a trait than a coping response (e.g. Taylor, Repetti and Seeman 1997). This view raises the question of whether hostility is also indirectly associated with disease by virtue of a relationship with social deprivation (see Chapter 2).

Type C personality

The search for a disease-prone personality in relation to CHD (cf. Friedman and Booth-Kewley 1987), which led to identification and examination of type A and hostility, stimulated research into whether or not there was a cancer-prone personality type.

Earlier work that considered the existence of disease-prone personality types includes that of Eysenck (1988) and Grossarth-Maticek (Grossarth-Maticek, Bastiaans and Kanazin 1985). They hypothesised that personality played an important part in the development of cancer and CHD and identified four personality 'types'. Their 'cancer-prone personality', type 1, was characterised by suppression of emotion and inability to cope with inter-personal stress, leading to feelings of hopelessness, helplessness and finally depression, whereas a CHD-prone personality, type 2, was characterised by strong reactions of frustration, anger, hostility and emotional arousal (similar to TAB described above). Eysenck and Grossarth-Maticek (1989), following a large-scale community survey in Yugoslavia, reported evidence to show that type 1 increased individual risk of cancer by 120 times and type 2 increased CHD risk 25 times. These figures obviously suggest that phenomenal amounts of risk can be conferred on personality variables, for example greater risk than that elicited even by smoking. The claims of these authors inevitably led to much scrutiny of their work, and the survey and its findings have now been heavily criticised on the grounds of inappropriate analyses, insufficient methodological detail being provided in their paper, and a general inability of others to replicate their findings in either CHD studies or cancer studies (Amelang and Schmidt-Rathjens 1996; Pelosi and Appleby 1992, 1993; Smedslund and Rundmo 1999).

In contrast, Temoshok's typology (Temoshok and Fox 1984; Temoshok 1987), following a fifteen-year follow-up of women with breast cancer, did generate a robust finding of an association between passive and helpless coping style and poor disease prognosis. They described a **Type C personality** as having the following characteristics:

- cooperative and appeasing
- compliant and passive
- stoic
- unassertive and self-sacrificing
- tendency to inhibit negative emotions, particularly anger.

Type C personality
a cluster of personality characteristics manifested in stoic, passive and non-emotionally expressive coping responses. Thought to be associated with an elevated cancer risk.

Several studies have offered support for the Type C typology and elevated cancer risk. For example, Shaffer, Graves, Swank *et al.* (1987) conducted a thirty-year prospective study of 972 physicians and found that participants who exhibited high levels of emotional expression and 'acting out' had less than a 1 percent risk of developing cancer, whereas those who inhibited emotional expression were sixteen times more likely than this group to develop cancer. In contrast to the passive, emotionally suppressed behaviour of these participants is evidence pointing to positive outcomes among cancer patients showing 'fighting spirit' (see 'What is adaptive coping?' section above).

Type D personality

Type D personality
a personality type characterised by high negative affectivity and social inhibition.

More recent than research into elevated CHD risk through Type A behaviour and hostility is the notion of a **Type D personality**, considered to be detrimental to cardiovascular disease prognosis and outcomes (Denollet and Potter 1992; Denollet, Sys, Stroobant *et al.* 1996; Denollet 1998). This personality type is best described as a 'distressed' personality, with individuals scoring highly on negative affectivity (NA) and social inhibition (SI, defined as 'the avoidance of potential dangers involved in social interaction such as disapproval or nonreward by others' (Denollet 1998: 209)). Type D individuals therefore experience negative emotions but inhibit them while also avoiding social contact, and these characteristics have been associated with increased mortality following a heart attack or other cardiac event, even when controlling for other biomedical risk factors (e.g. Denollet *et al.* 1996). The effect was found in both women and men who had pre-existing heart disease.

In an attempt to identify physiological correlates of Type D personality, Habra, Linden, Anderson *et al.* (2003) examined cardiovascular reactivity (blood pressure, heart rate and salivary cortisol levels) of undergraduate students completing a mental arithmetic task while being harassed. Socially inhibited males showed heightened blood pressure reactivity; negative affectivity was associated with dampened heart rate changes during the task in males; and salivary cortisol levels were positively associated with both Type D dimensions (but not in final, more stringent analyses). However, unlike Denollet's studies, where NA and SI were only predictive jointly, Habra's findings suggested that NA and SI operated independently. These differences may be due to clear differences in the samples (older adults with CHD versus healthy undergraduate students), but further research is obviously warranted with this Type D construct.

Neuroticism

Neuroticism is a broad dimension of individual differences characterised by the tendency to experience negative emotions and to exhibit associated beliefs and behaviours (Costa and McCrae 1987). Individuals high on neuroticism often display anxious beliefs and behaviour disproportionate to the situation. Neuroticism was one of the three personality dimensions identified by Eysenck (1982). It is thought to be a trait, and therefore relatively unchangeable. As described in Chapter 9, neuroticism is related to increased attention to internal states and increased somatic complaints, and it has been thought to underpin many stress–health associations (Costa and McCrae 1987; McCrae 1990). Watson and Clark (1984) proposed that a related construct, a pervasive trait known as negative affectivity (NA), would play a central role in the stress–health relationship. Trait NA is a personality dimension, with high-NA individuals characterised by a generalised negative outlook, greater introspection, low affect (mood) and low self-concept. In studies of a range of adult samples, NA was also found to be associated with lower self-rated health, greater health complaints, but generally not with objective ill-health indicators (Cohen *et al.* 1995; Watson and Pennebaker 1989; Evers *et al.* 2003). It is likely that neuroticism and negative affectivity influence the reporting of physical symptoms and health complaints because of their influence on somatisation and attention to internal bodily states. Anxious 'over-scanning', and the likelihood of interpreting bodily signs in a threatening manner, makes for excessive symptom perception, but in the absence of consistent evidence of an association with actual illness events, NA is described as a 'nuisance factor' (Watson and Pennebaker 1989: 248) that makes it necessary for researchers to interpret with caution self-reported outcomes of health complaints and self-reported predictors of stress or distress, as the relationship 'found' between stress and illness may be inflated by the reporting bias of participants high in NA. In spite of only weak longitudinal or predictive associations between NA and objective indicators of illness (e.g. Friedman and Booth-Kewley 1987), studies have still sought to identify whether any physiological pathway exists between NA and illness outcomes, with some suggestion that NA is associated with raised cortisol levels, which causes immune function to be suppressed (e.g. van Eck, Berkhof, Nicolson *et al.* 1996).

So far, we have presented personality concepts that are in some way associated with negative outcomes, but several other factors have been identified that can be considered as 'resource' variables, i.e. aspects of personality that may reduce the negative outcomes of stressful experiences.

Hardiness

The concept of hardiness was identified and tested by Kobasa (1979) when searching for factors that might differentiate those who respond to stress by becoming ill from those who stay healthy. Hardiness was defined as:

- experiencing rich, varied and rewarding experiences in childhood;
- manifest in feelings of commitment, control and challenge.

Commitment was defined as a person's sense of purpose or involvement in events and activities and with people in their lives. Committed individuals were thought to view potentially stressful situations as meaningful and interesting. Control was defined as a person's belief that they can influence events in their lives. Individuals high on control were thought to view stressors as potentially changeable. Challenge was defined as a person's tendency to view change as a normal aspect of life and as something that can be positive. Individuals scoring high on the challenge dimension would view change as an opportunity for growth rather than as a threat to security.

Rather than exerting a direct effect on health experience, it is thought that by possessing each of these characteristics a hardy person was equipped with characteristics that would buffer them against the experience of stress and thus enable them to remain healthy. Kobasa's first study was based on male executives who completed Holmes and Rahes' social readjustment rating scale (see Chapter 11) and a self-report checklist of symptoms and illness events. Correlational findings were upheld in subsequent longitudinal prospective studies (Kobasa, Maddi and Kahn, 1982), and the buffering effects are presented in Figure 12.3, where it is evident that hardiness has most effect in situations of high stress. Further evidence for this buffering effect was reported by Beasley, Thompson and Davidson (2003) in a study of 187 university students who retrospectively reported life stress. In addition to finding a direct relationship between hardiness and reduced distress, hardiness buffered the effects of negative life events on the psychological health of female participants. For both males and females, the negative effect of emotion-oriented coping on distress was lower in those scoring high on the hardiness measure. However, this study was cross-sectional and, in fact, several prospective studies have failed to find evidence of buffering effects of hardiness. It has also been suggested that it is a lack of hardiness that is important, rather than the presence of it. Rhodewalt and Zone (1989) came to this conclusion following a study of adult women, where non-hardy women had appraised life events more negatively than hardy women, and that even though they had not experienced more recent life events than had the hardy women, the non-hardy women did tend to rate more of the events as undesirable and requiring adjustment on their part. This has led to suggestions that non-hardiness may reflect underlying neuroticism (Funk 1992).

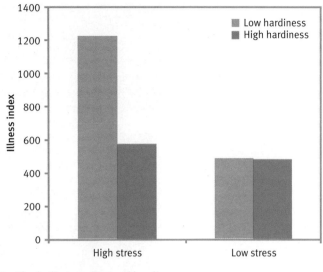

Figure 12.3   The buffering effects of hardiness.

Source: adapted from Kobasa *et al.* (1982)

Optimism

Another 'protective' resource that may be beneficial when dealing with stress is that of dispositional optimism, i.e. having a generally positive outlook and positive outcome expectations. Scheier and colleagues (Scheier, Weintraub and Carver 1986; Scheier and Carver 1992) proposed that dispositional optimists are predisposed towards believing that desired outcomes are possible, and that this motivates optimistic individuals to cope more effectively and persistently with stress or illness events, thus reducing their risk of negative outcomes. Dispositionally optimistic persons are less likely to make internal ('it is my fault'), stable ('it is an aspect of my personality that I can not change') and global attributions for negative events; i.e. they are more likely to appraise stress as changeable and specific and coming from external sources that are potentially more changeable or ignorable than internal ones. Pessimism, on the other hand, is a generalised negative outlook associated with denial and distancing responses to stress. Pessimism among cancer patients, for example, was found to have independent effects to optimism and was associated with mortality among younger patients even when controlling for the related construct of depression (Schulz, Bookwala, Knapp *et al.* 1996).

In a meta-analysis of studies using the life orientation test (the measure of optimism developed by Scheier and Carver 1985; see Table 12.2) Andersson (1996) reports that optimism was significantly associated with coping, with reduced symptom reporting and with reduced negative mood or depression, with this latter relationship being strongest. Of the studies reviewed by Andersson, examples include Aspinwall and Taylor's (1992) findings that optimism predicted active coping responses among students during times of stress; and, among a clinical sample, Taylor, Kemeny, Aspinwall *et al.*'s (1992) findings that optimism predicted better psychological and physical functioning in HIV-positive men. Optimism has therefore had reported

Plate 12.1   How optimistic are you? Is this glass half-empty or half-full?

Source: Alamy/Steve Hamblin

Table 12.2   Measuring optimism: the life orientation test

Please be as honest and accurate as you can be throughout. Try not to let your response to one statement influence your responses to other statements. There are no 'correct' or 'incorrect' answers. Answer according to your *own* feelings rather than how you think 'most people' would answer. Using the scale below, write the appropriate letter in the box beside each statement.

A	B	C	D	E
I agree a lot	I agree a little	I neither agree nor disagree	I disagree a little	I disagree a lot

1. In uncertain times, I usually expect the best   ☐
2. It's easy for me to relax*   ☐
3. If something can go wrong for me, it will   ☐
4. I always look on the bright side   ☐
5. I'm always optimistic about my future   ☐
6. I enjoy my friends a lot*   ☐
7. It's important for me to keep busy*   ☐
8. I hardly ever expect things to go my way   ☐
9. Things never work out the way I want them to   ☐
10. I don't get upset easily*   ☐
11. I'm a believer in the idea that 'every cloud has a silver lining'   ☐
12. I rarely count on good things happening to me   ☐

* these are 'filler' items, which have the function of disguising the focus of the test

benefits for both healthy populations dealing with stressful events and patient populations dealing with various aspects of their illness.

Optimism seems to lead to better functioning and outcomes because optimistic people appraise events in a way that makes it more likely that they will employ problem-focused coping strategies (Taylor and Armor 1996). For example, a study of law students found that optimistic students exhibited less avoidance coping and lower perceived stress than non-optimistic students, although the authors (Segestrom, Taylor, Kemeny *et al.* 1998) do point out that situational rather than dispositional optimism was associated with the lowered stress appraisals. This distinction between different types of optimism is important, particularly given that the different measures of optimism predicted different outcomes – situational optimism predicted elevated mood and immune function, where dispositional optimism did not.

Such beneficial effects of optimism as have been relatively consistently reported in the literature raises the question of the feasibility of interventions to enhance optimistic beliefs. If optimism is stable, how could this be achieved? Folkman and Moskowitz (2000) have suggested that optimistic beliefs can be maintained by successful coping outcomes. This leads to a consideration of whether coping skills training and positive feedback on successful efforts may build optimism. If so, optimism would then become closer to what is termed self-efficacy, i.e. a belief that one has the capacity to do what is required in a given situation (see Chapter 5). Another construct related to dispositional optimism, is that of unrealistic optimism, i.e. the view that unpleasant events are more likely to happen to others than to oneself, and that pleasant events are more likely to happen to oneself than to others (Weinstein 1982; also discussed in Chapter 5). Unrealistic optimism is sometimes referred to as 'defensive optimism' (Schwarzer 1993) as it may operate as an emotional buffer against the recognition or acceptance of possible negative outcomes, i.e. it may protect people from a depressing reality.

How is dispositional optimism related to the two constructs of unrealistic optimism and self-efficacy, and do they each have independent effects on adaptation to illness? The relationship between these three related constructs has been addressed by Fournier, de Ridder and Bensing (2002), who examined predictors of self-care in people with either insulin-dependent diabetes or multiple sclerosis (MS). They hypothesised that people with diabetes – a disease generally controllable by self-management – would have better mood and self-care if they were high on positive **efficacy** and dispositional optimism, as this would lead to better self-care strategies, perceived positive benefits to their condition and thus lower levels of anxiety and depression. In contrast, positive efficacy expectations in the MS patients were thought to be less important to self-care, as this disease is less controllable. In MS patients, it was hypothesised that unrealistic optimism would instead benefit mood, because these beliefs were maintained in the face of health deterioration, and therefore the individual is not facing negative feedback from unrealistically optimistic expectations and attempts to control their illness. Both hypotheses were confirmed by their data, highlighting the fact that optimistic beliefs work in different ways depending on context and the controllability of the disease. They also report that dispositional optimism and self-efficacy beliefs remained relatively stable over the twelve-month follow-up period in comparison with unrealistic optimism, which decreased over time. Stable, dispositional variables such as optimism may offer more limited opportunity

efficacy
Bandura's technical term analogous to confidence.

for intervention than do cognitions, such as situational and unrealistic optimism or perceptions of control, and it is to this latter construct that we now turn our attention.

Stress and cognitions

Perceived control

Early work on the construct of control considered it to be a personality trait. Locus of control, derived from Rotter's social learning theory, proposed LoC as a generalised belief that would influence behaviour as greater reinforcements (e.g. rewarding outcomes) were expected when responsibility for events was placed internally rather than externally (Rotter 1966). Furthermore, internal locus of control beliefs would only predict behaviour in situations where the rewards/outcomes were valued. LoC therefore refers to the trait-like expectation that personal actions will be effective in controlling or mastering the environment, with individuals falling on the side of either internality or externality.

According to Rotter, an 'internal' individual would take responsibility for what happens to them; for example, they would attribute successes to their own efforts and their failures to their own laziness. An 'external' individual would be more likely to believe that outside forces or chance circumstances control their lives, and both success and failures would be likely to be attributed to luck or chance. These beliefs would therefore influence a person's behaviour. It is considered that internal individuals have more efficient cognitive systems and that they expend energy on obtaining information that will enable them to influence events of personal importance. In other words, internally oriented individuals would engage in more problem-focused coping efforts when faced with personal or social stressors.

Relating locus of control to more specific outcomes, that of health, Wallston and colleagues (e.g. Wallston, Wallston and deVellis 1978) described a health locus of control construct, assessed using the multidimensional health locus of control scale. The MHLC assesses the extent to which a person believes that they themselves, external factors or 'powerful others' (e.g. friends, health professionals) are responsible for their health and health outcomes. This measure therefore assesses three subscales and includes items such as:

- 'I am in control of my health' – internal;
- 'No matter what I do, if I am going to get sick I will get sick' – external;
- 'Regarding my health, I can only do what my doctor tells me to do' – powerful others.

The MHLC has been used extensively, and internal, external and powerful others beliefs have been found to be associated with a range of coping, emotional and behavioural outcomes (including health behaviour itself). For example, among two longitudinal studies of patients with lower back pain, internal HLC was associated with reduced physical disability at follow-up, and patients with stronger internal control beliefs gained more from their treatment and exercised more often (distress was associated with poorer exercise behaviour) (Fisher and Johnston 1998; Härkäpää, Järvikoski, Mellin *et al.* 1991). Using an HLC measure specific to recovery from disability (the recovery locus of control scale; Partridge and Johnston 1989), Johnston, Morrison, MacWalter *et al.* (1999) also found that perceptions of internal control predicted better recovery from disability six months after an acute stroke. However, when attempting to reveal how perceived control may have influenced physical recovery (measured in terms of the ability to perform a range of activities such as walking, dressing and toileting), the authors did not find that internal PC led to an increase in exercise behaviour, as reported by the Finnish study (Härkäpää *et al.* 1991). Importantly, these authors reassessed this group of stroke survivors at three years following their stroke to examine whether the beneficial effects of PC persisted long term, and results confirmed that perceived control beliefs, as assessed at baseline (10–20 days post-stroke onset) were significantly predictive of long-term physical recovery but not emotional recovery in terms of reduced distress (Johnston *et al.* 2004; Morrison *et al.* 2005).

The importance of this type of finding is that, unlike neurological impairment or age (both predictors of outcome following stroke), control beliefs can be modified. For example, Fisher and Johnston (1996) showed how a simple letter-based intervention increased internal control beliefs and reduced pain reports in a chronic pain sample. Such findings suggest that enhancing internal control beliefs is a useful intervention approach when the outcome concerned is physical. However, few studies have found perceived control to be predictive of disease course, for example cancer relapse or survival (DeBoer, Ryckman, Pruyn *et al.* 1999).

Furthermore, there is evidence that internal control is not always adaptive in that it can lead to optimistic biases such as unrealistic optimism, although the direction of causality is unclear (do optimists perceive control, or does perceiving control make you optimistic? e.g. Klein and Helweg-Larsen 2002). Furthermore, maintaining beliefs in internal control in situations where such beliefs are unrealistic (e.g. severe and permanent disability following traumatic brain injury), may lead to problem-focused coping efforts that fail. This perceived failure could in turn contribute to feelings of depression and helplessness, whereas accepting the reality of having no control may lead to more adaptive emotion-focused coping responses (Folkman 1984; Thompson 1981).

One important question to be asked in this regard is 'control over what?' Various types of control have been described:

- *Behavioural*: the belief that one has behaviour available that would reduce the negative impact of a stressor, e.g. using controlled breathing techniques prior to and during a painful dental procedure.

- *Cognitive*: the belief that one has certain thought processes or strategies available that would reduce the negative impact of a stressor, e.g. distracting oneself from surgical pain by focusing on pleasant thoughts of a forthcoming or past holiday.

- *Decisional*: having the opportunity to choose between options, e.g. having a local anaesthetic prior to a tooth extraction (bearing in mind that the after-effects can last for hours!) or having the tooth removed without anaesthetic.

- *Informational*: having the opportunity to find out about the stressor; i.e. get knowledge of what, why, when, where, likely outcomes, possibilities, etc. Information allows preparation (see Chapter 13).

■ *Retrospective*: attributions of cause or control over an event made after it happens: i.e. searching for a meaning for an event can give some sense of order in life; e.g. blaming a birth defect on a defective gene (internal) may be more adaptive than attributing blame externally, although this is not clear-cut.

Each of these types of control can reduce the stressfulness of an event by altering the appraisal a person makes of the stressor, by reducing emotional arousal or by influencing the coping responses adopted (e.g. Parkes 1984). Thompson, Sobolew-Shubin, Galbraith *et al.* (1993), in a study of seventy-one adult cancer patients, showed that, even in generally uncontrollable circumstances in terms of disease progression, perceiving control over day-to-day emotions and physical symptoms significantly reduced distress, and that these perceptions of control remained associated with adjustment even in those with poorer physical functioning. This highlights that while control over outcome may not be realistic, control over aspects of the event or responses to it remain beneficial to adjustment

Self-efficacy and perceived locus of control are the two main control concepts used in health psychology, and they could be considered as spanning different phases of the coping process; for example, locus of control is an appraisal of the extent to which an individual believes they can control outcomes, whereas self-efficacy addresses appraisal of the resources and skills an individual believes they can use in order to achieve desired outcomes. Also related to control beliefs are **causal attributions**. A review of sixty-four datasets exploring associations between attributions of cause in a wide range of conditions (including arthritis, cancer, heart disease, burns, AIDS, infertility, stroke and pregnancy loss) and adjustment (Hall and Marteau 2003), 80 percent of studies reported no association between internal (behavioural self-blame) attributions or external (other-blame) attributions and adjustment. In fact, no particular attribution was strongly associated with achieving a better outcome. Characterological self-blame (e.g. it is something in my nature that I can't change that caused me to become ill) was most often associated with poorer outcomes. This type of self-blame has been associated with negative emotions such as depression.

causal attribution
where a person attributes the cause of an event, feeling or action to themselves, to others, to chance or to some other causal agent.

Stress and emotions

Depression and anxiety

The role of depression in increasing the incidence/likelihood of disease experience is controversial and depends on the disease concerned. The Alameda County study discussed in Chapter 3 (where we listed the seven types of 'healthy behaviour') did not find any effect of depressed mood upon CHD incidence; however, other studies have associated depression with hypertension, even when taking other risk factors into consideration. For example, the Framingham heart study found that depression, as well as anxiety, predicted twenty-year incidence of hypertension even controlling for age, smoking and obesity (Markowitz *et al.* 1993). In relation to cancer, a major study showed that recurrent major depression among an elderly sample predicted a higher incidence of breast cancer (Penninx, Guralnik, Pahor *et al.* 1998).

Booth-Kewley and Friedman (1987), in their meta-analysis of studies exploring the psychological predictors of heart disease, highlighted several studies that found a significant association between depression and CHD outcomes (heart attack, angina, cardiac death, as well as global CHD). More recently, a review by Hemingway and Marmot (1999) found that eleven out of eleven longitudinal prospective studies in healthy populations presented results supportive of a role of depression and/or anxiety in the aetiology (development) of CHD, and that six out of six prospective studies among CHD patients reported a significant prognostic role for depression.

A significant association between depressed mood and mortality from heart attack (myocardial infarction, MI), has also been reported. For example, Frasure-Smith, Lespérance and Talajic (1995) found that depression was more predictive of death than was either the degree of heart damage or having had a previous heart attack. Subsequent work has confirmed such findings; for example, an impressive longitudinal study of 237 healthy men (Vaillant 1998) found that 45 percent of those with a depressive episode at or before the baseline assessment were dead by the time of follow-up – a massive fifty-five years later – compared with only 5 percent of those who had not experienced such an episode. Neither depression nor anxiety were predictive of (non-)survival in two longitudinal studies of stroke patients carried out in Scotland (Johnston, Pollard, Morrison *et al.* 2004; Lewis, Dennis, O'Rourke and Sharpe 2001; Morrison, Pollard, Johnston *et al.* 2005), although other studies with longer follow-ups have found a significant relationship (Morris, Robinson, Andrzejewski, Samuels and Price 1993).

Depressed mood may reflect an underlying state of negative affectivity (see earlier section on personality), which is what has been suggested through the work of Denollet and his colleagues (Denollet and dePotter 1992; Denollet 1998). These researchers have found that cardiovascular disease outcomes (recovery, death, further heart attacks) can be partially explained by high NA scores combined with social inhibition ('type D' personality; see earlier section), and while there is no suggestion that such characteristics predict disease onset, the evidence is mounting as to their role in cardiovascular disease outcomes.

Research has also attempted to identify emotions associated with increased cancer risk. One such study is the Western Electric study (WES; Persky, Kempthorne-Rawson and Shekelle 1987), which conducted seventeen- and twenty-year follow-ups and found that those participants who initially scored highly on the global depression subscale of the MMPI (Minnesota multiphasic personality inventory) had a greater incidence of cancer at follow-up. However, this was later attributed to environmental factors. Another large-scale longitudinal study – the Alameda County study – did not replicate these findings (Kaplan and Reynolds 1988). Although there is some suggestion that feelings of hopelessness and helplessness associated with depression are implicated in cancer onset (Everson *et al.* 1996), the evidence appears to be, as with CHD, more strongly in support of depression influencing outcomes rather than aetiology. The subject of depression as an outcome itself is addressed in Chapter 14.

Depression has also been found to be associated with the behaviour a person engages in when dealing with a stressful event such as illness. Depression is seen to reduce the likelihood of healthy behaviour or cessation of unhealthy behaviour. For example, people who had experienced a heart attack (MI) and who exhibited subsequent depression had lower rates of smoking cessation than those who did not show signs of depression five months after the MI (Huijbrechts, Duivenvoorden, Deckers *et al.* 1996). Depressed individuals were also less likely to attend cardiac rehabilitation classes than non-depressed individuals (Lane, Carroll, Ring *et al.* 2001), and generally research findings suggest that adherence to therapeutic interventions or treatments such as exercise or medication is lower among depressed individuals than those who are not depressed (e.g. DiMatteo, Lepper and Crogan 2000; Wing, Phelan and Tate 2002). Such non-adherent behaviour can expose individuals to adverse health outcomes, such as future illness, poorer recovery from illness, or even mortality (McDermott, Schmitt and Wallner 1997).

As well as possibly operating on disease outcomes via an effect on non-adherence, depression and anxiety have been shown to influence the appraisals that individuals make when facing stressful events (appraisals of threat, as opposed to appraisals of challenge), thus influencing the coping actions a person engages in. For example, Lowe, Vedhara, Bennett *et al.* (2003), drawing from the stress–emotion–coping framework of Smith and Lazarus (1993; see Chapter 11 for theoretical explanation) examined whether the emotion of depression was attached to secondary appraisals of low problem-focused coping potential and pessimistic future expectations, and whether anxiety was attached to appraisals of low emotion-focused coping potential. Results from 148 women with suspected breast cancer confirmed expectations in relation to stress appraisals and also found that confrontation coping, avoidance coping and acceptance-resignation coping were all positively associated with anxiety, whereas depression was negatively associated with confrontation and not related to the other two coping responses.

IN THE SPOTLIGHT below highlights the fact that coping with stress is not all about negative emotions and that there is a growing body of research pointing to the importance of thinking and acting positively.

Emotional disclosure

One possible moderator of coping receiving increased attentions in recent years is that of **emotional disclosure** – the opposite of emotional suppression, or repressive coping, commonly found to be detrimental to health (see also 'type C' section under Personality and stress). A leading figure in this area is Pennebaker (e.g. Pennebaker, Kiecolt-Glaser and Glaser 1988; Pennebaker 1993), who with various colleagues has developed a paradigm whereby writing about one's recent trauma is found to have long-term benefits in terms of immune functioning (Pennebaker *et al.* 1988; Petrie, Booth, Pennebaker *et al.* 1995), and healthcare use (Pennebaker and Beall 1986).

expressed emotion
the disclosure of emotional experiences as a means of reducing stress; often achieved by describing the experience in writing.

Disclosure of emotional experiences is not to be confused with work on **expressed emotion** (EE; can include the expression of negative as well as positive emotion), which although often studied using a similar expressive writing paradigm has been associated with poorer prognosis among psychiatric populations and is showing contradictory findings among the physically ill (interested readers can see the recent meta-analysis by Panagopoulou,

IN THE SPOTLIGHT

Positivity and meaningful lives

There has been a growth in studies in what is being called 'positive psychology' (Folkman and Moskowitz 2000: Seligman and Csikszentmihalyi 2000). Basically, what these authors, among others, are suggesting is that we need to move away from a focus on how to reduce or avoid negative thoughts and emotions and turn more attention towards the benefits to health and wellbeing offered by thinking and acting positively. For example, in addition to optimism, which we have discussed in this chapter, hope, happiness and joy are thought to contribute to what Seligman, in a special edition on positive psychology in *The Psychologist* (2003), calls desirable lives: the pleasant life, the good life and the meaningful life. A pleasant life arises from one that pursues positive emotions about present, past and future experiences and involves the simple pleasures and gratifications or rewards that we get out of life. A good life arises from being and doing and being involved in life and all its activities so as to get the best out of it. A meaningful life is when we use our strengths and skills to benefit more than just ourselves.

To feel that life is pleasant, good or meaningful would imply that a person would therefore be happy, but little research has actually addressed happiness in relation to health outcomes, more often than not assessing subjective 'wellbeing', which may not be quite the same. Veenhoven (2003) states that happiness can be defined and measured and that by simply asking people about their levels of happiness we could explore questions such as is quality of life associated with happiness or can we have a quality of life without it? What makes a good life? Think about your own life and what makes you happy – it may help you live longer!

---

congestive heart failure a disorder in which the heart loses its ability to pump blood efficiently. As a consequence, many organs do not receive enough oxygen and nutrients, leading to the potential for them to become damaged and, therefore, not work effectively.

Kersbergen and Maes 2002). For example, Coyne and colleagues (2003) found that EE among couples where one had experienced **congestive heart failure** was associated with poorer marital quality and increased distress. Other authors suggest that EE assists in emotional self-regulation by allowing the patient or their carer to develop greater mental control over their illness and a coherent narrative of events in their head, which facilitates 'closure' and reduces distress. However, the evidence on the benefits and 'dis-benefits' of emotional writing, disclosure, and emotional expression remain mixed and will no doubt continue to develop as an avenue of research enquiry.

Social support and stress

The final topic in this chapter is that of social support, a potential resource available to most but not all of us that has been shown to be strongly associated with health and illness outcomes. Evidence exists that people who have strong (in both size and usage) networks of social support are healthier and live longer than the socially isolated, but what actually is meant by 'social support'?

Table 12.3 Types and functions of social support

	Provider	Recipient
Emotional support:	empathy caring concern	reassurance sense of comfort and belongingness
Esteem support	positive regard encouraging person positively comparing	builds self-worth sense of competence being valued
Tangible/instrumental support	direct assistance financial/practical aid	reduces strain/worry
Informational support:	advice, suggestions feedback	communication self-efficacy/self-worth
Network support	Welcoming Shared experiences	Sense of belonging Affiliation

Definition, types and functions of social support

Social support can be actual or perceived. People with social support believe they are loved and cared for, esteemed and valued, and part of a social network of communication and mutual obligation, such as that often shared with family, friends or members of a social organisation. The social network facilitates the provision of goods, services and mutual defence in times of need or danger (Cobb 1976). Social support is a resource that when perceived as being available will affect how individuals appraise and respond to events, with individuals who perceive support levels as high being likely to appraise events as less stressful than individuals who do not perceive they have any support (i.e. social support acting as a 'buffer' against stress). Social isolation in terms of having a low level of social support and activity has been associated with heart disease mortality, for example among middle-aged men followed up for ten years (Orth-Gomér, Undén and Edwards 1988).

There are various types of social support and their functions in terms of what the social support provider provides and in terms of what is received by the recipient (see Table 12.3). Five basic types have been described, although some authors only distinguish between instrumental, emotional and informational, and most studies do not attempt to record what the recipient actually 'gets' from the support but rather assume that it is all helpful. (Chapter 15 challenges this assumption when carer and patient relationships are examined.)

Social support and mortality

Since Cobb's early work, many years have been spent trying to establish whether social support is causally implicated in mortality, and early support was obtained from the Alameda County study (Berkman and Syme 1979), even when health status and self-reported health-risk behaviour were controlled for. Early work also reported a twofold increase in mortality for those with low levels of social relationships (House *et al.* 1982). More recent studies have confirmed these associations. For example, Vogt, Mullooly, Ernst *et al.* (1992), from a fifteen-year follow-up of 2,603 adults, concluded that social 'networks' (assessed by size, number of supportive domains (scope) and frequency of use) strongly predicted mortality from ischaemic heart disease, cancer and stroke. A large-scale study of French employees (Melchior, Berkman, Niedhamer *et al.* 2003) also found that a lack of social support and dissatisfaction with social relationships predicted poor health status.

Social support and disease

Evidence of a relationship between life stress and health status has pointed to social support as a moderator. For example, Rosengren, Orth-Gomer, Wedel and Wilhelmsen (1993) found that among middle-aged men, the association between an accumulation of critical life changes and subsequent heart attack was moderated by the quality of social support. More recently, among individuals suffering from rheumatoid arthritis, social support in terms of a limited social network was predictive of disease activity three years later, even when coping behaviour was controlled for (Evers *et al.* 2003). It has been suggested that social relationships are particularly important in diseases where physical dependence on others, and decreased social activity resulting from the disease, are present (Penninx *et al.* 1999). Furthermore, social support may buffer the impact of depression on mortality following a heart attack (Frasure-Smith, Lespérance, Gravel *et al.* 2000).

How does social support influence health status?

We all need support. There is ample evidence that social support effectively reduces distress during times of stress (e.g. Cutrona and Russell 1987, 1990), and furthermore the lack of social support during times of need can itself be very stressful, particularly for people with high needs for social support but insufficient opportunities to obtain it, e.g. the elderly, the recently widowed and other victims of sudden, severe or uncontrollable life events (e.g. Penninx *et al.* 1999). Although there is more evidence for the benefit of social support in reducing stress and distress during illness than there is on actually preventing it occurring, Greenwood, Muir, Packham and Madeley (1996), following a review of empirical studies, also concluded that poor social support had a stronger effect on CHD incidence than did stressful life events.

Two theories as to how social support might operate have been proposed (Cohen, 1988):

1. *Direct effects hypothesis*: social support is beneficial regardless of the amount of stress people experience, and a lack of social support is detrimental to health even in the absence of stress. High levels of social support provide a greater sense of belonging and self-esteem than low levels, thus producing a positive outlook and healthier lifestyles. Alternatively, social support has a physiological route to health by virtue of either reduced blood pressure reactivity, thought to arise from positive stress appraisals and emotions, or possibly via enhanced endocrine or immune system functions, although there are less consistent findings in this area. (For a comprehensive review, see Uchino, Cacioppo and Kiecolt-Glaser 1996.)

2. *Buffering hypothesis*: social support protects the person against negative effects of high stress. Social support acts as a buffer by either (1) influencing the person's *cognitive appraisals* of a situation so they perceive their resources as being greater to meet threat; or (2) modifying the person's *coping response* to a stressor after it has been appraised as stressful (i.e. they do not cope alone) (Cohen and Wills 1985).

Seeking social support is generally considered an active coping strategy, whether the support is sought for informational and practical reasons or with the goal of emotional support. Kyngaes, Mikkonnen, Nousiainen *et al.* (2001) reported on the coping strategies of young people within two months of developing cancer. This sample engaged in emotion-, appraisal- and problem-focused coping strategies, but accessing social support was one of the most common strategies. Support was sought from health professionals in terms of obtaining information about their disease and its treatment, and emotional support was sought from their families.

In terms of receiving support, Turner-Cobb, Sephton, Koopman *et al.* (2000) found that breast cancer patients who assessed social support as present and helpful had lower morning cortisol levels than those who did not assess social support in this way, suggesting a physiological route by which social support may enact its benefits. Cognitive-behavioural interventions that have provided breast cancer patients with group support have also reported reduced cortisol levels (e.g. Creuss, Antoni, McGregor *et al.* 2000). We outlined the immunological effects of cortisol in Chapter 11 whereby increased cortisol is associated with immune down-regulation and is perhaps implicated in tumour growth.

Plate 12.2   From an early age, social support is a powerful moderator of stress response.

■ Can social support be bad for you?

It is worth noting that there are some instances where high levels of social support can be detrimental. For example, among pain patients it was found that high social support in terms of providing practical assistance with every-day tasks caused poor adaptation due to operant conditioning (e.g. Gil *et al.* 1987). Over-caring (see also Chapter 15) can cause the care recipient to become overly dependent on the carer and overly passive in terms of their own recovery (see Chapter 15). In addition, the type of social support provided may not always be received as supportive, or, more importantly, the help offered may not match the needs of the patient: e.g. instrumental support is helpful if aspects of the event are controllable; emotional support may be more helpful when things are uncontrollable, e.g. after a death (e.g. Cutrona and Russell 1990).

Finally, there is a caveat in social support research. Given the subjectivity of the construct in that it is defined in terms of 'how much social support do you perceive?', studies have to rely on self-report. As noted elsewhere, there are inherent biases in gathering self-report data, and it is likely that individual difference variables, such as neuroticism, may influence not only an individual's perceptions of the nature and level of social support they have received but also their satisfaction with it (Uchino *et al.* 1996). Additionally, personality in itself might interfere with social resources and in effect prevent or enhance a person's ability to access support, or gain from it (see discussion of hostility, for example).

Summary

The evidence reviewed in Chapter 11 suggested that stress can increase the risk of artery damage, which in turn encourages the development of CHD. This is a direct effect proposal, which implies that simply reducing stress exposure would reduce the likelihood of that disease. However, this chapter has shown this to be overly simplistic. Many factors moderate the impact of stress on health, or the impact of stressful illness upon longer-term outcomes such as disability, distress and survival. This chapter has described how factors attributed to a person's personality, control beliefs, emotions and use of social support can affect stress responses and outcomes. Such variables can be studied in terms of the direct relationships they have with stress outcomes, or as variables that need to be controlled for when examining other predictors. For example, one study might examine whether trait neuroticism predicts psychological distress following surgery, where another study might control for neuroticism in examining the effects of a pre-surgical information sheet on patient distress following surgery. Whatever the research question, it has become increasingly clear that many variables influence the relationship between a stressful event and its outcomes and that biological, psychological and social factors work together in the stress–illness experience.

Further reading

Adler, N.E. and Matthews, K.A. (1994). Health psychology: why do some people get sick and some stay well? *Annual Review of Psychology*, 45: 229–59.
A useful overview of many of the moderating variables discussed in this chapter.

Rice, P.L. (1992). *Stress and Health*. California: Brooks/Cole.
A clearly written book addressing most if not all of the topics discussed in this chapter.

Uchino, B.N., Cacioppo, J.T. and Kiecolt-Glaser, J.K. (1996). The relationship between social support and physiological processes: a review with emphasis on underlying mechanisms and implications for health. *Psychological Bulletin*, 119: 488–533.
An excellent and well-presented review of social support and its effects on cardio-vascular, endocrine and immune system functioning. Very useful summaries are provided of key studies.

CHAPTER 13

Managing stress

Learning outcomes

By the end of this chapter, you should have an understanding of:

- ways of intervening at a population or organisational level to reduce work stress
- the elements of a cognitive behavioural approach to stress management
- the nature and treatment of post-traumatic stress disorder in response to the onset of illness
- interventions of value in helping people to cope with the stress associated with a surgical operation

CHAPTER OUTLINE

Stress, they say, is all around us. Indeed, one of the most frequently reported problems in general practitioners' surgeries is tiredness – often as a symptom of stress. Other chapters in this book comment on the role of stress in the development of illness (Chapter 11), or how learning to manage stress effectively can enhance mood, improve the outcome of a number of diseases and reduce the experience of pain (Chapters 16, 17). What they do not consider in any detail is how such changes can be achieved. This chapter addresses this issue from a number of perspectives. First, it considers approaches used to minimise stress in healthy individuals, both in the public at large and in the workplace. In this, it complements Chapters 5 and 6 and their consideration of health-promotion strategies. The chapter then considers the nature of stress management interventions used when working with individuals who are experiencing stress. This section builds on Chapters 11 and 12, which examined the relationship between stress, coping and illness and will prepare you for Chapters 16 and 17, which include sections on how stress management can help people to cope with illness and pain. The chapter then examines how we treat an extreme response – known as post-traumatic stress – that can occur in response to the onset of illness. Finally, we consider how stress may be minimised when people face a specific stressor – in this case a surgical intervention – in hospital, using relatively simple interventions. This flow of the chapter moves us from discussion of stress management in preventive settings to those where an individual is coping with the stress of having a disease or its treatment. It also moves from highly complex systemic interventions involving whole organisations to much simpler interventions that can be conducted by nursing and other health professionals in general conversations with patients.

Preventing stress

Teaching stress management strategies

Perhaps the simplest way that we can help to minimise stress among the general population is to teach them stress management techniques. These can be taught in night school or even at health fairs using the approach adopted by Brown, Cochrane and Hancox (2000). They ran eight free full- or half-day stress management workshops in a leisure centre following a publicity drive as part of the 'Healthy Birmingham 2000' programme. These workshops taught attenders relaxation and other strategies for controlling their stress (which we describe later in the chapter). Their comparison groups comprised people who took part in a day-long programme focusing on sessions on healthy eating, alcohol awareness and physical exercise, and a group of people on a waiting list for future workshops. The event proved very popular and attracted both people who had seen a health professional, usually their general practitioner, about stress-related problems and those who had not. The intervention also proved successful. Compared with baseline levels, participants in the full-day workshops showed significantly greater reductions in stress and anxiety three months following the workshop than those in the control groups – an impressive result given the relative brevity of the

intervention and the wide range of people attending. This type of approach has the potential to provide significant benefit to those who take part – but only a very small proportion of the public are likely to attend such workshops. Health psychologists and others have therefore turned to other methods of attempting to reduce the stress of significant parts of the general population. One of the most important approaches they have adopted is to develop strategies for reducing stress in more 'captive audiences', the most important of which has been people at work.

Stress management at an organisational level

There is significant and rising pressure on employers to provide staff with the skills to manage stress effectively. In the UK, this has become increasingly important as the Health and Safety Executive, which determines safety standards in the workplace, has now stated that employers have a legal obligation to protect the emotional as well as physical wellbeing of their employees. Their reasons for this policy include data from their own sources (e.g. Jones, Huxtable, Hodgson *et al.* (2003)), which indicated that:

- In 2002, over half a million individuals in Britain reported experiencing work-related stress at a level that was making them ill, while nearly one in five thought their job was very or extremely stressful.
- Work-related stress, depression or anxiety accounts for an estimated 13.5 million lost working days per year in Britain.
- Levels of work stress are rising.
- Teachers and nurses have particularly high prevalence of work-related stress.

Most published attempts to reduce stress in the workplace have involved running stress management training at the workplace using similar methods to those of Brown and colleagues described above. That is, they have tried to help attenders to cope more effectively with the demands placed upon them. These appear to be effective. Eriksen, Ihlbaek, Mikkelsen *et al.* (2002), for example, randomly allocated a large group of employees to one of three intervention conditions: physical exercise, stress management training, or an integrated health programme involving physical exercise and health information. None of the interventions influenced health complaints, sick leave or job stress. However, each of the interventions did appear to impact on its target. Participants in the physical activity intervention showed improvements in general health and physical fitness, while the stress management group reported reductions in their levels of general stress. Despite this level of success, Oldenburg and Harris (1996) suggested that there are a number of factors that limit the benefits of workplace stress management programmes. Their main concern was over the number and type of people who attend such programmes. They noted that this type of programme usually attracts only between 10 and 40 percent of the workforce – and even less if it is not given a 'high profile' in the workplace. In addition, the majority of people who do attend seem to have relatively few stress-related problems, while many anxious individuals do not attend, perhaps because they feel that they will gain little from such courses or do not want to air their problems in front of their

Plate 13.1   The London Stock Exchange typifies an environment that encourages stress and high levels of aggressive behaviour and adrenalin.

Source: Alamy/The Hoberman Collection

Table 13.1   Some of the sources of stress for hospital workers

Professional issues	Patient issues	Work issues
Over-promotion	Distressed patients or relatives	Shift work
Under-promotion	'Difficult' patients or relatives	Poor working conditions
Interactions with colleagues	Dying patients	Too high a workload
Interactions with management	Complaints made against staff	Work intruding on home time
Working beyond knowledge level		Lack of social support
Lack of management support		Inadequate equipment

Source: Bennett *et al.* (1999)

colleagues. The failure of Eriksen's intervention to influence either work-related stress or levels of sick leave also highlights the need to influence these issues more directly – by addressing the *causes* of stress.

Identifying organisational causes of stress is more complex than providing stress management classes and has potentially more significant implications for an organisation. Table 13.1, for example, indicates the variety of potential stressors that may influence the stress of people working in a hospital, some of which are common to many work situations, some of which are unique to working in healthcare settings.

Changing any of these factors may impact on the stress of hospital workers, and working out where and how to intervene at an organisational

level is not easy. However, the process used by one of the authors (PB) to reduce stress in a group of hospitals provides an example of how this might be done. The process involved:

- identifying causes of stress in the working environment;
- identifying solutions to this stress from those most involved;
- developing a process of change to address the issues raised.

The first two stages of the intervention involved running a series of focus groups with different staff throughout the organisation. These were led by a health psychologist, who worked with the management of the hospital but who was not part of the management team. Many focus groups were run with key hospital staff, including cleaners and porters, nurses, managers, clerical workers, and people from the paramedical professions such as occupational therapists and physiotherapists. In each of these meetings, comprising about six people, attenders were invited to identify factors in their working environments that adversely affected their 'quality of life' at work. If problems were identified – and they inevitably were – they were also asked to identify any solutions to those problems. These meetings were intended to last up to one hour but often went on longer, and they were extremely productive.

Each of the issues and solutions put forward in the groups were then arranged into a set of common problems (and perhaps solutions) in a document that formed the basis of the next phase of the intervention. Problems raised included major systemic problems, such as:

- a poor computer network system;
- poor timing of the hospital bus provision (it did not fit in with shift times);
- very poor parking facilities, making transport to and from work difficult;
- inadequate crèche facilities;
- the organisation of various groups of wards in the hospital into competing rather than cooperating units;
- a working culture among management that punished people who did not work significant overtime.

Interestingly, the solutions that some workers had used to manage their stress impacted on other workers by increasing their dissatisfaction and stress. One example of this was that the management team in one hospital had moved its offices away from the wards to avoid what they thought of as too much day-to-day contact with the ward staff and to allow them to concentrate on more long-term planning. As a result, the management group felt less stressed and more able to get on with their job effectively. By contrast, and unbeknown to the management team, the ward nurses were angry and disillusioned as they felt this was an example of management blocking off contact that they felt vital to their effective running of the ward.

Once the problems and solutions were documented, these were taken to a small committee of senior managers, which formed a response to the needs. It did so by grouping the issues raised into three broad categories:

1. likely to have minimal effect, but relatively easy to instigate;
2. likely to have a significant effect, but more difficult to instigate;
3. likely to have a significant effect, but impossible to instigate.

Clearly, the interventions focused on the first two of these categories. Changes made included increasing the size of the crèche and lengthening its opening hours so that it was more useful for shift workers, changing the times of the hospital buses to make them more user-friendly, and initiating a new hospital computer system – over a number of years. However, any interventions need not necessarily be on such a large scale. One example of this was provided by a nurse manager, who noted that her staff often arrived late or very close to the time of their morning shift. When she asked them why, she found that these were predominantly single mothers who had to leave their child with a childminder on their way to work. Because childminders would only take children from a time close to the beginning of the shift, this put these nurses under significant time pressure. If the traffic was good between the childminder and hospital, they got to work on time; if the traffic was busy or delayed, they were late to work. The simple solution to the problem was to start the shift fifteen minutes later.

Do organisational interventions work?

There have been relatively few empirical studies of the effectiveness of this type of intervention. However, those that have been reported suggest they may be of benefit. Maes, Kittel, Scholten *et al.* (1990), for example, changed the nature of the working environment by redesigning jobs to avoid short and repetitive performance tasks, giving workers some control over the organisation of work and enhanced social contact. They also trained managers in communication and leadership skills and encouraged them to develop strategies for reducing stress in their area of work. This intervention resulted in increased quality of work and lower absenteeism rates in comparison with the control sites, which received no intervention.

A second intervention to use such an approach was reported by Mikkelsen and Saksvik (1999). They intervened in two offices in the Norwegian Post Office. The intention of their intervention was to increase employees' learning opportunities and decision-making authority in order to improve the work environment and health. In order to decide what changes to make, they ran discussion groups with the workers, which 'diagnosed' their present problems, then planned and enacted changes to the working environment to remedy them. They reported that work conditions in the larger organisation actually deteriorated over the course of the study, a process that was reversed in one but not both intervention offices. They attribute the failure of the latter to organisational restructuring and turbulence interfering with potential benefits of the intervention. A third, and much simpler, intervention was reported by Dababneh, Swanson and Shell (2001). They evaluated the impact of short rest breaks on productivity and wellbeing in a meat-processing factory. In one condition, workers were given thirty-six minutes of extra breaks by adding to their present breaks – one by adding four nine-minute break schedules distributed evenly throughout the day; the other by adding twelve three-minute breaks. Neither additional break lowered production, but both resulted in significant reductions in psychological discomfort. Workers preferred the nine-minute rest interval.

IN THE SPOTLIGHT

School kids learn anger control

The *Sunday Times* (11 January 2004) reported the use of a variant of stress management known as anger management in a school. The article was an interesting leap from the cynical to the convinced. It began:

> We have become so used to laughing at psychobabble, or at least I hope we have, that the phrase anger management training can usually be relied on to raise a titter. The news on Thursday that a school in north London is offering anger management classes for six-year-olds must have provoked a full-throttle guffaw in anyone who spotted it.

What it went on to describe was indeed unusual, describing an anger resolution and conflict management scheme developed at St Ann's Church of England primary school in Tottenham, London. In it, patrols of children – some as young as 6 – wearing badges and red caps marked 'Mentor' were learning how to stop bullying. They had weekly role play sessions in which they practised anger management and conflict resolution training. They were taught ways of helping other children to walk away from arguments and fights and to control their anger with breathing techniques (see below). The aim was that when anyone became angry or aggressive in the school playground, the mentors could help them to 'stop, think and listen and deal with their anger'.

The article goes on to state:

> This sounded perfectly absurd at first. Role play is yet another of those maddening phrases that immediately makes one think of Ricky Gervais and *The Office* (a British comedy involving an absurd office manager and his pathetic attempts to manage his staff while ingratiating himself with them). But slowly I began to believe that this scheme is perhaps not such a silly idea.

Because it seemed to work. Pupils in this school were achieving more than in comparable schools. Behaviour in the school had improved, and the academic performance of the school was above the national average, despite being in a deprived and violent area, where children frequently lacked good role models at home.

Perhaps psychological methods have some benefits after all.

Working with individuals

Stress theory – a quick review

stress management training
a generic term for interventions designed to teach participants how to cope with stress.

In this section, we examine some of the components of a set of interventions that are collectively often referred to as **stress management training**. They are based on cognitive behavioural theories of stress, which consider stress to be the outcome of a variety of environmental and cognitive processes (see Chapter 11). Stress is seen as a negative emotional and physiological state resulting from our cognitive responses to events that occur around us. That is, stress can be seen as a process rather than an outcome. We feel 'stressed', but we also have thoughts that contribute to this feeling, and associated

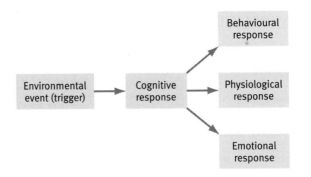

Figure 13.1 A simplified representation of the event–stress process suggested by Beck and other cognitive therapists.

physiological and behavioural responses, all of which form part of the 'stress response'. We discussed appraisal and transactional theories of stress in Chapter 11. Stress management approaches are in part based on these theories and in part based on more clinical theories, the two most prominent of which are those of Aaron Beck (1976) and Albert Ellis (1977). Both assumed that our cognitive response to events – not the events themselves – determines our mood, and that feelings of distress or other negative emotional states are a consequence of 'faulty' or 'irrational' thinking (see Figure 13.1). That is, they considered stress to be the result of *misinterpretations* of environmental events or cognitions that exaggerate the negative elements within them and lose focus on any positive aspects of the situation.

Beck referred to the thoughts that drive negative emotions as automatic negative assumptions. They come to mind automatically as the individual's first response to a particular situation and are without logic or grounding in reality. Despite this, their very automacity means they are unchallenged and taken as true. He identified two levels of cognition. Surface cognitions are those we are aware of. We can access them and report them relatively easily. Underlying them are a set of unconscious beliefs about ourselves and the world, known as **cognitive schemata** (singular, schema), that influence our surface cognitions, which, in turn, influence our emotions, behaviour and levels of physiological arousal. Stress-evoking thoughts, for example, result in an increase in sympathetic nervous system arousal (see Chapter 8), behaviour that may be more or less helpful in resolving the problem an individual is facing, and feelings of distress, pressure or anxiety. Beck identified a number of categories of thoughts that lead to negative emotions, including:

cognitive schema (schemata)
set of unconscious beliefs about the world and ourselves that shape more conscious cognitive responses to events that impinge on us.

■ *Catastrophic thinking*: considering an event as completely negative, and potentially disastrous: 'That's it – I've had a heart attack. I'm bound to lose my job, and I won't be able to earn enough to pay the mortgage'.

■ *Over-generalization*: drawing a general (negative) conclusion on the basis of a single incident: 'That's it – my pain stopped me going to the cinema – that's something else I can't do'.

■ *Arbitrary inference*: drawing a conclusion without sufficient evidence to support it: 'The pain must indicate I have a tumour. I just know it'.

- *Selective abstraction*: focusing on a detail taken out of context: 'OK, I know I was able to cope with going out, but my joints ached all the time, and I know that will stop me going out in future'.

A good example of how long-term schemata drive very stressful ways of responding to external events is provided by Price's (1988) cognitive model of type A behaviour. From her clinical work with type A men, she concluded that the schemata underlying type A behaviour were low self-esteem and a belief that one can gain the esteem of others only by continually proving oneself as an 'achiever' and a capable individual. These underlying beliefs underpinned more conscious competitive, time-urgent or hostile thoughts.

Surface cognitions associated with type A behaviour include:

- *Time-urgent thoughts*: 'Come on – we haven't got all day – I'm going to be late! Why is he so slow? Am I the only person who gets things done around here?'

- *Hostile thoughts*: 'That person cut me up deliberately! I'll sort him out. Why is everyone else so incompetent – they really are pretty stupid'.

Deeper (unconscious) schemata include:

- 'I can't say no to her request or I will look incompetent and I will lose her respect'.

- 'I must get to the meeting on time – whatever the cost – or people will think I'm incompetent and I will lose their respect'.

- 'People only respect you for what you do for them – not for who you are'.

What do YOU think?

The cognitive-behavioural model of stress assumes that stress lies within the individual. Stress arises from the misinterpretation of events that happen to us. But is this really true? It is possible to argue that while some stress may be the result of faulty thinking, stress can also be triggered by truly stressful circumstances. Most people would consider having a surgical operation, for example, to be a stressful event. Theorists such as Hobfoll have argued that many more general factors, such as being a single mother or holding down a demanding job, are universally stressful events. Arguments that socio-economic status influences health through psychological processes discussed in Chapter 2 also implicitly suggest that there are broad differences in the degree of stress experienced across different social groups.

If these assertions are true, then, at least in some cases, stress truly does result from environmental circumstances and not from an individual's interpretation of a situation. Such arguments may lead us to question how relevant stress management techniques based on the cognitive-behavioural models described above can be in these contexts.

The argument that cognitive-behavioural therapists would marshal against this critique is that even acknowledging that there are environmental factors that influence stress, some people cope with them better than others. There is individual variability in our ability to cope with similar demands placed on us. The role of stress management is not to deny the role of the environment but to help people to cope with the stressful circumstances they face as effectively as they can and with the least possible emotional distress. This seems to be a reasonable argument, but it leaves a number of questions for health psychologists. One particularly pertinent issue is how much effort we should put into changing the sources of stress and how much into changing people's responses to potentially stressful environments. Should we put our emphasis on reducing social inequalities by changing the environment, or on helping people to cope better with the demands of their environment here and now? Should we help some people to cope better with operations, or try to make the processes before and after an operation less stressful for all? Often, teaching people to cope better with stressful situations is easier and cheaper than changing the causes of stress. But is it the best approach?

Stress management training

The model of the stress response described above suggests a series of factors that can be changed in order to reduce an individual's stress. These include:

- environmental events that trigger the stress response – or series of triggers to longer-term stress;
- inappropriate behavioural, physiological or cognitive responses that occur in response to this event.

Most stress management programmes focus on changing people's reactions to events that happen around them or to them. Many simply teach relaxation to minimise the high levels of arousal associated with stress (see Chapter 8). More complex interventions try to change participants' cognitive (and therefore emotional) reactions to these events. Few address the factors that trigger the stress response in the first place. This can be considered a serious limitation – the most effective way of reducing stress is to stop it occurring in the first place. Accordingly, we incorporate into our overview of stress management training a process of both identifying and changing triggers to stress as well as strategies for dealing with stressful thoughts, feelings, emotions and behaviour once initiated:

- Triggers can be identified and modified using problem-solving strategies.
- Cognitive distortions can be identified and changed through a number of cognitive techniques, such as **cognitive restructuring** (see below).

cognitive restructuring
a reconsideration of automatic negative or catastrophic thoughts to make them more in line with reality.

- High levels of muscular tension and other signs of high arousal can be reduced through relaxation techniques.
- 'Stressed' behaviour can be changed through consideration and rehearsal of alternative behavioural responses.

■ Changing triggers

This is an often neglected part of stress management training, perhaps because there is no standard intervention that can be applied. The triggers to each person's stress necessarily differ, as will any strategies they develop to reduce the frequency of such triggers. Changing triggers involves first identifying situations that add to an individual's stress and then either changing their nature or reducing the frequency with which they occur. A simple strategy to reduce an individual's level of stress or anger while driving to work, for example, may be to start the journey earlier than previously so they feel less pressure during the journey.

One of the most frequently used approaches to identifying and changing triggers to stress was developed by Gerard Egan (1998). His model of problem-focused counselling involves three phases, through which the identification and change of any stress triggers can be achieved:

1. *Problem exploration and clarification*: what are the triggers to stress?
2. *Goal setting*: which triggers does the individual want to change?
3. *Facilitating action*: how do they set about changing the triggers to stress?

While this sequence may appear somewhat logical and obvious, when first used in the early 1960s this approach actually represented a significant shift from the rather unfocused counselling previously (and indeed still) practised by many therapists based on Roger's (1961) client-led counselling approach. This approach can also form part of the self-management programmes discussed in Chapter 17.

Problem exploration and clarification

The goal of the first stage of counselling is to help an individual to identify the problems he or she is facing that may be contributing to their stress. Some of these may be immediately obvious; some require a more detailed exploration around what is happening in that individual's life. The goal of this stage is to clarify *exactly* what problems the individual is facing, and in some detail: only then can appropriate problem-solving strategies be applied. Some therapist skills or strategies that are particularly pertinent to this stage of counselling are listed below:

- direct questioning and prompts
- silence and minimal prompts
- empathic feedback

The most obvious way of eliciting information is to ask direct questions. These should be open-ended in order to discourage one-word answers. Questions such as 'What aspects of your job contribute to your stress?' are likely to elicit much more information than 'Does your job cause you any stress?' A second approach similar to direct questioning is known as prompting. Here, requests for information take the form of prompts and probes requesting information: 'Tell me about . . .', 'Describe . . .'.

It is important to mix direct questioning with other techniques for encouraging the person to explore relevant issues. One such method involves the use of silence or minimal prompts ('uh-huh'). By its very nature, problem exploration leads individuals to consider matters they have not previously addressed. The process cannot be rushed, and filling silences with new questions may interrupt their thoughts and impede the proper exploration of problems. A further method of encouraging problem exploration is through the use of what Egan termed 'empathic feedback'. Reflecting back to people an understanding of their situation or feelings through a simple phrase can be highly effective: 'So, you are telling me that you felt very lonely when your partner refused to talk about . . .'. Such feedback also shows that the counsellor understands the situation.

Goal setting

Once particular problems have been identified, some people may feel they are able to deal with them and need no further help in making appropriate changes. However, others may need further support in determining what they want to change and how to change it. The first stage in this process is to help the individual to decide the goals he or she wishes to achieve, and to frame these goals in specific rather than general terms (e.g. 'I will try to relax more' versus 'I will take 20 minutes out each day to practise some yoga'). If the final goal seems too difficult to achieve in one step, the identification of sub-goals working towards the final goal should be encouraged. Consider the possibilities for reducing various 'life stresses':

- Do less work about the house – let my partner do more of the work!
- Set off to work ten minutes earlier so I don't have to rush.
- Learn to relax by going to yoga class once a week.
- Join up with friends to form an exercise group.
- Say 'no' to requests at work that seem impossible to achieve.
- Talk to friends more.
- Work on my relationship with my partner – try to have fewer rows.

Some goals may be apparent following the problem exploration phase. However, should this not be the case, Egan identified a series of strategies designed to help the patient to identify and set goals. One of the most important is to challenge the individual to explore new perspectives – to think about new ways of doing things. It is particularly useful when the person appears locked into old ways of thinking or feels that little can be done. Direct challenges or advice giving, however well phrased ('Well, why don't you take some time out each day to relax?'), are likely to result in resistance to change or feelings of defeat. Accordingly, challenge in this context involves inviting the individual to explore new solutions, using phrases such as:

- 'Perhaps it would be useful to look at some different ways of looking at solutions to this problem'.
- 'I wonder if there are any other things you could do to deal with this problem'.

Facilitating action

Once goals have been established in the second phase of this problem-focused approach, some individuals may feel that they need no further support to achieve them. Others, who by this stage may have a good idea of *what* they want to achieve, can remain unsure of *how* to achieve them – how do you negotiate doing less work around the house and letting your partner do more? Accordingly, the final stage of this element of stress management is to plan ways of achieving the identified goals.

Stress may have multiple sources, and some areas of stress may be easier to change than others. It can be helpful to work towards relatively easy goals at the beginning of any attempt at change before working towards more serious or difficult-to-change goals as the individual gains skills or confidence in their ability to change. Some goals can be achieved using the personal resources already available to the individual – once they have planned how they will achieve them, they feel confident in their ability to put the plan into action. Other plans may require the individual to learn new skills in order to manage their stress more effectively. They may, for example, benefit from learning to relax or reducing the frequency or type of any stress-provoking thoughts that contribute to their stress. It is to these taught skills that we now turn.

Relaxation training

The goal of teaching relaxation skills is to enable the individual to relax as much as is possible and appropriate both throughout the day and at times of particular stress. This contrasts with procedures such as meditation, which provide a period of deep relaxation and 'time out' as sufficient in themselves. As well as the physical benefits, effective use of relaxation techniques leads to an increase in actual and perceived control over the stress response. This can be a valuable outcome in itself, as perceptions of loss of control can themselves contribute to feelings of stress. Relaxation may also increase access to calm and constructive thought processes, although this is a relatively weak effect, reflecting the reciprocity between each of the different stress components. Relaxation skills are best learned through three phases:

1. learning basic relaxation skills;
2. monitoring tension in daily life;
3. using relaxation at times of stress.

■ Learning relaxation skills

The first stage of learning relaxation skills is to practise them under optimal conditions, such as in a comfortable chair in a quiet room, where there are no distractions and it is relatively easy to relax. Initially, a trained practitioner should teach the process of deep relaxation. This can then be added to by continued practice at home, typically using taped instructions. Regular practice over a period of days – and sometimes weeks – is important at this stage, as the skills need to be well practised and relatively automatic before they can be used effectively in 'real life' contexts.

The relaxation process most commonly taught is based on Jacobson's (1938) deep muscle relaxation technique. This involves alternately tensing and relaxing muscle groups throughout the body in an ordered sequence. Over time, the emphasis of practice shifts towards relaxation without prior tension, or relaxing specific muscle groups while using others, to mimic use of relaxation in the 'real world'. The order in which the muscles are relaxed varies, but a typical exercise may involve the following stages (the tensing procedure is described in brackets):

- hands and forearms (making a fist);
- upper arms (touching fingers to shoulder);
- shoulders and lower neck (pulling up shoulders);
- back of neck (touching chin to chest);
- lips (pushing them together);
- forehead (frowning);

- abdomen/chest (holding deep breath);
- abdomen (tensing stomach muscles);
- legs and feet (push heel away, pull toes to point at head: not lifting leg).

■ Monitoring physical tension

At the same time as practising relaxation skills, individuals can begin to monitor their levels of physical tension throughout the day. Initially, this serves as a learning process, helping them to identify how tense they are at particular times of the day and what triggers any excessive tension. This process may also help to identify likely future triggers to stress and provide clues as to when the relaxation procedures may be particularly useful. This frequently involves the use of a 'tension diary', in which the individual records their level of tension on some form of numerical scale (0 = no tension, 100 = the highest tension possible) at regular intervals throughout the day or at times of particular stress. As a prelude to cognitive or behavioural interventions, such diaries may also focus on the thoughts, emotions or behaviour experienced at such times. Figure 13.2 provides an excerpt from a typical stress diary. As the individual begins to use additional strategies to combat their stress, they may add in columns measuring their level of tension after the use of relaxation, the thoughts they used to deal with their stressful thoughts, and so on.

■ *In vivo* relaxation

After a period of learning relaxation techniques and monitoring tension, individuals can begin to integrate relaxation into their daily lives. At this stage, relaxation involves reducing tension to appropriate levels while engaging in everyday activities. Initially, this may involve trying to keep as relaxed as possible and appropriate at times of relatively low stress and then, as the individual becomes more skilled, using relaxation at times of increasing stress. The goal of relaxation at these times is not to escape from the cause of stress but to remain as relaxed as possible while dealing with the particular stressor. An alternative strategy involves relaxing at regular intervals (such as coffee breaks) throughout the day.

Time	Situation	Tension	Behaviours	Thoughts
8.32	Driving to work – late!	62	Tense – gripping steering wheel Cutting up other drivers Cursing at traffic lights	Late again!! . . . the boss is bound to notice . . . Come on – hurry up – I haven't got all day! Why do these bloody traffic lights always take so long to change?!
10.00	Presenting work to colleagues	75	Spoke too quickly Rushed	I'm not looking good here . . . why can I never do this properly? They must think I'm a fool! I feel a wreck!

Figure 13.2 Excerpt from a stress diary noting stress triggers, levels of tension, and related behaviours and thoughts

> OK, now we're nice and relaxed, the next stage is flying.....

Cognitive interventions

self-talk

talking to oneself (internally). Can be negative and thus add to stress. Therapeutically, individuals are taught to use self-talk in a way that helps them to keep calm.

Two strategies for changing cognitions are frequently employed. The simpler, known as self-instruction training, was developed by Meichenbaum (1985) and is targeted at surface cognitions. It involves interrupting the flow of stressogenic (stress-provoking) thoughts and replacing them with pre-rehearsed stress reducing or 'coping' thoughts – so-called positive '**self-talk**'. These typically fall into one of two categories. The first are reminders to use any stress-coping techniques the person has learned ('You're winding yourself up here – come on, take it easy, remember to relax, deep breathe, relax your muscles'). The second form of self-instruction acts as a form of reassurance, reminding the individual that they have previously coped effectively with their feelings of distress ('Come on, you've dealt with this before – you should be able to again – keep calm – things will not get out of control') and will be able to now. To make sure these are relevant to the individual, and to help to actually evoke these thoughts at times of stress, Meichenbaum suggested that particular coping thoughts should be rehearsed, wherever possible, before the stressful events occur – whether in a therapy session or minutes before an anticipated stressor is likely to occur. At a minimum, such thoughts interrupt the flow of stressful thoughts; at best, they actively reduce an individual's levels of stress.

A more complex intervention, cognitive restructuring, involves identifying and challenging the accuracy of stress-engendering thoughts (*ibid.*). It asks the individual to consider them as hypotheses, not facts, and to assess their validity without bias. This process may involve consideration of both surface cognitions and cognitive schemata – although the latter require significant insight and may best be achieved in the context of therapy. The best way of challenging stressogenic thoughts may initially be taught in therapy sessions. In this, the therapist uses a process known as the Socratic method or 'guided discovery' (Beck 1976) to help patients to identify distorted patterns of thinking that are contributing to their problems. The therapist then encourages the individual to consider and evaluate different sources of information that provide evidence of the reality or unreality of the beliefs they hold. Patients may be challenged to question their stressful assumptions by asking key questions such as:

- What evidence is there that supports or denies my assumption?
- Are there any other ways I can think about this situation?
- Could I be making a mistake in the way I am thinking?

Once the individual can engage in this process in the therapy session, they are encouraged to use the Socratic process at times when they feel hooked into feelings of stress – to question the basis of those feelings. One technique that has been developed specifically to help to identify and challenge core beliefs is known as the downward arrow technique. When patients express what seems to be inappropriate thoughts or reactions to events, the downward arrow technique can be used to identify distortions in core beliefs that are contributing to their problems. Key questions include:

- What is your concern about . . . ?
- What would the implications be . . . ?
- What would the consequences be . . . ?
- What would the ultimate consequences be . . . ?

Behavioural interventions

The goal of behavioural change is to help the individual to respond to any stress triggers in ways that maximise their effectiveness in dealing with the trigger and that do so in a way that causes them minimal stress. Some behaviour can be relatively simple. Behaviour that reduces the stress of driving may involve driving within the speed limits, putting the handbrake on when stopped at traffic lights and taking time to relax, and not cutting in front of other cars. Others may take practice – a person who becomes excessively angry, for example, may role play assertive responses in therapy sessions to prepare them for doing the same in 'real life'. Still others may have to be thought through at the time of the stress. Here, the goal of stress management training may be to teach the individual to plan their response to any potential stressor to be one that minimises their personal stress. A simple rule of thumb that can be useful here is to encourage individuals to stop and plan what they are going to do – even if this takes a few seconds – rather than to jump into action without thought, as this typically leads to more rather than less stress.

Stress inoculation training

stress inoculation training
a form of stress-reducing intervention in which participants are taught to control stress by rehearsing prior to going into stressful situations. Participants are taught to relax and use calming self-talk. The approach was developed by Donald Meichenbaum.

In his approach called **stress inoculation training**, Meichenbaum (1985) suggested that the various strands of cognitive therapy described above could be combined so that when an individual is facing a stressor, they concentrate on:

- checking that their behaviour is appropriate to the circumstances;
- maintaining relaxation;
- giving themselves appropriate self-talk.

In addition, he suggested that where a particular stressor can be anticipated, the opportunity should be taken to rehearse these actions before the event itself. Once in the situation, the planned strategies should be enacted. Finally, after the situation has occurred, time should be given to review what occurred and successes or failures learned from – rather than treated as disasters that should be forgotten.

RESEARCH FOCUS

Hockmeyer, J. and Smyth, J. (2002). Evaluating the feasibility and efficacy of a self-administered manual-based stress management intervention for individuals with asthma: results from controlled study. *Behavioral Medicine*, 27: 161–72.

Background

Teaching stress management skills may significantly improve the health and wellbeing of many people with chronic disease (see Chapter 17). However, these interventions are expensive, and for this reason many of the interventions described in this chapter are conducted relatively infrequently even in hospitals that are considered to be 'centres of excellence'. One way of reducing the cost is to teach these techniques to small groups of people at once. An alternative is to provide a teaching manual and to allow patients to learn techniques with minimal contact with healthcare professionals. Hockmeyer and Smyth adopted the latter approach in developing an intervention for people with asthma. The programme had two elements. The first involved teaching people to manage their stress through the use of stress management techniques. The second involved encouraging people to express any negative emotions that they may be experiencing through the use of a simple 'expressive writing' technique (see Chapter 17). They hoped to:

- improve lung function; and
- reduce self-reported stress levels.

Method

Participants

The sample comprised twenty-five men and twenty-nine women, with a mean age of 20.7, who had been diagnosed with asthma for an average of almost 11 years.

Procedure

Participants were randomly allocated to either a four-week active intervention group or a placebo intervention. They completed measures at baseline and four weeks later, including:

- *lung function*: the amount of expired air and speed of exhalation using spirometry;
- *perceived stress scale*: the degree to which participants perceived events or circumstances in their lives as stressful in the previous 30 days.

Intervention

Participants in the active intervention were given a workbook. This had three components:

1. a tape-recorded deep-breathing exercise, which participants were asked to practise regularly;
2. a cognitive-behavioural treatment;
3. a 20-minute exercise in which participants wrote about a stressful life event.

The stress management exercises involved a brief reading each week to help participants to become aware of their 'thoughts, feelings, and emotions' about stressful experiences. Each of the four weeks' readings had a corresponding application, which participants were encouraged to spend 30 minutes working on. The applications focused on recording thoughts and completing cognitive restructuring exercises. Participants were asked to complete the 20-minute writing exercise at the beginning of each week. This involved writing about an experience that was causing them significant stress, including the feelings and thoughts it

continued

aroused, and then to challenge any beliefs that they may have developed as a consequence of the experience. The placebo intervention involved the same elements: a tape recording containing educational material about asthma, and a series of brain teasers said to 'warm up' their thinking in preparation for a series of time management exercises. Participants were asked to complete the brain teasers before writing about issues around time management at the beginning of each week.

Results

Perfect compliance was reported by 78 percent of the active intervention and 74 percent of the placebo intervention. The former listened to their relaxation tape an average of 2.28 times per week. Those in the placebo group listened to it an average of 2.16 times per week. Key outcomes were:

- the intervention group made greater improvements on the measure of lung function;
- measures of perceived stress did not fall in either condition.

Discussion

The study suggested that a combination of breathing exercise and emotional expression can impact on lung function, but which element of the intervention brought about these changes was not clear. The intervention may have proved to be 'too minimal' to achieve any difference in stress ratings between the two conditions in this population. However, as participants were not selected for the study because of their high levels of stress, it is also possible that the intervention may have proved more effective in a more 'stressed' population. Accordingly, although the study provided an interesting attempt to help people to manage their stress and asthma more effectively, the results are inconclusive. It is important to target interventions at appropriate populations. Stress management procedures simply will not work if they are implemented with people who have low levels of stress. Overall, therefore, this may be considered an interesting study, but also one that was perhaps inappropriately targeted.

Helping people to cope with trauma

Post-traumatic stress disorder

post-traumatic stress disorder
a disorder that forms a response to experiencing a traumatic event. The key elements are unwanted repetitive memories of the event, often in the form of flashbacks, attempts at avoidance of such memories, and a generally raised level of arousal.

The American Psychiatric Association (American Psychiatric Association 2000) states that for a person to be given a diagnosis of **post-traumatic stress disorder** (PTSD) they must have experienced or witnessed an event that involved actual or threatened death or serious injury, or a threat to the physical integrity of self or others, and that their immediate response involved intense fear, helplessness or horror. In the longer term, the individual must have experienced three clusters of symptoms lasting one month or more:

1. *Intrusive memories*: the trauma is re-experienced through intrusive thoughts, flashbacks or nightmares. Flashbacks often feel as real as the event but may be fragmentary or partial. Emotions and sensations associated with the trauma may be relived with similar intensity to those felt at the time. Images are often described as if being in a film of the incident.

Initially, the person may feel that they are actually 'in' the film: as they recover, their perspective may shift to that of outside observer watching a film. That is, they begin to, almost literally, feel more detached from the trauma.

2. *Avoidance*: this may involve mental defence mechanisms such as being unable to recall aspects of the trauma, emotional numbness or detachment from others, as well as physically avoiding reminders of the trauma.

3. *Arousal*: persistent feelings of over-arousal that may be evidenced by irritability, being easily startled or hyper-vigilant, suffering insomnia, or having difficulty concentrating.

Symptoms often begin within days or a few weeks of the precipitating event, but can recur after symptoms have faded as a result of further trauma or life events as diverse as trauma anniversaries, interpersonal losses and changes in health status.

Many health workers may witness other people at times of either threatened or actual death. Emergency ambulance workers, for example, are frequently involved in incidents involving serious trauma, death and high levels of personal distress. For this reason, the prevalence of PTSD in this group is alarming high. Bennett, Williams, Page *et al.* (2004), for example, found that 21 percent of their sample of working emergency ambulance personnel were experiencing some degree of PTSD. Many patients also experience PTSD as a consequence of events that led them to hospital or which occurred in hospital, although the exact prevalence of PTSD among such people is difficult to determine, as some studies use much stricter criteria for a 'diagnosis' of PTSD than others. Among cancer patients, for example, two studies using very rigorous criteria for the diagnosis of PTSD have reported a 3 percent prevalence among women with breast cancer (Green, Rowland, Krupnick *et al.* 1998) and 5 percent of people undergoing bone marrow transplant in the treatment of cancer (Widows, Jacobsen and Fields 2000). Using less rigid criteria, Meeske, Ruccione and Globe (2001) reported that 20 percent of their sample of adults who had been treated successfully for cancer an average of eleven years previously still met the full criteria for PTSD. A small percentage of people may have residual symptoms of PTSD twenty years after diagnosis and treatment (Kornblith, Herndon, Weiss *et al.* 2003). About 10 percent of people who have had a myocardial infarction may also experience PTSD (Bennett, Owen, Koutsakis *et al.* 2002). Post-traumatic stress may not just affect those with the condition. High rates of PTSD have also been found among the parents of children diagnosed as having cancer. Landolt, Vollrath, Ribi *et al.* (2003), for example, found that 16 percent of the fathers and 24 percent of the mothers of children diagnosed with either cancer or diabetes met the diagnostic criteria for PTSD five–six weeks after the diagnosis was given.

■ Preventing PTSD: psychological debriefing

psychological debriefing a procedure in which people who have been through a particular trauma talk through the trauma in a structured way with a counsellor.

Because of the serious, and potentially long-term, impact that PTSD can have for an individual, a significant amount of research and clinical work has been done to try to prevent PTSD occurring following traumatic incidents. The most frequently used approach is called **psychological debriefing**. Many hospitals and other services such as the ambulance and police services regularly use psychological debriefing to help staff to cope following traumatic incidents (Smith and Roberts 2003). This usually comprises a single-session interview conducted close to the time of a traumatic event. It involves the individual talking about the event and their emotional reactions to it in a detailed and systematic manner. The therapist leads the person through the event in a very structured manner, asking them to talk about the events that have occurred and their emotional, cognitive and behavioural responses to those events. It is hoped that this procedure helps the individual to come to terms with any emotional trauma they have experienced and prevent the development of PTSD.

The procedure is at least partly justified by theorists such as Brewin and Holmes (2003), who have suggested that the symptoms of PTSD result from traumatic memories remaining isolated from the general memory system, with flashbacks and other unwanted recall of events being the result of cognitive attempts to integrate isolated traumatic memories into general memory. Once such memories are fully integrated into the memory system, they lose their emotional charge and are no more salient than other more general memories. This process of integration is facilitated by thinking and rethinking about the memories until full integration has been achieved. Debriefing may encourage the integration of memories into general memory from the outset and prevent them becoming isolated and emotionally distressing.

How effective psychological debriefing is in achieving its goals is, unfortunately, somewhat questionable. In a meta-analysis of trials using debriefing, Rose, Bisson and Wessely (2001) concluded that it may not only be ineffective in preventing PTSD, it may actually *increase* risk for the disorder. None of the studies they analysed found that debriefing lowered risk for PTSD in the three–four months following a traumatic incident. More worrying were the results of the two studies that reported longer-term findings. Both found that those who received debriefing were at nearly twice the risk of developing PTSD than those who did not receive the intervention. That is, debriefing seemed to inhibit long-term recovery from psychological trauma. A number of explanations have been proposed for these findings:

■ 'Secondary traumatisation' may occur as a result of further exposure to a traumatic incident within a short time of the event.

■ Debriefing may 'medicalise' normal distress and increase the expectancy of developing psychological symptoms in those who would otherwise not have done so.

■ Debriefing may prevent the potentially protective responses of denial and distancing that may occur in the immediate aftermath of a traumatic incident.

These findings seem particularly worrying given the continued widespread use of debriefing. It may well be that in the immediate aftermath of a trauma, the person may benefit from some degree of avoidance of thinking about the trauma, only allowing themselves to think about it and deal with it over a longer period.

■ Treating PTSD

Following a traumatic incident, many people experience PTSD-like symptoms for a limited period. Many will also recover from them in the weeks following the incident. However, where these are persistent and distressing (for at least one month), people may be diagnosed as having PTSD. In such cases, the optimum treatment seems to be very similar to debriefing, as it involves repeated exposure to memories of the event. This may take place over a period of several sessions, until integration of isolated memories into general memory is achieved and the symptoms no longer occur. This type of intervention, known as **exposure therapy**, may lead to an initial increase in distress as upsetting images, previously avoided where possible, are deliberately recollected. To minimise this distress, Leskin, Kaloupek and Keane (1998) recommended a graded exposure process in which the individual initially recalls and talks about particular elements of a traumatic event at a level of detail they choose over several occasions until they no longer find them upsetting. Any new and potentially more distressing memories remain the focus of the next stages of the intervention.

exposure therapy
a form of therapy involving exposure to traumatic memories, based on the theoretical assumption that continued exposure will result in a gradual reduction in the level of fear associated with such memories.

Reactivation of memories by this procedure involves describing the experience in detail, focusing on what happened, the thoughts and emotions experienced at the time, and any memories that the incident triggered. This approach can be augmented by a variety of cognitive behavioural techniques, including relaxation training and cognitive restructuring. Relaxation helps the individual to control their arousal when recalling distressing events or at other times in the day when they are feeling tense or on edge. Cognitive restructuring can help them to change any distorted cognitions they had in response to the event and make them less threatening ('I'm going to die! It felt like I was going to die, but actually most people survive a diagnosis of . . .').

A number of studies have found exposure-based therapy to be superior to no treatment and interventions such as supportive counselling and relaxation therapy without exposure. Foa, Rothbaum, Riggs *et al.* (1991), for example, compared the effectiveness of a waiting list control condition, self-instruction training as developed by Meichenbaum (see above), supportive counselling, and an exposure programme. Participants in each of the active interventions experienced more improvements than those in the waiting list condition. However, by the three-month follow-up, people in the exposure programme reported the least intrusive memories and arousal.

eye movement desensitisation and reprocessing
a form of therapy for post-traumatic stress disorder involving exposure to traumatic memories while repeatedly moving the eyes. Its method of working is not clear. However, the most popular theory is that when the eyes move back and forth this creates brain activity similar to that which occurs during REM (rapid eye movement) sleep. This may help the brain to process the 'stuck' material, enabling the person to arrive at an adaptive resolution.

Eye movement desensitisation and reprocessing

The most recent treatment for PTSD is known as **eye movement desensitisation and reprocessing** (EMDR). This approach was discovered by chance by Shapiro (1995). In a now famous story of how the approach was initially developed, she noticed that while walking in the woods her disturbing thoughts began to disappear and were less upsetting than before. She linked this change to her eyes spontaneously moving rapidly backwards and forwards in an upward diagonal while walking. Since then, the procedure has been developed into a standardised intervention, and its effectiveness has been evaluated in a number of clinical trials. The intervention involves recall of trauma memories as visual images. The participant is then asked to link these images with a negative cognition associated with the memory but framed in the present tense ('I am terrified'). The individual rates the strength of emotion evoked by this process on a scale of 0–100. They are then asked to track the therapist's finger as it is moved increasingly quickly across their line of vision. After twenty-four such movements, the patient is instructed to 'blank it out' or 'let it go' and asked to rate their level of emotion. This procedure is repeated until the patient experiences minimal distress to the presence of the image and negative cognition. If no changes occur, the direction of eye movements is changed.

EMDR incorporates exposure to elements of the trauma stimulus. It is therefore important to determine whether the addition of the eye movements enhances the effect of exposure. This does not seem to be the case. While EMDR is certainly more effective than no treatment, it may be no more effective than standard exposure methods. Reviewing the evidence, Davidson and Parker (2001) used meta-analysis to compare the effectiveness of EMDR with no treatment, non-specific treatments and the exposure methods described above. While their analyses indicated a benefit for EMDR when compared with no treatment or non-specific treatments, its benefits were similar to or less than those resulting from exposure approaches.

Minimising stress in hospital settings

Pre-operational preparation

Having an operation is a stressful event, whether it is a small operation conducted under local anaesthetic or a larger one involving a period of unconsciousness and a significant period of recovery. It should not be surprising, therefore, that levels of anxiety can be high both before and after an operation. This anxiety is both unpleasant for the individual concerned and can add to the complications they experience. It may increase the amount of painkilling medication they take, the degree to which they need reassurance both before and after the operation, and even the period necessary for them to stay in hospital (Johnston and Vogele 1993). As a consequence, a number of researchers have attempted to identify simple means of preparing people psychologically for an operation in order to minimise its associated distress. While the stress management approaches described above may be appropriate under such circumstances, healthcare staff and patients rarely have the time (or the inclination) to teach or learn these strategies. Accordingly, a very different approach has been taken to help people to cope with this specific type of stress.

Many studies have shown that we feel less anxiety when faced with potentially stressful circumstances if we can be given some degree of control over them (e.g. Lok and Bishop 1999). These findings have led health psychologists to examine whether giving patients undergoing surgery more control over their situation will reduce the amount of stress they experience. Clearly, patients cannot have much control over their anaesthetics or surgery – such things really should be left to the experts! So, in this case, 'giving control' has been interpreted as 'keeping people informed about what is happening to them'. This is thought to reduce anxiety by minimising the fear of the unknown. If patients know what to expect, they may understand better and be less alarmed by any experiences they have. If patients are told, for example, that they will experience some pain after their surgery they will be

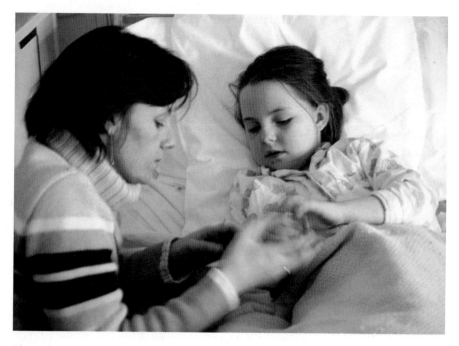

Plate 13.2 The calming presence of a parent can help children to relax and cope better with any concerns they may have about their operation.

Source: John Cole/Science Photo Library

less alarmed and less likely to think that things have gone wrong if they do experience any pain. A number of studies have examined the effectiveness of providing two sorts of information to patients prior to them having surgery:

1. *Procedural information*: telling patients about the events that will occur before and after surgery, such as having a pre-medication injection, waking in the recovery room and having a drip in their arm.
2. *Sensory information*: telling patients what they will feel before and after surgery; e.g. that it is normal to feel some pain following surgery, or that they may feel confused when they come round from the anaesthetic.

The overall picture is that these interventions work. Most of the research evaluating the effectiveness of this type of intervention was conducted in the 1980s and early 1990s. In a review of this literature, Johnston and Vogele (1993) conducted a series of meta-analyses, the results of which indicated that these types of intervention resulted in improvements on measures including reported pain and discomfort, distress about pain, use of painkillers, time to get out of bed following surgery, and physiological indices of stress such as heart rate. However, no one intervention appeared to be consistently better than any other, and the optimal intervention would appear to be a combination of both types of information.

avoidant coping
a style of coping that involves emotional regulation by avoiding confrontation with a stressful situation. Analogous to emotion-focused coping.

■ ## Matching patient needs

What may be as important as the type of intervention is matching it to the characteristics of the patients receiving it. Patients who typically cope using **avoidant coping** strategies may benefit, for example, from receiving less information than those who typically cope with stress by using problem-focused strategies (see Chapter 11) or seeking relevant information. One study to examine this issue was reported by Wilson (1981). She allocated patients undergoing surgery to either routine care, a combination of procedural and sensory information, relaxation training, or a combination of both active interventions. All those in the active interventions fared better than those in the routine care group. However, they also found that patients given the procedural and sensory information who typically used **problem-focused coping** strategies to deal with stress did better than those who used emotion-focused strategies on various measures of recovery and use of painkillers. It seems that giving information to people who typically seek information and try to think their way through problems appears beneficial; such information may be unwanted by people who typically avoid such issues and may even make things worse for them.

This hypothesis was tested more recently by Morgan, Roufeil, Kaushik *et al.* (1998), who reported a study in which they gave people identified as primarily 'information seekers' or 'avoiders' either sensory information about the nature of a forthcoming **colonoscopy** or no information. Patients who were given information congruent with their coping style (i.e. no information for avoiders; information for 'seekers') reported less anxiety prior to the procedure than those who were given incongruent information. They also scored lower on a measure of 'pain behaviour' made by nursing staff during the procedure, although participants did not report any differences in pain during the procedure or differ in their use of sedative drugs. These data suggest that:

■ People who usually cope using problem-focused strategies benefit from information that helps them to understand their experience and to actively interpret their experience in relation to information they are given.

■ People who usually cope using avoidant, emotion-focused strategies benefit most from not being told what to expect, and perhaps being helped to develop strategies that help them to be distracted from the situation.

Levels of anxiety may also influence the impact of pre-operative preparation. Hathaway (1986), for example, concluded from a meta-analysis that patients with low levels of anxiety benefited most from the provision of procedural information, while those with high levels of anxiety gained most from unstructured discussion. Anxiety inhibits new learning, partly because people who are anxious may not attend to whatever they are being told, partly as a direct inhibition of memory processes. It is possible, therefore, that anxious patients may benefit most when they are given relatively little information, but the information they are given matches their needs.

Studies of the effects of teaching relaxation to anxious patients have reported mixed results. Wilson (1981) found that patients who had relatively low levels of anxiety seemed to benefit most from learning relaxation skills. By contrast, those patients with particularly high levels of anxiety did not benefit from being taught relaxation – perhaps because their anxiety prevented them learning and implementing their relaxation skills sufficiently well. By contrast, Wilson *et al.* (1982) found that relaxation was of benefit to some anxious patients while undergoing **endoscopy**. Together, these results suggest that people with moderately raised levels of anxiety may benefit most

problem-focused coping
a style of coping that involves active planning and dealing with any source of stress.

colonoscopy
a minor surgical procedure in which a small piece of bowel wall is cut from the colon. This can then be tested for the presence of malignant cells.

endoscopy
the use of a thin, lighted tube (called an endoscope) to examine the inside of the body.

from the use of relaxation, as they may be able to implement the skills more easily than those with high levels of anxiety.

More complex interventions have taught people cognitive restructuring techniques (see above) to help to minimise anxiety-provoking thoughts both before and after surgery. Ridgeway and Mathews (1982), for example, assigned women having gynaecological surgery to one of three conditions: a placebo condition, in which they received general information about the hospital ward; procedural and sensory information; and training in cognitive restructuring methods. Following surgery, there were no differences between the groups on measures of pain, nausea or sleep duration. However, participants in the cognitive restructuring condition used less analgesia while in hospital and reported less pain following discharge from hospital than either of the other groups. Despite the success of the cognitive intervention, the simplicity of the informational-based interventions makes them more likely to be carried out in the 'real world' of a busy ward.

■ Working with children and parents

Much of the recent work in preparing people for surgery has focused on helping children and their parents. Studies that have focused on children have shown a variety of techniques that may be of benefit. Mahajan, Wyliie, Steffen *et al.* (1998), for example, randomly allocated children aged between 6 and 19 to one of two conditions prior to gastrointestinal endoscopy. The first received routine preparation. The second received procedural preparation, involving a demonstration of materials that would be used during the endoscopy and the use of a doll or a book of photographs showing the procedure. Compared with the no-preparation condition, participants in the procedural information condition reported less anxiety both before and during the procedure, used less anaesthetic and had lower heart rates, suggesting that they were more relaxed. Hatava, Olsson and Lagerkranser (2000) randomly assigned children and parents to one of two interventions designed to reduce anxiety before an ear, nose or throat (ENT) operation. In the first condition, they were given written or verbal information by a nurse two weeks prior to surgery. This included information about general hospital rules, routines and the date of the operation. This acted as a form of **placebo intervention** as there is little here that would have been expected to reduce anxiety other than meeting the nurse that may be involved in their care. The second group were given a more complex intervention comprising the same information two weeks prior to the operation followed by a visit to the ENT department the day before surgery. During this visit, each child and parent met the anaesthetist who would be at the operation. Following this, they took part in a group session led by a nurse in which they were shown the operating theatre and lay on the operating table. They were also shown the equipment that would be used during anaesthesia, with which they were encouraged to play in order to minimise threat and increase familiarity. They were then shown the procedure that would occur on the day through role play using a doll. This complex intervention resulted in significant benefits – particularly for the youngest children in the programme, those under 5 years old. Both younger and older children reported less fear and anxiety prior to the surgery. In addition, their parents reported more satisfaction and less anxiety than those who did not receive the intervention.

placebo intervention
an intervention designed to simulate a psychological intervention but not believed to be a specific therapy for the target condition.

bone marrow biopsy
usually performed under local anaesthetic by making a small incision into the skin. A biopsy needle is then pushed through the bone and takes a sample of marrow from the centre of the bone. Marrow contains platelets, phagocytes and lymphocytes.

Jay, Elliott and Fitzgibbons (1995) provided an unusual comparison between medical and psychological methods of reducing distress in children undergoing **bone marrow biopsy**, which can be, and often is, conducted under local anaesthetic. It can also be distressing for both the children and parents involved. They compared two approaches to minimising this distress in a sample of children aged between 3 and 12. The first was simply to fully anaesthetise the children. While this approach evokes some degree of anxiety, they reasoned that it may be less distressing than experiencing the process while under local anaesthetic. They compared this approach with conducting the procedure under local anaesthetic after teaching the children both relaxation and cognitive restructuring as a means of controlling their distress. One can only imagine that this was taught at a very simple level, particularly to the younger children. Perhaps not surprisingly, the children who received training in stress management methods experienced more distress than those who were anaesthetised at the beginning of the procedure (i.e. before the children in the anaesthetic condition were completely unconscious). However, their parents' ratings suggested that they were the least distressed in the following days. Interestingly, neither the children nor their parents showed any preference for either intervention.

Interventions that target parents may also benefit both parent and child. Campbell, Kirkpatrick, Berry *et al.* (1992), for example, prepared mothers of pre-school age children for a cardiac operation during which their child would be conscious in one of three ways: supportive counselling, education about the hospital and procedure, and relaxation and positive self-talk (stress management). The latter interventions proved most effective. Mothers and children who received the stress management training coped better with the procedure itself, and their children adapted more positively at home following discharge from hospital than those in the other conditions. The women who received the educational intervention reported less anxiety and tension during the procedure than those in the other conditions. Again, it seems that a combination of interventions including education and teaching coping strategies may provide the optimal intervention.

Summary

This chapter has examined a variety of approaches to stress management and contexts in which it has been conducted. Systemic interventions that target whole organisations can be used as a preventive approach. More individual approaches based around specific therapeutic approaches may benefit people experiencing mild stress to highly traumatic stress. Finally, simple procedural information may benefit people facing the stress of an operation where there is little time (or need) to use these more complex interventions.

We noted that while stress management 'classes' provide a potentially useful and effective way of reaching the public, attendance is likely to be limited, and health psychologists and others have targeted larger and more 'captive audiences' in organisations.

Managing stress at this level can involve a variety of approaches depending on the organisational causes of stress. Stress management interventions should follow an audit of stressors and target environmental issues that both contribute to stress and can realistically be changed in the context of the particular workplace.

Cognitive behavioural interventions targeted at reducing stress involve changing:

- triggers to stress, using, for example, the problem-focused approach of Egan;
- the cognitive precursors to stress, using the self-instruction and cognitive restructuring approaches of Beck, Meichenbaum and Ellis;
- the physiological response to stress using relaxation methods, including the modified Jacobsen technique;
- the behavioural reactions to stressful situations using Meichenbaum's stress inoculation and role play techniques.

Treatments of trauma include those that are thought to be preventive and those that help people to cope with longer-term conditions such as post-traumatic stress disorder.

- Clinical debriefing close to the time of the incident does not appear to be preventive.
- Exposure-based interventions seem to be effective in the treatment of established PTSD.
- EMDR seems to provide no additional benefit to these approaches.

Finally, providing relevant information to help people to understand and cope with the stress of hospital procedures such as operations may reduce distress and pain and facilitate rehabilitation following surgery. However, its benefits vary according to individual differences in coping style.

- Patients who are typically problem solvers benefit most from the provision of information.
- Patients who typically cope with stress using avoidant strategies may be helped best by teaching them distraction techniques.

Further reading

Elkin, A. (1999). *Stress Management for Dummies*. New York: Wiley.
An irreverent but useful guide to managing your own stress.

Meichenbaum, D. (1985). *Stress Inoculation Training*. Longman Higher Education.
A more academic review of stress management techniques for working with individuals. It's a bit old now, but it remains one of the best introductory texts there is.

Barlow, D.H. and Mostofsky, D.I. (2000). *The Management of Stress and Anxiety in Medical Disorders*. Allyn and Bacon.
A more up-to-date review of stress management in relation to health problems.

Williams, S. and Cooper, L. (2002). *Managing Workplace Stress*. Chichester: Wiley.
A good and practical review of stress management issues at an organisational level. It was sponsored by the 'bosses' (the Confederation of British Industry), so they should know what they are talking about.

PART 3

Being ill

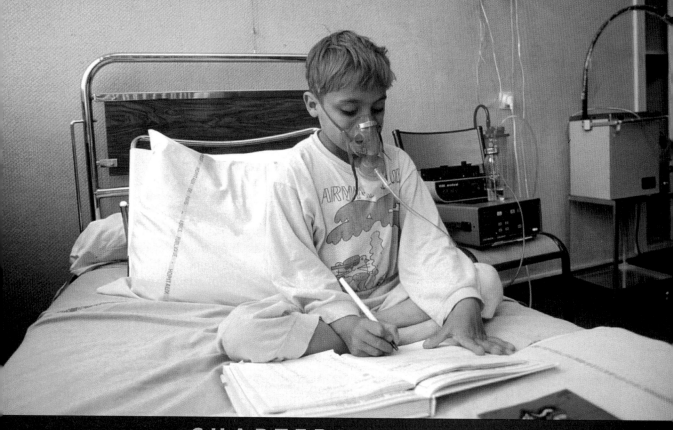

CHAPTER 14

The impact of illness on quality of life

Learning outcomes

By the end of this chapter, you should have an understanding of:

- domains of quality of life
- quality of life as a multidimensional, dynamic and subjective construct
- demographic, clinical and psychosocial influences on perceptions of quality of life
- benefits and disadvantages of common methods of assessing quality of life
- the need to consider specific populations when developing measurement tools

CHAPTER OUTLINE

Illness is a dynamic process, beginning with perception of symptoms or a diagnosis and continuing or changing over time as a function of the disease pathology, treatment possibilities and the responses to illness by the person affected and those around them. We have shown in previous chapters that many individual and social factors exist that influence the responses to a stressful experience, and in this chapter we turn our attention to the impact of illness. We address the impact of illness on an individual's emotional wellbeing and adjustment, on their global and health-related functioning, in other words, their quality of life (QoL). It is first necessary to define this broad construct, before exploring how demographic, disease and treatment, and psychosocial factors can influence perceptions of QoL. Having described what QoL is (if that is fully possible given the subjectivity of the concept), we turn attention to issues of how to measure this multidimensional, dynamic and subjective concept.

Illness and quality of life

While the primary goal of medicine and healthcare is to improve health and/or treat and cure illness and its symptoms, there is a need to address more global outcomes of healthcare treatments and services, such as patient wellbeing. Unlike clinical outcomes, which can be assessed in an objective manner (such as observing improved physical functioning or reduced symptomatology), assessing patient wellbeing requires that the view of the patient be sought. For example, in clinical trials (such as those conducted to test the efficacy of a new drug) and intervention studies (psychological or clinical), it is important to evaluate clinical outcomes such as symptom reduction but also the individual's own perceptions of how the treatment or intervention has influenced their illness experience and their general psychosocial functioning. QoL research has become a major area of multidisciplinary research for a variety of reasons. One may be that due to technological advances medicine can effectively treat more conditions and thus people are living longer than in previous generations. Related to this is growing acceptance, primarily within the medical domain, of the importance of knowing about and understanding the psychosocial as well as the clinical outcomes of treatments or interventions. Having this fuller knowledge has implications for future care, treatment and service provision. As Boini, Briançon, Guillemin *et al.* (2004: 4) succinctly put it, 'physicians now have the opportunity to add life to years, as well as adding years to life'. Furthermore, patients may derive great benefit from certain treatments or interventions in terms of enhanced quality of life, even though these same treatments or interventions may not extend survival or quantity of life (see IN THE SPOTLIGHT below).

To illustrate the growth of QoL research in both the psychological and medical literature, Garratt, Schmidt, Mackintosh *et al.* (2002) published a review in the *British Medical Journal*, where it was revealed that between 1990 and 1999 there were over 23,000 QoL records in the literature engines searched, 4,000 of which were specifically about scale development and testing. What is this construct that has received so much research attention?

What do YOU think?	How would you define quality of life? Think about you 'now' compared perhaps with your parents and your friends. Do you think you see 'quality of life' differently to them? Consider why this may be. Consider what you see as being important to your quality of life in the future. Have you ever experienced something which has challenged your quality of life? If so, in what way did it challenge it, and how did you deal with it?

What is quality of life?

In general terms, quality of life (QoL) can be referred to as an individual's evaluation of their overall life experience at a given time (global quality of life), with the term 'health-related QoL' emerging to refer to evaluations of life experience and how they are affected by disease, accidents or treatments. A health-related quality of life is therefore associated with 'optimal levels of mental, physical, role (e.g. work, parent, carer) and social functioning, including relationships, and perceptions of health, fitness, life satisfaction and well-being. It should also include some assessment of the patient's level of satisfaction with treatment, outcome and health status and with future prospects' (Bowling 1995: 3).

According to the World Health Organization Quality of Life (WHOQOL) working group (1993, 1994), QoL is a person's perceptions of their position in life in relation to their cultural context and the value systems of that context in relation to their own goals, standards and expectations. Quality of life is considered to be a broad concept affected by an individual's physical and mental health, level of independence, quality of social relationships, social integration and, added subsequently (WHOQOL 1998), their personal, religious and spiritual beliefs. This working group has produced a generic and cross-culturally valid assessment tool (WHOQOL-100), which addresses twenty-five different facets of QoL grouped into one of six domains:

1. *physical health*: pain and discomfort; energy and fatigue; sleep and rest;
2. *psychological*: positive feelings; self-esteem; thinking, memory, learning and concentration; bodily image and appearance; negative feelings;
3. *level of independence*: activities of daily living (e.g. self-care); mobility; medication and treatment dependence; work capacity;
4. *social relationships*: personal relationships; practical social support; sexual activity;
5. *relation to environment*: physical safety and security; financial resources; home environment; availability and quality of health/social care; learning opportunities; leisure participation and opportunities; transport; physical environment;
6. *Spirituality, religion and personal beliefs.*

This generic tool provides core items for use across all conditions, with disease- and population-specific versions being developed subsequently, including the WHOQOL-HIV. This measure is used to assess the QoL of individuals with HIV and AIDS and includes illness-specific facets, such as concern with HIV/AIDS symptoms, the HIV testing and results process, disclosure of HIV status, the meaning and purpose of life, and death and dying (O'Connell, Skevington and Saxena on behalf of WHOQOL-HIV group 2003).

■ Disease, disability and handicap

One of the aims of assessing QoL is to assess the impact of disease on an individual's functioning, and initially this led to studies being somewhat tied to assessment of physical function, even though this is only one domain thought to reflect QoL. Many studies use measures of disease or symptom severity, disability or physical functioning as outcome measures that are considered as indicative of quality of life. However, the WHO model of impairment, disability and handicap (see Chapter 1; WHO 1980) described how illness had more than just physical consequences by defining handicap as disadvantages and limitations in performing social roles that resulted directly from impairment and/or disability. Johnston and Pollard (2001), in testing the WHO model, further concluded that the linear relationship between impairment, disability and handicap was not inevitable but depended on psychological factors. Further support for this comes from studies of individuals suffering from rheumatoid arthritis, where the link between pathophysiology and disability outcomes is often found to be indirect and moderated by psychosocial and environmental factors (see Walker, Jackson and Littlejohn 2004 for a review).

Rather than considering disease, disability and handicap as indicative of quality of life, they could therefore be considered as potential influences upon it (McKenna, Whalley and Doward 2000; McKenna 2004) that may or may not affect a person's perceived QoL, depending on the extent to which that individual rates them as important to that judgement (e.g. Cox 2003). For some individuals, the inability to perform valued activities as a result of impairment or disability may be considered a 'fate worse than death' (e.g. Ditto, Druley, Moore *et al.* 1996); however, for others they will continue to find meaning and purpose in life in spite of disablement. IN THE SPOTLIGHT (below) raises the question of whether the outcomes important to the person concerned are the same as the outcomes valued by the health profession or, in particular, health economists.

What influences quality of life?

Many factors influence QoL:

■ demographics: e.g. age, culture;

■ the condition itself: e.g. symptoms, presence or absence of pain, functional disability, neurological damage with associated motor, emotional or cognitive impairment, sensory or communicative impairment;

■ treatment (availability, nature, extent, toxicity, side-effects, etc.);

■ psychosocial factors: e.g. emotions (anxiety, depression), coping, social context, goals and support.

Which health outcomes are important to whom?

For most people, the choice between a treatment without major side-effects and a treatment with major side-effects would be an easy decision, i.e. that without the side-effects. However, the decision becomes more complex if the choice is now between a treatment without major side-effects but with only moderate proven success in eradicating the illness concerned, and a treatment with significant side-effects but with excellent success rates. Which would you choose? These types of decision are faced daily by many cancer patients, who are fighting for survival but facing often toxic treatments in terms of their side-effects. The quantity of life may be added to by these treatments, but what about life quality? These questions raise the issue of which outcomes are best for the individual being treated.

If economics also enters the debate, as it increasingly does in terms of treatment costs, costs of hospital stays, costs of follow-up care, etc., then decisions about which treatment outcomes are best often fall into the hands of doctors and hospital managers who are responsible for spending. The outcome of mortality has little healthcare cost, whereas prolonged morbidity does and therefore treatment efficacy is central to these decisions. The ideal outcome from a medical standpoint is likely to be optimal functioning, but few treatments come with that guarantee, and if they do then they are likely to be very expensive! Decisions are generally made in terms of weighing up the costs of treatment (e.g. financial costs, costs to the person in terms of side-effects) against the objective benefits of treatment (e.g. financial savings from reduced further treatment needs, projected quantity of life gain for the individual).

Time trade-off techniques used by health economists can examine the utility (importance) attached to health states. Health practitioners and patients can be asked to imagine living with a certain condition for a couple of years, compared with living in better health for a shorter length of time if given a certain treatment, although they may die or be very ill after this time. The actual periods in normal health are adjusted until the person can no longer choose between the states. For example, if you were indifferent to whether you lived in poor health for six months or in optimal health for three months with treatment, then this would indicate the utility of that treatment for that individual. Basically, these kinds of judgement require individuals to consider how much time in terms of current QoL they would be willing to trade for post-treatment QoL; for example, how many days of treatment would you willingly trade for how many months of improved health? (See Bowling 1995a: 12–14 for a fuller discussion of the complexities of such techniques).

The point is that such decisions, and the values placed on outcomes such as pain, disability, distress and even death, are subjective: i.e. different individuals value different aspects of life, and as this chapter will show, what is valued may change over the lifespan. For example, will a 75-year-old cancer patient consider the treatment options such as eight weeks of intensive chemotherapy, the anticipated benefits in terms of extended lifespan, and the likely side-effects (nausea, hair loss, etc.) in the same way as a 45-year-old parent? This is why it is so important to assess individuals' perceptions of what makes their life 'quality'.

■ Age and quality of life

Age has been shown to influence the aspects of life considered to be important to people. Studies of QoL in child populations remain relatively limited,
and where studies exist they tend to have focused on chronic illnesses such as
asthma and epilepsy, where illness has the potential to have a broad psychosocial impact but is not generally life-threatening. As Bowling (1995b)
notes, some illnesses and their treatments and side-effects can have 'extra'
effects on children's functioning that are unlikely to be a factor in the
attainment of life quality of adults; for example, some cancer treatments can
impact upon desire and/or the ability to play with friends, participate in
sporting activities or attend school. Illnesses such as childhood epilepsy have
been found to impede social functioning, independence and relationships
with peers as well as, in some cases, self-esteem and mood (McEwan, Espie
and Metcalfe 2004). Jirojanakul, Skevington and Hudson (2003) note that
understanding of childhood QoL is additionally important because effects of
impaired QoL may be cumulative and affect development, and therefore
identifying QoL difficulties early in their experience might enable interventions to be put in place that prevent later problems. Eiser and Morse (2001)
conducted a review of the literature concerning assessing childhood QoL and
noted that QoL judgements are made by assessing present lifestyle relative
to one's expectations. A fruitful avenue of work might therefore examine

Plate 14.1 The experience of certain illnesses during childhood can lead to social
exclusion if the child is unable to join in physical activities with their friends. These
children can become withdrawn or depressed as a result.

Source: Joe Vaughn/Getty Images

whether children with chronic disease modify their future life expectations as a result of QoL being compromised in their childhood; to date we are unaware of any such studies.

While the majority of studies have relied on parental 'proxy' reports of their child's QoL (see Measuring quality of life, below), several interesting studies have employed qualitative methods to elicit domains of importance in QoL and factors that influence it, for example by carrying out focus group discussions with the children themselves. Cramer, Westbrook, Devinsky *et al.* (1999, cited in McEwan *et al.* 2004) conducted focus groups with adolescents with epilepsy and identified eight subscales that related to the health-related QoL:

1. general epilepsy impact
2. memory/concentration problems
3. attitudes towards epilepsy
4. physical functioning
5. stigma
6. social support
7. school behaviour
8. general health perceptions.

These findings reflect a broad range of influences on the QoL of young people (aged 11–17), and quantitative results from the same study found that seizure severity was the main predictor of health-related quality of life, independent of age of onset of the illness. In other words, length of time that the illness had been present did not appear to reduce the impact of severe seizures on QoL. In another focus group study that examined health-related QoL and its relation to distress among children with epilepsy aged 6–12, distress was mainly associated with loss of independence and restrictions in daily activities, concern about the reactions of others to their illness and seizures, treatment by peers, and concerns about the side-effects of medication (Ronen *et al.* 1999, as cited in McEwan *et al.* 2004).

Generic QoL, as opposed to QoL specifically in relation to illness (health-related QoL), in children has, perhaps surprisingly, been found to be less affected by health states (chronic, acute or severe illness) than by socio-economic factors (Jirojanakul, Skevington and Hudson 2003). These authors report that, among children aged 5–8 either attending school or working alongside construction worker parents (permitted in Thailand, where the study took place), social background variables such as parental income, education, and occupational status, type of housing, and extent of child's extracurricular activities significantly explained QoL (assessed with a child-friendly form as well as by proxy), whereas health status was not. While this study was conducted in Thailand, and among predominantly healthy children, the findings are considered consistent with studies in Western child populations, where current life circumstances (and the expectations they bring with them) are important to QoL (e.g. Eiser and Morse 2001).

One factor that may influence the impact of illness on QoL is whether or not it occurs at an earlier age than is typical of that disease onset. For example, an adult experiencing a stroke at a time in life when they are still professionally or reproductively active may report effects on different QoL domains from those reported by elderly, retired stroke patients (e.g. Ferro and Crespo 1994). However, age was not found to be a predictor of quality of life in a one-year longitudinal study of stroke survivors ranging from 32 to 90 years old (Carod-Artal, Egido, Gonzalez *et al.* 2000), with other factors being important such as physical disability, depressed mood and gender (females had poorer QoL).

Being unable to return to work has been associated with a deterioration in QoL among younger people who have suffered an acute stroke (e.g. Niemi *et al.* 1988), and while returning to the workforce is not an issue facing most elderly individuals, there is increasing medical and social interest in how to maintain activity among the elderly. Maintaining QoL and promoting healthy, positive and successful ageing has become increasingly important given the ageing population of most societies (Baltes and Baltes 1990; Grundy and Bowling 1999). The goal of healthy ageing approaches is to minimise dependency (physical and/or emotional), which, in turn, it is hoped, will reduce the 'costs' to society of healthcare provision for an increasingly ageing population. Studies of older people have found the life domains of importance to be good physical functioning, having relationships with others, and maintaining health and social activity. Compared with younger samples, older people are more likely to mention independence, or the fear of losing it and becoming dependent (Bowling 1995b). Blane, Higgs, Hyde and Wiggins (2004) examined influences on QoL in over 300 individuals aged between 65 and 75 and found that serious and limiting health problems were most strongly predictive of QoL, with housing security, receipt of welfare or non-pension income and (for men only) years out of work also predictive. When a limiting illness is involved, the domains of importance become more focused on physical functioning and activity, social support and social contact. The type of illness is often found to be less important to

Plate 14.2   Social isolation increases the risk of physical and psychological ill-health.
Source: Jerry Cooke/Corbis

QoL than the level of resultant physical disability, with limitations in activity or role being a negative predictor of both mental and physical QoL scores. Non-limiting chronic disease did not affect QoL in Blane *et al.*'s study. An important global aim of interventions to enhance QoL, regardless of disease type (although the physical role may be more challenged by some conditions than others), should therefore be the improvement and maintenance of physical and role functioning. In old age, therefore, QoL continues to be multidimensional, and even among the 'oldest old' (i.e. 85 or older), QoL encompasses psychological, social and environmental wellbeing (Grundy and Bowling 1999). ISSUES (below) addresses the question of whether or not QoL is attainable at the end of life, as a result of either ageing or terminal illness.

ISSUES

End-of-life QoL

While the majority of deaths in the UK take place in hospitals, the care of the dying more often takes place in patients' homes, until the point is reached where some home carers can no longer provide the necessary care or medication and hospitalisation in nursing homes or hospices ensues. The hospice movement developed in the late 1960s out of recognition that traditional hospitals with their routines, emphasis on treatment and depersonalised atmosphere were not best placed to provide care to the dying (Saunders and Baines, 1983). Elizabeth Kubler-Ross (1969) at this time also highlighted the psychological and emotional aspects of dying and the need to 'listen to the dying patient'. The hospice movement therefore developed with a view to providing care that facilitates an optimal QoL for both patients and their families as death approaches. This requires that patients are pain-free, experience little distress, maintain some dignity and control, and can maintain relationships with loved ones in a caring and compassionate environment. A good QoL at the end of life has also been found to encompass patients' need to remain as independent as possible so as not to 'burden' (see later section) their carer (e.g. Gill, Kaur, Rummans, Novotny and Sloan 2003). It is also important for carers' needs to be supported in order that they are able to provide the patient with whatever support is needed during the final days and weeks of their life (World Health Organization Expert Committee 1990). Hospices therefore provide this kind of environment, although hospice beds remain predominantly for cancer patients (Seale 1991). However, do hospices make a difference?

Carers of patients who had died in hospices reported that 'their' patients were more aware that they were dying than did carers of those who had died in hospital, perhaps reflecting the ethos of openness encouraged in hospices (*ibid.*). This openness regarding dying may enable greater preparation for death and bereavement among patients and spouse carers, which has, in turn, been associated with reduced levels of emotional distress (e.g. Chochinov, Tataryn, Wilson *et al.* 2000). The positive differences attributed to hospice care are not consistently reported, however; for example, Seale and Kelly (1997) did not find a difference between hospice and hospital care in terms of the care and support provided to spouses. Thinking positively, this may reflect the changing nature of hospital care towards more holistic, psychosocial care, or thinking less positively, perhaps a growing medicalisation of hospices (Crossley and Small 1998).

Whenever a person is facing death as a result of a longstanding illness, issues such as 'a good death' and 'dying with dignity' become salient and bring with them many ethical and

continued

moral debates. When should treatment be stopped? How much pain can a person endure, and for how long? Should a dying person who has been experiencing great pain be resuscitated if they become unconscious? Should a person facing a terminal illness and inevitable decline towards death (such as the highly publicised case of Diane Petty, who faced full physical paralysis while remaining mentally intact as a result of motor neurone disease) be allowed to invite assisted suicide? Research has consistently shown that older people do not fear death itself, as younger people do, but are more concerned about the process of dying and the fear of dying in pain or without dignity and self-control (e.g. Chochinov, Hack, Hassard *et al.* 2002; McKiernan 1996; Strang and Strang 2002).

How, and even where, an ill person chooses to die is inevitably a personal decision. Choosing 'when' to die is altogether more contentious. 'Advance directives' are becoming increasingly common, whereby people indicate their wishes for medical intervention (or not) when and if the time comes that they are unable to communicate their wishes. The practice of non-treatment of a dying person – passive euthanasia – is generally acknowledged as an inevitable part of medicine; however, active euthanasia in terms of carrying out an action that effectively ends that life (such as administering a fatal dose of adrenaline) is much less common. Van der Heide *et al.* (2003), in a study of end-of-life decision-making practices in six European countries, found that the explicit hastening of death varied from less than 1 percent in Denmark, Italy, Sweden and Switzerland, through to 1.82 percent in Belgium and 3.4 percent in the Netherlands. The legality of assisted suicide or euthanasia also varies from being fully prohibited (e.g. Italy) to prohibited except in specific circumstances (e.g. Belgium, the Netherlands).

Human rights legislation, the desire for control over our lives and the fact that the world is facing an ageing population, many of whom will live many years with chronic ill-health, suggests that issues regarding euthanasia are going to remain, and possibly grow.

Have your own personal experiences of death, if you have experienced any, influenced your thoughts on how you would choose to die, if that choice were available? What do you think would provide 'quality of life' at the end of life?

■ Culture and quality of life

Chapter 1 described how health itself is viewed slightly differently in Western and non-Western cultures, with individualistic Western views and more collectivist Eastern views of health being identified. Yan and Sellick (2004) point out that culture influences many factors relevant to quality of life judgements, such as responses to pain, attitudes towards and use of traditional versus Western medicines and treatments, concepts of dependency, and the culture of communication. While their longitudinal study of Chinese cancer patients revealed many of the same physical, psychosocial and emotional responses to gastrointestinal cancer reported in Western studies, the authors note that their sample differed from Western samples in their emphasis on family support, and in the patients' indirect indication of distress through symptom report rather than through direct interpersonal communication. The role of culture and the underlying values and beliefs about health, illness and QoL must therefore be considered in terms of their influence on self-reported QoL. As Bullinger (1997: 816) observed: 'If disease, as anthropological research suggests, is so very much culture-bound, how could quality of life be culture free?' Conceptually, the meaning of health and illness has been shown to be affected by cultural norms and experiences of health, illness and healthcare, as well as by different belief systems, such as the Chinese belief in the need to maintain a balance between *yin* and *yang*, or as in some tribal beliefs in the supernatural. We described many such different beliefs in the opening chapter. Cultural differences also affect how QoL can be assessed (see Measuring quality of life section below).

■ Aspects of the illness and quality of life

It is quite common for QoL not to be predicted by objectively determined severity of illness and associated symptoms. Furthermore, among carers, it has also been shown that the severity of symptoms or disability of the cared-for does not inevitably reduce carer QoL. We return to this issue in Chapter 15. The finding that symptom severity or extent of disability does not consistently predict QoL highlights the subjective nature of this concept, and it should come as no surprise to readers that QoL judgements, as with stress and illness discussed in previous chapters, are influenced by individual differences in the appraisal of, and subsequent coping with, ill-health. It also highlights the fact that QoL is by definition about the things that people value in life, and that illness or physical disability may or may not change such perceptions. Most available measures assume that illness will disrupt many domains of QoL, yet, as noted by Carr and Higginson (2001: 1,359): 'if they [standardised measures] do not cover domains that are important to individual patients they may not be valid measures for those patients'.

In many instances, however, illness does affect QoL. For example, pervasive and persistent pain and disability are generally found to be associated with a lower QoL, for example as reflected in depression levels, disability and use of healthcare (see Chapter 16). Ferrucci, Baldasseroni, Bandinelli *et al.* (2000) investigated the extent to which disease severity in stroke, Parkinson's disease or coronary heart disease patients was associated with their health-related QoL. They found that the relationship between disease severity and health-related QoL was non-linear in the stroke and CHD patients, and that only in the least severe stroke and most severe CHD cases was QoL in fact associated. In Parkinson's disease, however, there was a linear relationship reported whereby severe PD associated with lower health-related QoL. In other words, severity of illness is not inevitably or consistently associated with lower health-related QoL, and disease-specific relationships need to be explored.

In those with neurological illnesses such as Parkinson's disease, cognitive dysfunction such as memory impairment or attentional deficits can disrupt key QoL domains such as physical and psychosocial functioning. Furthermore, memory deficits can make it hard for some individuals to evaluate their current status against their former status in order to make meaningful QoL judgements (Murrell 2001). Perhaps for this reason patients with cognitive impairments have been the subject of less research attention (see also Measuring quality of life section below).

■ Aspects of treatment and quality of life

Treatment itself also influences QoL. Most studies that examine the effects of treatment on QoL do so in order to either determine its impact on specific populations or to compare which of several treatment alternatives is associated with the greatest QoL outcomes. In cancer, for example, scores on the

POQOLS (pediatric oncology (child cancer) QoL scale; Goodwin, Boggs and Graham-Pole 1994) differed across groups receiving different treatments; for example, children undergoing intensive treatment showed poorer QoL than those in remission (Bijttebier, Vercruysse, Vertommen *et al.* 2001).

Many treatment evaluations carried out as part of randomised controlled trials of new or comparable treatments include some indicator of QoL such as symptomatology, physical functioning or return to work. However, few as yet have adopted 'patient-centred' measures, which invite patients to describe outcomes important to them in terms of their QoL (Carr and Higginson 2001). However, this is an area of research and evaluation that is becoming more widespread, particularly in studies of cancer or pain. For example, several studies have been carried out to ascertain the impact of bone marrow transplantation in leukaemia patients. In a UK study, Watson, Buck, Wheatley *et al.* (2004) examined the QoL outcomes of a large number (481) of patients who had participated in a randomised trial of one of two types of bone marrow transplantation (BMT) (both preceded by intensive chemotherapy) compared with a course of intensive chemotherapy alone. On following participants up after one year, those patients who received BMT reported greater fatigue, more problems in sexual and social relationships, and disruptions to work and leisure activities. In addition, having BMT from a related sibling had a greater negative impact on the QoL indices than either unrelated donor transplantation or the chemotherapy group. A Dutch study of psychological functioning and QoL following BMT found that a quarter of patients still experienced significant functional limitations when followed up after three years, although almost 90 percent of the total sample (thus including many of those with functional limitations) reported their quality of life to be good to excellent (Broers, Kaptein, Le Cessie *et al.* 2000). Although effects of BMT on quality of life appear from these data to be long-lasting, another study of Dutch patients by Helder, Bakker, de Heer *et al.* (2004) found that the majority of QoL domain scores in young adults who had been children (an average age of 11) at the time of their BMT were not significantly lower than that found in a comparison group of healthy young adults. For example, those who had undergone childhood BMT between six and twelve years previously did not score lower in terms of physical or role functioning, pain or vitality, mental health, social and emotional functioning than the healthy participants, although their general health was rated lower (using the SF36 measure – see below). These findings would suggest that the childhood experience of a serious illness requiring intensive treatment and a prolonged period of adjustment does not have long-lasting effects into adulthood, although such conclusions have to be tempered by the fact that the study involved a relatively small sample, was cross-sectional and did not assess a number of other factors that may have contributed to the QoL of BMT survivors, such as social support resources.

■ Psychosocial influences on quality of life

Among physically healthy populations, the presence of anxiety symptoms or disorder has been associated with poor QoL (e.g. Mendlowicz and Stein 2001). Among those with physical illness, emotional responses have also been shown to impact upon quality of life. For example, both depression and anxiety symptoms measured within fifteen days of a heart attack were found to predict low QoL at four months, although depression was the strongest predictor (Lane, Carroll, Ring *et al.* 2000). Similarly, among 568 cancer patients, anxiety and depression were both related to the QoL dimensions of emotional, physical and social functioning, pain, fatigue (depression only), and global QoL, although as in Lane's study, depression was more strongly associated (Skarstein, Aass, Fossa *et al.* 2000).

Studies of the impact of pain on patient wellbeing may offer some explanation as to why depression is commonly associated with QoL, as pain is strongly associated with depressed mood (see Chapter 16). One study that examined both pain and depression is that of Rosenfeld, Breitbart, McDonald *et al.* (1996) who conducted a prospective survey of over 400 AIDS patients in New York; 63 percent of participants reported frequent or persistent pain in the preceding two weeks. Comparing scores across a range of QoL indices between those who were and those who were not currently experiencing pain revealed significant differences between the groups in terms of psychological distress, depression, feelings of hopelessness and global QoL. The analyses controlled for other possible influences on the QoL indices, such as age or gender, and social support (which itself was an independent predictor of distress). These results are consistent with many pain studies, showing that pain affects a broad range of psychosocial functioning. Also of importance is the finding that race was significantly related to QoL and distress, with non-white patients reporting poorer QoL and more distress. The authors consider whether this may be due to differences in access to pain management, or whether it reflects other factors not considered in their study, such as socio-economic or life stress, which may be detrimental to the QoL evaluations these individuals made. These findings highlight that several factors need to be taken into account when attempting to establish what 'predicts' QoL: the presence or absence of pain; the presence or absence of depressed mood; levels of social support, ethnicity and other background stressors that may be happening independently of the disease process under study.

In terms of coping response, Carver, Scheier and Pozo (1992) point out that avoidant coping is likely to be beneficial to QoL in situations where a person is unable to exert control, and they suggest that approach coping in these situations could lead to frustration when control is not forthcoming. Others suggest that maintaining a good QoL in relatively unalterable situations, such as that faced by individuals with chronic pain, may require individuals to cope by means of acceptance coping or positive reinterpretation (McCracken 1998). For example, McCracken and Eccleston (2003), in a study of 230 adults with chronic pain, found that coping was weakly related to pain acceptance and unreliably associated with adjustment, but that among those who did show acceptance of their pain, many QoL indicators were higher, including reduced pain symptomatology and disability, less depression and pain-related anxiety, a higher amount of time per day spent up and about, and a greater likelihood to be working. Such findings underscore the fact that, as discussed in Chapter 12, there is no one coping strategy that is inherently better than another and that coping is individual and contextual and will change over time and place depending on the demands and resources available to the person.

In terms of resources upon which individuals may draw when faced with stress or the demands of illness, previous chapters have highlighted the crucial role of social support. Perceived social support is generally considered

important to personal wellbeing, and many positive relationships between perceived social support, coping and adjustment to chronic disease have been reported. However, the direction of causality between variables is not always clear. Disentangling the direction of relationships between resource or coping variables and illness outcomes such as QoL requires studies with several waves of data collection, where change in the levels of support and adjustment, changes in coping responses, etc., can be assessed. In an attempt to do just this, Burgoyne and Renwick (2004) assessed forty-one Canadian adults with HIV three times over a four-year period and examined whether changes or stability in social support was associated with changes or stability in QoL. Although it had a relatively small sample size, this well-designed study considers the dynamic associations between disease symptomatology, social support and QoL and explores the direction of causality between these factors; for example, do changes in social support lead to changes in QoL, or do changes in QoL lead to changes in social support? Slightly contrary to expectations, analyses revealed that both social support and QoL remained relatively stable over the four-year period, although social support did decrease significantly for 40 percent of the sample. Poorer mental functioning QoL scores tended to predict subsequent lower perceived emotional and informational support, but the directional relationship between physical functioning QoL and social support was unclear. However, results did not show any strong longitudinal association between social support and subsequent QoL. In terms of linked changes over time in QoL or social support, results did not reveal that changes in either were linked in the longer term (i.e. from year 1 to year 4), but there was evidence of a link between year 1 and 2, and certainly the two measures were associated within each time point, with positive or negative changes in social support corresponding to positive or negative changes in QoL domains. However, the disappointing longitudinal predictive results means that social support and its effects on QoL, at least in this disease group, remains open to debate and in need of a similarly designed study to be conducted with a much larger sample.

■ Goals and QoL

QoL research has sometimes been criticised for the absence of a theoretical model around which to develop and test the QoL concept. One attempt to bring theory to bear has employed Carver and Scheier's self-regulation theory (see Chapter 9), which describes a process of goal attainment in the face of a disturbance such as illness (1992). It is proposed that the disturbance of personal goal attainment caused by chronic illness and its consequences is likely to influence a person's perceived QoL (e.g. Echteld, Maes and van Elderen 1998). Within the self-regulatory framework, event appraisal, appraisals of goal disturbance, outcome expectancies, appraisals of resources and coping processes all combine to influence QoL (e.g. Maes, Leventhal and de Ridder 1996). Echteld, van Elderen and van der Kamp (2003), for example, found that among 158 patients who had undergone **coronary angioplasty**, disease-specific quality of life and positive affect three months after surgery were predicted by pre-surgery QoL, low stress appraisals and avoidant coping. Goal disturbance predicted disease-specific QoL and negative affect. Boersma, Maes and Joekes (in press) also found that disturbance in 'higher-order' goals such as fulfilling duties to others, or having fun, following a heart attack was associated with anxiety, depression and a lower health-related quality of life. It may be that goals indirectly influence QoL outcomes by altering the 'meaning' a person attaches to their illness (Taylor 1983; theory of cognitive adaptation to illness, see below). The 'meaning' of illness has been defined as 'an individual's understanding of the implications an illness has on self, relationships with others, priorities, and future goals', and as such has been shown to influence wellbeing and adjustment, for example among those with cancer (e.g. Fife 1995, cited in Walker *et al.* 2004, p. 467). Examining personal goals (both day-to-day and higher-order goals) and their attainment or non-attainment as a result of ill-health is therefore potentially a useful avenue of research.

coronary angioplasty
a procedure where a small balloon is inserted into the blocked coronary artery of a person with **atheroma**.

Measuring quality of life

Several main reasons have been suggested as to why QoL assessment is a useful clinical practice (e.g. Higginson and Carr 2001). These include:

■ *Measure to inform*: to increase understanding about the multidimensional impact of illness and factors that moderate impact, in order to (1) inform interventions and best practice, and (2) inform patients about treatment outcomes or possible side-effects in order that they are prepared, or that supportive resources can be put in place. For example, Ganz *et al.* (1993) interviewed 227 women newly diagnosed with breast cancer and again a year later. Some of the difficulties that these women identified included excessive weight gain and sexual dysfunction. If these consequences were discussed with patients at an early stage, they could mentally 'prepare' for them and as a result minimise their impact. Descriptive studies can also be used to inform patients and their families about likely treatment experiences so that treatment choices can be made. For example, Fallowfield *et al.* (1990) concluded, following a review of the breast cancer surgery literature, that there is no definite evidence that breast-sparing procedures have more favourable QoL and psychosocial outcomes than mastectomy (although some studies did find better body image and sexual functioning in those with breast-conserving therapy). This information can be presented by healthcare providers to aid patient decision making.

■ *Measure to evaluate alternatives*: QoL measures may be used as a form of clinical 'audit' to identify which interventions have the 'best' outcomes – for the patient, but also often in relation to costs. In medicine (and health economics), a related concept has emerged, called quality-adjusted life years, or QALYs. Different treatments may be considered as increasing length of life and QoL to varying degrees, and if weightings are attached to certain treatments and assessed against the actual cost of the treatment, QALYs can be used to inform medical treatment decisions. For example, two cancer treatments may offer the same survival benefits, but QoL and QALYs may be poorer during and after one treatment than the other; or one treatment may be cheaper than the other where both have the same effect on improved QoL. Brewster, Hackett, Morrison *et al.* (2004) surveyed the influences upon health professionals and general public attitudes towards treating cancer in the elderly and found that hypothetical decisions to offer treatment were most commonly influenced by life gain, followed by quality of life gain, severity of side-effects and finally patient age. The financial cost of treatment was not examined in this study.

■ *Measure to promote communication*: while this is unlikely to be the primary motive for conducting a QoL assessment in a clinical setting, engaging patients in QoL assessment may require health professionals to address areas that they may not otherwise have done, for example about treatment satisfaction, family interactions, hobbies or sexual functioning. This will provide health professionals with a more holistic view of the impact that illness or treatment has had upon their patient and may help future treatment decision making or healthcare.

Whatever the motive for assessing QoL, a major issue faced by researchers or clinicians is which instrument or method of assessment to use. If we accept that QoL is a multidimensional, dynamic and subjective construct, measurement is inevitably going to face many challenges!

Leventhal and Colman (1997) state that QoL should be considered not only in terms of outcomes but also as a process that is influenced by individuals' perceptions of various domains of their lives, including their perceptions of any illness and its treatment (see Chapter 9), and the weightings or importance they attach to their perceptions at any given point in time. They do not argue that QoL should be assessed separately from all its possible component parts, e.g. physical, emotional and social functioning, but that each should be seen as separate factors, as possible determinants of QoL. Changes in any of these determinants will influence changes in QoL (see Figure 14.1). This process model has generally been accepted in psychological research studies where multiple measures of determinants are used, as well as generic or specific QoL measures, as will be seen in the discussion of measures below.

Generic versus specific QoL measures

While the global domains of QoL described by the WHOQOL group and outlined at the start of the chapter have been supported in many empirical

Status pre-disease   Status post-disease and treatment

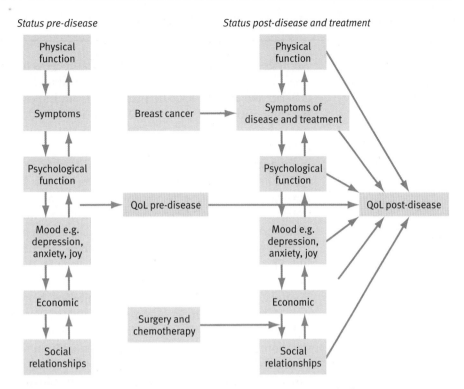

Figure 14.1 The quality-of-life process prior to and subsequent to breast cancer. Baseline QoL is changed by the impact of the disease and treatment upon each of the domains. Changes in functioning post-disease are weighted and will lead to changes in post-disease onset QoL.

Source: Leventhal and Coleman (1997: 759). Reproduced by permission of Taylor & Francis Ltd. www.tandf.co.uk/journals

studies, a question remains as to whether to adopt a generic, or global, measure of QoL such as the WHOQOL, or a measure specific to the illness being studied. Commonly employed generic measures include the Medical Outcome study short form 36, usually referred to as the SF36 (Stewart and Ware 1992); the Nottingham health profile (NHP; Hunt, McEwan and McKenna 1986); and the EUROQOL (Euroqol group 1990). In terms of disease-specific measures an increasing number are available, such as those developed for people with cancer (e.g. EORTC; Aaronson 1993), asthma (e.g. Hyland, Bellesis, Thompson *et al.* 1996), arthritis (e.g. AIMS-1, 2; Meenan and Mason 1990) or Parkinson's disease (see review by Marinus, Ramaker, van Hilten *et al.* 2002).

There are disadvantages and advantages to both types of measure. Generic measures, while allowing for comparison between different illness groups, often fail to address some of the unique QoL issues for that illness: in cancer, for example, issues regarding fears of recurrence or the side-effects of chemotherapy; and in HIV infection issues such as HIV testing and self-disclosure of a positive diagnosis to others (as addressed by WHOQOL-HIV). Disease-specific measures therefore have 'added value' in that such issues are addressed, but they do not allow for the same amount of cross-illness comparability. This comparability allows questions such as 'Is the quality of life reduced more by cancer than by heart disease?' – a question that is of interest perhaps in terms of targeting community support resources.

Individualised QoL measures

Another option available to health researchers is to use individualised measures of QoL. Individual QoL instruments abandon the dimensions of many generic and disease-specific instruments and allows respondents to choose the dimensions and concerns relevant and of value to them (see RESEARCH FOCUS). One example is the schedule for the evaluation of individual quality of life (SEIQoL; O'Boyle, McGee, Hickey *et al.* 1992, 1993), which invites individuals to identify five aspects of life that are important to them (i.e. 'What are the five most important areas of your life at present – the things that make your life a relatively happy or sad one at the moment . . . the things that you feel determine your quality of life?'). Individuals then rate their current level of functioning on each, attach a weighting of importance to each aspect and rate how satisfied they are currently with that aspect of life. The aspects of life mentioned most often by the hip replacement patients in the original study were family, leisure activities, independence, happiness, finances and religion; with control subjects being very similar, although nominating health more often than patients. Perhaps it was important to the healthy participants to retain health and therefore these participants mentioned it, whereas it featured less strongly in the patient sample perhaps because they had had to readjust their life goals and values and no longer rated health as one of the most important domains in their lives, although this was not explored in the study.

RESEARCH FOCUS

Generating individualised QoL beliefs

Stenner, Cooper and Skevington (2003). Putting the Q into quality of life: the identification of subjective constructions of health-related quality of life using Q methodology. *Social Science and Medicine*, 57: 2161–72.

Background aims

Measures of QoL need to tap into individual patients' points of view. This makes 'standardisation' of measurement a difficult goal, as the factors that make up perceived quality of life for one person may be very different to the factors that make up the same 'level' of quality of life for another. This issue has been addressed in an interesting study by Stenner, Cooper and Skevington (2003), who employed an idiographic technique, i.e. one where each participant identifies aspects of QoL important to them.

Method

The specific technique adopted was 'Q' methodology, whereby participants sort a collection of fifty-two statements about QoL (developed from WHOQOL and other sources) into piles according to their importance to them (least important, neutral, most important) and then return to the three piles and sort each item within the piles on a scale ranging from –5 least important, through 0 neutral, to +5 extremely important. In this way, ninety healthy participants produced what is known as their own Q sort. They then examine their Q sort and discuss why they ranked some items as more important than others, and whether they believe it is an accurate reflection of their personal view about QoL.

Results

When analysed statistically, eight significant factors emerged that were interpreted as reflecting distinct constructs of the meaning and personal relevance of QoL:

1. *Happy families* (fifteen participants): the factor onto which the Q sorts of older (mean 49 years), married individuals (thirteen) fell. Relationships within and support from the family were crucial to these individuals, with relationships and support from non-family members being considered less important. Family relationships and support were considered important to good health, contentment and QoL, as were, to a lesser degree, financial concerns. These individuals valued physical health and independence more than either psychological wellbeing or spiritual concerns.

2. *Stand on my own two feet*: this factor included fourteen participants of a younger mean age (34.4 years) with a mix of married, single and cohabiting individuals. For these individuals, psychological wellbeing was central, with aspects of QoL that maintain independence rated highly. A need to feel in control was important, in terms of life and work issues, and financial issues following from work success related to feelings of self-worth, life satisfaction and control. Although relationships with friends and family were considered important, independence and personal control over achievements were more important. Physical states such as pain were not highly important to the perceived QoL of this group, although physical independence was.

3. *Emotional independence*: ten participants (mean age 30.5 years, majority (six) single, five were university educated) loaded onto this factor, exemplified by a need for mental wellbeing and stability and for physical functioning not to be interfered with by negative emotions. Spiritual calmness and inner peace were considered important to wellbeing, although not religion *per se*. This inner peace and happiness was thought to come from oneself, and from self-control of negative feelings, rather than from reliance on relationships with others, or from physical states.

4. *Just do it*: nine participants loaded on this factor (similar age to the previous group, 30.4 years, majority (five) single, and majority (six) university educated). This group placed high importance on being active and having a meaningful life, which was brought about by 'doing' things considered to be important to them, e.g. being active, engaging in leisure activities, having a good sex life. Friends were more central to this group than family. Personal beliefs rather than religion were important to overall wellbeing, with self-esteem being derived from self-control and action.

5. *Life as a positive challenge*: five participants (mean age 22.8 years, three single, all educated to university level) on this factor highlighted learning and knowledge as important, whereas money was considered less important. Negative emotions functioned as a means of enabling a person to experience life, and for these individuals meaningfulness in life was more important than personal control. Relationships with others, friends and family, were rated more important than both health and overall QoL, although health became important if it impacted on daily functioning (NB: this relates nicely to the surveys of health perceptions reported in Chapter 1, where health becomes more important when ill-health is experienced).

6. *In God we trust*: four participants loaded onto this factor, all of whom were young females (mean age 25.3 years) who reported practising religion. For these individuals, the dominant theme was that life is controlled by 'something' or 'someone' else and that faith in this is crucial. Personal beliefs and meaningfulness in life were also important, with the next

continued

most important aspect being supportive relationships with others. Health and overall QoL were not ranked highly by this group.

7. *Staying healthy enough to bring home the bacon*: four participants loaded onto this factor, three of whom were male (mean age 44, three married, one separated, none university educated). For these individuals, physical health was crucial, as was sex and mobility, treatment for health problems, and external appearance. Good health was considered functional and central to a sense of pride, although money was important to providing for home and family.

8. *You can't choose your family*: three participants (mean age 23 years, two undergraduate, one postgraduate). Similar to the 'life as a positive challenge' group in terms of age and educational level, this group differed in that they placed high importance on relationships and the support of friends, whereas family lacked importance. Importance was attached to not experiencing negative feelings or letting them interfere with daily functioning. Self-esteem and satisfaction were important, with mental health, rather than physical health, crucial to this.

Discussion

This study was selected for attention because results such as these highlight that while there are certain commonalities in what people think is important in their lives (such as the importance of relationships, control and independence), many differences exist (e.g. the extent to which spirituality is a self-belief or based on a religion; the extent to which friends and/or family support is valued; the extent to which mental wellbeing is valued in comparison to physical health; and the extent to which control is considered to be an internal or external resource). These findings also highlight that the different strands of QoL interact and causal sequencing seems likely; in other words, psychological aspects may influence the reported social, financial and physical aspects, and vice versa. Interesting differences are suggested for age, gender and educational status, although this study is limited by not including participants over the age of 64, anyone who was unemployed, or anyone not of white English origin. (The influence of ageing on perceived QoL was addressed earlier in the chapter.) Gender, age and educational attainment differences may influence an individual's current and future life goals, and it has been suggested that goal direction and attainment may be important influences upon a person's QoL. The role of goals and QoL has been addressed in several studies working within the self-regulation framework of Carver and Scheier (e.g. Carver and Scheier, 1981; Carver, Scheier and Pozo, 1992).

While individualised methods of assessment acknowledge the subjectivity of QoL, such methods are time-consuming and relatively complex processes that critics suggest may exclude their use in certain populations. Addressing this point, Jenkinson, Fitzpatrick, Garrat *et al.* (2001) adopted technology to make QoL assessment quicker, portable and possibly more adaptable to clinical situations. They describe a method of assessment known as the dynamic health assessment (DYNHA) system (see www.qualitymetric.co), which is a short computer-based instrument based on the SF36. Items for assessment are selected from a pool, dependent upon participants' earlier responses to global questions. The benefit of this method is that assessment is more adapted to uniquely individual problems, while the use of SF36 items still enables comparison with other groups assessed with SF36. More studies are required using this method, but results from Jenkinson's study with neurological populations are encouraging.

Practicality of measures

Where assessment circumstances allow, most studies use multiple measures, and as well as assessing generic and/or illness-specific multidimensional QoL will generally also include unidimensional outcome measures such as assessments of mood, pain or disability that address only one specific aspect of QoL. There is a natural limit to how many questionnaires can be 'inflicted' on an ill individual, and it is important for researchers to be sensitive to this. A good research tool may not be an appropriate tool to administer in a clinical setting. For example, the functional limitations profile (Patrick and Peach 1989) (or its American precursor the sickness impact profile; Bergner, Bobbitt, Carter *et al.* 1981) while a well-validated and commonly employed outcome measure, has 136 items assessing twelve domains of potential illness impact (e.g. self-care, mobility, social functioning, communication and emotion), and it takes twenty–thirty minutes to complete, which is potentially impractical in many clinical settings.

In addition, certain conditions make it difficult to carry out assessments of subjective perceptions, such as QoL. Illnesses that elicit a communication deficit, such as the receptive and expressive aphasias that are common following a stroke, often results in such patients being excluded from self-report studies (e.g. Morrison, Pollard, Johston *et al.* 2005) and the use of proxy measures often results, the limitations of which are described below.

Overall, there has been a proliferation of QoL measures and assessment methods available to researchers in this area, and the choice of which to use will be determined by the aims of the study and by the practicalities offered by the research situation and the population to be studied. This makes it quite difficult to compare across studies, and quite difficult to translate research findings into clinical practice. While the growth of the WHOQOL group measures may go some way towards achieving consistency in measurement, the standardisation of quantitative measures and methods bring with them the risk of losing information as to the very personal and individualised meaning of QoL (see RESEARCH FOCUS above).

Two final factors that warrant consideration in the development of new measures or in the choice made from existing instruments (see Bowling 1995a for coverage of many QoL instruments) is that of participant age and culture.

■ Culture

Measures of health-related QoL have been developed predominantly in the English language, meaning that for use in non-English-speaking countries, measures have to be translated. Bowden and Fox-Rushby (2003) reviewed the process of translating measures, generally developed in English, in twenty-three countries across Africa, Asia, Eastern Europe, the Middle East and South America. These authors concluded that in the process of translation the meaning of items may be lost, and that using measures that have been generated predominantly from samples of Western populations assumes that words and concepts have equivalent meaning in different cultures, and that domains have equal salience. Furthermore, the nature of disease varies considerably between countries, with, for example, the authors citing the fact that in Europe only 6 percent of mortality is attributable to communicable diseases (such as HIV, TB), whereas in Africa and Southeast Asia communicable diseases account for 71 and 39 percent of deaths, respectively. Differences in disease experience such as these are likely to have an effect on illness and QoL expectations. The WHOQOL group is addressing these culturally relevant questions in its many studies.

■ Age

McEwan, Espie and Metcalfe (2004: 4) point out that adapting an adult questionnaire into a child version 'fails to acknowledge important aspects of child and adolescent development and functioning'. The young child may, for example, have cognitive limitations that make it difficult for them to understand abstract questions such as those concerning life satisfaction or global wellbeing. Although some measures have been developed specifically to assess QoL in child populations (e.g. Eiser and Morse 2001), not many have been validated, and this fact, alongside a common assumption of cognitive limitation in children, has led to many studies using parents to complete questionnaires on behalf of their children (e.g. Bijttebier *et al.* 2001). This is known as proxy measurement. However, parental 'proxy' reports in effect go against the principle of QoL being a personal subjective belief, as a parent may not share the same views as their child. This point was well illustrated by Eiser and Morse (2001) when they reviewed studies of chronically ill samples where both child reports and parental proxy reports were generated. Parent–child agreement was greater for observable aspects of QoL such as physical functioning but less for emotional or perceived social functioning. In Bijttebier *et al.*'s (2001) study of QoL among young cancer patients (using parental proxy reports), predominantly observable aspects of QoL were assessed in relation to:

- *physical restriction*: e.g. my child has been able to perform as usual;
- *emotional distress*: e.g. my child has anger outbursts;
- *discomfort from medical treatment*: e.g. my child complained of pain after a medical procedure.

As such, the data on child QoL obtained in this study may be more reliable than if 'non-behavioural' aspects of QoL had been assessed; however, whole domains of QoL are not examined.

As further illustration of possible discrepancies between proxy and 'real' reports, a study of 100 children with congenital heart disease and their parents found that while both parents and children reported reduced child motor functioning and autonomy when compared with healthy children, the children reported lower levels of emotional QoL than did their parents. Overall, parents reported that more problems were faced by their children than the children themselves reported (Krol, Grootenhuis, Destrée-Vonk *et al.* 2003). Healthy children, by contrast, have been reported to show less agreement with their parents regarding their physical status than they do in other domains (e.g. Theunissen, Vogels, Koopman *et al.* 1998).

Additionally, it has been shown following a review of findings of six studies where two sets of ratings were obtained that significant discrepancies exist in the perceptions of patient wellbeing and QoL during the course of long-term (primarily cancer) treatment reported by their physicians and that reported by the patients themselves, or in the case of children, parental perceptions (Janse, Gemke, Uiterwaal *et al.* 2004).

The findings reviewed here highlight that parent–child dyads may converge and diverge in terms of their beliefs, depending on various factors including the child's current health status. In the context of a child with illness, parental over- or underestimation of a child's problem areas can have implications for parental caring behaviour (see Chapter 15). Furthermore, we have presented evidence that patient (or parent) ratings often diverge from health professionals' ratings of that patient's QoL, and this could lead to misunderstandings about treatment or its usefulness in terms of QoL gain, which may, as Janse *et al.* note, have implications for non-adherence.

Summary

This chapter has provided evidence that QoL is an important concept that encompasses a person's subjective belief about the quality of various life domains of importance to them. We have described a range of influences on the experience of quality of life, including aspects of the disease and its treatment, as well as aspects of the individual such as their age, mood or levels of social support. We have also shown that, in spite of difficulties in clearly defining and measuring QoL, there is a growing recognition of the need to do so and for research and practice to look beyond traditionally clinical outcomes of illness, such as disability, symptomatology, and mortality, to more holistic psychosocial outcomes. While there is increasing evidence of the inclusion of QoL assessment in clinical trials of treatments or in psychosocial interventions, the debate as to whether it is best assessed objectively or subjectively, generically or specifically, remains.

Further reading

Bowling, A. (1991). *Measuring Health: A Review of Quality of Life*. Buckingham: Open University Press.

Bowling, A. (1995). *Measuring Disease: A Review of Disease-specific Quality of Life Measurement Scales*. Buckingham: Open University Press.
These two well-written books provide the reader with a comprehensive overview of issues in both health- and illness-related quality of life. Additionally, the majority of QoL scales available at the time are outlined and useful examples provided. While they have become dated as many new scales appear, such as the WHOQOL, these books provide essential background reading.

Carr, A.J. and Higginson, I.J. (2001). Are quality of life measures patient centred? *British Medical Journal*, 32: 1357–60.
This brief paper addresses the crucial issues of how to measure QoL, and who should take the measurements – doctors, patients or other proxy reporters? The

fact that this paper was published in the *British Medical Journal* is encouraging testimony to the fact that QoL is on the medical profession's agenda.

Eiser, C. and Morse, R. (2001). The measurement of quality of life in children: past and future perspectives. *Journal of Developmental and Behavioral Pediatrics*, 22: 248–56.
An important and clearly written paper considering the specific issues of QoL in children.

CHAPTER 15

The impact of illness on patients and their families

Learning outcomes

By the end of this chapter, you should have an understanding of:

- the many emotional consequences of physical illness, particularly those of anxiety and depression
- the impact of physical illness in the family on the wellbeing of close family members or informal carers
- evidence showing that neither being ill nor caring for a sick relative or friend is inevitably a negative experience
- how some caring is not beneficial to the recipient

CHAPTER OUTLINE

In previous chapters, although describing many individual and social factors that influence the responses to a stressful experience such as illness, the focus has predominantly been on the person experiencing the stress or suffering the illness. In this chapter, we turn our attention to the impact of illness on the individual's emotional wellbeing but also on the wellbeing and quality of life of family members, many of whom act as informal carers.

This chapter highlights that while illness or caring for an ill person has many potentially negative consequences, positive outcomes are also forthcoming; and that research needs to attend increasingly to the perceptions held within dyads where one is ill, as evidence is growing that shared or discrepant perceptions play a predictive role in patient outcomes.

Illness, emotions and adjustment

Illness presents individuals with many challenges and issues that change over time, depending upon the illness, the treatment, the individual's cognitive, behavioural and emotional responses, and the social and cultural context in which the illness occurs. Illness is a complex process, illustrated by Morse and Johnson (1991) in their generic model of the emotional and coping responses from the onset of symptoms through to living with a chronic illness. Individuals facing illness are considered as having to deal with:

1. *Uncertainty*: this is a period in which the individual tries to understand the meaning and severity of the first symptoms.

2. *Disruption*: this occurs when it becomes evident to the individual that they have a significant illness. At this time, they experience a crisis characterised by intense stress and a high level of dependence on health professionals and/or other people who are emotionally close to the individual.

3. *Striving for recovery*: this period is typified by the individual attempting to gain some form of control over their illness by means of active coping.

4. *Restoration of wellbeing*: in this phase, the individual achieves a new emotional equilibrium based on an acceptance of the illness and its consequences.

In relation to cancer, a similar series of stages of response to diagnosis has been proposed (Holland and Gooen-Piels 2000):

1. *Initial response*: can include a range of responses, including disbelief, denial and shock. Some people may challenge the diagnosis or the ability of the health professional. At this stage, individuals try to defend themselves from the implications of the diagnosis and may not process information clearly.

2. *Dysphoria*: this phase may last one–two weeks and involves individuals gradually coming to terms with the reality of their diagnosis. Simultaneously, they may experience significant distress and related symptoms

such as insomnia, reduced appetite, poor concentration, anxiety and depression. As information about treatment is gradually presented and processed, hope and optimism may emerge to compete with the more distressing thoughts.

3. *Adaptation*: this period may last for weeks, or months, and involves the person adapting more positively to their diagnosis and developing long-term coping strategies in order to maintain equilibrium.

Although these models propose a staged adaptive process, not all individuals will move through the stages smoothly and achieve emotional equilibrium or a stage of acceptance and adaptation. For example, among cancer patients, some will enter the terminal phase still 'in denial' of their impending death. Hinton (1999) found that by the time of their death, only half of the people followed in their study were 'accepting' of death, and 18 percent of patients and 24 percent of relatives actually became less accepting of death as they moved towards it. It is likely that elements from different 'stages' may co-occur; for example, a person may still experience significant distress even when actively coping with their illness. Individuals may also move backwards and forwards between stages and reactions, for example shifting their focus from one of cure to one of 'healing', in which they try to resolve life issues and achieve some completion of their life's achievements. They may still maintain hope at this time, but rather than hope for a cure they may shift towards hope for a 'good' or pain-free death (Little and Sayers 2004). Religion and spirituality are frequently important factors in maintaining this type of hope. A transition from curative to palliative treatment, if the former is unsuccessful, can be extremely distressing for patients. Overall, the rates of anxiety and/or depression are high among people who are dying, although this is by no means universal (e.g. Heaven and Maguire (1999) reported only 17 percent prevalence of clinical levels of distress in their sample). The certainty of death commonly brings with it emotional and existential crises alongside concerns about the process of dying and about pain control (Strang and Strang 2002), and fears about a loss of dignity, which can raise distress and even lower the will to live (Chochinov, Hack, Hassard *et al.* 2002). Kubler-Ross (1969) described a staged reactive process to dying, with initial shock and numbness following a terminal diagnosis being followed by a stage of denial and feelings of isolation, at which point individuals may become angry, blame others or even attempt to 'bargain' for goals they wish to meet before dying. Kubler-Ross describes the final stage as one of acceptance, although as we have already noted, this is not always reached.

Several authors have criticised such 'staged' approaches for the manner in which they categorise patients and create expectations of responses to serious illness events or to dying, whereas people's experiences and reactions vary hugely and are unique (e.g. Hale 1996; Crossley 2000). However, such theories should be considered a useful starting point for those working with the ill or dying, on the understanding that individuals may not neatly fit into any one of the defined stages and that caring responses therefore need to be individually tailored.

Not all illnesses bring with them an imminent threat to mortality, and many individuals live with illness. Living with chronic illness (including many treatable cancers) or the fear of recurrence of an acute illness can itself be distressing, however.

Negative emotional reactions to illness

■ **Reactions to diagnosis**

Many studies have been conducted with patients with cancer, from diagnosis through active treatment to terminal stages, or to survival (e.g. Kornblith 1998). Most studies find that reactions to a cancer diagnosis are frequently catastrophic and highly emotional (e.g. O'Connor, Wicker and Germino 1990), with some individuals describing themselves quite literally as 'fighting for their life' (Landmark and Wahl 2002). This qualitative study reports how one woman, recently diagnosed with breast cancer, described herself as standing 'with one foot in the grave, the other on the edge' (p. 115). In the early stages of cancer, Montgomery, Pocock, Titley *et al.* (2003) found moderate to severe or severe levels of depression in 51 percent of their sample of people with leukaemia and lymphoma, with 14 percent reporting similarly high levels of anxiety. Negative emotional reactions are also common among those with sudden-onset heart disease (e.g. Lane, Carroll, Ring *et al.* 2002), stroke (e.g. Astrom 1996; Hosking, Marsh and Friedman 1996), or following a positive HIV diagnosis (Valente 2003). In terms of heart disease and heart attack, it has been estimated that one-third or more of sufferers will experience levels of depression above cut-offs indicating clinical disorder; and among stroke patients the figures have been reported as anywhere between 18 and 60 percent (House, Dennis, Mogridge *et al.* 1991).

■ **Emotional reactions to illness or its treatment**

It would be impossible to address reactions to all illnesses, or even all chronic illnesses, so what follows is a representative selection of common and potentially life-changing illnesses: cancer, HIV, heart attack, stroke and diabetes.

While initial levels of distress among cancer patients generally fall to levels comparable with healthy populations (e.g. Cassileth *et al.* 1985), they are seen to become elevated at certain points during treatment, or when awaiting test results, and when end-stage illness is reached and treatment ended with no further hope for a cure. During the active treatment phase of their illness, cancer patients may have to cope with a variety of stressors, including significant side-effects such as potentially debilitating and distressing nausea, fatigue and weight loss. At this time, individuals may weigh up the unwanted effects of treatment against the benefits of symptom reduction and survival gains, and while the majority choose to continue with treatment, a small minority do opt to withdraw from treatment. Even when at risk of illness, not everyone will opt for treatment when it is offered. For example, Lovegrove, Rumsey, Harcourt *et al.* (2000) found that 50 percent of 106 women at high familial risk of breast cancer attending a breast care clinic and who were asked to take part in a trial of tamoxifen, a synthetic, non-steroidal agent with tumour-limiting benefits in an unaffected breast, refused to participate. Those refusing tended to be younger, found the information about tamoxifen as a potential preventive treatment harder to understand than those who took part, knew more about lifestyle risk factors, and saw fewer benefits of the drug.

For many stroke patients, significant levels of emotional distress (anxiety and/or depression) persist for many months, with psychosocial factors in

addition to disease features predicting long-term outcome. For example, patient satisfaction with healthcare and confidence in recovery predicted depression at six months and three years following acute stroke (Morrison, Johnston and MacWalter 2000; Morrison, Pollard, Johnston and MacWalter 2005). Depression and anxiety are also found in heart attack patients following hospital discharge, which often persist for up to a year later (Lane, Carroll, Ring *et al.* 2002). In terms of living with HIV and AIDS, Valente (2003) concluded from a summary of existing data that between 20 and 30 percent of people with HIV are clinically depressed at some stage in their illness. Among women with HIV, Morrison *et al.* (2002) reported depression levels four times higher than that expected among age-matched control subjects, although among this female-only sample, anxiety levels were not raised significantly. Other studies of both genders have reported 70 percent having moderate to high anxiety (Cohen, Hoffman, Cromwell *et al.* 2002). As with depression among physically healthy individuals, high levels of background stress, low levels of personal resources and social support, and poor coping skills all contribute to depression (e.g. Catz, Gore-Felton and McClure 2002). Among those with HIV infection, the presence of what have been identified as 'punishment beliefs' (i.e. where HIV infection is considered by the individual to be a 'punishment' for 'inappropriate' behaviour) was associated with relatively high levels of depression and relatively low self-esteem (Safren, Radomsky, Otto *et al.* 2002). Such beliefs reflect possible internalisation of early beliefs or prejudices about HIV and likely routes of infection, such as injecting drug use or unprotected homosexual sex.

Finally, among those living with diabetes – a chronic illness requiring ongoing self-management (diet, taking insulin, etc.) – emotional distress is also prevalent. A systematic review of studies with a combined population of over 2,500 adults with diabetes and almost 1,500 control participants found a 14 percent prevalence of generalised anxiety disorder, compared with population norms of around 3–4 percent, and elevated anxiety symptoms in 40 percent (Grigsby, Anderson, Freedland *et al.* 2002). Anderson, Freidland, Clouse *et al.* (2001) report that depression is twice as likely in adults with diabetes than in those without.

Chronic illness can also bring about a sense of 'loss of self' (Charmaz 1983, 1991) to the sufferer, a condition exacerbated by the necessity of living a restricted life due to symptoms, or by social isolation due to physical limitations or fears of others' response to their 'new state'. Negative responses of others can sometimes lead to perceptions of the self being discredited, or to perceiving oneself as being a burden on others by being unable to fulfil ones 'normal' social roles and tasks. As Radley (1994: 148) notes: 'The problems of chronic illness are to do with retention and loss, not just of "self" but of a way of life'. Given this, it is perhaps surprising to discover that for some individuals, illness is perceived as bringing benefits (see below).

■ Reactions at the end of treatment

In the immediate period following treatment, cancer patients and their families may experience a degree of emotional ambivalence: on the one hand, the treatment and its side-effects have stopped, but on the other hand, a sense of vulnerability and of being abandoned can result from decreased contact with the health professional staff, with whom relationships have inevitably built

up during treatment. This feeling of 'abandonment' following treatment discharge has been reported in other patient groups, for example, stroke patients (e.g. Pound, Bury, Gompertz *et al.* 1994). However, Wiles, Ashburn, Payne *et al.*'s (2004) qualitative study of stroke patients' experience on discharge from physiotherapy noted that where discharge is 'managed well', disappointment can be contained to disappointment at cessation of physiotherapy but not disappointment in terms of a loss of expectation of further potential recovery.

■ The effect of negative emotional reactions to illness

Unfortunately, the presence of depression and anxiety can impede engagement in treatment or rehabilitation efforts. Depressed people, for example, are less likely to attend cardiac rehabilitation classes than non-depressed ones (Lane, Carroll, Ring *et al.* 2001), and anxiety is often associated with poor control of blood glucose levels among those with diabetes (e.g. Niemcryk, Speers, Travis *et al.* 1990). Depression and anxiety have also been shown to impede behavioural change. For example, Huijbrechts, Duivenvoorden, Deckers *et al.* (1996) reported lower rates of smoking cessation following a heart attack in people who were depressed or anxious than among those who reported no distress five months after the event; and among HIV-positive homosexual males, depression was associated with more than twice the rate of engagement in unprotected anal sex with partners than that reported by non-depressed HIV-positive homosexual males (Rogers, Curry, Oddy *et al.* 2003).

Depression also exerts a significant influence on whether such patients resume pre-illness functioning, particularly in terms of return to work and social activities, and this may in part be due to the symptom inflation commonly witnessed among depressed people (see Chapter 9).

Depressive illness is a significant cause of morbidity, disability and reduced survival among the physically ill (Morris, Robinson, Andrzejewski *et al.* 1993; Peveler, Carson and Rodin 2002), although this association has not been found in all studies.

Positive responses to illness

Although studies of positive outcomes remain relatively rare, a growing number of studies are reporting that positive outcomes can be experienced by those facing significant health stressors. Evidence of finding benefit, for example, comes from Petrie, Buick, Weinman and Booth (1999), who found that 60 percent of those who had had a heart attack or had developed breast cancer reported some personal gains over the first three months following illness onset, and 58 percent reported specific positive effects of their illness (see Figure 15.1). The most commonly endorsed benefits were improved close relationships, increased empathy among women with breast cancer, and a healthier lifestyle for men following a heart attack.

As with the negative consequences of illness, the experiencing of benefits is influenced by personal and social resources and by coping responses. For example, Schulz and Mohamed (2004) carried out a prospective study of 105 cancer patients, interviewed at one, six and twelve months following tumour

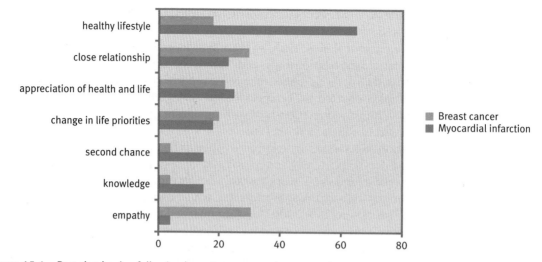

Figure 15.1 Perceived gains following breast cancer or a heart attack.
Source: Petrie, Buick, Weinman and Booth (1999)

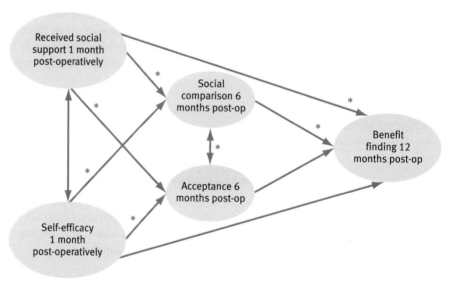

Figure 15.2 The direct and indirect effects of internal (self-efficacy) and external (social support) resources upon benefit finding in the twelve months following cancer surgery.
Source: adapted from Schulz and Mohamed (2004: 659)

acceptance coping
accepting the reality of a situation and that it cannot easily be changed.

social comparison
the process by which a person or group of people compare themselves (their behaviour or characteristics) with others.

surgery and found that finding benefit at twelve months was directly predicted by levels of self-efficacy (a personal resource) and social resources (amount of social support received) at 1 month. However, as can be seen in Figure 15.2 (in which the arrowed lines with asterisks reflect significant associations), when examining whether coping mediated the relationship between these internal and external resources and benefit finding, individuals with high social support resources exhibited greater benefit finding regardless of whether **acceptance coping** or **social comparison** coping was used, whereas the beneficial effect of self-efficacy appeared to be mediated by

coping (as the direct association between self-efficacy and finding benefit was insignificant).

Benefits of illness, such as becoming more accepting of things in life or having closer relationships with family or friends, could actually lead to reported QoL levels higher than those reported by healthy individuals (as, for example, reported by Tempelaar *et al.* 1989, cited in Schulz and Mohamed 2004). Improved relationships with significant others is a commonly reported 'benefit' of illness, although there is a need for more research to investigate relationship factors in relation to their influence on emotions and adjustment. De Vellis, Lewis and Sterba (2003) suggested that good relationships between couples may work towards the creation and maintenance of positive emotions (in patients and/or carers), which may benefit adjustment.

Fredrickson (1998, 2001) has summarised the key benefits of maintaining positive emotions:

■ the promotion of psychological resilience and more effective problem solving;
■ the dispelling of negative emotions;
■ the triggering of an upward spiral of positive feelings.

However, emotions form only part of a person's response to illness. The coping strategies that a person adopts to help them to cope with the disease and its consequences may be as important as the emotions they experience in determining illness outcomes (see also Chapters 9, 11 and 12 for a discussion of Leventhal's self-regulation model of illness and Lazarus's stress-coping theory).

Coping with illness

The coping strategies used to cope with illness do not differ from those used to cope with any other problem that an individual faces; in other words, illness does not trigger unique coping strategies, and as such the theory and concepts of coping outlined in Chapter 11 are as relevant here as they are to consideration of stress coping. However, coping with illness does raise a number of illness-specific issues, such as:

■ the symptoms of the disease;
■ the possibility of pain;
■ an uncertain future;
■ changes in self-image and possibly self-esteem;
■ issues of maintaining control over health and life in general;
■ maintaining control over illness, such as symptom management, treatment, or prevention of progression;
■ changes in relationships with family and friends.

Moos and Schaefer (1984) attributed many of these factors to the experience of illness as a 'crisis', whereby individuals face potential changes in identity (healthy person to sick person, for example), location (home to nursing home), role (e.g. independent breadwinner to dependant), and changes to aspects of social support (e.g. from socially integrated to socially isolated). Moos and Schaefer describe three processes that result from the crisis of illness:

1. *Cognitive appraisal*: the individual appraises the implications of the illness for their lives.

2. *Adaptive tasks*: the individual performs illness-specific tasks such as dealing with symptoms or with treatment, and general tasks such as preserving emotional balance, self-image and relationships with others.

3. *Coping skills*: the individual engages in coping strategies defined as either appraisal-focused (e.g. denial or minimising, positive reappraisal, mental preparation/planning); problem-focused (e.g. information and support seeking, taking direct action to deal with a problem, identifying alternative goals and rewards); and emotion-focused coping (e.g. mood regulation, emotional discharge such as venting anger, or passive and resigned acceptance).

▪ Coping by denial or avoidance

Of the many studies conducted in relation to coping, a common initial response to diagnosis or illness onset is either conscious or unconscious denial of its occurrence. Denial appears to be adaptive in the short term as it enables the individual to cope with the distress felt. In the longer term, however, denial and the related strategy of avoidance tend to interfere with active coping efforts and are associated with increased long-term distress. Many, but not all, studies report negative outcomes of avoidant coping and denial; for example:

- Avoidant coping and emotion-focused strategies were associated with greater depression than problem-focused coping among a sample of HIV-positive homosexual men (Safren, Radomsky, Otto *et al.* 2002).

- Among a sample of women experiencing breast biopsy and assessed prior to diagnosis, cognitive avoidance was associated with greater distress, as was scoring low on optimism and high on perceived threat (Stanton and Snider 1993).

- Among adolescents with chronic disease (asthma, juvenile arthritis, cystic fibrosis, eczema), positive adjustment was predicted by seeking social support and confrontational coping, negative adjustment was predicted by depressive coping (e.g. passivity), but avoidance coping was not a strong predictor (Meijer, Sinnema, Bijstra *et al.* 2002).

- Among patients with rheumatoid arthritis, scoring highly on the avoidance/denial subscale of the Vanderbilt multidimensional pain coping inventory, was positively correlated with active coping and positive outcomes (Smith, Wallston, Dwyer *et al.* 1997). This unusual finding is thought to reflect the specific context of coping with pain (see Chapter 16).

▪ Problem-focused and acceptance coping

Generally speaking, after the initial period following illness onset or diagnosis has passed, problem-focused coping, such as making use of social support resources or planning how to deal with the problems faced, and acceptance coping are associated with more positive adaptation. Lowe, Norman and Bennett (2000) examined levels of distress six months following a heart attack in relation to the coping and emotions reported in hospital and at two months. Acceptance-focused coping (e.g. accepting things as they are, reinterpreting things in a positive light) was the most prevalent form of coping, followed by problem-focused, emotion-focused and, least of all, avoidance coping. Acceptance coping was associated with lower levels of distress, problem-focused coping was associated with high levels of positive mood, and emotion-focused coping was associated with low mood. Longitudinal analyses confirmed a prospective relationship between problem-focused coping and improved health outcomes, suggesting that effort directed to changeable aspects of the situation resulted in improved health outcomes (either perceived or actual).

People engage in all sorts of coping efforts and do not generally use strategies defined as only emotion-focused, only problem-focused or only avoidant. This is because situations are generally dynamic and multidimensional, and therefore responses also need to be dynamic and multidimensional. As evidence of this, a study of young people within two months of developing cancer (Kyngaes, Mikkonen, Nouisiainen *et al.* 2001) found that emotion-focused, appraisal-focused and problem-focused strategies were employed. The strategies most frequently used were accessing social support (seeking information from health professionals as well as emotional support from families), believing in recovery and returning to 'normal' life (positive reframing). Some authors point to a 'time X strategy interaction' whereby different strategies are adopted at different periods in the illness 'crisis'. For example, Heim, Augustiny, Blaser *et al.* (1987) suggested that cancer patients use more active and problem-focused strategies earlier in the disease, with a shift to more passive and avoidant strategies as the disease progresses. This shift may be highly functional. Stanton, Danoff-Burg and Huggins (2002) reported a complex relationship between positive future expectancies, coping and outcomes of women with early-stage breast cancer. Active acceptance at the time of diagnosis predicted better adjustment in terms of mood and reduced fear of recurrence than did avoidant strategies. Pessimism about the future was associated with coping by turning to religion, whereas those women who retained high amounts of hope for the future generally benefited from the use of more active coping strategies.

The coping responses of people facing illness are therefore individual and dynamic and, reflecting Lazarus's transactional model of stress and coping (see Chapter 11), change over time as a result of changing demands and resources and of coping appraisal (what seems to work best for the person). The factors that moderate this relationship may also change over time; for example, social support may fluctuate. The crisis theory of Moos and Schaefer (1984) mentioned earlier assumes that individuals cope out of a motivation to restore equilibrium and normality to their lives. One of the key resources that most individuals have to aid in that process is that of family support yet, as we describe in the next section, illness also impacts on these individuals, which can have additional effects on the adjustment of the individual facing the illness.

Illness: a family affair

People do not get ill in a vacuum: their illness exists within their immediate personal context and within their larger social network and culture. Not surprisingly, many of the wide-ranging effects of illness on the 'sufferer' described earlier in this chapter can also be experienced by those closest to the ill person. The growing trend towards home care and day treatments places further pressures on families.

Family systems

The families of people who develop an illness also need to adapt to changes that an illness brings to their family member and to their own life. Theories of adjustment to illness by patients such as that proposed by Morse and Johnson (1991), described at the start of this chapter, generally posit a staged approach towards adjustment. For example, McCubbin and Patterson (1982) noted that stress in the family is a pressure that can disrupt or change the 'family system', and they observed three stages in a continuum of adaptation:

1. *Stage of resistance*: where family members try to deny or avoid the reality of what has happened.
2. *Stage of restructuring*: where family members begin to acknowledge reality and start to reorganise their lives around the notion of a changed family.
3. *Stage of consolidation*: where newly adopted roles may have to become permanent, for example if recovery is not forthcoming; and where new ways of thinking (about life/health/behaviour) may emerge.

Relevant to this continuum of adaptation are the three integrated dimensions of family system functioning highlighted by Olson and Stewart (1991): cohesion, adaptability and communication. Olson provided evidence that families who were balanced on these dimensions (i.e. they work together and are affiliated and emotionally bonded with each other, they adapt roles and rules in face of new situations, and they communicate effectively) showed better adaptation to life stressors, including illness. These broad dimensions can be seen in a study by McCubbin and Patterson (1983) of parental coping in relation to having a child with cystic fibrosis, where three specific factors within parental coping strategies were identified, each of which held different implications for family functioning:

1. coping by maintaining and focusing on family life and the relationships therein;
2. coping by trying to maintain wellbeing through the use of social relationships;
3. coping by having relationships with medical staff and parents of other ill children.

Drawing on this model, Eiser and Havermans (1992) studied children with either asthma, diabetes, epilepsy, leukaemia or heart conditions and revealed four factors within parental coping, which they labelled:

1. autonomy (similar to McCubbin's second factor)
2. medical care (use of and beliefs in effectiveness)
3. social support–information
4. family support.

Gender, disease type, length of illness and the extent to which the parent was experiencing family or social functioning difficulties, all affected which forms of coping were found most useful. For example, parents of older children, regardless of illness, experienced fewer difficulties; social support coping was used less the longer the illness lasted; parents of children with heart conditions or leukaemia used more medical care support coping than parents of children with other conditions; mothers endorsed all types of coping more than fathers; mothers who coped through maintaining autonomy and social support reported more difficulties than those who did not cope in this way; and fathers also reported more difficulties if they used autonomy coping, and if they used less medical care coping. The influence of context, in terms of the length of time since the onset of illness, upon parental coping is highlighted further in RESEARCH FOCUS below.

While family members are generally involved in providing support to the family member with an illness, some also become that person's primary (main) carer; i.e. they are required to provide assistance above and beyond that which is 'normal' for their role (preparing a meal for a partner may be usual, whereas helping them to bathe may not be) (e.g. Schulz and Quittner 1998).

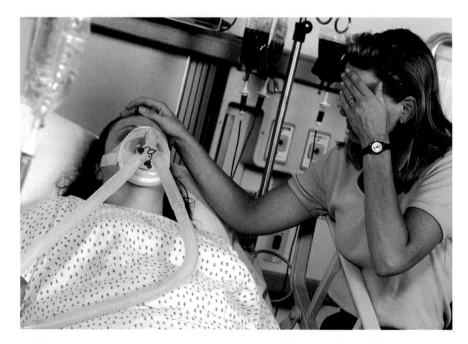

Plate 15.1   Illness impacts on more than just the patient.

Source: Alamy/Agency Photo Network

How do parents cope with cancer in their child?

Norberg, A.L., Lindblad, F. and Boman, K.K. (2005). Coping strategies in parents of children with cancer. *Social Science and Medicine*, 60: 965–75.

Background

Receiving a diagnosis at any point in one's life can be inherently stressful. In spite of advances in treatment, many forms of cancer remain life-threatening, and where treatment is available it is generally intensive, intrusive on one's life, and can bring with it undesirable side-effects. It is difficult to imagine any family that would not be affected by a member receiving such a diagnosis. It is likely to be even more distressing when the diagnosis is received by a child. Evidence to date highlights how watching their child suffer and dealing with the reactions of others pose many challenges for parents in terms of their own coping and in terms of helping their child to cope.

Aims of study

This paper addresses the impact of childhood cancer on parental coping where children are dealing with various types of cancer at various stages following diagnosis. It also examines whether the parents of children with cancer coped with general life stresses any differently than parents of a healthy child.

Methods

395 parents (224 mothers and 171 fathers) of children either undergoing (44.3 percent) or having completed cancer treatment (55.2 percent) were recruited from two Swedish paediatric oncology units. The overall response rate for study participation was an excellent 73 percent, reflecting the interest that parents had in being provided with an opportunity to talk about their experience. 59 percent of non-responders were fathers, which is similar to that found previously and points to an area of need for further investigation. The average total number of children in these families was 2.5.

In terms of cancer type, the two largest diagnostic groups were leukaemia (44 percent) and brain tumours (14.9 percent). Parents were excluded from the study if their child had an incurable diagnosis or if their child was currently receiving palliative treatment. In terms of time since diagnosis, there was a wide range from 0 months to 21 years, but for analysis purposes only three groups were compared: one–eight weeks (86 parents); 18–30 months (72 parents) and 60–120 months (60 parents). A third of the children had been diagnosed while under 3 years of age; 23 percent had been 3–6 years old, 13.9 percent 6–9 years old; 18.5 percent 9–15 years old; and 10.6 percent 15–21 years old.

A comparison group of 184 parents of healthy children aged 0–16 (58 percent mothers) was also recruited from the same geographical area. The average total number of children per family was 2.2. Questionnaires included the Utrecht coping list, and as measures of outcome, state anxiety using Spielberger's state–trait anxiety scale and the Zung self-rating depression scale. The coping measure required parents to respond in relation to general stressful events on seven subscales of coping strategies: *active problem focusing* (e.g. goal-oriented sorting things out); *palliative reaction pattern* (e.g. behavioural distraction, relaxation); *avoidance behaviour* (e.g. withdrawing from difficult situations); *social support seeking*; *passive reaction pattern* (isolating self from others, fantasy escape); *expression of emotion* (annoyance and anger); and *comforting cognition* (looking on bright side, positive comparison).

continued

Results
Both state anxiety and state depression were higher among parents of children with cancer (PCC) than among parents of healthy children (PHC). Mothers of both healthy children and those with cancer reported significantly higher levels of anxiety and depression than did the fathers. Overall, coping, perhaps surprisingly, was not found to differ between PCC and PHC, although PCC showed a significant tendency towards the use of passive reaction coping.

When coping was compared across only the two main cancer sites, no significant differences in coping strategies emerged, and furthermore the three groupings according to length of time since diagnosis also showed no differences. Whether or not the child was currently undergoing treatment, or had completed it, did not affect coping responses or the levels of anxiety and depression in PCC.

Given the lack of between-group differences in coping, the authors then explored the within-group associations; in other words, they examined which coping strategies were correlated with greater anxiety or depression. Among both PCC and PHC, the more frequent use of active problem focusing and less use of avoidance and passive reaction coping was associated with lower levels of anxiety and depression. Given the gender differences found in anxiety and depression, analyses were rerun controlling for gender (partial correlations), and the negative effects of these coping strategies persisted.

Finally, the relationship between coping and anxiety and depression was examined according to groupings of length of time since diagnosis, and in terms of the two main diagnostic groupings, and these factors were found to make some significant differences. For example, active problem focusing was associated with less emotional distress in parents of children with leukaemia, but not those with brain tumours; and avoidance behaviour was not related to anxiety or depression in the recently diagnosed group (1–8 weeks), whereas in parents of those diagnosed 60–120 months previously it related to both anxiety and depression.

Discussion
This is a fascinating study, which although cross-sectional, manages to address questions related to illness stage and parental coping through the use of different 'cohorts' of parents, i.e. different lengths of time since the child was diagnosed. Perhaps surprisingly, PCC did not differ in terms of how they coped with general stress from PHC, even though they were experiencing greater distress. This may in part be because coping was assessed in terms of general stress, whereas mood measures reflected current mood. In addition, while disease group differences did have some effect on which coping strategies were related to anxiety and depression, no disease group differences affected the coping strategies reported. Patterns of association between coping, anxiety and depression reflected, for both sets of parents, what is generally reported in the literature: i.e. active, problem-focused forms of coping appear to be more adaptive to dealing with stress than passive or emotion-focused responses.

In conclusion, results highlight the value of subgroup analysis where sample size allows this. One crucial finding, which reflects what has been said in Chapter 14 regarding the use of avoidance coping, is that it appears less beneficial when being used by parents who are further removed in time from the cancer diagnosis than when it is reported by parents who have recently received their child's diagnosis. The ideal next stage to address questions raised by this study more fully would inevitably be a prospective longitudinal study of parents and children from as soon as possible following diagnosis.

Caring

There are approximately 5.7 million UK-based informal (unpaid, non-professional) carers, aged predominantly between 45 and 64, 3.3 million of whom are female (Department of Health 1999). The 'problems' carers are providing care for are predominantly those of chronic diseases (approximately 40 percent), with significant proportions caring for problems relating to ageing: dementia, problems of mobility, and mental, emotional or neurological problems. As noted by Kalra, Evans, Perez *et al.* (2004: 1,099) in relation to stroke management: 'Although the physical, psychological, emotional, and social consequences of care-giving and its economic benefit to society are well recognised, care-givers' needs are often given low priority'. These authors go on to present positive effects of carer training in providing physical care to the stroke survivor, in terms of reduced carer burden, reduced anxiety and depression, and improved QoL for both the carers and their patients. Addressing carer issues is therefore crucial to both patient and carer outcomes, and therefore the remainder of this chapter is dedicated to their experience or their relationship with the person they care for.

What do YOU think?

We live in an ageing society, but increasing life expectancy brings with it increasing needs for care of the elderly. We also live in a society where chronic diseases are of growing prevalence due to medical successes. This means that disability and dependence is increasing, not only among those considered 'elderly' but also in those in late middle age who may live for a further ten, twenty or thirty years in a dependent condition. More and more societies seem to be turning to families as sources of care. Although the gender imbalance in terms of who provides care has shifted away from being predominantly female towards being more balanced, gender roles have generally changed hugely over past decades. Ask your mother or your grandmother about their views on staying at home to care for a sick or dependent relative, and then consider your own situation. Are you already, or likely to be facing in the future, the need to provide informal and unpaid care for a relative? How does this make you feel? How do you imagine you will balance your various life roles if you take on an additional caring role? Are your projected life goals likely to be constrained by anticipated caring needs? Do you already worry about what will happen to your parents if they become chronically ill or develop dementia?

Questions such as these need to be asked, and answers need to be found. Are family members, particularly women, due to societal change in employment and social status, less willing to care for a dependent, possibly ageing, family member than previous generations? If so, what are the likely consequences for their mental and physical wellbeing if providing care becomes a necessity? What are the implications for health and social care policy? Such questions require wider social and political answers, but they have significant psychological implications.

Supportive relationships

There is a clear need to evaluate the effects of supportive relationships, because, as Evans and Bishop (1990) noted in relation to acute stroke outcomes, 'the patient's support system 1) is ultimately responsible for long-term care and 2) may influence poststroke psychosocial outcomes dramatically' (p. II-48). As described in Chapter 12, there is consistent evidence as to the benefits of being part of a functional supportive network as opposed to being socially isolated. For example, benefits of social support include:

- increased adherence to treatment and self-care (e.g. Lo 1999; Toljamo and Hentinen 2001);
- better emotional adjustment and coping with stressful events (e.g. Hallaråker *et al*. 2001; Thoits 1995);
- better physiological functioning (e.g. Taylor, Klein, Grunewald *et al.* 2003; Uchino, Cacioppo and Kiecolt-Glaser 1996);
- reduced mortality or increased survival (e.g. Greenwood, Muir, Packham *et al.* 1996; Vogt, Mullooly, Ernst, *et al.* 1992).

Consensus exists that it is not simply the absolute number of supports a person has available to them (structural) but the perceived quality and function of these supports (functional) and satisfaction with the support provided that is critical in predicting such outcomes (e.g. Quick, Nelson, Matusek *et al.* 1996; Vogt *et al.* 1992). However, social support is not always helpful, even if intended as such by the carer.

■ Helpful and unhelpful caring

Studies of caring for people with a range of illnesses, such as AIDS, diabetes, and cancer, have found that there are common caring actions that are perceived as helpful, such as practical assistance and expressions of love, concern and understanding, and relative consistency in terms of actions considered to be unhelpful, for example minimising the situation, being unrealistically cheerful, underestimating the illness effects on the patient, or being critical or over-demanding. Patients who perceived their carers' actions as unhelpful have been found to have more negative perceptions of themselves and their spouses, and greater depression (Clark and Stephens 1996). Although helpful actions have generally been shown to occur more frequently than unhelpful actions, unhelpful actions appear to have a more strongly negative effect on wellbeing than helpful actions have a positive effect (e.g. Norris, Stephens and Kinney 1990). Additionally, over-caring or being overly helpful and solicitous (e.g. taking over a person's chores, encouraging them to rest) can act as a form of operant conditioning in which patients are rewarded for exhibiting 'sick role' behaviour (see Chapter 1). For example, among a sample of 119 patients with chronic fatigue syndrome and their significant other, 'over-helped' care recipients exhibited greater fatigue and pain than those receiving punishing (e.g. carer expresses irritation at patient) or distracting (e.g. carer involves patient in activities) carer responses (Schmaling, Smith and Buchwald 2000). Over-protected patients may also experience reduced perceptions of self-efficacy, self-esteem and recovery motivation, and elevated depression (e.g. Thomson and Pitts 1992) and, among pain patients, increased disability (e.g. Flor, Breitenstein, Birbaumer *et al.* 1995; Williamson, Robinson and Melamed 1997).

Several studies have identified social interactions that are unsupportive and detrimental to the care receiver's wellbeing. For example, a study of 271 individuals living with HIV identified four types of unsupportive interaction:

1. insensitivity
2. disconnecting or disengaging behaviour
3. blaming or fault finding
4. forced optimism.

The first three of these interaction types were significantly predictive of patient depression, above and beyond the prediction offered by patient physical functioning and positive social support (Ingram, Jones, Fass *et al.* 1999). Similarly, Kerns, Haythornwaite, Southwick *et al.* (1990) found that what they termed 'punishing' spousal responses (such as ignoring the patient or expressing impatience or anger with them) was predictive of increased distress and depressive symptoms.

These types of findings highlight the need to assess positively perceived support separately from negatively perceived support rather than assessing on a continuum of overall support without addressing how that support is evaluated. Given the evidence as to the presence of helpful and unhelpful caring actions, it is not perhaps surprising that when initially faced with a caring role, care providers ask themselves questions such as 'What is "good" care?' 'Am I suitably equipped to deal with the demands of the person I am caring for?' The act of caring for a person with a chronic illness presents many challenges to carers, and not surprisingly research attention has increasingly turned to the examination of the impact of caring on the carers themselves.

Consequences of caring

Many different terms have been used to describe carer outcomes of providing care, and just as many different outcome measures are used, some of which assess mental health, some physical health and some global psychosocial wellbeing. A commonly employed term is that of 'carer burden', defined as the objective and subjective 'costs' of caring to the carer (e.g. Zarit, Reever and Bach-Peterson 1980). This term covers a broad-based outcome of caring that encompasses physical, psychological, financial and social costs of caring, and many studies have explored burden as an outcome, rather than focusing solely on emotional distress or physical outcomes (e.g. Scholte op Reimer, de Haan, Rijners *et al.* 1998; Schulz, O'Brien, Bookwala *et al.* 1995).

■ Emotional impact of caring

Research has suggested that up to three-quarters of carers experience clinically significant distress, a level significantly higher than that found in age-matched controls. Similarly, carers' physical health and life satisfaction are generally found to be lower than in non-carers. Feelings of loss, anxiety or depression are common among partners of those who have had a heart attack (e.g. Arefjord, Hallarakeri, Havik *et al.* 1998), and among those caring for a relative following a stroke, levels of depression have been shown to be two to three times that found in a comparable group of non-carers (Scholte op Reimer, de Haan, Rijners *et al.* 1998). It is not just spouses or partners that experience the distress of caring but also the parents of ill children. For example, parents of children with cancer showed relatively stable but high levels of distress, with 51 percent of mothers and 39 percent of fathers exhibiting levels above the cut-off for emotional disorder, and distress remained high even after treatment had been completed, reflecting parental fears of recurrence (Sloper 2000). (See RESEARCH FOCUS above for details of a study of parental coping with a child with cancer.)

Studies suggest that emotional distress is most marked among women carers (e.g. Pinquart and Sörensen 2003; van den Heuvel, de Witte, Schure *et al.* 2001), although some of the reported gender differences may be confounded by the fact that about 70 percent of carers are women, which is reflected in study samples. Gender bias in the caring role may be a result of the greater life expectancies for women, as well as perhaps a questionable societal expectation of caring being a 'natural' role for women, who are 'expected' to find it fulfilling, even in the absence of financial reward (e.g. Lee 2001; Yee and Schulz 2000). Hagedoorn, Sanderman, Buunk *et al.* (2002), in a comparison of male and female carers of a partner with cancer, found that elevated distress among female carers was found only in those who reported low levels of carer efficacy (not believing in one's ability to care effectively) and perceived challenges to their role identity resulting from a perception of not 'caring well'.

■ Physical effects of caring

The stress of caring may also impact on some, but perhaps not all, people's physical health. Among cancer carers, for example, female carers experienced a decline in their own physical health in the six months following their partner's diagnosis of colorectal cancer, whereas male carers did not (Nijboer, Tempelaar, Triemstra *et al.* 2001), perhaps relating to the higher levels of distress or lower levels of carer-perceived efficacy reported among women carers in other studies, although this study did not explore these issues. Interestingly, an extremely large study of the physical health, psychological wellbeing and quality of life of over 11,000 Australian women aged from 70 to 75 (Lee 2001) did not find a significant difference in physical health between the 10 percent identified as carers and the majority of the elderly sample. However, the carers did differ significantly in terms of their emotional wellbeing and perceived stress levels, supporting the reasonably consistent findings as to the emotional impact of caring.

■ Immunological effects of caring

There is a large body of evidence that points to immunosuppressant effects of long-term caring. For example, a study comparing elderly carers of a spouse with Alzheimer's disease with control subjects found that carers had lower immune function and reported more days of illness over the previous year (Kiecolt-Glaser, Malarkey, Cacioppo *et al.* 1994). The immune-compromising effects of caring for a person with Alzheimer's has generally been confirmed (e.g. reviews by Bourgeois, Schulz and Burgio 1996; Schulz *et al.* 1995). Kiecolt-Glaser, Glaser, Gravenstein *et al.* (1996) also conducted a study where similar carers were given an influenza vaccination, and they found that carers showed less appropriate immune responses to the vaccination than did control participants, suggesting that these carers had less resistance to infection. This evidence derives predominantly from elderly carers, whereas several studies in younger populations report inconsistent effects of chronic caring on the immune function and resistance to infection. For example, Vedhara, McDermott, Evans *et al.* (2002) did not find that carers of a spouse with multiple sclerosis (a condition equally as chronic as Alzheimer's) differed in their immune responses following an influenza vaccination from non-carers. However, this sample of younger carers appeared to be less distressed about their caring than that reported among other carer groups, which may in part explain their 'preserved' immune responses following vaccination.

Finally, it is unclear whether the damaging effects of caring on carer immune function are confined to those individuals caring for spouses with chronic and degenerative conditions such as Alzheimer's disease or multiple sclerosis, as few studies have examined carer responses in situations where the illness event is an acute one, with potential for recovery.

■ Positive aspects of the caring role

In spite of the negative aspects of caring considered above, many studies have identified positive aspects of the caring role. Orbell, Hopkins and Gillies (1993) noted that caring 'may be appraised by the carer as negative, benign or positive. Caring may be appraised as an intrusion on personal lifeplans,

Plate 15.2 Having more time to spend with a partner as a result of illness can lead to a sharing of activities previously lost to the other demands of life. Spending 'quality time' together can strengthen some relationships.

Source: © Reg Charity/Corbis

but may also be appraised as positive, to the extent that it provides affirmation of valued aspects of the self' (p. 153). For example, studies have identified caring satisfaction such as feeling a sense of fulfilment, feeling useful, increased feelings of closeness or increased day-to-day interactions as a result of patients and carers spending more leisure time together (e.g. Kinney, Stephens, Franks *et al.* 1995; Kramer 1997). Kinney *et al.* (1995) investigated the daily hassles and uplifts (stresses and satisfactions) reported by seventy-eight family carers of stroke patients and found that carers generally reported more uplifts (such as the care recipient cooperating with them, having pleasant interactions with care recipient) on a day-to-day basis than they did hassles (such as care recipient complaining or criticising, care recipient being unresponsive). However, this did vary depending on the care recipient's level of impairment, with care recipients who had greater impairment generally having carers who reported more hassles. While hassles were strong predictors of poor carer wellbeing, when the overall number of uplifts outweighed the number of hassles reported, carers were less depressed and had better social relations than when hassles outweighed uplifts. Such protective or buffering effects of uplifts, even in the face of concurrent hassles, highlights the need for studies to assess both negative and positive aspects of caring and to examine the interaction between them in order to further understanding of the effects of such counterbalancing on carer wellbeing.

Influences on caring outcomes

■ Features of the illness or of the cared-for

The illness or behavioural features of the care recipients have important but complex influences on carer outcome. Studies of carers of people with Alzheimer's disease, for example, have shown that distress is more clearly associated with demanding or disruptive behaviour than with the level of physical impairment or disability of the care recipient (e.g. Gaughler, Davey, Pearlin *et al.* 2000; Morrison 1999). Carer distress is subject to further fluctuations dependent on the care recipient's physical and mental wellbeing at any point in time (e.g. Beach, Schulz, Lee *et al.* 2000).

Among carers of stroke survivors, while the severity of stroke impairment during the acute phase (i.e. approximately ten days post-stroke) predicted their future expectancies, it was their appraisals of the consequences of the illness and of their coping resources that predicted their psychological wellbeing (Forsberg-Wärleby, Möller and Blomstrand 2001). Subjective appraisals of the situation made by the carer therefore differ from objective features of the illness, such as disability, in the extent to which they determine carer outcomes. To illustrate this further, again among those caring for stroke survivors, depression at six months was predicted primarily by an increase in negative characteristics of the care recipient (such as demanding behaviour), by reductions in carers perceiving that they had a reciprocal confiding relationship with the person they cared for, by the age and health of the care recipient (but not the carer's own age and health), and by income and a change in living standards. In contrast, carer burden was explained by the age of the carer (older carers were less burdened), a decline in the positive characteristics of the care recipient, reduced satisfaction with their own

---

Table 15.1 Potential causes of carer distress

- The financial drain of caring caused by caring interference in employment
- The emotional demands of providing long-term care for a relative who often provides little in return
- The physically tiring nature of some caring roles
- The inability to replenish personal resources due to social isolation or poor utilisation of support resources and leisure time

or more deep-seated, even unacknowledged sources of stress:

- Feelings of anger (e.g. with the person for becoming ill, for them being born handicapped)
- Feelings of guilt (e.g. that they may have directly/indirectly contributed to the situation)
- Feelings of grief (e.g. that they have 'lost' who they used to have)

These latter are indicative of extremely complex feelings that are difficult to voice, but if they are suppressed they can cause increased stress and distress.

---

social contacts, and increased concern for future care (Schulz, Tompkins and Rau 1988). This study, while somewhat dated, remains important because it examined changes in objective and subjective predictor variables over time, reflecting how the demands of caring are dynamic and fluctuating. It is worth noting that an increase in negative characteristics of the care recipient predicted carer depression, whereas a decrease in their positive characteristics predicted carer perceived burden. This reflects that burden is not equivalent to depression (as some studies imply) but is perhaps more tied up with the relationship between the carer and care recipient.

■ The influence of carer characteristics and responses

It is generally accepted that the underlying source of carer distress or strain appears to result from subjective appraisals of an imbalance between the demands of caring and the resources perceived to be available to the carer (e.g. Orbell and Gillies 1993), which may include what Wallander and Varni (1998) refer to as 'resistance factors'. Resistance factors include intrapersonal factors such as personality and motivation, socio-ecological factors such as the carer's family environment and support resources, and stressprocessing factors, which include an individual's cognitive appraisals of a situation and their coping responses (akin to Lazarus's theory, Chapter 11).

The role of carer appraisal in predicting carer stress was highlighted in one of the few prospective studies of carer health carried out with 122 family carers of persons with Alzheimer's disease: in this sample, improvements in carer physical or mental health were not directly associated with a reduction in caring demands but with the carer's appraisal of the stressors as benign, with approach rather than avoidant coping, and with greater levels of the personal resource of social support (Goode, Haley, Roth *et al.* 1998). Vedhara, Shanks, Anderson *et al.* (2000), similarly, did not find an association between perceived caring difficulties and carer anxiety and depression, and they propose that carer mood is perhaps mediated by factors other than qualitative difficulties in caring, such as coping strategies and the use of social support. McClenahan and Weinman (1998) have also shown that a carer's illness perceptions (see Chapter 9) are associated with carer distress, in particular when their perceived timeline for the illness is chronic.

Shewchuck, Richards and Elliott (1998) found that adjustment to caring for a person with a spinal cord injury varied significantly over the first caring year and was influenced by patient and carer characteristics, such as age, the carer's own health, and also by the carer's behaviour in terms of their use of support. Using social support as a coping strategy has emerged as an important predictor of carer outcomes. For example, in a study of male heart attack patients and their spouses, Bennett and Connell (1999) found that the primary causes of carer anxiety were the perceived consequences of the heart attack, with many wives becoming hyper-vigilant, watching for signs that their partner may have a further MI, and that the lack of a confidant with whom they could discuss these concerns was an important factor in maintaining anxiety.

Other carer behaviour, such as that made in response to the patient's situation, may also influence their emotional wellbeing; for example, wives of heart attack patients have been found to inhibit angry or sexual feelings in order to 'protect' their husbands, although in doing so they may increase their own distress (e.g. Coyne and Smith 1991).

Finally, other studies have highlighted the role of carer personality variables such as optimism (generally a positive resource) and neuroticism (generally a negative characteristic), showing that these characteristics had direct effects on carer mental health, as well as indirect effects via their influence on perceived stress, and on the perceptions and appraisals of the care recipient's level of impairment (e.g. Hooker, Monahan, Shifren *et al.* 1992; Shifren and Hooker 1995).

■ The relationship between carer and patient

Some studies have examined spousal carers, where the relationship is characterised by being full-time, interdependent and intimate (cf. Coyne and Fiske 1992) and thus uniquely supportive. Other studies have shown less control over the carer 'types' recruited to the study and have included informal carers with varying degrees of association – mothers, fathers, siblings, daughters, friends. Pinquart and Sörensen (2003) hypothesised that differences in psychological and physical health would be greater among spousal carers than non-spousal carers, for female rather than male carers, and for older rather than younger carers. Whilst a study of caring for an older adult only, their results did support these hypotheses. What is becoming increasingly clear is that as well as the nature of the carer–patient relationship, the quality of the relationship between these individuals influences the outcomes of caring for both parties.

■ Relationship quality

DeVellis, Lewis and Sterba (2003) consider that increased research into the nature and processes in dyadic relationships will benefit our understanding of adjustment to illness. They note that social support research does not

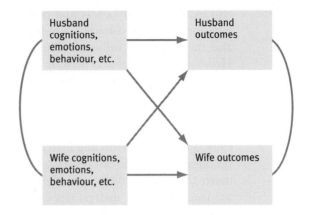

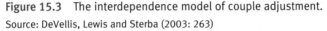

Figure 15.3   The interdependence model of couple adjustment.

Source: DeVellis, Lewis and Sterba (2003: 263)

necessarily explore the relationship between those studied in terms of the nature and quality of the interaction, and that more studies are required that address the reciprocal and interdependent relationships that people engage in. This reciprocity is represented in Figure 15.3, where the relationship depicted is that of a marriage.

Banthia, Malcarne, Varni, *et al.* (2003) reported that the quality of a relationship may moderate the effects of individual coping. They measured coping and dyadic adjustment in couples where the male had prostate cancer and found that while low patient mood was generally associated with avoidant coping and high levels of intrusive thinking, patients in strong relationships experienced less distress than those in less strong relationships, even when they engaged in these maladaptive coping strategies.

The quality of the spousal relationship was also an important determinant of the effects of caring on carer functioning in a cross-sectional study of seventy-five carers of cancer patients (Williamson, Shaffer and Schulz 1998). In this study, a distinction was drawn between depressed carers and resentful carers: depressed carers reported close, communal and intimate relationships with the patient, and this closeness created the restrictions on their own activities (i.e. they wanted to be with the person they cared for), whereas resentful carers reported less close relationships and reported their activity restriction to be predicted by severity of patient symptoms (they were restricted out of the necessity to provide care). This important, but subtle, distinction between depressed and resentful carers may help to explain differences in longer-term carer outcomes. Thompson, Galbraith, Thomas *et al.* (2002) also found that resentful carers tend to provide overly controlling and over-protective care, and they suggest that such caring styles may undermine patient autonomy and progress. More research that explores the causes of carer resentment is required as it may offer potential opportunites for intervention, to the benefit of both parties.

■ **Dyadic perceptions, shared and discrepant beliefs**

Given the individual nature of health and illness beliefs, stress appraisal and coping responses, it cannot be assumed that carers and those they care for will exhibit similar beliefs and responses. A growing avenue of research is exploring whether differences in the beliefs and responses of informal carers and their partners influence illness outcomes (e.g. Coyne and Fiske 1992; Heijmans, de Ridder and Bensing 1999; Morrison 2001). Carers provide support to their ill partner, primarily because they think it is needed. However, this does not mean that care recipients will perceive the care and social support received as positive or helpful. This discrepancy is important: e.g. differences in perceived care needs between the carer and the patient may exist. Sarason, Sarason and Pierce (1990) have shown that carer and patient perceptions often do not correlate, with carers perceiving that they are giving more than the patients feel they are receiving. This has inevitable consequences for carer distress (see earlier).

In addition to divergent perception of patient needs, individuals in caring dyads may hold different and diverging beliefs about the illness itself. For example, the illness representations (see Chapter 9) of identity, timeline, causes, consequences and control/cure may also differ between patients, carer spouses and significant others. In a recent longitudinal study Weinman *et al.* (2000) found that following a heart attack, participation in rehabilitation exercises could be predicted more from spousal beliefs, particularly where the spouse attributed the heart attack to the patient's poor health habits (internal cause) than by the patient's own attributions. Figueras and Weinman (2003) further examined the illness representations of seventy patient–partner dyads following a heart attack and distinguished between couples who shared 'similar positive' perceptions, 'similar negative' perceptions or 'conflicting'. The most negative perceptions and conflicting perceptions emerged in relation to perceptions of control/cure, with shared positive perceptions more evident in relation to the identity, timeline and consequences dimensions. Dyads with shared positive perceptions fared better in terms of lower disability, fewer sexual functioning difficulties, less health-related distress, greater vitality and better global adjustment than dyads with negative or conflicting perceptions. In a similar vein, Heijmans *et al.* (1998) compared the illness representations of married couples in chronic fatigue syndrome (CFS) and Addison's disease (AD) and found that couples in both disease groups differed in terms of perceived consequences and timeline of the disease (AD carers perceived greater and longer-lasting consequences than patients; CFS patients perceived greater consequences but a shorter timeline than carers). Perceptions of identity and cause of the illnesses were relatively similar within couples. Although this cross-sectional study reported only minimal association between discrepant illness perceptions and coping behaviour, consistent relationships were found between discrepancies and the patient outcomes of physical and social functioning, psychological adjustment, and vitality. Spousal minimisation of CFS and its consequences was predictive of poorer patient outcomes, and perhaps surprisingly, spousal pessimism about timeline was associated with better outcomes in AD.

It is not just spouses' perceptions that may influence patient outcomes; for example, a recent study (Urquhart-Law 2002) of thirty adolescents with type 1 diabetes and their mothers showed that illness representations of severe and negative consequences and emotional representations were greater in the mothers than in the adolescents. However, analysis showed that this 'maximising' (as opposed to 'minimising' found in the CFS study reported above) on the part of the mothers was not associated with adolescent wellbeing. However, this was a small-scale study that also suffered from being cross-sectional.

Reviewing the available evidence would lead to a conclusion that both maximising and minimising on the part of carers can have adverse consequences, whereas shared perceptions are more adaptive, but there remains a need for further study within both adult and parent–child dyads to address the prospective impact (positive and negative) of such discrepancies on patient outcomes, and on the psychosocial outcomes of the carers.

Summary

This chapter has described two broad areas where illness has an impact: on the emotional wellbeing of the patient; and the QoL, and on emotional and physical wellbeing of informal carers. It should have become clear that physical illness has potentially many and varied consequences, and that this complexity of influence places many challenges in front of a researcher or practitioner wishing to assess illness outcomes. We have described a large evidence base as to the effects of caring for a sick relative or friend. Acknowledging and identifying the consequences of caring enables interventions to be implemented for the benefit of carers and those they care for, as well as potentially for society in terms of reduced social and healthcare costs of caring for carers who themselves experience significant stress, burden or ill-health.

Importantly, we have highlighted that caring, or being ill, does not bring with it inevitable negative consequences. We have also addressed a new and important area of research that highlights that perceptions of illness and its consequences can vary in couples living with illness, and how such discrepancies and the interdependence in relationships can influence a range of outcomes. It is intended that the breadth of consequences and moderating factors described in this chapter provide the reader with a strong foundation on which to study the psychology of illness.

Further reading

Suls, J. and Wallston, K.A. (eds) (2003). *Social Psychological Foundations of Health and Illness*. Malden, Mass., Blackwell.
This comprehensive text presents material that is central to many chapters in our textbook. For the current chapter, you could look particularly at chapters 16–19, where psychological, social and relationship influences on adjustment to illness are described.

Pinquart, M. and Sörensen, S. (2003). Differences between caregivers and non-caregivers in psychological health and physical health: a meta-analysis. *Psychology and Aging*, 18: 250–67.

This paper reviews the data from many key studies of the relationship between caring and health outcomes and is a valuable source of referenced information should you wish to pursue this topic further.

Lee, C. (1999). Health, stress and coping among women caregivers: a review. *Journal of Health Psychology*, 4: 27–40.
This review paper describes and discusses some of the gendered issues in caring.

CHAPTER 16

Pain

Learning outcomes

By the end of this chapter, you should have an understanding of:

- different types of pain
- the prevalence of chronic pain
- psychological factors that influence the experience of pain
- the gate theory of pain
- the neuromatrix theory of pain
- behavioural and cognitive-behavioural treatments of acute and chronic pain

CHAPTER OUTLINE

This chapter examines a number of physiological and psychological explanations for our differing experiences of pain. It first examines the experience of pain: how various types of pain are defined, how prevalent they are, and how we respond to acute and chronic pain. It then considers the role of emotion, cognitions and attention in mediating the experience of pain. The next section describes the gate theory of pain developed by Melzack and Wall, which explains how both biological and psychological factors combine to create our experience of pain. Finally, the chapter goes on to consider a number of psychological interventions used in the treatment of both acute and chronic pain.

The experience of pain

Pain is a familiar sensation for most of us. It is functional. It is unpleasant, and it warns us of potential damage to the body. A reflex action when we feel pain is to pull away from the cause of that pain or to try to reduce the pain. Pain may also signal the onset of disease – and is the symptom most likely to lead an individual to seeking medical help. People with a condition known as congenital universal insensitivity to pain (CUIP), who cannot feel pain, usually die at a young age (Nagasako, Oaklander and Dworkin 2003) because they fail to respond to illnesses of which the main symptom is pain (such as appendicitis) or to avoid situations that risk their health. They could, for example, receive extensive burns by being too close to a hot fire without experiencing the warning signs that most of us take for granted.

Despite its survival benefits, when pain lasts for a long time, it feels destructive and problematic. It can be so difficult to ignore that it takes over our lives. Chronic pain may be the result of long-term conditions such as rheumatoid arthritis, but pain may also endure long after the time of any physical damage, or may even be experienced in areas of the body that no longer exist. Many people who have had an arm or leg amputated go on to experience **phantom limb pain**, in which they feel pain in their non-existent limb – sometimes for many years. Accordingly, pain can also be maladaptive and contribute to long-term problems for an affected individual.

phantom limb pain
a phenomenon that occurs following amputation of a limb, in which the individual feels like they still have their limb, and the limb is in pain.

Types of pain

migraine
a headache with symptoms including nausea, vomiting, or sensitivity to light. Associated with changes in vascular flow within the brain.

Medical definitions have categorised various types of pain, including:

- *Acute pain*: despite most people's experience of acute pain as lasting only a few minutes, acute pain is defined as pain lasting less than three to six months. Some episodes of acute pain, usually involving some form of injury, may occur only once, and generally the pain disappears once the damaged tissue has healed. Examples include toothache and childbirth. However, acute pain may be recurrent. Conditions such as **migraine**,

trigeminal neuralgia
a painful inflammation of the trigeminal nerve that causes sharp and severe facial pain.

headaches or **trigeminal neuralgia** may involve repeated episodes of pain, each one of which can be defined as 'acute' but which are also part of a longer-term condition.

- *Chronic pain*: this is pain that continues for more than three to six months. Chronic pain generally begins with an episode of acute pain that fails to improve over time. In this category, there are two broad types of pain: (1) pain with an identifiable cause such as rheumatoid arthritis or a back injury, and (2) pain with no identifiable cause. The latter is not unusual – 85 percent of cases of back pain have no known physical cause (Deyo 1991). Chronic pain can, itself, be divided into two types:

    1. *Chronic benign pain*: in which long-term pain is experienced to a similar degree over time. An example of this may be lower back pain.
    2. *Chronic progressive pain*: here, the pain becomes progressively worse over time due to the progression of a disease such as rheumatoid arthritis.

Another way of thinking about types of pain is to think about the nature of the pain. Here, three dimensions of experience are frequently used:

1. *the type of pain*: including stabbing, shooting, throbbing, aching, piercing, sharp and hot;
2. *the severity of pain*: from mild discomfort to excruciating;
3. *the pattern of pain*: including brief, continuous and intermittent.

The prevalence of pain

It would be difficult to find many people who had not experienced some degree of acute pain in the last month or so, but chronic pain is also remarkably common. Blyth, March and Cousins (2003), for example, found that 21 percent of a large community sample reported some degree of chronic pain. The most frequently reported causes of pain were injury (38 percent), sports injury (13 percent) and a 'health problem' (29 percent). Nearly 80 percent of those who reported having chronic pain had consulted a doctor about it in the six months before the survey. Eriksen, Jensen, Sjogren *et al.* (2003) reported similar prevalence levels: 19 percent of their community sample had some degree of chronic pain. Older people were more likely to report pain than younger ones (perhaps reflecting higher levels of illness in an older population). Divorced or separated people were more likely to report having pain than married people. Not surprisingly, perhaps, people with jobs that involved 'high physical strain' were more likely to report chronic pain than those in more sedentary jobs.

Pain is a primary reason for visiting a doctor. Mantyselka *et al.* (2001), for example, reported that 40 percent of primary care visits were the result of pain; 21 percent of their sample of people who attended their doctor with a primary symptom of pain had experienced pain for more than six months, and 80 percent reported limited physical function as a consequence of their pain. The most common areas of pain were in the lower back, abdomen and head. Among particular patient groups, levels of pain can be even higher. Potter, Hami, Bryan *et al.* (2003), for example, reported that 64 percent of people receiving care from a hospice, the majority of whom had a diagnosis of terminal cancer, reported pain as one of their primary symptoms. The cost of pain is not only physical and psychological, it is economic. Maniadakis and Gray (2000), for example, estimated the direct costs to the British health service of treating back pain in 1998 to be £1,632 million. The *indirect* costs of back pain to the economy in terms of days off sick, production losses in industry, the costs of 'informal' care of people with back pain, and so on, were even greater – an estimated £10,668 million.

Living with pain

To say that chronic pain is unpleasant is understating its potential effects. Pain can have a profound effect on an affected individual and those close to them, so much so that many people with chronic pain organise their day around their pain. They may be prevented from engaging in physical, social and even work activities. Some may even find looking after themselves on a day-to-day basis difficult. It may affect social and marital relationships, resulting in conflict between couples – which may itself exacerbate the pain (Lang, Joyce, Spiegel *et al.* 1996). It may also affect an individual's financial situation, as they may lose their job because of pain-related disability. It is noteworthy that people who have physically demanding jobs are more likely to experience pain than those in sedentary jobs – and most likely to lose them due to any physical limitations caused by pain (Eriksen, Jensen, Sjogren *et al.* 2003).

Not surprisingly, levels of depression are high among people with chronic pain (Bair, Robinson, Katon and Kroenke 2003). However, the direction of association between depression and pain is not always clear. It is possible that some people who are depressed focus on bodily symptoms or minor aches and pains and are more likely to perceive them as painful 'symptoms' of disease than people who are not depressed. That is, depression may lead to high levels of reporting of pain symptoms. In other cases, the strain of living with pain and the restrictions on life that it imposes may lead to depression. There may indeed be a *reciprocal* relationship between depression and pain. People who are depressed may feel unable to cope with their pain and thus limit their activity to minimise any pain they experience. This lack of activity may lead to a stiffening of joints and muscles, which results in increased pain when they do attempt activities. This, in turn, may restrict their activity further and increase their depression. And so the cycle continues.

A further factor that may influence how people respond to pain comes from their interactions with their social environment. Pain brings a number of costs – it may also bring a number of (often unconscious) benefits to both the person in pain and those around them. Bokan, Ries and Katon (1981), for example, identified three kinds of 'gain' or reward associated with pain:

1. *primary (intrapersonal) gain*: occurs when expressions of pain (wincing, clutching painful areas, and so on) results in the cessation or reduction of an aversive consequence – for example, someone taking over a household chore that causes pain;

2. *secondary (interpersonal) gain*: occurs when pain behaviour results in a positive outcome, such as expressions of sympathy or care;

3. *tertiary gain*: involves feelings of pleasure or satisfaction that someone other than the individual in pain may experience when they help them.

A further type of gain may stem from an individual's beliefs about their pain. If they believe that when they do certain things the pain they experience indicates they are causing themselves physical harm, the relief gained from avoiding activity may also reinforce inaction and lack of activity.

These various reward systems can lead to considerable problems. If an individual in pain experiences an environment in which their expressions of pain are rewarded by outcomes that they desire and that those around them gain satisfaction from providing, this may result in them doing less and less to help themselves, leading to increasing inactivity, muscle stiffness and wastage, which exacerbate any problems they may have. Imagine, for example, Mr Jones, who has had chronic backache for a number of months. Over this time, he has found that certain activities increase his pain. Activities such as standing while raising his hands and lifting prove particularly difficult. Unfortunately, these activities correspond to those involved in washing the dishes following a meal. Because of this, he worries that any pain he experiences is because of the position he is having to adopt while washing up. As a result, although he does not complain about doing the washing up, he shows his pain through winces and an awkward stance at the sink. His wife, alert to his non-verbal behaviour and not wishing her husband to be in pain, offers to do the washing up for him on a couple of occasions, and soon he stops doing it altogether. As a result, Mr Jones feels better because he is avoiding his worries and a boring task, and Mrs Jones feels better because she cares about her husband and wants to do the best she can for him. It seems like a win–win situation. However, both parties may eventually lose as a result of this process: Mr Jones because his increasing inactivity will lead to further back problems; Mrs Jones because she will potentially become overburdened and resentful of her role as a 'carer'.

Brena and Chapman (1983) described the so-called 'five Ds' that may result from such an environment:

1. dramatization of complaints;

2. disuse through inactivity;

3. drug misuse as a result of over-medication in response to pain behaviour;

4. dependency on others due to learned helplessness and impaired use of personal coping skills;

5. disability due to inactivity.

However, many people cope well with chronic pain for significant periods of time without encountering such problems, and many environments will encourage activity and minimise the pain experience. Evers, Kraaimaat, Geenen et al. (2003), for example, found that patients with rheumatoid arthritis who had good social support reported less pain and better physical functioning than those who were less well supported. This may be the result of a number of factors. People who are well supported may be encouraged by friends to take part in more activities, which may maintain function and prevent joint stiffening and other factors that contribute to pain. The emotional support that such people provide may also influence the experience of pain. However, the process described by Bokan and Brena and colleagues indicates how some people may lose control over their pain and health – and may benefit from some of the pain management interventions discussed later in the chapter. The RESEARCH FOCUS below in this chapter also illustrates some of the problems of living with sickle cell disease – a painful and debilitating condition experienced by people of African or Caribbean descent.

RESEARCH FOCUS

Elander, J., Lusher, L., Bevan, B. and Telfer, P. (2003). Pain management and symptoms of substance dependence among patients with sickle cell disease. *Social Science and Medicine*, 57: 1683–96.

Background

Sickle cell disease (SCD) is an inherited disorder mainly affecting people of African or Caribbean origin. People with SCD make an unusual form of red blood cells, called haemoglobin S (for sickle). For much of the time they have no symptoms. However, they may have episodes when their red blood cells 'sickle'. At these times, they become stiff, distorted in shape and have difficulty passing through the body's small blood vessels. As a result, they may block them, preventing blood reaching parts of the body close to the area of blockage – causing severe pain. These episodes are treated using strong analgesics including intravenous pethidine, morphine or diamorphine – all members of the opiate family of drugs. The severity of pain experienced by people with SCD may result in many of them self-medicating with illegal and addictive drugs – to help them to control their pain on a day-to-day basis and to prevent their going into hospital. This study examined the prevalence of addiction to painkillers in a group of people with SCD and tried to gain an understanding of issues surrounding the use of these drugs.

Method

The study involved interviewing patients with SCD about their pain management away from hospital.

Participants

Participants were fifty-one patients with SCD living in London. Their average age was 34, and they averaged 8.7 painful episodes they had managed at home in the previous year and 1.8 hospital admissions over the same period.

Procedure

The interviews were semi-structured. Questions were used that allowed a diagnosis of either drug abuse or drug dependence to be made.

Participants were asked whether these symptoms reflected attempts at controlling pain or whether they were a consequence of other reasons (e.g. recreational drug use).

Results

Key results of the study were:

- 37 percent of participants met the criteria for drug abuse in the previous year as a result of attempts to control their pain.

- 31 percent of participants achieved the diagnostic criteria for drug dependence in the previous year as a result of attempts to control pain.

In addition, five themes related to drug use emerged from the interviews:

1. *Drug use as active coping attempts*: described how attempts to stop pain quickly or manage pain at home and avoid going into hospital resulted in behaviour 'resembling' that of drug dependence.

2. *Seeking a more normal life*: drugs were used, sometimes despite side-effects, to maintain everyday activities.

3. *Awareness of dependence*: many participants expressed a dislike of medication and showed awareness of the risk of dependence even when their only use was related to pain control.

4. *Psychological disturbance*: many people used analgesic drugs to control negative psychological consequences of their pain, such as depression, stress and lack of sleep.

5. *Impaired activities*: using analgesics helped to control pain but brought with it a number of negative aspects, such as drowsiness, that interfered with everyday activities.

Discussion

This paper highlights some of the problems that people face when trying to control extreme pain, which may occur at any time, while maintaining a 'normal' life. The tensions between controlling pain, trying to stay out of hospital and the impairment of activities and awareness of an unwanted dependence speak eloquently of the difficulties these people face. The high prevalence of drug dependence and abuse specifically related to pain control shows the lengths that they went through to control their pain in a way that was acceptable to them and avoided their being admitted to hospital. These authors suggested that data indicated the doctors may have been too conservative and unwilling to provide pain medication at a level that many people felt they needed. This demonstrates the tension that doctors may feel – between providing 'sufficient' medication to meet the needs of patients and over-prescribing and causing dependence.

Biological models of pain

Perhaps the simplest biological theory of pain is that there are 'pain receptors' in the skin and elsewhere in the body that when activated transmit information to a centre in the brain that processes pain-related information. Once activated, this 'pain centre' produces the sensory experience of pain. This type of theory, known as a specificity theory, was first proposed in the third century BC by Epicurus and was later taken up by Descartes and others in the seventeenth century. Von Frey (1894; see Norrsell, Finger and Lajonchere 1999) added to this theory by suggesting that our skin includes three different types of nerve, each of which responds to touch, warmth or pain. These theories were further elaborated by Goldscheider (1884; see Norrsell, Finger and Lajonchere 1999), whose pattern theory of pain suggested that pain sensations occurred only when the degree of nerve stimulation crossed a certain threshold. These basic biological models of pain, with some elaboration, remained dominant until the 1960s. They were supported by the identification of nerves that were sensitive to different types of pain, and nerve tracts that led from the skin to the spine, where they linked with other nerves before leading to the brain (see below).

These theories have one common tenet: that the sensation of pain is a direct representation of the degree of physical damage or sensation sustained by the individual. This tenet has the benefit of simplicity. Unfortunately, it can easily be shown to be wrong. We have already hinted at a number of factors that influence our experience of pain. Three other sets of evidence have been used to challenge these simple biological theories of pain:

1. pain in the absence of pain receptors;
2. 'pain receptors' that do not transmit pain;
3. evidence of the impact of psychological factors on the experience of pain.

Pain in the absence of pain receptors

Perhaps the most obvious evidence to counter these simple biological models is the evidence that many people experience pain in the absence of any nerve pain receptors. The most dramatic example of this phenomenon is known as 'phantom limb pain', which involves sensations, sometimes extremely painful, that feel located in the patient's missing limb following amputation. These range from feelings of pressure or tickling to intense pain, burning or cramping, in a limb that does not exist. Up to 70 percent of amputees report phantom limb pain a week after amputation, and over half of these people still experience phantom limb pain for many months or even years after their surgery (Dijkstra, Geertzen, Stewart *et al.* 2002). Interestingly, people who have their upper limb amputated are far less likely to experience phantom limb pain than those who have had a leg amputated. Similar experiences are reported by people with spinal cord injuries and paralysis. Unfortunately, phantom limb pain is difficult to treat and can have a significant negative impact on those with the condition.

'Pain receptors' that do not transmit pain

A second physical phenomenon that presents problems for the theories stems from the experiences of people with CUIP referred to above. Individuals with this condition may experience painless bone fractures and ulceration to their hands and feet, which may go unnoticed. They may also fail to identify pain as a symptom of severe disease and sustain dramatic injuries as a result of a failure to respond to danger signals. Some people with CUIP may even experience ulceration of the cornea of the eye as they fail to protect against strong sunlight (Nagasako, Oaklander and Dworkin 2003). Individuals with CUIP appear to have intact pain pathways, so they present the opposite problem to that posed by phantom limbs: a failure to perceive pain in the presence of an apparently intact pain pathway.

Psychological influences on pain

A number of psychological factors have been found to influence the experience of pain. Three of the key ones are:

1. *Mood and pain*: anxiety and depression reduce pain tolerance and increase the reporting of pain.
2. *Attention and pain*: focusing on pain increases the experience of pain.
3. *Cognitions and pain*: expectations of increases or reductions in pain can be self-fulfilling.

■ Mood and pain

Mood influences the perception of pain – and pain influences mood. Evidence of the influence of mood on the experience of pain can be found in studies in which participants are asked to rate or tolerate pain until their discomfort is too great to tolerate the pain any further. These have shown that depressed or anxious participants report the equivalent pain stimulus as more painful than people without any mood disorder (e.g. Mel'nikova 1993). Similarly, Pinerua-Shuhaibar, Prieto-Rincon, Ferrer *et al.* (1999) found that depressed people would tolerate acute pain for slightly less than half the time that non-depressed individuals were willing or able to do so.

Short-term changes in mood may also affect the experience of pain. Fisher and Johnston (1996b), for example, gave patients with lower back pain a simple mood induction procedure in which they were asked either about upsetting aspects of their condition or to report more positive aspects of their condition and how they were coping with it. Before and after this procedure, participants were given a plastic bag into which were placed as many packets of rice as they felt able to tolerate and then to hold the bag until it felt uncomfortable. In comparison with their performance at baseline, participants who reported the upsetting issues (and were therefore assumed to be more depressed) performed less well. By contrast, those whose mood was improved were able to hold the same weights for a longer period than baseline. This was an important study, as it used real patients faced with a task similar to their everyday activities.

Evidence of the reciprocal relationship between pain and mood suggested earlier has also been reported in a number of studies. Moldofsky and Chester (1970), for example, followed a group of people with joint pain, measuring their pain levels and mood twice daily for just over one month. They found two distinct patterns of relationship between mood and pain. One group was characterised by increases in anxiety or anger preceding increases in pain. The other reported increases on a measure of depression following a period of increased pain. That is, in one group a worsening of mood appeared to result in increased perceptions of pain: in the other, increases in pain resulted in a worsening of mood. Magni, Moreschi, Rigatti-Luchini *et al.* (1994) reached similar conclusions in their longitudinal study of over 2,000 participants whom they followed for a period of eight years. They found that particip-ants who reported chronic pain at the beginning of the study were nearly three times more likely to become depressed over the follow-up period than those without this problem. By contrast, another group of people who were depressed and free of pain at the beginning of the study were over twice as likely to report having had a significant period of pain over the follow-up period. The authors speculated that depression may predict some 'pain conditions' while some 'pain conditions' may predict depression, although the nature of these two groups was not clear. Suffice it to say that there is an interaction between pain and mood that can operate in both directions.

■ Attention and pain

One of the ways that mood may influence our perception of pain is by influen-cing the attention we pay to any pain sensations. Depressed or anxious people may pay more attention to any pain sensations than other people, and this focus may significantly influence the pain experience. Focusing on pain seems to increase its impact: focusing on other things seems to reduce it. Many people who experience injuries while playing sports requiring effort and concentration, for example, do not notice the extent of any injuries until after the game has finished. Less anecdotally, there is evidence that fewer people experience pain following physical trauma at times of intense stress, such as being on the battlefield, than when similar levels of injury are sustained in less stressful situations (Beecher 1946). This may be because of attentional factors – in the battlefield there are many important distractions from one's own pain. However, other factors may also have been involved. It is possible, for example, that the soldiers were simply pleased to be alive following battle and thought that their injury would result in them being sent away from the battlefield. Civilians would be more likely to view their injuries as unwelcome and likely to interfere with their day-to-day activities. The issue here, therefore, may be the meaning ascribed to the injury and pain as much as the degree of attention paid to it.

Plate 16.1   The experience of pain differs according to context. Terry Butcher (in photograph) probably experienced no pain when clearly injured while playing football for England. After the match, it may have been a different story.

Source: David Cannon/Allsport/Getty

However, attention, and perhaps other emotional and cognitive factors, does seem to influence the degree of pain experienced by individuals taking part in mutilating religious rituals. Perhaps the most dramatic example of this is a fertility ritual held in northern India in which men are carried from village to village while suspended from ropes and hooks placed through the skin in their backs attached to carrying frames (Melzack 1973). A similar process seems to have occurred in the traditional sun dance of some Native American tribes, which involved pierced dancers tied to a ceremonial pole with thongs slipped through cuts in their chest dancing for hours to tear their flesh and break free (Morris 1999). Both sets of rituals occurred in the absence of any apparent pain among their participants.

A number of experimental studies have also reported reductions in pain following the use of distraction techniques, while experimental manipulations that increase attention to painful stimuli result in increased reporting of pain. James and Hardardottir (2002), for example, asked patients to place their lower arm in freezing cold water (an exquisitely painful procedure known as the **cold pressor test**) and to either concentrate on a computer-based task or the pain sensations. Those who focused on the pain were least able to tolerate it and pulled their arm out of the water significantly earlier than those in the distraction task.

cold pressor test
procedure in which participants place their arm in a mixture of water and ice maintaining the water temperature at between 0 and 3°C.

Attentional bias may also explain why some people with acute pain go on to develop chronic pain, while others do not. Vlaeyen, Kole-Snijders, Boeren *et al.* (1995), for example, suggested that people who develop chronic pain in the absence of any clear physical injury or inflammation may respond to acute pain with a degree of fear, worry about its consequences and begin to check themselves for any pain sensations, which because they are now paying attention to a variety of aches and pains that may pass unnoticed in other people they begin to notice and label as pain that is symptomatic of an underlying problem. They also stop engaging in activities that may trigger an episode of pain. This leads to increased disability and chronic pain. This hypothesis has gained support from studies such as that reported by Dehghani, Sharpe and Nicholas (2003). Their study, which used the dot probe task to explore attentional bias towards pain-related stimuli, found that people with chronic pain were more attentive to words describing the sensory experience of pain than neutral words or words describing its emotional or behavioural consequences. Their results also indicated that people with high levels of fear of pain both attended to these words more quickly and then had difficulty in focusing their attention away from these words. Both results support the attentional hypothesis of chronic pain.

■ Cognition and pain

Mood may influence pain by influencing our thoughts about the nature and consequences of any pain. The types of thought that may influence the pain experience include:

- attributions of the cause of pain;
- beliefs about the ability to tolerate pain;
- beliefs about the ability to control pain;
- expectations of pain relief – the placebo effect.

Causal attributions

A simple example of how attributions of the cause of pain may influence the pain experience was described by Cassell (1982) in a case report in which one patient's pain was easily controlled with codeine when they attributed it to **sciatica** but required strong opiate analgesia when they attributed the same pain to having cancer. Walsh and Radcliffe (2002) found that the beliefs of people with chronic back pain influenced their willingness to take part in an exercise programme. Those people who believed their pain was the result of physical damage to their spine were more reluctant to engage in exercise than those who attributed it to 'psychological' factors – as a result of their fear that exercise would exacerbate their damaged back and increase their pain. Similarly, Murphy, Lindsay and Williams (1997) found that the activities of people with lower back pain were more restricted by their expectations of pain than by the actual pain they experienced. They were most restricted when the pain they experienced exceeded the level of pain they expected to experience. The greater the discrepancy between their expectations of pain and their actual level of pain, the less likely they were to continue exercising, presumably because they considered this additional pain as indicating some physical damage as a result of their exercise.

Tolerating pain

A second set of beliefs that influence the pain experience involve individuals' beliefs in their ability to tolerate or cope with pain. People with high expectations of being able to tolerate or cope with pain appear to do just that. In a clinical example of this phenomenon, Bachiocco, Scesi, Morselli *et al.* (1993) measured a number of variables in patients prior to their having surgery, including previous pain behaviour, familial pain tolerance, locus of control and their expected ability to cope with pain. Each independently predicted the degree to which they experienced pain during their recovery period.

sciatica

pain down the leg, which is caused by irritation of the main nerve into the leg, the sciatic nerve. This pain tends to be caused where the nerves pass through and emerge from the lower bones of the spine (lumbar vertebrae).

Controlling pain

People who feel able to control their pain seem to experience less pain than those who do not hold this belief. In a clinical study of this phenomenon, Jensen, Turner and Romano (2001) found that among a group of patients with chronic pain involved in a pain management programme, increased perceptions of control over pain accompanied reductions in reported pain. This type of study, while of interest, can be interpreted in different ways: reductions in control could have led to increased control over pain as much as perceived ability to control led to reductions in pain, or changes on both measures may have occurred independently. Experimental studies allow us to explore this issue with more clarity. In one such study, van den Hout, Vlaeyen, Peters *et al.* (2000) randomly assigned healthy participants to one of three preparatory conditions before they were given a cold pressor task. The preparatory condition involved a task during which they were given feedback indicating high levels of control over the task, low levels of control and no feedback. Despite the fact that the initial task was not pain-related, it seemed to have some carry-over to the cold pressor task. In this, participants who received the high control feedback tolerated the cold pressor task for significantly longer than those who received low control feedback.

Perceived control may also influence pain-related behaviour in patient populations. In a partial replication of their study of the effect of mood on pain behaviour described above, Fisher and Johnston (1996) allocated patients with chronic pain to conditions in which their perceptions of control over their pain were experimentally increased or decreased. Control was increased by asking patients to talk about times when they had been in control of their pain and decreased by asking them to recount periods when their control was low. Patients in the increased control condition performed their lifting task for longer than those in the decreased control condition.

Expectations of pain relief

Expectations about the potential pain relief provided by certain drugs or other treatments may significantly influence the experience of pain. The best example of this can be found in work into the placebo effect. A placebo (from the Latin, 'I please') is an inert preparation that has no pharmacological effects. Despite this, they are regularly found to have a profound influence on the experience of pain – partly as a result of attributions of medical power given to them. Two of hundreds of studies of the placebo effect provide examples of its impact. Verdugo and Ochoa (1994) examined the placebo response to injection of saline (salt water) close to the area of maximum pain in patients with neuropathic pain – that is, pain that seems to be generated by the nerves themselves – which can be difficult to treat with conventional analgesia. Following this simple intervention, nearly two-thirds of the patients reported a 50 percent or greater reduction in pain. In a similar study, Fine, Roberts, Gillette *et al.* (1994) tested a placebo injected into patients with chronic lower back pain. All participants in the study reported significant reductions in pain beginning between fifteen minutes and one hour after the injection and lasting up to several days.

Although neither study directly measured beliefs about the nature of the interventions, this type of study provides indirect evidence that patients' expectations of relief from pain, and the power of an injection to provide this, can significantly influence the pain experience. By contrast, many people who are seeking compensation for injury are likely to report more pain and be more disabled by their pain than those not seeking such compensation (Suter 2002). These factors may make the treatment of painful conditions where there is ongoing litigation somewhat complicated!

IN THE SPOTLIGHT

Ethnicity and pain

An anaesthetist who had worked in a variety of countries was describing the amount of anaesthetic he had to give to people having the same operation in different countries across Europe and the USA. He suggested that if the UK acted as a sort of 'baseline' against which to compare other countries, then people in the USA liked to be knocked out completely and not to experience any pain at all – so they needed more anaesthetic than people in the UK. By contrast, he suggested that people from Scandinavian countries expected to experience a reasonable amount of pain following surgery, so they needed less anaesthetic than people from the UK. Whether his story is true or not, it raises issues about whether there are differences in pain expectations and tolerance across countries and cultures.

A number of studies have recently examined similar issues, studying ethnic differences in the experience of both acute and chronic pain in the USA. Sheffield, Biles, Orom *et al.* (2000), for example, found that African American participants in their study rated a series of thermal stimuli as more unpleasant and showed a tendency to rate it as more intense than whites. Incidentally, women also showed a tendency to rate the stimuli as more unpleasant and more intense than men. Similarly, Riley, Wade, Myers *et al.* (2002) found that African American patients experiencing chronic pain reported significantly higher levels of pain unpleasantness, emotional response to pain and pain behaviour, but not pain intensity, than their white counterparts. Differences were largest for measures of unpleasantness and measures of depression and fear. In a similar study, Green, Baker, Sato *et al.* (2003) reported that African Americans with chronic pain reported more pain, sleep disturbance and depression than their white counterparts.

These data evoke a number of questions. The first question that has to be asked is why are we interested in this type of issue? Why should we expect such differences, and what if anything do they tell us? Are any differences biological or genetic? Are they the result of socio-cultural factors? Are they cognitively mediated? Are they the results of biased reporting of results – are there studies out there that have found no differences in pain experiences and responses between different social and ethnic groups that do not get reported? The data tell us very little about the origins of any between-group differences – and lead to dangers of negative stereotyping.

Ironically, these emerging stereotypes conflict with at least some health professionals' beliefs about ethnic differences in pain thresholds. What evidence there is suggests that African Americans are likely to be offered less analgesic than their white counterparts, at least in some US hospitals (see Chapter 2). But stereotypes do seem to influence our expectations of different social groups and how they are treated. Morris (1999), for example, noted that the least powerful groups within any culture are the most likely for their pain to be disregarded – and the most powerful are likely to have access to good pain relief should it be required. He cited historical examples of the disregard of pain among insane people in the eighteenth century, black American women in the nineteenth century. One interesting belief noted by Morris, was that in the eighteenth and nineteenth century labourers were thought to have 'coarse' nerves that freed them from pain while undertaking hard manual work, while upper-class men and women were thought to have 'refined' nervous systems that would not allow them to engage in such labour without harm. Care should be taken not to establish more racial or ethnic stereotypes.

A psycho-biological theory of pain

**gate control theory
of pain**
a theory of pain
developed by Melzack
and Wall in which
a 'gate' is used as
a metaphor for the
chemicals, including
endorphins, that
mitigate the experience
of pain.

The evidence considered previously suggests that two sets of processes are involved in the experience of pain: one involving sensory information from the site of the painful stimulation, the other involving emotional and cognitive processes. The **gate control theory of pain** proposed by Melzack and Wall (e.g. 1965) takes both processes into account and is generally recognised as the best theoretical account of pain we now have. Melzack and Wall used the analogy of a gate to explain the pain experience. The essence of their gate control theory of pain is that the degree of pain we experience is the result of two sets of processes:

1. Pain receptors in the skin and organs transmit information about physical damage to a series of 'gates' in the spinal column (see Figure 16.1). Within the gates, these nerves link to other nerves along the spinal column that transmit information up to pain centres in the brain.

2. At the same time as we experience physical damage, we also experience related cognitions and emotions – fear, alarm, and so on. This information results in the activation of nerve fibres taking information from the brain down the spinal column to the gate at which the incoming pain signals enter the spinal column.

The degree of pain we experience is a result of differing levels of activation in these two systems. Activation of the sensory nerves from the site of the pain to the spinal column 'opens' the gate. This activates the nerves leading to the

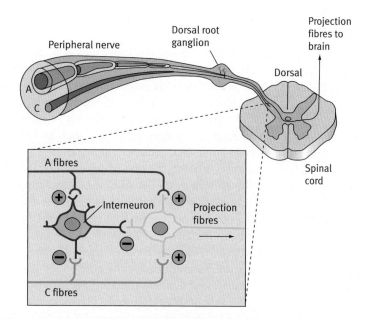

Figure 16.1   The transmission of information along the A and C fibres to the gelatinosa substantia in the spinal cord and upwards to the brain.

Source: adapted from Rosenzweig, Leiman and Breedlove (1996: 272)

pain centres and is recognised as pain – that is the essence of the biological theories of pain described above. However, the downward pathways activated by emotional and cognitive factors can also influence the position of the gate. Anxious thoughts or focusing attention on pain 'open' the gate and increase our experience of pain; calming or distracting thoughts 'close' the gate. This, in effect, prevents neural impulses travelling up through the spinal cord to the brain and reduces the experience of pain. The intensity of pain we experience at any time will be a function of these two sometimes competing and sometimes complementary processes.

Pain sensations are transmitted from the site of an injury to the spinal gate by nerves known as nociceptors, three types of which have been identified:

- A delta fibres (types I and II):
  - respond to light touch, mechanical and thermal stimuli. Carry information about brief sharp pain;
  - very strong noxious stimuli related to potential or actual damage to tissues. The experience is short-lasting.
- C polymodal fibres:
  - slow conducting;
  - carry information about dull, throbbing, pain – which is experienced for a longer period than that from the A delta fibres.

Perhaps the most important characteristic of these different fibres is that they transmit information at different speeds. As a result, our response to injury usually involves two phases:

1. The first, mediated by A delta fibres, involves the experience of sharp pain.
2. This is followed by a more chronic throbbing pain mediated by the C polymodal fibres.

A second set of nerves, known as A beta fibres, also transmit tactile information, particularly related to gentle touch. These fibres can work to our advantage as they provide information competing with the A delta and C fibres at the spinal column. When we receive an injury, activation of the A delta fibres is initiated and sends 'pain signals' via the spinal column to the brain. The first instinct we have following such an injury is to rub the site of the injury. This simple act reduces the amount of pain we experience. This occurs because rubbing the site of injury activates A beta fibres responding to this mild stimulation. Because they transmit information more quickly than C fibres, this information also reaches the brain more quickly and reduces the degree of activation that would have been triggered by the C fibres alone. Thus, in the terms of Melzack and Wall, activation of A beta fibres to touch and gentle stimuli can close the pain gate. Activation of A delta and C fibres to painful stimuli opens the gate.

The A and C fibres transmit information to areas in the spinal cord known as the substantia gelatinosa. These lie within the dorsal horn of each part of the spinal column (see Figure 16.1). Nerve impulses here trigger the release of a chemical known as substance P into the substantia gelatinosa. This, in turn, activates nerve fibres known as T(ransmitter) fibres, which transmit the sensation of pain to the brain:

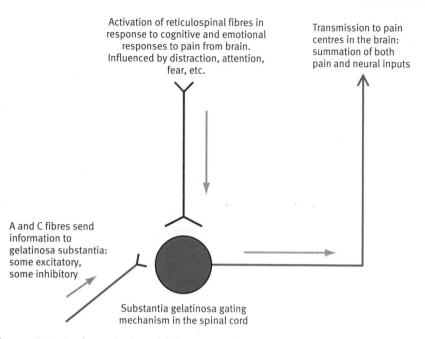

Activation of reticulospinal fibres in response to cognitive and emotional responses to pain from brain. Influenced by distraction, attention, fear, etc.

Transmission to pain centres in the brain: summation of both pain and neural inputs

A and C fibres send information to gelatinosa substantia: some excitatory, some inhibitory

Substantia gelatinosa gating mechanism in the spinal cord

Figure 16.2   A schematic view of the gate control mechanism postulated by Melzack and Wall.

thalamus
area of the brain that links the basic functions of the hindbrain and midbrain with the higher centres of processing, the cerebral cortex. Regulates attention and contributes to memory functions. The portion that enters the limbic system is involved in the experience of emotions.

limbic system
a series of structures in the brain, often referred to as the 'emotional computer' because of its role in coordinating emotions. It links sensory information to emotionally relevant behaviour, in particular responses to fear and anger.

hypothalamus
area of the brain that regulates appetite, sexual arousal and thirst. Also appears to have some control over emotions.

endorphins
naturally occurring opiate-like chemicals released in the brain and spinal cord. They reduce the experience of pain and can induce feelings of relaxation or pleasure. Associated with the so-called 'runner's high'.

catastrophising
the act of constructing **catastrophic thoughts**.

■ Information from A fibres is taken to the **thalamus** and on to the cortex, where the individual can plan and initiate action to remove them from the source of the pain.

■ Information from the C fibres follows a pathway to the **limbic system, hypothalamus** and autonomic nervous system (see Chapter 8). Activity within the limbic system adds an emotional content, such as fear or alarm, to the experience of pain. The hypothalamus controls activity within the autonomic nervous system (see Chapter 8), which allows us to respond quickly to remove ourselves from harm.

The results of this neural activity are transmitted *down* the spinal column through nerve pathways known as reticulospinal fibres to the spinal gate mechanism (see Figure 16.2). These may trigger the release of a variety of chemicals into the 'soup' of chemicals in the substantia gelatinosa (and brain), the most important of which are naturally occurring opiate-like substances called **endorphins**. These 'close' the gate and moderate the degree of pain experienced. Activity in this system is mediated by a number of factors, each of which influences the release of endorphins. These include:

■ *Focusing on the pain*: worrying, or **catastrophising**, reduces the amount of endorphins released and opens the gate.

■ *Emotional and cognitive factors*: feeling optimistic and unconcerned about the 'meaning' of the pain increases endorphin release and closes the gate – anxiety, worry, anger or depression opens the gate.

■ *Physical factors*: relaxation increases endorphin release and lessens the experience of pain.

Pain medication will also 'close' the pain gate.

<table>
<tr><td>

What do YOU think?

</td><td>

We have already identified a number of factors that influence our experience of pain. Think how *you* react to pain. Do these factors reflect your own experience of pain? And how do we come to respond to pain in the way we do? Do you rub yourself if you are bruised to ease the pain? If so, why? Did you learn to do it as a response to previous pain experiences – or were you told to do so by a parent or friend. Are you stoic in the face of pain? If so, is this a result of how others have expected you to respond? 'Big boys don't cry': cultural and childhood experiences may encourage different ways of expressing both emotional and physical pain in men and women. Do they affect how you respond to pain? Or do you respond in ways determined by your personality? People who are generally anxious or neurotic may be more prone to respond to pain with anxiety and high levels of physiological arousal – resulting in a relatively high experience of pain (and other labelling of bodily sensations as 'symptoms' of disease: see Chapter 9). People who are more relaxed and optimistic may have a less emotional response to pain and experience relatively less pain. Is this the case for you?

</td></tr>
</table>

Future understandings of pain – the neuromatrix

Despite the success of the gate theory of pain, it has still struggled to account for one important type of pain – phantom limb pain. The theory cannot account for pain in the absence of stimulation by the A and C fibres. In response to these limitations, Melzack (1999) has developed a more complex theory of the mechanisms of pain that attempts to explain this mysterious phenomenon. His model has three key assumptions:

1. The same neural processes that are involved in pain perception in the intact body are involved in pain perception in the phantom limb.
2. All the qualities that we normally feel from the body, including pain, can be felt in the absence of inputs from the body.
3. The body is perceived as a unity and is identified as the 'self', distinct from other people and the surrounding world.

Melzack contended that the anatomical substrate of the 'body-self' is a large, widespread network of neurons linking the thalamus, cortex and limbic system in the brain. He termed this system the 'neuromatrix'. We process and integrate pain-related information within the neuromatrix. Related information about a pain experience (physical elements of the injury, emotional reactions to the injury, and so on) combine to form a 'neurosignature' or network of information about the nature and emotional reaction to a pain stimulus. Neurosignatures have two components:

1. *the body-self matrix*: processes and integrates incoming sensory and emotional information;
2. *the action neuromatrix*: develops behavioural responses in response to these networks.

Behavioural responses to pain can only occur after information about the nature of the pain, its cause, and physical and emotional consequences have been, at least, partially processed and integrated. We do not move away from a hot object, for example, until we realise that it is the cause of pain and continuing to be near it will cause further pain and potential injury. We only become consciously aware of pain after this integrated network of information is then projected to what Melzack terms the 'sentient neural hub': the seat of consciousness. Here, the stream of nerve impulses is converted into a continually changing stream of awareness.

So far, Melzack's new theory does not explain the experience of phantom limb pain. This moves us from an explanation of how we feel pain from external sources to one explaining how we feel pain generated by the body itself. Melzack suggested that the neuromatrix is pre-wired to 'assume' that the limbs can move. Accordingly, in people who have had limbs removed, the body still sends signals to try to move them. When they do not move in response to these signals, stronger and more frequent messages may be sent to the muscles, and these are perceived as pain. Melzack's theory of pain is still relatively new and has only recently been subjected to empirical research. However, what data there are provide broad support for the existence of a neuromatrix, but we have yet to locate it within any particular brain area (Derbyshire 2000).

Helping people to cope with pain

The first-line treatment for *acute* pain is generally some form of pharmacological treatment – varying in strength from aspirin to some form of opium derivative such as pethidine. Psychological interventions generally form a second-level intervention. The American Agency for Health Care Policy (1992), for example, suggested that these should be used for those who find this type of intervention 'appealing', where patients may benefit from reducing or avoiding pharmacological treatment, have high levels of anxiety, would need prolonged pain relief and/or who have incomplete pain relief following pharmacological intervention. By contrast, increasing numbers of patients with *chronic* pain resulting from conditions as varied as rheumatoid arthritis and lower back pain are being taught to manage their pain using psychological approaches in order to minimise the amount of painkilling medication they need to take and to maintain or improve their quality of life. It is important that the effectiveness of these interventions is evaluated as part of the day-to-day care of patients as well as in research studies. So, before we look at some of the approaches used to treat both acute and chronic pain, we examine some simple, and not so simple, ways of measuring pain.

Measuring pain

The simplest measure of pain involves the use of a simple linear visual analogue or numerical rating scales – typically varying from a score of 0, registering no pain, to 100, rating the most pain you could imagine. This type of measure is quick to administer and score and is frequently used in clinical settings. A limitation of the approach is that patients often find it quite difficult to consider pain in numerical terms. Another simple approach involves patients rating their pain on a series of adjectives denoting increasing pain: mild, distressing, excruciating, and so on. This has the advantage of being more easily comprehensible to patients than numeric scales – it uses concepts patients are more familiar with. However, this approach has its disadvantages, as many patients tend to rate themselves somewhere in the middle of such scales, making them less sensitive to subtle differences in pain than analogue scales.

One important limitation of these measures is that they simply measure the sensation of pain. However, we have already noted that the experience of pain is multidimensional. It involves emotional, cognitive and behavioural responses as well as sensory experiences. A number of measures have tried to address these inadequacies. Perhaps the best known of these is the McGill pain questionnaire (e.g. Melzack 1975). This is more complicated to administer and interpret than the simple scales described above. However, it provides a multidimensional understanding of the nature of the pain that an individual is experiencing. In its various forms, it measures:

- *the type of pain*: including throbbing, shooting, stabbing, cramping, gnawing, hot, tender and so on, using a four-point scale from 'none' to 'severe';
- *the emotional response to the pain*: including tiring, exhausting, fearful and punishing;
- *the intensity of the pain*: on a scale from 'no pain' to 'worst possible pain';
- *the timing of pain*: whether it is brief, continuous or intermittent.

While this measure extends our assessment of pain, it does not address all the responses to it. It does not, for example, measure pain in relation to movement or measure an individual's behavioural response to pain. How much does it restrict their daily life? Can they walk up stairs, or lift heavy weights? These may all have to be measured separately. Turk and Okifuji (1999) suggested that one can also measure the pain behaviour in which an individual engages. They suggested measuring:

- verbal/vocalisations
  - sighs, moans
  - complaints
- motor behaviour
  - facial grimacing
  - distorted gait (limping)
  - rigid or unstable posture
  - excessively slow or laboured movement
  - seek help/pain reducing behaviour
- taking medication
  - use of protective device – cane, cervical collar, etc.
  - visit doctor
- functional limitations
  - resting
  - reduced activity.

Each of these may become a target for some of the interventions discussed below.

Acute pain

A number of approaches have been used to help people to cope with acute pain. Any procedures used need to be relatively easy to learn and use. Accordingly, most approaches to acute pain control have focused on:

■ increasing patients' sense of control over the pain experience and medical procedures;
■ teaching coping skills, including distraction techniques and relaxation;
■ hypnosis.

Some of these and other approaches to pain control are discussed further in the context of preparing people for the experience of surgery in Chapter 10. Here, we address other ways of achieving these goals.

■ Increasing control: patient-controlled anaesthesia

The experience of a patient experiencing pain in acute settings following trauma or surgical operations can be made worse by their fears that they cannot control their pain. They may be frightened that when they are in significant pain the nurses may be too busy to give them painkillers, that the pain will be so bad that it will not be controlled by the type of painkiller they will be given, and so on. To alleviate such fears, patients may exaggerate reports of pain or pester healthcare professionals to give them painkillers in order to avoid periods of inadequate analgesia. This may result in them experiencing unnecessary anxiety and higher levels of medication than would actually have been necessary.

patient-controlled analgesia (PCA)
a technique through which small doses of analgesic drugs, usually opioids, are administered (usually by an intravenous drip and controlled by a pump) by patients themselves. It is mostly used for the control of post-operative pain.

One way that each of these issues can be addressed is through the use of **patient-controlled anaesthesia** (PCA). Using this method, the patient controls how much analgesic drug they receive through an intravenous drip – albeit with some controls built into the delivery system so they cannot exceed a specified dosage. It is assumed that because patients can control the timing of their pain relief, they will be less anxious about the control of their pain, be more satisfied with their analgesia and use less analgesic. Systematic reviews of this approach, summarised in *Bandolier* (2003), suggest that this is the case. The majority of studies that have compared levels of satisfaction with PCA against healthcare-professional-controlled anaesthesia have found higher levels of satisfaction with PCA. There is also consistent evidence that PCA may result in less use of analgesics than when health professionals have control over pain control. Van der Vyver *et al.* (2002), for example, reported a systematic review of the use of analgesia and pain control during childbirth. In all cases of comparison between PCA and doctor-controlled anaesthesia, they found that women used less analgesia. Even children can use PCA systems. Birmingham, Wheeler, Suresh *et al.* (2003) reported data from over a hundred children for whom PCA was used for acute post-operative pain control. Satisfactory analgesia was obtained in 90 percent of cases, with no evidence of toxicity or serious adverse effects. It therefore seems to be a safe, beneficial form of treatment for a wide range of people.

■ Teaching coping skills

Distraction

We have already noted in the chapter that focusing on pain tends to increase the experience of pain, while distraction decreases it. Given the apparent simplicity of teaching distraction techniques, these would seem to be sensible strategies to teach patients who are in acute pain or who have to undergo painful procedures. The procedure seems to work. Callaghan and Li (2002), for example, taught women undergoing a hysterectomy to distract themselves from worrisome thoughts prior to their operation. Compared with women only given information about the procedure, they reported less pain and evidenced less distress after the operation.

Fauerbach, Lawrence, Haythornwaite *et al.* (2002) also reported success after teaching distraction skills – but only if patients actively focused on something other than the pain experience rather than simply trying not to think of the pain. Their study involved a comparison of an intervention designed to reduce the negative emotional aspects of a painful procedure and one designed to distract completely from the procedure – both of which should reduce the intensity of any pain (see above). In their study, patients receiving regular, extremely painful, dressing changes to burns were randomly assigned to an emotional control or distraction condition. In the first, participants were asked to focus on the sensory experience of their dressing change 'while noticing subtle variations in the sensory experience and the ebb and flow of pain sensations' (p. 1007), to focus on the present and not to anticipate or dwell on future and past pain, limiting thoughts to those about the sensory experience and not its implications or other potentially **catastrophic thoughts**. In the distraction condition, participants were given a choice of music to listen to and taught to focus on the melody, style or emotional tone, different instruments, and lyrics. Their analyses focused on the degree of tension the patients experienced during the dressing change and the number of intrusive and catastrophic thoughts they had during and after the procedures. The distraction procedure resulted in fewer intrusive thoughts and less tension during the procedure than the emotion-focusing procedure. However, patients who did not focus on the tasks assigned, but tried to ignore the sensations without this focus, experienced the most intrusive thoughts and tension during the dressing change. It seems that having a focused concentration on something other than the pain is beneficial – but unfocused attempts simply to ignore it are less so.

catastrophic thoughts
automatic thoughts that exaggerate the negative aspects of any situation.

Relaxation

A second relatively simple approach that can be taught to patients is the use of relaxation. This involves teaching people to relax the muscles throughout their body, particularly those close to the site of the pain (see Chapter 13). This has a number of advantages. First, it can be used to reduce any muscular tension that can contribute to the experience of pain. Second, because relaxation instructions may explicitly involve thinking about pleasant images or at least images inconsistent with the painful situation, it may act as a form of distraction. The concentration involved in relaxing may also distract from pain sensations even when it focuses exclusively on physical sensations. Finally, there is evidence that relaxation promotes endorphin release and thus has a direct impact on the pain experience. There is ample evidence that relaxation procedures can help to reduce levels of pain and distress associated with post-operative pain. Renzi, Peticca and Pescatori (2000), for example, reported that patients undergoing major bowel surgery experienced less pain, less distress and better sleep following surgery than a control group receiving 'standard care'. The evidence in support of relaxation is so consistent that the American National Institutes of Health consensus panel (National Institutes of Health Technology Assessment Panel 1996) concluded that relaxation procedures should be adopted for general use.

■ Hypnosis

Hypnosis is a procedure during which a health professional suggests that a patient experience changes in sensations, perceptions, thoughts or behaviour. The hypnotic context is generally established by an induction procedure. Although there are many different hypnotic inductions, most include suggestions for relaxation, calmness and wellbeing. Instructions to imagine or think about pleasant experiences are also commonly included in hypnotic inductions. It has been shown to have a reliable and significant effect on acute pain (Patterson and Jensen 2003).

Not only can hypnosis reduce pain following operations, it may also aid patients' physical recovery. Ginandes, Brooks, Sando *et al.* (2003) examined the effects of hypnosis on pain and wound healing following breast surgery. They allocated women to three interventions following surgery: usual care (normal analgesia); sessions with a counsellor providing unstructured support; and hypnosis, in which they focused on relaxation and 'accelerated wound healing' as part of the instructions ('Imagine your wound healing well'). They measured the women's pain and level of wound healing one week and seven weeks following the interventions and found that the wounds of the women in the hypnosis healed significantly more quickly than those in the other conditions. They also experienced less pain over the course of their recovery. Hypnosis can also reduce distress and pain during painful medical procedures. Lang, Joyce, Spiegel *et al.* (1996), for example, reported that patients taught self-hypnosis were less distressed, needed fewer painkillers and were less likely to interrupt a variety of uncomfortable or painful medical procedures than controls not taught these techniques. Children may also benefit from hypnosis. Zelter and LeBaron (1982) found that children and adolescents who underwent hypnotic procedures reported less pain and were less distressed during a variety of painful medical procedures than controls.

Chronic pain

■ Behavioural interventions

Behavioural interventions are based on operant conditioning processes. The treatment model, initially developed by Fordyce (1976), is based on the premise that we cannot truly understand the pain experience of others; all we can do is observe 'pain behaviour'. Fordyce argued that this behaviour should, therefore, form the target of any intervention, not the unobservable inner experience. Operant theory states that pain behaviour may be established and controlled not only by the experience of pain but also by how others respond to expressions of pain. Pain behaviour may be as subtle as gentle winces or as obvious as lying down unable to move as a result of apparently unbearable pain. It may be reinforced by expressions of sympathy, being 'let off' tasks about the home, given analgesia, and so on (see Bokan *et al.* 1981, earlier in the chapter).

The aim of behavioural interventions is to reduce disability by changing the environmental contingencies that influence pain behaviour – to remove the individual from any reinforcement of their pain behaviour. Instead, non-pain-related, adaptive behaviour is reinforced. The methods used include:

■ reinforcement of adaptive behaviour such as appropriate levels of exercise;
■ withdrawal of attention or other rewards that were previous responses to pain behaviour;
■ providing analgesic medication at set times rather than in response to behaviour.

In this way, new forms of behaviour are encouraged through appropriate reinforcement, and older maladaptive behaviour is extinguished through non-reinforcement. The approach may involve both health professionals and others with whom the patient interacts, including their partner or even friends.

Depending on the nature of the presenting problem, these processes may be added to by other interventions. In the case of lower back pain, for example, where disuse may have resulted in a weakening of the back muscles, patients may take part in exercise programmes. In these, patients will typically engage in a number of exercise trials to identify their tolerance for various lifting activities and movements. The programme will then advance them through a series of progressively more difficult steps towards full mobility and strength. Success at each stage of the intervention is positively rewarded by the healthcare professionals involved in the treatment programme.

Early studies of this approach were often case histories, as the approaches used to treat individual cases were necessarily quite different. Fordyce (1976), for example, reported a case in which they moved a hospital patient who was engaging in excessive pain behaviour into a single room, the door of which could be closed if necessary. This prevented the patient trying to attract the attention of nurses in the ward. Rewards for non-pain behaviour and 'punishments' for pain-related behaviour were achieved by entering and leaving the room if the patient inappropriately demanded pain medication or staying for social chat if they did not do so. These various case reports indicated the potential for this type of treatment. More recently, the development of standardised behavioural programmes in the treatment of a variety of disorders, including back pain, has meant that their effectiveness can be assessed using group designs.

Back pain is frequently treated using behavioural methods, possibly because it is a common disorder that often has no obvious pathology but which can cause significant impairment. They are also very effective in treating the disorder. Van Tulder, Ostelo, Vlaeyen *et al.* (2003), for example, reported a meta-analysis of the effects of behavioural programmes on lower back pain. They considered interventions that had targeted people with lower back pain that had lasted for twelve weeks or more and for which there was no obvious physical pathology, such as infection, cancer or osteoporosis. They concluded that there was strong evidence that behavioural treatments were of significant benefit on measures of reported pain, improvements in mobility and lifting capacity, and on behaviour away from the clinic.

■ Cognitive-behavioural interventions

Behavioural interventions clearly work by changing behaviour, but such changes may also affect other parts of the pain experience. Active engagement in activities may distract patients from negative cognitive and emotional responses to pain. Re-engaging in activities previously stopped may increase self-efficacy beliefs and optimism ('Wow – I didn't think I was going to be able to do that. Perhaps I can do some other things I've stopped doing'.). That is, behavioural programmes may *indirectly* change pain-related cognitions, and these changes may contribute to any improvements that patients make. Cognitive-behavioural approaches tackle these issues more directly. They focus on the role of cognitions in mediating our emotional and behavioural responses to pain. Cognitions are seen as central to our experience of pain, and our reactions to it. As such, the model does not contradict the model of pain provided by the gate control model – it focuses on one group of variables that influence the gate. The goals of cognitive-behavioural therapy for pain are threefold:

1. To help patients to alter their beliefs that their problems are unmanageable. To help them to become 'resourceful problem solvers' and move away from feeling unable to cope with their pain.

2. To help patients to identify the relationship between their thoughts, emotions, and behaviour, and in particular how catastrophic or other negatively biased thoughts can lead to increased perceptions of pain, emotional distress and psychosocial difficulties.

3. To provide patients with strategies to manage their pain, emotional distress and psychosocial difficulties, and in particular to help them to develop effective and adaptive ways of thinking, feeling and behaving.

Cognitive-behavioural interventions can be provided as both individual and group interventions. Cognitive change is brought about in a number of stages (see also the discussion of stress management skill in Chapter 13). In these, patients are helped to identify any maladaptive thoughts that are increasing their experience of pain or their disability. This can be achieved by discussion in therapy sessions in which patients reflect back on periods of pain or when they have been frightened to engage in particular behaviour. Any thoughts that occurred at such times are identified and discussed. Patients may also be asked to monitor their thoughts during their day-to-day activities by completing a diary in which they record their level of pain, accompanying thoughts and mood.

Once patients have begun to identify how their thoughts influence the level of pain they experience, their behaviour and their mood, they are taught to change the nature of their thoughts to more adaptive ones. This may involve two types of cognitive intervention. The first is known as self-instruction training. In this, patients are taught to change the commentary in their head at times of worry or concern about their pain or activities to a more positive commentary. This can be pre-rehearsed and thought through with the therapist. Such thoughts include reassuring commentaries, such as 'I've had pain like this before and it didn't do me any harm in the long run' or 'The pain only means I'm extending myself, not doing myself any damage'. Other thoughts may involve reminders to use other strategies to help to control the pain: 'OK! When the pain starts, remember to relax so I don't add to it with tension', and so on.

A more complex cognitive process involves trying to identify the thoughts that are driving any emotional distress or inhibiting behaviour and challenging them. This involves treating them not as truths but as hypotheses, and challenging the hypotheses by looking for contrary evidence. In practice, these types of challenge may not be that different to the self-instructions, but they may be more targeted at particular worries or concerns:

> Oh no! My back's beginning to hurt again. I *know* that means I'm going to be in pain for hours – I'd better stop now and take it easy. Hang on! Remember the last time this happened; I didn't feel that bad, particularly after relaxing and slowing down a bit. So take it easy and keep going and I'll feel better in myself for trying.

These cognitive interventions are often accompanied by a programme of gradually increasing exercise. This may have a number of advantages. First, and most obviously, it will increase fitness and minimise restriction of activities. In addition, it allows patients to learn from their actual experience that they will not be harmed by exercising – and therefore confirm some of the new beliefs that the cognitive therapy is trying to instil.

Other interventions may also be provided. One frequently used intervention involves teaching people to relax their muscles throughout their body and particularly close to the site of the pain (see above in the case of acute pain). Hanson and Gerber (1990) summarised some other strategies for coping with periods of particularly intense pain that can be taught in a cognitive behavioural programme, including:

- stop and ask myself if I can identify the pain trigger or learn anything from this pain;
- begin slow, deep breathing and remind myself to keep calm; review my alternatives;
- identify some distracting activities – a conversation with my partner about anything but the pain, a crossword puzzle, baking biscuits, etc.;
- take a long, hot shower;
- listen to relaxation or self-hypnosis tape;
- use positive **self-talk** – 'The pain won't last. I can handle this on my own';
- use pain-modification imagery – imagine a block of ice resting on my back, see my endorphins working, and so on.

Cognitive-behavioural interventions have proved very effective in the treatment of chronic pain. Morley, Eccleston and Williams (1999), for example, found twenty-five trials suitable for meta-analysis that examined their effectiveness in the treatment of pain resulting from a number of medical conditions, including back problems, arthritis and musculo-skeletal problems but excluding headaches. Overall, cognitive-behavioural treatments proved more effective than no treatment on measures of reported pain, mood, cognitive coping and appraisals, behavioural activity and social engagement.

self-talk
talking to oneself (internally). Can be negative and thus add to stress. Therapeutically, individuals are taught to use self-talk in a way that helps them to keep calm.

They proved more effective than pharmacological, educational and occupational therapy interventions on measures of reported pain, cognitive coping and appraisal, and in reducing the frequency of pain-related behaviour. Perhaps surprisingly, however, cognitive-behavioural interventions were no more effective than the others in reducing negative, fearful or catastrophic thoughts. Nor were they more effective in changing mood. This may be because the most important therapeutic process in these interventions is that patients engage in higher levels of activity than they previously had. As discussed above, this may change their beliefs about their ability to exercise, to control their pain while doing so, and their mood. Cognitive-behavioural interventions may speed this process up – but the best proof of one's ability to change for the better is actually doing so.

Evidence for this line of argument can be found in the results of a number of studies. In the first, Burns, Kubilus, Bruehl *et al.* (2003) found that the cognitive changes patients made in the early stages of a cognitive-behavioural programme were strongly predictive of pain outcomes later in therapy. They took measures of catastrophising and pain at the beginning, end and middle of a four-week cognitive-behavioural pain management programme. Early changes on each of these measures were predictive of pain measures taken at the end of therapy. By contrast, early changes in pain did not predict changes in these cognitive measures. They took this pattern of results to indicate that cognitive changes are central to changing how well people cope with their pain, at least in the early stages of therapy. In the longer term, these advantages may dissipate. Turner and Clancy (1988), for example, found a cognitive-behavioural approach to be more effective than a behavioural one on measures of physical and psychosocial functioning immediately after treatment, but that the two interventions were equally effective at a six- and twelve-month follow-up.

■ Relaxation and biofeedback

Relaxation can be used to relax the whole body or to relax specific muscles groups such as those on the forehead or back, which contribute to headaches and back pain, respectively. The latter may be of particular benefit in some patients. Turk (1986), for example, noted that many patients taught general relaxation for the treatment of back pain generally reported reductions in pain. However, one small subgroup of individuals reported either no benefit or even an increase in pain following the intervention. Closer assessment revealed that while many people in this group had been able to relax most of their muscles, they had been unable to relax the particular muscles in their back that were contributing to their pain. To do this, they needed guidance on relaxing these specific muscles. This can be achieved through the use of **biofeedback** techniques, including electromyographic biofeedback, galvanic skin response and thermal biofeedback:

1. *Electromyographic (EMG) biofeedback*: measures the small amount of electrical current in the muscles. The voltage equates with muscle tension: higher voltage = higher tension. Uses electrodes stuck to the skin over specific muscles that contribute to pain.

2. *Galvanic skin response (GSR)*: measures general tension in the body by measuring subtle changes in the moisture (sweat) typically of the hand.

biofeedback
technique of using monitoring devices to provide information regarding an autonomic bodily function, such as heart rate or blood pressure. Used in an attempt to gain some voluntary control over that function.

Increased sweat relates to increased general muscle tension – although the relationship is far from one to one.

3. *Thermal biofeedback*: based on a theory that warming the skin can reduce the pain of headaches. Skin temperature is measured by a thermistor, often placed on the back of the fingers to avoid sweat and to provide a more accurate gauge of body temperature.

Whatever the mode of measurement, biofeedback helps patients to make changes (relax, increase finger temperature) guided by auditory or visual feedback on any physiological changes they produce. In the case of auditory feedback, for example, a tone may become lower as the person relaxes their muscles. Visual feedback may involve moving an indicator along a scale as they do the same. In this way, changes in physiology that the patient may not recognise are made apparent and the patient can learn how to change their muscle tension.

One area in which biofeedback has been used with some success is the treatment of chronic headaches. Holroyd and Lipchik (1999) summarised the literature as indicating that EMG-guided relaxation led to an average 50 percent reduction in headache activity in people who experience tension headaches. Thermal biofeedback has been shown to lead to a similar reduction in migraine activity. These improvements are about three times as large as any gains following some form of placebo intervention. However, while a number of people have suggested that although biofeedback may be an effective intervention, it is generally no more effective than relaxation alone (e.g. Stuckey, Jacobs and Goldfarb 1986). As relaxation is both simpler and cheaper to implement, this should perhaps be the first-line treatment rather than biofeedback.

If relaxation techniques are to be augmented. It may be better to do so using strategies that address other aspects of the pain experience than the physiological ones. More complex cognitive-behavioural interventions, for example, may add to the benefits of relaxation in the treatment of tension headaches, particularly where an individual is facing significant stresses in their lives which add to an their overall stress or inhibit their use of simple relaxation strategies (Tobin, Holroyd, Baker *et al.* 1988).

An alternative strategy has been to combine relaxation with anti-depressant medication. No one has fully explained why anti-depressant medication helps to reduce pain, but it has consistently been shown to do so. With this in mind, Holroyd, O'Donnell, Stensland *et al.* (2001) compared treatment with anti-depressant medication, training in relaxation techniques aimed at preventing the stress thought to trigger the headaches and help to manage the pain following its onset, a combination of the two, and a placebo drug therapy. The results were encouraging for both interventions. Both anti-depressant and cognitive-behavioural techniques proved to be more effective than the placebo on measures including the frequency of headaches, analgesic medication use and restrictions in activity as a result of the headache. Although both single active interventions were equally effective, patients who received the pharmacological medication experienced these changes more quickly than those in the cognitive-behavioural intervention. The combined therapy proved the most effective. This resulted in clinically significant reductions on a combined index of headache severity in

Plate 16.2   Biofeedback has proven to be an excellent treatment for specific pain due to muscle tension. However, in many cases, simple relaxation may prove as effective.

Source: Will & Deni Mcintyre/Science Photo Library

64 percent of participants in this condition. This compared with 38 percent of those in the anti-depressant condition, 35 percent of those receiving stress management and 29 percent of those in the placebo condition.

Pain management clinics

So far, we have considered treatments for pain in isolation, without considering who provides the treatment or where patients may go for treatment. Nowadays, many hospitals provide services specifically for people with chronic pain – of whatever origin. These services will involve a number of people. Doctors, usually anaesthetists, provide expertise in the pharmacological and even surgical treatment of pain. Physiotherapists work with patients to develop exercise programmes that they can realistically expect to be able to engage in. Occupational therapists may work with patients to consider how they can improve their day-to-day activities around the home if their mobility is restricted. Specialist nurses may work with patients to develop pain management plans for individuals or groups of individuals. Psychologists may also contribute to and develop such programmes. Table 16.1 shows the outline of a typical out-patient pain management programme – conducted at the Gloucester Royal Hospital in the UK.

Table 16.1 Outline of a typical pain management programme, in this case run at the Gloucester Royal Hospital in the UK

WEEK 1	Welcome, introduction and housekeeping Pain management philosophy What is chronic pain? – questions answered Introduction to exercise – sitting and standing Pacing everyday activities The stress response and introduction to diaphragmatic breathing
WEEK 2	Recap pacing Goal setting and action plans Introduction to exercise – lying Sitting and chairs Introduction to stretch and relax Video patients doing exercises for comparison at end of group
WEEK 3	How pain works: the gate control theory of pain How pain works: pain pathways Thoughts and feelings about pain Exercises Stretch and relax Action plans
WEEK 4	Recommended use of medication for chronic pain Communication and relationships Pain management graduate perspective talk Exercises Introduction to relaxing your mind Action plans
WEEK 5	Lifting and bending Managing everyday activities Sexual relationships The benefits of exercise Exercise Relaxing your mind Action plans
WEEK 6	Introduction to fitness and fitness equipment Doctor's talk: medication, treatments and surgery for chronic pain, sleeping and beds / positions to ease pain Action plans Relaxation
WEEK 7	Flare-ups and setbacks Helpful sleep habits Video exercises and compare with the beginning of the course Introduction to brief relaxation techniques Reviewing progress, and setting goals for the follow-up sessions

Summary

Pain is a widely prevalent phenomenon. Over 20 percent of the general population are experiencing chronic pain at any one time, and the personal and social consequences of chronic pain are significant. Various types of pain have been identified:

- *acute*: lasting up to between three and six months;
- *chronic*: lasting more than three to six months; can be further categorised as chronic benign and chronic progressive pain.

Pain can also be defined in terms of its nature: its type, severity, and pattern.

The experience of pain is moderated by a variety of physical and psychological factors, including:

- the degree of attention paid to the pain;
- the mood of the individual;
- the person's beliefs about the nature of the pain, including its cause and controllability.

Early specificity and pattern theories that did not take account of these psychological factors proved to be unsuccessful in explaining the various ways in which pain can be experienced. A more complex model, developed by Melzack and Wall, known as the gate theory of pain, has superseded these models of pain. This suggests that pain is the outcome of a number of complementary or competing processes. Any model of pain has to take into account how psychological factors affect the perception of pain. The gate theory of pain suggests that:

- Afferent nerves carry pain messages up to the substantia gelatinosa and then through the spinal gate mechanism to the brain.
- At the same time, psychological processes influence the activity of nerves leading from the brain to the spinal gate.
- Activation of both systems results in a variety of chemicals being produced within the gate (substantia gelatinosa) some of which 'open' the pain gate, some of which 'close' it. The main chemicals involved in reducing pain sensations in the substantia gelatinosa are endorphins.

Melzack has developed a more complex neurological model of pain, known as the neuromatrix, which accounts for phenomena previously difficult to account for by the gate theory (including phantom limb pain).

Both behavioural and cognitive behavioural interventions have proved to be effective in the treatment of both acute and more chronic pain.

Biofeedback interventions can help to reduce pain, but their overall effectiveness is no greater than more general relaxation procedures. They may be best used when there are individual muscle groups contributing to the pain that are not relaxed following more general relaxation instructions.

Psychological interventions may be combined (at least in some cases) with anti-depressant medication to provide maximal benefit.

Further reading

Melzack, R. and Wall, P.D. (1996). *The Challenge of Pain*. Penguin.
A classic. The most up-to-date text by the originators of the gate control theory. Written in a non-technical way for the interested 'lay' reader.

Morley, S., Eccleston, C. and Williams, A. (1999). Systematic review and meta-analysis of randomized controlled trials of cognitive behaviour therapy and behaviour therapy for chronic pain in adults, excluding headache. *Pain*, 80: 1–13. A relatively up-to-date review of intervention studies to treat pain.

Morris, D.B. (1999). Sociocultural and religious meanings of pain. In R.J. Gatchel and D.C. Turk (eds), *Psychosocial Factors in Pain*. New York: Guilford Press. Extends the discussion from psychology to other perspectives on pain.

CHAPTER 17

Improving health and quality of life

Learning outcomes

By the end of this chapter, you should have an understanding of a number of psychological interventions that aim to:

- *reduce distress*: focusing on information provision, stress management training and providing social support
- *improve disease management*: focusing on information provision, self-management training, stress management training, facilitating family and social support, and the use of written emotional expression
- *reduce the risk of future disease or disease progression*: focusing on counselling, stress management and providing social support

CHAPTER OUTLINE

This chapter focuses on a number of psychological interventions used to help people to cope with and manage serious illnesses. Such interventions have a number of goals. Some seek to reduce the distress associated with having a serious illness. Others aim to help people to manage their illness as effectively as possible and to minimise its impact on their daily life. Yet others are designed to prevent the progression of an illness and minimise the risk of further health problems in the future. This chapter considers a number of interventions designed to achieve these goals in the context of a number of chronic diseases, such as cancer, coronary heart disease and arthritis.

Coping with chronic illness

The onset of a serious illness has many implications for both the individual concerned and those around them. Following the onset of symptoms, the person with the illness may experience the anxiety of waiting for and being given a serious diagnosis, the possibility of having to come into hospital, with its discomfort and disruption of normal life, and so on. In the longer term, they may have to come to terms with restrictions or handicaps associated with their condition and the possibility of a gradual decline in health. They may have to learn how to manage their condition or take action to prevent their health deteriorating further. Having a chronic illness presents the individual with a number of 'tasks'. People who are HIV-positive have to take many drugs each day at carefully determined times; people with arthritis may benefit from engaging in a variety of exercises to maintain joint mobility; and so on. Other diseases, such as coronary heart disease (CHD), may or may not be apparent on a day-by-day basis. However, changing risk factors such as diet or smoking may help to prevent the disease progressing further. A third issue that patients often have to deal with is the significant emotional distress that may accompany a diagnosis of severe or chronic disease.

The interventions considered include different approaches to helping people to cope with each of these challenges. This chapter examines the effectiveness of a number of approaches used to help people to reduce any distress they experience, to manage their disease and to prevent it developing further. The therapeutic approaches we consider include:

- providing relevant information
- stress management training
- the use of social support
- self-management training
- enhancing social support
- the use of written emotional expression.

Each type of intervention may have multiple benefits. In cardiac patients, for example, changes in mood may increase the likelihood of their participation in an exercise programme, and therefore impact on both their mood and their physical health. Conversely, taking part in an exercise programme may reduce depression or anxiety as the individual feels they are gaining control over their illness and their life. Providing social support has been used to help people to cope emotionally with an illness and is also thought to impact on the prognosis of some illnesses, perhaps because it encourages appropriate behavioural change. Similarly, stress management training may reduce the distress associated with an illness as well as prevent progression of some illnesses, as reductions in distress may affect immune function and sympathetic nervous system activity, both of which may impact adversely on a number of disease processes (see Chapter 8). So, separating the specific outcomes of the various interventions is a little artificial. Nevertheless, we try to tease out each of these multiple end-points and consider how well each intervention achieves each of these separate goals.

Reducing distress

Information provision

Many people with serious illnesses experience significant levels of distress. They may have concerns about their prognosis and treatment, the potential effects of their illness on their quality of life, and so on. Levels of distress are perhaps highest in the early stages of an illness or at times when the nature of an illness changes. We discuss these issues in more detail in Chapter 12. However, as an example of the levels of distress linked to the onset of disease, about one-third of patients with cancer and a quarter of those who have had a myocardial infarction (MI) report clinically significant levels of distress at some time in the course of their illness (e.g. Zabora, BrintzenhofeSzoc, Curbow *et al.* 2001). Distress can be reduced by a number of types of information, some of which do not necessarily specifically target distress, including information about:

- the nature of a disease and/or its treatment;
- how to cope with disease and/or its treatment;
- how to change behaviour in order to reduce risk of disease or disease progression.

Perhaps the simplest form of information provision involves keeping patients informed about the progress of their condition and its treatment. Uncertainty can increase distress – providing information can reduce it. Wells, McQuellon, Hinkle *et al.* (1995), for example, found that giving people with cancer information about their chemotherapy, showing them around the clinic in which they would receive the treatment and giving them the opportunity to ask questions to a specialist counsellor was highly effective in reducing their levels of distress.

More complex interventions may also be relevant at the beginning of a serious illness. One particular issue that needs to be dealt with particularly sensitively is telling patients and relatives when they have a disease with a poor or fatal prognosis – a process often known as 'breaking bad news'. The way that this information is given at this time may have important implications for how people cope and come to terms with their prognosis. Clearly, the communication skills of the person giving the bad news are important in the success of this process – we discuss these issues in more detail in Chapter 10. However, a simple informational strategy may also facilitate this process. Hogbin and Fallowfield (1989) gave patients an audiotape of the consultation in which people were given their 'bad news'. They were encouraged to play the tape in their own time to help them to recall the information given. This simple procedure helped them to be able recall more information than a control group who did not receive the tape and to be more confident about telling their family and friends about their illness and prognosis. As a result of findings such as this, this simple strategy is now frequently used when telling people bad news. However, it should be noted that not all patients may benefit from it. McHugh, Lewis, Ford *et al.* (1995) found that in the months following this type of information provision, patients with a particularly poor prognosis who were given the tape were more likely to be depressed than those not given the tape.

Providing people with information about how to cope emotionally with medical procedures can add to the benefits of providing information about the nature of the procedures they will experience (see also discussion of pre-operative information discussed in Chapter 10). Marteau, Kidd, Cuddeford *et al.* (1996), for example, considered the effectiveness of two booklets given to women referred for **colposcopy** following an abnormal **cervical smear**:

colposcopy
a method used to identify cells that may develop into cancer of the cervix. Sometimes follows a cervical smear if abnormalities are found. A colposcope is a low-power microscope.

cervical smear
smear of cells taken from the cervix to examine for the presence of cell changes indicating risk of cancer.

1. A coping booklet provided brief information about the procedure they were about to experience, information on the likely outcomes of the procedure, and instructions on relaxation and distraction techniques (see Chapter 13) they could use to help them to cope before and during the procedure.

2. A medical information booklet provided more details on the nature of cervical abnormalities, the procedure and its likely outcomes than the information booklet. However, it did not suggest any coping strategies that the women might use.

The results suggested a specific effect of each aspect of the information given. All patients who received the leaflets knew more about issues around the colposcopy than a group of patients who received no information. However, the women who received the medical leaflet did not experience any reductions in anxiety as a consequence. By contrast, those patients given the coping leaflet were less anxious when they attended the hospital for their operation than those who either received no booklet or the medical one.

New technologies may be used to help the provision of information. Rawl, Given, Given *et al.* (2002) evaluated the effect of a computer-based intervention that provided women newly diagnosed with breast cancer with information on the disease, its treatment and strategies for symptom management. This was combined with support from a nurse specialising in the care of people with cancer. Following the intervention, participants reported less depression and anxiety than those who did not receive the intervention, although combining the two elements of the intervention makes it difficult to work out which aspect of the intervention proved the more effective.

Educational programmes whose primary intention is to help people to manage a disease and to reduce risk of further disease may also impact on mood. Why this should happen is not clear. The two examples we cite here relate to cardiac patients. In each of these studies, it is possible that the interventions provided patients with a sense of control over their illness and reduced anxieties about their long-term health. They also encouraged participants to re-establish old habits and not to overly restrict their lives as a result of their disease. This may also have resulted in improved mood. The first of these studies was an important study of rehabilitation of people following an MI. In this, Lewin, Roberston, Irving *et al.* (1992) compared the effectiveness of a six-week home-based education package known as the 'Heart Manual' with a placebo package of information and informal counselling. The Heart Manual focused on guiding patients through a progressive change of risk factors for CHD, including changes in diet, exercise and relaxation techniques. Patients followed the manual at home for a period of six weeks. Over this time, they also received three telephone calls from expert nurses to discuss their progress and any problems they were experiencing. Over the following year, participants who received the Heart Manual reported lower levels of anxiety and depression than those in the control group. They were also less likely than people in the control group to go to their doctor with concerns over their heart condition in the first six months following their discharge from hospital.

In a similar type of programme, Hartford, Wong and Zakaria (2002) used a telephone contact programme for patients who had had a **coronary artery bypass graft** and their partners. The programme provided information on a number of issues to aid recovery, including a graded activity and exercise plan, coping with pain, and dealing with psychosocial problems, diet and medication use. The programme began with a meeting between a specialist nurse and the patient and their partner on the day of discharge, when they were provided with information about medication for pain, distances to walk, rest stops on the way home, the nurse's 24-hour telephone number, and a time when they would phone again. This was followed by six telephone calls at increasing intervals over the next seven weeks, during which problems were assessed and relevant information provided. Despite its emphasis on changing behaviour, it also proved effective in reducing both patient and partner levels of anxiety.

coronary artery bypass graft
surgical procedure in which veins or arteries from elsewhere in the patient's body are grafted from the aorta to the coronary arteries, bypassing blockages caused by atheroma in the cardiac arteries and improving the blood supply to the heart muscle.

Stress management training

Stress management training involves teaching individuals directly how to cope with stress, using strategies including:

■ *problem-solving*: to prevent or minimise external problems that contribute to stress;

■ *cognitive restructuring*: to identify and challenge stress-provoking thoughts, which may initiate or exacerbate the stress response;

■ *relaxation*: to reduce the physiological arousal that forms part of the stress response.

We discuss these approaches in more detail in Chapter 13. Given that these strategies are directly targeted at reducing distress, one would hope that they are effective in doing so – and this does seem to be the case. A meta-analysis of forty-five studies involving some form of stress management procedure (Meyer and Mark 1995) concluded that the average person was up to 60 per-cent better off than those not receiving the intervention. They have proved effective at various stages in the process of care, including:

- waiting for a diagnosis;
- during treatment;
- coping with the emotional stress of living with a long-term illness.

Here, stress management procedures used to help people to cope with three illnesses, HIV/AIDS, cancer and heart disease, provide examples of their effectiveness.

Nowadays, it is possible to obtain the results of HIV tests within a few hours. However, this was not always the case, and early attempts to help people to cope with the stress of testing often lasted several weeks. In one of these, Antoni, Baggett, Ironson *et al.* (1991) examined the effect of a ten-week stress management programme in which participants received their HIV status result halfway through the programme. The first part of the programme focused on coping with the uncertainty of waiting for results; the second part focused on coping with knowledge of having the HIV. Men in the control group who were found to be HIV-positive reported significant increases in anxiety and depression over the waiting period. The same scores of those who were in the intervention group actually fell over the same period. Not such positive results were reported by Coates, McKusick, Kuno *et al.* (1989). They found that men waiting for a result of HIV testing reported increased anxiety after a stress management programme. The authors specu-lated that the programme may have repeatedly reminded those taking part about the potential problems of being HIV-positive more than it helped them to cope with their stress levels.

Other studies of stress management have attempted to reduce distress among people living with HIV. Chesney, Folkman and Chambers (1996), for example, compared a three-month programme of what they termed **coping effectiveness training** with an education-only group and a waiting list control. Coping effectiveness training taught participants to identify the nature of particular stresses they were facing:

- If the stressor was potentially changeable, participants were encouraged to plan and adopt strategies to change the nature of the stressor, using some of the problem-solving approaches described in Chapter 13.

- If the stressor was evaluated as unchangeable, participants were encouraged to engage in more emotion-focused coping strategies such as relaxation or distraction to manage their personal response to the stress in a way that minimised the level of stress experienced.

The intervention proved effective, with people in the active intervention group reporting significantly greater reductions in stress and increases in self-efficacy than those in either of the other conditions.

The carers of people who are HIV-positive may themselves experience significant stress and may thus also benefit from being taught stress man-agement techniques. But is it better to work with such people individually, or as part of a couple and include the cared-for person in the intervention? Pakenham, Dadds and Lennon (2002) addressed this issue, comparing a

coping effectiveness training
a specialist form of stress management in which participants are taught to alter the nature of their coping efforts to suit the particular type of demands they are facing: using emotion-focused coping where the situation cannot be changed and problem-focused coping where it can.

stress management intervention targeted at carers individually or as a dyad, comparing the effectiveness of both with a waiting list control group. The intervention included strategies to help the resolution of problems through problem-solving techniques as well as strategies to help participants to cope with any distress they experienced. Although working with individuals proved better than no intervention, the most effective intervention involved working with both members of the couple in the programme.

A second group of patients for whom stress management has proved an effective intervention are people with a diagnosis of cancer. One early study in this population was reported by Fawzy, Fawzy, Hyun *et al.* (1993), who compared a stress management programme with usual care in a group of patients with **malignant melanoma** whose tumours had been surgically excised. The intervention comprised three active components:

1. *health education*: focusing on the nature of melanoma, and appropriate nutrition, exercise and sun exposure;
2. *stress management techniques*: in particular relaxation and enhancement of problem-solving skills;
3. '*general coping alternatives*'.

Only the active intervention group reported any improvements in mood both immediately after the intervention and at six-month follow-up. More recently, Antoni, Lehman, Kilbourn *et al.* (2001) found that stress management interventions resulted in significant decreases in levels of depression and increases in what they termed '**benefit finding**' (finding positive aspects of their disease) among women in the early stages of breast cancer when compared with a one-day educational seminar. Typical benefits included:

- a greater enthusiasm to live life to the full;
- making positive life choices as a result of illness;
- a greater appreciation of being alive;
- improved relationships with partner.

Of note was that the women who fared best following the intervention were those who had relatively low levels of optimism at the start of therapy.

A more specific stress management programme has been developed for use with cancer patients at the Royal Marsden Hospital in London, which called its approach 'adjuvant psychological therapy'. It is a brief, focused therapy that identifies significant problems and teaches cognitive and behavioural strategies for solving them. It attempts to engender what the group termed a 'fighting spirit': that is, a positive and active approach to dealing with their illness and its associated problems. Moorey, Greer and Watson (1994) compared this approach with routine care (i.e. no psychological intervention) in a population of women with breast cancer. By the end of therapy, participants in the active intervention reported significantly less psychological distress than those in the control group. At one-year follow-up, rates of anxiety were 19 percent in the active intervention group and 44 percent among control patients: rates for depression were 11 and 18 percent, respectively. A subsequent study by the same group (Moorey, Greer, Bliss *et al.* 1998) found that their approach was also more effective than a generic counselling approach in reducing distress.

A third group in which we consider the effectiveness stress management programmes is cardiac patients. Most of these interventions have targeted

malignant melanoma
a rare but potentially lethal form of skin cancer.

benefit finding
a process of finding beneficial outcomes as a consequence of what is normally seen as a negative event, such as developing cancer or being infected with the HIV.

levels of anxiety, usually with significant effect (Rees, Bennett, Vedhara *et al.* 2004). However, given the increasing emphasis on the role of depression in increasing risk of further MI (see Chapter 8), some studies have begun to target depression levels. Freedland, Carney, Hance *et al.* (1996), for example, reported that a cognitive-behavioural intervention – using strategies similar to those used in stress management programmes – resulted in significant reductions in depression after an average of nine sessions.

It is not only the individual who has experienced the MI who may become distressed – so too do their family and friends. They may worry about the implications of the MI for their partner's health, their income, and so on. They may also have to take on more roles and responsibilities in the home. As a consequence, they may sometimes become more distressed following an MI than the patient. For this reason, family members are frequently invited to many cardiac rehabilitation programmes. One of the few studies to evaluate an intervention targeted at both patients and their partners was reported by Nelson, Baer and Cleveland (1998), who compared an individually targeted stress management programme and a partner-oriented programme with standard care. The partner programme provided partners with information on disease process, physical functioning and what they could expect their partners to be able to do socially and in relation to work. In addition, they encouraged them to express how they felt when they were anxious or angry. People in the family intervention fared better than the standard care on measures of distress and reported higher levels of adherence to medical treatment regimens. However, patients who took part in the stress management programme reported greater involvement in their work and social activities in addition to these gains. Accordingly, while the provision of information may be of significant benefit to partners, these benefits may still be augmented by the addition of a cognitive stress management programme.

RESEARCH FOCUS

Shapiro, S.L., Bootzin, R.R., Figueredo, A.J., Lopez, A.M. and Schwartz, G.E. (2003). The efficacy of mindfulness-based stress reduction in the treatment of sleep disturbance in women with breast cancer. An exploratory study. *Journal of Psychosomatic Research*, 54: 85–91.

Background
A diagnosis of breast cancer can elicit significant distress. One of the problems that may result from this distress is significant difficulties in sleeping. Between 31 and 54 percent of patients with breast cancer report sleep difficulties close to the time of the diagnosis, and many experience continued difficulties. The present study evaluated the role of a meditation-based stress management programme, known as mindfulness, in reducing sleep disturbances in this population.

The use of mindfulness as a means of stress reduction has been championed by Kabat-Zinn since the 1970s. However, its origins are much older and stem from Buddhist teaching. According to this, mindfulness (*sati*) is non-judgemental observation. It is that ability of the mind to observe without criticism. With this ability, one sees things without condemnation or judgement. One is surprised by nothing. One simply takes a balanced interest in things exactly as they are in their natural states. One does not decide and does not judge. One just observes. In terms of coping with cancer, it involves a dislocation between knowledge of having cancer and any negative emotions – the patient learns to observe their thoughts and emotions without being overwhelmed by them.

The present study examined the impact of the use of mindfulness on sleep in patients with breast cancer. Specifically, they hypothesised that:

- Sleep complaints would be associated with psychological distress.
- Participants in the mindfulness programme would demonstrate significantly greater reported sleep quality and efficiency compared with a 'free choice' coping condition.
- Within those who took part in the mindfulness programme, improvement would be greatest among those who practise mindfulness the most.

Method
Participants were sixty-three women recruited from oncologists in Tucson, Arizona. They were aged 18–80, had a history of stage II breast cancer (an early stage where breast cancer has spread to underarm lymph nodes and/or the tumour is 1–2 inches across) a maximum of two years ago and were currently in remission.

Measures included:

- *the Profile of Mood States*: measuring a variety of mood states, including anxiety and depression;
- *the Beck Depression Inventory*: measuring depression;
- *the State–Trait Anxiety Inventory*: measuring characteristic (trait) and present (state) levels of anxiety;
- *sleep diary*: included measures of naps, time taken to get to sleep, number and duration of awakenings, quality of sleep, feelings upon wakening, and total sleep. Sleep efficiency was calculated as the ratio of the time asleep divided by the total time in bed from the time the individual intended to sleep until their final awakening. Ratings of sleep quality were based on ten-point daily ratings taken on arising on items 'Rate the quality of your sleep last night' and 'Rate how rested/refreshed you feel now'.

Participants completed the questionnaires two weeks before the intervention began, and one week, three months and nine months after the intervention. In addition, they completed the sleep diary for one week before the intervention and throughout the six weeks of the intervention.

The interventions
The mindfulness intervention comprised six two-hour sessions and one six-hour silent retreat. Participants received training in the following meditation practices:

- *sitting meditation*: involved awareness of body sensations, thoughts and emotions while continually returning the focus of attention to the breath;
- *body scan*: a progressive movement of attention through the body from toes to head, observing any sensations in different regions of the body;
- *hatha yoga*: consists of stretches and postures designed to enhance awareness and balance and strengthen the musculo-skeletal system;
- *loving kindness meditation*: directing compassionate attention to oneself and others.

The free-choice coping strategy involved participants 'freely choosing' their own stress management techniques to engage in each week (including talking to a friend, taking a warm bath). Participants received a workbook including support resources available in the community, poetry and a diary for writing a journal. They were asked to monitor and record their use of

continued

stress management strategies they used each day. They received no formal or structured intervention or instruction.

Results

Of the sixty-three women randomised to each condition, one dropped out from the free-choice coping condition before baseline assessment due to family constraints, and one left the mindfulness condition due to a recurrence of her cancer. So sixty-one women actually took part in the intervention phase of the study. Of these, fifty-four (86 percent) completed the post-intervention questionnaires, forty-one (65 percent) completed the three-month follow-up assessment, and forty-nine (78 percent) completed the nine-month follow-up assessment. Adherence to the mindfulness programme was acceptable: 84 percent of the women completed at least four of the seven sessions: 80 percent completed five or more.

Baseline scores on the outcome measures of sleep efficiency and quality indicated moderate sleep problems. The average sleep efficiency score was 0.88, time asleep was 6 hours and 53 minutes, 'restful' ratings were 6.1, and quality of sleep ratings were 6.6 out of 10.

The study used multiple regression analyses to examine factors that contributed significantly to changes on each of the key outcomes. Accordingly, they did not report mean scores at each time of the study. Instead, they reported which variables independently predicted the key independent variables – that is, the various measures of sleep – in a series of multiple regressions. Their key findings, according to each of their hypotheses were:

■ Sleep efficiency was not significantly associated with baseline distress. However, participants with greater baseline distress had significantly lower levels of sleep quality and refreshing sleep throughout the period of the study – regardless of the type of intervention received.

■ Sleep quality did not improve over the time of the experiment in either condition. Feeling refreshed following sleep fell significantly over the period of the study, regardless of the type of intervention received. Sleep efficiency increased in both groups over time, but these changes were not statistically significant.

■ Neither sleep efficiency nor sleep quality was significantly related to the amount of mindfulness practice. However, feelings of being refreshed after sleep were positively associated with increasing practice of mindfulness.

Discussion

The key findings of the study were that people who had high levels of anxiety and/or depression slept less well than those who were less distressed. The interventions had marginal effects on sleep. Both interventions were associated with marginal improvements on the measure of sleep efficiency. However, overall, sleep quality remained unchanged, and the degree to which participants felt refreshed after sleep actually fell over the study period. The effects of mindfulness practice were equally modest. Increased use of the technique appeared to have little impact on sleep efficiency and quality. Only feelings of being refreshed after sleep increased with the degree of practice of mindfulness.

These must be seen as somewhat disappointing findings. In defence of mindfulness, the authors note that even at 'peak compliance', participants in the mindfulness intervention were using the method for an average of five minutes per day – significantly below that recommended for optimal effectiveness of the technique. So the problem here may not be the potential effectiveness of the technique but rather the willingness of people to actually utilise the technique in the 'real world' of their busy and demanding lives. Future research may involve developing a more user-friendly intervention or examining the effectiveness of the intervention if used by people who are motivated and can find the time to use the approach to its optimum.

Social support

We discussed in Chapter 12 how social support can improve or maintain both mental and physical health. With this in mind, a number of studies have evaluated the impact of support groups designed to provide social support from people experiencing similar health problems. Many of these have been led by professionals and include an element of group therapy or working towards group goals. One of the first studies to evaluate the effectiveness of this approach was reported by Spiegel, Bloom, Kraemer *et al.* (1989). They randomly assigned women with breast cancer to either a usual treatment control or weekly support groups led by health professionals. These focused on a number of issues, including:

- building strong, supportive bonds;
- expressing emotions;
- dealing directly with fears of dying;
- improving relationships within the family;
- active involvement in decisions concerning treatment.

Only those in the active intervention evidenced any improvements on measures of depression and anxiety.

More recently, Classen, Butler, Koopman *et al.* (2001) reported on the effectiveness of a year-long series of weekly support groups in which patients with breast cancer were encouraged to explore their emotional reactions to their illness and to gain support from the group. Compared with participants in a control group provided with educational materials, participants in the active intervention reported significantly greater reductions in traumatic stress symptoms and better mood in the long term. In a later report (Giese-Davis, Koopman, Butler *et al.* 2002), the same research team reported that women who went through the groups reported less suppression of negative moods while also showing less aggressive, inconsiderate, impulsive and irresponsible behaviour in comparison with the no-treatment group. They therefore concluded that this form of intervention can help women to become more expressive of their emotions without becoming more hostile. This type of intervention may also work in non-Western settings. Montazeri, Jarvandi, Haghighat *et al.* (2001) reported similar benefits following participation in support groups for breast cancer among Iranian women. Group involvement was found to be the most important factor that contributed to improved wellbeing.

Comparing new age and traditional approaches to support, Targ and Levine (2002) investigated the effects of a twelve-week course in complementary and alternative medicine including the use of meditation, affirmation, imagery and ritual with attendance at a breast cancer support group. The group support included teaching cognitive-behavioural stress management skills as well as providing social support. Both intervention approaches proved effective in improving a number of outcomes, including measures of anxiety, helplessness/hopelessness, depression and confusion. However, the complementary intervention group made gains on a measure of 'spiritual wellbeing' not found in the cognitive-behavioural support group. Support groups have also been used to help people who are HIV-positive come to terms with their condition and its consequences. Goodkin, Tuttle, Blaney *et al.* (1998), for example, evaluated the effect of such a group with both

HIV-positive and HIV-negative men who had recently experienced the loss of a loved one. The intervention focused on bereavement-related issues, including ventilation of feelings and moving on one's life. The intervention proved successful, with participants in the intervention group reporting less distress and grief than those in a no-treatment control group.

Managing illness

A second set of interventions can be used to help people to gain the skills and motivation to manage the symptoms of an illness as effectively as possible: to maintain an exercise and mobility programme in rheumatoid arthritis, an insulin regimen in diabetes, and so on. The goal of the intervention here is not to prevent the development of a disease but to minimise its negative impact on the affected individual.

Information provision

There is a significant body of evidence to show that patient education programmes can enhance knowledge about a condition or its management, at least in the short term (e.g. Gibson *et al.* 2000; van den Arend, Stolk and Rutten 2000). However, even where increases in knowledge are achieved they may not always impact on behaviour or symptom control. Indeed, a number of studies have found only a marginal relationship between educational programmes and behavioural change. In a systematic review of eleven educational programmes for people with asthma, for example, Gibson, Coughlan, Wilson *et al.* (2000) concluded that while such programmes increased knowledge, there was no evidence that they impacted on measures of medication use, doctor visits, hospitalisation and lung function. That said, high-quality programmes that provide patients with relevant information can help patients to manage their condition.

The best type of written information not only gives information about a condition and its management but also engages the reader in a programme of change or planning their own care. When this is done, written information can provide a powerful and cost-effective intervention. In one study of this approach, Lewin, Furze, Robinson *et al.* (2002) evaluated a written intervention to help people to manage their angina. They compared a standard educational package providing information but no strategies of change with a written behavioural programme showing participants how best to manage their angina and encouraging them to plan new activities and to limit the impact of angina on their lives. Six months after the end of the intervention, patients in the behavioural intervention reported lower levels of angina, used drugs to control their angina less frequently and reported fewer physical restrictions on their activities than patients in the control group. An interactive programme in the treatment of diabetes was reported by Piette, Weinberger and McPhee (2000), who evaluated the impact of an 'automated telephone disease management programme' (ATDM) in which low-income participants received a telephone call from a nurse educator every two weeks.

In the course of the call, they were asked to report on their health and their self-care, and they received relevant self-care education. Compared with people who did not receive the intervention, patients in the ATDM condition reported fewer symptoms of depression, greater confidence in their ability to engage in self-care behaviour and fewer days spent in bed due to illness.

The Internet now provides a key source of information for many patients. This provides both formal 'official' sites and 'unofficial' sites, many of which advocate the use of a variety of treatment approaches or condemn them as dangerous and unacceptable. Given the plethora of, often contradictory, information on the Internet, access to this information can both benefit the patient and carry the potential for confusion and even harm. It also presents significant challenges for doctors when giving information about a particular condition. Witness one anecdotal story in which a UK doctor prescribed tamoxifen, a drug treatment known to significantly reduce the risk of cancer recurrence in women that have had breast cancer (see Buzdar 2004). In the consultation, he described both the benefits and the common side-effects and health risks of taking the drug to one patient. With this knowledge, she decided to take the drug on a preventive basis. The next day she telephoned the doctor to say that she was no longer willing to take the drug as she had searched a number of US websites, and their descriptions of the health risks associated with the drug made her decide against its use. While in one way this may be seen as the power of truly informed consent, what had frightened this woman was reading a list of diseases that had occurred in women taking the drug. What she did not have was the data to contextualise this list, which included many conditions that may have occurred in only a very small percentage of those taking the drug, or which may not even have been the result of taking it.

Healthcare providers are now responding to this sort of challenge by providing their own web-based information that patients can easily access and that can provide appropriate information. One of many web-based health information sites is now provided by the American Heart Association (AHA: Yancy 2002). Heart Profilers (www.americanheart.org/profilers) provides a web-based interactive tool through which patients can obtain a personalised report of 'scientifically accurate' treatment options, a list of questions to ask their doctor on their next visit (which has been shown to improve doctor–patient communication and patient satisfaction – see Chapter 10), and key information that they need to participate in their treatment. In the site, menus lead to information related to heart failure and CHD, hypertension, high cholesterol, and **atrial fibrillation**. The effectiveness of this type of intervention is difficult to assess. However, people who access health- and illness-related websites are generally more knowledgeable than those who do not (Kalichman, Benotsh, Weinhardt *et al.* 2003), although this may be the result of better-informed people being more likely to access Internet sites relevant to their illness. Nevertheless, these data suggest that the Internet may prove a useful resource for people with many chronic conditions.

atrial fibrillation
a heart rhythm disorder (arrhythmia). It involves a very rapid heart rate, in which the atria (upper chambers of the heart) contract in a very rapid and disorganised manner and fail to pump blood effectively through the heart.

Self-management training

Perhaps the best-known approach to helping patients to gain control over the illness is known as self-management training (Lorig 1996). This involves teaching affected individuals how to manage their illness in a way that maximises control over symptoms and quality of life. It is based on social cognition theory (e.g. Bandura 2001), which suggests that patients can learn self-management skills from practice and watching others, and that success in achieving control leads, in turn, to increased confidence and continued application of new skills. Accordingly, the core of self-management training is a structured, progressive, skills-training programme that ensures success at each stage before progression to the next. Self-management programmes are often, but not uniquely, run as group interventions, facilitating the process of learning from observation of others. The approach is specifically targeted at the effective management of disease. It does not focus on the emotional sequelae of disease; nor is it intended to be a preventive intervention. Self-management programmes began by focusing on helping people cope with arthritis, typically addressing issues such as:

- exercising with arthritis
- managing pain
- eating healthily
- preventing fatigue
- protecting joints
- taking arthritis medication
- dealing with stress and depression
- working with the doctor and healthcare team
- evaluating alternative treatments
- outsmarting arthritis: problem solving.

These programmes proved extremely effective. A review by SuperioCabuslay, Ward and Lorig (1996), for example, reported gains in excess of drug treatment alone of:

- 20 to 30 percent on measures of pain relief;
- 40 percent in functional ability;
- 60 to 80 percent in the reduction in tender joint counts.

The original self-management programmes addressed all issues with all people. However, it is possible that some issues were more relevant than others. As a result, a number of programmes have now moved from a 'one size fits all' approach to tailored programmes that provide a number of modules that participants can select according to their particular needs. Evers, Kraaimaat, van Riel *et al.* (2002) evaluated the effectiveness of one such programme targeted at people with rheumatoid arthritis. Modules included those targeted at helping people to cope with fatigue, negative mood and pain, and to maintain or improve social relationships. The programme resulted in mid- to long-term gains on a number of psychological measures, including the use of active coping strategies, mood, fatigue and helplessness in comparison with a no-treatment condition.

Following their success with arthritis, self-management programmes are now used to help people to manage a number of long-term conditions. Gifford, Laurent, Gonzales *et al.* (1998), for example, randomly assigned men with symptomatic HIV or AIDS to either a seven-session group self-management programme or usual care. The intervention used interactive methods to provide information about living with HIV/AIDS and a number of disease self-management skills, including symptom assessment and management, medication use (see Chapter 10), physical exercise and relaxation skills. Over the course of the study, participants who did not enter the programme reported increases in the number of 'troubling symptoms' they experienced and an increased feeling of lack of control over their health. By contrast, participants in the self-management condition reported more control over their health and fewer 'troubling symptoms'. One other programme (Inouye, Flannelly and Flannelly 2001) reported short-term gains on measures of mood, including anger, and increases in perceived control over their condition following an HIV self-management intervention compared with a waiting list control group.

A third example of self-management programmes involves the control of blood sugar levels in diabetes. Langewitz, Wossmer, Iseli *et al.* (1997) reported a particularly interesting study of the effectiveness of what they termed intensified functional insulin therapy. Not only did their intervention involve an educational component, it also taught participants how factors such as additional exercise and eating meals with varying levels of carbohydrate may influence their blood sugar levels by them actually experiencing these situations in the programme. Participants were taught coping strategies and practised them while in these conditions. This approach should provide more realistic learning than conventional approaches and therefore provide more benefit – should problems arise. In comparison with baseline measures, participants in the intervention evidenced significant improvements in blood sugar levels and a reduction in the frequency with which they experienced **hypoglycaemic episodes** in the following year.

hypoglycaemic episode occurs when the body's glucose level is too low. It frequently occurs when too much insulin or oral diabetic medication is taken, not enough food is eaten, or following exercise without appropriate food intake. Symptoms include excessive sweating, paleness, fainting and eventually loss of consciousness.

atopic dermatitis a number of conditions, including eczema, involving an inflammatory response of the skin.

Self-management programmes can be implemented simply and cheaply using information technology. Glasgow, Toobert and Hampson (1996), for example, combined the use of a touch-screen computer-based programme with phone calls and interactive video or videotape instruction to teach people with diabetes how to cope with challenges to their dietary control, to solve problems and to set goals in terms of future dietary targets. People who received this intervention evidenced greater improvements on a number of measures of dietary choice than those in a control condition who did not receive the intervention. Taking this approach one step further, the same research group (Glasgow, Boles, McKay *et al.* 2003) evaluated a self-management programme for diabetes control, called the 'Diabetes Network (D-Net)', provided on the Internet. The trial compared the effects of tailored self-management training or peer support components with a basic, Internet-based, information-focused intervention in a population of 'relatively novice' Internet users. The intervention was implemented well, and improvements were observed across a variety of patients. However, there were difficulties in maintaining use of the system over time, and the addition of the tailored self-management and peer support components did not significantly improve results. Nevertheless, the programme supports the basic use of easily gained information over the Internet as a viable and potentially useful intervention.

Stress management training

A number of interventions have focused on teaching stress management procedures in an effort to control the symptoms of disorders as diverse as rheumatoid arthritis and **atopic dermatitis**. Some of the relevant literature is reviewed below, focusing on the treatment of irritable bowel syndrome, angina and diabetes.

Irritable bowel syndrome (IBS; see Chapter 8) includes the symptoms of alternating diarrhoea and constipation and abdominal pain. Interest in treating the condition using stress management techniques stems from early ideas that the condition is a direct consequence of stress, the strongest hypothesis being that IBS is an alternative presentation of anxiety disorder (Latimer, Sarna, Campbell *et al.* 1981). Latimer suggested that people who have high levels of anxiety but little psychological insight may report the physical symptoms of stress, including IBS, rather than their feelings of anxiety. This model has now been strongly questioned, and the role of food sensitivities is now more widely acknowledged, although stress remains an important trigger to IBS symptoms in many patients who have the condition (e.g. Locke, Weaver, Melton *et al.* 2004).

Most studies of the effectiveness of psychological treatments of IBS have proved equally or more effective than medical treatments. Kennedy, Jones *et al.* (2005), for example, reported a study in which they examined whether stress management could add to the effectiveness of a drug that slows down the gut's activity and is generally used to treat IBS. All the people in the study were first given the drug treatment. Those who continued to have IBS symptoms six weeks later were either entered into a stress management programme intended to reduce stress and teach them how best to manage their symptoms or continued on the drug regimen they were already on in the hope that additional time on the drug would improve their symptoms. Of this group, patients in the cognitive-behavioural programme fared best, reporting significant improvements in a variety of measures of IBS symptoms as well as reductions in measures of emotional distress.

Episodes of angina may be triggered by emotional as well as by physical stresses (see Chapter 8). Accordingly, a number of studies have explored the potential benefits of stress management procedures in people with this condition. One of the first studies was reported by Bundy, Carroll, Wallace *et al.* (1994), who found that patients who took part in a stress management programme reported greater reductions in the frequency of angina symptoms, were less reliant on medication and performed better on a standardised exercise known as a **treadmill test** than a control group who did not receive the intervention. A much larger study, involving hundreds of participants, was reported by Gallacher, Hopkinson, Bennett *et al.* (1997), who compared a less intensive intervention, involving a stress management programme delivered in booklet form and three group meetings, with a no-treatment control condition. At six-month follow-up, patients in the intervention condition reported significantly fewer episodes of angina triggered by stress, but not exercise – a finding consistent with the intervention impacting directly on the stress mechanisms that led to the episodes of angina.

The potential benefits of stress management for the control of diabetes are perhaps less obvious than those related to either IBS or angina. Nevertheless, there are reasons to presume that they could form an effective element in any programme of diabetes control. Stress often precedes periods of reduced adherence to self-care behaviour and may be associated with inappropriate changes in eating patterns (Viner, McGrath and Trudinger 1996). In addition, high levels of stress hormones such as cortisol reduce the body's sensitivity to insulin and may be accompanied by elevations in blood sugar

treadmill test
a test of cardiovascular fitness in which participants gradually increase the level of exercise on a treadmill while having their heart monitored with an electrocardiogram.

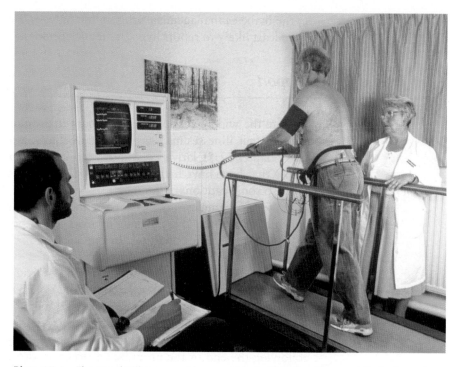

Plate 17.1   The treadmill can provide a good test of cardiac fitness while in the safety of a medical setting.

Source: Simon Fraser/Coronary Care Unit/Hexham General Hospital/Science Photo Library

(Surwit and Schneider 1993). Accordingly, some studies have found relaxation to be an effective intervention in keeping blood sugar levels within the optimum range. Surwit, van Tilburg, Zucker *et al.* (2002), for example, reported a study comparing the effectiveness of a diabetes education group and a combined education plus stress management group in the long-term control of high blood sugar levels. Their main outcome measure was a substance known as HbA(1c), which indicates levels of blood sugar over the previous three months. One year following the intervention, patients in the combined intervention had lower levels of HbA(1c) than those in the education-only group. Interestingly, Aikens, Kiolbasa and Sobel (1997) found that those people who reported the most stress and who felt that their levels of insulin were most susceptible to changes in stress levels were, paradoxically, least likely to use the relaxation methods they were taught. However, those who did practise relaxation did benefit in terms of diabetic control.

Perhaps the best interventions are those that combine teaching stress management techniques with other strategies to help to control diabetes. Grey, Boland, Davidson *et al.* (2000), for example, compared an intensive diabetes management programme combined with a stress management programme with the diabetes management programme alone in young people with diabetes. By one-year follow-up, participants in the combined intervention had lower blood sugar levels and a higher belief in their ability to control diabetes and general health than those in the single condition. In addition, participants in the combined intervention were less likely to gain weight than those in the diabetes management programme only, and women in this condition were least likely to report hypoglycaemic episodes.

Social and family support

Despite the widely acknowledged impact that family and friends of people with chronic illnesses may have on their behaviour and emotional wellbeing (see Chapter 12), relatively few interventions have targeted such individuals. Those that have have had generally positive results – although among them are also some cautionary findings.

Some programmes have worked with peers to help people to cope with chronic conditions. These usually involve peer experts showing how best to manage a particular condition. In one such programme, Lorig, Ritter and Gonzalez (2003) reported the outcomes of a peer-led education programme among a Hispanic community teaching participants self-management strategies for a variety of chronic conditions – CHD, lung disease and type 2 diabetes. The intervention proved successful, with attenders reporting better health status, health behaviour and confidence in their ability to manage their condition than controls who did not attend the sessions for up to one year following the end of the programme. Another project, described by Greco, Pendley, McDonell et al. (2001), reported outcomes of an intervention in which young people with diabetes and their best friends took part in a group intervention aimed at increasing diabetes-related knowledge in both participants and increasing the friend's support of the patient's diabetes care behaviour. In this, the intervention proved successful. In addition, the adolescents' wider groups of friends also reported an improved understanding of diabetes, and parents reported less diabetes-related conflict.

Involving partners in any intervention may also be of value – and may be done quite simply. Taylor, Bandura, Ewart et al. (1985), for example, compared the effects of wives' differing levels of involvement in testing the exercise tolerance of cardiac patients. In their study, wives were allocated to one of three conditions:

1. observing their partners taking part in a treadmill test to assess their cardiac fitness;

2. observing their partners take the test and also taking part in it themselves;

3. no observation of the test.

All the women were fully informed of their partner's level of fitness in a counselling session. The key measure in the study was the wives' ratings of their partners' physical and cardiac efficiency. Partners who both observed and took part in the treadmill exercise were more reassured of their husbands' ability to exercise than women in either other group. Although we do not know from the results of this study, it is hoped that this confidence would result in the women being less restrictive of their levels of exercise and less anxious when they did so. However, involving partners in educational programmes may not always be successful. Riemsma, Taal and Rasker (2003) reported that when both patients and their partners attended a cardiac group education programme, participants reported decreases in self-efficacy and increased fatigue. By contrast, patients participating in group education without partners showed increases in self-efficacy and decreased fatigue.

Emotional expression

Perhaps the most unexpected therapeutic approach now being developed for people with physical health problems is variously termed narrative or written emotional expression. The work stems from the findings of Pennebaker in the 1980s (see Pennebaker, Colder and Sharp 1990) of the psychological effects of a writing task in which healthy participants, usually students, wrote about an event or issue from the past that had caused them upset or distress in a way that explored their emotional reaction to that event for about fifteen–twenty minutes on three consecutive days. Typical instructions for this exercise were:

1. Find a place where you will not be disturbed. You can write by hand or on a computer – whatever you are most comfortable with. If you don't want to write, you can also talk into a tape recorder.

2. Plan on your writing for a minimum of three days and a minimum of 15 minutes a day. The only rule is that you write continuously. If you run out of things to say, simply repeat what you have already written.

3. Instructions: really let go and write about your very deepest thoughts and feelings about X. How does X relate to other parts of your life? For example, how do they tie into issues associated with your childhood, your relationship with your family and friends, and the life you have now. How might they be related to your future, your past, or who you are now? Why are you feeling the ways you are and what other issues are being brought up by this?

4. You can write about the same general topic every day or a different one each day. Don't worry about spelling or grammar. Your writing is for you and you alone. Many people throw away their writing samples as soon as they are finished. Others keep them and even edit them.

5. Be your own experimenter. Try writing in different ways. If you find that you are getting too upset in your writing, then back off and change directions. Your goal here is to better understand your thoughts and feelings associated with X. See which approach to writing works best for you.

Following this process, participants typically reported short-term increases in depression or distress but in the mid to long term to have experienced better mood, and importantly in this context, seemed to have better physical health as measured by immune function and the frequency of visiting a doctor (see Esterling, L'Abate, Murray *et al.* 1999). It took some time for this approach to be tested in patient populations. However, the interventions that have been conducted appear to show benefits following this approach. Smyth, Stone, Hurewitz *et al.* (1999), for example, compared the effects of written expressed emotion and a neutral writing task in patients with rheumatoid arthritis and asthma. Those in the intervention condition were asked to write about the 'most stressful experience they had ever undergone'; those in the control group were asked to write about time management issues as an exercise to reduce stress. Both types of patient in the intervention group fared better than their equivalents in the control group at four-month follow-up: patients with asthma showed improvements in lung function, while patients with rheumatoid arthritis showed improvements on a combined index measuring physician-rated factors such as disease activity, joint swelling and tenderness, and the presence and severity of joint deformities as well as patient reports of any constraints on daily living tasks. Accordingly, the gains reported cannot be attributed to changes in self-report of symptoms as a function of improved mood following the intervention: they appear to be 'objective' gains in disease activity.

A more recent study of the same approach was reported by Stanton, Danoff-Burg, Sworowski *et al.* (2002), who assigned participants, all of whom were in the early stages of breast cancer, to write about either (1) their deepest thoughts and feelings regarding breast cancer (the emotional expression condition); (2) positive thoughts and feelings regarding breast cancer; or (3) facts about their experience of having breast cancer (the neutral task). Once again, the emotional expression seemed to be of benefit. In comparison with the neutral task, participants in the emotional expression condition reported fewer somatic symptoms and fewer visits to the doctor with worries about cancer or related medical conditions. Of interest was that women who typically did not use avoidant coping strategies appeared to benefit most from the emotional expression condition. The positive emotional expression task appeared to benefit those women who were typically avoidant, presumably because it did not force them to confront their fears and other issues raised by their disease.

What do YOU think?

The premise of the emotional expression paradigm is that it can be useful to think about, and somehow process, emotional issues. This has proved effective in a number of settings, but are there times when this may not be an optimal, or even a desirable approach. It has been suggested that there may be times when the opposite approach may be of benefit. It was reasoned that people waiting for medical information – some of which may have powerful implications for the individual, such as their HIV status or risk of developing cancer – may benefit more by being distracted from any worries they may have than dwelling on them. At this time, they have no information to process emotionally – rather, they are lacking any relevant information. At such times, it may be best to distract from any intrusive worries rather than focus on them using the Pennebaker approach. Their approach proved effective in helping women going through assessment of their risk of developing breast cancer, although it was not compared with the emotional expression approach. This suggests that there may be some conditions or situations in which emotional expression is likely to be of benefit, some where other approaches may be of benefit. This addresses a frequently raised issue of targeting interventions at appropriate times and at individuals most likely to benefit from them. So what sort of conditions, situations or individuals may be best helped by emotional expression? Are there situations where this approach should be avoided, and other approaches considered?

Preventing disease progression

Counselling

One particular form of counselling has been used with cardiac patients in an attempt to prevent disease progression – with somewhat mixed results. The Life Stress Monitoring Program (LSMP: Frasure-Smith and Prince 1985) targeted middle-aged men who had experienced an MI and who were struggling to cope in the year following their infarction. In the study, a cohort of over 450 patients who had experienced an MI were allocated into a no-intervention control group or a low-contact 'counselling' intervention. In this, they received monthly telephone contact from a nurse for a period of one year, during which they completed a measure of psychological distress. If they scored above a criterion score, indicating significant stress, they were offered a home visit by a specialist nurse. The action taken by this nurse could vary according to the circumstances they encountered: the majority of contacts involving teaching and providing reassurance by supplying information, but the intervention could involve changes in medication and referral to a cardiologist if necessary.

Half the participants in the intervention condition were visited by the nursing team over the period of the intervention, with an average of six hours contact per patient. By the end of the intervention, the total death rate in the control group was 9 percent, while that of the intervention group was 5 percent – a significant difference. Four years following baseline, although a similar percentage of patients in the intervention and control groups had a further MI, patients in the intervention group were less likely to have died from their MI, suggesting a smaller but still significant benefit from having taken part in the counselling intervention. While these data were encouraging, they should be viewed with some caution. Unfortunately, the proportion of white-collar workers in the intervention group was significantly greater than that in the control group. Accordingly, many of those in the intervention group may have been at less risk of re-infarction than those in the control group simply as a consequence of socio-economic differences (see Chapter 2). As a consequence of methodological constraints, these differences could not be statistically partialled out in their analyses, and the interpretation of the results must therefore be considered with some caution.

Such caution may be justified by the results of a later attempt to replicate these findings by the same team (Frasure-Smith, Lesperance, Prince *et al.* 1997). The Montreal heart attack readjustment trial (M-HART) study evaluated the same form of intervention, this time including interventions with women and an older population. Unfortunately, the intervention resulted in no benefits for men – re-infarction rates in the first year were 2.4 percent in the intervention group and 2.5 percent in the control group. Worse, women in the intervention group proved to be *more* at risk of re-infarction than those in the control group, with re-infarction rates of 10.3 percent and 5.4 percent, respectively – an effect maintained up to five-year follow-up (Frasure-Smith, Lesperance, Gravel *et al.* 2002). In retrospect, these findings may have been a consequence of inadequately trained nurses attempting to cope with extremely distressed individuals and thus perhaps exacerbating rather than moderating their problems.

Stress management training

The impact of more traditional cardiac rehabilitation programmes that provide some form of intervention to all patients has been reviewed by Dusseldorp, van Elderen, Maes *et al.* (1999) and Linden, Stossel and Maurice (1996), who conducted meta-analyses of the effect of 'psychosocial' and 'psycho-educational' interventions on twenty-three and thirty-seven programmes, respectively. These interventions typically combined some form of **exercise programme** involving graded increases in activity with an educational programme about risk factor change, medication and other issues relevant to patients being discharged home following an MI. Both reviews came to some positive conclusions. Linden and colleagues, for example, reported that patients who did not enter a psychosocial programme were significantly more likely to experience a death or have further cardiac problems in the two years following their infarction than those who did. After this, any protective effect was weaker. Dusseldorp *et al.* similarly reported that psycho-educational interventions resulted in a 34 percent reduction in cardiac mortality, a 29 percent reduction in recurrence of MI, and significant positive effects on blood pressure, cholesterol, body weight, cigarette smoking, physical exercise and eating habits. However, both reports did not separate the effects of different psychosocial interventions such as counselling, risk behaviour education and what they term 'stress management trials'.

Perhaps the strongest evaluation of the effectiveness of stress management alone was provided by Friedman, Thoresen, Gill *et al.* (1986), who reported on a trial known as the Recurrent Coronary Prevention Program. This targeted men high on a measure of **Type A behaviour** who had experienced an MI. Participants were allocated to one of three groups: cardiac rehabilitation, cardiac rehabilitation plus type A management, and a usual care control. The rehabilitation programme involved small group meetings over a period of four and half years, in which participants received information on medication, exercise and diet, as well as social support from the group. The type A management group received the same information in addition to engaging in a sustained programme of behavioural change involving training in relaxation, cognitive techniques and specific behavioural change plans in which they reduced the frequency of their type A behaviour. Evidence of the effectiveness of this process was compelling. Over the four and a half years of the intervention, those in the type A management programme were at half the risk of further infarction than those in the traditional rehabilitation programme, with total infarction rates over this time of 6 and 12 percent in each group, respectively. This remains one of the most convincing studies of the effectiveness of stress management on survival following an MI (Schneiderman, Antoni and Saab 2001), although whether most healthcare services could provide such an expensive long-term intervention is debatable.

A follow-up study (Friedman, Powell, Thoresen *et al.* (1987) followed participants in the intervention arm of the trial for a further year and

exercise programme
a key element of most cardiac rehabilitation, including a progressive increase in exercise usually starting in a gym, sometimes developing into exercise in the home and beyond.

Type A behaviour (TAB)
a constellation of characteristics, mannerisms and behaviour including competititiveness, time urgency, impatience, easily aroused hostility, rapid and vigorous speech patterns and expressive behaviour. Extensively studied in relation to the aetiology of coronary heart disease, where hostility seems central.

also reported the outcomes of a group of patients who were initially in the control group and who then took part in a year-long type A management programme. This latter group also showed a significantly reduced intensity of type A behaviour and a significant decrease in the number of people to have a further infarction and to die over this follow-up period. One other study of this approach was reported by Burell (1996). Project New Life worked with type A patients who had undergone a coronary artery bypass operation. They were randomly allocated into a type A management programme involving seventeen group meetings over a period of one year and a usual care control. By between five and six and a half years following surgery, the prognoses of those patients who had taken part in the intervention programme were much better than those in the control group. By this time, a significantly higher proportion of those in the control group than in the intervention group had died from a variety of causes. In addition, the intervention group had suffered significantly fewer **cardiac events**, including further MI, re-operation and cardiac death, than those in the control group.

cardiac event
generic term for a variety of end-points of coronary heart disease, including a myocardial infarction, angina and cardiac arrest.

Smaller studies have also shown positive gains following stress management interventions targeted at more general responses to stress. Blumenthal, Jiang, Babyak *et al.* (1997) assigned cardiac patients to either a 'usual care' group involving regular out-patient appointments with a cardiologist, a four-month programme of exercise, or a programme of stress management training. Those in the stress management group were least likely to have a cardiac event over the following year. Interestingly, despite the emphasis placed on exercise programmes as part of cardiac rehabilitation, the risk of further cardiac problems among patients in the exercise group was not significantly lower than for those in the control group. Appels, Bar, Lasker *et al.* (1997) used a simpler intervention programme involving a relaxation and controlled breathing course for patients following heart surgery. The intervention resulted in a 50 percent reduction in risk of further cardiac surgery or infarction in comparison with that of participants in a no-treatment group.

Depression substantially increases risk of infarction or re-infarction (see Frasure-Smith, Lespérance and Talajic 1995 and discussion in Chapter 8). Such a relationship suggests that interventions that reduce depression should reduce the risk of re-infarction. However, evidence in support of this hypothesis is still lacking. In one of the first studies to examine this issue, Black *et al.* (1998) allocated MI patients found to be experiencing significant distress to either usual care or to one to seven sessions of behavioural therapy. They found that 35 percent of participants in the active intervention were hospitalised with cardiac symptoms in the following year, in comparison with 48 percent of those in the usual care group. However, whether this difference was a consequence of physiological or psychological changes such as less anxiety over cardiac symptoms is not clear.

Unfortunately, evidence from the largest trial of any form of cardiac rehabilitation, known as the ENRICHD study (Berkman *et al.* 2003) suggests that interventions targeted at depression may not prove as effective as this early study may have suggested. The ENRICHD study was a large multicentre study involving 2,481 patients, providing an intervention that may have lasted up to one year for people identified as depressed immediately following their MI. All participants in the active intervention arm received two or three treatment components, each aimed at improving their emotional state:

- group cognitive behaviour therapy;
- social support enhanced by training participants in the social skills needed to develop their social support network;
- anti-depressant medication for people who did not evidence any improvement in mood received.

A comparison group received the usual care provided by the institutions in which the study took place. Unfortunately, the results of the study were disappointing. Although the ENRICHD intervention did result in lower levels of depression than those achieved in the usual care condition, there were no differences in survival between the two groups over the two years following infarction. These data have led some to claim that there are no benefits to treating depression in MI patients – and they certainly seem to indicate this to be the case. However, the sheer size of the study meant that the investigators had limited control over the interventions received by patients in both arms of the study. This meant that the usual care received by some people in the control condition was, in fact, very similar to that provided by the ENRICHD study. In addition, attendance at the ENRICHD intervention was less than optimal, with most patients attending about eleven sessions – an attendance not that different to many of the control group interventions. Perhaps because of these factors, the differences in levels of depression between the two interventions, although statistically significant, were not that great, and it remains possible that the ENRICHD intervention did not result in a sufficiently large reduction in depression compared with that of the control condition to impact on the health of those who took part in the intervention.

IN THE SPOTLIGHT

Reading the report of the ENRICHD study, which was published in the prestigious *Journal of the American Medical Association*, it is clear that the readers of this journal had one interest. Did treating depression save lives? This is a question that has excited many health psychologists as well as medical doctors – and it is very important. But because it did not save lives, many psychologists consider the ENRICHD study to be a failure. But was it? Yes, from a biomedical stance, the results of the ENRICHD study were disappointing. But what about a more psychological perspective?

Depression is a potentially disabling condition that has significant implications for the quality of life and rehabilitation outcomes of both patients and people involved with them. While psychologists should be involved in the questions of the impact of disease on physiological processes, they should also be careful not to lose sight of other psychological questions and adopting too strong a biomedical stance in the questions they address. Changes in depression are an important outcome in themselves – not just a vehicle to reduce mortality. From this perspective, the ENRICHD intervention proved a costly one that fared moderately better than the care usually provided. As such, it provides a wealth of information about how to identify and treat depression in cardiac patients, with potentially significant benefits to future cardiac patients. We should be careful not to throw out the 'psychological baby' when we throw out the 'medical bath water'.

Disease progression in patients with immune-system-mediated diseases may also be influenced by stress management procedures. One condition in which these issues have been explored is that of HIV/AIDS. Antoni, Cruess, Klimas *et al.* (2002), for example, followed the immunological outcomes in twenty-five HIV-positive men randomly allocated to either a ten-week stress management intervention or a waiting list control condition. Their measures particularly focused on the impact of the intervention on the level of CD4+ cells in participants' blood. Immediately following the intervention, those who took part had higher CD4+ cell counts than those in the control group, despite their being no pre-treatment differences, suggesting that the stress management influenced levels of a key process in HIV disease, one that may slow down the disease progress and place an individual at less risk of other opportunistic infections.

A second set of studies has examined whether stress management procedures can influence the health outcomes of people with cancer. Outcomes following the intervention conducted by Fawzy *et al.* (1993) described earlier in the chapter were impressive. In a series of studies, they reported the percentage of people in a stress management group and a no-treatment control group to show progression of malignant melanoma six months, five–six years and ten years after the intervention. At the first of the long-term follow-up periods, participants were significantly less likely to have died of cancer than those in the control group and were marginally less likely to have had a longer period free of disease. By the ten-year follow-up (Fawzy, Canada and Fawzy 2003), these differential effects remained. By this time, eleven of the thirty-four people in the control group had had recurrences and had died of cancer: three others had had non-fatal recurrences. In the stress management group, nine of thirty-four had died of cancer, and two had survived recurrences. Overall, these differences were not significantly different between the groups. However, after statistically controlling for differences in the severity of the presenting melanoma, more of those who took part in the stress management intervention survived up to ten years after their initial diagnosis than those who were in the control group. Similar gains following stress management training or similar interventions have been found in two large studies of patients with gastrointestinal cancer (Kuchler, Henne-Bruns, Rappat *et al.* 1999) and a mixture of cancers (McCorkle, Strumpf, Nuamah *et al.* 2000), although some smaller studies have reported null findings. However, Boesen, Dalton and Ross (2002) pointed out that the effects of these interventions may have been stronger if patients had been selected for any of the studies as a result of their having some distress to ameliorate rather than simply having a diagnosis of cancer.

Social support

Providing additional social support may impact on health outcomes. One of the earliest studies of this issue was reported by Spiegel, Bloom and Yalom (1981). In a study intended to influence quality of life in cancer patients, they randomly assigned women with breast cancer to either an active treatment programme or a no-treatment control. The active intervention involved weekly support groups that emphasised building strong supportive bonds, expressing emotions, dealing directly with fears of dying, improving relationships within the family and active involvement in decisions concerning treatment. To the surprise of the investigators, women in this group lived an average of eighteen months longer than those in the no-treatment control, despite being well matched for disease status at the beginning of the trial. These findings generated a great deal of excitement in the research and clinical community when published. Unfortunately, an attempted replication of the study met with only modest success. Gellert, Maxwell and Siegel (1984) compared the effectiveness of the programme developed by Spiegel with a standard treatment condition in a matched sample of breast cancer patients. Although their data showed trends towards a survival gain in the intervention group (by an average of eleven months: ninety-six versus eighty-five months), these differences were not statistically significant. Other negative findings have also been reported (e.g. Goodwin, Leszcz, Ennis *et al.* 2001). Accordingly, increasing social support has yet to be convincingly shown to impact on illness outcomes in patients with cancer.

Social support has proved a useful adjunct to other interventions targeted at risk behaviour change. West, Edwards and Hajek (1998), for example, reported on the benefits of a 'buddy system' for individuals attempting to quit smoking. All those involved in the study attended a nurse-led smokers' clinic.

Plate 17.2   Serious injury or disability need not interfere with quality of life, as these wheelchair basketball players illustrate. Players may also gain informal social support from this sort of group activity, which may contribute to their wellbeing.

Source: Glyn Kirk/Action Plus

Smokers in the buddy condition were paired with another smoker trying to give up at the same time to provide mutual support between clinic sessions. The percentage of smokers still abstinent at the end of treatment was significantly higher in the buddy condition than the solo condition: 27 versus 12 percent. A further study by Digiusto and Bird (1995) randomly allocated smokers to either social support or self-control interventions. Their findings emphasised the need to tailor interventions to the specific needs and characteristics of the target population: the social support treatment proved most effective for participants who already had high baseline self-control orientation scores and participants with high self-efficacy scores. Increasing social support has yet to be shown to reduce morbidity, but it still has a role to play in helping people to change their behaviour.

Summary

The chapter considered psychological interventions designed to achieve three interacting goals in patients with serious chronic diseases:

- to reduce distress
- to improve disease management
- to reduce risk of future disease or disease progression.

A number of approaches have been successfully used in each case.
Reductions in distress have been achieved by the use of:

- appropriate information (including information about a condition or coping strategies to minimise distress or improve control over the condition);
- stress management training while waiting for a diagnosis, during treatment and while coping with the emotional stress of living with a long-term illness;
- providing social support – often in the guise of professionally run support groups.

Improvements in the management of illness have been achieved by:

- providing information – particularly information that provides a structure to achieve symptom control rather than simply providing information about a condition or its treatment;
- training in self-management programmes, with emphasis shifting from the provision of general 'one size fits all' programmes to more bespoke programmes specifically developed to suit participants' needs;
- stress management training in conditions in which stress is involved in their aetiology (e.g. irritable bowel syndrome) or may exacerbate symptoms (e.g. angina, diabetes);
- improving social and family support;
- written emotional expression.

Finally, a number of interventions may impact on longer-term health:

- Counselling may be of benefit in cardiac patients, but results of the M-HART study have made people cautious in adopting this model.

- Stress management appears to be of benefit in improving health in a number of conditions, including CHD and HIV/AIDS.

- Treatment of depression in cardiac patients may impact on prognosis, although the ENRICHD study suggests that this approach should be viewed with caution.

- Social support may be of benefit, although the promise of some early studies has not been repeated in later studies.

Overall, there is significant evidence that psychological interventions can be of great value in helping people to come to terms with the emotional consequences of having a serious chronic illness. They may also be of benefit in aiding day-to-day symptoms and even longer-term prognoses in a more limited set of conditions.

Further reading

The entire volume of the *Journal of Consulting and Clinical Psychology* for June 2002 (volume 70, part 3) provides an excellent overview of the types of intervention that may be used with a variety of health conditions.

Berkman, L.F., Blumenthal, J., Burg, M. *et al.* (2003). Effects of treating depression and low perceived social support on clinical events after myocardial infarction: the Enhancing Recovery in Coronary Heart Disease Patients (ENRICHD) randomized trial. *Journal of the American Medical Association*, 289: 3106–16.
An important study, although a disappointing one, certainly from the perspective of the authors.

Esterling, B.A., L'Abate, L., Murray, E.J. and Pennebaker, J. (1999). Empirical foundations for writing in prevention and psychotherapy: mental and physical health outcomes. *Clinical Psychology Review*, 19: 79–96.
A good review of written emotional expression as a means of improving physical and emotional health status.

SuperioCabuslay, E., Ward, M.M. and Lorig, K.R. (1996) Patient education interventions in osteoarthritis and rheumatoid arthritis: a meta-analytic comparison with nonsteroidal antiinflammatory drug treatment. *Arthritis Care and Research*, 9: 292–301.
A review of self-management interventions by one of their originators, Kate Lorig.

PART 4

Futures

CHAPTER 18

Futures

Learning outcomes

By the end of this chapter, and building on what you have learned from the rest of this book, you should have an understanding of:

- the importance of evidence to inform effective clinical and healthcare practice
- some of the key areas where health psychology has provided a strong evidence base, based on summaries regarding:
    - psychosocial predictors of health and risk behaviour
    - psychosocial predictors of disease outcomes
    - psychosocial predictors of the use of healthcare and adherence
- some of the key areas in which health psychology research has added to the evidence base by developing, delivering or evaluating a range of psychosocial interventions:
    - health professional–patient communication and adherence
    - uptake of health screening
    - health behaviour change
    - coping with disease and improving outcomes (including carers)
- areas where health psychology could contribute fruitfully in the future

CHAPTER OUTLINE

In this final chapter, we draw together much of the work described in this book by exploring the question of where health psychology is now and where it is going in the future. To do this, we have subdivided the chapter into two broad sections, which we have called 'Getting evidence into practice' and 'Futures'. The first is concerned with external influences on the profession and discipline of health psychology, that of the health professionals who need to provide 'evidence-based practice', to implement 'clinical guidelines' and to evaluate their successes and failures. These expectations open the door for health psychologists to provide strong, theoretically derived evidence to practitioners and brings with it many issues relating to how best to get such research findings into practice. We provide examples of areas of relative success in terms of providing an evidence base upon which effective interventions have been built, and we focus in particular on health behaviour change and coping with chronic disease. Given that this is the final chapter, we also introduce some critical evaluation of our successes and point to some limitations that require addressing in the future if health psychologists are to better inform practice.

The second, shorter, section describes the status of health psychology as a discipline and as a profession and argues that, in order to move forward, there is a need for health psychologists to engage more politically and to 'sell' themselves and their 'goods' more effectively to policy makers and health practitioners. It is only by doing so that we will be able to maximise the impact of the health psychology evidence base on actual healthcare practice to the benefit of patients, families, health professionals and, ultimately, society!

This chapter should therefore be of benefit to students who are considering a future career in this domain, working perhaps in a clinical setting, as well as those who are studying it as an academic subject and wish to learn about the subject's past successes and future potential.

Getting evidence into practice

Clinical effectiveness depends upon the health service environment and its internal organisation and upon issues of clinical governance or policy, which require all health organisations to work towards quality improvements in healthcare delivery. In most countries, clinical guidelines are published that detail standards of care and treatment for specific conditions (e.g. British Thoracic Society, 1997), and in the United Kingdom the National Institute for Clinical Excellence (NICE) is responsible for producing guidelines and recommendations to the National Health Service as to how best to pursue a policy of improved care. For example, guidelines have been produced in relation to chronic lung disease, or chronic obstructive pulmonary disease as it is known (National Collaborating Centre for Chronic Conditions 2004). MacNee (2004), in reviewing the new guidelines for this group of lung diseases, concluded that they are 'truly evidence based, wide ranging, and deal with diagnosis, assessment of severity, and treatment' (p. 361). The evidence that such guidelines draw upon will include an exhaustive array of results from drug trials or epidemiological surveys (of symptom or disease prevalence for example), but they may not consider individual or social factors that may interfere with a patient's uptake of, or adherence to, an evidence-based treatment programme. It is important therefore for health psychologists to disseminate their findings widely, otherwise opinions such as that of Weller in an editorial comment in the *European Journal of Cancer* (2004: 314) will persist: 'there is a paucity of behavioural and social science research to underpin approaches to more effective, behaviourally-focussed preventive strategies for cancer, and improved psychosocial support for cancer patients. Patients with unmet needs typically show higher psychological and symptom distress'. Health psychology findings can provide some answers to fill these gaps.

Evidence of the psychosocial influences on uptake and response to screening, treatment or other interventions, or evidence of the effectiveness of non-pharmacological, psychosocial interventions on a range of clinical and non-clinical/psychosocial outcomes, needs to be widely available and accessible so as to build on the available biomedical knowledge. One useful resource in this instance is that of the Cochrane Library, which provides a regularly updated, electronically available database of results of all randomised controlled trials of healthcare interventions. However, as the eminent, now deceased, health psychologist Richard Lazarus (2000: 667) noted: 'The lack of collaboration and communication between researcher and clinician . . . is a familiar and painful topic for most psychologists'. He went on to say that 'It is disheartening that so few researchers accept the responsibility of making the relevance of their research clear to the practitioner, and so few clinicians pay attention to such research even when it has implications for clinical practice'. Although Lazarus was referring primarily to the situation in the USA, his comments also reflect the situation in Europe.

Even when a fully informed evidence base and written guidelines on best practice exist, there is no guarantee that they will actually be implemented by the health professions concerned (e.g. Lomas 1991). While there is some evidence that very specific recommendations, such as providing reminders to patients to attend screening appointments, have been successfully adopted (e.g. Mandelblatt and Kanesky 1995; Snell and Buck 1996), many barriers to implementing clinical guidelines have been identified. For example, the NHS Centre for Reviews and Dissemination report, *Effective Health Care: Getting Evidence into Practice* (1999) highlights the following:

■ weaknesses in communicating the evidence base to practitioners;

■ conflicting sources of information and opinion being available to practitioners (such as patient preferences, which can contradict global recommendations);

■ a tendency to individually tailor responses and make decisions that may not always adhere to guidelines;

■ difficulties in getting the right people to work together to implement change (for example to involve a health promotion advisor in a general practice making changes aimed at improving smoking cessation);

■ resistance to change, which is amplified by health professionals' stress levels.

Given these broad-ranging weaknesses in the system, it is not surprising that efforts are being made to try to address this situation.

Table 18.1 Barriers to change among health professionals

- *Environmental/organisational issues*: time, staffing and support, funding and costs, occupational stress
- *Transferability*: research tools are not necessarily feasible clinical tools
- *Information transfer*: deficient communication of information through health service hierarchy
- *Information content*: may not be seen as credible or applicable to one's patient/patient group
- *Personal characteristics of the professional*: age, gender, culture and ethnic values or norms
- *Personal attitudes and beliefs regarding*:
  - *the target behaviour* (their own and/or the patients')
  - *the treatment* (for example, attitudes towards HRT (hormone replacement therapy), chemotherapy, child immunisation, abortion)
  - towards *the condition* (e.g. obesity, drug use, heart disease, AIDS, chronic pain, chronic fatigue syndrome)

Implementing clinical guidelines

'Unless research-based evidence and guidance is incorporated into practice, efforts to improve the quality of care will be wasted. Implementing evidence may require health professionals to change long-held patterns of behaviour' (NHS Centre for Reviews and Dissemination 1999: 1). Table 18.1 identifies some of the specific barriers there may be to change.

However, simply providing research information alone has been shown to be insufficient to alter an individual practitioner's health practice. Having the information incorporated into circulated guidelines does not necessarily mean that it will be incorporated into a changed practice. For example, Oxman, Davis, Haynes *et al.* (1995) reviewed 102 studies of interventions to improve healthcare delivery. Examples of the studies reviewed included one that provided training to increase the offering and thus potential uptake of breast cancer screening services (Snell and Buck, 1996); and another that trained doctors in order to increase their skills in offering smoking cessation advice (Lancaster, Silagy, Fowler and Spiers 1999). Oxman and colleagues found that those interventions where information on what to do had been distributed passively to health professionals resulted in little evidence of behaviour change (i.e. the health professionals' behaviour did not suggest successful implementation of the guidelines). Even more complex interventions had only moderate effects on behaviour, for example training that provided practice information/education as well as feedback on practice. Furthermore, these multifaceted interventions tend to cost more, which is a further barrier to change, and one that needs to be overcome by politicians and funders.

The need for theory-driven practice

This textbook has described a wide body of contemporary evidence as to the importance of psychological theory and psychosocial factors in explaining health and illness behaviour and outcomes. Health psychology (and indeed social psychology, which has provided the origins for many health psychology theories) has offered health and social care practitioners a wealth of theoretically derived scientific evidence on which they can draw when generating their practice.

Theory and health behaviour change

Consider, for example, the evidence as to the important role played by the range of social cognitions, defined and described by psychological models, such as the theory of planned behaviour. A significant body of evidence points to the role of individual cognitions in influencing health behaviour such as treatment adherence, the uptake of screening or immunisation, or smoking cessation described in Chapter 5. For example, when attempting to treat health problems resulting from a health-risk behaviour such as smoking, practitioners could examine findings from studies based on learning theory, socio-cognitive theory, or those that have more specifically examined self-efficacy.

Evidence has been amassed that does not simply describe associations between social factors, health beliefs and health behaviours but has also proved that behaviour can be *predicted* from many of these factors, either individually or in combination. Prediction is the first step towards intervention. Knowing what factors influence behaviour can provide the foundations for individually targeted interventions to change health behaviour (Chapters 6, 13, 17) and for societal-level interventions (Chapter 7).

The teaching of such models and their components to health professionals could provide them with a framework of factors to explore with their

Plate 18.1　Psychologists have a lot to offer in terms of healthy eating programmes for young children.

Source: University of Wales Bangor

patients; for example, they can establish the beliefs about smoking that maintain smoking behaviour (such as high social norms and low self-efficacy beliefs) in order to identify the best approaches to cessation. But methods of eliciting such beliefs need to be practical. For example, implementing evidence drawn from research into clinical practice would require health professionals to administer any measures, or any intervention, in exactly the same format and manner as was used in the research study – and, as we point out in a later section, this is not always possible in the clinical setting.

■ Theory and perceiving and responding to symptoms and illness

Consider Leventhal's self-regulation theory and how it describes how symptoms are interpreted and responded to (Chapter 9) or theories of stress and coping such as that developed by Lazarus, which have highlighted the crucial role played by cognitive appraisal and emotions in an individual's interaction with their potentially stressful environment (Chapter 11). Studies working within these theoretical frameworks have provided longitudinal prospective evidence of, for example, relationships between symptom or event appraisals, illness representations, positive and negative emotions, coping responses, and a wide range of illness outcomes for both patients and their family carers (as described in Chapters 14 and 15).

Coping research has shown that it is almost impossible to state categorically what makes a 'good' coping response and what makes a 'bad' one, as coping has consistently been shown to be dynamic, individual and flexible, but there is relatively strong evidence to state that avoidance coping, when used in the long term, tends to be maladaptive. Furthermore, as Lazarus noted in his influential book *Stress and Emotion: A New Synthesis* (1999), both those strategies described as problem-focused and those described as emotion-focused can work well and interact together to influence health outcomes (see Chapter 12). Coping skills training programmes and interventions work on the premise that coping mitigates the negative impact of stressful events, including illness events, on adaptive outcomes, such as enhanced quality of life, physical and social functioning, and reduced distress. We have reviewed evidence of such interventions in Chapter 17, and some further examples are provided in a later section.

Evidence as to the effectiveness of learning theory and specifically operant conditioning techniques also exists in the realm of recovery from illness or injury, predominantly from studies conducted with pain patients (see Chapter 16). For example, Fordyce (1982) showed that having staff regulate analgesia (painkiller) administration to fixed timings such as every four hours, rather than giving it on demand in response to pain behaviour, (such as patient groaning, staying in bed), and speaking to the patients independently of when they were complaining of distress or pain, successfully reduced counterproductive pain behaviour. More recent work on the importance of perceived control has shown that patient-controlled analgesia (PCA, where patients can activate the analgesia drip themselves, although the total amount delivered in one go, and over a fixed period of time, e.g. 24 hours, is carefully set up and controlled) can help to reduce patient distress and pain symptoms. PCA has been adopted in many hospital settings.

Although a lot of the research in health psychology has focused on what 'not' to do and what not to 'think' in order to enhance health or improve illness outcomes, research in the developing positive psychology tradition (e.g. Folkman and Moskowitz 2000; Seligman and Csikszentmihalyi 2000) has highlighted the role of positive emotions and thoughts in stress, coping and health research. It is not simply that positive emotions, such as hope or optimism, irrevocably lead to positive health outcomes, because unfounded hope or optimism can be detrimental when one's coping efforts do not meet with success, and in some situations hope may raise anxiety. However, harnessing more positive emotions such as hope or optimism, can be beneficial (see, for example, Chapter 12).

■ Theory and health professional practice

Health professional practice can be constrained at times by the biomedical standpoint. Wade and Halligan (2004) note that biomedical models of illness over-focus on the disease pathology rather than on understanding it, and that quite often the person's role in their own illness is disregarded – as long as they are cooperative! If patients and health professionals have different 'models' of illness (see Chapter 1), it is not particularly surprising that doctor–patient communication sometimes stumbles, and that patient adherence is, to many treatments, lower than is recommended (see Chapter 10).

Psychological theories in this domain would suggest that rather than health professionals examining solely the nature, style and content of material they present to patients in an attempt to gain 'control' or encourage self-management of that patient's illness, they also consider the models of illness or health beliefs of the patient as well as addressing their own attitudes and beliefs. Health professional beliefs about illness, attitudes towards a treatment or towards a patient and their expectancies of patients may act as barriers towards change. For example, the theory of planned behaviour and the health action process approach highlight the crucial role of self-efficacy beliefs in translating intention (to behave in a certain way) into action. Hayes and Morrison (under review) found that the self-efficacy beliefs of junior doctors, in relation to breaking bad news about dying to patients and families, was low, and that this, combined with negative attitudes towards death and dying, influenced the health professional's own attitudes towards working with dying patients. Social cognition theory (cf. Bandura 1986) highlights the need for individuals to believe that they have the skills required to engage in

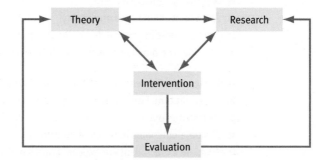

Figure 18.1   From theory to practice and back again.

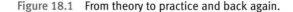

the relevant behaviour (i.e. self-efficacy; see Chapter 5). There is, for example, limited likelihood that training in doctor–patient communication or in 'breaking bad news effectively' (e.g. Faulkner *et al.* 1995; Faulkner 1998; Maguire and Faulkner, 1988; Parle, Maguire and Heaven 1997) will lead to improvements in communication behaviour if a health professional simply does not believe that they are able to 'empathise' with patients or even talk about death (Hayes and Morrison – under review).

Psychological research can also aid in the development of psychometrically robust assessment tools of, for example, patient needs, quality of life, satisfaction with care and emotional distress, which can be used in the clinical setting as a means of better assessing patient outcomes. However, as has been noted elsewhere in this book, a well-validated and commonly employed research tool is not necessarily a good practical clinical tool.

Evidence that has implications for practice

Table 18.2 presents the ideal framework for conducting interventional research and following it through to application, although in presenting this list we are not claiming that all studies presented in this textbook or in this chapter have progressed through all of these stages! A wealth of studies have been presented in this book, but in this concluding chapter we want to highlight a few areas where health psychology research has developed potential for evidence-based intervention and practice. Opinions may vary, but we have chosen to include healthcare communication and adherence to medication, uptake of health screening, health behaviour change, coping and adjustment to chronic disease (including the needs of carers).

■ Communication and adherence

Adherence is a difficult behaviour to change, and although adhering in the past has commonly emerged as the best predictor of current adherence (Sherbourne, Hays, Ordway *et al.* 1992), there is evidence that communications that are patient-friendly and that consider the belief structures of patients can improve adherence further. In an informed review of factors

Table 18.2   From theory to intervention

- Identify the 'problem'.
- Analyse available data and theory.
- Develop aims of intervention and outcomes sought.
- Consider the processes by which the intervention may act and ensure these are assessed.
- Design the intervention with built-in evaluative components.
- Implement the intervention – with robust control groups.
- Assess outcomes.
- Evaluate outcomes in terms of objectives.
- Evaluate expected and unexpected outcomes in terms of costs, implications, drop-out.
- Disseminate to those for whom the findings have implications, e.g. theoreticians, practitioners.

important to adherence among children, diMatteo (2004) highlights the following:

- the provision of both written and verbal information about the treatment regime to child and parents and evidence that it has been understood;
- the building of trust between health professional, child patient and parent through supportive and sensitive interactions and discussion of perspectives on treatment needs and goals;
- the consideration of specific beliefs and attitudes about treatment needs and goals, including areas of discrepancy between child and parent, and in particular identifying child health beliefs;
- identification and discussion of norms and expectations regarding adherence behaviour that the child is exposed to: for example, parental adherence behaviour and treatment anxieties, cultural and social norms of treatment adherence;
- gaining and encouraging family commitment to treatment and within-family communication if problems with treatment arise by providing social support to the child and family, possibly via illness-specific support groups;
- working together to overcome barriers and increase belief in ability to adhere/support the child in adhering (self-efficacy);
- tailoring wherever possible the treatment regime to the lifestyles of the family unit.

These are ideal standards for improving adherence, not just among child populations but in all age groups, as very few individuals face illness in isolation; thus involving partners or other family members is crucial. There is a consistent body of evidence showing that alongside patient involvement in healthcare decision making (Department of Health 2001), healthcare professional communication with patients is central to achieving adherence (or compliance) to healthcare recommendations regarding behaviour change or to following treatment or medication regimes (e.g. Ley 1999). Kok and Schaalma (1998) distinguish between blindly following healthcare recommendations (adherence or compliance) and communications and information presentation that empowers a patient to make good decisions about their disease self-management. Leaflets and other written materials are available on many health topics, written with the well-intentioned purpose of increasing knowledge and understanding about a condition or procedure, and in some cases it also aims to increase adherence (for example, leaflets about the need to complete a course of antibiotics even when symptoms disappear). However, the readability of some such material is poor, with overuse of jargon and technical terms being common, hence its usefulness has been questioned (e.g. Smith, Gooding, Brown *et al.* 1998). Written information is not always an ideal substitute for face-to-face verbal discussion. For example, Michie, Miles and Weinman (2003), in a review of health communications research, report that six out of eight studies in which doctor–patient consultations elicited and responded to patient views and perspectives about their illness and treatment found a positive association with treatment adherence, although four of these studies were limited by being cross-sectional. In five out of seven studies where consultations additionally took the form of empowering patients to take some control or an active part in the consultation, positive associations with adherence were reported, although all were cross-sectional.

Health psychology has contributed much to our understanding of lay perceptions of health, illness and treatment and the cognitions that may facilitate or impede health behaviour, such as adherence (see Chapters 5–7, 9–10). Knowledge of this type can be easily integrated into the questions asked by health professionals, such as:

- 'What, if any, barriers do you perceive in your life that might interfere with you taking this medication?' (perceived barriers, cf. health belief model).

- 'Do other people around you want you to stop smoking?' (subjective norms, cf. theory of planned behaviour).

- 'To what extent do you believe you are capable of doing what is required of you in order to change this behaviour (self-efficacy, cf. HAPA).

- Discussions around 'how do you think about your illness/treatment?' based on Leventhal's self-regulation theory and illness perceptions.

- Or even the use of formal brief assessments of illness perceptions and beliefs about medication.

As Sutton (2002) notes, interventions to change existing belief structures into ones more likely to potentiate behaviour change need to address both an individual's *beliefs about the behaviour* in question (e.g. from 'I'm not ill enough to keep taking these pills' to 'I need to keep taking these pills or my symptoms will return') and their *normative beliefs* (e.g. from 'my family won't mind if I don't take the pills' to 'my family would be happier if I were symptom-free because I took the pills'). The cognitive changes aimed for might include:

- increasing the positive evaluation of likely positive outcomes of adherence (e.g. improved health is important);

- decreasing the value placed on unlikely positive outcomes of adherence (e.g. improved mood is not crucial);

- increasing the positive value placed on likely negative outcomes of adherence (e.g. the side-effects won't last for ever);

- increasing the negative value placed on negative outcomes considered unlikely (e.g. if symptoms get worse on medication, I need to see a doctor).

Normative beliefs and the motivation to comply with those from whom the norms of behaviour are drawn need to be positive, and if not (for example, friends or family promote the non-use of medicines) then the individual has to learn not to be motivated to comply with these influences. Unfortunately, few models in health or social psychology go on to describe *how* an intervention should go about trying to change such beliefs. This has tended to be the domain of clinical psychologists, who have formulated various forms of cognitive–behavioural or behavioural intervention and applied them to behaviour change.

One exception is the Dutch study by Theunissen and colleagues (e.g. Theunissen, de Ridder, Bensing and Rutten 2003) which, drawing from Leventhal's self-regulation theory, suggests that conversations between GP trainees and their patients with hypertension could beneficially be designed to include either a discussion of the patients' perceptions of their illness and treatment or a discussion of their action plans and self-efficacy regarding adherence. In an experimental study comparing standard care consultation with a consultation focused on illness and treatment perceptions, or one addressing action plans regarding adherence to hypertension medication, both types of experimental intervention influenced patient perceptions, but not consistently in the anticipated direction. For example, in the group discussing illness perceptions, while they became less likely to perceive their illness as a mystery and had fewer concerns about the harmful side-effects of medication, they also became less confident in their ability to take the medicine as prescribed. In the group describing action plans regarding adherence, concerns about the harmful effects of medication increased, but confidence in communicating these concerns to their physicians decreased. The authors conclude that a combined intervention, with conversations between doctors and their patients addressing both their illness perceptions and their action plans regarding adherence, would be preferable. Neither intervention method changed actual adherence behaviour, however, possibly because the sample contained individuals already high in adherence, with little room for improvement. Such an intervention package needs further tailoring before it would be recommended as standard practice; however, this study is promising in that it brings to bear another theoretical framework on which health practitioners could potentially base their communications with patients.

■ Screening uptake and impact

Health psychological research has explored both structural and personal variables influential in the initial uptake of screening programmes such as those offering cancer screening. This research has shown that a range of factors, including the method and source of the screening invitation, personal health beliefs and risk perceptions, and demographic variables such as age and socio-economic status, can be influential and as such are worthy targets for health education and promotion (see Chapters 5 and 6). More recently, the identification of individualised implementation intentions (II) (the when, where and how a behaviour will be performed) has shown how the simple requirement of forming an II can increase the likelihood of screening behaviour taking place. For example, Orbell and Sheeran (2002) described three longitudinal studies aimed at increasing the practice of breast self-examination, cervical screening uptake and vitamin C supplement use where the formation of an II was manipulated in a questionnaire otherwise based on the theory of planned behaviour components (see Chapter 5). They report significant effects of the II manipulation in the intervention group, with each of the three types of behaviour increasing relative to the control groups. Intentions did not differ between the groups at baseline; nor did changes in intention differ over time between follow-up assessments, suggesting that motivation to perform the behaviour in question was similar and therefore the study concluded that it is the formation of the II that made a crucial difference as to whether the behaviour was carried out or not. These studies are important in that the formation of an II is such a simple task, yet it can have significant effects on translating healthy intentions into health actions. It is not a big step for health practitioners to ask patients to form an II during a consultation.

Apart from focusing on IIs, other studies have examined beliefs associated with screening behaviour. For example, following a study identifying the determinants of interest in bowel cancer screening, Williamson and Wardle (2002) developed a psycho-educational intervention based primarily on the health belief model and components of the TPB, targeted at individuals aged between 55 and 64 with the aim of increasing uptake of bowel cancer screening using flexible sigmoidoscopy (FS). This procedure requires a sigmoidoscope to be inserted into the bowel to check for the presence of pre-malignant polyps, or if the disease is present at a later stage, cancerous growths; if polyps are present they can often be removed at the same time, making this an intrusive yet effective technique for both the detection and treatment of this condition. The intervention booklet addressed potentially modifiable determinants of screening identified in their earlier study and aimed to increase positive beliefs about FS at the same time as reducing perceived barriers to taking the screening test (e.g. seeing the test as embarrassing, uncomfortable, time-consuming, worrying or tempting fate) and increasing awareness of the potential benefits of screening. Solutions to how to cope and use social support during the decision-making process regarding screening uptake were also modelled in the booklet using humour and cartoon conversations between a hypothetical couple and relevant others, such as the GP. The sample consisted of 2,966 individuals who had expressed 'probable interest' in FS screening, with 1,453 randomly allocated to receiving the booklet (the remaining 1,513 acted as a control group, receiving only standard care). Only 53.7 percent of those individuals returned a questionnaire covering demographic information, health, perceived bowel cancer risk, and screening beliefs and intention, which had been despatched with the booklet with instructions to complete it after reading the booklet (NB: no control over whether this instruction was followed or not). Preliminary results of this trial found that the 'booklet' group showed an increased intention to attend FS screening, along with more positive screening attitudes and beliefs. It is to be hoped that when this group publishes its follow-up findings, the booklet intervention effects persist in terms of intention turning into actual screening uptake behaviour.

In spite of many studies published in the psychological literature, an Expert Group (2004) reviewing the evidence base in order to provide a strategy for development of behavioural and social science research in cancer, concluded that: 'Little is known of the behavioural and social factors which lead to a limited uptake of such [screening] programmes' (p. 320). This group points to many as yet unexplored questions regarding non-uptake, such as the extent to which non-participation reflects informed choice on the part of an individual as opposed to the presence of social or physical barriers to attendance. The group also comments on a lack of systematic evidence related to the response to screening: 'There is a clear need for the systematic study of: the psychological consequences associated with the screening process . . . taking account of the ways in which these are modulated by social, cultural and educational factors' (p. 322). So, although health psychology research has provided some evidence as to the role of socio-cognitive and emotional influences on screening uptake and response, the 'audience' for these findings perhaps needs to be widened.

However, it is important to note that research has not provided clear and consistent answers to questions such as increasing screening uptake. In spite of several individual studies reporting significant effects of having patients form implementation intentions, or action plans, such as that of Orbell and Sheeran (2002) referred to at the start of this section, or the majority of studies reviewed in a meta-analysis by Sheeran (2002), several more recent studies have produced findings that question their utility. For example, Michie, Dormandy and Marteau (2004) carried out an experimental study of an intervention aimed at increasing antenatal screening uptake among women who had expressed the intention to do so. Eighty-eight pregnant women were allocated to either standard care or a group asked to write down an action plan for attending or making the screening appointment. No difference in subsequent attendance was found. In the intervention group itself, however, only 63 percent actually made an action plan, and these women *were* more likely to attend screening (84 percent of them attended) than the women in this group who had not done so (47 percent attended). The authors conclude that evidence of the effectiveness of making action plans among clinical populations is limited. Much previous evidence as to the efficacy of making action plans had been drawn from studies of non-clinical populations. Although the sample size was quite small, this study makes a very important point: if research findings are to be relevant to clinical practice, the research findings need to be obtained from clinical populations.

■ Health promotion and health behaviour change

Health psychology has contributed greatly to the understanding of the wide array of factors that play a role in the initiation, maintenance and cessation of behaviour damaging to health or of behaviour beneficial to health. Sociocognitive and emotional factors pertinent to the development of health promotion activities at both the individual and societal level in the areas of smoking cessation, safe sex practices and health screening have been heavily studied. If interventions based on identified predictors are successful, this should become evident through a downturn over time in the incidence and prevalence of risk behaviour or in the diseases associated with it. We have yet to reach this stage and may in fact never do so. If this 'ideal' downturn in the prevalence or incidence of health-damaging behaviour occurred, it would not imply that health psychology-led interventions would then become redundant; for example, even if smoking initiation in the young was to stabilise at a minimal level, greater attention could then turn to the promotion of healthy functioning in the elderly (given our ageing society), perhaps through the promotion of dietary change or exercise regimes. Where health psychology has perhaps traditionally focused on the prevention of disease associated with high risk of mortality, such as heart disease, population trends will increasingly require that attention be turned to chronic diseases and their associated morbidity in terms of disability, impaired social functioning or productivity. The costs of chronic disease to society in terms of health and social care are enormous, and these costs will grow as our elderly population grows.

In the meantime, however, sufficient unhealthy behaviour remains in society for health psychology research and practice to be kept busy! While many theories of health behaviour change fail to outline how health beliefs, attitudes or expectations can be changed, there are one or two clear exceptions:

in relation to the concept of self-efficacy, and in relation to stage models and processes of change (such as the trans-theoretical model described in Chapter 5). We shall briefly address both of these in turn.

Bandura (1997) has provided some guidance, specifying how 'guided mastery' involving practice and feedback of the behaviour required can enhance individual self-efficacy beliefs. One example of an intervention to enhance self-efficacy carried out by Armitage and Connor (2002) in an attempt to change fat intake among hospital workers, succeeded in a modest 1 percent reduction in fat intake among those with high (but not low) fat intake. However, this study failed to build into its manualised (leaflet) intervention any elements of individually tailored feedback or guidance over time as the behaviour change was adopted; had it done so, its effects may have been greater (although the intervention would have been more costly). Nonetheless a 1 percent reduction in fat intake is worthwhile if one considers the number of high-fat consumers whose health would benefit from even this small reduction. This highlights the importance of not losing sight of the 'clinical significance' of findings that may appear to be of weak statistical significance.

The transtheoretical model (TTM), commonly known as the stages of change model, was developed by Prochaska and di Clemente in 1982. Since then there has been a mass of research that has supported the existence of a staged process of change, with people first being unaware or not concerned about their behaviour or the need for change (pre-contemplators). Then for some reason, perhaps a health scare or media campaign, they begin to consider the need for change (contemplators); some then make preparations to change, and some then take action. Action, such as a dietary change or smoking cessation, may or may not be maintained depending on individual and social factors. Interventions aimed at promoting healthy behaviour that adopted this model led to reports of many successes (e.g. review by Ashworth 1997), although as noted in Chapter 6, there were also some failures. Very recently, the stages of change model has come under scrutiny in terms of stage-based activity interventions (Adams and White 2005). These authors considered the negative evidence presented in two review papers and attempted to come up with some explanations as to why long-term changes were not being reported. Their conclusions, primarily that exercise is a more complex form of behaviour than is often acknowledged in interventions, that the methods for determining the stage at which a person is at are flawed, and that processes may exist other than those defined in the TTM (i.e. decisional balance, self-efficacy and processes of change) that determine movement between stages (e.g. action plans, goals), have themselves come under scrutiny in a series of five commentaries (see Further reading). It is debates such as these that will move health psychology theory, research and practice onwards.

■ Coping with, and adjustment to, chronic disease

We have shown throughout this textbook, but most particularly in the latter half (Chapter 9 onwards) that individual differences in thoughts, feelings and behaviour make a significant difference to how individuals respond to illness, from first sensing a bodily change and perceiving it as a symptom through to facing terminal illness. Whether research has operated under the stress-coping theory of Richard Lazarus, which highlights appraisals, or self-regulation theories such as Leventhal's, which highlights illness perceptions, coping has been viewed as central. Scores of studies have pointed to associations between individual cognitions or emotions, coping and disease outcomes, yet Coyne and Racioppo (2000: 656), in an article questioning whether the gap between coping research and intervention research will ever be closed, comment that 'a cursory examination of the bulk of the results of descriptive coping research reveals that these results have little or no direct relevance to the specifics of intervention'.

However, this perhaps overly negative view can be seen in the fact that, in spite of a seemingly large evidence base, interventions such as those described in Chapter 17 do not regularly include coping skills training or coping effectiveness training components. De Ridder and Schreurs (2001) point to three reasons why there is a seeming lack of coping-based interventions:

1. The evidence base relies heavily on academically oriented surveys that may not easily be translated into practice (Coyne points out that, for example, coping checklists do not often address why people cope in the way they do, i.e. coping goals, which may be better targets of intervention).

2. Many studies address healthy rather than clinical populations and therefore findings are often not generalisable.

3. Many therapists are behavioural in orientation, rather than cognitive, and given that health psychology models of coping are heavily cognitive in focus, therapists may feel insufficiently skilled to base their interventions on cognitive components.

However, coping-based interventions do exist that have been shown to be effective in increasing adherence, reducing chronic pain, reducing distress associated with undergoing medical procedures and improving general adjustment to illness (see Chapter 17).

Many other interventions indirectly address coping by focusing on the cognitions and/or the emotions that help to shape the coping response. Clear examples of such interventions can be seen in those that target patient perceptions of control. This implementation of research evidence in practice is perhaps best seen in the work of Kate Lorig and her manualised approach to the self-management of arthritis (e.g. Lorig and Holman 1989; Lorig, Sobel *et al.* 1999). Based on research evidence drawn from many years of study in arthritic populations, patient cognitions of (pain) control and self-efficacy were highlighted as important in the attainment of positive illness outcomes, such as reduced pain or fatigue and increased self-management behaviour such as exercise. The resulting intervention – the Arthritis Self-Management Programme (ASMP) – is run in groups that are led by either health professionals or lay tutors who themselves have chronic conditions. The groups are accompanied by a self-management manual, which requires individual patients to read information about their condition and symptoms and how to manage them (e.g. pain management, avoiding triggers), and which sets tasks such as the making of an exercise plan. This intervention has recently been adopted in various healthcare trusts in the UK, following positive results of a randomised controlled trial of the ASMP (Barlow, Turner and Wright 2000; Barlow, Wright, Sheasby *et al.* 2002). While this research has been conducted in a particular population (arthritis pain), the hope is that a 'core' intervention can be developed to be delivered to mixed patient groups. In other words, what started as an intervention for a specific group of patients experiencing condition-specific problems can become a generic intervention appropriate for use in, and acceptable to, many patient populations. Obviously, such a generic approach would need to acknowledge many factors, including the influence of demographic factors such as age. For example, does a 30-year-old cancer patient have the same illness experience and consequences as an 80-year-old? And are their needs the same in terms of what would reduce their distress?

In the area of illness perceptions, coping responses and illness outcomes, a large body of evidence has been built up over recent years (e.g. Scharloo *et al.* 1998; and see Chapter 9), but researchers are only beginning to draw from these findings in developing interventions. One example is that of Petrie, Cameron, Ellis, Buick and Weinman (2002), where an intervention based on Leventhal's self-regulation theory and the development of illness perceptions was conducted among a sample of 65 heart attack patients randomly assigned to either receive the intervention or standard care (control participants). The findings of this study were positive; for example, those receiving the illness-perception based intervention had:

- more positive perceptions of the consequences of their heart attack;
- greater beliefs in control over symptoms;
- greater preparedness to leave hospital;
- returned to work quicker;
- a lower rate of angina symptoms than controls.

However, it is necessary to avoid overdrawing conclusions from this small trial, because in any area of research there is a need for initial findings to be replicated in a larger trial. Furthermore, it is hard to conclude which aspect(s) of the intervention were most effective given that the intervention contained components that did not solely address the changing of illness representations. For example, the intervention also contained elements of social support and encouraged the making of action plans. Additionally, the intervention was not compared with the effects of any alternative intervention. However, Petrie *et al.*'s intervention is a brief hospital-based intervention, and therefore there is perhaps no obvious alternative with which to compare it. While the findings of this study are nonetheless encouraging, the 'evidence base' on which to develop more interventions in this or in other conditions based only on targeting illness representations is as yet limited.

As a final criticism of this approach, the illness representation model is very cognitive in emphasis, and although there are signs that the emotional representation component is being developed (see Chapter 9), contextual factors important to the experience of health, illness and healthcare also need to be addressed if a fuller picture of influences on health outcomes is to be obtained.

Carers' needs

McPherson, McNaughton and Pentland (2000) note that it is not just in relation to patient care and patient outcomes that guidance is needed for practitioners in order for them to implement best care, but also in relation to carers. They describe a study of carers of those with traumatic brain injury, where information needs were high following discharge of the 'patient' into their care. Information needs were independent of the severity of brain injury or the level of functional impairment and suggest that guidance for practitioners is required in order that they are able to provide the range of information that carers require. In a similar vein, Zinovieff, Morrison, Coles *et al.* (2005) have conducted a survey of cancer patient and carer needs and have found that needs range from a general need among both patients and carers for information about the illness and associated treatments to specific needs such as having someone to talk to about sexual concerns, or about sources of financial help to make home modifications.

We described in Chapter 15 how illness can impact on family members in very similar ways to how it impacts on those with the illness. Carer strain, distress, burden and reduced quality of life are detrimental not only to the carer but also to the person they are caring for. Increasingly, interventions are acknowledging that carer wellbeing is important. Visser-Meily, van Heugten, Post *et al.* (2005), following a review of the effectiveness of interventions directed at stroke carers, concluded that of the four types of intervention identified – specialist service provision such as family support workers, (psycho)education, counselling and peer support – counselling-based interventions that examined problem-solving or coping strategies and goal setting appeared to be the most effective. They also note that many of the twenty-two studies identified and reviewed had the patient's outcome as their primary goal and that the problems experienced by carers and the needs such problems elicited were insufficiently assessed and addressed. This is an area of research and intervention that clearly needs further investment.

Individual or group approaches to intervention

Putting some of these theory-led research findings into practice presents a challenge for health professionals as there is no definitive answer to many psychological questions. For example, health professionals cannot simply attempt to transform emotion-focused copers into problem-focused copers or pessimistic thinkers into optimists as a means of improving adherence or adjustment to illness. Instead, health professionals need to work at an individual level to explore the event appraisals, expectations and functions of coping for that individual at that point in time, and further they need to identify the beliefs and emotions that underlie the appraisals and coping responses made. Any intervention therefore becomes multifaceted, as illustrated in the many examples of effective interventions described in Chapters 6, 7, 13 and 17. Clinical guidelines generally take the 'group' scenario, whereas psychologists tend to emphasise the need to address the individual and their unique set of characteristics and circumstances. However, such an individual approach can be costly in terms of time, effort and the mix of services that may be identified as required.

Futures

Over the past twenty-five or so years, health psychology has grown rapidly across many academic centres in Europe (including in the UK), in the USA and in Australasia, and the subject is now taught at undergraduate level to most psychology undergraduates. Increasingly, health psychology has become a core subject on the curricula of health professional students; for example, one of the authors (Morrison) taught health psychology in the early to mid 1990s to future nurses, dieticians, occupational and physiotherapists, speech and language therapists, podiatrists (formerly known as chiropodists), and medical students. While for many of the allied professions (primarily the therapists), employing a biopsychosocial approach to health and illness was not totally alien, health psychology teaching to biomedically oriented medical students was, at times, something of a challenge! Over the last ten years, however, things have changed and a more holistic approach to health, illness and healthcare has been acknowledged as offering many new and useful insights into patient processes and outcomes.

As health psychology has grown in popularity among undergraduates who wish to pursue an applied profession but prefer 'physical health' issues to the more mental health orientation of clinical psychologists, a need has developed for postgraduate-level training courses. Different countries have their own programmes of training, and you are referred to the companion website for fuller details of some of these opportunities. Currently, many health psychologists are also clinically qualified, having done so before health psychology emerged as a discipline. Some still choose to follow the clinical psychology route because it is perceived as having a more clearly defined career structure and better pay than academically based research or teaching, and a clinical psychologist can, upon qualification, choose to specialise in a 'health psychology' topic area anyway. However, things are changing, and it is important for aspiring health psychologists to keep checking the relevant professional body for their country to be aware of professionalisation developments (for example, the British Psychological Society accredits masters-level courses in order for postgraduates to move towards accreditation as a chartered health psychologist – see companion website). However, at the time of writing, many jobs are advertised that recognise the clinical background of individuals interested in health psychology and use the term 'clinical health psychologist' to describe a clinically qualified individual who has also studied the theories and methods of health psychology and how to apply them to the clinical setting.

Across Europe, there are particular centres of excellence in both research and teaching at both undergraduate and postgraduate level in the UK, Netherlands, Germany, Spain, France, Sweden and Finland; in Bulgaria, health psychology is addressed within the departments of social and applied psychology, with a particular emphasis on stress research; and in other countries health psychology is seen in courses better described as behavioural medicine in terms of emphasis. In some countries, those doing the 'work' of 'health psychologists' are not always described as such. For example, in Sweden in 1989 'district psychologists' were introduced into primary health care with responsibility for psychological health, and continuing developments of this role should result in these psychologists being considered as analogous to general practice physicians.

Apart from teaching and training psychology undergraduates to become 'health psychologists', disseminating health psychology to other professions, most of all the medical profession, is paramount.

Health psychology and undergraduate medical training

The General Medical Council's recommendations for *Tomorrow's Doctors* (General Medical Council 2002) followed the Department of Health's (2001c) report *Involving Patients and the Public in Healthcare*, where the clear argument was presented for a healthcare system that brings patients in from the 'outside' to the inside, where their views are sought and responded to. If patients are to be encouraged, by means of patient liaison services or patients forums, to express their views, needs and concerns, health professionals need to be able to encourage, to listen, to empathise and to react appropriately whenever possible. Communication skills that enable the development and maintenance of good relationships with patients and their carers (e.g. Maguire and Pitceathly 2002) are set down as a core requirement of undergraduate medical training and of subsequent medical practice. Alongside these skills, *Tomorrow's Doctors* states that graduates should 'know about, understand and be able to apply and integrate the clinical, basic, behavioural and social sciences on which medical practice is based' (p. 4). This is crucial

Plate 18.2 To make an increasing difference to the health of our nations, health psychologists need to disseminate their findings to a wide audience, including health professionals, educators and policy makers.

Source: Bananastock/Photolibrary.com

as it highlights a shift from a biomedical view of medicine, i.e. identify and treat symptoms (see Chapter 1), to one that places health and illness within a wider social context and acknowledges human variability in response to illness and healthcare. Patients' view and beliefs are to be taken into account.

Academic health psychologists are increasingly employed as lecturers in medical faculties, where they offer core behavioural science teaching to our future doctors. Health psychology is also a core component of nursing and therapeutic professional education. Health psychology as a discipline has moved from theory building and theory testing to application – intervention and evaluation – and it is commonly taught to health professional students as well as psychology and social science students. In this way, health psychology is well placed to influence the future practice of health professionals on matters concerned with responses to illness and healthcare, and to influences on health-protective and -enhancing behaviour. However, there is still some room for improvement, as is summarised below.

Issues for the future

■ Making statistical significance in health psychological research clinically significant

Sterne and Davey-Smith (2001) present a strong case for why statistical significance tests, traditionally using the $p < 0.05$ convention to reject a null hypothesis (i.e. that no difference or no association exists between examined variables that could not exist purely by chance), are limiting, partly because the interpretation of p values is subjective, and partly because many null hypotheses are in fact meaningless. In other words, generating a null hypothesis that simply states that there will be no effect in terms of associations between variables examined, or in terms of differences between groups examined, or in terms of differences between an intervention group and a control group, sets research up in such a way as to conduct analysis that will hopefully allow us to reject the null hypothesis, rather than simply to confirm a hypothesis. Clark-Carter (2003) states that this is because one can never claim to have produced enough evidence to state that something is 'true', whereas we can claim to have demonstrated that something is unlikely to be the case if we find no evidence for it. There is a growing requirement (for example from both the American Psychological Association and the British Psychological Society) for those publishing scientific findings to report 'effect sizes' in their data. This statistical debate has been well described in a special issue of *The Psychologist* (December 2003), which those readers who are likely to be pursuing independent research are encouraged to read. The general implication of this debate is that there is a need for research to avoid interpreting significant p values as clinically meaningful, or interpreting non-significant p values as of no clinical significance, as this is not always the case when working at an individual level.

■ The need for health psychologists to engage politically

For health psychologists to turn their research evidence into practice, they need to engage in appropriate dissemination to healthcare practitioners and, ideally, to policy makers. Having greater professional 'status', as implied in the British example of stage 2 professional recognition for example (see companion website), and the increasing presence of health psychology 'practitioners' in healthcare settings, will go some way towards making health psychology voices 'heard'. However, there is some concern that psychologists are reluctant to use their carefully collected evidence to provide 'guidelines' for practice. Johnson (1999) suggests that this wariness is in part due to a psychologist's training in being critically aware of limitations in a knowledge base; for example, we typically encourage our students to become increasingly critical in their thinking and in their interpretation of research methodologies and evidence. Johnson concludes that: 'I sometimes think we spend more time criticizing each other than we do promoting our accomplishments. In the meantime, other health professionals are more than willing to write practice guidelines and identify standards of care in areas where psychology has greater expertise' (p. 330). To 'sell' our findings to practitioners and policy makers, we need to have confidence in both our findings and ourselves.

In addition to learning how to better 'sell' the findings of health psychology research to health professions and policy makers, Murray and Campbell (2003) argue that health psychologists also need to engage more effectively on a socio-political level. To do so, they argue, health psychology needs to broaden its approaches to encompass socio-cultural, economic and political aspects of health and healthcare. (This book has acknowledged this need in a whole chapter addressing social inequalities in health, and integrated elsewhere in the book are many of the criticisms targeted at mainstream health psychologists by critical health psychologists.) The perception of psychology, and by default, health psychology, is that we develop and test our theories and methods at an individual level. This traditional narrowness in focus has, Murray and Campbell note, perhaps held back the effectiveness of strategies to improve health on a large scale (such as reducing HIV infection in sub-Saharan Africa, promoting healthier diets in the West), because salient aspects of the micro and macro socio-economic and political environment that act to maintain inequalities in health are ignored. Health psychology, Murray and Campbell propose, needs to engage in some reflection in order to move forward in a more 'actionable' manner. Schwarz and Carpenter (1999, cited in Davey-Smith, Ebrahim and Frankel 2001), point out that focusing on individual-level determinants of health instead of macro-level determinants (such as income or poverty levels), leads to individualised interventions that fail to address the question, or the solution, appropriately.

Further relating to this point about the individual or the group, it is worth noting that most outcomes of intervention studies are summarised in terms of group effects, and conclusions are often drawn that state that the 'intervention was effective'. However, group successes obscure the individuals for whom the intervention has not worked. There is a need for psychological research to more fully address the process questions, for example to explore subgroups for whom interventions are more or less effective, and to examine drop-out and any reasons for it. By doing so, researchers may be better placed to formulate what might be a better-tailored intervention for some individuals (a 'pragmatic' approach; e.g. Pocock 1983 cited in Richardson 2000).

■ The need to remain positive

While this textbook has highlighted many of the challenges faced by our discipline (such as definitional clarity, choice of assessment techniques and tools, inclusion and consideration of socio-cultural influences on health and illness), it has highlighted the many domains in which it can be considered that health psychology has contributed significantly to understanding (e.g. health behaviour and behaviour change, stress and coping, illness processes and outcomes, psychosocial interventions). There is a lot to be positive about, although not complacent, as some of the reviews referred to in this chapter have shown. For example, do implementation intentions work in clinical samples? Do stage-based activity interventions work in the long term? Does coping really make a difference? As well as opportunities for improvement arising out of critical review, developments in the field of 'positive psychology' (cf. Seligman and Csikszentmihalyi 2000) bring with them many other opportunities for health psychology to strengthen its evidence base. Research in the 'positive psychology' tradition has shown that out of many potentially negative situations come positives (for example, reaffirmed love, or the discovery of unknown personal strengths, caused by entering a spousal caring role), and that positive affect and the finding of 'meaning' in stressful situations can be adaptational (e.g Folkman and Moscowitz 2000). Underlying many psychosocial interventions to improve adjustment or behavioural change has been the assumption that certain stressors (e.g. illness, caring) inevitably elicit negative affect and cognition, and that these need to be reduced in order to improve outcome. In contrast, positive psychology encourages thinking to turn to enhancement of positive affect (particularly that which is congruent with one's current situation), such as hope or optimism in a situation where goals are attainable, humour or positive reappraisal where goals are not so easily reached. Furthermore, in the area of preventive health, health psychology research has identified 'protective' factors for health as well as risk factors for morbidity. For example, think of the research supporting positive associations between social support, or optimism, and positive adjustment to stressful events. Such findings provide opportunities for interventions that are quite different in emphasis from those offered by the findings of negative associations between hostility, stress responses and coronary heart disease. We must not fall into the trap of assuming that we can only advise on 'what not to do' .

Health psychology will not stand still. Its contribution to the health of society is likely to grow as our knowledge base and our confidence in it grows, and as external bodies grow in confidence as to the important role health psychologists can play. New developments in the professional and academic practice of this discipline will be highlighted and updated annually on the companion website to this text: www.pearsoned.co.uk/morrison.

Summary

This final chapter has attempted to draw together much of the work described in this book and to give the reader a picture of the ways in which health psychology research can contribute to health practice. Although health psychology is a theory led discipline, its goals are applied, and we have attempted in this chapter to make the links between theory and practice evident. As well as describing many of what could be called 'successes', we have also presented evidence of limitations in our work to date. Critically appraising 'where we are now' will enable the discipline and practice to move forward effectively, and we have outlined some of the areas that would benefit from further development. Finally, to reiterate what was said at the outset of this chapter: there is a need for health psychologists to engage more politically and to 'sell' themselves and their 'goods' more effectively to policy makers and health practitioners. In doing so, we would hope to maximise the impact of health psychology as a discipline upon health psychology as a practice. Our final aim should be to strengthen the links between health psychology and health professional practice in order to benefit all of us who will at some point in their lives enter the healthcare system.

Further reading

Adams, J. and White, M. (2005). Why don't stage-based activity promotion interventions work? *Health Education Research*, 20: 237–43.

Brug, J., Conner, M., Harre, N., Kremers, S., McKellar, S. and Whitelaw, S. (2005). The transtheoretical model and stages of a change: a critique. Observations by five commentators on the paper by Adams, J. and White, M. Why don't stage-based activity promotion interventions work? *Health Education Research*, 20: 244–58.
These two papers (or sets of papers in the latter instance) are an essential read for anyone interested in stage-based interventions. The initial paper questions the value of such interventions, and the latter selection of commentaries re-reviews the evidence and considers whether there is a future for such interventions or not.

De Ridder, D. and Schreurs, K. (2001). Developing interventions for chronically ill patients: is coping a helpful concept? *Clinical Psychology Review*, 21: 205–240.
A well-resourced and clear overview of the goals of coping-based interventions, and a review of thirty-five intervention studies. The authors consider strengths, weaknesses and potential for future interventions in chronically ill populations.

Rutter, D. and Quine, L. (2002). *Changing Health Behaviour*. Buckingham: Open University Press.
This well-written text highlights many areas of intervention in which health and social psychologists have been at the forefront. Chapters describe specific theory-based interventions including those directed at safer sex practices, smoking cessation, reduced fat intake, uptake of screening for colorectal or cervical cancer, the use of cycling helmets by schoolchildren and pedestrian safety. It also includes a useful chapter by Steve Sutton that raises some of the difficulties in turning research findings into effective interventions.

GLOSSARY

A

acceptance coping: accepting the reality of a situation and that it cannot easily be changed.

acetylcholine: a white crystalline derivative of choline that is released at the ends of nerve fibres in the parasympathetic nervous system and is involved in the transmission of nerve impulses in the body.

adrenal glands: endocrine glands, located above each kidney. Comprises the cortex, which secretes several steroid hormones, and the medulla, which secretes noradrenaline.

adrenaline: a neurotransmitter and hormone secreted by the adrenal medulla that increases physiological activity in the body, including stimulation of heart action and an increase in blood pressure and metabolic rate. Also known as epinephrine.

affective: to do with affect or mood and emotions.

age-specific mortality: typically presented as the number of deaths per 100,000, per annum, according to certain age groups, for example comparing rates of death from cancer in 2001 between those aged 45–54 with those aged 55–64.

agonist: a drug that simulates the effects of neurotransmitters, such as the serotonin agonist fluoxetine, which induces satiety (reduces hunger).

Alcoholics Anonymous: a worldwide self-help organisation for people with alcohol-related problems. Based on the belief that alcoholism is a physical, psychological and spiritual illness and can be controlled by abstinence. The twelve steps provide a framework for achieving this.

ambivalence: the simultaneous existence of both positive and negative evaluations of an attitude object, which could be both cognitive and emotional.

angina: severe pain in the chest associated with a temporary insufficient supply of blood to the heart.

antibodies: immunoglobulins produced in response to an antigen.

antigen: unique protein found on the surface of a pathogen that enables the immune system to recognise that pathogen as a foreign substance and therefore produce antibodies to fight it. Vaccinations introduce specially prepared viruses or bacteria into a body, and these have antigens.

antioxidant: oxidation of low-density lipoprotein (LDL or 'bad') cholesterol has been shown to be important in the development of fatty deposits in the arteries; anti-oxidants are chemical properties (polyphenols) of some substances (e.g. red wine) thought to inhibit the process of oxidation.

anti-retroviral drugs: drugs that prevent the reproduction of a type of virus known as a retrovirus. Most well known in the treatment of the HIV.

appraisals: interpretations of situations, events or behaviour that a person makes.

arteriosclerosis: loss of elasticity and hardening of the arteries.

atherosclerosis: formation of fatty plaque in the arteries.

atheroma: fatty deposit in the intima (inner lining) of an artery.

atopic dermatitis: a number of conditions, including eczema, involving an inflamma-tory response of the skin.

atrial fibrillation: a heart rhythm disorder (arrhythmia). It involves a very rapid heart rate, in which the atria (upper chambers of the heart) contract in a very rapid and disorganised manner and fail to pump blood effectively through the heart.

attention: generally refers to the selection of some stimuli over others for internal processing.

attributions: a person's perceptions of what causes beliefs, feelings, behaviour and actions (based on attribution theory).

aorta: the main trunk of the systemic arteries, carrying blood from the left side of the heart to the arteries of all limbs and organs except the lungs.

autoimmune condition: a group of diseases, including type 1 diabetes, Crohn's disease and rheumatoid arthritis, characterised by abnormal functioning of the immune system in which it produces antibodies against its own tissues – it treats 'self' as 'non-self'.

avoidant coping: a style of coping that involves emotional regulation by avoiding confrontation with a stressful situation. Analogous to emotion-focused coping.

B

bad news (interview): conversation between health professional (usually a doctor) and patient in which they are told 'bad news', usually that their illness has a very poor prognosis and they may die.

baroreceptors: sensory nerve endings that are stimulated by changes in pressure. Located in the walls of blood vessels such as the carotid sinus.

basal ganglia: area of the brain responsible for complex motor coordination.

B cell: a form of lymphocyte involved in destruction of antigens. Memory B cells provide long-term immunity against previously encountered pathogens.

behavioural immunogen: a behavioural practice considered to be health-protective, e.g. exercise.

behavioural pathogen: a behavioural practice thought to be damaging to health, e.g. smoking.

behaviourism: the belief that psychology is the study of observables and therefore that behaviour, not mental processes, is central.

benefit finding: a process of finding beneficial outcomes as a consequence of what is normally seen as a negative event, such as developing cancer or being infected with the HIV.

benign (tumour): tumour that cannot spread by invasion or metastasis. It does not carry the risk to health that a malignant tumour carries.

β-blocker medication: a form of medication that acts to slow down and strengthen the heart contractions. Acts on the adrenergic receptors within the heart muscle.

bile: a digestive juice, made in the liver and stored in the gallbladder. Involved in the digestion of fats in the small intestine.

biofeedback: technique of using monitoring devices to provide information regarding an autonomic bodily function, such as heart rate or blood pressure. Used in an attempt to gain some voluntary control over that function.

biomedical model: a view that diseases and symptoms have an underlying physiological explanation.

biopsy: the removal of a small piece of tissue for microscopic examination and/or culture, usually to help to make a diagnosis.

biopsychosocial: a view that diseases and symptoms can be explained by a combination of physical, social, cultural and psychological factors (cf. Engel 1977).

blunters: a general coping style that involves minimising or avoiding the source of threat or stress, i.e. avoiding threat-relevant information (as opposed to **monitors**).

body mass index: a measurement of the relative percentages of fat and muscle mass in the human body, in which weight in kilograms is divided by height in metres and the result used as an index of obesity.

bone marrow biopsy: usually performed under local anaesthetic by making a small incision into the skin. A biopsy needle is then pushed through the bone and takes a sample of marrow from the centre of the bone. Marrow contains platelets, phagocytes and lymphocytes.

C

cardiac arrest: situation in which the heart ceases to beat.

cardiac event: generic term for a variety of end-points of coronary heart disease, including a myocardial infarction, angina and cardiac arrest.

cardiovascular: pertaining to the heart and blood vessels.

carotid artery: the main artery that takes blood from the heart via the neck to the brain.

catastrophic thoughts: automatic thoughts that exaggerate the negative aspects of any situation.

catastrophising: the act of constructing **catastrophic thoughts**.

catecholamines: these chemical substances are brain neurotransmitters and include adrenaline and noradrenaline.

causal attribution: where a person attributes the cause of an event, feeling or action to themselves, to others, to chance or to some other causal agent.

CD4+ cells: otherwise known as helper T cells, these are involved in the proliferation of cytotoxic T cells as part of the immune response. HIV infection impairs their ability to provide this function.

cell suicide: a type of cell death in which the cell uses specialised cellular machinery to kill itself.

central nervous system: that part of the nervous system consisting of the brain and spinal cord.

cervical smear: smear of cells taken from the cervix to examine for the presence of cell changes indicating risk of cancer.

chronic bronchitis: an inflammation of the bronchi, the main air passages in the lungs, which persists for a long period or repeatedly recurs. Characterised by excessive bronchial mucus and a cough that produces sputum for three months or more in, at least two consecutive years.

chronic obstructive airways disease: a persistent airway obstruction associated with combinations of chronic bronchitis, small airways disease, asthma and emphysema.

clot busters: drugs which dissolve clots associated with myocardial infarction and can prevent damage to the heart following such an event. Are best used within one hour of the infarction.

cognitive dissonance: a state in which conflicting or inconsistent cognitions produce a state of tension or discomfort (dissonance). People are motivated to reduce the dissonance, often by rejecting one set of beliefs in favour of the other.

cognitive restructuring: a reconsideration of automatic negative or catastrophic thoughts to make them more in line with reality.

cognitive schema (schemata): set of unconscious beliefs about the world and ourselves that shape more conscious cognitive responses to events that impinge on us.

cold pressor test: procedure in which participants place their arm in a mixture of water and ice maintaining the water temperature at between 0 and 3°C.

collectivist: a cultural philosophy that emphasises the individual as part of a wider unit and places emphasis on actions motivated by collective, rather than individual, needs and wants.

colonoscopy: a minor surgical procedure in which a small piece of bowel wall is cut from the colon. This can then be tested for the presence of malignant cells.

colostomy: a surgical procedure that creates an opening (stoma) in the abdomen for the drainage of stool from the large intestine (colon). It may be temporary or permanent.

colposcopy: a method used to identify cells that may develop into cancer of the cervix. Sometimes follows a cervical smear if abnormalities are found. A colposcope is a low-power microscope.

comparative optimism: initially termed 'unrealistic optimism', this term refers to an individual's estimate of their risk of experiencing a negative event compared with similar others (Weinstein and Klein 1996).

congestive heart failure: a disorder in which the heart loses its ability to pump blood efficiently. As a consequence, many organs do not receive enough oxygen and nutrients, leading to the potential for them to become damaged and, therefore, not work effectively.

coping effectiveness training: a specialist form of stress management in which participants are taught to alter the nature of their coping efforts to suit the particular type of demands they are facing: using emotion-focused coping where the situation cannot be changed and problem-focused coping where it can.

coping self-efficacy: the belief that one can carry out a particular coping response in a given set of circumstances.

coronary angioplasty: a procedure where a small balloon is inserted into the blocked coronary artery of a person with **atheroma**.

coronary artery bypass graft: surgical procedure in which veins or arteries from elsewhere in the patient's body are grafted from the aorta to the coronary arteries, bypassing blockages caused by atheroma in the cardiac arteries and improving the blood supply to the heart muscle.

coronary heart disease: a narrowing of the blood vessels that supply blood and oxygen to the heart. Results from a build-up of fatty material and plaque (**atherosclerosis**). Can result in **angina** or **myocardial infarction**.

corticosteroids: potent anti-inflammatory hormones (including cortisol) made naturally in the body or synthetically for use as drugs.

cortisol: a stress hormone that increases the availability of energy stores and fats to fuel periods of high physiological activity. It also inhibits inflammation of damaged tissue.

Crohn's disease: autoimmune disease that can affect any part of the gastrointestinal tract but most commonly occurs in the ileum (the area where the small and large intestine meet).

cross-sectional design: a study that collects data from a sample on one occasion only. Ideally, the sample should be selected to be representative of the population under study.

D

decisional balance: where the costs of behaviour are weighed up against the benefits of that behaviour.

defibrillator: a machine that uses an electric current to stop any irregular and dangerous activity of the heart's muscles. It can be used when the heart has stopped (**cardiac arrest**) or when it is beating in a highly irregular (and ineffective) manner.

denial response: taking a view that denies any negative implications of an event or stimulus. If subconscious, it is considered a defence mechanism.

diabetes (type 1 and 2): a lifelong disease marked by high levels of sugar in the blood and a failure to transfer this to organs that need it. It can be caused by too little insulin (type 1) resistance to insulin (type 2), or both.

diastolic blood pressure: the minimum pressure of the blood on the walls of the arteries between heart beats (measured in relation to **systolic blood pressure**).

distancing response: taking a detached view, often a scientific view, of an event or stimulus in order to reduce emotional activation.

drug abuse: involves use of a drug that results in significant social or work-related problems.

drug dependence: usually a progression from drug abuse. Involves dependence on the drug to achieve a desired psychological state, withdrawal symptoms in the absence of the drug, and social and work-related problems.

dualism: the idea that the mind and body are separate entities (cf. Descartes).

E | **efficacy**: Bandura's technical term analogous to confidence.

egocentric: self-centred, such as in the pre-operational stage (age 2–7) of children, when they see things only from their own perspective (cf. Piaget).

emphysema: a late effect of chronic infection or irritation of the bronchial tubes. When the bronchi become irritated, some of the airways may be obstructed or the walls of the tiny air spaces may tear, trapping air in the lung beyond them. As a result, the lungs may become enlarged, at the same time becoming less efficient in exchanging oxygen for carbon dioxide.

empiricism: arising from a school of thought that all knowledge can be obtained through experience.

endocrine glands: glands that produce and secrete hormones into the blood or lymph systems. Includes the pituitary and adrenal glands, and the islets of Langerhans in the pancreas. These hormones may affect one organ or tissue, or the entire body.

endorphins: naturally occurring opiate-like chemicals released in the brain and spinal cord. They reduce the experience of pain and can induce feelings of relaxation or pleasure. Associated with the so-called 'runner's high'.

endoscopy: the use of a thin, lighted tube (called an endoscope) to examine the inside of the body.

epidemiology: the study of patterns of disease in various populations and the association with other factors such as lifestyle factors. Key concepts include mortality, morbidity, prevalence, incidence, absolute risk and relative risk. Type of question: Who gets this disease? How common is it?

erythrocyte: a mature blood cell that contains **haemoglobin** to carry oxygen to the bodily tissues.

exercise programme: a key element of most cardiac rehabilitation, including a progressive increase in exercise usually starting in a gym, sometimes developing into exercise in the home and beyond.

exogenous: relating to things outside the body.

exposure therapy: a form of therapy involving exposure to traumatic memories, based on the theoretical assumption that continued exposure will result in a gradual reduction in the level of fear associated with such memories.

expressed emotion: the disclosure of emotional experiences as a means of reducing stress; often achieved by describing the experience in writing.

eye movement desensitisation and reprocessing: a form of therapy for post-traumatic stress disorder involving exposure to traumatic memories while repeatedly moving the eyes. Its method of working is not clear. However, the most popular theory is that when the eyes move back and forth this creates brain activity similar to that which occurs during REM (rapid eye movement) sleep. This may help the brain to process the 'stuck' material, enabling the person to arrive at an adaptive resolution.

F

false positive result: a situation in which an individual is told that they may have a disease or are at risk of disease, but subsequent tests show that they are not at risk or do not have the disease.

fine needle aspiration: entails placing a very thin needle into a mass within the breast and extracting cells for microscopic evaluation. It takes seconds, and the discomfort is comparable with that of a blood test.

G

gallbladder: a structure on the underside of the liver on the right side of the abdomen. It stores the bile that is produced in the liver before it is secreted into the intestines. This helps the body to digest fats.

gate control theory of pain: a theory of pain developed by Melzack and Wall in which a 'gate' is used as a metaphor for the chemicals, including **endorphins**, that mitigate the experience of pain.

general adaptation syndrome: a sequence of physiological responses to prolonged stress, from the alarm stage through the resistance stage to exhaustion.

H

haemoglobin: the main substance of the red blood cell. When oxygenated in the lungs, it is converted to oxyhaemoglobin, thus allowing the red blood cells to carry oxygen from the air in our lungs to all parts of the body.

health behaviour: behaviour performed by an individual, regardless of their health status, as a means of protecting, promoting or maintaining health, e.g. diet.

health differential: a term used to denote differences in health status and life expectancy across different groups.

health hardiness: the extent to which a person is committed to and involved in health-relevant activities, perceives control over their health and responds to health stressors as challenges or opportunities for growth.

health locus of control: the perception that one's health is under personal control; controlled by powerful others such as health professionals; or under the control of external factors such as fate or luck.

heart failure: a state in which the heart muscle is damaged or weakened and is unable to generate a cardiac output sufficient to meet the demands of the body.

high-density lipoprotein (HDL): lipoproteins are fat protein complexes in the blood that transport cholesterol, triglycerides and other lipids to various tissues. The

main function of HDL appears to be to carry excess cholesterol to the liver for 're-packaging' or excretion in the bile. Higher levels of HDL seem to be protective against CHD, so HDL is sometimes referred to as 'good' cholesterol.

holistic: root word 'wholeness', holistic approaches are concerned with the whole being and its wellbeing, rather than addressing the purely physical or observable.

hypertension: chronically high blood pressure (considered to be high if systolic pressure exceeds 160 and diastolic exceeds 120).

hypoglycaemic episode: occurs when the body's glucose level is too low. It frequently occurs when too much insulin or oral diabetic medication is taken, not enough food is eaten, or following exercise without appropriate food intake. Symptoms include excessive sweating, paleness, fainting and eventually loss of consciousness.

hypothalamus: area of the brain that regulates appetite, sexual arousal and thirst. Also appears to have some control over emotions.

I

illness behaviour: behaviour that characterises a person who is sick and who seeks a remedy, e.g. taking medication. Usually precedes formal diagnosis, when behaviour is described as **sick role behaviour**.

illness cognition: the cognitive processes involved in a person's perception or interpretation of symptoms or illness and how they represent it to themselves (or to others) (cf. Croyle and Ditto 1990).

illness representations: beliefs about a particular illness and state of ill health – commonly ascribed to the five domains described by Leventhal: identity, timeline, cause, consequences and control/cure.

incidence: the number of new cases of disease occurring during a defined time interval – not to be confused with prevalence, which refers to the number of established cases of a disease in a population at any one time.

individual differences: aspects of an individual that distinguish them from other individuals or groups (e.g. age, personality).

individualism: a cultural philosophy that places responsibility at the feet of the individual; thus behaviour is often driven by individual needs and wants rather than by community needs or wants.

inflammatory bowel disease: a group of inflammatory conditions of the large intestine and, in some cases, the small intestine. The main forms of IBD are **Crohn's disease** and **ulcerative colitis**.

irritable bowel syndrome: a disorder of the lower intestinal tract. Symptoms include pain combined with altered bowel habits resulting in diarrhoea, constipation or both. It has no obvious physiological abnormalities, so diagnosis is by the presence and pattern of symptoms.

ischaemic heart disease: a heart disease caused by a restriction of blood flow to the heart.

K

Kaposi's sarcoma: a malignant tumour of the connective tissue, often associated with AIDS. The tumours consist of bluish-red or purple lesions on the skin. They often appear first on the feet or ankles, thighs, arms, hands and face.

L

lay referral system: an informal network of individuals (e.g. friends, family, colleagues) turned to for advice or information about symptoms and other health-related matters. Often but not solely used prior to seeking a formal medical opinion.

life events: a term used to describe occurrences in a person's life which may be viewed positively or negatively but which inherently require some adjustment on the part of the person (e.g. marriage, loss of job). Such events are implicated in the experience of stress.

limbic system: a series of structures in the brain, often referred to as the 'emotional computer' because of its role in coordinating emotions. It links sensory information to emotionally relevant behaviour, in particular responses to fear and anger.

locus of control: a personality trait thought to distinguish between those who attribute responsibility for events to themselves (i.e. internal LoC) or to external factors (external LoC).

longitudinal (design): responses assessed in a study that have been taken on more than one occasion over time, either prospectively (future-oriented) or retrospectively (based on recall of past events). Prospective longitudinal studies are more powerful, and such methods are important to studies where assessment of change is important.

low-density lipoprotein (LDL): the main function of LDLs seems to be to carry cholesterol to various tissues throughout the body. LDLs are sometimes referred to as 'bad' cholesterol because elevated levels of LDL correlate most directly with **coronary heart disease**.

lower respiratory tract infection: infection of the parts of the respiratory system including the larynx, trachea, bronchi and lungs.

lumpectomy: a surgical procedure in which only the tumour and a small area of surrounding tissue are removed. Contrasts with mastectomy, in which the whole breast is removed.

lymphocyte: a type of white blood cell. Lymphocytes have a number of roles in the immune system, including the production of antibodies and other substances that fight infection and disease. Includes T and B cells.

M

malignant melanoma: a rare but potentially lethal form of skin cancer.

mammography: a low-dose X-ray procedure that creates an image of the breast. The X-ray image can be used to identify early stages of tumours.

mechanistic: a reductionist approach that reduces behaviour to the level of the organ or physical function. Associated with the **biomedical** model.

mediate/mediator: some variables may mediate the effects of others upon an outcome, for example, individual beliefs may mediate the effects of gender upon behaviour, thus gender effects would be said to be indirect, rather than direct, and beliefs would be mediator variables.

melanoma: a form of skin cancer that arises in melanocytes, the cells that produce pigment. Usually begins in a mole.

meta-analysis: a review and re-analysis of pre-existing quantitative datasets that combines the analysis so as to provide large samples and high statistical power from which to draw reliable conclusions about specific effects.

migraine: differs from other headaches because it involves symptoms such as nausea, vomiting or sensitivity to light. Their exact cause is not known. However, they appear to be related to problems with blood flow through parts of the brain. At the start of a migraine, blood vessels in certain areas of the brain constrict, leading to symptoms including visual disturbances, difficulty in speaking, weakness or numbness. Minutes to hours later, the blood vessels dilate, leading to increased blood flow in the brain and a severe headache.

monitors: a generalised coping style that involves attending to the source of stress or threat and trying to deal with it directly, e.g. through information gathering/attending to threat-relevant information (as opposed to **blunters**).

morbidity: costs associated with illness such as disability, injury.

mortality: death. Generally presented as mortality statistics, i.e. the number of deaths in a given population and/or in a given year ascribed to a given condition (e.g. number of cancer deaths among women in 2000).

motivation: memories, thoughts, experiences, needs and preferences that act together to influence (drive) the type, strength and persistence of our actions.

motivational interview: developed by Miller and Rollnick, a set of procedures designed to increase motivation to change behaviour.

multiple sclerosis: a disorder of the brain and spinal cord caused by progressive damage to the myelin sheath covering of nerve cells. This results in decreased nerve functioning, which can lead to a variety of symptoms, including weakness, paralysis, tremor, pain, tingling, numbness and decreased coordination.

myelin sheath: a substance that contains both protein and fat (lipid) and surrounds all nerves outside the brain. It acts as a nerve insulator and helps in the transmission of nerve signals.

myocardial infarction: death of the heart muscle due to a stoppage of the blood supply. More often known as a heart attack.

N   **natural killer (NK) cells:** cells move in the blood and attack cancer cells and virus-infected body cells.

negative affectivity: a dispositional tendency to experience persistent and pervasive negative or low mood and self concept (related to **neuroticism**).

neophobia: a persistent and chronic fear of anything new (places, events, people, objects).

neuroticism: a personality trait reflected in the tendency to be anxious, feel guilty and experience generally negative thought patterns.

neurotransmitter: a chemical messenger (e.g. adrenaline, acetylcholine) used to communicate between neurons and other neurons and other types of cell.

nicotine replacement therapy (NRT): replacement of nicotine to minimise withdrawal symptoms following the cessation of smoking. Delivered in a variety of ways, including a transdermal patch placed against the skin, which produces a measured dose of nicotine over time.

noradrenaline: this **catecholamine** is a neurotransmitter found in the brain and in the **sympathetic nervous system**. Also known as norepinephrine.

O

objective: i.e. real, visible or systematically measurable (e.g. adrenaline levels). Generally pertains to something outside the body that can be seen by others (as opposed to **subjective**).

operant conditioning: attributed to Skinner, this theory is based on the assumption that behaviour is directly influenced by its consequences (e.g. rewards, punishments, avoidance of negative outcomes).

oral hypoglycaemic agents: various drug types, all of which reduce circulating blood sugar.

outcome expectancies: the outcome that is expected to result from behaviour, e.g. exercise will make me fitter.

P

pain threshold: the minimum amount of pain intensity that is required before it is detected (individual variation).

pancreas: gland in which the islets of Langerhans produce insulin. Also produces and secretes digestive enzymes. Located behind the stomach.

parasympathetic nervous system: arm of the autonomic nervous system that is responsible for rest and recuperation.

pathogen: a collective name for a variety of challenges to our health and immune system, including bacteria and viruses.

patient-controlled analgesia (PCA): a technique through which small doses of analgesic drugs, usually opioids, are administered (usually by an intravenous drip and controlled by a pump) by patients themselves. It is mostly used for the control of post-operative pain.

perceived behavioural control: one's belief in personal control over a certain specific action or behaviour.

phagocyte: an immune system cell that can surround and kill micro-organisms and remove dead cells. Phagocytes include macrophages.

phantom limb pain: a phenomenon that occurs following amputation of a limb, in which the individual feels like they still have their limb, and the limb is in pain.

placebo intervention: an intervention designed to simulate a psychological intervention but not believed to be a specific therapy for the target condition.

platelets: tiny bits of protoplasm found in the blood that are essential for blood clotting. These cells bind together to form a clot and prevent bleeding at the site of injury.

post-traumatic stress disorder: a disorder that forms a response to experiencing a traumatic event. The key elements are unwanted repetitive memories of the event, often in the form of flashbacks, attempts at avoidance of such memories, and a generally raised level of arousal.

predisposing factors: factors that increase the likelihood of a person engaging in a particular behaviour, such as genetic influences on alcohol consumption.

premature mortality: death before the age it is normally expected. Usually set at deaths under the age of 75.

prevalence: the number of established cases of a disease in a population at any one time. Often described as a percentage of the overall population or cases per 100,000 people.

primary prevention: intervention aimed at changing risk factors prior to disease development.

problem-focused coping: a style of coping that involves active planning and dealing with any source of stress.

problem-focused counselling: a counselling approach developed by Gerard Egan that attempts to foster a collaborative and structured approach between counsellor and client to solving life problems.

procedural information: telling patients about the events that will occur before and after surgery, such as having a pre-medication injection, waking in the recovery room, and having a drip in their arm.

prognosis: the predicted outcome of a disease.

prosocial behaviour: behavioural acts that are positively valued by society and that may elicit positive social consequences, e.g. offering sympathy, helping others.

psychological debriefing: a procedure in which people who have been through a particular trauma talk through the trauma in a structured way with a counsellor.

psychosocial: an approach that seeks to merge a psychological (more micro- and individually oriented) approach with a social approach (macro-, more community- and interaction-oriented), for example to health.

Q **qualitative methodologies**: qualitative methods are concerned with describing (qualifying) the experience, beliefs and behaviour of a particular group of people. Data elicited is non-numerical, may or may not be generalisable to the wider population, but may generate themes of response that can be examined in further samples. The depth of material gained through qualitative work is great and allows insight into the meaning behind people's responses. Methods may include open-ended interviews, focus group discussions, taped transactions and conversations. Samples are generally small given the time demands of data collection and analysis.

quantitative methodologies: unlike **qualitative** methods, quantitative methods are concerned with counting (quantifying), i.e. data describes the frequency with which a set of beliefs are held or behaviour actioned and means of scores can be obtained and compared statistically. Larger and more representative samples can be obtained, as the method of data collection is predominantly paper-based questionnaires that are self-completed (or can be completed in the presence of a researcher). Criticised for reducing data to numerical categories at the expense of breadth of illustrative meaning.

R **reinforcers**: factors that reward or provide a positive response following a particular behaviour or set of behaviours (positive reinforcer); or enable the removal or avoidance of an undesired state or response (negative reinforcer).

relapse prevention: a set of skills taught to people needing to achieve long-term behavioural change that prepare them to resist temptation and how to minimise the impact of any relapse should it occur. Often used with people taking addictive drugs.

repression: a defensive coping style that serves to protect the person from negative memories or anxiety-producing thoughts by preventing their gaining access to consciousness.

rheumatoid arthritis: a chronic autoimmune disease with inflammation of the joints and marked deformities. Something (possibly a virus) triggers an attack of the synovium in the joint by the immune system, which stimulates an inflammatory reaction that can lead to destruction of the joint.

risk ratio: a way of comparing whether the probability of a certain event is the same for two groups. A risk ratio of 1 implies that the event is equally likely in both groups. A risk ratio greater than 1 implies that the event is more likely in the first group. A risk ratio of less than 1 implies that the event is less likely in the first group.

S

salience: strength and importance.

sciatica: pain down the leg, which is caused by irritation of the main nerve into the leg, the sciatic nerve. This pain tends to be caused where the nerves pass through and emerge from the lower bones of the spine (lumbar vertebrae).

self-concept: those conscious thoughts and beliefs about yourself that allow you to feel are distinct from others and that you exist as a separate person.

self-efficacy: the belief that one can perform particular behaviour in a given set of circumstances.

self-regulation: the process by which individuals monitor and adjust their behaviour, thoughts and emotions in order to maintain a balance or a sense of normal function.

self-talk: talking to oneself (internally). Can be negative and thus add to stress. Therapeutically, individuals are taught to use self-talk in a way that helps them to keep calm.

sensitivity (of a test): the probability that a test is correctly positive or correctly negative; for example, a sensitive test may have 95 percent success in detecting a disease among patients known to have that disease, and 95 percent success in not detecting a disease among disease-free individuals.

seropositive: the presence of the HIV in the bloodstream.

sick role behaviour: the activities undertaken by a person diagnosed as sick in order to try to get well.

social cognition: a model of social knowledge and behaviour that highlights the explanatory role of cognitive factors (e.g. beliefs and attitudes).

social comparison: the process by which a person or group of people compare themselves (their behaviour or characteristics) with others.

social desirability bias: the tendency to answer questions about oneself or one's behaviour in a way that is thought likely to meet with social (or interviewer) approval.

social identity: a person's sense of who they are at a group, rather than personal and individual, level (e.g. you are a student, possibly a female).

socialisation: the process by which a person learns – from family, teachers, peers – the rules, norms and moral codes of behaviour that are expected of them.

social learning theory: a theory that has at its core the belief that a combination of outcome expectancy and outcome value will shape subsequent behaviour. Reinforcement is an important predictor of future behaviour.

socio-economic status: a measure of the social class of an individual. Different measures use different indicators, including income, job type or years of education. Higher status implies a higher salary or higher job status.

Socratic dialogue: exploration of an individual's beliefs, encouraging them to question their validity.

specificity (of a test): the likelihood that a test will produce a few false positive results and a few false negatives; i.e. does not produce a positive result for a negative case, and vice versa.

stages of change model: developed by Prochaska and di Clemente, this identifies five stages through which an individual passes when considering behavioural change: pre-contemplation, contemplation, preparation, change and maintenance/relapse.

stem cell: a 'generic' cell that can make exact copies of itself indefinitely. In addition, such cells have the ability to produce specialised cells for various tissues in the body, including blood, heart muscle, brain and liver tissue. Found in the bone marrow.

stem cell transplant: stem cells are given to the person after chemotherapy to help the bone marrow to recover and continue producing healthy blood cells.

stress inoculation training: a form of stress-reducing intervention in which participants are taught to control stress by rehearsing prior to going into stressful situations. Participants are taught to relax and use calming self-talk. The approach was developed by Donald Meichenbaum.

stress management training: a generic term for interventions designed to teach participants how to cope with stress.

stress reactivity: the physiological arousal, such as increased heart rate or blood pressure, experienced during a potentially stressful encounter.

stroke: involves damage to the brain as a result of either bleeding into the brain tissue or a blockage in an artery, which prevents oxygen and other nutrients reaching parts of the brain. More scientifically known as a cerebro-vascular accident (CVA).

subjective: personal, i.e. what a person thinks and reports (e.g excitement) as opposed to what is **objective**. Subjective is generally related to internal interpretations of events rather than observable features.

subjective expected utility (seu) theory: a decision-making model where an individual evaluates the expected utility (cf. desirability) of certain actions and their outcomes and selects the action with the highest seu.

subjective norm: a person's beliefs regarding whether important others (referents) would think that they should or should not carry out a particular action. An index of social pressure, weighted generally by the individual's motivation to comply with the wishes of others (see theory of planned behaviour).

sympathetic nervous system: the part of the autonomic nervous system involved in mobilising energy to activate and maintain arousal (e.g. increased heart rate).

synapse: junction between two neurons or between a neuron and target organ. Nerve impulses cross a synapse through the action of neurotransmitters.

systolic blood pressure: the maximum pressure of blood on the artery walls, which occurs at the end of the left ventricle output/contraction (measured in relation to **diastolic blood pressure**).

T

T cell: a cell that recognises antigens on the surface of a virus-infected cell, binds to that cell and destroys it.

thalamus: area of the brain that links the basic functions of the hindbrain and midbrain with the higher centres of processing, the cerebral cortex. Regulates attention and contributes to memory functions. The portion that enters the limbic system is involved in the experience of emotions.

theory: a general belief or beliefs about some aspect of the world we live in or those in it, which may or may not be supported by evidence. For example, women are worse drivers than men.

transdermal patch: a method of delivering a drug in a slow release form. The drug is impregnated into a patch, which is stuck to the skin and gradually absorbed into the body.

transient ischaemic attack: a short period of reduced blood flow to the brain, resulting in symptoms including short periods of confusion, weakness and other minor neurological symptoms.

treadmill test: a test of cardiovascular fitness in which participants gradually increase the level of exercise on a treadmill while having their heart monitored with an electrocardiogram.

trigeminal neuralgia: a painful inflammation of the trigeminal nerve that causes sharp and severe facial pain.

Type A behaviour (TAB): a constellation of characteristics, mannerisms and behaviour including competititiveness, time urgency, impatience, easily aroused hostility, rapid and vigorous speech patterns and expressive behaviour. Extensively studied in relation to the aetiology of coronary heart disease, where hostility seems central.

Type C personality: a cluster of personality characteristics manifested in stoic, passive and non-emotionally expressive coping responses. Thought to be associated with an elevated cancer risk.

Type D personality: a personality type characterised by high negative affectivity and social inhibition.

type 1 diabetes: see **diabetes**.

type 2 diabetes: see **diabetes**.

U

ulcerative colitis: a chronic inflammatory disease of the large intestine, characterised by recurrent episodes of abdominal pain, fever and severe diarrhoea.

ultrasound: the use of ultra high-frequency sound waves to create images of organs and systems in the body.

unrealistic optimism: also known as 'optimistic bias', whereby a person considers themselves as being less likely than comparable others to develop an illness or experience a negative event.

V **variable:** (noun). Something that can be measured or is reported and recorded as data, such as age, mood, smoking frequency or physical functioning.

vasospasm: a situation in which the muscles of artery walls in the heart contract and relax rapidly, resulting in a reduction of the flow of blood through the artery.

vicarious learning: learning from observation of others.

volition: action or doing (the post-intentional stage highlighted in the HAPA model of health behaviour change).

W **written emotional expression:** a writing technique in which participants write about upsetting incidents either in their past or related to specific issues.

REFERENCES

Abbott, S. (1988). Talking about AIDS. Report for AIDS Action Council, Canberra. *National Bulletin*, August, 24–7.

Abraham, C., Krahé, B., Dominic, R. and Fritsche, I. (2002). Do health promotion messages target cognitive and behavioural correlates of condom use? A content analysis of safer sex promotion leaflets in two countries. *British Journal of Health Psychology*, 7: 227–46.

Abraham, S.C.S., Sheeran, P., Abrams, D. and Spears, R. (1996). Health beliefs and teenage condom use: a prospective study. *Psychology and Health*, 11: 641–55.

Abramsky, L. and Fletcher, O. (2002). Interpreting information: what is said, what is heard – a questionnaire study of health professionals and members of the public. *Prenatal Diagnosis* 22: 1188–94.

Absetz, P., Aro, A.R. and Sutton, S.R. (2003). Experience with breast cancer, pre-screening perceived susceptibility and the psychological impact of screening. *Psycho-Oncology*, 12: 305–18.

Achat, H., Kawachi, I., Byrne, C., Hankinson, S. and Colditz, G.A. (2000). Prospective study of job strain and risk of breast cancer. *International Journal of Epidemiology*, 29: 622–8.

Acheson, D. (1998). *Independent Inquiry into Inequalities in Health*. Report. London: HMSO.

Adams, J. and White, M. (2005). Why don't stage-based activity promotion interventions work? *Health Education Research*, 20: 237–43.

Ader, R. and Cohen, N. (1993). Psychoneuroimmunology: conditioning and stress. *Annual Review of Psychology*, 44: 53–85.

Ader, R. (2001). Psychoneuroimmunology. *Current Directions in Psychological Science*, 10: 94–8.

Adler, N.E. and Matthews, K.A. (1994). Health psychology: why do some people get sick and some stay well? *Annual Review of Psychology*, 45: 229–59.

Affleck, G., Tennen, H., Croog, S. and Levine, S. (1987). Causal attributions, perceived benefits, and morbidity after a heart attack: an 8-year study. *Journal of Consulting and Clinical Psychology*, 55: 29–35.

Agency for Health Care Policy and Research (1992). *Acute Pain Management, Clinical Practice Guideline*. Silver Spring, Md: AHCPR.

Ager, A., Carr, S., Maclachlan, M. and Kaneka-Chilongo, B. (1996). Perceptions of tropical health risks in Mponda, Malawi: attributions of cause, suggested means of risk reduction and preferred treatment. *Psychology and Health*, 12: 23–31.

Agostinelli, G. and Grube, J.W. (2002). Alcohol counter-advertising and the media. A review of recent research. *Alcohol Research and Health*, 26: 15–21.

Aikens, J.E., Kiolbasa, T.A. and Sobel, R. (1997). Psychological predictors of glycemic change with relaxation training in non-insulin-dependent diabetes mellitus. *Psychotherapy and Psychosomatics*, 66: 302–6.

Ajzen, I. (1985). From intentions to actions: a theory of planned behavior. In J. Kuhl and J. Beckman (eds), *Action-control: From Cognition to Behavior*. Heidelberg: Springer Verlag.

Ajzen, I. (1991). The theory of planned behaviour. *Organizational Behavior and Human Decision Processes*, 50: 179–211.

Ajzen, I. and Fishbein, M. (1970). The prediction of behavior from attitudinal and normative beliefs. *Journal of Personality and Social Psychology*, 6: 466–87.

Ajzen, I. and Madden, T.J. (1986). Prediction of goal-directed behavior: attitudes, intentions, and perceived behavioral control. *Journal of Experimental Social Psychology*, 22: 453–74.

Alaranta, H., Rytokoski, U., Rissanen, A., Talo, S., Ronnemaa, T., Puukka, P., Karppi, S.L., Videman, T., Kallio, V. and Slatis, P. (1994). Intensive physical and psychosocial training program for patients with chronic low back pain. *Spine*, 19: 1339–49.

Alexander, F. (1950). *Psychosomatic Medicine: Its Principles and Application*. New York: W.W. Norton.

Alexander, D.A. and Walker, L.G. (1994). A study of methods used by Scottish police officers to cope with work-induced stress. *Stress Medicine*, 10: 131–8.

Alexander, R.E. (2000). Readability of published dental educational materials. *Journal of the American Dental Association*, 131: 937–42.

Alfredsson, L., Spetz, C.-L. and Theorell, T. (1985). Type of occupational and near-future hospitalization for myocardial infarction and some other diagnoses. *International Journal of Epidemiology*, 4: 378–88.

Allen, J.D., Stoddard, A.M., Mays, J. and Sorensen, G. (2001). Promoting breast and cervical cancer screening at the workplace: results from the Woman to Woman study. *American Journal of Public Health*, 91: 584–90.

Allen, J.K., Scott, L.B., Stewart, K.J. and Young, D.R. (2004). Disparities in women's referral to and enrollment in outpatient cardiac rehabilitation. *Journal of General Internal Medicine*, 19: 747–53.

Allied Dunbar National Fitness Survey (1992). *A Report on Activity Patterns and Fitness Levels*. London: Sports Council and Health Education Authority.

Allport, G.W. (1920). The influence of the group upon association and thought. *Journal of Experimental Psychology*, 3: 159–82.

Allport, G.W. (1935). Attitudes. In C. Murchison (ed.), *Handbook of Social Psychology*, Worcester, Mass.: Clark University Press.

Allport, G.W. (1961). *Pattern and Growth in Personality*. New York: Holt, Rinehart & Winston.

Allport, G.W. (1966). Traits revisited. *American Psychologist*, 21: 1–10.

Aloise-Young, P.A., Hennigan, K.M. and Graham, J.W. (1996). Role of self-image and smoker stereotype in smoking onset during early adolescence: a longitudinal study. *Health Psychology*, 15: 494–7.

Amelang, M. and Schmidt-Rathjens, C. (1996). Personality, cancer and coronary heart disease: further evidence on a controversial issue. *British Journal of Health Psychology*, 1: 191–205.

American Agency for Health Care Policy (1992). *Acute Pain Management: Operative or Medical Procedures and Trauma. Clinical Practice Guideline No. 1*. AAHCP: Washington, DC.

American Heart Association (1995). *Heart and Stroke Facts: 1995 Statistical Supplement*. American Heart Association, Dallas.

American Psychiatric Association (2000). *Diagnostic and Statistical Manual of Mental Disorders*, 4th edn with revised text. Washington.

Ames, G.M. and Janes, C.R. (1987). Heavy and problem drinking in an American blue-collar population: implications for prevention. *Social Science and Medicine*, 25: 949–60.

Andersen, B.L., Cacioppo, J.T. and Roberts, D.C. (1995). Delay in seeking a cancer diagnosis: delay stages and psychophysiological comparison processes. *British Journal of Social Psychology*, 34: 33–52.

Andersen, R. and Newman, F. (1973). Societal and individual determinants of medical care utilization in the United States. *Millbank Memorial Fund Quarterly*, 51: 95–107.

Anderson, R.J., Friedland, K.E., Clouse, R.E. and Lustman, P.J. (2001). The prevalence of comorbid depression in adults with diabetes: a meta-analysis. *Diabetes Care*, 24: 1069–78.

Andersson, G. (1996). The benefits of optimism: a meta-analytic review of the Life Orientation Test. *Personality and Individual Differences*, 21: 719–25.

André, M., Borgquist, L. and Molstad, S. (2002). Asking for 'rules of thumb': a way to discover tacit knowledge in general practice. *Family Practice*, 19: 617–22.

Ansari, M., Shlipak, M.G., Heidenreich, P.A., Van Ostaeyen, D., Pohl, E.C., Browner, W.S. and Massie, B.M. (2003). Improving guideline adherence: a randomized trial evaluating strategies to increase beta-blocker use in heart failure. *Circulation*, 107: 2799–804.

Antoni, M.H. (1987). Neuroendocrine influences in psychoimmunology and neoplasia: A review. *Psychology and Health*, 1: 3–24.

Antoni, M.H., Baggett, L., Ironson, G. and LaPerriere, A. (1991). Cognitive behavioral stress management intervention buffers distress responses and immuno-logical changes following notification of HIV-1 seropositivity. *Journal of Consulting and Clinical Psychology*, 59: 906–15.

Antoni, M.H., Cruess, D.G., Klimas, N., Maher, K., Cruess, S.E., Kumar, M., Lutgendorf, S., Ironson, G., Schneiderman, N. and Fletcher, M.A. (2002). Stress management and immune system reconstitution in symptomatic HIV-infected gay men over time: effects on transitional naive T-cells (CD4+CD45RA+CD29+). *American Journal of Psychiatry*, 159: 143–5.

Antoni, M.H., Lehman, J., Kilbourn, K., Boyers, A.E., Culver, J.L., Alferi, S.M., Yount, S.E., McGregor, B.A., Arena, P.L., Harris, S.D., Price, A.A. and Carver, C.S. (2001). Cognitive-behavioral stress management intervention decreases depression and enhances optimism and the sense of positive contribu-tions among women under treatment for early-stage breast cancer. *Health Psychology*, 20: 20–32.

Antonovsky, A. (1987). *Unravelling the Mystery of Health: How People Manage Stress and Stay Well*. San Francisco: Jossey-Bass.

Appels, A., Bar, F., Lasker, J., Flamm, U. and Kop, W. (1997). The effect of a psychological intervention program on the risk of a new coronary event after angioplasty: a feasibility study. *Journal of Psychosomatic Medicine*, 43: 209–17.

Arefjord, K., Hallarakeri, E., Havik, O.E. and Maeland, J.G. (1998). Myocardial infarction: Emotional Con-sequences for the wife. *Psychology and Health*, 13: 135–46.

Armitage, C.J. (2003). The relationship between multi-dimensional health locus of control and perceived behavioural control: how are distal perceptions of control related to proximal perceptions of control? *Psychology and Health*, 18: 723–38.

Armitage, C. and Conner, M. (1998). Extending the theory of planned behaviour: a review and avenues for further research. *Journal of Applied Social Psychology*, 28: 1429–64.

Armitage, C.J. and Conner, M. (2002). Reducing fat intake: interventions based on the theory of planned behaviour. In D. Rutter and L. Quine (eds), *Changing Health Behaviour*. Buckingham: Open University Press.

Armitage, C.J., Conner, M., Loach, J. and Willetts, D. (1999). Different perceptions of control: applying an extended theory of planned behaviour to legal and illegal drug use. *Basic and Applied Social Psychology*, 21: 301–16.

Arora, N.K. and McHorney, C.A. (2000). Patient pre-ferences for medical decision making: who really wants to participate? *Medical Care*, 38: 335–41.

Aspinwall, L.G. and Brunhart, S.M. (1996). Disting-uishing optimism from denial: optimistic beliefs predict attention to health threats. *Personality and Social Psychology Bulletin*, 22: 993–1003.

Aspinwall, L.G. and Taylor, S.E. (1992). Modeling cog-nitive adaptation: a longitudinal investigation of the impact of individual differences and coping on college adjustment and performance. *Journal of Personality and Social Psychology*, 61: 755–65.

Astin, J.A. (1998). Why patients use alternative medicine: results of a national study. *Journal of the American Medical Association*, 279: 1548–53.

Astrom, M. (1996). Generalized anxiety disorder in stroke patients: a 3 year longitudinal study. *Stroke*, 17: 270–5.

Atkinson, R.M. (1994). Late onset problem drinking in older adults. *International Journal of Geriatric Psychiatry*, 9: 321–6.

Audrain, J., Boyd, N.R., Roth, J., Main, D., Caporaso, N.F. and Lerman, C. (1997). Genetic susceptibility testing in smoking-cessation treatment: one-year out-comes of a randomized trial. *Addictive Behaviors*, 22: 741–51.

Austoker, J. (1994). Screening for ovarian, prostrate and testicular cancers. *British Medical Journal*, 309: 315–20.

Ayanian, J.Z., Cleary P.D., Weissman J.S. and Epstein, A.M. (1999). The effect of patients' preferences on racial differences in access to renal transplantation. *New England Journal of Medicine*, 341: 1661–9.

Bachiocco, V., Scesi, M., Morselli, A.M. and Carli, G. (1993). Individual pain history and familial pain tolerance models: relationships to post-surgical pain. *Clinical Journal of Pain*, 9: 266–71.

Bagozzi, R.P. (1993). On the neglect of volition in con-sumer research: a critique and proposal. *Psychology and Marketing*, 10: 215–37.

Baider, L., Andritsch, E., Uziely, B., Goldzwieg, G., Ever-Hadani, P., Hofman, G., Krenn, G. and Samonigg, H. (2003). Effects of age on coping and psychological distress in women diagnosed with breast cancer: review of literature and analysis of two different geographical settings. *Critical Reviews in Oncology/Hematology*, 46: 5–16.

Bair, M.J., Robinson, R.L., Katon, W. and Kroenke, K. (2003). Depression and pain comorbidity: a literature review. *Archives of Internal Medicine*, 163: 2433–45.

Bajekal, M., Primatesta, P. and Prior, G. (2003). *Health Survey for England 2001: Fruit and Vegetable Con-sumption*. London: Stationery Office.

Baker, A.H. and Wardle, J. (2003). Sex differences in fruit and vegetable intake in older adults. *Appetite*, 40: 269–75.

Balarajan, R. and Raleigh, V. (1993). *Ethnicity and Health in England*. London: HMSO.

Balldin, J., Berglund, M., Borg, S., Mansson, M., Bendtsen, P., Franck, J., Gustafsson, L., Halldin, J., Nilsson, L.H., Stolt, G. and Willander, A. (2003). A 6-month controlled naltrexone study: combined effect with cognitive behavioral therapy in outpatient treatment of alcohol dependence. *Alcoholism Clinical and Experimental Research*, 27: 1142–9.

Baltes, P.B. and Baltes, M.M. (1990). *Successful Aging: Perspectives from the Behavioral Sciences*. New York: Cambridge University Press.

Bandolier (1999). Transcutaneous electrical nerve stimulation (TENS) in postoperative pain. *Bandolier*, July. Available from www.bandolier.com.

Bandolier (2003). Acute pain. *Bandolier* extra, February. Available from www.ebandolier.com.

Bandura, A. (1977). Self-efficacy: toward a unifying theory of behavioral change. *Psychological Review*, 84: 191–215.

Bandura, A. (1986). *Social Foundations of Thought and Action*. New Jersey: Prentice Hall.

Bandura, A. (1997). *Self-Efficacy: The Exercise of Control*. New York: W.H. Freeman.

Bandura, A. (2001). Social cognitive theory: an agentic perspective. *Annual Review of Psychology*, 52: 1–26.

Banks, S.M., Salovey, P., Greener, S., Rothman, A.J., Moyer, A., Beauvais, J. and Epel, E. (1995). The effects of message framing on mammography utilization. *Health Psychology*, 14: 178–84.

Banthia, R., Malcarne, V.L., Varni, J.W., Ko, C.M., Sadler, G.R. and Greenberg, H.L. (2003). The effects of dyadic strength and coping styles on psychological distress in couples faced with prostrate cancer. *Journal of Behavioral Medicine*, 26: 31–52.

Barefoot, J.C., Dahlstrom, G. and Williams, R.B. (1983). Hostility, CHD incidence, and total mortality: a 25-year follow-up study of 255 physicians. *Psychosomatic Medicine*, 45: 59–63.

Barlow, J., Turner, A.P. and Wright, C.C. (2000). A randomised controlled study of the Arthritis Self-Management Programme in the UK. *Health Education Research Theory and Practice*, 15: 665–80.

Barlow, J.H., Wright, C., Sheasby, J., Turner, A. and Hainsworth, J. (2002). Self-management approaches for people with chronic conditions: a review. *Patient Education and Counselling*, 48: 177–87.

Baron-Epel, O. and Kaplan, G. (2001). General subjective health status or age-related subjective health status: does it make a difference? *Social Science and Medicine*, 53: 1373–81.

Bartley, M., Sacker, A. and Clarke, P. (2004). Employment status, employment conditions, and limiting illness: prospective evidence from the British household panel survey 1991–2001. *Journal of Epidemiology and Community Health*, 58: 501–6.

Baum, A. (1990). Stress, intrusive imagery and chronic distress. *Health Psychology*, 9: 665–75.

Baum, A., Garofalo, J.P. and Yali, A.M. (1999). Socioeconomic status and chronic stress. Does stress account for SES effects on health? *Annals of the New York Academy of Science*, 896: 131–44.

Baum, A., Gatchel, R.J. and Krantz, D.S. (1997). *An Introduction to Health Psychology*, 3rd edition, New York: McGraw-Hill.

Baum, A. and Grunberg, N.E. (1991). Gender, stress and health. *Health Psychology* 10: 80–5.

Bauman, B. (1961). Diversities in conceptions of health and fitness. *Journal of Health and Human Behavior*, 2: 39–46.

Beach, S.R., Schulz, R., Lee, J.L. and Jackson, S. (2000). Negative and positive health effects of caring for a disabled spouse: longitudinal findings from the Caregiver Health Effects study. *Psychology and Aging*, 15: 259–71.

Beadsmoore, C.J. and Screaton, N.J. (2003). Classification, staging and prognosis of lung cancer. *European Journal of Radiology*, 45: 8–17.

Beasley, M., Thompson, T. and Davidson, J. (2003). Resilience in response to life stress: the effects of coping style and cognitive hardiness. *Personality and Individual Differences*, 34: 77–95.

Beaver, K., Bogg, J. and Luker, K.A. (1999). Decision-making role preferences and information needs: a comparison of colorectal and breast cancer. *Health Expectations*, 2: 266–76.

Beaver, K., Luker, K.A., Owens, R.G., Leinster, S.J., Degner, L.F. and Sloan, J.A. (1996). Treatment decision making in women newly diagnosed with breast cancer. *Cancer Nursing*, 19: 8–19.

Beck, A.T. (1976). *Cognitive Therapy and the Emotional Disorders*. New York: International Universities Press.

Beck, A. (1977). *Cognitive Therapy of Depression*. New York: Guilford Press.

Beck, A.T., Ward, C.H., Mendelson, M., Mock, J.E. and Erbaugh, J.K. (1962). Reliability of psychiatric diagnoses: 2. A study of consistency of clinical judgements and ratings. *American Journal of Psychiatry*, 119: 351–7.

Beck, A.T., Wight, F.D., Newman, C.F. and Liese, B.S. (1993). *Cognitive Therapy for Substance Abuse*. New York: Guilford Press.

Becker, M.H. (ed.) (1974). The health belief model and personal health behavior, *Health Education Monographs*, 2: 324–508.

Becker, M.H., Haefner, D.P. and Maiman, L.A. (1977). The health belief model in the prediction of dietary compliance: a field experiment. *Journal of Health and Social Behavior*, 18: 348–66.

Becker, M.H. and Maiman, L.A. (1975). Socio-behavioral determinants of compliance with health and medical care recommendations. *Medical Care*, 13: 10–14.

Becker, M.H. and Rosenstock, I.M. (1987). Comparing social learning theory and the health belief model. In W.B. Ward (ed.), *Advances in Health Education and Promotion*. Greenwich, Conn.: JAI Press.

Beecher, H.K. (1946). Pain in men wounded in battle. *Annals of Surgery*, 123: 96–105.

Beeney, L.J., Bakry, A.A. and Dunn, S.M. (1996). Patient psychological and information needs when the diagnosis is diabetes. *Patient Education and Counselling*, 29: 109–16.

Bell, D.E. (1982). Regret in decision-making under uncertainty. *Operations Research*, 21: 961–81.

Bellaby, P. (2003). Communication and miscommunication of risk: understanding UK parents' attitudes to combined MMR vaccination. *British Medical Journal*, 327: 725–8.

Belloc, N.B. and Breslow, L. (1972). Relationship between physical health status and health practices. *Preventive Medicine*, 1: 409–21.

Benight, C.C., Ironson, G., Klebe, K., Carver, C.S., Wynings, C., Burnett, K., Greenwood, D., Baum, A. and Schneiderman, N. (1999). Conservation of resources and coping self-efficacy predicting distress following a natural disaster: a causal model analysis where the environment meets the mind. *Anxiety, Stress and Coping*, 12: 107–26.

Bennett, P. (2000). *Introduction to Clinical Health Psychology*. Oxford: Oxford University Press.

Bennett, P. (2003). *Abnormal and Clinical Psychology: An Introductory Text*. Buckingham: Open University Press.

Bennett, P. (2005a). Gastric and duodenal ulcers. In S. Ayers, A. Baum, C. McManus, S. Newman, K. Wallston, J. Weinman and R. West (eds) *Cambridge Handbook of Psychology, Health and Medicine* (2nd Edition). Cambridge: Cambridge University Press.

Bennett, P. (2005b). Irritable Bowel Syndrome. In S. Ayers, A. Baum, C. McManus, S. Newman, K. Wallston, J. Weinman and R. West (eds) *Cambridge Handbook of Psychology, Health and Medicine* (2nd Edition). Cambridge: Cambridge University Press.

Bennett, P., Ahmed, A. and Lowe, R. (in revision). Linking appraisals, emotions and coping in response to work-related stress. *British Journal of Clinical Psychology*.

Bennett, P. and Connell, H. (1999) Dyadic responses to myocardial infarction. *Psychology, Health and Medicine*, 4: 45–55.

Bennett, P. and Murphy, S. (1997). *Psychology and Health Promotion*. Buckingham: Open University Press.

Bennett, P., Owen, R.L., Koutsakis, S. and Bisson, J. (2002). Personality, social context and cognitive predictors of post-traumatic stress disorder in myocardial infarction patients. *Psychology and Health*, 17: 489–500.

Bennett, P. and Smith, C. (1992). Parents' attitudinal and social influences on childhood vaccination. *Health Education Research: Theory and Practice*, 73: 341–8.

Bennett, P., Smith, P. and Gallacher, J.E.J. (1996). Vital exhaustion, neuroticism and symptom reporting in cardiac and non-cardiac patients. *British Journal of Health Psychology*, 1: 309–13.

Bennett, P., Williams, Y., Page, N., Hood, K. and Woollard, M. (2004). Levels of mental health problems among UK emergency ambulance personnel. *Emergency Medical Journal*, 21: 235–6.

Benyamini, Y., Leventhal, E.A. and Leventhal, H. (2003). Elderly people's ratings of the importance of health-related factors to their self-assessments of health. *Social Science and Medicine*, 56: 1661–7.

Bergner, M., Bobbitt, R.A., Carter, W.B. *et al.* (1981). The sickness impact profile: development and final revision of a health status measure. *Medical Care*, 19: 787–805.

Berkman, L.F. (1984). Assessing the physical health effects of social networks and social support. *Annual Review of Public Health*, 5: 413–32.

Berkman, L.F., Blumenthal, J., Burg, M., Carney, R.M., Catellier, D., Cowan, M.J., Czajkowski, S.M., DeBusk, R., Hosking, J., Jaffe, A., Kaufmann, P.G., Mitchell, P., Norman, J., Powell, L.H., Raczynski, J.M. and Schneiderman, N. (2003). Effects of treating depression and low perceived social support on clinical events after myocardial infarction: the Enhancing Recovery in Coronary Heart Disease (ENRICHD) patients randomized trial. *Journal of the American Medical Association*, 289: 3106–16.

Berkman, L.F. and Syme, S.L. (1979). Social networks, lost resistance and mortality: a nine-year follow-up of Alameda County residents. *American Journal of Epidemiology*, 109: 186–204.

Bibace, R., Schmidt, L.R. and Walsh, M.E. (1994). Children's perceptions of illness. In G.N. Penny, P. Bennett and M. Herbert (eds), *Health Psychology: A Lifespan Perspective*. Switzerland: Harwood Academic Publishers.

Bibace, R. and Walsh, M.E. (1980). Development of children's conceptions of illness, *Pediatrics*, 66: 912–17.

Biddle, S. (1995). Exercise and psychosocial health. *Research Quarterly for Exercise and Sport*, 66: 292–7.

Biddle, S., Fox, K. and Boutcher, S. (2000). *Physical Activity and Psychological Wellbeing*. London: Routledge.

Biddle, S. and Murtrie, N. (1991). *Psychology of Physical Activity: A Health Related Perspective*. London: Springer Verlag.

Biggam, F.H., Power, K.G., MacDonald, R.R., Carcary, W.B. and Moodie, E. (1997). Self-perceived occupational stress and distress in a Scottish police force. *Work and Stress*, 11: 118–33.

Biglan, A., Duncan, T.E., Ary, D.A. and Smolkovski, K. (1995). Peer and parental influences on adolescent tobacco use. *Journal of Behavioural Medicine*, 18: 315–30.

Bijttebier, P., Vercruysse, T., Vertommen, H., van Gool, S.W., Uyttebroeck, A. and Brock, P. (2001). New evidence on the reliability and validity of the pediatric oncology quality of life scale. *Psychology and Health*, 16: 461–9.

Billings, A.G. and Moos, R.H. (1981). The role of coping responses and social resources in attenuating the stress of life events. *Journal of Behavioural Medicine*, 4: 139–57.

Billings, A.G. and Moos, R.H. (1984). Coping, stress, and resources among adults with unipolar depression. *Journal of Personality and Social Psychology*, 46: 877–91.

Bird, J.E. and Podmore, V.N. (1990). Children's understanding of health and illness. *Psychology and Health*, 4: 175–85.

Birmingham Health Authority (1995). *Birmingham Annual Public Health Report: Closing the Gap*. Birmingham: Birmingham Health Authority.

Birmingham, P.K., Wheeler, M., Suresh, S., Dsida, R.M., Rae, B.R., Obrecht, J., Andreoni, V.A., Hall, S.C. and Cote, C.J. (2003). Patient-controlled epidural analgesia in children: can they do it? *Anesthesia and Analgesia*, 96: 686–91.

Bishop, G.D. and Teng, C.B. (1992). Cognitive organization of disease information in young Chinese Singaporeans. Paper presented at First Asian Conference in Psychology, Singapore.

Bjordal, J.M., Johnson, M.I. and Ljunggreen, A.E. (2002). Transcutaneous electrical nerve stimulation (TENS) can reduce postoperative analgesic consumption. A meta-analysis with assessment of optimal treatment parameters for postoperative pain. *European Journal of Pain*, 7: 181–8.

Black, J.L., Allison, T.G., Williams, D.E., Rummans, T.A. and Gau, G.T. (1998). Effect of intervention for psychological distress on rehospitalization rates in cardiac rehabilitation patients. *Psychosomatics*, 39: 134–43.

Blair, S. and Brodney, S. (1999). Effects of physical inactivity and obesity on morbidity and mortality: current evidence and research issues. *Medicine and Science in Sports and Exercise*, 31(suppl.): S646–62.

Blalock, J.E. (1994). The syntax of immune-neuro-endocrine communication. *Immunology Today*, 15: 504–11.

Blane, D., Higgs, P., Hyde, M. and Wiggins, R.D. (2004). Life course influences on quality of life in early old age. *Social Science and Medicine*, 58: 2171–9.

Blaxter, M. (1987). Evidence on inequality in health from a national survey, *The Lancet*, ii: 30–3.

Blaxter, M. (1990). *Health and Lifestyles*. London: Routledge.

Blenkinsop, S., Boreham, R. and McManus, S. (NFER) (2003). *Smoking, Drinking and Drug Use among Young People in England in 2002*. London: Stationery Office.

Block, G., Patterson, B. and Subar, A. (1992). Fruit, vegetables and cancer prevention: a review of the epidemiological evidence. *Nutrition and Cancer*, 18: 1–29.

Blumenthal, J.A., Jiang, W., Babyak, M.A., Williams, D.E., Rummans, T.A. and Gau, G.T. (1997). Stress management and exercise training in cardiac patients with myocardial ischemia. *Archives of Internal Medicine*, 157: 2213–17.

Blyth, F.M., March, L.M. and Cousins, M.J. (2003). Chronic pain-related disability and use of analgesia and health services in a Sydney community. *Medical Journal of Australia*, 179: 84–7.

Boersma, S.N., Maes, S. and van Elderen, T.M.T. (in press). Goal disturbance predicts health-related quality of life and depression four months after myocardial infarction. *British Journal of Health Psychology*

Boersma, S.N., Maes, S. and Joekes, K. (in press). Goal disturbance in relation to anxiety, depression, and health-related quality of life after myocardial infarction. *Quality of Life Research*,

Boini, S., Briançon, S., Guillemin, F., Galan, P. and Hercberg, S. (2004). Impact of cancer occurrence on health-related quality of life: a longitudinal pre-post assessment. *Health and Quality of Life Outcomes*, 2: 4–19.

Bokan, J.A., Ries, R.K. and Katon, W.J. (1981). Tertiary gain and chronic pain. *Pain*, 10: 331–5.

Booth-Kewley, S. and Friedman, H.S. (1987). Psychological predictors of heart disease: a quantitative review. *Psychological Bulletin*, 101: 343–62.

Booth-Kewley, S. and Vickers, R.R., Jr (1994). Associations between major domains of personality and health behaviour. *Journal of Personality*, 62: 281–98.

Boreham, R. and Shaw, A. (2001). *Smoking, Drinking and Drug Use Among Young People in England in 2000*. London: Stationery Office.

Borland, R. (1997). Tobacco health warnings and smoking related cognitions and behaviours. *Addiction*, 92(11): 1427–35.

Bourdeaudhuij, I. de. and Van Oost, P. (1998) Family characteristics and health behaviours of adolescents and families. *Psychology and Health*, 13: 785–804.

Boureaudhuij, I.D. (1997). Family food rules and healthy eating in adolescents. *Journal of Health Psychology*, 2: 45–56.

Bourgeois, M., Schulz, R. and Burgio, L. (1996). Interventions for caregivers of patients with Alzheimer's disease: a review and analysis of content, process and outcomes. *International Journal of Aging and Human Development*, 43: 35–92.

Bowden, A. and Fox-Rushby, J.A. (2003). A systematic and critical review of the process of translation and adaptation of generic health-related quality of life measures in Africa, Asia, Eastern Europe, the Middle East, South America. *Social Science and Medicine*, 57: 1289–306.

Bowland, L., Cockburn, J., Cawson, J., Christensen Anderson, A., Moorehead, S. and Kenny, M. (2003). Counselling interventions to address the psychological consequences of screening mammography: a randomised trial. *Patient Education and Counseling*, 49: 189–98.

Bowling, A. (1991). *Measuring Health: A Review of Quality of Life*. Buckingham: Open University Press.

Bowling, A. (1995a). *Measuring Disease: A Review of Disease-specific Quality of Life Measurement Scales*. Buckingham: Open University Press.

Bowling, A. (1995b). The most important things in life. Comparisons between older and younger population age groups by gender. Results from a national survey of the public's judgements. *International Journal of Health Sciences*, 6: 169–75.

Boyer, C.B., Friend, R., Chlouverakis, G. and Kaloyanides, G. (1990). Social support and demographic factors influencing compliance of hemodialysis patients. *Journal of Applied Social Psychology*, 20: 1902–18.

Bracken, P. and Thomas, P. (2002). Time to move beyond the mind–body split (editorial). *British Medical Journal*, 325: 1433–4.

Brain, K., Gray, J., Norman, P., France, E., Anglim, C., Barton, G., Parsons, E., Clarke, A., Sweetland, H., Tischkowitz, M., Myring, J., Stansfield, K., Webster, D., Gower-Thomas, K., Daoud, R., Gateley, C., Monypenny, I., Singhal, H., Branston, L., Sampson, J., Roberts, E., Newcombe, R., Cohen, D., Rogers, C., Mansel, R. and Harper, P. (2000). Randomized trial of a specialist genetic assessment service for familial breast cancer. *Journal of the National Cancer Institute*, 92: 1345–51.

Braithwaite, D., Sutton, S. and Steggles, N. (2002). Intention to participate in predictive genetic testing for hereditary cancer: the role of attitude toward uncertainty. *Psychology and Health*, 17: 761–72.

Bratzler, D.W., Oehlert, W.H. and Austelle, A. (2002). Smoking in the elderly – It's never too late to quit. *Journal of the Oklahoma State Medical Association*, 95: 185–91.

Brawley, O.W. and Freeman, H.P. (1999). Race and outcomes: is this the end of the beginning for minority health research? *Journal of the National Cancer Institute*, 91: 1908–9.

Brena, S.F. and Chapman, S.L. (1983). *Management of Patients with Chronic Pain*. Great Neck, NY: PMA Publications.

Breslow, L. (1983). The potential of health promotion. In D. Mechanic (ed.), *Handbook of Health, Health Care and the Health Professions*. New York: Free Press.

Brett, J. and Austoker, J. (2001). Women who are recalled for further investigation for breast screening: psychological consequences 3 years after recall and factors affecting re-attendance. *Journal of Public Health Medicine*, 23: 292–300.

Brewer, B.W., Manos, T.M., McDevitt, A.V., Cornelius, A.E. and van Rallte, J.L. (2000). The effect of adding lower intensity work on the perceived aversiveness of exercise. *Journal of Sport and Exercise Psychology*, 22: 118–30.

Brewin, C., Dalgleish, T. and Joseph, S. (1996). A dual representation theory of post-traumatic stress disorder. *Psychological Review*, 103: 670–86.

Brewin, C.R. and Holmes E.A. (2003). Psychological theories of posttraumatic stress disorder. *Clinical Psychology Review*, 23: 339–76.

Brewster, A.E., Hackett, P., Morrison, V., White-Gwenin, C., Branston, L., Price, P., Robbé, I., O'Mahony, S., Adams-Jones, D. and Maughan, T. (under review). Attitudes of the general public and professional health care staff towards cancer treatment in the elderly.

British Medical Association (2003a). *Adolescent Health*. British Medical Association, Board of Science and Education: BMA Publications Unit.

British Medical Association (2003b). *Childhood Immunisation: A Guide for Healthcare Professionals*. British Medical Association, Board of Science and Education: BMA Publications Unit.

British Thoracic Society (1997). Guidelines for the management of chronic obstructive pulmonary disease. *Thorax*, 52 (suppl. 5): 1–26.

Briviba, K., Pan, L. and Rechkemmer, G. (2002). Red wine polyphenols inhibit the growth of colon carcinoma cells and modulate the activation pattern of mitogen-activated protein kinases. *Journal of Nutrition*, 132: 2814–18.

Broadbent, E., Petrie, K.J., Alley, P.G. and Booth, R.J. (2003). Psychological stress impairs early wound repair following surgery. *Psychosomatic Medicine*, 65: 865–9.

Broers, S., Kaptein, A.A., Le Cessie, S., Fibbe, W. and Hengevel, M.W. (2000). Psychological functioning and quality of life following bone marrow transplantation: a 3-year follow-up study. *Journal of Psychosomatic Research*, 48: 11–21.

Brosschot, J.F. and Thayer, J.F. (1998). Anger inhibition, cardiovascular recovery, and vagal function: a model of the link between hostility and cardiovascular disease. *Annals of Behavioral Medicine*, 20: 326–32.

Brown, J., Cooper, C. and Kirkcaldy, B. (1996). Occupational stress among senior police officers. *British Journal of Psychology*, 87: 31–41.

Brown, J.E., Brown, R.F., Miller, R.M., Dunn, S.M., King, M.T., Coates, A.S. and Butow, P.N. (2000). Coping with metastatic melanoma: the last year of life. *Psycho-Oncology*, 9: 283–92.

Brown, J.S.L., Cochrane, R. and Hancox, T. (2000). Large-scale health promotion stress workshops for the general public: a controlled evaluation. *Behavioural and Cognitive Psychotherapy*, 28: 139–51.

Brownson, R., Koffman, D., Novotny, T., Hughes, R. and Eriksen, M. (1995). Environmental and policy interventions to control tobacco use and prevent cardiovascular disease. *Health Education Quarterly*, 22: 478–98.

Bruce, J. and van Teijlingen, E. (1999). A review of the effectiveness of Smokebusters: community-based smoking prevention for young people. *Health Education Research*, 14: 109–20.

Bruera, E., Sweeney, C., Willey, J., Palmer, J.L., Tolley, S., Rosales, M. and Ripamonti, C. (2003). Breast cancer patient perception of the helpfulness of a prompt sheet versus a general information sheet during outpatient consultation: a randomized, controlled trial. *Journal of Pain and Symptom Management*, 25: 412–19.

Brug, J., Conner, M., Harre, N., Kremers, S., McKellar, S. and Whitelaw, S. (2005). The transtheoretical model and stages of a change: a critique. Observations by five commentators on the paper by Adams, J. and White, M. Why don't stage-based activity promotion interventions work? *Health Education Research*, 20: 244–58.

Brunton, G., Harden, A., Rees, R., Kavanagh, J., Oliver, S. and Oakley, A. (2003). *Children and Physical Activity: A Systematic Review of Barriers and Facilitators.* London: EPPI-Centre, Social Science Research Unit, Institute of Education, University of London.

Bryan, A.D., Aiken, L.S. and West, S.G. (1996). Increasing condom use: evaluation of a theory-based intervention to prevent sexually transmitted diseases in young women, *Health Psychology*, 15: 371–82.

Bryan, A.D., Aiken, L.S. and West, S.G. (1997). Young women's condom use: the influence of acceptance of sexuality, control over the sexual encounter, and perceived susceptibility to common STDs. *Health Psychology*, 16: 468–79.

Bryon, M. (1998). Adherence to treatment in children. In L.B. Myers and K. Midence (eds), *Adherence to Treatment in Medical Conditions*, Netherlands: Harwood Academic Publishers.

Buckman, R. (1992). Who's for CPR? *Journal of the Royal College of Physicians of London*, 26: 461–2.

Budd, R.J. (1987). Response bias and the theory of reasoned action. *Social Cognition*, 5: 95–107.

Budd, R. and Rollnick, S. (1996). The structure of the readiness to change questionnaire: a test of Prochaska and di Clemente's transtheoretical model. *Health Psychology*, 15: 365–76.

Buick, D. and Petrie, K. (2002). 'I know just how you feel': the validity of healthy women's perceptions of breast cancer patients receiving treatment. *Journal of Applied Social Psychology*, 32: 110–23.

Bullinger, M. (1997). The challenge of cross-cultural quality of life assessment. *Psychology and Health*, 12: 815–26.

Bundy, C., Carroll, D., Wallace, L. and Nagle, R. (1994). Psychological treatment of chronic stable angina pectoris. *Psychology and Health*, 10: 69–77.

Burack, J.H., Barrett, D.C., Stall, R.D., Chesney, M.A., Ekstrand, M.L. and Coates, T.J. (1993). Depressive symptoms and CD4 lymphocyte decline among HIV infected men. *JAMA*, 270(21): 2568–73.

Burell, G. (1996). Group psychotherapy in project New Life: treatment of coronary-prone behaviors for patients who had coronary bypass graft surgery. In S. Scheidt and R. Allan (eds), *Heart and Mind*. American Psychological Association.

Burgoyne, R. and Renwick, R. (2004). Social support and quality of life over time among adults living with HIV in the HAART era. *Social Science and Medicine*, 58: 1353–66.

Burns, J.W., Kubilus, A., Bruehl, S., Harden, R.N. and Lofland, K. (2003). Do changes in cognitive factors influence outcome following multidisciplinary treatment for chronic pain? A cross-lagged panel analysis. *Journal of Consulting and Clinical Psychology*, 71: 81–91.

Burns, V.E., Carroll, D., Drayson, M., Whitham, M. and Ring, C. (2003). Life events, perceived stress and antibody response to influenza vaccination in young, healthy adults. *Journal of Psychosomatic Research*, 55: 569–72.

Bury, J., Morrison, V. and MacLachlan, S. (1992). *Working with Women and AIDS: Medical, Social and Counselling Issues.* London: Routledge.

Buzdar, A.U. (2004). Hormonal therapy in early and advanced breast cancer. *Breast Journal*, 10 (suppl. 1): S19–21.

Byrne, D.G. and Mazanov, J. (2003). Adolescent stress and future smoking behaviour: a prospective investigation. *Journal of Psychosomatic Research*, 54: 313–21.

Byrne, P. and Long, B. (1976). *Doctors Talking to Patients: A Study of the Verbal Behaviour of General Practitioners Consulting in their Surgeries*. London: HMSO.

Cacioppo, J.T., Andersen, B.L., Turnquist, D.C. and Petty, R.E. (1986). Psychophysiological comparison processes: Interpreting cancer symptoms. In B.L. Andersen (ed.), *Women with Cancer: Psychosocial Perspectives*. New York: Springer Verlag.

Cacioppo, J.T., Andersen, B.L., Turnquist, D.C. and Tassinary, L.G. (1989). Psychophysiological comparison theory: on the experience, description and assessment of signs and symptoms. *Patient Education and Counselling*, 13: 257–70.

Cacioppo, J.T., Poehlmann, K.M., Kiecolt-Glaser, J.K., Malarkey, W.B., Burelson, M.H., Berntson, G.G. and Glaser, R. (1998). Cellular immune responses to acute stress in female caregivers of dementia patients and matched controls. *Health Psychology*, 17: 182–9.

Callaghan, P. and Li, H.C. (2002). The effect of pre-operative psychological interventions on post-operative outcomes in Chinese women having an elective hysterectomy. *British Journal of Health Psychology*, 7: 247–52.

Calnan, M. (1987). *Health and Illness: The Lay Perspective*. London: Tavistock.

Camp, D.E., Klesges, R.C. and Relyea, G. (1993). The relationship between bodyweight concerns and adolescent smoking. *Health Psychology*, 12: 24–32.

Campbell, J.D., Mauksch, H.O., Neikirk, H.J. and Hosokawa, M.C. (1990). Collaborative practice and provider styles in delivering health care. *Social Science and Medicine*, 30: 1359–65.

Campbell, L.A., Kirkpatrick, S.E., Berry, C.C. and Lamberti, J.J. (1992). Psychological preparation of mothers of pre-school children undergoing cardiac catheterization. *Psychology and Health*, 7: 175–85.

Campbell, M.K., Tessaro, I., DeVellis, B. Benedict, S., Kelsey, K. and Belton, L. (2002). Effects of a tailored health promotion program for female blue-collar workers: health works for women. *Preventive Medicine*, 4: 313–23.

Cannon, W.B. (1932). *The Wisdom of the Body*. New York: W.W. Norton.

Carlson, N. (2003) *Physiology of Behaviour*, 8th edition, Boston MA: Allyn and Bacon.

Carlson, L.E., Taenzer, P., Koopmans, J. and Casebeer, A. (2003). Predictive value of aspects of the transtheoretical model on smoking cessation in a community-based, large-group cognitive behavioral program. *Addictive Behaviors*, 28: 725–40.

Caro, J.J., Speckman, J.L., Salas, M., Raggio, G. and Jackson, J.D. (1999). Effect of initial drug choice on persistence with antihypertensive therapy: the importance of actual practice data. *Canadian Medical Association Journal*, 160: 41–6.

Carod-Artal, J., Egido, J.A., González, J.L. and de Seijas, E.V. (2000). Quality of life among stroke survivors evaluated 1 year after stroke. *Stroke*, 31: 2995–3005.

Carr, A.J. and Higginson, I.J. (2001). Are quality of life measures patient centred? *British Medical Journal*, 32: 1357–60.

Carr, D. (2003). A 'good death' for whom? Quality of spouse's death and psychological distress among older widowed persons. *Journal of Health and Social Behavior*, 44: 215–32.

Carroll, D., Davey-Smith, G. and Bennett, P. (1996). Some observations on health and socioeconomic status. *Journal of Health Psychology*, 1: 1–17.

Carroll, D., Moore, R.A., McQuay, H.J., Fairman, F., Tramer, M. and Leijon, G. (2001). Transcutaneous electrical nerve stimulation (TENS) for chronic pain. In *The Cochrane Library*, issue 4. Oxford: Update Software.

Carroll, K.M., Libby, B., Sheehan, J. and Hyland, N. (2001). Motivational interviewing to enhance treatment initiation in substance abusers: an effectiveness study. *American Journal of Addiction*, 10: 35–9.

Carver, C.S. and Scheier, M.F. (1981). *Attention and Self-Regulation: A Control Theory Approach to Human Behavior*. New York: Springer.

Carver, C.S., Pozo, C., Harris, S.D., Noriega, V., Scheier, M.F., Robinson, D.S., Ketchan, A.S., Moffat, F.L., Jr and Clark, K.C. (1993). How coping mediates the effect of optimism on distress: a study of women with early stage breast cancer. *Journal of Personality and Social Psychology*, 65: 375–90.

Carver, C.S., Scheier, M.F. and Pozo, C. (1992). Conceptualizing the process of coping with health problems. In H.S. Friedman (ed.), *Hostility, Coping and Health*. Washington: American Psychological Association.

Carver, C.S., Scheier, M.F. and Weintraub, J.K. (1989). Assessing coping strategies: a theoretically based approach. *Journal of Personality and Social Psychology*, 56: 267–83.

Cassel, J. (1974). An epidemiological perspective of psychosocial factors in disease etiology. *American Journal of Public Health*, 64: 1040–3.

Cassell, E.J. (1976). Disease as an 'it': concepts of disease revealed by patients' presentation of symptoms. *Social Science and Medicine*, 10: 143–6.

Cassell, E.J. (1982). Paracetamol plus supplementary doses of codeine. An analgesic study of repeated doses. *European Journal of Clinical Pharmacology*, 23: 315–19.

Cassileth, B.R., Lusk, E.J., Brown, L.L. and Cross, P.A. (1985). Psychosocial status of cancer patients and next of kin: normative data from the profile of mood states. *Journal of Psychosocial Oncology*, 3: 99–105.

Catz, S.L., Gore-Felton, C. and McClure, J.B. (2002). Psychological distress among minority and low-income women living with HIV. *Behavioral Medicine*, 28: 53–60.

Cavelaars, A.E.J.M., Kunst, A.E. and Mackenbach, J.P. (1997). Socio-economic differences in risk factors for morbidity and mortality in the European Community. *Journal of Health Psychology*, 2: 353–72.

Centers for Disease Control and Prevention (1996). Community-level prevention of human immunodeficiency virus infection among high-risk populations: the AIDS Community Demonstration Projects. *MMWR Morbidity and Mortality Weekly Reports*, 45 (RR-6): 1–24.

Centers for Disease Control and Prevention (2004). Impact of a smoking ban on restaurant and bar revenues – El Paso, Texas. *MMWR Morbidity and Mortality Weekly Reports*, 53: 150–1.

Chalmers, B. (1996). Western and African conceptualisations of health. *Psychology and Health*, 12: 1–10.

Champion, V.L. (1990). Breast self-examination in women 35 and older: a prospective study. *Journal of Behavioural Medicine*, 13: 523–38.

Champion, V.L. and Miller, T.K. (1992). Variables related to breast self-examination. *Psychology of Women Quarterly*, 16: 81–96.

Chan, D.K.-S. and Fishbein, M. (1993). Determinants of women's intentions to tell their partner to use condoms. *Journal of Applied Social Psychology*, 23: 1455–70.

Charmaz, K. (1983). Loss of self: a fundamental form of suffering in the chronically ill. *Sociology of Health and Illness*, 5: 168–95.

Charmaz, K. (1991). *Good Days, Bad Days: The Self in Chronic Illness and Time*. New Brunswick, NJ: Rutgers University Press.

Charmaz, K. (1994). Identity dilemmas of chronically ill men. *Sociological Quarterly*, 35: 269–88.

Chassin, C., Presson, C.C., Rose, J.S. and Sherman, S.J. (1996). The natural history of cigarettes from adolescence to adulthood: demographic predictors of continuity and change. *Health Psychology*, 15: 478–84.

Cheing, G.L., Tsui, A.Y., Lo, S.K. and Hui-Chan, C.W. (2003). Optimal stimulation duration of TENS in the management of osteoarthritic knee pain. *Journal of Rehabilitation Medicine*, 35: 62–8.

Chen, S.Y., Gibson, S., Katz, M.H., Klausner, J.D. and Dilley, S. (2002). Continuing increases in sexual risk behavior and sexually transmitted diseases among men who have sex with men: San Francisco, Calif., 1999–2001. *American Journal of Public Health*, 92: 1387–8.

Cheng, C. (2000). Seeking medical consultation: perceptual and behavioural characteristics distinguishing consulters and nonconsulters with functional dyspepsia. *Psychosomatic Medicine*, 62: 844–52.

Cheng, T.L., Savageau, J.A., Sattler, A.L. and DeWitt, T.G. (1993). Confidentiality in health care: a survey of knowledge, perceptions, and attitudes among high school students. *Journal of the American Medical Association*, 269: 1404–7.

Chesney, M.A. (2003). Adherence to HAART regimes. *AIDS Patient Care and STDs*, 17: 169–77.

Chesney, M.A., Folkman, S. and Chambers, D. (1996). Coping effectiveness training for men living with HIV: preliminary findings. *International Journal of STDs and AIDS*, suppl. 2: 75–82.

Chochinov, H.M., Hack, T., Hassard, T., Kristjanson, L.J., McClement, S. and Harlos, M. (2002). Dignity in the terminally ill: a cross-sectional, cohort study. *The Lancet*, 360: 2026–30.

Chochinov, H.M., Tataryn, D.J., Wilson, K.G., Ennis, M. and Lander, S. (2000). Prognostic awareness and the terminally ill. *Psychosomatics*, 41: 500–4.

Choi, W.S., Harris, K.J., Okuyemi, K. and Ahluwalia, J.S. (2003). Predictors of smoking initiation among college-bound high school students. *Annals of Behavioral Medicine*, 26: 69–74.

Christensen, A.J., Edwards, D.L., Wiebe, J.S., Benotsch, E.G., McKelevey, L., Andrews, M. and Lubaroff, D.M. (1996). Effect of verbal self-disclosure on natural killer cell activity: moderating influence of cynical hostility. *Psychosomatic Medicine*, 58: 150–5.

Christensen, C., Larson, J.R., Jr, Abbott, A., Ardolino, A., Kranz, T. and Pfeiffer, C. (2000). Decision making of clinical teams: communication patterns and diagnostic error. *Medical Decision Making*, 20: 45–50.

Cioffi, D. (1991). Beyond attentional strategies: a cognitive-perceptual model of somatic interpretation. *Psychological Bulletin*, 109: 25–41.

Clark, D.B. and Sayette, M.A. (1993). Anxiety and the development of alcoholism: clinical and scientific issues. *American Journal on Addictions*, 2: 59–76.

Clark, S.L. and Stephens, M.A.P. (1996). Stroke patients' well-being as a function of caregiving spouses' helpful and unhelpful actions. *Personal Relationships*, 3: 171–84.

Clark-Carter, D. (2003). Effect sizes; the missing piece in the jigsaw. *The Psychologist*, 16: 636–8.

Clarke, R. (2000). Perceptions of interethnic group racism predict increased vascular reactivity to a laboratory challenge in college women. *Annals of Behavioral Medicine*, 22: 214–22.

Classen, C., Butler, L.D., Koopman, C., Miler, E., DiMiceli, S., Giese-Davis, J., Fobair, P., Carlson, R.W., Kraemer, H.C. and Spiegel, D. (2001). Supportive-expressive group therapy and distress in patients with metastatic breast cancer: a randomized clinical intervention trial. *Archives of General Psychiatry*, 58: 494–501.

Coates, T.J., McKusick, L., Kuno, R. and Stites, D.P. (1989). Stress management training reduced numbers of sexual partners but did not improve immune function in men infected with HIV. *American Journal of Public Health*, 79: 885–7.

Cobb, S. (1976). Social support as a moderator of life stress. *Psychosomatic Medicine*, 38: 300–14.

Cockburn, J., Paul, C., Tzelepis, F., McElduff, P. and Byles, J. (2003). Delay in seeking advice for symptoms that potentially indicate bowel cancer. *American Journal of Health Behavior*, 27: 401–7.

Cohen, F. and Lazarus, R. (1979). Coping with the stresses of illness. In G.C. Stone, F. Cohen and N.E. Adler (eds), *Health Psychology: A Handbook*. San Francisco: Jossey-Bass.

Cohen, H.J., Pieper, C.F., Harris, T., Rao, K. and Currie, M.M.K. (1997). The association of plasma IL-6 levels with functional disability in community-dwelling elderly. *Journal of Gerontology. A: Biological Science and Medical Science*, 52: M201–8.

Cohen, L.A. (1987). Diet and cancer. *Scientific American*, 102: 42–8.

Cohen, M., Hoffman, R.G., Cromwell, C., Schmeidler, J., Ebrahim, F., Carrera, G., Endorf, F., Alfonso, C.A. and Jacobson, J.M. (2002). The prevalence of distress in persons with human immunodeficiency virus infection. *Psychosomatics*, 43: 10–15.

Cohen, S. (1988). Psychosocial models of the role of social support in the etiology of physical disease, *Health Psychology*, 7: 269–97.

Cohen, S., Doyle, M.J., Skoner, D.P., Fireman, P., Gwaltney, J.M., Jr and Newsom, J.T. (1995). State and trait negative affect as predictors of objective and subjective symptoms of respiratory viral infections. *Journal of Personality and Social Psychology*, 68: 159–69.

Cohen, S., Evans, G.W., Stokols, D. and Krantz, D.S. (1986). *Behavior, Health and Environmental Stress*. New York: Plenum.

Cohen, S., Frank, E., Doyle, W.J., Skoner, D.P., Rabin, B.S. and Gwaltney, J.M., Jr (1998). Types of stressors that increase susceptibility to the common cold in healthy adults. *Health Psychology*, 17: 214–23.

Cohen, S. and Herbert, T.B. (1996). Health psychology: psychological factors and physical disease from the perspective of human psychoneuroimmunology. *Annual Review of Psychology*, 47: 113–42.

Cohen, S. and Hoberman, H. (1983). Positive events and social support as buffers of life change stress. *Journal of Applied Social Psychology*, 13: 99–125.

Cohen, S., Kamarck, T. and Mermelstein, R. (1983). A global measure of perceived stress. *Journal of Health and Social Behaviour*, 24: 385–96.

Cohen, S., Tyrell, D.A. and Smith, A.P. (1993a). Life events, perceived stress, negative affect and susceptibility to the common cold. *Journal of Personality and Social Psychology*, 64: 131–40.

Cohen, S., Tyrell, D.A. and Smith, A.P. (1993b). Psychological stress and susceptibility to the common cold. *New England Journal of Medicine*, 325: 606–12.

Cohen, S. and Williamson, G.M. (1991). Stress and infectious disease in humans. *Psychological Bulletin*, 109: 5–24.

Cohen, S. and Wills, T.A. (1985). Stress, social support and the buffering hypothesis. *Psychological Bulletin*, 98: 310–57.

Cole, S.W., Kemeny, M.E., Taylor, S.E. and Visscher, B.R. (1996). Elevated physical health risk among gay men who conceal their homosexual identity. *Health Psychology*, 15: 23–51.

Coleman, D.L. (1979). Obesity genes: beneficial effects in heterozygous mice. *Science*, 203: 663–5.

Coleman, P.G. (1999). Identity management in later life. In R.T. Woods (ed.), *Psychological Problems of Ageing: Assessment, Treatment and Care*. Chichester: Wiley.

COMMIT (1995). Community intervention trial for smoking cessation (COMMIT): II. Changes in adult cigarette smoking prevalence. *American Journal of Public Health*, 85: 193–200.

Compas, B.E., Stoll, M.F., Thomsen, A.H., Oppedisano, G., Epping-Jordan, J.A. and Krag, D.N. (1999). Adjustment to breast cancer: age-related differences in coping and emotional distress. *Breast Cancer Research and Treatment*, 54: 195–203.

Conner, M. and Armitage, C.J. (1998). Extending the theory of planned behaviour: a review and avenues for further research. *Journal of Applied Social Psychology*, 28: 1429–64.

Conner, M. and Norman, P. (1996). *Predicting Health Behaviour: Research and Practice with Social Cognition Models*. Buckingham: Open University Press.

Constans, J.I., Mathews, A., Brantley, P.J. and James, T. (1999). Attentional reactions to an MI: the impact of mood state, worry, and coping style. *Journal of Psychosomatic Research*, 46: 415–23.

Cooper, C.L. and Payne, R. (eds), (1988). *Causes, Coping and Consequences of Stress at Work*. Chichester: Wiley.

Cordova, M., Andrykowski, M., Kenady, D., McGrath, P., Sloan, D. and Redd, W. (1995). Frequency and correlates of posttraumatic-stress-disorder-like symptoms after treatment for breast cancer. *Journal of Consulting and Clinical Psychology*, 63: 981–6.

Costa, P.T., Jr and McCrae, R.R. (1987). Neuroticism, somatic complaints and disease: is the bark worse than the bite? *Journal of Personality*, 55: 299–316.

Costa, P.T. and McCrae, R.R. (1992a). Four ways five factors are basic. *Personality and Individual Differences*, 13: 653–65.

Costa, P.T. and McCrae, R.R. (1992b). *Revised NEO Personality Inventory (NEO PI-R) and NEO five-factor inventory (NEO FFI) professional manual*. Odessa, Fla: Psychological Assessment Resources.

Cotman, C.W. and Engesser-Cesar, C. (2002). Exercise enhances and protects brain function. *Exercise Sport Science Reviews*, 30: 75–9.

Courtenay, W.H. (2000). Constructions of masculinity and their influence on men's well-being: a theory of gender and health. *Social Science and Medicine*, 50: 1385–1401.

Cox, K. (2003). Assessing the quality of life of patients in phase I and II anti-cancer drug trials: interviews versus questionnaires. *Social Science and Medicine*, 56: 921–34.

Cox, K.L., Gorely, T.J., Puddey, I.B., Burke, V. and Beilin, L.J. (2003). Exercise behaviour change in 40- to 65-year-old women: the SWEAT study (Sedentary Women Exercise Adherence Trial). *British Journal of Health Psychology*, 8: 477–95.

Cox, W.M. and Klinger, E. (2004). A motivational model of alcohol use: Determinants of use and change. In: W.M. Cox and E. Klinger (eds), *Handbook of Motivational Counselling: Concepts, Approaches, and Assessments*. (121–38). Chichester: John Wiley.

Coyne, J. and Fiske, V. (1992). Couples coping with chronic and catastrophic illness. In T.J. Akamatsu, M.A.P. Stephens, S.E. Hobfoll and J.H. Crowther (eds), *Family Health Psychology*. Washington: Hemisphere Publishing.

Coyne, J.C., Benazon, N.R., Rohrbaugh, M.J. and Shoham, V. (2003). Patient and spousal attitude in couples living with chronic heart failure. Symposium paper presented at the 17th Conference of the European Health Psychology Society, September, Kos.

Coyne, J.C. and Racioppo, M.W. (2000). Never the twain shall meet? Closing the gap between coping research and clinical intervention research. *American Psychologist*, 55: 655–64.

Coyne, J.C. and Smith, D.A.F (1991). Couples coping with a myocardial infarction: A contextual perspective on wive's distress. *Journal of Personality and Social Psychology*, 61: 404–12.

Cramer, J.A. (1998). Enhancing patient compliance in the elderly. Role of packaging aids and monitoring. *Drugs and Aging*, 12: 7–15.

Cramer, J.A. (2004). A systematic review of adherence with medications for diabetes. *Diabetes Care*, 27: 1218–24.

Creuss, D.G., Antoni, M.H., McGregor, B.A., Kilbourn, K.M., Boyers, A.E., Alferi, S.M., Carver, C.S. and Kumar, M. (2000). Cognitive-behavioral stress management reduces serum cortisol by enhancing benefit finding among women being treated for early stage breast cancer. *Psychosomatic Medicine*, 62: 304–8.

Crisp, A., Sedgwick, P., Halek, C., Joughin, N. and Humphrey, H. (1999). Why may teenage girls persist in smoking? *Journal of Adolescence*, 22: 657–72.

Crossley, M.L. (2000). *Rethinking Health Psychology*. Buckingham: Open University Press.

Crossley, M.L. and Small, N. (1998). Evaluation of HIV/AIDS Education Training Services Provided by London Lighthouse at St. Ann's Hospice. Stockport Health Authority.

Croyle, R.T. and Barger, S.D. (1993). Illness cognition. In S. Maes, H. Leventhal and M. Johnston (eds), *International Review of Health Psychology*, Vol. II. Chichester: Wiley.

Croyle, R.T. and Ditto, P.M. (1990). Illness cognition and behavior: an experimental approach. *Journal of Behavioral Medicine*, 13: 31–52.

Cummings, J.H. and Bingham, S.A. (1998). Diet and the prevention of cancer. *British Medical Journal*, 317: 1636–40.

Curbow, B., Somerfield, M.R., Baker, F., Wingard, J.R. and Legro, M.W. (1993). Personal changes, dispositional optimism, and psychological adjustment to bone marrow transplantation. *Journal of Behavioral Medicine*, 16: 423–43.

Curry, S.J. and Emmons, K.M. (1994). Theoretical models for predicting and improving compliance with breast cancer screening. Mini-series: advances in behavioural medicine research on breast cancer. *Annals of Behavioral Medicine*, 16: 302–16.

Cutrona, C.E. and Russell, D.W. (1987). The provision of social relationships and adaptation to stress. In W.H. Jones and D. Perlman (eds), *Advances in Personal Relationships*, Vol. 1. Greenwich, Conn.: JAI Press.

Cutrona, C.E. and Russell, D.W. (1990). Type of social support and specific stress: toward a theory of optimal matching. In B.A. Sarason, I.G. Sarason and G.R. Pierce (eds), *Social Support: An Interactional View*. New York: Wiley.

Dababneh, A.J., Swanson, N. and Shell, R.L. (2001). Impact of added rest breaks on the productivity and well being of workers. *Ergonomics*, 44: 164–74.

Dalton, S.O., Boesen, E.H., Ross, L., Schapiro, I.R. and Johansen, C. (2002). Mind and cancer: do psychological factors cause cancer? *European Journal of Cancer*, 38: 1313–23.

Dancey, C.P., Taghavi, M., Fox, R.J. The relationship between daily stress and symptoms of irritable bowel: a time-series approach. *Journal of Psychosomatic Research*. May, 1998. 44(5): 537–45.

Dantzer, R. and Kelley, K.W. (1989). Stress and immunity: an integrated view of relationships between the brain and the immune system. *Life Sciences*, 44: 1995–2008.

Darnley, S.E., Kennedy, T., Jones, R., Chalder, T. and Wessley, S. (2002). A randomised controlled trial of the addition of cognitive behavioural therapy (CBT) to antispasmodic therapy for irritable bowel syndrome (IBS) in primary care. *Gastroenterology*, 122: A-69.

Davey-Smith, G., Ebrahim, S. and Frankel, S. (2001). How policy informs the evidence: 'evidence-based' thinking can lead to debased policy making (editorial). *British Medical Journal*, 322: 184–5.

Davey-Smith, G. and Philips, A.N. (1991). Socioeconomic conditions in childhood and ischaemic heart disease in middle age. *British Medical Journal*, 302: 113–14.

Davey-Smith, G., Wentworth, D., Neaton, J.D., Stamler, R. and Stamler, J. (1996). Socio-economic differentials in mortality risk among men screened for the Multiple Risk Factor Intervention Trial, 2: black men. *American Journal of Public Health*, 86: 497–504.

David, J.P. and Suls, J. (1996). Coping efforts in daily life: role of big five traits and problem appraisals. *Journal of Personality*, 67: 265–94.

Davidson, P.R. and Parker, K.C.H. (2001). Eye movement desensitization and reprocessing (EMDR): a meta-analysis. *Journal of Consulting and Clinical Psychology*, 69: 305–16.

Davies, J.B. and Baker, R. (1987). The impact of self-presentation and interviewer bias on self-reported heroin use. *British Journal of Addiction*, 82: 907–12.

Dearing, J.W., Rogers, E.M., Meyer, G., Casey, M.K., Rao, N., Campo, S. and Henderson, G.M. (1996). Social marketing and diffusion-based strategies for communicating with unique populations: HIV prevention in San Francisco. *Journal of Health Communication*, 1: 343–63.

Deary, I.J., Clyde, Z. and Frier, B.M. (1997). Constructs and models in health psychology: the case of personality and illness reporting in diabetes mellitus. *British Journal of Health Psychology*, 2: 35–54.

DeBoer, M.F., Ryckman, R.M., Pruyn, J.F. and Van den Borne, H.W. (1999). Psychosocial correlates of cancer relapse and survival: a literature review. *Patient Education and Counselling*, 37: 215–30.

DeFoe, J.R. and Breed, W. (1989). Consulting to change media contents: two cases in alcohol education. *International Quarterly of Community Health Education*, 4: 257–72.

DeFriese, G. and Woomert, A. (1983). Self-care among the US elderly. *Research on Aging*, 5: 3–23.

De Haes, H. and Koedoot, N. (2003). Patient centered decision making in palliative cancer treatment: a world of paradoxes. *Patient Education and Counselling*, 50: 43–9.

Dehghani, M., Sharpe, L. and Nicholas, M.K. (2003). Selective attention to pain-related information in chronic musculoskeletal pain patients. *Pain*, 105: 37–46.

de Lange, A.H., Taris, T.W., Kompier, M.A., Houtman, I.L. and Bongers, P.M. (2003). 'The very best of the millennium': longitudinal research and the demand–control–(support) model. *Journal of Occupational Health Psychology*, 8: 282–305.

Dembrowski, T.M., MacDougall, J.M., Costa, P.T., Jr and Grandits, G.A. (1989). Components of hostility as predictors of sudden death and myocardial infarction in the Multiple Risk Factor Intervention Trial. *Psychosomatic Medicine*, 51: 514–22.

De Moor, C., Sterner, J., Hall, M., Warneke, C., Gilani, Z., Amato, R. and Cohen, L. (2002). A pilot study of the effects of expressive writing on psychological and behavioral adjustment in patients enrolled in a phase II trial of vaccine therapy for metastatic renal cell carcinoma. *Health Psychology*, 21: 615–19.

Denollet, J. (1998). Personality and coronary heart disease: the type-D scale-16 (DS16). *Annals of Behavioral Medicine*, 20: 209–15.

Denollet, J. and dePotter, B. (1992). Coping subtypes for men with coronary heart disease: relationship to well-being, stress and type-A behavior. *Psychological Medicine*, 22: 667–84.

Denollet, J., Sys, S.U., Stroobant, N., Rombouts, H., Gillebert, T.C. and Brutsaert, D.L. (1996). Personality as an independent predictor of long-term mortality in patients with coronary heart disease. *The Lancet*, 347: 417–21.

de Nooijer, J., Lechner, L. and de Vries, H.A. (2001). Qualitative study on detecting cancer symptoms and seeking medical help; an application of Andersen's model of total patient delay. *Patient Education and Counseling*, 42: 145–57.

Department of Health (1991). *The Health of the Nation*. London: HMSO.

Department of Health (1992). *The Health of the Nation: A Strategy for Health in England*. London: HMSO.

Department of Health (1995). *Obesity: Reversing the Increasing Problem of Obesity in England*. Report from the Nutrition and Physical Activity Task Forces. London: HMSO.

Department of Health (1998a). *Health Survey for England: The Health of Young People 1995–1997.* London: Department of Health.

Department of Health (1998b). *Report of the Scientific Committee on Tobacco and Health.* London: Department of Health.

Department of Health (1999a). *Caring about Carers: A National Strategy for Carers.* London: Department of Health.

Department of Health (1999b) *Saving Lives: Our Healthier Nation.* London: Department of Health.

Department of Health (2000) Statistics on Smoking: England 1978 onwards. *Statistical Bulletin* 200/17. London: Department of Health.

Department of Health (2001a). *The 2000 Health Survey for England: The Health of Older People (aged 65+).* London: Department of Health.

Department of Health (2001b). *The Expert Patient: A New Approach to Chronic Disease Management for the 21st Century.* London: Department of Health.

Department of Health (2001c). *Involving Patients and the Public in Healthcare,* www.dh.gov.uk/ PolicyAndGuidance/OrganisationPolicy/PatientAnd PublicInvolvement/InvolvingPatientsPublicHealthcare/ fs/en.

Department of Health and Human Services (1996). Report of final mortality statistics, 1994. *Monthly Vital Statistics Report,* 45 (3 suppl.). Hyattsville, Md: Public Health Service.

Department of Health and Human Services (1998). *Health, United States, 1998: Socio-economic Status and Health Chartbook.* Hyattsville, Md: National Centre for Health Statistics.

Derbyshire, S.W. (2000). Exploring the pain 'neuromatrix'. *Current Reviews of Pain,* 4: 467–77.

De Ridder, D., Fournier, M. and Bensing, J. (2004). Does optimism affect symptom report in chronic disease? What are its consequences for self-care behaviour and physical functioning? *Journal of Psychosomatic Research,* 56: 341–50.

De Ridder, D. and Schreurs, K. (2001). Developing interventions for chronically ill patients: Is coping a helpful concept? *Clinical Psychology Review,* 21: 205–40.

Descartes, R. (1664). *Traite de l'homme.* Paris: Angot.

Detweiler, J.B., Bedell, B.T., Salovey, P., Pronin, E. and Rothman, A.J. (1999). Message framing and sunscreen use: gain framed messages motivate beachgoers. *Health Psychology,* 18: 189–96.

De Vellis, R.F., Lewis, M.A. and Sterba, K.R. (2003). Interpersonal emotional processes in adjustment to chronic illness. In J. Suls and K.A. Wallston (eds), *Social Psychological Foundations of Health and Illness.* Malden, Mass.: Blackwell.

Dey, P., Bundred, N., Gibbs, A., Hopwood, P., Baildam, A., Boggis, C., James, M., Knox, F., Leidecker, V. and Woodman, C. (2002). Costs and benefits of a one stop clinic compared with a dedicated breast clinic: randomised controlled trial. *British Medical Journal,* 324: 507.

Deyo, R.A. (1986). Early diagnostic evaluation of lower back pain. *Journal of General Internal Medicine,* 1: 328–38.

Deyo, R.A. (1991). Fads in the treatment of low back pain. *New England Journal of Medicine,* 325: 1039–40.

di Clemente, C.C. and Prochaska, J.O. (1982). Self-change and therapy change of smoking behavior: a comparison of processes of change in cessation and maintenance. *Addictive Behaviours,* 7: 133–42.

di Clemente, C.C. and Velicer, W.F. (1997). The transtheoretical model of health behavior change. *American Journal of Health Promotion,* 12: 11–12.

di Clemente, C.C., Prochaska, J.O., Fairhurst, S.K., Velicer, W.F., Velasquez, M.M. and Rossi, J.S. (1991). The process of smoking cessation: an analysis of precontemplation, contemplation, and preparation stages of change. *Journal of Consulting and Clinical Psychology,* 59: 295–304.

Didlake, R.H., Dreyfus, K., Kerman, R.H., Van Buren, C.T. and Kahan, B.D. (1988). Patient noncompliance: a major cause of late graft failure in cyclosporine-treated renal transplants. *Transplant Proceedings,* 20: 63–9.

Diefenbach, M.A., Leventhal, E.A., Leventhal, H. and Patrick-Miller, L. (1995). Negative affect relates to cross-sectional but not longitudinal symptom reporting: data from elderly adults. *Health Psychology,* 15: 282–8.

Digiusto, E. and Bird, K.D. (1995). Matching smokers to treatment: self-control versus social support. *Journal of Consulting and Clinical Psychology,* 63: 290–295.

Dijkstra, P.U., Geertzen, J.H., Stewart, R. and van der Schans, C.P. (2002). Phantom pain and risk factors: a multivariate analysis. *Journal of Pain Symptom Management,* 24: 578–85.

Dillay, J.W., McFarland, W., Woods, W.J., Sabatino, J., Lihatsh, T., Adler, B., Swig, L. and Dark, T. (2002). Thoughts associated with unprotected anal intercourse among men at high risk in San Francisco 1997–1999. *Psychology and Health,* 17: 235–46.

DiMatteo, R. (2004). The role of effective communication with children and their families in fostering adherence to pediatric regimes. *Patient Education and Counselling,* 55: 339–44.

DiMatteo, R.M., Lepper, H.D. and Croghan, T.W. (2000). Depression is a risk factor for noncompliance with medical treatment: meta-analysis of the effects of anxiety and depression on patient adherence. *Archives of Internal Medicine*, 160: 2101–7.

Dimigen, G. and Ferguson, K. (1993). An investigation into the relationship of children's cognitive development and their concepts of illness. *Psychologia*, 36: 97–102.

Ditto, P.H., Druley, J.A., Moore, K.A. *et al.* (1996). Fates worse than death: the role of valued life activities in health state evaluations. *Health Psychology*, 15: 332–43.

Ditto, T.T. and Jemmott, J.B., III (1989). From rarity to evaluative extremity: effects of prevalence information on evaluations of positive and negative characteristics. *Journal of Personality and Social Psychology*, 57: 16–26.

Dodds, J. and Mercey, D. (2002). *London Gay Men's Survey: 2001 Results*. London: Department of STDs, Royal Free and University College Medical School.

Dodds, J.P., Mercey, D.E., Parry, J.V. and Johnson, A.M. (2004). Increasing risk behaviour and high levels of undiagnosed HIV infection in a community sample of homosexual men. *Sexually Transmitted Infections*, 80: 236–40.

Dohrenwend, B.S. and Dohrenwend, B.P. (1982). Some issues in research on stressful life events. In T. Millon, C. Green and R. Meagher (eds), *Handbook of Clinical Health Psychology*, New York: Plenum.

Doll, R. and Hill, A.B. (1954). The mortality of doctors in relation to their smoking habits: a preliminary report. *British Medical Journal*, 1: 1451–5.

Doll, R. and Peto, R. (1981). *The Cause of Human Cancer*. Oxford: Oxford University Press.

Doll, R., Peto, R., Hall, E. and Gray, R. (1994). Mortality in relation to consumption of alcohol: 13 years observation on male British doctors. *British Medical Journal*, 309: 911–18.

Dooley, D., Fielding, J. and Levi, L. (1996). Health and unemployment. *Annual Review of Public Health*, 17: 449–65.

Doyal, L. (2001). Sex, gender, and health: the need for a new approach. *British Medical Journal*, 323: 1061–3.

Droomers, M., Schrijvers, C.T.M. and Mackenbach, J.P. (2002). Why do lower educated people continue smoking? Explanations from the longitudinal GLOBE study. *Health Psychology*, 21: 263–72.

Drossaert, C.H., Boer, H. and Seydel, E.R. (1996). Health education to improve repeat participation in the Dutch breast cancer screening programme: evaluation of a leaflet tailored to previous participants. *Patient Education and Counselling*, 8: 121–31.

Duffy, L.C., Zielezny, M.A., Marshall, J.R., Byers, T.E., Weiser, M.M., Phillips, M.D., Calkins, B.M., Ogra,

P.L. and Graham, S. (1991). Relevance of major stress events as an indicator of disease activity prevalence in inflammatory bowel disease. *Behavioral Medicine*, fall: 101–10.

Dunbar-Jacob, J., Burke, L.E. and Pucznski, S. (1995). Clinical assessment and management of adherence to medication regimens. In P.M. Nicassio and T.W. Smith (eds), *Managing Chronic Illness: A Biopsychosocial Perspective*. Washington: American Psychological Association.

Dutta-Bergman, M.J. (2003). A descriptive narrative of healthy eating: a social marketing approach using psychographics in conjunction with interpersonal, community, mass media and new media activities. *Health Marketing Quarterly*, 20: 81–101.

Dusseldorp, E., van Elderen, T., Maes, S., Meulman, J. and Kraaij, V. (1999). A meta-analysis of psycho-educational programs for coronary heart disease patients. *Health Psychology*, 18: 506–19.

Dzewaltowski, D.A. (1989). Toward a model of exercise motivation. *Journal of Sport and Exercise Psychology*, 11: 251–69.

Eagly, A.H. and Chaiken, S. (1993). *The Psychology of Attitudes*. Orlando, Fla: Harcourt Brace Jovanovich.

Echabe, A.E., Guillen, C.S. and Ozamiz, J.A. (1992). Representations of health, illness and medicines: coping strategies and health promoting behaviour. *British Journal of Clinical Psychology*, 31: 339–49.

Echteld, M.A., Maes, S. and van Elderen, T.M.T. (1998). Predictors of quality of life in PTCA* patients: avoiding stressors increases quality of life. In R. Schwarzer (ed.), *Advances in Health Psychology Research*. Berlin: Berlin Free University. [* percutaneous transluminal coronary angioplasty]

Echteld, M.A., van Elderen, T.M.T. and van der Kamp, L.J.T. (2001). How goal disturbance, coping and chest pain relate to quality of life: a study among patients waiting for PTCA. *Quality of Life Research*, 10: 487–501.

Edelmann, R. (1999). *Psychosocial aspects of the health care process*. Harlow: Prentice Hall.

Edwards, G., Anderson, P., Babor, T., Casswell, S., Ferrence, N., *et al.*, (1994) *Alcohol Policy and the Public Good*. Oxford: Oxford University Press.

Edwards, W. (1954). The theory of decision making. *Psychological Bulletin*, 51: 380–417.

Egan, G. (1998). *The Skilled Helper: Models, Skills, and Methods for Effective Helping*. Monterey, Calif.: Brooks/Cole.

Egan, G. (2001). *The Skilled Helper: A Problem-Management and Opportunity-Development Approach to Helping*. Wadsworth.

Eiser, C. (1985). *The Psychology of Childhood Illness*. New York: Springer Verlag.

Eiser, C. and Havermans, T. (1992). Mothers' and fathers' coping with chronic childhood disease. *Psychology and Health*, 7: 249–57.

Eiser, C. and Morse, R. (2001). The measurement of quality of life in children: past and future perspectives. *Journal of Developmental and Behavioral Pediatrics*, 22: 248–56.

Eiser, C., Patterson, D. and Tripp, J.H. (1984). Diabetes and developing knowledge of the body. *Archives of Disease in Childhood*, 59: 167–9.

Eiser, J.R. (1996). Reconnecting the individual and the social in health psychology. *Psychology and Health*, 11: 605–18.

Eiser, J.R., Eiser, C. and Pauwels, C. (1993). Skin cancer: assessing perceived risk and behavioral attitudes. *Psychology and Health*, 8: 393–404.

Ellis, A. (1977). The basic clinical theory of rational–emotive therapy. In A. Ellis and R. Grieger (eds), *Handbook of Rational–Emotive Therapy*. New York: Springer Verlag.

Elmer, P.J., Grimm, R., Jr, Laing, B., Grandits, G., Svendsen, K., Van Heel, N., Betz, E., Raines, J., Link, M. and Stamler, J. (1995). Lifestyle intervention: results of the Treatment of Mild Hypertension Study (TOMHS). *Preventive Medicine*, 24: 378–88.

Elstein, A.S. and Schwarz, A. (2002). Clinical problem solving and diagnostic decision making: selective review of the cognitive literature. *British Medical Journal*, 324: 729–32.

Elwyn, G., Edwards, A., Kinnersley, P. and Grol, R. (2000). Shared decision making and the concept of equipoise: the competences of involving patients in healthcare choices. *British Journal of General Practice*, 50: 892–9.

Ely, J.W., Levinson, W., Elder, N.C., Mainous, A.G., III and Vinson, D.C. (1995). Perceived causes of family physicians' errors. *Journal of Family Practice*, 40: 337–44.

Endler, N.S. and Parker, J.D.A. (1993). The multidimensional assessment of coping: Concepts, issues, measurement. In G.L. Van Heck, P. Bonaiuto, I.J. Deary and W. Nowack (eds), *Personality Psychology in Europe*, Vol. 4. Netherlands: Tilburg University Press.

Endler, N.S., Parker, J.D.A. and Summerfeldt, L.J. (1998). Coping with health problems: developing a reliable and valid multidimensional measure. *Psychological Assessment*, 10: 195–205.

Engel, G.L. (1977). The need for a new medical model: a challenge for biomedicine. *Science*, 196: 129–36.

Engel, G.L. (1980). The clinical application of the biopsychosocial model. *American Journal of Psychiatry*, 137: 535–44.

Epstein, R.M., Quill, T.E. and McWhinney, I.R. (1999). Somatization reconsidered: incorporating the patient's experience of illness. *Archives of Internal Medicine*, 159: 215–22.

Eriksen, H.R., Ihlebaek, C., Mikkelsen, A., Gronningsaeter, H., Sandal, G.M. and Ursin, H. (2002). Improving subjective health at the worksite: a randomized controlled trial of stress management training, physical exercise and an integrated health programme. *Occupational Medicine*, 52: 383–91.

Eriksen, J., Jensen, M.K., Sjogren, P., Ekholm, O. and Rasmussen, N.K. (2003). Epidemiology of chronic non-malignant pain in Denmark. *Pain*, 106: 221–8.

Erikson, E.H. (1959). Identity and the life cycle. *Psychological Issues*, 1: 1–171.

Erikson, E.H. (1980). *Identity and the Life Cycle: A Reissue*. New York: W.W. Norton.

Erikson, E.H., Erikson, J.M. and Kivnick, H.Q. (1986). *Vital Involvement in Old Age: The Experience of Old Age in Our Time*. New York: W.W. Norton.

Esterling, B.A., Kiecolt-Glaser, J.K. and Glaser, R. (1996). Psychosocial modulation of cytokine induced natural killer cell activity in older adults. *Psychosomatic Medicine*, 58: 264–72.

Esterling, B.A., L'Abate, L., Murray, E.J. and Pennebaker, J.W. (1999). Empirical foundations for writing in prevention and psychotherapy: mental and physical health outcomes. *Clinical Psychology Review*, 19: 79–96.

European Commission (1999). *A Pan-EU Survey of Consumer Attitudes to Physical Activity, Body Weight and Health*. Luxembourg: EC. DGV/F.3.

Euroqol Group (1990). Euroqol: a new facility for the measurement of health related quality of life. *Health Policy*, 16: 199–208.

Evans, D. and Norman, P. (2002). Improving pedestrian road safety among adolescents: an application of the theory of planned behaviour. In D. Rutter and L. Quine (eds), *Changing Health Behaviour*. Buckingham: Open University Press.

Evans, R.L. and Bishop, D.S. (1990). Psychosocial outcomes in stroke survivors. *Stroke*, 21 (suppl. II): II-48–II-49.

Evans, S., Fishman, B., Spielman, L. and Haley, A. (2003). Randomized trial of cognitive behaviour therapy versus supportive psychotherapy for HIV-related peripheral neuropathic pain. *Psychosomatics*, 44: 44–50.

Evers, A.W., Kraaimaat, F.W., Geenen, R., Jacobs, J.W. and Bijlsma, J.W. (2003). Pain coping and social support as predictors of long-term functional disability and pain in early rheumatoid arthritis. *Behaviour Research and Therapy*, 41: 1295–310.

Evers, A.W., Kraaimaat, F.W., van Riel, P.L. and de Jong, A.J. (2002). Tailored cognitive-behavioral therapy in early rheumatoid arthritis for patients at risk: a randomized controlled trial. *Pain*, 100: 141–53.

Everson, S.A., Goldberg, D.E., Kaplan, G.A., Cohen, R.D., Pukkala, E., Tuomilehto, J. and Salonen, J.T. (1996). Hopelessness and risk of mortality and incidence of myocardial infarction and cancer. *Psychosomatic Medicine*, 58: 113–24.

Everson, S.A., McKey, B.S. and Lovallo, W.R. (1995). Effects of trait hostility on cardiovascular responses to harassment in young men. *International Journal of Behavioral Medicine*, 2: 172–91.

Expert Group (2004). Research in the behavioural and social sciences to improve cancer control and care: a strategy for development. *European Journal of Cancer*, 40: 316–25.

Eysenck, H.J. (1970). *The Structure of Human Personality*, 3rd edn. London: Methuen.

Eysenck, H.J. (1982). *Personality, Genetics and Behaviour*. New York: Praeger.

Eysenck, H.J. (1991). Dimensions of personality: 16, 5, or 3? Criteria for a taxonomic paradigm. *Personality and Individual Differences*, 12: 773–90.

Eysenck, H.J. and Grossarth-Maticek, R. (1989). Prevention of cancer and coronary heart disease and the reduction in the cost of the National Health Service. *Journal of Social, Political and Economic Studies*, 14: 25–47.

Faller, H. and Bülzebruck, H. (2002). Coping and survival in lung cancer: a 10-year follow-up. *American Journal of Psychiatry*, 159: 2105–7.

Fallowfield, L.J., Hall, A., Maguire, G.P. and Baum, M. (1990). Psychological outcomes of different treatment policies in women with early breast cancer outside a clinical trial. *British Medical Journal*, 301: 575–80.

Fallowfield, L., Jenkins, V., Farewell, V., Saul, J., Duffy, A. and Eves, R. (2002). Efficacy of a Cancer Research UK communication skills training model for oncologists: a randomised controlled trial. *The Lancet*, 359: 650–6.

Family Heart Study Group (1994). Randomised controlled trial evaluating cardiovascular screening and intervention in general practice: principal results of British family heart study. *British Medical Journal*, 308: 313–20.

Farber, N.J., Urban, S.Y., Collier, V.U., Weiner, J., Polite, R.G., Davis, E.B. and Boyer, E.G. (2002). The good news about giving bad news to patients. *Journal of General Internal Medicine*, 17: 914–22.

Farooqi, I.S., Jebb, S.A., Langmack, G., Lawrence, E., Cheetham, C.H., Prentice, A.M., Hughes, I.A., McCamish, M.A. and O'Rahilly, S. (1999). Effects of recombinant leptin therapy in a child with congenital leptin deficiency. *New England Journal of Medicine*, 341: 879–84.

Farquhar, J., Fortmann, S., Flora, J., Taylor, B., Haskell, W., Williams, P., Maccoby, N. and Wood, P. (1990a). Effects of community-wide education on cardiovascular disease risk factors. *Journal of the American Medical Association*, 264: 359–65.

Farquhar, J.W., Fortmann, S.P., Flora, J.A., Taylor, C.B., Haskell, W.L., Williams, P.T., Maccoby, N. and Wood, P.D. (1990b). Effects of community-wide education on cardiovascular disease risk factors. The Stanford Five-City Project. *Journal of the American Medical Association*, 264: 359–65.

Farquhar, J., Maccoby, N. and Wood, P. (1977). Community education for cardiovascular disease. *The Lancet*, 1: 1192–5.

Faulkner, A. (1998). *When the News is Bad*. Cheltenham: Stanley Thorne.

Faulkner, A., Argent, J., Jones, A. and O'Keeffe, C. (1995). Improving the skills of doctors in giving distressing information. *Medical Education*, 29: 303–7.

Fauerbach, J.A., Lawrence, J.W., Haythornthwaite, J.A. and Richter, L. (2002). Coping with the stress of a painful medical procedure. *Behaviour Research and Therapy*, 40: 1003–15.

Fawzy, F.I., Canada, A.L. and Fawzy, N.W. (2003). Malignant melanoma: effects of a brief, structured psychiatric intervention on survival and recurrence at 10-year follow-up. *Archives of General Psychiatry*, 60: 100–3.

Fawzy, F.I. and Fawzy, N.W. (1998). Psychoeducational interventions. In J. Holland (ed.), *Textbook of Psycho-Oncology*. New York: Oxford University Press.

Fawzy, F.I., Fawzy, N.W., Hyun, C.S., Elashoff, R., Guthrie, D., Fahey, J.L. and Morton, D.L. (1993). Malignant melanoma: effects of an early structured psychiatric intervention, coping, and affective state on recurrence and survival 6 years later. *Archives of General Psychiatry*, 50: 681–9.

Feldman, P.J., Cohen, S., Doyle, W.J., Skoner, D. and Gwaltney, J.M., Jr (1999). The impact of personality on the reporting of unfounded symptoms and illness. *Journal of Personality and Social Psychology*, 77: 370–8.

Felsten, G. (2004). Stress reactivity and vulnerability to depressed mood in college students. *Personality and Individual Differences*, 36: 789–800.

Fenton, K.A., Korovessis, C., Johnson, A.M., McCadden, A., McManus, S., Wellings, K., Mercer, C.H., Carder, C., Copas, A.J., Nanchahel, K., Macdowall, W., Ridgeway, G., Field, J. and Erens, B. (2001). Sexual behaviour in Britain: reported sexually transmitted infections and prevalence of genital *Chlamydia trachomatir* infection. *The Lancet*, 358: 1851–4.

Ferrie, J.E., Martikainen, P., Shipley, M.J., Marmot, M.G. and Smith, G.D. (2001). Employment status and health after privatisation in white collar civil servants: prospective cohort study. *British Medical Journal*, 322: 647.

Ferro, J.M. and Crespo, M. (1994). Prognosis after transient ischemic attack and ischemic stroke in young adults. *Stroke*, 25: 1611–16.

Ferruci, L., Baldasseroni, S., Bandinelli, D., De Alfieri, W., Cartei, A., Calvani, D., Baldini, A., Masotti, G. and Marchionni, N. (2000). Disease severity and health-related quality of life across different chronic conditions, *Journal of the American Geriatrics Society*, 48: 1490–95.

Festinger, L. (1957). *A Theory of Cognitive Dissonance*. Stanford, Calif.: Stanford University Press.

Figueiras, M.J. and Weinman, J. (2003). Do similar patient and spouse perceptions of myocardial infarction predict recovery? *Psychology and Health*, 18: 201–16.

Filakti, H. and Fox, J. (1995). Differences in mortality by housing tenure and by car access from the OPCS Longitudinal Study. *Population Trends*, 81: 27–30.

Fine, P.G., Roberts, W.J., Gillette, R.G. and Child, T.R. (1994). Slowly developing placebo responses confound tests of intravenous phentolamine to determine mechanisms underlying idiopathic chronic low back pain. *Pain*, 56: 235–42.

Finnegan, J.R., Jr, Meischke, H., Zapka, J.G., Leviton, L., Meshack, A., Benjamin-Garner, R., Estabrook, B., Hall, N.J., Schaeffer, S., Smith, C., Weitzman, E.R., Raczynski, J. and Stone, E. (2000). Patient delay in seeking care for heart attack symptoms: findings from focus groups conducted in five U.S. regions. *Preventive Medicine*, 31: 205–13.

Finney, L.J. and Iannotti, R.J. (2002). Message framing and mammography screening: a theory-driven intervention. *Behavioral Medicine*, 28: 5–14.

Fishbein, M. (1967). Attitude and the prediction of behavior. In M. Fishbein (ed.), *Readings in Attitude Theory and Measurement*. New York: Wiley.

Fishbein, M. and Ajzen, I. (1985). *Belief, Attitude, Intention and Behavior: An Introduction to Theory and Research*. Reading, Mass.: Addison-Wesley.

Fisher, J.D., Bell, P.A. and Baum, A. (1984). *Environmental Psychology*, 2nd edn. New York: Holt, Rinehart & Winston.

Fisher, K. and Johnston, M. (1996a). Emotional distress as a mediator of the relationship between pain and disability: an experimental study. *British Journal of Health Psychology*, 1: 207–18.

Fisher, K. and Johnston, M. (1996b). Experimental manipulation of perceived control and its effect on disability. *Psychology and Health*, 11: 657–69.

Fisher, K. and Johnston, M. (1998). Emotional distress and control cognitions as mediators of the impact of chronic pain on disability. *British Journal of Health Psychology*, 3: 225–36.

Fiske, S.T. and Taylor, S.E. (1991). *Social Cognition*, 2nd edn. New York: McGraw-Hill.

Fleishman, J.A., Sherbourne, C.D., Cleary, P.D., Wu, A.W., Crystal, S. and Hays, R.D. (2003). Patterns of coping among persons with HIV infection: configurations, correlates, and change. *American Journal of Community Psychology*, 32: 187–204.

Fletcher, S.W., Black, W., Harris, R., Riner, B.K. and Shapiro, S. (1993). Report of the international workshop on screening for breast cancer. *Journal of the National Cancer Institute*, 85: 1644–56.

Fletcher, S.W., Harris, R.P., Gonzalez, J.J., Degnan, D., Lannin, D.R., Strecher, V.J., Pilgrim, C., Quade, D., Earp, J.A. and Clark, R.L. (1993). Increasing mammography utilization: a controlled study. *Journal of the National Cancer Institute*, 20: 112–20.

Flor, H., Breitenstein, C., Birbaumer, N. and Fuerst, M. (1995). A psychophysiological analysis of spouse solicitousness towards pain behaviours, spouse interaction and physical consequences. *Behavior Therapy*, 26: 255–72.

Foa, E.B., Rothbaum, B.O., Riggs, D.S. and Murdock, T.B. (1991). Treatment of posttraumatic stress disorder in rape victims: a comparison between cognitive and behavioural procedures and counselling. *Journal of Consulting and Clinical Psychology*, 59: 715–23.

Folkman, S. (1984). Personal control and stress and coping processes: a theoretical analysis. *Journal of Personality and Social Psychology*, 46: 839–52.

Folkman, S. and Chesney, M. (1995). Coping with HIV infection. In M. Stain and A. Baum (eds), *Chronic Diseases. Perspectives in Behavioral Medicine*. Hillsdale, NJ: Lawrence Erlbaum.

Folkman, S. and Lazarus, R.S. (1988). *Manual for the Ways of Coping Questionnaire*. Palo Alto, Calif.: Consulting Psychologists Press.

Folkman, S.K. and Moskowitz, J.T. (2000). Positive affect and the other side of coping. *American Psychologist*, 55: 647–54.

Food Standards Agency (2000). *National Diet and Nutrition Survey: Young People Aged 4–18 Years*. London: Stationery Office.

Ford, S., Fallowfield, L. and Lewis, S. (1996). Doctor–patient interactions in oncology. *Social Science and Medicine*, 42: 1511–19.

Ford, S., Schofield, T. and Hope, T. (2003). What are the ingredients for a successful evidence-based patient choice consultation? A qualitative study. *Social Science and Medicine*, 56: 589–602.

Fordyce, W.E. (1976). *Behavioural Methods for Chronic Pain and Illness*. St Louis: Mosby.

Fordyce, W.E. (1982). The modification of avoidance learning in pain behaviors. *Journal of Behavioral Medicine*, 5: 405–14.

Fordyce, W.E. (1986). Learning processes in pain. In R.A. Sternbach (ed.), *The Psychology of Pain*, 2nd edn. New York: Raven Press.

Forsberg-Wärleby, G., Möller, A. and Blomstrand, C. (2001). Spouses of first-ever stroke patients: psychological well-being in the first phase after stroke. *Stroke*, 32: 1646–56.

Forwell, G.D. (1993). *Glasgow's Health: Old Problems – New Opportunities*. A report by the Director of Public Health. Glasgow: Department of Public Health.

Fournier, M., de Ridder, D. and Bensing, J. (2002). Optimism and adaptation to chronic disease: the role of optimism in relation to self-care options in type 1 diabetes mellitus, rheumatoid arthritis and multiple sclerosis. *British Journal of Health Psychology*, 7: 409–32.

Franzkowiak, P. (1987). Risk taking and adolescent development. *Health Promotion*, 2: 51–60.

Frasure-Smith, N. (1991). In-hospital symptoms of psychological stress as predictors of long-term outcome after acute myocardial infarction in men. *American Journal of Cardiology*, 67: 121–7.

Frasure-Smith, N., Lespérance, F., Gravel, G., Masson, A., Juneau, M., Talajic, M. and Bourassa, M.G. (2000). Social support, depression, and mortality during the first year after myocardial infarction. *Circulation*, 101: 1919–24.

Frasure-Smith, N., Lespérance, F., Gravel, G., Masson, A., Juneau, M. and Bourassa, M.G. (2002). Long-term survival differences among low-anxious, high-anxious and repressive copers enrolled in the Montreal heart attack re-adjustment trial. *Psychosomatic Medicine*, 64: 571–9.

Frasure-Smith, N., Lespérance, F., Prince, R.H., Verrier, P., Garber, R.A., Juneau, M., Wolfson, C. and Bourassa, M.G. (1997). Randomised trial of home-based psychosocial nursing intervention for patients recovering from myocardial infarction. *The Lancet*, 350: 473–9.

Frasure-Smith, N., Lespérance, F. and Talajic, M.E. (1995). Coronary heart disease/myocardial infarction: depression and 18-month prognosis after myocardial infarction. *Circulation*, 91: 999–1005.

Frasure-Smith, N. and Prince, R. (1985). The ischemic heart disease life stress monitoring program: impact on mortality. *Psychosomatic Medicine*, 47: 431–45.

Fredrickson, B.L. (1998). What good are positive emotions? *Review of General Psychology*, 2: 300–19.

Fredrickson, B.L. (2001). The role of positive emotions in positive psychology: the broaden-and-build theory of positive emotions. *American Psychologist*, 56: 218–26.

Fredrickson, M. and Matthews, K.A. (1990). Cardiovascular responses to behavioral stress and hypertension: a meta-analytic review. *Annals of Behavioral Medicine*, 12: 30–9.

Freedland, K.E., Carney, R.M., Hance, M.L. and Skala, J.A. (1996). Cognitive therapy for depression in patients with coronary artery disease. *Psychosomatic Medicine*, 58: 93.

Freidson, E. (1961). *Patients' Views of Medical Practice*. New York: Russell Sage Foundation.

French, D.P., Senior, V., Weinman, J. and Marteau, T. (2001). Causal attributions for heart disease. *Psychology and Health*, 16: 77–98.

French, D.P., Marteau, T., Senior, V. and Weinman, J. (2002). The structure of beliefs about the causes of heart attack: a network analysis. *British Journal of Health Psychology*, 7: 463–79.

French, J.R.P., Jr, Caplan, R.D. and Van Harrison, R. (1982). *The Mechanisms of Job Stress and Strain*. Chichester, Wiley.

French, S.A., Perry, C.L., Leon, G.R. and Fulkerson, J.A. (1994). Weight concerns, dieting behaviour, and smoking initiation among adolescents: a prospective study. *American Journal of Public Health*, 84: 1818–20.

Freud, S. and Breuer, J. (1895). Studies on hysteria. In J. Strachey (ed.), *The Standard Edition of the Complete Psychological Works of Sigmund Freud*. London: Hogarth Press.

Friedman, H.S. (2003). Healthy life-style across the life-span: the heck with the Surgeon General! In J. Suls and K.A. Wallston (eds), *Social Psychological Foundations of Health and Illness*. Malden, Mass.: Blackwell.

Friedman, H.S. and Booth-Kewley, S. (1987). The 'disease-prone personality'. A meta-analytic view of the construct. *American Psychologist*, 42: 539–55.

Friedman, H.S., Tucker, J.S., Schwartz, J.E., Martin, L.R., Tomlinson-Keasey, C., Wingard, D.L. and Criqui, M.H. (1995). Childhood conscientiousness and longevity: health behaviors and cause of death. *Journal of Personality and Social Psychology*, 68: 696–703.

Friedman, M. and Rosenman, R.H. (1959). Association of specific overt behavior pattern with blood and cardiovascular findings. *Journal of American Medical Association*, 169: 1286–97.

Friedman, M. and Rosenman, R.H. (1974). *Type A Behavior and Your Heart*. New York: A.A. Knopf.

Friedman, M., Thoresen, C.E., Gill, J.J., Ulmer, D., Powell, L.H., Price, V.A., Brown, B., Thompson, L., Rabin, D.D. and Breall, W.S. (1986). Alteration of Type A behavior and its effect on cardiac recurrences in post myocardial infarction patients: summary results of the Recurrent Coronary Prevention Project. *American Heart Journal*, 112: 653–65.

Funk, S.C. (1992). Hardiness: a review of theory and research. *Health Psychology*, 11: 335–45.

Furnham, A. (1990). The Type A behaviour pattern and perception of self. *Personality and Individual Differences*, 11: 841–51.

Gadsby, J.G. and Flowerdew, M.W. (2000). Transcutaneous nerve stimulation and acupuncture-like transcutaneous nerve stimulation for chronic low back pain. In *The Cochrane Library*, issue 2. Oxford: Update Software.

Galavotti, C., Pappas-DeLuca, K.A. and Lansky, A. (2001). Modeling and reinforcement to combat HIV: the MARCH approach to behavior change. *American Journal of Public Health*, 91: 1602–7.

Gallacher, J.E.J., Hopkinson, C.A., Bennett, P., Burr, M.L. and Elwood, P.C. (1997). Effect of stress management on angina. *Psychology and Health*, 12: 523–32.

Gander, P.H., Merry, A., Millar, M.M. and Weller, J. (2000). Hours of work and fatigue-related error: a survey of New Zealand anaesthetists. *Anaesthetics and Intensive Care*, 28: 178–83.

Garratt, A., Schmidt, L., Mackintosh, A.M. and Fitzpatrick, R. (2002). Quality of life measurement: bibliographic study of patient assessed health outcome measures. *British Medical Journal*, 324: 1417–21.

Gascoigne, P., Mason, M.D. and Roberts, E. (1999). Factors affecting presentation and delay in patients with testicular cancer: results of a qualitative study. *Psycho-Oncology*, 8: 144–54.

Gauce, A.M., Comer, J.P. and Schwartz, D. (1987). Long-term effect of a systems orientated school prevention program. *American Journal of Orthopsychiatry*, 57: 127–31.

Gaughler, J.E., Davey, A., Pearlin, L.I. and Zarit, S.H. (2000). Modeling caregiver adaptation over time: the longitudinal impact of behaviour problems. *Psychology and Aging*, 15: 437–50.

Gawande, A.A., Zinner, M.J., Studdert, D.M. and Brennan, T.A. (2003). Analysis of errors reported by surgeons at three teaching hospitals. *Surgery*, 133: 614–21.

Gellert, G., Maxwell, R.M. and Siegel, B.S. (1993). Survival of breast cancer patients receiving adjunctive psychosocial support therapy: A 10-year follow-up study. *Journal of Clinical Oncology*, 11: 66–9.

General Medical Council (2002). *Tomorrow's Doctors, Recommendations on Undergraduate Medical Education*. London: General Medical Council.

Gerbert, B. (1984). Perceived likeability and competence of simulated patients: influence on physician's management plans. *Social Science and Medicine*, 18: 1053–60.

German, J.B. and Walzem, R.L. (2000). The health benefits of wine. *Annual Review of Nutrition*, 20: 561–93.

Gibson, D.R., Flynn, N.M. and Perales, D. (2001). Effectiveness of syringe exchange programs in reducing HIV risk behavior and HIV seroconversion among injecting drug users. *AIDS*, 15: 1329–41.

Gibson, P.G., Coughlan, J., Wilson, A.J., Abramson, M., Bauman, A. and Hensley, M.J. (2000). Limited (information only) patient education programs for adults with asthma. *Cochrane Database Systematic Review*, 2: CD001005.

Giese-Davis, J., Koopman, C., Butler, L.D., Classen, C., Cordova, M., Fobian, P., Benson, J., Kraemer, H.C. and Speigel, D. (2002). Change in emotion-regulation strategy for women with metastatic breast cancer following supportive-expressive group therapy. *Journal of Consulting and Clinical Psychology*, 70: 916–25.

Gifford, A.L., Laurent, D.D., Gonzales, V.M., Chesney, M. and Lorig, K.R. (1998). Pilot randomized trial of education to improve self-management skills of men with symptomatic HIV/AIDS. *Retrovirology*, 18: 136–44.

Gil, K.M., Keefe, F.J., Crisson, J.E. and VanDalfsen, P.J. (1987). Social support and pain behavior. *Pain*, 29: 209–17.

Gil, K.M., Williams, D.A., Keefe, F.J. and Beckham, J.C. (1990). The relationship of negative thoughts to pain and psychological distress. *Behavior Therapy*, 21: 349–62.

Gill, P., Kaur, J.S., Rummans, T., Novotny, P.J. and Sloan, J.A. (2003). The hospice patient's primary caregiver. What is their quality of life? *Journal of Psychosomatic Research*, 55: 445–51.

Gillam, S., Jarman, B., White, P. and Law, R. (1989). Ethnic differences in consultation rates in urban general practice. *British Medical Journal*, 299: 953–7.

Gillies, P.A. (1991). HIV infection, alcohol and illicit drugs. *Current Opinion in Psychiatry*, 4: 448–53.

Ginandes, C., Brooks, P., Sando, W., Jones, C. and Aker, J. (2003). Can medical hypnosis accelerate post-surgical wound healing? Results of a clinical trial. *American Journal of Clinical Hypnosis*, 45: 333–51.

Glanz, K., Grove, J., Lerman, C., Gotay, C. and Le Marchand, L. (1999). Correlates of intentions to obtain genetic counseling and colorectal cancer gene testing among at-risk relatives from three ethnic groups. *Cancer Epidemiology Biomarkers and Prevention*, 8: 329–36.

Glanz, K., Lankenau, B., Foerster, S., Temple, S., Mullis, R. and Schmid, T. (1995). Environmental and policy approaches to cardiovascular disease prevention through nutrition: opportunities for state and local action. *Health Education Quarterly*, 22: 512–27.

Glaser, R., Rice, J., Sheridan, J., Fertel, R., Stout, J., Speicher, C., Pinsky, D., Kotur, M., Post, A., Beck, M. and Kiecolt-Glaser, J. (1987). Stress-related immune suppression: health implications. *Brain, Behavior and Immunity*, 1: 7–20.

Glasgow, R.E., Boles, S.M., McKay, H.G. and Barrera, M. (2003). The D-Net diabetes self-management program: long-term implementation, outcomes, and generalization results. *Preventive Medicine*, 36: 410–19.

Glasgow, R.E., Hollis, J.F., Ary, D.V. and Boles, S.M. (1993). Results of a year-long incentives based work-site smoking cessation program. *Addictive Behaviors*, 18: 209–16.

Glasgow, R.E., Toobert, D.J. and Hampson, S.E. (1996). Effects of a brief office-based intervention to facilitate diabetes dietary self-management. *Diabetes Care*, 19: 835–42.

Glenister, D. (1996). Exercise and mental health: a review. *Journal of the Royal Society of Health*, 116: 7–13.

Glenton, C. (2002). Developing patient-centred information for back pain sufferers. *Health Expectations*, 5: 319–29.

Goddard, M. and Smith, P. (1998). *Equity of Access to Health Care*. York: University of York.

Godfrey, C. (1990). Modelling demand. In A. Maynard and P. Tether (eds), *Preventing Alcohol and Tobacco Problems. 1.* Avebury: ESRC.

Godin, G., Gagné, C., Maziade, J., Moreault, L., Beaulieu, D. and Morel, S. (2001). Breast cancer: the intention to have a mammography and a clinical breast examination – application of the theory of planned behavior. *Psychology and Health*, 16: 423–41.

Godin, G. and Kok, G. (1996). The theory of planned behavior: a review of its applications to health-related behaviours. *American Journal of Health Promotion*, 11: 87–98.

Godin, G., Lambert, L.-D., Owen, N., Nolin, B. and Prud'homme, D. (2004). Stages of motivational readiness for physical activity: a comparison of different algorithms of classification. *British Journal of Health Psychology*, 9: 253–67.

Godin, G. and Shephard, R.J. (1986). Normative beliefs of school children concerning regular exercise. *Journal of School Health*, 54: 443–5.

Godin, G., Valois, P., Lepage, L. and Desharnais, R. (1992). Predictors of smoking behaviour – an application of Ajzen's theory of planned behaviour. *British Journal of Addiction*, 87: 1335–43.

Goldberg, D. (1997). *General Health Questionnaire (GHQ–12)*. Windsor: NFER-Nelson.

Goldberg, D. and Williams, P. (1988). *A User's Guide to the General Health Questionnaire*. Windsor: NFER-Nelson.

Goldberg, L.R. and Strycker, L.A. (2002). Personality traits and eating habits: the assessment of food preferences in a large community sample. *Personality and Individual Differences*, 32: 49–65.

Goldberg, R.J., Steg, P.G., Sadiq, I., Granger, C.B., Jackson, E.A., Buda, J.A., Brieger, D., Avezum, A. and Goodman, S. (2002). Extent of, and factors associated with, delay to hospital presentation in patients with acute coronary disease (the GRACE registry). *American Journal of Cardiology*, 89: 791–6.

Goldman, S.L., Whitney-Saltiel, D., Granger, J. and Rodin, J. (1991). Children's representations of 'everyday' aspects of health and illness. *Journal of Pediatric Psychology*, 16: 747–66.

Gollwitzer, P.M. (1993). Goal achievements: the role of intentions. In E.T. Higgins and R.M. Sorrentino (eds), *Handbook of Motivation and Cognition: Foundations of Social Behaviour*, Vol. 2. New York: Guilford Press.

Gollwitzer, P.M. (1999). Implementation intentions: strong effects of simple plans. *American Psychologist*, 54: 493–503.

Gollwitzer, P.M. and Brandstätter, V. (1997). Implementation intentions and effective goal pursuit. *Journal of Personality and Social Psychology*, 73: 186–99.

Gollwitzer, P.M. and Oettingen, G. (1998). The emergence and implementation of health goals. *Psychology and Health*, 13: 687–715.

Gollwitzer, P.M. and Oettingen, G. (2000). The emergence and implementation of health goals, In: P. Norman and C. Abraham (eds), *Understanding and changing health behaviour: From health beliefs to self regulation* (229–60). Amsterdam: Harwood Academic Press.

Gollwitzer, P.M. and Schaal, B. (1998). Metacognition in action: the importance of implementation intentions. *Personality and Social Psychology Review*, 2: 124–36.

Gomel, M., Oldenburg, B., Simpson, J.M. and Owen, N. (1993). Work-site cardiovascular risk reduction: a randomized trial of health risk assessment, education, counseling, and incentives. *American Journal of Public Health*, 83: 1231–8.

Goode, K.T., Haley, W.E., Roth, D.L. and Ford, G.R. (1998). Predicting longitudinal changes in caregiver physical and mental health: a stress process model. *Health Psychology*, 17: 190–8.

Goodkin, K., Feaster, D.J., Asthana, D., Blaney, N.T., Kumar, M., Baldewicz, T., Tuttle, R.S., Maher, K.J., Baum, M.K., Shapshak, P. and Fletcher M.A. (1998). A bereavement support group intervention is longitudinally associated with salutary effects on the CD4 cell count and number of physician visits. *Clinical and Diagnostic Laboratory Immunology*, 5: 382–91.

Goodkin, K., Baldewicz, T.T., Asthana, D., Khamis, I., Blaney, N.T., Kumar, M., Burkhalter, J.E., Leeds, B. and Shapshak, P. (2001). A bereavement support group intervention affects plasma burden of human immunodeficiency virus type 1. Report of a randomized controlled trial. *Journal of Human Virology*, 4: 44–54.

Goodwin, D., Boggs, S. and Graham-Pole, J. (1994). Development and validation of the Pediatric Oncology Quality of Life Scale. *Psychological Assessment*, 6: 321–8.

Goodwin, P.J., Leszcz, M., Ennis, M., Koopmans, J., Vincent, L., Guther, H., Drysdale, E., Hundleby, M., Chochinov, H.M., Navarro, M., Speca, M. and Hunter, J. (2001). The effect of group psychosocial support on survival in metastatic breast cancer. *New England Journal of Medicine*, 345: 1719–26.

Goyder, E.C., McNally, P.G. and Botha, J.L. (2000). Inequalities in access to diabetes care: evidence from a historical cohort study. *Quality in Health Care*, 9: 85–9.

Graham, H. (1994). Gender and class as dimensions of smoking behaviour in Britain: insights from a survey of mothers. *Social Science and Medicine*, 38: 691–8.

Graham, J., Ramirez, A., Love, S., Richards, M. and Burgess, C. (2002). Stressful life experiences and risk of relapse of breast cancer: observational cohort study. *British Medical Journal*, 324: 1420–3.

Greco, P., Pendley, J.S., McDonell, K. and Reeves, G. (2001). A peer group intervention for adolescents with type 1 diabetes and their best friends. *Journal of Pediatric Psychology*, 26: 485–90.

Green, B.L., Rowland, J.H., Krupnick, J.L., Epstein, S.A., Stockton, P., Stern, N.M., Spertus, I.L. and Steakley, C. (1998). Prevalence of posttraumatic stress disorder in women with breast cancer. *Psychosomatics*, 39: 102–11.

Green, C.R., Baker, T.A., Sato, Y., Washington, T.L. and Smith, E.M. (2003). Race and chronic pain: a comparative study of young black and white Americans presenting for management. *Journal of Pain*, 4: 176–83.

Greenwood, C.R., Carta, J.J. and Kamps, D. (1990). Teacher versus peer-mediated instruction: a review of educational advantages and disadvantages. In H. Foot, M. Morgan and R. Shute (eds), *Children Helping Children*. Chichester: Wiley.

Greenwood, D.C., Muir, K.R., Packham, C.J. and Madeley, R.J. (1996). Coronary heart disease: a review of the role of psychosocial stress and social support. *Journal of Public Health Medicine*, 18: 221–31.

Greer, S. (1999). Mind–body research in psycho-oncology. *Advances in Mind–Body Medicine*, 15: 236–81.

Greer, S., Morris, T. and Pettingale, K. (1979). Psychological responses to breast cancer: effect on outcome. *The Lancet*, 2: 940–9.

Greer, S., Morris, T., Pettingale, K. and Haybittle, J. (1990). Psychological response to breast cancer and 15 year outcome. *The Lancet*, 335: 49–50.

Grey, M., Boland, E.A., Davidson, M., Li, J. and Tamborlane, W.V. (2000). Coping skills training for youths with diabetes mellitus has long-lasting effects on metabolic control and quality of life. *Journal of Pediatrics*, 137: 107–13.

Grigsby, A.B., Anderson, R.J., Freedland, K.E., Clouse, R.E. and Lustman, P.J. (2002). Prevalence of anxiety in adults with diabetes. A systematic review. *Journal of Psychosomatic Research*, 53: 1053–60.

Griva, K., Myers, L.B. and Newman, S. (2000). Illness perceptions and self-efficacy beliefs in adolescents and young adults with insulin dependent diabetes mellitus. *Psychology and Health*, 15: 733–50.

Grodstein, F., Chen, J. and Willett, W.C. (2003). High-dose antioxidant supplements and cognitive function in community-dwelling elderly women. *American Journal of Clinical Nutrition*, 77: 975–84.

Grossarth-Maticek, R., Bastiaans, J. and Kanazin, D.T. (1985). Psychosocial factors as strong predictors of mortality from cancer, ischemic heart disease and stroke: the Yugoslav prospective study. *Journal of Psychosomatic Research*, 29: 167–76.

Grundy, E. and Bowling, A. (1999). Enhancing the quality of extended life years. Identification of the oldest old with a very good and very poor quality of life. *Aging and Mental Health*, 3: 199–212.

Grunfeld, E.A., Hunter, M.S., Ramirez, A.J. and Richards, M.A. (2003). Perceptions of breast cancer across the lifespan. *Journal of Psychosomatic Research*, 54: 141–6.

Gudmunsdottir, H., Johnston, M., Johnston, D. and Foulkes, J. (2001). Spontaneous, elicited and cued causal attributions in the year following a first myocardial infarction. *British Journal of Health Psychology*, 6: 81–96.

Gulland, A. (2002). BMA steps up call for ban on smoking in public places. *British Medical Journal*, 325: 1058.

Guthrie, R.M. (2001). The effects of postal and telephone reminders on compliance with pravastatin therapy in a national registry: results of the first myocardial infarction risk reduction program. *Clinical Therapeutics*, 23: 970–80.

Haan, M.H. (2003). Can vitamin supplements prevent cognitive decline and dementia in old age? (editorial). *American Journal of Clinical Nutrition*, 77: 762–3.

Haan, M.N. and Kaplan, G.A. (1985). The contribution of socio-economic position to minority health. In M. Heckler (ed.), *Report of the Secretary's Task Force on Black and Minority Health: Crosscutting Issues in Health and Human Services*. Washington: US DHHS.

Haberman, D. and Bloomfield, D.S.F. (1988). Social class differences in mortality in Great Britain around 1981. *Journal of the Institute of Actuaries*, 115: 495–517.

Habra, M.E., Linden, W., Anderson, J.C. and Weinberg, J. (2003). Type D personality is related to cardiovascular and neuroendocrine reactivity to acute stress. *Journal of Psychosomatic Research*, 55: 235–45.

Hagedoorn, M., Sandermann, R., Buunk, B.P. and Wobbes, T. (2002). Failing in spousal caregiving: the 'identity-relevant stress' hypothesis to explain sex differences in caregiver distress. *British Journal of Health Psychology*, 7: 481–94.

Hagger, M., Chatzisarantis, N., Biddle, S.J.H. and Orbell, S. (2001). Antecedents of children's physical activity intentions and behaviour: predictive validity and longitudinal effects. *Psychology and Health*, 16: 391–407.

Hagger, M.S. and Orbell, S. (2003). A meta-analytic review of the common-sense model of illness representations. *Psychology and Health*, 18: 141–84.

Hakim, A.A., Petrovitch, H., Burchfield, C.M., Webster-Ross, G., Rodriguez, B.L., White, L.R., Yano, K., Curb, J.D. and Abbott, R.D. (1998). Effects of walking on mortality among non-smoking retired men. *New England Journal of Medicine*, 338: 94–9.

Hale, G. (1996). The social construction of grief. In N. Cooper, C. Stevenson and G. Hale (eds), *Integrating Perspectives on Health*. Buckingham: Open University Press.

Halford, J.C.G. and Blundell, J.E. (2000). Serotonin drugs and the treatment of obesity. In T.G. Heffner and D.H. Lockwood (eds), *Obesity: Pathology and Therapy*. Berlin: Springer Verlag.

Hall, E.E., Ekkekakis, P. and Petruzzello, S.J. (2002). The affective beneficence of vigorous exercise revisited. *British Journal of Health Psychology*, 7: 47–66.

Hall, J.A., Roter, D.L. and Katz, N.R. (1988). Meta-analysis of correlates of provider behavior in medical encounters. *Medical Care*, 26: 657–75.

Hall, J.A. and Roter, D.L. (2002). Do patients talk differently to male and female physicians? A meta-analytic review. *Patient Education and Counseling*, 48: 217–24.

Hall, S. and Marteau, T.M. (2003). Causal attributions following serious unexpected negative events: a systematic review. *Journal of Social and Clinical Psychology*, 22: 515–36.

Hall, S.M., Tunstall, C., Rugg, D., Jones, R.T. and Benowitz, N. (1985). Nicotine gum and behavioral treatment in smoking cessation. *Journal of Consulting and Clinical Psychology*, 53: 256–8.

Hallaråker, E., Arefjord, K., Havik, O.E. and Maeland, J.G. (2001). Social support and emotional adjustment during and after a severe life event: a study of wives of myocardial infarction patients. *Psychology and Health*, 16: 343–56.

Halm, M., Penque, S., Doll, N. and Beahrs, M. (1999). Women and cardiac rehabilitation: referral and compliance patterns. *Journal of Cardiovascular Nursing*, 13: 83–92.

Halstead, M.T. and Fernsler, J.I. (1994). Coping strategies of long-term cancer patients. *Cancer Nursing*, 17: 94–100.

Hampson, S.E., Glasgow, R.E. and Toobert, D.J. (1990). Personal models of diabetes and their relation to self-care activities. *Health Psychology*, 9: 632–46.

Hampson, S.E., Glasgow, R.E. and Zeiss, A. (1994). Personal models of osteoarthritis and their relation to self-management activities and quality of life. *Journal of Behavioural Medicine*, 17: 143–58.

Han, K.S. (2002). The effect of an integrated stress management program on the psychologic and physiologic stress reactions of peptic ulcer in Korea. *International Journal of Nursing Studies*, 39: 539–48.

Hanson, R.W. and Gerber, K.E. (1990). *Coping with Chronic Pain. A Guide to Patient Self-management*. New York: Guilford Press.

Harburg, E.J.C., Chape, C., Erfurt, J.C., Hauenstein, L.S., Schull, W.J. and Schork, M.A. (1973). Socio-ecological stressor areas and black and white blood pressure: Detroit. *Journal of Chronic Disease*, 26: 595–611.

Harcourt, D., Ambler, N., Rumsey, N. and Cawthorn, S.J. (1998). Evaluation of a one-stop breast lump clinic: a randomised controlled trial. *The Breast*, 7: 314–19.

Harding, S. and Maxwell, R. (1997). Differences in mortality of migrants. In F. Drever and M. Whitehead (eds), *Health Inequalities: Decennial Supplement*. London: HMSO.

Härkäpää, K., Järvikoski, A., Mellin, G., Hurri, H. and Luoma, J. (1991). Health locus of control beliefs and psychological distress as predictors for treatment outcome in low-back pain patients: results of a 3-month follow-up of a controlled intervention study. *Pain*, 46: 35–41.

Harland, J., White, M., Drinkwater, C., Chinn, D., Farr, L. and Howel, D. (1999). The Newcastle exercise project: a randomised controlled trial of methods to promote physical activity in primary care. *British Medical Journal*, 319: 828–32.

Harris, D.M. and Guten, S. (1979). Health-protective behaviour: an exploratory study. *Journal of Health and Social Behavior*, 20: 17–29.

Harris, P. and Middleton, W. (1994). The illusion of control and optimism about health: on being less at risk but no more in control than others. *British Journal of Social Psychology*, 33: 369–86.

Harris, T., Ferrucci, L., Tracy, R., Corti, M., Wacholder, S., Ettinger, W.H., Jr, Hemovitz, H., Cohen, H.J. and Wallace, R. (1999). Associations of elevated interleukin-6 and C-reactive protein levels with mortality and the elderly. *American Journal of Medicine*, 106: 506–12.

Harrison, J.A., Mullen, P.D. and Green, L.W. (1992). A meta-analysis of studies of the health belief model with adults. *Health Education Research, Theory and Practice*, 7: 107–16.

Hart, C.L., Davey-Smith, G., Hole, D.J. and Hawthorne, V.M. (1999). Alcohol consumption and mortality from all causes, coronary disease, and stroke: results from a prospective cohort study of Scottish men with 21 years of follow-up. *British Medical Journal*, 318: 133–40.

Hartford, K., Wong, C. and Zakaria, D. (2002). Randomized controlled trial of a telephone intervention by nurses to provide information and support to patients and their partners after elective coronary artery bypass graft surgery: effects of anxiety. *Heart and Lung*, 31: 199–206.

Haste, H. (2004). *My Body, My Self: Young People's Values and Motives about Healthy Living*, Report 2. London: Nestlé Social Research Programme.

Hatava, P., Olsson, G.L. and Lagerkranser, M. (2000). Preoperative psychological preparation for children undergoing ENT operations: a comparison of two methods. *Paediatric Anaesthesia*, 10: 477–86.

Hathaway, D. (1986). Effect of preoperative instruction on postoperative outcomes: a meta-analysis. *Nursing Research*, 35: 269–75.

Hausenblas, H.A. and Symons Downs, D. (2002). How much is too much? The development and validation of the Exercise Dependence Scale. *Psychology and Health*, 17: 387–404.

Havik, O.E. and Maeland, J.G. (1988). Changes in smoking behavior after a myocardial infarction. *Health Psychology*, 7: 403–20.

Hayes, J. and Morrison, V. (under review). Attitudes towards breaking bad news among junior doctors.

Haynes, B. and Haines, A. (1998). Barriers and bridges to evidence-based clinical practice. *British Medical Journal*, 317: 273–6.

Haynes, G. and Feinleib, M. (1980). Women, work, and coronary heart disease: prospective findings from the Framingham heart study. *American Journal of Public Health*, 70: 133–41.

Haynes, R.B., McKibbon, A. and Kanani, R. (1996). Systematic review of randomized trials of interventions to assist patients to follow prescriptions for medications. *The Lancet*, 384: 383–5.

Haynes, S.G., Feinleib, M. and Kannel, W.B. (1980). The relationship of psychosocial factors to coronary heart disease in the Framingham study. III. Eight year incidence of coronary heart disease. *American Journal of Epidemiology*, 111: 37–58.

Health Education Authority (1997). *Guidelines: Promoting Physical Activity with Black and Minority Ethnic Groups*. London: Health Education Authority.

Health Education Authority (1998). *Young and Active? Policy Framework for Young People and Health – Enhancing Physical Activity*. London: Health Education Authority.

Health Promotion Authority for Wales (1996). *Lifestyle Changes in Wales. Health in Wales Survey 1996*, Technical Report no. 27. Cardiff: Health Promotion Authority for Wales.

Heather, N. and Robertson, I. (1997). *Problem Drinking*. Oxford: Oxford University Press.

Heaven, C.M. and Maguire, P. (1998). The relationship between patients' concerns and psychological distress in a hospice setting. *Psycho-Oncology*, 7: 502–7.

Heckhausen, H. (1991). *Motivation and Action*. Berlin: Springer Verlag.

Heijmans, M. (1998). Coping and adaptive outcome in chronic fatigue syndrome: importance of illness cognitions. *Journal of Psychosomatic Research*, 45: 39–51.

Heijmans, M. and de Ridder, D. (1998). Structure and determinants of illness representation in chronic disease: a comparison of Addison's disease and chronic fatigue syndrome. *Journal of Health Psychology*, 3: 523–37.

Heijmans, M., de Ridder, D. and Bensing, J. (1999). Dissimilarity in patients' and spouses' representations of chronic illness: explorations of relations to patient adaptation. *Psychology and Health*, 14: 451–66.

Heim, E., Augustiny, K., Blaser, A. and Burki, C. (1987). Coping with breast cancer: a longitudinal prospective study. *Psychotherapy and Psychosomatics*, 48: 44–59.

Hein, H.O., Suadicani, P. and Gyntelberg, F. (1992). Ischaemic heart disease incidence by social class and form of smoking: the Copenhagen male study – 17 years follow-up. *Journal of Internal Medicine*, 231: 477–83.

Heine, S.J. and Lehman, D.R. (1995). Cultural variation in unrealistic optimism: does the West feel more invulnerable than the East? *Journal of Personality and Social Psychology*, 68: 595–607.

Helder, D.I., Bakker, B., deHeer, P., van der Veen, F., Vossen, J.M.J.J., Wit, J.M. and Kaptein, A.A. (2004). Quality of life in adults following bone marrow transplantation during childhood. *Bone Marrow Transplantation*, 33: 329–336.

Helman, C. (1978). Feed a cold starve a fever – folk models of infection in an English suburban community and their relation to medical treatment. *Culture, Medicine and Psychiatry*, 2: 107–37.

Heloma, A. and Jaakola, M.S. (2003). Four-year follow-up of smoke exposure, attitudes and smoking behaviour following enactment of Finland's national smoke-free work-place law. *Addiction*, 98: 1111–17.

Hemingway, H. and Marmot, M. (1999). Psychosocial factors in the aetiology and prognosis of coronary heart disease: systematic review of prospective cohort studies. *British Medical Journal*, 318: 1460–7.

Hendry, L.B. and Kloep, M. (2002). *Lifespan Development: Resources, Challenges, Risks*. London: Thomson Learning.

Herbert, T.B. and Cohen, S. (1993). Stress and immunity in humans: a meta-analytic review. *Psychosomatic Medicine*, 55: 364–79.

Herzlich, C. (1973). *Health and Illness: A Social Psychological Analysis*. London: Academic Press.

Hewitt, D., McDonald, M., Portenoy, R., Rosenfield, B., Passik, S. and Breitbart, W. (1997). Pain syndromes and etiologies in ambulatory AIDS patients. *Pain*, 70: 117–23.

Higginson, I.J. and Carr, A.J. (2001). Using quality of life measures in the clinical setting. *British Medical Journal*, 322: 1297–300.

Hinton, J. (1999). The progress of awareness and acceptance of dying assessed in cancer patients and their caring relatives. *Palliative Medicine*, 13: 19–35.

Hobfoll, S.E. (1989). Conservation of resources: a new attempt at conceptualizing stress. *American Psychologist*, 44: 513–24.

Hobfoll, S. (1991). Traumatic stress: a theory based on rapid loss of resources. *Anxiety Research*, 4: 187–97.

Hobfoll, S.E. (2001). The influence of culture, community, and the nested-self in the stress processes: advancing conservation of resources theory. *Applied Psychology: An International Review*, 50: 337–421.

Hobfoll, S.E., Jackson, A.P., Lavin, J., Britton, P.J. and Shepherd, J.B. (1994). Women's barriers to safer sex. *Psychology and Health*, 9: 233–52.

Hobfoll, S.E. and Lilly, R.S. (1993). Conservation of resources; a new attempt at conceptualising stress. *American Psychologist*, 44: 513–24.

Hodgson, S. and Maher, E. (1999). *A Practical Guide to Human Cancer Genetics*. Cambridge: Cambridge University Press.

Hogbin, B. and Fallowfield, L. (1989). Getting it taped: the 'bad news' consultation with cancer patients. *British Journal of Hospital Medicine*, 41: 330–3.

Holland, J.C. and Gooen-Piels, J. (2000). Principles of psycho-oncology. In J.C. Holland and E. Frei (eds), *Psychological Care of the Patient with Cancer*. New York: Oxford University Press.

Hollis, J.F., Connett, J.E., Stevens, V.J. and Greenlick, M.R. (1990). Stressful life events, Type A behaviour, and the prediction of cardiovascular disease and total mortality over six years. *Journal of Behavioral Medicine*, 13: 263–81.

Holmes, T.H. and Rahe, R.H. (1967). The social readjustment rating scale. *Journal of Psychosomatic Research*, 11: 213–18.

Holmes, T.H. and Masuda, M. (1974). Life change and illness susceptibility. In B.S. Dohrenwend and B.P. Dohrenwend (eds), *Stressful Life Events: Their Nature and Effects*. New York: Wiley.

Holroyd, K.A. and Lipchik, G.L. (1999). Psychological management of recurrent headache disorders: progress and prospects. In R.J. Gatchel and D.C. Turk (eds), *Psychosocial Factors in Pain*. New York: Guilford Press.

Holroyd, K.A., O'Donnell, F.J., Stensland, M., Lipchik, G.L., Cordingley, G.E. and Carlson, B.W. (2001). Management of chronic tension-type headache with tricyclic antidepressant medication, stress management therapy, and their combination. *Journal of the American Medical Association*, 285: 2208–15.

Hooker, K., Monahan, D., Shifren, K. and Hutchinson, C. (1992). Mental and physical health of spouse caregivers: the role of personality. *Psychology and Aging*, 7: 367–75.

Hooper, L., Bartlett, C., Davey-Smith, G. and Ebrahim, S. (2002). Systematic review of long-term effects of advice to reduce dietary salt in adults. *British Medical Journal*, 325: 628–32.

Hoorens, V. and Buunk, B.P. (1993). Social comparisons of health risks: locus of control, the person-positivity bias, and unrealistic optimism. *Journal of Applied Social Psychology*, 23: 291–302.

Hopwood, P. (1997). Psychological issues in cancer genetics: current research and future priorities. *Patient Education and Counselling*, 32: 19–31.

Horne, R. (1997). Representations of medication and treatmen: advances in theory and measurement. In K.J. Petrie and J. Weinman (eds) *Perceptions of health and illness*. Chur: Harwood.

Horne, P.J., Tapper, K., Lowe, C.F., Hardman, C.A., Jackson, M.C. and Woolner, J. (2004). Increasing children's fruit and vegetable consumption: a peer modelling and rewards-based intervention. *European Journal of Clinical Nutrition*, 58: 1649–60.

Horne, R. (1999). Patients' beliefs about treatment: the hidden determinant of treatment outcome? *Journal of Psychosomatic Research*, 47: 491–5.

Horne, R. and Weinman, J. (1999). Patients' beliefs about prescribed medicines and their role in adherence to treatment in chronic physical illness. *Journal of Psychosomatic Research*, 47: 555–67.

Horne, R. and Weinman, J. (2002). Self-regulation and self-management in asthma: exploring the role of illness perceptions and treatment beliefs in explaining non-adherence to preventer medication. *Psychology and Health*, 17: 17–32.

Hosking, S.G., Marsh, N.V. and Friedman, P.J. (1996). Post-stroke depression: prevalence, course and associated factors. *Neuropsychological Review*, 6: 107–33.

House, A., Dennis, M., Mogridge, L., Warlow, C., Hawton, K. and Jones, L. (1991). Mood disorders in the year after first stroke. *British Journal of Psychiatry*, 2: 211–21.

House, J.S. (1987). Chronic stress and chronic disease in life and work: conceptual and methodological issues. *Work and Stress*, 1: 129–34.

House, J.S., Kessler, R., Herzog, A.R., Mero, R., Kinney, A. and Breslow, M. (1991). Social stratification, age, and health. In K.W. Scheie, D. Blazer and J.S. House (eds), *Aging, Health Behaviours, and Health Outcomes*. Hillsdale, NJ: Lawrence Erlbaum.

House, J.S., Robbins, C. and Metzner, H.L. (1982). The association of social relationships and activities with mortality: prospective evidence from the Tecumseh Community Health Study. *American Journal of Epidemiology*, 116: 123–40.

Houston, B.K., Chesney, M.A., Black, G.W., Cates, D.S. and Hecker, M.H.L. (1992). Behavioral clusters and coronary heart disease. *Psychosomatic Medicine*, 54: 447–61.

Houston, M. (2004). Commissioner denies plans for a Europe-wide smoking ban. *British Medical Journal*, 328: 544.

Hu, F.B., Willett, W.C., Colditz, G.A., Ascherio, A., Speizer, F.E., Rosner, B., Hennekens, C.H. and Stampfer, M.J. (1999). Prospective study of snoring and risk of hypertension in women. *American Journal of Epidemiology*, 150: 806–16.

Hu, F.B., Willett, W.C., Manson, J.E., Colditz, G.A., Rimm, E.B., Speizer, F.E., Hennekens, C.H. and Stampfer, M.J. (2000). Snoring and risk of cardiovascular disease in women. *Journal of the American College of Cardiology*, 35: 308–13.

Hu, T.-W., Sung, H.-Y. and Keeler, T.E. (1995). Reducing cigarette consumption in California: tobacco taxes vs. an anti-smoking media campaign. *American Journal of Public Health*, 85: 1218–22.

Hudzinski, L.G. and Frohlich, E.D. (1990). One-year longitudinal study of a no-smoking policy in a medical institution. *Chest*, 97: 1198–202.

Hulse, G.K. and Tait, R.J. (2002). Six-month outcomes associated with a brief alcohol intervention for adult in-patients with psychiatric disorders. *Drug and Alcohol Review*, 21: 105–12.

Hunt, S.M. and Martin, C.J. (1988). Health related behaviour change – a test of a new model. *Psychology and Health*, 2: 209–30.

Hunt, S.M., McEwan, J. and McKenna, S.P. (1986). *Measuring Health Status*. Beckenham: Croom Helm.

Hunter, M.S., Grunfeld, E.A. and Ramirez, A.J. (2003). Help-seeking intentions for breast-cancer symptoms: a comparison of self-regulation model and the theory of planned behaviour. *British Journal of Health Psychology*, 8: 319–34.

Hyland, M.E., Bellesis, M., Thompson, P.J. and Keenyon, C.A.P. (1996). The constructs of asthma quality of life: psychometric, experimental and correlational evidence. *Psychology and Health*, 12: 101–21.

Ingledew, D.K. and McDonagh, G. (1998). What coping functions are served when health behaviours are used as coping strategies? *Journal of Health Psychology*, 3: 195–213.

Ingram, K.M., Jones, D.A., Fass, R.J., Neideig, J.L. and Song, Y.S. (1999). Social support and unsupportive social interactions: their association with depression among people living with HIV. *AIDS Care*, 11: 313–29.

Inoue, S., Saeki, T., Mantani, T., Okamura, H. and Yamawaki, S. (2003). Factors related to patients' mental adjustment to breast cancer: patient characteristics and family functioning. *Support Care Cancer*, 11: 178–84.

Inoyue, J., Flannelly, L. and Flannelly, K.J. (2001). The effectiveness of self-management training for individuals with HIV/AIDS. *Journal of the Association of Nurses in AIDS Care*, 12: 71–82.

International Center for Alcohol Policies (ICAP) (1998). Report 5. Washington: ICAP.

International Obesity Taskforce and European Association for the Study of Obesity (2002). *Obesity in Europe: The Case for Action*. London: International Obesity Taskforce.

Isen, A.M. (1987). Positive affect, cognitive processes, and social behaviour. In L. Berkowitz (ed.), *Advances in Experimental Social Psychology 20*. New York: Academic Press.

Jackson, R., Scragg, R. and Beaglehole, R. (1991). Alcohol consumption and risk of coronary heart disease. *British Medical Journal*, 303: 211–16.

Jacobs, D.R., Jr, Luepker, R.V., Mittelmark, M.B., Folsom, A.R., Pirie, P.L., Mascioli, S.R., Hannan, P.J., Pechacek, T.F., Bracht, N., Carlaw, R., Kline, F.G. and Blackburn, H. (1986). Community-wide prevention strategies: evaluation design of the Minnesota Heart Health Program. *Journal of Chronic Diseases*, 39: 775–88.

Jacobsen, P.B. and Hahn, D.M. (1998). Cognitive behavioral programmes. In J. Holland (ed.), *Textbook of Psycho-Oncology*. New York: Oxford University Press.

Jacobson, E. (1938). *Progressive Relaxation*. Chicago: University of Chicago Press.

Jaffe, H. (1997). Dying for dollars. *Men's Health*, 12: 132–7.

Jaffe, L., Lutter, J.M., Rex, J., Hawkes, C. and Bucaccio, P. (1999). Incentives and barriers to physical activity for working women. *American Journal of Health Promotion*, 13(4): 215–18.

James, J.E. (2004). Critical review of dietary caffeine and blood pressure: a relationship that should be taken more seriously. *Psychosomatic Medicine*, 66: 63–71.

James, J.E. and Hardardottir, D. (2002). Influence of attention focus and trait anxiety on tolerance of acute pain. *British Journal of Health Psychology*, 7: 149–62.

James, S.A., LaCroix, A.Z., Kleinbaum, D.G. and Strogatz, D.S. (1984). John Henryism and blood pressure differences among black men. II. The role of occupational stressors. *Journal of Behavioral Medicine*, 7: 259–75.

Janlert, U., Asplund, K. and Weinehall, L. (1992). Unemployment and cardiovascular risk indicators. Data from the MONICA survey in northern Sweden. *Journal of Social Medicine*, 20: 14–18.

Janse, A.J., Gemke, R.J.B.J., Uiterwaal, C.S.P.M., van der Tweel, I., Kimpen, J.L.I. and Sinnema, G. (2004). Quality of life: patients and doctors don't always agree. *Journal of Clinical Epidemiology*, 57: 653–61.

Janz, N.K. and Becker, M.H. (1984). The health belief model: a decade later. *Health Education Quarterly*, 11: 1–17.

Janz, N.K., Zimmerman, M.A., Wren, P.A., Israel, B.A., Freudenberg, N. and Carter, R.J. (1996). Evaluation of 37 AIDS prevention projects: successful approaches and barriers to program effectiveness. *Health Education Quarterly*, 23: 80–97.

Janzon, E., Hedblad, B., Berglund, G. and Engstrom, G. (2004). Changes in blood pressure and body weight following smoking cessation in women. *Journal of Internal Medicine*, 255: 266–72.

Jarvis, M.J. (2004). Why people smoke. *British Medical Journal*, 328: 277–9.

Jay, S.M., Elliott, C.H. and Fitzgibbons, I. (1995). A comparative study of cognitive behavior therapy versus general anaesthesia for painful medical procedures in children. *Pain*, 62: 3–9.

Jeffery, R.W., Forster, J.L., French, S.A., Kelder, S.H., Lando, H.A., McGovern, P.G., Jacobs, D.R., Jr. and Baxter, J.E. (1993). The Healthy Worker Project: A work-site intervention for weight control and smoking cessation. *American Journal of Public Health*, 83: 395–401.

Jellinek, E.M. (1960). *The Disease Concept of Alcoholism*. New Haven, Conn.: Hillhouse Press.

Jemmott, J.B., Croyle, R.T. and Ditto, P.H. (1988). Commonsense epidemiology: self-based judgements from laypersons and physicians. *Health Psychology*, 7(1): 55–73.

Jenkins, P.R., Jenkins, R.A., Nannis, E.D., McKee, K.T., Jr and Temoshok, L.R. (2000). Reducing risk of sexually transmitted disease (STD) and human immunodeficiency virus infection in a military STD clinic: evaluation of a randomized preventive intervention trial. *Clinical Infectious Diseases*, 30: 730–5.

Jenkins, R.L., Lewis, G. and Bebbington, P. (1997). The National Psychiatric Morbidity Surveys of Great Britain: initial findings from the household survey. *Psychology and Medicine*, 27: 775–89.

Jenkinson, C., Fitzpatrick, R., Garrat, A., Peto, V. and Stewart-Brown, S. (2001). Can item response theory reduce patient burden when measuring health status in neurological disorders? Results from Rasch analysis of the SF36 physical functioning scale (PF-10). *Journal of Neurology, Neurosurgery and Psychiatry*, 71: 220–4.

Jensen, M.P., Turner, J.A. and Romano, J.M. (2001). Changes in beliefs, catastrophizing, and coping are associated with improvement in multidisciplinary pain treatment. *Journal of Consulting and Clinical Psychology*, 69: 655–62.

Jerram, K.L. and Coleman, P.G. (1999). The big five personality traits and reporting of health behaviours and health problems in old age. *British Journal of Health Psychology*, 4: 181–92.

Jerusalem, M. and Schwarzer, R. (1992). Self-efficacy as a resource factor in stress appraisal process. In R. Schwarzer (ed.), *Self Efficacy: Thought Control of Action*. Washington: Hemisphere.

Jessor, R. and Jessor, S.L. (1977). *Problem Behavior and Psychosocial Development: A Longitudinal Study of Youth*. New York: Academic Press.

Jirojanakul, P., Skevington, S.M. and Hudson, J. (2003). Predicting young children's quality of life. *Social Science and Medicine*, 57: 1277–88.

Johnson, J.V., Hall, E.M. and Theorell, T. (1989). Combined effects of job strain and social isolation on cardiovascular disease morbidity and mortality in a random sample of the Swedish male working population. *Scandinavian Journal of Work, Environment, and Health*, 15: 271–9.

Johnson, M.I. (2001). Transcutaneous electrical nerve stimulation (TENS) and TENS-like devices: do they provide pain relief? *Pain Reviews*, 8: 121–58.

Johnson, S.B. (1999). Commentary: psychologists' resistance to showcasing the profession's accomplishments: What is all the fuss about? *Journal of Pediatric Psychology*, 24: 329–30.

Johnsson, K.O. and Berglund, M. (2003). Education of key personnel in student pubs leads to a decrease in alcohol consumption among patrons: a randomized controlled trial. *Addiction*, 98: 627–33.

Johnston, M. and Kennedy, P. (1998). Editorial: special issue on clinical health psychology in chronic conditions. *Clinical Psychology and Psychotherapy*, 5: 59–61.

Johnston, M., Morrison, V., MacWalter, R. and Partridge, C. (1999). Perceived control, coping and recovery from disability following stroke, *Psychology and Health*, 14: 181–92.

Johnston, M. and Pollard, B. (2001). Consequences of disease: testing the WHO International Classification of Impairments, Disability and Handicap (ICIDH) model. *Social Science and Medicine*, 53: 1261–73.

Johnston, M., Pollard, B., Morrison, V. and MacWalter, R. (2004). Functional limitations and survival following stroke: psychological and clinical predictors of 3 year outcome. *International Journal of Behavioral Medicine*, 11: 187–96.

Johnston, M. and Vogele, K. (1993). Benefits of psychological preparation for surgery: a meta-analysis. *Annals of Behavioral Medicine*, 15: 245–56.

Joint Health Surveys Unit (2001). *Health Survey for England: The Health of Minority Ethnic Groups 1999*. London: HMSO.

Jonas, B.S. and Mussolino, M.E. (2000). Symptoms of depression as a prospective risk factor for stroke. *Psychosomatic Medicine*, 62: 463–71.

Jones, E. and Morrison, V. (2004). Patient–carer interactions following stroke: the effect on distress. BPS Division of Health Psychology Annual Conference, Edinburgh, September.

Jones, J.R., Huxtable, C.S., Hodgson, J.T. and Price, M.J. (2003). *Self-reported Illness in 2001/02: Results from a Household Survey*. London: Health and Safety Executive.

Jones, R.A. (1990). Expectations and delay in seeking medical care. *Journal of Social Issues*, 46: 81–95.

Jones, R., Pearson, J., McGregor, S., Barrett, A., Gilmore, W.H., Atkinson, J.M., Cawsay, A.J. and McEwen, J. (2002). Does writing a list help cancer patients ask relevant questions? *Patient Education and Counseling*, 47: 369–71.

Jørgensen, K.J. and Gøtzsche, P.C. (2004). Presentation on websites of possible benefits and harm from screening for breast cancer: a cross-sectional study. *British Medical Journal*, 328: 148–53.

Jousilahti, P., Vartiainen, E., Tuomilehto, J., Pekkenen, J. and Puska, P. (1995). Effect of risk factors and changes in risk factors on coronary mortality in three cohorts of middle aged people in eastern Finland. *American Journal of Epidemiology*, 141: 50–60.

Julien, R.M. (1996). *A Primer of Drug Action: A Concise, Nontechnical Guide to the Actions, Uses and Side Effects of Psychoactive Drugs*, 7th edn. New York: W.H. Freeman.

Kahn, K.L., Pearson, M.L., Harrison, E.R., Desmond, K.A., Rogers, W.H., Rubenstein, L.V., Brook, R.H. and Keeler, E.B. (1994). Health care for black and poor hospitalized Medicare patients. *Journal of the American Medical Association*, 271: 1169–74.

Kalichman, S.C., Benotsch, E.G., Weinhardt, L., Austin, J., Luke, W. and Cherry, C. (2003). Health-related internet use, coping, social support, and health indicators in people living with HIV/AIDS: preliminary results from a community survey. *Health Psychology*, 22: 111–16.

Kalichman, S.C., Cherry, C. and Browne-Sperling, F. (1999). Effectiveness of a video-based motivational skills-building HIV risk-reduction intervention for inner-city African American men. *Journal of Consulting and Clinical Psychology*, 67: 959–66.

Kalnins, I.H.C., Ballantyne, P. and Quartaro, G. (1994). School based community development as a health promotion strategy for children. *Health Promotion International*, 9: 269–79.

Kalra, L., Evans, A., Perez, I., Melbourn, A., Patel, A., Knapp, M. and Donaldson, N. (2004). Training carers of stroke patients: randomised controlled trial. *British Medical Journal*, 328: 1099–104.

Kanner, A.D., Coyne, J.C., Schaefer, C. and Lazarus, R.S. (1981). Comparison of two models of stress management: daily hassles and uplifts versus major life events. *Journal of Behavioral Medicine*, 4: 1–39.

Kaplan, G. and Baron-Epel, O. (2003). What lies behind the subjective evaluation of health status? *Social Science and Medicine*, 56: 1669–76.

Kaplan, G.A. and Reynolds, P. (1988). Depression and cancer mortality and morbidity: prospective evidence from the Alameda County study. *Journal of Behavioral Medicine*, 11: 1–14.

Karasek, R.A. (1979). Job demands, job decision latitude and mental strain: implications for job redesign. *Administrative Science Quarterly*, 24: 285–308.

Karasek, R. (1996). Lower health risk with increased job control among white collar workers. *Journal of Organizational Behavior*, 11: 171–85.

Karasek, R.A., Baker, D., Marxer, F., Ahlbom, A. and Theorell, T. (1981). Job decision latitude, job demands and cardiovascular disease: a prospective study of Swedish men. *American Journal of Public Health*, 71: 694–705.

Karasek, R.A. and Theorell, T. (1990). *Healthy Work: Stress, Productivity and the Reconstruction of Working Life*. New York: Basic Books.

Kasl, S.V. (1996). Theory of stress and health. In C.L. Cooper (ed.), *Handbook of Stress, Medicine and Health*. London: CRC Press.

Kasl, S.V. and Cobb, S. (1966a). Health behavior, illness behavior, and sick role behavior I. Health and illness behavior. *Archives of Environmental Health*, 12: 246–66.

Kasl, S.V. and Cobb, S. (1966b). Health behavior, illness behavior, and sick role behavior II. Sick role behavior. *Archives of Environmental Health*, 12: 531–41.

Katz, M.H. (1997). AIDS epidemic in San Francisco among men who report sex with men: successes and challenges of HIV prevention. *Journal of Acquired Immune Deficiency Syndrome and Human Retrovirology*, 14: S38–S46.

Keefe, F.J., Caldwell, D.S., Williams, D.A., Gil, K.M., Mitchell, D., Robertson, C., Martinez, S., Nunley, J., Beckham, J.C. and Helms, M. (1990). Pain coping skills training in the management of osteoarthritic knee pain – II: Follow-up results. *Behavior Therapy*, 21: 435–47.

Keinan, G., Carmil, D. and Rieck, M. (1991). Predicting women's delay in seeking medical care after discovery of a lump in the breast: the role of personality and behaviour patterns. *Behavioral Medicine*, 17: 177–83.

Kelly, J.A., Murphy, D.A., Sikkema, K.J. and Kalichman, S.C. (1993). Psychological interventions to prevent HIV infection are urgently needed. *American Psychologist*, 48: 1023–34.

Kelly, J.A., Murphy, D.A., Sikkema, K.J., McAuliffe, T.L., Roffman, R.A., Solomon, L.J., Winett, R.A., Kalichman, S.A. and Community HIV Prevention Research Collaborative (1997). Randomised, controlled, community-level HIV-prevention intervention for sexual-risk behaviour among homosexual men in US cities. *The Lancet*, 350: 1500–5.

Kelly, J.A., Murphy, D.A., Washington, C.D. and Wilson, T.S. (1994). The effects of HIV/AIDS intervention groups for high-risk women in urban clinics. *American Journal of Public Health*, 84: 225–37.

Kelly, J.A., St Lawrence, J.S., Stevenson, L.Y., Hauth, A.C., Kalichman, S.C., Diaz, Y.E., Brasfield, T.L., Koob, J.J. and Morgan, M.G. (1992). Community AIDS/HIV risk reduction: the effects of endorsements by popular people in three cities. *American Journal of Public Health*, 82: 1483–9.

Kemeny, M.E., Weiner, H., Taylor, S.E., Schneider, S., Visscher, B. and Fahey, L. (1994). Repeated bereavement, depressed mood, and immune parameters in HIV seropositive and seronegative homosexual men. *Health Psychology*, 13: 14–24.

Kennedy, T., Jones R., Darnley, S., Seed P., Wessely, S. and Chalder T. (2005) Cognitive behaviour therapy in addition to antispasmodic treatment for irritable bowel syndrome in primary care: randomised controlled trial. *British Medical Journal*, 331: 435.

Kentsch, M., Rodemerk, U., Muller-Esch, G., Schnoor, U., Munzel, T., Ittel, T.H. and Mitusch, R. (2002). Emotional attitudes toward symptoms and inadequate coping strategies are major determinants of patient delay in acute myocardial infarction. *Zeitschrift zu Kardiologie*, 91: 147–55.

Kerns, R.D., Haythornwaite, J., Southwick, S. and Giller, E.L. (1990). The role of marital interaction in chronic pain and depressive symptom severity. *Journal of Psychosomatic Research*, 34: 401–8.

Key, T.J., Fraser, G.E., Thorogood, M., Appleby, P.N., Beral, V., Reeves, G., Burr, M.L., Chang-Claude, J., Frentzel-Beyme, R., Kuzma, J.W., Mann, J. and McPherson, K. (1998). Mortality in vegetarians and non-vegetarians: a collaborative analysis of 8,300 deaths among 76,000 men and women in five prospective studies. *Public Health Nutrition*, 1: 33–41.

Khantzian, E.J. (2003). Understanding addictive vulnerability: an evolving psychodynamic perspective. *Neuro-psychoanalysis*, 5: 3–35.

Kickbusch, I. (2003). The contribution of the World Health Organization to a new public health and health promotion. *American Journal of Public Health*, 93: 383–8.

Kiechl, S., Egger, G., Mayr, M., Wiederman, C.J., Bonora, E., Oberhollenzer, F.M., Muggeo, M., Xu, Q., Wick, G. and Willeit, J. (2001). Chronic infections and the risk of carotid atherosclerosis: prospective results from a large population study. *Circulation*, 103: 1064–70.

Kiecolt-Glaser, J.K., Dura, J.R., Speicher, C.E., Trask, C.E. and Glaser, R. (1991). Spousal caregivers of dementia victims: longitudinal changes in immunity and health. *Psychosomatic Medicine*, 53: 345–62.

Kiecolt-Glaser, J.K., Garner, W., Speicher, C., Penn, G.M., Holliday, J.E. and Glaser, R. (1984). Psychosocial modifiers of immunocompetence in medical students. *Psychosomatic Medicine*, 46: 7–14.

Kiecolt-Glaser, J.K. and Glaser, R. (1995). Psychological influences on immunity. *Psychosomatics*, 27: 621–4.

Kiecolt-Glaser, J.K. and Glaser, R. (1999). Psychoneuroimmunology and cancer: fact or fiction? *European Journal of Cancer*, 35: 1603–7.

Kiecolt-Glaser, J.K., Glaser, R., Gravenstein, S., Malarkey, W.B. and Sheridan, J. (1996). Chronic stress alters the immune response to influenza virus vaccination in older adults. *Proceedings of the National Academy of Science USA*, 93: 3043–7.

Kiecolt-Glaser, J.K., Glaser, R., Williger, D. *et al.* (1985). Psychosocial enhancement of immunocompetence in a geriatric population. *Health Psychology*, 4: 25–41.

Kiecolt-Glaser, J.K., Malarkey, W.B., Cacioppo, J.T. and Glaser, R. (1994). Stressful personal relationships: Immune and endocrine function. In R. Glaser and J.K. Kiecolt-Glaser (eds), *Handbook of Human Stress and Immunity*. San Diego: Academic Press.

Kiecolt-Glaser, J.K., Marucha, P.T., Malarkey, W.B., Mercado, A.M. and Glaser, R. (1995). Slowing wound healing by psychosocial stress. *The Lancet*, 4: 1194–6.

Kiernan, P.J. and Isaacs, J.B. (1981). Use of drugs by the elderly. *Journal of the Royal Society of Medicine*, 74: 196–200.

Kinmonth, A.L., Woodcock, A., Griffin, S., Spiegal, N. and Campbell, M.J. (1998). Randomised controlled trial of patient-centred care of diabetes in general practice: impact on current wellbeing and future disease risk. The Diabetes Care from Diagnosis Research Team. *British Medical Journal*, 317: 1202–8.

Kinney, J.M., Stephens, M.A.P., Franks, M.M. and Norris, V.K. (1995). Stresses and satisfactions of family caregivers to older stroke patients. *The Journal of Applied Gerontology*, 14: 3–21.

Kirby, S.D., Ureda, J.R., Rose, R.L. and Hussey, J. (1998). Peripheral cues and involvement level: influences on acceptance of a mammography message. *Journal of Health Communication*, 3: 19–35.

Kirkcaldy, B.D. and Cooper, C.L. (1992). Managing the stress of change: Occupational stress among senior police officers in Berlin. *Stress Medicine*, 8: 219–31.

Kivimäki, M., Elovainio, M., Kokko, K., Pulkinnen, L., Kortteinen, M. and Tuomikoski, H. (2003). Hostility, unemployment and health status: testing three theoretical models. *Social Science and Medicine*, 56: 2139–52.

Kivimäki, M., Vahtera, J., Kosekenvuo, M., Uutela, A. and Pentti, J. (1998). Response of hostile individuals to stressful changes in their working lives: test of a psychosocial vulnerability model. *Psychological Medicine*, 28: 903–13.

Klein, C.T.F. and Helweg-Larsen, M. (2002). Perceived control and the optimistic bias: a meta-analytic review. *Psychology and Health*, 17: 437–46.

Kline, K.N. and Mattson, M. (2000). Breast self-examination pamphlets. A content analysis grounded in fear appeals research. *Health Communication*, 12: 1–21.

Kline, P. (1993). *Personality – the Psychometric View*. London: Routledge.

Klonoff, E.A. and Landrine, H. (1994). Culture and gender diversity in commonsense beliefs about the causes of six illnesses. *Journal of Behavioral Medicine*, 17: 407–18.

Knowler, W.C., Barrett-Connor, E., Fowler, S.E., Hamman, R.E., Lachin, J.M., Walker, E.A. and Nathan, D.M. (2002). Reduction in the incidence of type 2 diabetes with lifestyle intervention or metformin. *New England Journal of Medicine*, 346: 393–403.

Kobasa, S.C. (1979). Stressful life events, personality and health: an inquiry into hardiness. *Journal of Personality and Social Psychology*, 37: 1–11.

Kobasa, S.C., Maddi, S. and Kahn, S. (1982). Hardiness and health: a prospective study. *Journal of Personality and Social Psychology*, 42: 168–77.

Koffman, D.M., Lee, J.W., Hopp, J.W. and Emont, S.L. (1998). The impact of including incentives and competition in a workplace smoking cessation program on quit rates. *American Journal of Health Promotion*, 13: 105–11.

Kohl, H.W. (2001). Physical activity and cardiovascular disease: evidence for a dose–response. *Medicine and Science in Sports and Exercise*, 33: S472–S487.

Koikkalainen, M., Lappalainen, R. and Mykkanen, H. (1996). Why cardiac patients do not follow the nutritionist's advice: barriers in nutritional advice perceived in rehabilitation. *Disability and Rehabilitation*, 13: 619–23.

Kok, G. and Schaalma, H. (1998). Theory-based and data-based health education intervention programmes. *Psychology and Health*, 13: 747–51.

Kole-Snijders, A.M.J., Vlaeyen, J.W.S. and Goossens, M.E.J., *et al.* 1999. Chronic low back pain: what does cognitive coping skills training add to operant behavioural treatment? Results of a randomized trial. *Journal of Consulting and Clinical Psychology*, 67: 931–44.

Kolk, A.M., Hanewald, G.J.F.P., Schagen, S. and Gijsbers van Wijk, C.M.T. (2003). A symptom perception approach to common physical symptoms. *Social Science and Medicine*, 57: 2343–54.

Kop, N., Euwema, M. and Schaufeli, W. (1999). Burnout, job stress and violent behaviour among Dutch police officers. *Work and Stress*, 13: 3226–340.

Kop, W.J. and Krantz, D.S. (1997). Type A behaviour, hostility and coronary artery disease. In A. Baum, S. Newman, J. Weinman, R. West and C. McManus (eds), *Cambridge Handbook of Psychology, Health and Medicine*. Cambridge: Cambridge University Press.

Kornblith, A.B. (1998). *Psychosocial Adaptation of Cancer Survivors*. In J.C. Holland, W. Breibart and P.B. Jacobsen (eds), *Psycho-Oncology*. New York: Oxford University Press.

Kornblith, A.B., Herndon, J.E., II, Weiss, R.B., Zhang, C., Zuckerman, E.L., Rosenberg, S., Mertz, M., Payne, D., Jane Massie, M., Holland, J.F., Wingate, P., Norton, L. and Holland, J.C. (2003). Long-term adjustment of survivors of early-stage breast carcinoma, 20 years after adjuvant chemotherapy. *Cancer*, 98: 679–89.

Korotkov, D. and Hannah, T.E. (2004). The five factor model of personality: strengths and limitations in predicting health status, sick role and illness behaviour. *Personality and Individual Differences*, 36: 187–99.

Kraft, P., Sutton, S. and McCreath-Reynolds, H. (1999). The transtheoretical model of behaviour change: are the stages qualitatively different? *Psychology and Health*, 14: 433–50.

Kramer, B.J. (1997). Gain in the caregiving experience. Where are we? What next? *The Gerontologist*, 37: 218–32.

Krantz, D.S., Glass, D.C., Shaeffer, M.A. and Davia, J.E. (1982). Behavior patterns and coronary disease: a critical evaluation. In J.T. Cacioppo and R.E. Petty (eds), *Perspectives in Cardiovascular Psychophysiology*. New York: Guilford Press.

Krantz, G. and Orth, P. (2000). Common symptoms in middle-aged women: their relation to employment status, psychosocial work conditions and social support in a Swedish setting. *Journal of Epidemiology and Community Health*, 54: 192–9.

Krause, N.M. and Jay, G.M. (1994). What do global self-rated health items measure? *Medical Care*, 32: 930–42.

Krieger, N., Quesenberry, C. and Peng, T. (1999). Social class, race/ethnicity, and incidence of breast, cervix, colon, lung, and prostate cancer among Asian, black, Hispanic, and white residents of the San Francisco Bay area. *Cancer Causes Control*, 10: 525–37.

Kristensen, T.S. (1995). The demand–control–support model: methodological challenges for future research. *Stress Medicine*, 11: 17–26.

Krohne, H.W. (1993). Vigilance and cognitive avoidance as concepts in coping research. In H.W. Krohne (ed.), *Attention and Avoidance: Strategies in Coping with Aversiveness*. Seattle: Hogrefe and Huber.

Krol, Y., Grootenhuis, M.A., Destrée-Vonk, A., Lubbers, L.J., Koopman, H.M. and Laast, B.F. (2003). Health-related quality of life in children with congenital heart disease. *Psychology and Health*, 18: 251–60.

Kubler-Ross, E. (1969). *On Death and Dying*. New York: Macmillan.

Kuchler, T., Henne-Bruns, D., Rappat, S., Graul, J., Holst, K. and Williams, J.I. (1999). Impact of psychotherapeutic support on gastrointestinal cancer patients undergoing surgery: survival results of a trial. *Hepato-gastro-enterology*, 46: 322–35.

Kuntzleman, C.T. (1985). Enhancing cardiovascular fitness of children and youth: the Feelin' Good Program. In J.E. Zins, D.I. Wagner and C.A. Maher (eds), *Health Promotion in the Schools: Innovative Approaches to Facilitating Physical and Emotional Well-being*. New York: Hawthorn Press.

Kurtz, S. and Silverman, J. (1996). The Calgary–Cambridge observation guides: an aid to defining the curriculum and organising the teaching in communication training programmes. *Medical Education*, 30: 83–9.

Kyngaes, H., Mikkonen, R., Nousiainen, E.M., Rytilahti, M., Seppaenen, P., Vaattovaara, R. and Jaemsae, T. (2001). Coping with the onset of cancer. Coping strategies and resources of young people with cancer. *European Journal of Cancer Care*, 10: 6–11.

Lacroix, J.M., Martin, B., Avendano, M. and Goldstein, R. (1991). Symptom schemata in chronic respiratory patients. *Health Psychology*, 10: 268–73.

Lahelma, E., Martikainen, P., Rahkonen, O. and Silventoinen, K. (1999). Gender differences in ill-health in Finland: patterns, magnitude and change. *Social Science and Medicine*, 48: 7–19.

Lancaster, T., Silagy, C., Fowler, G. and Spiers, I. (1999). Training health professionals in smoking cessation. In *The Cochrane Library*, issue 1. Oxford: Update Software.

Landmark, B.T. and Wahl, A. (2002). Living with newly diagnosed breast cancer: a qualitative study of 10 women with newly diagnosed breast cancer. *Journal of Advanced Nursing*, 49: 112–21.

Landolt, M.A., Vollrath, M., Ribi, K., Gnehm, H.E. and Sennhauser, F.H. (2003). Incidence and associations of parental and child posttraumatic stress symptoms in pediatric patients. *Journal of Child Psychology and Psychiatry*, 44: 1199–207.

Landrine, H. and Klonoff, E.A. (1992). Culture and health-related schema: a review and proposal for interdisciplinary integration. *Health Psychology*, 11: 267–76.

Landrine, H. and Klonoff, E.A. (1994). Cultural diversity in causal attributions for illness: the role of the supernatural. *Journal of Behavioral Medicine*, 17: 181–93.

Lane, D., Carroll, D., Ring, C., Beevers, D.G. and Lip, G.Y. (2000). Effects of depression and anxiety on mortality and quality-of-life 4 months after myocardial infarction. *Journal of Psychosomatic Research*, 49: 229–38.

Lane, D., Carroll, D., Ring, C., Beevers, D.G. and Lip, G.Y. (2001a). Predictors of attendance at cardiac rehabilitation after myocardial infarction. *Journal of Psychosomatic Research*, 51: 497–501.

Lane, D., Carroll, D., Ring, C., Beevers, D.G. and Lip, G.Y. (2002). The prevalence and persistence of depression and anxiety following myocardial infarction. *British Journal of Health Psychology*, 7: 11–21.

Lang, E.V., Joyce, J.S., Spiegel, D., Hamilton, D., Lee, K.K., Schwartz, L., Slater, M.A. and Birchler, G.R. (1996). The role of pain behaviors in the modulation of marital conflict in chronic pain couples. *Pain*, 65: 227–33.

Lang, T., Nicaud, V., Slama, K., Hirsch, A., Imbernon, E., Goldberg, M., Calvel, L., Desobry, P., Favre-Trosson, J.P., Lhopital, C., Mathevon, P., Miara, D., Miliani, A., Panthier, F., Pons, G., Roitg, C. and Thoores, M. (2000). Smoking cessation at the workplace. Results of a randomised controlled intervention study. Worksite physicians from the AIREL group. *Journal of Epidemiology and Community Health*, 54: 349–54.

Langewitz, W., Wossmer, B., Iseli, J. and Berger, W. (1997). Psychological and metabolic improvement after an outpatient teaching program for functional intensified insulin therapy. *Diabetes Research and Clinical Practice*, 37: 157–64.

Larsen, R.J. and Kasimatis, M. (1991). Day-to-day physical symptoms: individual differences in the occurrence, duration, and emotional concomitants of minor daily illnesses. *Journal of Personality*, 59: 387–423.

Larson, J. (1999). The conceptualization of health. *Medical Care and Review*, 56: 123–236.

Latimer, P. (1981). Irritable bowel syndrome: a behavioral model. *Behaviour Research and Therapy*, 19: 475–83.

Latimer, P., Sarna, S., Campbell, D., Latimer, M., Waterfall, W. and Daniel, E.E. (1981). Colonic motor and myoelectric activity: a comparative study of normal subjects, psychoneurotic patients and patients with the irritable bowel syndrome. *Gastroenterology*, 80: 893–901.

Lau, R.R. and Hartman, K.A. (1983). Common sense representations of common illnesses. *Health Psychology*, 2: 167–85.

Lau, R.R., Bernard, T.M. and Hartman, K.A. (1989). Further explorations of common sense representations of common illnesses. *Health Psychology*, 8(2): 195–219.

Lauby, J.L., Smith, P.J., Stark, M., Person, B. and Adams, J. (2000). A community-level HIV prevention intervention for inner-city women: results of the Women and Infants Demonstration Projects. *American Journal of Public Health*, 90: 216–22.

Laugesen, M. and Meads, C. (1991). Tobacco restrictions, price, income and tobacco consumption in OECD countries, 1960–1986. *British Journal of Addiction*, 86: 1343–54.

Laux, L. and Weber, H. (1991). Presentation of self in coping with anger and anxiety: an intentional approach. *Anxiety Research*, 3: 233–55.

Lavery, J.F. and Clarke, V.A. (1996). Causal attributions, coping strategies and adjustment to breast cancer. *Cancer Nursing*, 19: 20–8.

Law, M.R., Frost, C.D. and Wald, N.J. (1991). By how much does dietary salt lower blood pressure? I – Analysis of observational data among populations. *British Medical Journal*, 302: 811–15.

Law, M.R., Wald, N.J. and Thompson, S.G. (1994). By how much and how quickly does reduction in serum cholesterol concentration lower risk of ischemic heart disease? *British Medical Journal*, 308: 367–72.

Lazarus, R.S. (1966). *Psychological Stress and the Coping Process*. New York: McGraw-Hill.

Lazarus, R.S. (1991a). *Emotion and adaptation*. New York: Oxford University Press.

Lazarus, R.S. (1991b). Psychological stress in the workplace. In P. Perrewe (ed.), *Handbook on Job Stress*.

Special issue of *Journal of Social Behavior and Personality*, 6: 1–13.

Lazarus, R.S. (1993a). From psychological stress to the emotions: a history of changing outlooks. *Annual Review of Psychology*, 44: 1–21.

Lazarus, R.S. (1993b). Coping theory and research: past, present and future. *Psychosomatic Medicine*, 55: 234–47.

Lazarus, R.S. (1999). *Stress and Emotion: A New Synthesis*. New York: Springer Verlag.

Lazarus, R.S. (2000). Toward better research on stress and coping. *American Psychologist*, 55: 665–73.

Lazarus, R.S. and Folkman, S. (1984). *Stress, Appraisal, and Coping*. New York: Springer Verlag.

Lazarus, R.S. and Launier, R. (1978). Stress related transactions between person and environment. In L.A. Pervin and M. Lewis (eds), *Perspectives in International Psychology*, New York: Plenum.

Lee, C. (1999). Health, stress and coping among women caregivers: a review. *Journal of Health Psychology*, 4: 27–40.

Lee, C. (2001). Experiences of family caregiving among older Australian women. *Journal of Health Psychology*, 6: 393–404.

Lee, I.-M., Rexrode, K.M., Cook, N.R., Manson, J.E. and Buring, J.E. (2001). Physical activity and coronary heart disease in women: is 'no pain, no gain' passé? *Journal of the American Medical Association*, 285: 1447–54.

Lee, S.J., Back, A.L., Block, S.D. and Stewart, S.K. (2002). Enhancing physician–patient communication. *Hematology*, 464–83.

Lefkowitz, R.J. and Willerson, J.T. (2001). Prospects for cardiovascular research. *Journal of the American Medical Association*, 285: 581–7.

Lerman, C. and Croyle, R. (1994). Psychological issues in genetic testing for breast cancer susceptibility. *Archives of Internal Medicine*, 154: 609–16.

Lerman, C., Hughes, C., Croyle, R.T., Main, D., Durham, D., Snyder, C. *et al.* (2000). Prophylactic surgery and surveillance practices one year following BRCA1/2 genetic testing. *Preventative Medicine*, 1: 75–80.

Lerman, C., Marshall, J. and Caminerio, A. (1996). Genetic testing for colon cancer susceptibility: anticipated reactions of patients and challenges to providers. *International Journal of Cancer*, 69: 58–61.

Leserman, J., Jackson, E.D., Petitto, J.M. *et al.* (1999). Progression to AIDS: The effects of stress, depressive symptoms, and social support. *Psychosom Med* 61(3): 397–406.

Leskin, G.A., Kaloupek, D.G. and Keane, T.M. (1998). Treatment for traumatic memories: review and recommendations. *Clinical Psychology Review*, 18: 983–1002.

Letherman, C., Blackburn, D. and Davidhizar, R. (1990). How postpartum women explain their lack of obtaining adequate prenatal care. *Journal of Advanced Nursing*, 15: 256–67.

Leventhal, E.A., Hansell, S., Diefenbach, M., Leventhal, H. and Glass, D.C. (1996). Negative affect and self-report of physical symptoms: two longitudinal studies of older adults. *Health Psychology*, 15: 193–9.

Leventhal, E.A. and Prohaska, T.R. (1986). Age, symptom interpretation and health behavior. *Journal of the American Geriatric Society*, 34: 185–91.

Leventhal, H. and Coleman, S. (1997). Quality of life: a process view. *Psychology and Health*, 12: 753–67.

Leventhal, H. and Diefenbach, M. (1991). The active side of illness cognition. In J.A. Skelton and R.T. Croyle (eds), *Mental Representations in Health and Illness*. New York: Springer Verlag.

Leventhal, H., Diefenbach, M. and Leventhal, E. (1992). Illness cognition: using common sense to understand treatment adherence and effect cognitive interactions. *Cognitive Therapy and Research*, 16(2): 143–63.

Leventhal, H., Easterling, D.V., Coons, H., Luchterhand, C. and Love, R.R. (1986). Adaptation to chemotherapy treatments. In B. Anderson (ed.), *Women with Cancer*. New York: Springer Verlag.

Leventhal, H., Meyer, D. and Nerenz, D. (1980). The common sense model of illness danger. In S. Rachman (ed.), *Medical Psychology*, Vol. 2. New York: Pergamon.

Leventhal, H., Nerenz, D.R. and Steele, D.J. (1984). Illness representations and coping with health threats. In A. Baum, S.E. Taylor and J.E. Singer (eds), *Handbook of Psychology and Health: Social Psychological Aspects of Health*, Vol. 4. Hillsdale, NJ: Lawrence Erlbaum.

Leventhal, H., Patrick-Miller, L. and Leventhal, E.A. (1998). It's long-term stressors that take a toll: comment on Cohen *et al.* (1998). *Health Psychology*, 17: 211–13.

Leventhal, H. and Tomarken, A. (1987). Stress and illness: perspectives from health psychology. In S.V. Kasl and C.L. Cooper (eds), *Research Methods in Stress and Health Psychology*. London: Wiley.

Levinson, D.J., Darrow, C.N., Klein, E.B., Levinson, M.H. and McKee, B. (1978). *The Seasons of a Man's Life*. New York: A.A. Knopf.

Levine, R.M. and Reicher, S. (1996). Making sense of symptoms: self categorization and the meaning of illness/injury. *British Journal of Social Psychology*, 35: 245–56.

Levy, L., Patterson, R.E., Kristal, A.R. and Li, S.S. (2000). How well do consumers understand percentage daily value of food labels? *American Journal of Health Promotion*, 14: 157–60.

Lewin, B., Robertson, I.H., Irving, J.B. and Campbell, M. (1992). Effects of self-help post-myocardial-infarction rehabilitation on psychological adjustment and use of health services. *The Lancet*, 339: 1036–40.

Lewin, R.J., Furze, G., Robinson, J., Griffith, K., Wiseman, S., Pye, M. and Boyle, R. (2002). A randomised controlled trial of a self-management plan for patients with newly diagnosed angina. *British Journal of General Practice*, 52: 194–6, 199–201.

Lewis, C.L. and Brown, S.C. (2002). Coping strategies of female adolescents with HIV/AIDS. *The Association of Black Nursing Faculty*, 13: 72–7.

Lewis, G., Bebbington, P., Brugha, T., Farrell, M., Gill, B., Jenkins, R. and Meltzer, H. (1998). Socioeconomic status, standard of living, and neurotic disorder. *The Lancet*, 352: 605–9.

Lewis, S.C., Dennis, M.D., O'Rourke, S.J. and Sharpe, M. (2001). Negative attitudes among short-term stroke survivors predict worse long-term survival. *Stroke*, 32: 1640–5.

Lewit, E., Coates, D. and Grossman, M. (1981). The effects of governmental regulation on teenage smoking. *Journal of Law and Economics*, 24: 545–69.

Ley, P. (1997). Compliance among patients. In A. Baum, S. Newman, J. Weinman, R. West and C. McManus (eds), *Cambridge Handbook of Psychology, Health and Medicine*. Cambridge: Cambridge University Press.

Ley, P. (1988). *Communicating with patients. Improving communication, satisfaction, and compliance*. London: Chapman Hall.

Lichtenstein, P. and Pedersen, N.L. (1995). Social relationships, stressful life events, and self-reported physical health: genetic and environmental influences. *Psychology and Health*, 10: 295–319.

Lim, A.S.H. and Bishop, G.D. (2000). The role of attitudes and beliefs in differential health care utilisation among Chinese in Singapore. *Psychology and Health*, 14: 965–77.

Linden, W., Stossel, C. and Maurice, J. (1996). Psychosocial treatment for cardiac patients: a meta-analysis. *Archives of Internal Medicine*, 156: 745–62.

Linegar, J., Chesson, C. and Nice, D. (1991). Physical fitness gains following simple environmental change. *American Journal of Preventive Medicine*, 7: 298–310.

Linn, S., Carroll, M., Johnson, C., Fulwood, R., Kalsbek, W. and Briefel, R. (1993). High density lipoprotein cholesterol and alcohol consumption in US white and black adults: data from NHANES II. *American Journal of Public Health*, 83: 811–16.

Lipkus, I.M., Barefoot, J.C., Williams, R.B. and Siegler, I.C. (1994). Personality measures as predictors of smoking initiation and cessation in the UNC Alumni heart study. *Health Psychology*, 13: 149–55.

Lipton, A.A. and Simon, F.S. (1985). Psychiatric diagnosis in a state hospital: Manhattan state revisited. *Hospital and Community Psychiatry*, 36: 368–73.

Litt, M.D., Nye, C. and Shafer, D. (1995). Preparation for oral surgery: evaluating elements of coping. *Journal of Behavioral Medicine*, 18: 435–59.

Little, M. and Sayers, E-J. (2004). While there's life . . . hope and the experience of cancer. *Social Science and Medicine*, 59: 1329–37.

Livingston, G. and Hinchliffe, A.C. (1993). The epidemiology of psychiatric disorders in the elderly. *International Review of Psychiatry*, 5: 317–29.

Lo, R. (1999). Correlates of expected success at adherence to health regimen of people with IDDM. *Journal of Advanced Nursing*, 30: 418–24.

Lobb, E.A., Butow, P.N., Kenny, D.T. and Tattersall, M.H. (1999). Communicating prognosis in early breast cancer: Do women understand the language used? *Medical Journal of Australia*, 171: 290–4.

Lobchuk, M.M. and Vorauer, J.D. (2003). Family care-giving, perspective-taking, and accuracy in estimating cancer patient symptom experiences. *Social Science and Medicine*, 57: 2379–84.

Locke, E.A. and Latham, G.P. (2002). Building a practically useful theory of goal setting and task motivation: a 35-year odyssey. *American Psychologist*, 57: 705–17.

Locke, G.R., III, Weaver, A.L., Melton, L.J., III and Talley, N.J. (2004). Psychosocial factors are linked to functional gastrointestinal disorders: a population based nested case-control study. *American Journal of Gastroenterology*, 99: 350–7.

Lodder, L., Frets, P.G., Trijsburg, R.W., Meijers-Heijboer, E.J., Klijn, J.G., Duivenvoorden, H.J., Tibben, A., Wagner, A., van der Meer, C.A., van den Ouweland, A.M. and Niermeijer, M.F. (2001). Psychological impact of receiving a BRCA1/BRCA2 test result. *American Journal of Medical Genetics*, 98: 15–24.

Logan, T.K., Cole, J. and Leukefeld, C. (2002). Women, sex, and HIV: social and contextual factors, meta-analysis of published interventions, and implications for practice and research. *Psychological Bulletin*, 128: 851–85.

Lok, C.F. and Bishop, G.D. (1999). Emotion control, stress, and health. *Psychology and Health*, 14: 813–27.

Lomas, J. (1991). Words without action? The production, dissemination, and impact of consensus recommendations. *Annual Reviews in Public Health*, 12: 41–65.

Longabaugh, R. and Morgenstern, J. (1999). Cognitive-behavioural coping-skills therapy for alcohol dependence. *Alcohol Research and Health*, 23: 78–85.

Longo, D.R., Johnson, J.C., Kruse, R.L., Brownson, R.C. and Hewett, J.E. (2001). A prospective investigation of the impact of smoking bans on tobacco cessation and relapse. *Tobacco Control*, 10: 267–72.

Lorig, K. (1996). *Patient Education: A Practical Approach*. Newbury Park, Calif.: Sage.

Lorig, K. and Holman, H. (1989). Long-term outcomes of an arthritis self-management study: effects of reinforcement efforts. *Social Science and Medicine*, 29: 221–4.

Lorig, K.R., Ritter, P.L. and Gonzalez, V.M. (2003). Hispanic chronic disease self-management: a randomized community-based outcome trial. *Nursing Research*, 52: 361–9.

Lorig, K., Sobel, D.S., Stewart, A.L., Brown, B.W., Jr, Bandura, A., Ritter, P. *et al.* (1999). Evidence suggesting that a chronic disease self-management program can improve health status while reducing hospitalisation. *Medical Care*, 37: 5–14.

Louria, D. (1988). Some concerns about educational approaches in AIDS prevention. In R. Schinazi and A. Nahmias (eds), *AIDS children, adolescents and heterosexual adults*. New York: Elsevier Science.

Lovallo, W.R. (1997). *Stress and Health: Biological and Psychological Interactions*. Newbury Park, Calif.: Sage.

Lovallo, W.R., Pincomb, G.A., Brackett, D.J. and Wilson, M.F. (1990). Heart rate reactivity as a predictor of neuroendocrine responses to aversive and appetitive challenges. *Psychosomatic Medicine*, 52: 17–26.

Lovegrove, E., Rumsey, N., Harcourt, D. and Cawthorn, S.J. (2000). Factors implicated in the decision whether or not to join the tamoxifen trial in women at high familial risk of breast cancer. *Psycho-Oncology*, 9: 193–202.

Lowe, C.F., Horne, P.J., Tapper, K., Bowdery, M. and Egerton, E. (2004). Effects of a peer-modelling and rewards based intervention to increase fruit and vegetable consumption in children. *European Journal of Clinical Nutrition*, 58: 510–22.

Lowe, R., Norman, P. and Bennett, P. (2000). Coping, emotion and perceived health following myocardial infarction. *British Journal of Health Psychology*, 5: 337–50.

Lowe, R., Vedhara, K., Bennett, P., Brookes, E., Gale, L., Munnoch, K., Schreiber-Kounine, C., Fowler, C., Rayter, Z., Sammon, A. and Farndon, J. (2003). Emotion-related primary and secondary appraisals, adjustment and coping associations in women awaiting breast disease diagnosis. *British Journal of Health Psychology*, 8: 377–91.

Lowes, J. and Tiggemann, M. (2003). Body dissatisfaction and dieting awareness in young children. *British Journal of Health Psychology*, 8: 135–47.

Lundberg, U., de Chateau, P., Winberg, J. and Frankenhauser, M. (1981). Catecholamine and cortisol excretion patterns in three year old children and their parents. *Journal of Human Stress*, 7: 3–11.

Luszczynska, A. and Schwarzer, R. (2003). Planning and self-efficacy in the adoption and maintenance of breast self-examination: a longitudinal study on self-regulatory cognitions. *Psychology and Health*, 18: 93–108.

MacFadyen, L., Amos, A., Hastings, G. and Parkes, E. (2002). They look like my kind of people – perceptions of smoking images in youth magazines. *Social Science and Medicine*, 56: 491–9.

Macintyre, S. (1986). The patterning of health by social position in contemporary Britain: directions for sociological research. *Social Science and Medicine*, 23: 393–415.

Macintyre, S. (1993). Gender differences in the perceptions of common cold symptoms. *Social Science and Medicine*, 36: 15–20.

Macintyre, S. and Ellaway, A. (1998). *Ecological Approaches: Rediscovering the Role of the Physical and Social Environment*. Oxford: Oxford University Press.

MacNee, W. (2004). Guidelines for chronic obstructive pulmonary disease (editorial). *British Medical Journal*, 329: 361–3.

MacNicol, S.A.M., Murray, S.M. and Austin, E.J. (2003). Relationships between personality, attitudes and dietary behaviour in a group of Scottish adolescents. *Personality and Individual Differences*, 35: 1753–64.

Macrodimitris, D. and Endler, N.S. (2001). Coping, control, and adjustment in Type 2 diabetes. *Health Psychology*, 20: 208–16.

Maes, S., Kittel, F., Scholten, H. and Verhoeven, C. (1990). Effects of the Brabantia project, a Dutch wellness-health programme at the worksite. *American Journal of Public Health*, 88: 1037–41.

Maes, S., Leventhal, H. and de Ridder, D.T. (1996). Coping with chronic disease. In M. Zeidner and N.S. Endler (eds), *Handbook of Coping*. New York: Wiley.

Magarey, A., Daniels, L.A. and Smith, A. (2001). Fruit and vegetable intakes of Australians aged 2–18 years: an evaluation of the 1995 National Nutrition Survey data. *Australian and New Zealand Journal of Public Health*, 25: 155–61.

Mager, W.M. and Andrykowski, M.A. (2002). Communication in the cancer 'bad news' consultation: patient perceptions and psychological adjustment. *Psycho-Oncology*, 11: 35–46.

Maggiolo, F., Ripamonti, D., Arici, C., Gregis, G., Quinzan, G., Camacho, G.A., Ravasio, L. and Suter, F. (2002). Simpler regimens may enhance adherence to antiretrovirals in HIV-infected patients. *HIV Clinical Trials*, 3: 371–8.

Magni, G., Moreschi, C., Rigatti-Luchini, S. and Merskey, H. (1994). Prospective study on the relationship between depressive symptoms and chronic musculoskeletal pain. *Pain*, 56: 289–97.

Magnusson, J.E. and Becker, W.J. (2003). Migraine frequency and intensity: relationship with disability and psychological factors. *Headache*, 43: 1049–59.

Maguire, P. and Faulkner, A. (1988). How to improve the counselling skills of doctors and nurses in cancer care. *British Medical Journal*, 297: 847–9.

Maguire, P. and Pitceathly, C. (2002). Key communication skills and how to acquire them. *British Medical Journal*, 325: 697–700.

Mahajan, L., Wyllie, R., Steffen, R., Kay, M., Kitaoka, G., Dettorre, J., Sarigol, S. and McCue, K. (1998). The effects of a psychological preparation program on anxiety in children and adolescents undergoing gastrointestinal endoscopy. *Journal of Pediatric Gastroenterology and Nutrition*, 27: 161–5.

Maisto, S.A. and Connors, G.J. (1992). Using subject and collateral reports to measure alcohol consumption. In R.Z. Litten and J.P. Allen (eds), *Measuring Alcohol Consumption: Psychosocial and Biochemical Methods*. New Jersey: Humana Press.

Malfetti, J. (1985). Public information and education sections of the report of the Presidential Commission on Drunk Driving: a critique and a discussion of research implication. *Accident Analysis and Prevention*, 17: 347–53.

Maliski, S.L., Heilemann, M.V. and McCorkle, R. (2002). From 'death sentence' to 'good cancer': couples' transformation of a prostate cancer diagnosis. *Nursing Research*, 51: 391–7.

Mallion, J.M., Baguet, J.P., Siche, J.P., Tremel, F. and de Gaudemaris, R. (1998). Compliance, electronic monitoring and antihypertensive drugs. *Journal of Hypertension*, (suppl.)16: S75–9.

Malow, R.M., Baker, S.M., Klimas, N., Antoni, M.H., Schneiderman, N., Penedo, F.J., Ziskind, D., Page, B., McMahon, R. and McPherson, S. (1998). Adherence to complex combination antiretroviral therapies by HIV-positive drug abusers. *Psychiatric Services*, 49: 1021–2.

Mandelblatt, J. and Kanesky, P.A. (1995). Effectiveness of interventions to enhance physician screening for breast cancer. *Journal of Family Practice*, 40: 162–71.

Maniadakis, N. and Gray, A. (2000). The economic burden of back pain in the UK. *Pain*, 84: 95–103.

Manning, P.K. and Fabrega, H. (1973). The experience of self and body: health and illness in the Chiapas Highlands. In G. Psathas (ed.), *Phenomenological Sociology: Issues and Applications*. New York: Wiley.

Mannino, D.M. (2003). Chronic obstructive pulmonary disease: definition and epidemiology. *Respiratory Care*, 48: 1185–91.

Manson, J.E., Greenland, P., LaCroix, A.Z., Stefanick, M.L., Mouton, C.P., Oberman, A., Perri, M.G., Sheps, D.S., Pettinger, M.B. and Siscovick, D.S. (2002). Walking compared with vigorous exercise for prevention of cardiovascular events in women. *New England Journal of Medicine*, 347: 716–25.

Manstead, A.S.R. (2000). The role of moral norm in the attitude–behavior relationship. In D.J. Terry and M.A. Hogg (eds), *Attitudes, Behavior and Social Context: The Role of Norms and Group Membership*. Mahwah, NJ: Lawrence Erlbaum.

Mantyselka, P., Kumpusalo, E., Ahonen, R., Kumpusalo, A., Kauhanen, J., Viinamaki, H., Halonen, P. and Takala, J. (2001). Pain as a reason to visit the doctor: a study in Finnish primary health care. *Pain*, 89: 175–80.

Marcus, B.H., Rakowski, W. and Rossi, J.S. (1992). Assessing motivational readiness and decision-making for exercise. *Health Psychology*, 22: 3–16.

Marcus, B.H., Selby, V.C., Niaura, R.S. and Rossi, J.S. (1992). Self-efficacy and the stages of exercise behaviour change. *Research Quarterly in Exercise and Sport*, 63: 60–6.

Marinus, J., Ramaker, C., van Hilten, J.J. and Stiggelbout, A.M. (2002). Health related quality of life in Parkinson's disease: a systematic review of disease specific instruments. *Journal of Neurology, Neurosurgery and Psychiatry*, 72: 241–8.

Markovitz, J.H., Matthews, K.A., Kannel, W.B., Cobb, J.L. and D'Agostino, R.B. (1993). Psychological predictors of hypertension in the Framingham study: is there tension in hypertension? *Journal of the American Medical Association*, 270: 2439–43.

Marks, D.F. (ed.) (2002). *The Health Psychology Reader*. London: Sage Publications.

Marks, D.F., Murray, M., Evans, B. and Willig, C. (2000). *Health Psychology: Theory, Research and Practice*. London: Sage.

Marks, I., Lovell, K., Noshirvani, H., Livanou, M. and Thrasher, S. (1998). Treatment of post-traumatic stress disorder by exposure and/or cognition restructuring. *Archives of General Psychiatry*, 55: 317–25.

Marlatt, G.A., Baer, J.S., Donovan, D.M. and Kivlahan, D.R. (1986). Addictive behaviors: etiology and treatment. *Annual Review of Psychology*, 39: 223–52.

Marmot, M.G., Davey-Smith, G. and Stansfield, S. (1991). Health inequalities among British civil servants: the Whitehall study II. *The Lancet*, 337: 1387–93.

Marmot, M.G., Fuhrer, R., Ettner, S.L., Marks, N.F., Bumpass, L.L. and Ryff, C.D. (1998). Contribution of psychosocial factors to socioeconomic differences in health. *The Milbank Quarterly*, 76: 403–448.

Marmot, M.G. and Madge, N. (1987). An epidemiological perspective on stress and health. In S.V. Kasl and C.L. Cooper (eds), *Research Methods in Stress and Health Psychology*, London: Wiley.

Marmot, M., Ryff, C.D., Bumpass, L.L., Shipley, M. and Marks, N.F. (1997). Social inequalities in health: next questions and converging evidence. *Social Science and Medicine*, 44: 901–10.

Marmot, M.G., Shipley, M.J. and Rose, G. (1984). Inequalities in health – specific explanations of a general pattern? *The Lancet*, i, 1003–6.

Marteau, T.M. (1989). Framing of information: its influence upon decisions of doctors and patients. *British Journal of Social Psychology*, 28: 89–94.

Marteau, T.M., Kidd, J., Cuddeford, L. and Walker, P. (1996). Reducing anxiety in women referred for colposcopy using an information booklet. *British Journal of Health Psychology*, 1: 181–9.

Marteau, T.M. and Kinmouth, A.L. (2002). Screening for cardiovascular risk: public health imperative or matter for individual informed choice? *British Medical Journal*, 325: 78–80.

Martin, J., Sabugal, G.M., Rubio, R., Sainz-Maza, M., Blanco, J.M., Alonso, J.L. and Dominiguez, J. (2001). Outcomes of a health education intervention in a sample of patients infected by HIV, most of them injection drug users: possibilities and limitations. *AIDS Care*, 13: 467–73.

Martin, L.M., Calle, E.E., Wingo, P.A. and Heath, C.W., Jr (1996). Comparison of mammography and Pap test use from the 1987 and 1992 National Health Interview Surveys: are we closing the gaps? *American Journal Preventive Medicine*, 12: 82–90.

Martin, R., Rothrock, N., Leventhal, H. and Leventhal, E. (2003). Common sense models of illness: implications for symptom perception and health-related behaviours. In J. Suls and K.A. Wallston (eds), *Social Psychological Foundations of Health and Illness*. Oxford: Blackwell.

Marucha, P.T., Kiecolt-Glaser, J.K. and Favgehi, M. (1998). Mucosal wound healing is impaired by examination stress. *Psychosomatic Medicine*, 60: 362–5.

Maslach, C. (1982). *Burnout: The Cost of Caring*. Englewood Cliffs, NJ: Prentice Hall.

Maslach, C. (1997). Burnout in health professionals. In A. Baum, S. Newman, J. Weinman, R. West and C. McManus (eds), *Cambridge Handbook of Psychology, Health and Medicine*. Cambridge: Cambridge University Press.

Matano, R.A., Futa, K.T., Wanat, S.F., Mussman, L.M. and Leung, C.W. (2000). The Employee Stress and Alcohol Project: the development of a computer-based alcohol abuse prevention program for employees. *Journal of Behavioral Health Services Research*, 27: 152–65.

Matarazzo, J.D. (1982). Behavioral health's challenge to academic, scientific and professional psychology. *American Psychologist*, 37: 1–14.

Matarazzo, J.D. (1984). Behavioral health: a 1990 challenge for the health sciences professions. In J.D. Matarazzo, N.E. Miller, S.M. Weiss, J.A. Herd and S.M. Weiss (eds), *Behavioral Health: A Handbook of Health Enhancement and Disease Prevention*. New York: Wiley.

Mathews, C., Guttmacher, S.J., Coetzee, N., Magwaza, S., Stein, J., Lombard, C., Goldstein, S. and Coetzee, D. (2002). Evaluation of a video based health education strategy to improve sexually transmitted disease partner notification in South Africa. *Sexually Transmitted Infections*, 78: 53–7.

Matthews, K.A., Siegel, J.M., Kuller, L.H., Thompson, M. and Vanat, M. (1983). Determinants of decision to seek medical treatment by patients with acute myocardial infarction symptoms. *Journal of Personality and Social Psychology*, 44: 1144–56.

McCann, B.S., Retzlaff, B.M., Dowdy, A.A., Walden, C.E. and Knopp, R.H. (1990). Promoting adherence to low-fat, low-cholesterol diets: review and recommendations. *Journal of the American Dietetic Association*, 90: 1408–14.

McCann, J., Stockton, D. and Goddard, S. (2002). Impact of false-positive mammography on subsequent screening attendance and risk of cancer. *Breast Cancer Research*, 4: R11.

McCarron, P., Davey-Smith, G. and Wormsley, J. (1994). Deprivation and mortality in Glasgow: changes from 1980 to 1992. *British Medical Journal*, 309: 1481–2.

McCarthy, W.H. and Shaw, H.M. (1989). Skin Cancer in Australia, *Medical Journal of Australia*, 150: 469–70.

McClenahan, R. and Weinman, J. (1998). Determinants of carer distress in non-acute stroke. *International Journal of Language and Communication Disorders*, 33: 138–43.

McCorkle, R., Strumpf, N., Nuamah, I., Adler, D.C., Cooley, M.E., Jepson, C., Lusk, E.J. and Torosian, M. (2000). A specialized home care intervention improves survival among older post-surgical cancer patients. *Journal of the American Geriatric Society*, 48: 1707–13.

McCracken, L. (1998). Learning to live with the pain: acceptance of pain predicts adjustment in persons with chronic pain. *Pain*, 74: 21–7.

McCracken, L.M. and Eccleston, C. (2003). Coping or acceptance: what to do about chronic pain? *Pain*, 105: 197–204.

McCrae, R.E. and Costa, P.T. (1987). Validation of the five-factor model of personality across instruments and observers. *Journal of Personality and Social Psychology*, 52: 81–90.

McCrae, R.E. and Costa, P.T. (1990). *Personality in Adulthood*. New York: Guilford Press.

McCrae, R.E., Costa, P.T., Ostendorf, F., Angleitner, A., Hrebickova, M., Avia, M.D., Sanz, J., Sancez-Bernardos, M.L., Kusdil, M.E., Woodfield, R., Saunders, P.R. and Smith, P.B. (2000). Nature over nurture: temperament, personality and life-span development. *Journal of Personality and Social Psychology*, 78: 173–86.

McCrae, R.R. (1990). Controlling neuroticism in the measurement of stress. *Stress Medicine*, 6: 237–40.

McCubbin, H.I. and Patterson, J.M. (1982). Family adaptations to crisis. In H.I. McCubbin, A. Cauble and J. Patterson (eds), *Family Stress, Coping and Social Support*. Springfield, Ill.: Charles Thomas.

McCubbin, H.I. and Patterson, J.M. (1983). The family stress process: the double ABCX model of adjustment and adaptation. In H.I. McCubbin, M.B. Sussman and J.M. Patterson (eds), *Social Stress and the Family: Advances and Developments in Family Stress Theory and Research*. New York: Haworth Press.

McDermott, M.M., Schmitt, B. and Wallner, E. (1997). Impact of medication non-adherence on coronary heart disease outcomes. *Archives of Internal Medicine*, 157: 1921–9.

McDonald, H.P., Garg, A.X. and Haynes, R.B. (2002). Interventions to enhance patient adherence to medication prescriptions: scientific review. *Journal of the American Medical Association*, 288: 2868–79.

McElnay, J. and McCallion, C.R. (1998). Adherence and the elderly. In L.B. Myers and K. Midence (eds), *Adherence to Treatment in Medical Conditions*. Amsterdam: Harwood Academic.

McEwan, M.J., Espie, C.A. and Metcalfe, J. (2004). A systematic review of the contribution of qualitative research to the study of quality of life in children and adolescents with epilepsy. *Seizure*, 13: 3–14.

McGill, H.C. and Stern, M.P. (1979). Sex and atherosclerosis. *Atherosclerosis Review*, 4: 157–248.

McGuire, W. (1985). Attitudes and attitude change. In G. Lindzey and E. Aronson (eds), *Handbook of Social Psychology*, Vol. 2. New York: Random House.

McHugh, P., Lewis, S., Ford, S., Newlands, E., Rustin, G., Coombes, C., Smith, D., O'Reilly, S. and Fallowfield, L. (1995). The efficacy of audiotapes in promoting psychological well-being in cancer patients: a randomised, controlled trial. *British Journal of Cancer*, 71: 388–92.

McKenna, M.C., Zevon, M.A., Corn, B. and Rounds, J. (1999). Psychosocial factors and the development of breast cancer: a meta-analysis. *Health Psychology*, 18: 520–31.

McKenna, S.P. (2004). Assessing the quality of life in phases I and II anti-cancer drug trials: interviews versus questionnaires by Cox K (letter to the editor). *Social Science and Medicine*, 58: 659–60.

McKenna, S.P., Whalley, D. and Doward, L.C. (2000). Which outcomes are important in schizophrenia trials? *International Journal of Methods in Psychiatric Research*, 9 (suppl. 1): S58–67.

McKiernan, F.M. (1996). Bereavement and attitudes to death. In R.T. Woods (ed.), *Handbook of the Clinical Psychology of Ageing*. Chichester: Wiley.

McLeod, J.D. and Kessler, R.C. (1990). Socio-economic status differences in vulnerability to undesirable life events. *Journal of Health and Social Behaviour*, 31: 162–72.

McNair, D., Lorr, M. and Droppelman, L. (1971). *Manual for the Profile of Mood States*. San Diego: Educational and Industrial Testing Service.

McNeil, B.J., Pauker, S.G., Sox, H.C., Jr and Tversky, A. (1982). On the elicitation of preferences for alternative therapies. *New England Journal of Medicine*, 306: 1259–62.

McPherson, K.M., McNaughton, H. and Pentland, B. (2000). Information needs of families when one member of the family has a severe brain injury. *International Journal of Rehabilitation Research*, 23: 295–301.

Mechanic, D. (1962). The concept of illness behavior. *Journal of Chronic Disease*, 15: 189–94.

Mechanic, D. (1972). Social psychological factors affecting the presentation of bodily complaints. *New England Journal of Medicine*, 286: 1132–9.

Mechanic, D. (1978). *Medical Sociology*, 2nd edn. New York: Free Press.

Meechan, G., Collins, J. and Petrie, K. (2002). Delay in seeking medical care for self-detected breast symptoms in New Zealand women. *New Zealand Medical Journal*, 115: U257.

Meenan, R.F. and Mason, J.H. (1990). *AIMS2 Users Guide*. Boston University School of Medicine, Department of Public Health.

Meeske, K.A., Ruccione, K. and Globe, D.R. (2001). Posttraumatic stress, quality of life, and psychological distress in young adult survivors of childhood cancer. *Oncology Nursing Forum*, 28: 481–9.

Meichenbaum, D. (1985). *Stress Inoculation Training*. New York: Pergamon Press.

Meijer, S.A., Sinnema, G., Bijstra, J.O., Mellenbergh, G.J. and Wolters, W.H.G. (2002). Coping style and locus of control as predictors for psychological adjustment of adolescents with a chronic illness. *Social Science and Medicine*, 54: 1453–61.

Melchior, M., Berkman, L.F., Niedhammer, I., Chea, M. and Goldberg, M. (2003). Social relations and self-reported health: a prospective analysis of the French Gazel cohort. *Social Science and Medicine*, 56: 1817–30.

Mel'nikova, T.S. (1993). Thresholds of pain responses to electrical stimuli in patients with endogenous depression. *Patologichskaia Fiziologiia I Eksperimentalnaia Terapiia*, 4: 19–21.

Melzack, R. (1973). *The Puzzle of Pain*. London: Penguin Education.

Melzack, R. (1975). The McGill pain questionnaire: major properties and scoring methods. *Pain*, 1: 277–99.

Melzack, R. (1999). From the gate to the neuromatrix. *Pain*, suppl. 6: S121–6.

Melzack, R. and Wall, P.D. (1965). Pain mechanisms: a new theory. *Science*, 50: 971–9.

Mendlowicz, M.V. and Stein, M.B. (2001). Quality of life in individuals with anxiety disorders. *American Journal of Psychiatry*, 157: 669–82.

Merritt, M.M., Bennett, G.G., Williams, R.B., Sollers, J.J., III and Thayer, J.F. (2004). Low educational attainment, John Henryism, and cardiovascular reactivity to and recovery from personally relevant stress. *Psychosomatic Medicine*, 66: 49–55.

Merzel, C. and D'Afflitti, J. (2003). Reconsidering community-based health promotion: promise, performance, and potential. *American Journal of Public Health*, 93: 557–74.

Meyer, J.M. and Stunkard, A.J. (1993). Genetics and human obesity. In A.J. Stunkard and T.A. Wadden (eds), *Obesity: Theory and Therapy*. New York: Raven Press.

Meyer, T.J. and Mark, M.M. (1995). Effects of psychosocial interventions with adult cancer patients: a meta-analysis of randomized experiments. *Health Psychology*, 12: 101–8.

Michell, L. and Amos, A. (1997). Girls, pecking order, and smoking. *Social Science and Medicine*, 44: 1861–9.

Michie, S., Dormandy, E. and Marteau, T.M. (2004). Increasing screening uptake among those intending to be screened: the use of action plans. *Patient Education and Counselling*, 55: 218–22.

Michie, S., Miles, J. and Weinman, J. (2003). Patient-centredness in chronic illness: what is it and does it matter? *Patient Education and Counselling*, 51: 197–206.

Mikkelsen, A. and Saksvik, P.O. (1999). Impact of a participatory organizational intervention on job characteristics and job stress. *International Journal of Health Services Research*, 29: 871–93.

Miller, S.M. (1987). Monitoring and blunting: validation of a questionnaire to assess styles of information seeking under threat. *Journal of Personality and Social Psychology*, 52: 345–53.

Miller, S.M., Brody, D.S. and Summerton, J. (1987). Styles of coping with threat: implications for health. *Journal of Personality and Social Psychology*, 54: 142–8.

Miller, S.M., Fang, C.Y., Manne, S.L., Engstrom, P.F. and Daly, M.B. (1999). Decision making about prophylactic oophorectomy among at-risk women: psychological influences and implications. *Gynaecological Oncology*, 75: 406–12.

Miller, S.M., Rodoletz, M., Mangan, C.E., Schroeder, C.M. and Sedlacek, T.V. (1996). Applications of the monitoring process model to coping with severe long-term medical threats. *Health Psychology*, 15: 216–25.

Miller, T.Q., Smith, T.W., Turner, C.W., Guijarro, M.L. and Hallet, A.J. (1996). A meta-analytic review of research on hostility and physical health. *Psychological Bulletin*, 119: 322–48.

Miller, T.Q., Turner, C.W., Tindale, R.S., Posavac, E.J. and Dugoni, B.L. (1991). Reasons for the trend towards null findings in research on Type A behavior. *Psychological Bulletin*, 110: 469–85.

Miller, W. and Rollnick, S. (2002). *Motivational Interviewing: Preparing People to Change Addictive Behaviour*. New York: Guilford Press.

Milne, S., Welch, V., Brosseau, L., Saginur, M., Shea, B., Tugwell, P. and Wells, G. (2001). Transcutaneous electrical nerve stimulation (TENS) for chronic low back pain. In *The Cochrane Library*, issue 4. Oxford: Update Software.

Ming, E.E., Adler, G.K., Kessler, R.C., Fogg, L.F., Matthews, K.A., Herd, J.A. and Rose, R.M. (2004). Cardiovascular reactivity to work stress predicts subsequent onset of hypertension: the Air Traffic Controller Health Change Study. *Psychosomatic Medicine*, 66: 459–65.

Misra, R., Crist, M. and Burant, C.J. (2003). Relationships among life stress, social support, academic stressors, and reactions to stressors of international students in the United States. *International Journal of Stress Management*, 10: 137–57.

Mitchell, A.J. and Kumar, M. (2002). Influence of psychological coping on survival – review is not systematic (letter to the editor). *British Medical Journal*, 326: 598.

Mitchell, J.B., Ballard, D.J., Matchar, D.B., Whisnant, J.P. and Samsa, G.P. (2000). Racial variation in treatment for transient ischemic attacks: impact of participation by neurologists. *Health Services Research*, 34: 1413–28.

Mittag, W. and Schwarzer, R. (1993). Interaction of employment status and self-efficacy on alcohol consumption: a two-wave study on stressful life transitions. *Psychology and Health*, 8: 7–87.

Moens, V., Baruch, G. and Fearon, P. (2003). Opportunistic screening for Chlamydia at a community based contraceptive service for young people. *British Medical Journal*, 326: 1252–5.

Moldofsky, H. and Chester, W.J. (1970). Pain and mood patterns in patients with rheumatoid arthritis. A prospective study. *Psychosomatic Medicine*, 32: 309–18.

Molyneux, A., Lewis, S., Leivers, U., Anderton, A., Antoniak, M., Brackenridge, A., Nilsson, F., McNeill, A., West, R., Moxham, J. and Britton, J. (2003). Clinical trial comparing nicotine replacement therapy (NRT) plus brief counselling, brief counselling alone, and minimal intervention on smoking cessation in hospital inpatients. *Thorax*, 58: 484–8.

Montazeri, A., Jarvandi, S., Haghighat, S., Vahdahni, M., Sajadian, A., Ebrahimi, M. and Haji-Mahmoodi, M. (2001). Anxiety and depression in breast cancer patients before and after participation in a cancer support group. *Patient Education and Counseling*, 45: 195–8.

Montgomery, C., Lydon, A. and Lloyd, K. (1999). Psychological distress among cancer patients and informed consent. *Journal of Psychosomatic Research*, 46: 241–5.

Montgomery, C., Pocock, M., Titley, K. and Lloyd, K. (2003). Predicting psychological distress in patients with leukaemia and lymphoma. *Journal of Psychosomatic Research*, 54: 289–92.

Moore, L. (2001). Are fruit tuck shops in primary schools effective in increasing pupils' fruit consumption? A randomised controlled trial. Abstract available from http://www.cf.ac.uk/socsi/whoswho/moore-tuckshop.html

Moore, L., Paisly, C.M. and Dennehy, A. (2000). Are fruit tuck shops in primary schools effective in increasing pupils' fruit consumption? A randomised controlled trial. *Nutrition and Food Science*, 30: 35–8.

Moore, S. and Rosenthal, D. (1993). *Sexuality in Adolescence*. London: Routledge.

Moore, S.M., Barling, N.R. and Hood, B. (1998). Predicting testicular and breast self-examination behaviour: a test of the theory of reasoned action. *Behaviour Change*, 15: 41–9.

Moorey, S. and Greer, S. (1994). Adjuvant psychological therapy for patients with cancer: outcome at one year. *Psycho-Oncology*, 3: 39–46.

Moorey, S., Greer, S., Bliss, J. and Law, M. (1998). A comparison of adjuvant psychological therapy and supportive counselling in patients with cancer. *Psycho-Oncology*, 7: 218–28.

Moorey, S., Greer, S., Watson, M. (1994). Adjuvant psychological therapy for patients with cancer: outcome at one year. *Psycho-oncology*, 3: 39–46.

Moos, R.H. and Schaefer, A. (1984). The crisis of physical illness: an overview and conceptual approach. In R.H. Moos (ed.), *Coping with Physical Illness: New Perspectives*, Vol. 2. New York: Plenum.

Mor, V., Malin, M. and Allen, S. (1994). Age differences in the psychosocial problems encountered by breast cancer patients. *Journal of the National Cancer Institute Monographs*, 16: 191–7.

Morgan, J., Roufeil, L., Kaushik, S. and Bassett, M. (1998). Influence of coping style and precolonoscopy information on pain and anxiety of colonoscopy. *Gastrointestinal Endoscopy*, 48: 119–27.

Morley, S., Eccleston, C. and Williams, A. (1999). Systematic review and meta-analysis of randomized controlled trials of cognitive behaviour therapy and behaviour therapy for chronic pain in adults, excluding headache. *Pain*, 80: 1–13.

Morris, C.D. and Carson, S. (2003). Routine vitamin supplementation to prevent cardiovascular disease: a summary of the evidence for the U.S. Preventive Services Task Force. *Annals of Internal Medicine*, 139: 56–70.

Morris, D.B. (1999). Sociocultural and religious meanings of pain. In R.J. Gatchel and D.C. Turk (eds), *Psychosocial Factors in Pain*. New York: Guilford Press.

Morris, J.N., Clayton, D.G., Everitt, M.G., Semmence, A.M. and Burgess, E.H. (1990). Exercise in leisure time: coronary attack and death rates. *British Heart Journal*, 63: 325–34.

Morris, P.L.P., Robinson, R.G., Andrzejewski, P., Samuels, J. and Price, T.R. (1993). Association of depression with 10-year poststroke mortality. *American Journal of Psychiatry*, 150: 124–9.

Morrison, M.F., Petitto, J.M., Ten Have, T., Gettes, D.R., Chiappini, M.S., Weber, A.L., Brinker-Spence, P., Bauer, R.M., Douglas, S.D. and Evans, D.L. (2002). Depressive and anxiety disorders in women with HIV infection. *American Journal of Psychiatry*, 159: 789–96.

Morrison, V. (1988). Observation and snowballing: useful tools for research into illicit drug use? *Social Pharmacology*, 2: 247–71.

Morrison, V. (1999). Predictors of carer distress following a stroke. *Reviews in Clinical Gerontology*, 9: 265–71.

Morrison, V. (2001). The need to explore discrepant illness cognitions when predicting patient outcomes. *Health Psychology Update*, 10: 9–13.

Morrison, V. (2003). Furthering the socio-cognitive explanation of addiction. *Neuro-Psychoanalysis*, 5: 39–42.

Morrison, V., Ager, A. and Willock, J. (1999). Perceived risk of tropical diseases in Malawi: evidence of unrealistic pessimism and the irrelevance of beliefs of personal control? *Psychology, Health and Medicine*, 4: 361–8.

Morrison, V., Cottrell, L., Dawson, J., Jere, C., Jones, V., and Waddon, A. (2002). Police force stress: Psychological and job feature characteristics. Paper presented at the *Annual Conference of the European Health Psychology Society*, September.

Morrison, V., Hutchinson, A. and McCarthy, M. (2000). Illness perceptions, perceived control and adherence in child asthmatics: are child–parent beliefs discrepant? Poster presentation at European Health Psychology Society annual conference, Leiden, The Netherlands.

Morrison, V., Johnston, M. and MacWalter, R. (2000). Predictors of distress following an acute stroke: disability, control cognitions and satisfaction with care. *Psychology and Health*, 15: 395–407.

Morrison, V. and Plant, M.A. (1991). Licit and illicit drug initiations and alcohol related problems among illicit drug users in Edinburgh. *Drug and Alcohol Dependence*, 27: 19–27.

Morrison, V., Pollard, B., Johnston, M. and MacWalter, R. (2005 in press) Anxiety and depression 3 years following stroke: demographic, clinical and psychological predictors. *Journal of Psychosomatic Research*.

Morrison, V.L. (1991a). The impact of HIV upon injecting drug users: a longitudinal study. *AIDS Care*, 3: 197–205.

Morrison, V.L. (1991b). Starting, switching, stopping: users' explanations of illicit drug use. *Drug and Alcohol Dependence*, 27: 213–17.

Morrison, V., White-Gwenin, C., a'ch Dafydd, N., Unwin, A., and Griffith, G. (2005 in revision). Can information modify people's intentions to undergo genetic testing:? an experimental study.

Morse, J.M. and Johnson, J.L. (1991). Towards a theory of illness. The illness constellation model. In J.M. Morse and J.L. Johnson (eds), *The Illness Experience: Dimensions of Suffering*. Newbury Park, Calif.: Sage.

Morse, S.R. and Fife, B. (1998). Coping with a partner's cancer: adjustment at four stages of the illness trajectory. *Oncology Nursing Forum*, 25: 751–60.

Moss-Morris, R. and Chalder, T. (2003). Illness perceptions and levels of disability in patients with chronic fatigue syndrome and rheumatoid arthritis. *Journal of Psychosomatic Research*, 55: 305–8.

Moss-Morris, R., Weinman, J., Petrie, K.J., Horne, R., Cameron, L.D. and Buick, D. (2002). The revised Illness Perception Questionnaire (IPQ-R). *Psychology and Health*, 17: 1–16.

Murgraff, V., McDermott, M.R., White, D. and Phillips, K. (1999). Regret is what you get: the effects of manipulating anticipated affect and time perspective on risky single occasion drinking. *Alcohol and Alcoholism*, 34: 590–600.

Murphy, D., Lindsay, S. and Williams, A.C. de C. (1997). Chronic low back pain: predictions of pain and relationship to anxiety and avoidance. *Behaviour Research and Therapy*, 35: 231–8.

Murray, D.F., Marks, M., Evans, B. and Willig, C. (2000). *Health Psychology: Theory, Research and Practice*. London: Sage.

Murray, M. (1997). A narrative approach to health psychology: background and potential. *Journal of Health Psychology*, 2: 9–20.

Murray, M. and Campbell, C. (2003). Beyond the sidelines: towards a more politically engaged health psychology. *Health Psychology Update*, 12: 12–17.

Murrell, R. (2001). Assessing the quality of life of individuals with neurological illness. *Health Psychology Update*, 10.

Myers, L.B. (1998). Repressive coping, trait anxiety and reported avoidance of negative thoughts. *Personality and Individual Differences*, 24: 299–303.

Myers, L.B. and Reynolds, D. (2000). How optimistic are repressors? The relationship between repressive coping, controllability, self-esteem and comparative optimism for health-related events. *Psychology and Health*, 15: 677–87.

Myers, J., Froelicher, V., Do, D., Partington, S. and Atwood, J.E. (2002). Exercise capacity and mortality among men referred for exercise testing. *New England Journal of Medicine*, 346: 793–801.

Nagasako, E.M., Oaklander, A.L. and Dworkin, R.H. (2003). Congenital insensitivity to pain: an update. *Pain*, 101: 213–19.

Naish, J., Brown, J. and Denton, B. (1994). Intercultural consultations: investigation of factors that deter non-English speaking women from attending their general practitioners for cervical screening. *British Medical Journal*, 309: 1126–8.

Naliboff, B.D., Munakata, J., Chang, L. and Mayer, E.A. (1998). Toward a biobehavioral model of visceral hypersensitivity in irritable bowel syndrome. *Journal of Psychosomatic Research*, 45: 485–93.

National Collaborating Centre for Chronic Conditions (2004). Chronic obstructive pulmonary disease. National clinical guidelines on management of chronic obstructive pulmonary disease in adults in primary and secondary care. *Thorax*, 59 (suppl. 1): 1–232.

National Diet and Nutrition Survey: Adults aged 19–64, Vol 1. (2000) Carried out in 2000 on behalf of the Food Standards Agency and Department of Health by the Social Survey Division of the Office for National Statistics and Medical Research Council Human Nutrition Research. London: Stationery Office.

National Institutes of Health Technology Assessment Panel (1996). Integration of behavioral and relaxation approaches into the treatment of chronic pain and insomnia. *Journal of the American Medical Association*, 276: 313–18.

Navas-Nacher, E.L., Colangelo, L., Beam, C. and Greenland, P. (2001). Risk factors for coronary heart disease in men 18 to 39 years of age. *Annals of Internal Medicine*, 134: 433–9.

Nazroo, J. (1997). *The Health of Britain's Ethnic Minorities: Findings from a National Survey*. London: Policy Studies Institute.

Nazroo, J.Y. (1998). *Genetic, Cultural or Socioeconomic Vulnerability? Explaining Ethnic Inequalities in Health*. Oxford: Blackwell.

Neaton, J.D., Blackburn, H., Jacobs, D. *et al.* (1992). Serum cholesterol and mortality findings for men screened in the Multiple Risk Factor Intervention Trial. *Archives of Internal Medicine*, 152: 1490–500.

Nelson, D.V., Baer, P.E. and Cleveland, S.E. (1998). Family stress management following acute myocardial infarction: an educational and skills training intervention program. *Patient Education and Counseling*, 34: 135–45.

Ness, A., Hooper, L., Egger, M., Powles, J.W. and Davey-Smith, G. (2003). Fruit and vegetables for cardiovascular disease. In *The Cochrane Library*, issue 1. Oxford: Update Software.

Ness, A.R. and Powles, J.W. (1997). Fruit and vegetables, and cardiovascular disease: a review. *International Journal of Epidemiology*, 26: 1–13.

Nestle, M. (1997). Alcohol guidelines for chronic disease prevention: from prohibition to moderation. *Nutrition Today*, 32: 86–92.

New, S.J. and Senior, M. (1991). 'I don't believe in needles': qualitative aspects of a study into the uptake of infant immunisation in two English health authorities. *Social Science and Medicine*, 33: 509–18.

Newhagen, J. and Reeves, B. (1987). Emotion and memory responses for negative political advertising: a study of television commercials used in the 1988 presidential campaign. In F. Biocca (ed.), *Television and Political Advertising*, Vol. 1. Hillsdale, NJ: Lawrence Erlbaum.

Ng, B., Dimsdale, J.E., Rollnick, J.D. and Shapiro, H. (1996). The effect of ethnicity on prescriptions for patient-controlled anaesthesia for post-operative pain. *Pain*, 66: 9–12.

NHS Centre for Reviews and Dissemination (1999). *Effective healthcare: getting evidence into practice*. NHS CRD, Vol. 5, No. 1. London: Royal Society of Medicine Press.

NHS Executive (1996). *Patient Partnership: Building a Collaborative Strategy*. Leeds: NHS Executive.

Nichols, K. (1993). *Psychological Care in Physical Illness*. Nelson Thornes.

Nicolson, N.A. and van Diest, R. (2000). Salivary cortisol levels in vital exhaustion. *Journal of Psychosomatic Research*, 49: 335–42.

Niemcryk, S.J., Speer, M.A., Travis, L.B. and Gary, H.E. (1990). Psychosocial correlates of haemoglobin A1c in young adults with type I diabetes. *Journal of Psychosomatic Research*, 34: 617–27.

Niemi, M., Laaksonen, R., Kotila, M. and Waltimo, O. (1988). Quality of life 4 years after stroke. *Stroke*, 19: 1101–7.

Nijboer, C., Tempelaar, R., Triemstra, M., Sanderman, R. and van den Bos, G.A.M. (2001). Dynamics in cancer caregiver's health over time: gender-specific patterns and determinants. *Psychology and Health*, 16: 471–88.

Noble, L.M. (1998). Doctor–patient communication and adherence to treatment. In L.B. Myers and K. Midence (eds), *Adherence to Treatment in Medical Conditions*. Amsterdam: Harwood Academic.

Norberg, A.L., Lindblad, F. and Boman, K.K. (2005). Coping strategies in parents of children with cancer. *Social Science and Medicine*, 60: 965–75.

Nordstrom, C.K., Dwyer, K.M., Merz, C.N., Shircore, A. and Dwyer, J.H. (2001). Work-related stress and early atherosclerosis. *Epidemiology*, 12: 180–5.

Norman, P. and Bennett, P. (1996). Health locus of control. In M. Conner and P. Norman (eds), *Predicting Health Behaviour*. Buckingham: Open University Press.

Norman, P., Bennett, P., Smith, C. and Murphy, S. (1998). Health locus of control and health behaviour. *Journal of Health Psychology*, 3: 171–80.

Norman, P., Conner, M. and Bell, S. (1999). The theory of planned behaviour and smoking cessation. *Health Psychology*, 18: 89–94.

Norman, P. and Smith, L. (1995). The theory of planned behaviour and exercise: an investigation into the role of prior behaviour, behavioural intentions and attitude variability. *European Journal of Social Psychology*, 25: 403–15.

Normandeau, S., Kalnins, I., Jutras, S. and Hanigan, D. (1998). A description of 5 to 12 year old children's conception of health within the context of their daily life. *Psychology and Health*, 13(5): 883–96.

Norris, V.K., Stephens, M.A. and Kinney, J.M. (1990). The influence of family interactions on recovery from stroke: help or hindrance? *The Gerontologist*, 30: 535–42.

Norrsell, U., Finger, S. and Lajonchere, C. (1999). Cutaneous sensory spots and the 'law of specific nerve energies': history and development of ideas. *Brain Research Bulletin*, 48: 457–65.

Nutbeam, D., Smith, C., Moore, L. and Bauman, A. (1993). Warning! Schools can damage your health: alienation from school and its impact on child behaviour. *Journal of Paediatrics and Child Health*, 29 (suppl. 1): S25–30.

O'Boyle, C.A., McGee, H., Hickey, A., O'Malley, K. and Joyce, C.R.B. (1992). Individual quality of life in patients undergoing hip replacement. *The Lancet*, 339: 1088–91.

O'Boyle, C.A., McGee, H., Hickey, A., Joyce, C.R.B., Browne, J., O'Malley, K. and Hiltbrunner, B. (1993). *The Schedule for the Evaluation of Individual Quality of Life (SEIQoL): Administration Manual*. Dublin: Department of Psychology, Royal College of Surgeons.

O'Brien, M.K., Petrie, K. and Raeburn, J. (1992). Adherence to medication regimens: updating a complex medical issue. *Medical Care Review*, 49: 435–54.

O'Carroll, R.E., Smith, K.B., Grubb, N.R., Fox, K.A. and Masterton, G. (2001). Psychological factors associated with delay in attending hospital following a myocardial infarction. *Journal of Psychosomatic Research*, 51: 611–14.

O'Cleirigh, C., Ironson, G., Antoni, M., Fletcher, M.A., McGuffey, L., Balbin, E., Schneiderman, N. and Solomon, G. (2003). Emotional expression and depth processing of trauma and their relation to long-term survival in patients with HIV/AIDS. *Journal of Psychosomatic Research*, 54: 225–35.

O'Connell, K., Skevington, S. and Saxena, S. on behalf of WHOQOL-HIV Group (2003). Preliminary development of the World Health Organization's Quality of Life HIV instrument (WHOQOL-HIV): analysis of the pilot version. *Social Science and Medicine*, 57: 1259–75.

O'Connor, A.P., Wicker, C.A. and Germino, B.B. (1990). Understanding the cancer patient's search for meaning. *Cancer Nursing*, 13: 167–75.

O'Donnell, C.R., O'Donnell, L., San Doval, A., Duran, R. and Labes, K. (1998). Reductions in STD infections subsequent to an STD clinic visit. Using video-based patient education to supplement provider interactions. *Sexually Transmitted Diseases*, 25: 161–8.

O'Donnell, L., San Doval, A., Duran, R. and O'Donnell, C.R. (1995). The effectiveness of video-based interventions in promoting condom acquisition among STD clinic patients. *Sexually Transmitted Diseases*, 22: 97–103.

O'Farrell, T.J. and Fals-Stewart, W. (2000). Behavioral couples therapy for alcoholism and drug abuse. *Journal of Substance Abuse Treatment*, 18: 51–4.

Office for National Statistics (1997). *Smoking among Secondary School Children in 1996: England*. London: Stationery Office.

Office for National Statistics (1998). *1996 Mortality Statistics: Cause*, Series DH2, 23. London: The Stationery Office.

Office for National Statistics (1999). *Social Trends 29*. London: Stationery Office.

Office for National Statistics (2000). *Results from the 1998 General Household Survey*. London: Stationery Office.

Ogden, J. (2003). Some problems with social cognition models: a pragmatic and conceptual analysis. *Health Psychology*, 22: 424–8.

Ogden, J., Fuks, K., Gardner, M., Johnson, S., McLean, M., Martin, P. and Shah, R. (2002). Doctors' expressions of uncertainty and patient confidence. *Patient Education and Counselling*, 48: 171–6.

Ogden, J. and Mtandabari, T. (1997). Examination stress and changes in mood and health related behaviours. *Psychology and Health*, 12: 288–99.

Ogden, J., Veale, D. and Summers, Z. (1997). The development and validation of the Exercise Dependence Questionnaire. *Addiction Research*, 5: 343–56.

Ohayon, M.M., Guilleminault, C., Priest, R.G., Zulley, J. and Smirne, S. (2000). Is sleep-disordered breathing an independent risk factor for hypertension in the general population (13,057 subjects)? *Journal of Psychosomatic Research*, 48: 593–601.

Oldenburg, B., Glanz, K. and French, M. (1999). The application of staging models to the understanding of health behaviour change and the promotion of health. *Psychology and Health*, 14: 503–16.

Oldenburg, B. and Harris, D. (1996). The workplace as a setting for promoting health and preventing disease. *Homeostasis*, 37: 226–32.

Olson, D.H. and Stewart, K.L. (1991). Family systems and health behaviours. In H.E. Schroeder (ed.), *New Directions in Health Psychology Assessment*. New York: Hemisphere.

Ong, L.M.L., de Haes, J.C.J.M., Hoos, A.M. and Lammes, F.B. (1995). Doctor–patient communication: a review of the literature. *Social Science and Medicine*, 40: 903–18.

Onwuanyi, A.E., Clarke, A. and Vanderbush, E. (2003). Cardiovascular disease mortality. *Journal of the National Medical Association*, 95: 1146–51.

Orbell, S. and Gillies, B. (1993). What's stressful about caring? *Journal of Applied Social Psychology*, 23: 272–90.

Orbell, S., Hopkins, N. and Gillies, B. (1993). Measuring the impact of informal caregiving. *Journal of Community and Applied Social Psychology*, 3: 149–63.

Orbell, S., Hodgkins, S. and Sheeran, P. (1997). Implementation intentions and the theory of planned behaviour. *Personality and Social Psychology*, 23: 945–54.

Orbell, S. and Sheeran, P. (2002). Changing health behaviours: the role of implementation intentions. In D. Rutter and L. Quine (eds), *Changing Health Behaviour*. Buckingham: Open University Press.

Orford, J. (2001). *Excessive Appetites: A Psychological View of Addictions*, 2nd edn. Chichester: Wiley.

Orrell, C., Bangsberg, D.R., Badri, M. and Wood, R. (2003). Adherence is not a barrier to successful antiretroviral therapy in South Africa. *AIDS*, 1369–75.

Orth-Gomér, K., Undén, A.-L. and Edwards, M.-E. (1988). Social isolation and mortality in ischemic heart disease. *Acta Medica Scandinavica*, 224: 205–15.

Orth-Gomér, K. and Undén, A.-L. (1990). Type A behaviour, social support, and coronary risk: interaction and significance for mortality in cardiac patients. *Psychosomatic Medicine*, 52: 59–72.

Osse, B.H.P., Myrra, J.F.J., Vernooj-Dassen, E.S., Schade, E., de Vree, B., van den Muilsenbergh, M.E.T.C. and Grol, R.P.T.M. (2002). Problems to discuss with cancer patients in palliative care: a comprehensive approach. *Patient Education and Counseling*, 47: 195–204.

OXCHECK Study Group (1994). Effectiveness of health checks conducted by nurses in primary care: results of the OXCHECK study after one year. Imperial Cancer Research Fund OXCHECK Study Group. *British Medical Journal*, 308: 308–12.

OXCHECK Study Group (1995). Effectiveness of health checks conducted by nurses in primary care: final results of the OXCHECK study. Imperial Cancer Research Fund OXCHECK Study Group. *British Medical Journal*, 310: 1099–104.

Oxman, A.D., Davis, D., Haynes, R.B. and Thomson, MA. (1995). No magic bullets: a systematic review of 102 trials of interventions to improve professional practice. *Canadian Medical Association Journal*, 153: 1423–31.

Pachter, L.M. (1994). Culture and clinical care: folk illness beliefs and behaviours and their implications for health care delivery. *Journal of the American Medical Association*, 7: 690–4.

Paffenbarger, R.S., Hyde, J.T., Wing, A.L. and Hsieh, C.C. (1986). Physical activity, all-cause mortality, and longevity of college alumni. *New England Journal of Medicine*, 314: 605–12.

Page-Shafer, K.A., Satariano, W.A., Winkelstein, W. Jr. (1996) Comorbidity and HIV disease progression in homosexual/bisexual men. The San Francisco Men's Health Study. *Annals of Epidemiology 1996*, 6: 420–30.

Pakenham, K.I., Dadds, M.R. and Lennon, H.V. (2002). The efficacy of a psychosocial intervention for HIV/AIDS caregiving dyads and individual caregivers: a controlled treatment outcome study. *AIDS Care*, 14: 731–50.

Pakenham, K.I., Pruss, M. and Clutton, S. (2000). The utility of sociodemographics, knowledge and health belief model variables in predicting reattendance for mammography screening: a brief report. *Psychology and Health*, 15: 585–91.

Panagopoulou, E., Kersbergen, B. and Maes, S. (2002). The effects of emotional (non-)expression in (chronic) disease: a meta-analytic review. *Psychology and Health*, 17: 529–45.

Papanicolaou, D.A., Wilder, R.L., Manolagas, S.C. and Chrousos, G.P. (1998). The pathophysiologic roles of interleukin-6 in human disease. *Archives of Internal Medicine*, 128: 127–37.

Paris, W., Muchmore, J., Pribil, A., Zuhdi, N. and Cooper, D.K. (1994). Study of the relative incidences of psychosocial factors before and after heart transplantation and the influence of posttransplantation psychosocial factors on heart transplantation outcome. *Journal of Heart Lung Transplantation*, 13: 424–30.

Park, D.C., Morrell, R.W., Frieske, D. and Kincaid, D. (1992). Medication adherence behaviors in older adults: effects of external cognitive supports. *Psychology and Aging*, 7: 252–6.

Parkes, K. (1984). Locus of control, cognitive appraisal, coping appraisal and coping in stressful episodes. *Journal of Personality and Social Psychology*, 46: 655–68.

Parle, M., Maguire, P. and Heaven, C. (1997). The development of a training model to improve health professionals' skills, self-efficacy and outcome expectancies when communicating with cancer patients. *Social Science and Medicine*, 44: 231–40.

Parsons, T. (1951). *The Social System*. New York: Free Press.

Partridge, C. and Johnston, M. (1989). Perceived control of recovery from physical disability: measurement and prediction. *British Journal of Clinical Psychology*, 28: 53–9.

Pate, R.R., Pratt, M., Blair, S.N., Haskell, W.L., Macera, C.A., Bouchard, C. *et al.* (1995). Physical activity and public health: a recommendation from the Centers for Disease Control and the American College of Sports Medicine. *Journal of the American Medical Association*, 273: 402–7.

Paterson, J., Moss-Morris, R. and Butler, S.J. (1999). The effect of illness experience and demographic factors on children's illness representations. *Psychology and Health*, 14: 117–29.

Paton, A. (1999). Reflections on alcohol and the young. Invited commentary. *Alcohol and Alcoholism*, 34: 502–5.

Patterson, B.K., Carlo, D.J., Kaplan, M.H., Marecki, M., Pawha, S. and Moss, R.B. (1999). Cell-associated HIV-1 messenger RNA and DNA in T-helper cell and monocytes in asymptomatic HIV-1-infected subjects on HAART plus an inactivated HIV-1 immunogen. *AIDS*, 13: 1607–11.

Patterson, D.R. and Jensen, M.P. (2003). Hypnosis and clinical pain. *Psychological Bulletin*, 129: 495–521.

Patton, G.C., Johnson-Sabine, E., Wood, K., Mann, A.H. and Wakeling, A. (1990). Abnormal attitudes in London schoolgirls – a prospective epidemiological study: outcome at twelve month follow-up. *Psychological Medicine*, 20: 383–94.

Patrick, D.L. and Peach, H. (1989). *Disablement in the Community*. Oxford: Oxford University Press.

Pearlin, L.I. (1983). Role strains and personal stress. In H.B. Kaplan (ed.), *Psychosocial Stress: Trends in Theory and Research*. New York: Academic Press.

Pearlin, L.I. and Mullan, J.T. (1992). Loss and stress in ageing. In M.L. Wykle, E. Kahara and J. Kowal (eds), *Stress and Health among the Elderly*. New York: Springer Verlag.

Peay, M.Y. and Peay, E.R. (1998). The evaluation of medical symptoms by patients and doctors. *Journal of Behavioral Medicine*, 21: 57–81.

Pelosi, A.J. and Appleby, L. (1992). Psychological influences on cancer and ischaemic heart disease (for debate). *British Medical Journal*, 304: 1295–8.

Pelosi, A.J. and Appleby, L. (1993). Personality and fatal diseases. *British Medical Journal*, 306: 1666–7.

Peltola, H., Patja, A., Leinikkii, P., Valle, M., Davidkin, I. and Paunio, M. (1998). No evidence for measles, mumps and rubella vaccine-associated inflammatory bowel disease or autism in a 14-year prospective study. *The Lancet*, 351: 1327–8.

Pendleton, D.A. (1983). Doctor–patient communication: a review. In D. Pendleton and J. Hasler (eds), *Doctor–Patient Communication*. London: Academic Press.

Pendleton, D., Schofield, T., Tate, P., Havelock, P. (1984). *The Consultation: An Approach to Learning and Teaching*. Oxford: Oxford University Press.

Pennebaker, J.W. (1982). Social and perceptual factors affecting symptom reporting and mass psychogenic illness. In M.J. Colligan, J.W. Pennebaker and L.R. Murphy (eds), *Mass Psychogenic Illness: A Social Psychological Analysis*. Hillsdale, NJ: Lawrence Erlbaum.

Pennebaker, J.W. (1992). *The Psychology of Physical Symptoms*. New York: Springer Verlag.

Pennebaker, J.W. (1993). Putting stress into words: health, linguistic and therapeutic implications. *Behavioral Research Therapy*, 31: 539–48.

Pennebaker, J.W. and Beall, S. (1986). Confronting a traumatic event: toward an understanding of inhibition and disease. *Journal of Abnormal Psychology*, 95: 274–81.

Pennebaker, J.W., Colder, M. and Sharp, L.K. (1990). Accelerating the coping process. *Journal of Personality and Social Psychology*, 58: 528–37.

Pennebaker, J.W., Kiecolt-Glaser, J. and Glaser, R. (1988). Disclosure of trauma and immune function: health implications for psychotherapy. *Journal of Consulting and Clinical Psychology*, 56: 239–45.

Pennebaker, J.W. and Skelton, J.A. (1981). Selective monitoring of bodily sensations. *Journal of Personality and Social Behaviour*, 35: 167–74.

Penninx, B., Guralnik, J.M., Pahor, M., Ferrucci, L., Cerhan, J.R., Wallace, R.B. and Havlik, R.J. (1998). Chronically depressed mood and cancer risk in older persons. *Journal of the National Cancer Institute*, 90: 1888–93.

Penninx, B.W.J.H., van Tilburg, T., Kriegsman, D.M.W., Boeke, A.J.P., Deeg, D.J.H. and van Eijk, J.T.M. (1999). Social network, social support, and loneliness in older persons with different chronic diseases. *Journal of Ageing and Health*, 11: 151–68.

Penny, G.N., Bennett, P. and Herbert, M. (eds) (1994). *Health Psychology: A Lifespan Perspective*. Switzerland: Harwood Academic.

Perloff, L.S. and Fetzer, B.K. (1986). Self–other judgements and perceived vulnerability to victimization. *Journal of Personality and Social Psychology*, 50: 502–10.

Perry, C.L. and Grant, M. (1988). Comparing peer-led to teacher-led youth alcohol education in four countries. (Australia, Chile, Norway and Swaziland). *Alcohol Health and Research World*, 12: 322–6.

Perry, K., Petrie, K.J., Ellis, C.J., Horne, R. and Moss-Morris, R. (2001). Symptom expectations and delay in acute myocardial infarction patients. *Heart*, 86: 91–2.

Persky, V.W., Kempthorne-Rawson, J. and Shekelle, R.B. (1987). Personality and risk of cancer: 20 year follow-up of the Western Electric study. *Psychosomatic Medicine*, 49: 435–49.

Perugini, M. and Bagozzi, R.P. (2001). The role of desires and anticipated emotions in goal-directed behaviours: broadening and deepening the theory of planned behaviour. *British Journal of Social Psychology*, 40: 79–98.

Peterson, T.R. and Aldana, S.G. (1999). Improving exercise behaviour: an application of the stages of change model in a worksite setting. *American Journal of Health Promotion*, 13: 229–32.

Peto, R., Darby, S., Deo, H., Silcocks, P., Whitley, E. and Doll, R. (2000). Smoking, smoking cessation, and lung cancer in the UK since 1950: combination of national statistics with two case-control studies. *British Medical Journal*, 321: 323–9.

Peto, R. and Lopez, A.D. (1990). Worldwide mortality from current smoking patterns. In B. Durston and K. Jamrozik (eds), *Tobacco and Health 1990: The Global War*. Proceedings of the 7th World Conference on Tobacco and Health. Perth: Health Department of Western Australia.

Peto, R., Lopez, A.D., Borehan, J., Thun, M. and Heath, C., Jr (1994). *Mortality from Smoking in Developed Countries 1950–2000*. Oxford: Oxford University Press.

Petrak, J.A., Doyle, A.-M., Smith, A., Skinner, C. and Hedge, B. (2001). Factors associated with self-disclosure of HIV serostatus to significant others. *British Journal of Health Psychology*, 6: 69–79.

Petrie, K.J., Booth, R.J., Pennebaker, J.W., Davison, K.P. and Thomas, M.G. (1995). Disclosure of trauma and immune response to hepatitis B vaccination program. *Journal of Consulting and Clinical Psychology*, 63: 787–92.

Petrie, K.J., Buick, D.L., Weinman, J. and Booth, R.J. (1999). Positive effects of illness reported by myocardial infarction and breast cancer patients. *Journal of Psychosomatic Research*, 47: 537–43.

Petrie, K.J., Weinman, J., Sharpe, N. and Buckley, J. (1996). Role of patients' view of their illness in predicting return to work and functioning after a myocardial infarction. *British Medical Journal*, 312: 1191–4.

Petrie, K.J. and Weinman, J. (2003). More focus needed on symptom appraisal (editorial). *Journal of Psychosomatic Research*, 54: 401–3.

Petruzzello, S.J., Jones, A.C. and Tate, A.K. (1997). Affective responses to acute exercise: a test of opponent-process theory. *Journal of Sports Medicine and Physical Fitness*, 37: 205–11.

Petticrew, A., Fraser, J. and Regan, M. (1999). Adverse life events and risk of breast cancer: a meta-analysis. *British Journal of Health Psychology*, 4: 1–17.

Petticrew, M., Bell, R. and Hunter, D. (2002). Influence of psychological coping on survival and recurrence in people with cancer: a systematic review. *British Medical Journal*, 325: 1066.

Petty, R. and Cacioppo, J. (1986). The elaboration likelihood model of persuasion. In L. Berkowitz (ed.), *Advances in experimental social psychology*, Vol. 19. Orlando, Fla: Academic Press.

Petty, R.E. and Cacioppo, J.T. (1996). *Attitudes and Persuasion: Classic and Contemporary Approaches*. Boulder, Colo.: Westview Press.

Peveler, R., Carson, A. and Rodin, G. (2002). Depression in medical patients. *British Medical Journal*, 325: 149–52.

PHLS Communicable Disease Surveillance Centre (2002). *HIV and AIDS in the United Kingdom 2001. An Update: November 2002*. London: PHLS, ICH (London) and SCIEH.

Piaget, J. (1930). *The Child's Conception of Physical Causality*. London: Routledge and Kegan Paul.

Piaget, J. (1970). Piaget's theory. In P.H. Mussen (ed.), *Carmichael's Manual of Child Psychology*, 3rd edn, Vol. 1. New York: Wiley.

Piette, J.D., Weinberger, M. and McPhee, S.J. (2000). The effect of automated calls with telephone nurse follow-up on patient-centered outcomes of diabetes care: a randomized controlled trial. *Medical Care*, 38: 218–30.

Pinel, J.P.J. (2003). *Biopsychology*, 5th edn. Boston: Allyn and Bacon.

Pinerua-Shuhaibar, L., Prieto-Rincon, D., Ferrer, A., Bonilla, E., Maixner, W. and Suarez-Roca, H. (1999). Reduced tolerance and cardiovascular responses to ischemic pain in minor depression. *Journal of Affective Disorders*, 56: 119–26.

Pinquart, M. and Sörensen, S. (2003). Differences between caregivers and noncaregivers in psychological health and physical health: A meta-analysis. *Psychology and Aging*, 18: 250–67.

Pirozzo, S., Summerbell, C., Cameron, C. and Glasziou, P. (2003). Advice on low-fat diets for obesity. In *The Cochrane Library*, issue 1. Oxford: Update Software.

Plante, T.G. and Rodin, J. (1990). Physical fitness and enhanced psychological health. *Current Psychology Research and Reviews*, 9: 3–24.

Potter, J., Hami, F., Bryan, T. and Quigley, C. (2003). Symptoms in 400 patients referred to palliative care services: prevalence and patterns. *Palliative Medicine*, 17: 310–14.

Potter, J.D., Slattery, M.L., Bostick, R.M. and Gapstur, S.M. (1993). Colon cancer: a review of the epidemiology. *Epidemiological Review*, 15: 499–545.

Pound, P., Bury, M., Gompertz, P. and Ebrahim, S. (1994). Views of survivors of stroke on the benefits of physiotherapy. *Quality in Health Care*, 3: 69–74.

Powell-Griner, E., Anderson, J.E. and Murphy, W. (1997). State and sex-specific prevalence of selected characteristics behavioural risk factor surveillance system, 1994 and 1995. *Morbidity and Mortality Weekly Report*, Centres for Disease Control, surveillance summaries, 46: 1–31.

Power, R., Koopman, C., Volk, J., Israelski, D.M., Stone, L., Chesney, M.A. and Spiegel, D. (2003). Social support, substance use, and denial in relationship to antiretroviral treatment adherence among HIV-infected persons. *AIDS Patient Care and STDs*, 17: 245–52.

Prentice, A.M. and Jebb, S.A. (1995). Obesity in Britain: gluttony or sloth. *British Medical Journal*, 311: 437–9.

Prescott-Clarke, P. and Primatesta, P. (1998). *Health survey for England: the health of young people 1995–97*. London: The Stationery Office.

Price, R.A. and Gottesman, I.I. (1991). Body fat in identical twins reared apart: roles for genes and environment. *Behavioral Genetics*, 21: 1–7.

Price, V.A. (1988). Research and clinical issues in treating Type A behavior. In B.K. Houston and C.R. Snyder (eds), *Type A Behavior Pattern: Research, Theory, and Practice*. New York: Wiley.

Prochaska, J.O. (1994). Strong and weak principles for progressing from precontemplation to action based on twelve problem behaviours. *Health Psychology*, 13: 47–51.

Prochaska, J.O. and di Clemente, C.C. (1984). *The Transtheoretical Approach: Crossing Traditional Boundaries of Therapy*. Homewood Ill.: Dow Jones Irwin.

Prochaska, J.O. and di Clemente, C.C. (1986). Towards a comprehensive model of change. In B.K. Houston and N. Heather (eds), *Treating Addictive Behaviours: Processes of Change*. New York: Plenum.

Prochaska, J.O. and Marcus, B.H. (1994). The transtheoretical model: applications to exercise. In R.K. Dishman (ed.), *Advances in Exercise Adherence*. Champaign, Ill.: Human Kinetics.

Prochaska, J.O., Norcross, J.C., Fowler, J.L. and Follick, M.J. (1992). Attendance and outcome in a worksite weight control program: processes and stages of change as process and predictor variables. *Addictive Behaviors*, 17: 35–45.

Prochaska, J.O., Velicer, W.F., Rossi, J.S. *et al.* (1994). Stages of change and decisional balance for 12 problem behaviours. *Health Psychology*, 13: 39–46.

Prohaska, T.R., Funch, D. and Blesch, K.S. (1990). Age patterns in symptom perception and illness behaviour among colorectal cancer patients. *Behavior, Health and Aging*, 1: 27–39.

Prohaska, T.R., Keller, M.L., Leventhal, E.A. and Leventhal, H. (1987). Impact of symptoms and aging attribution on emotions and coping. *Health Psychology*, 6: 495–514.

Project MATCH Research Group (1998). Matching alcoholism treatments to client heterogeneity: Project MATCH three-year drinking outcomes. *Alcoholism: Clinical and Experimental Research*, 22: 1300–11.

Ptacek, J.T.P. and Eberhardt, T.L. (1996). Breaking bad news: a review of the literature. *Journal of the American Medical Association*, 276: 496–502.

Ptacek, J.T., Ptacek, J.J. and Ellison, H. (2001). 'I'm sorry to tell you' – physicians' reports of breaking bad news. *Journal of Behavioral Medicine*, 24: 205–17.

Puska, P., Tuomilehto, J., Nissinen, A. and Vartiainen, E. (1985). *The North Karelia Project: 20 Year Results and Experiences*. Helsinki: National Public Health Institutem.

Quah, S.-H. and Bishop, G.D. (1996). Seeking help for illness: the roles of cultural orientation and illness cognition. *Journal of Health Psychology*, 1: 209–22.

Quick, J.D., Nelson, D.L., Matuszek, P.A.C., Whittington, J.L. and Quick, J.C. (1996). Social support, secure attachments and health. In C.L. Cooper (ed.), *Handbook of Stress, Medicine and Health*. London: CRC Press.

Qureshi, M., Thacker, H.L., Litaker, D.G. and Kippes, C. (2000). Differences in breast cancer screening rates: an issue of ethnicity or socioeconomics? *Journal of Women's Health and Gender Based Medicine*, 9: 1025–31.

Radley, A. (1994). *Making Sense of Illness: The Social Psychology of Health and Disease*. London: Sage.

Radley, A. (1996). Social psychology and health: framing the relationship. *Psychology and Health*, 11: 629–34.

Rafferty, Y., Friend, R. and Landsbergis, P.A. (2001). The association between job skill discretion, decision authority and burnout. *Work and Stress*, 15: 73–85.

Raftery, K.A., Smith-Coggins, R. and Chen, A.H. (1995). Gender-associated differences in emergency department pain management. *Annals of Emergency Medicine*, 26: 414–21.

Ragland, D.R. and Brand, R.J. (1988). Type A behaviour and mortality from coronary heart disease. *New England Journal of Medicine*, 318: 65–9.

Rahe, R. (1974). Life change and subsequent illness reports. In E.K.E. Gunderson and R. Rahe (eds), *Life Stress and Illness*. Springfield, Ill.: Charles Thomas.

Ramirez, A., Craig, T., Watson, J., Fentiman, I., North, W. and Rubens, R. (1989). Stress and relapse of breast cancer. *British Medical Journal*, 298: 291–3.

Ramirez, A.J., Westcombe, A.M., Burgess, C.C., Sutton, S., Littlejohns, P. and Richards, M.A. (1999). Factors predicting delayed presentation of symptomatic breast cancer: a systematic review. *The Lancet*, 353: 1119–26.

Rand, C.S. and Wise, R.A. (1994). Measuring adherence to asthma medication regimens. *American Journal of Respiratory and Critical Care Medicine*, 149 (suppl.): 69–76.

Rawl, S.M., Given, B.A., Given, C.W., Champion, V.L., Kozachik, S.L. and Barton, D. (2002). Intervention to improve psychological functioning for newly diagnosed patients with cancer. *Oncology Nursing Forum*, 29: 967–75.

Reddy, D.M., Fleming, R. and Adesso, V.J. (1992). Gender and health. In S. Maes, H. Leventhal and M. Johnston (eds), *International Review of Health Psychology*, Vol. 1. Chichester: Wiley.

Rees, K., Bennett, P., Vedhara, K., West, R., Davey-Smith, G. and Ibrahim, S. (2004). Stress management for coronary heart disease. *The Cochrane Library*.

Renner, B. and Schwarzer, R. (2003). Social-cognitive factors in health behaviour change. In J. Suls and K. Wallston (eds), *Social Foundations of Health and Illness*. Oxford: Blackwell.

Renzi, C., Peticca, L. and Pescatori, M. (2000). The use of relaxation techniques in the perioperative management of proctological patients: preliminary results. *International Journal of Colorectal Diseases*, 15: 313–16.

Resnicow, K., Jackson, A., Wang, T., De, A.K., McCarty, F., Dudley, W.N. and Baranowski, T.A. (2001). Motivational interviewing intervention to increase fruit and vegetable intake through black churches: results of the Eat for Life trial. *American Journal of Public Health*, 91: 1686–93.

Rhodes, F. and Wolitski, B. (1990). Perceived effectiveness of fear appeals in AIDS education: relationship to ethnicity, gender, age and group membership. *AIDS Education and Prevention*, 2: 1–11.

Rhodewalt, F. and Zone, J.B. (1989). Appraisal of life change, depression, and illness in hardy and non-hardy women. *Journal of Personality and Social Psychology*, 56: 81–8.

Ricciardelli, L.A. and McCabe, M.P. (2001). Children's body image concerns and eating disturbance: a review of the literature. *Clinical Psychology Review*, 21: 325–44.

Rice, P.L. (1992). *Stress and Health*. California, Brooks/Cole.

Richard, R., van der Pligt, J. and de Vries, N. (1996). Anticipated regret and time perspective: changing sexual risk-taking behaviour. *Journal of Behavioural Decision Making*, 9: 185–99.

Richards, J., Fisher, P. and Conner, F. (1989). The warnings on cigarette packages are ineffective. *Journal of the American Medical Association*, 261: 45.

Richards, M.A., Westcombe, A.M., Love, S.B., Littlejohns, P. and Ramirez, A.J. (1999). Influence of delay on survival in patients with breast cancer: a systematic review. *The Lancet*, 353: 1119–26.

Richardson, J. (2000). The use of randomised control trials in complementary therapies: exploring the issues. *Journal of Advanced Nursing*, 32: 398–406.

Richmond, R.L., Kehoe, L. and de Almeida Neto, A.C. (1997). Effectiveness of a 24-hour transdermal nicotine patch in conjunction with a cognitive behavioural programme: one year outcome. *Addiction*, 92: 27–31.

Ridgeway, V. and Mathews, A. (1982). Psychological preparation for surgery: a comparison of methods. *British Journal of Clinical Psychology*, 21: 271–80.

Riemsma, R.P., Taal, E. and Rasker, J.J. (2003). Group education for patients with rheumatoid arthritis and their partners. *Arthritis and Rheumatism*, 49: 556–66.

Rigby, K., Brown, M., Anagnostou, P., Ross, M.W. and Rosser, B.R.S. (1989). Shock tactics to counter AIDS: the Australian experience. *Psychology and Health*, 3: 145–59.

Riley, J.L., III, Wade, J.B., Myers, C.D., Sheffield, D., Papas, R.K. and Price, D.D. (2002). Racial/ethnic differences in the experience of chronic pain. *Pain*, 100: 291–8.

Rivis, A. and Sheeran, P. (2003). Social influences and the theory of planned behaviour: evidence for a direct relationship between prototypes and young people's exercise behaviour. *Psychology and Health*, 18: 567–83.

Roberts, C.S., Cox, C.E., Reintgen, D.S., Baile, W.F. and Gibertini, M. (1994). Influence of physician communication on newly diagnosed breast patients' psychologic adjustment and decision-making. *Cancer*, 74: 336–41.

Roberts, J. and Rowland, M. (1981). *Hypertension in Adults 25–74 years of age, United States, 1971–1975*. Hyattsville, Md: National Center for Health Statistics (Vital and Health Statistics, Series II: Data from the National Health Survey, No. 221). DHHS publication No. 81-1671.

Rogers, C.R. (1961). *On Becoming a Person*. Boston: Houghton Mifflin.

Rogers, E. (1983). *Diffusion of Innovations*. New York: Free Press.

Rogers, G., Curry, M., Oddy, J., Pratt, N., Beilby, J. and Wilkinson, D. (2003). Depressive disorders and unprotected casual anal sex among Australian homosexually active men in primary care. *HIV Medicine*, 4: 271–5.

Rogers, R.W. (1983). Cognitive and physiological responses to fear appeals and attitude change: a revised theory of protection motivation. In J.T. Cacioppo and R.E. Petty (eds), *Social psychophysiology: a source book*. New York: Guilford Press.

Romelsjö, A. and Branting, M. (2000). Consumption of illegal alcohol among adolescents in Stockholm county. *Contemporary Drug Problems*, 27: 315–33.

Rosch, P.J. (1994). Can stress cause coronary heart disease? (editorial). *Stress Medicine*, 10: 207–10.

Rose, J.S., Chassin, L., Presson, C.C. and Sherman, S.J. (1996). Prospective predictors of quit attempts and smoking cessation in young adults. *Health Psychology*, 15: 261–8.

Rose, S., Bisson, J. and Wessely, S (2001). Psychological debriefing for preventing post traumatic stress disorder (PTSD). *Cochrane Database Systematic Review*, 3.

Rosenfeld, B., Breitbart, W., McDonald, M.V., Passik, S.D., Thaler, H. and Portenoy, R.K. (1996). Pain in ambulatory AIDS patients II: impact of pain on psychological functioning and quality of life. *Pain*, 68: 323–8.

Rosengren, A., Orth-Gomér, K., Wedel, H. and Wilhelmsen, L. (1993). Stressful life events, social support, and mortality in men born in 1933. *British Medical Journal*, 307: 1102–5.

Rosenman, R.H. (1978). Role of Type A pattern in the pathogenesis of ischaemic heart disease and modi-fication for prevention. *Advances in Cardiology*, 25: 34–46.

Rosenman, R.H. (1996). Personality, behavior patterns, and heart disease. In C. Cooper (ed.), *Handbook of Stress, Medicine and Health*. Florida: CRC Press.

Rosenman, R.H., Brand, R.J., Jenkins, C.D., Friedman, M., Straus, R. and Wurm, M. (1975). Coronary heart disease in the Western Collaborative Group study; follow-up experience after 8 and a half years. *Journal of the American Medical Association*, 233: 872–7.

Rosenman, R.H., Brand, R.J., Sholtz, R.I. and Friedman, M. (1976). Multivariate prediction of coronary heart disease during 8.5 year follow-up in the Western Collaborative Group study. *The American Journal of Cardiology*, 37: 903–10.

Rosenstock, I.M. (1966). Why people use health services. Milbank *Memorial Fund Quarterly*, 44: 94–124.

Rosenstock, I.M. (1974). The health belief model and preventive health behaviour. *Health Education Monographs*, 2: 354–86.

Rotter, J.B. (1966). Generalized expectancies for the internal versus external control of reinforcement. *Psychological Monographs*, 90: 1–28.

Rovelli, M., Palmeri, D., Vossler, E., Bartus, S., Hull, D. and Schweizer, R. (1989). Noncompliance in organ transplant recipients. *Transplant Proceedings*, 21: 833–4.

Royal College of Physicians (1995). *Alcohol and the Public Health*. London: Macmillan.

Ruberman, W., Weinblatt, E., Goldberg, J.D. and Chaudhary, B.S. (1984). Psychosocial resilience and protective mechanisms. *American Journal of Orthopsychiatry*, 57: 316–30.

Rudat, K. (1994). *Black and Minority Ethnic Groups in England: Health and Lifestyles*. London: Health Education Authority.

Russell, M.A., Wilson, C. and Baker, C.D. (1979). Effect of general practitioners' advice against smoking. *British Medical Journal*, 2: 231–5.

Rutter, D.R. (2000). Attendance and reattendance for breast cancer screening: a prospective 3-year test of the theory of planned behaviour. *British Journal of Health Psychology*, 2: 199–216.

Rutter, D. and Quine, L. (2002). *Changing Health Behaviour*. Buckingham: Open University Press.

Safer, M.A., Tharps, Q.J., Jackson, T.C. and Leventhal, H. (1979). Determinants of three stages of delay in seeking care at a medical setting. *Medical Care*, 7: 11–29.

Safren, S.A., Otto, M.W. and Worth, J.L. (2001). Two strategies to increase adherence to HIV antiretroviral medication: Life-Steps and medication monitoring. *Behaviour Research and Therapy*, 39: 1151–62.

Safren, S.A., Radomsky, A.S., Otto, M.W. and Salomon, E. (2002). Predictors of psychological well-being in a diverse sample of HIV-positive patients receiving highly active antiretroviral therapy. *Psychosomatics*, 43: 478–84.

Sales, J., Duffy, J., Plant, M. and Peck, D. (1989). Alcohol consumption, cigarette sales and mortality in the United Kingdom: An analysis of the period 1970–1985. *Drug and Alcohol Dependence*, 24: 155–60.

Salovey, P., Rothman, A.J., Detweiler, J.B. and Steward, W.T. (2000). Emotional states and physical health. *American Psychologist*, 55: 110–21.

Samkoff, J.S. and Jacques, C.H. (1991). A review of studies concerning effects of sleep deprivation and fatigue on residents' performance. *Academic Medicine*, 66: 687–93.

Sanders, S.H., Brena, S.F., Spier, C.J., Beltrutti, D., McConnell, H. and Quintero, O. (1992). Chronic low back pain patients around the world: cross-cultural similarities and differences. *Journal of Clinical Pain*, 8: 317–23.

Sanderson, C. and Jemmott, J. (1996). Moderation and mediation of HIV-prevention interventions: relationship status, intentions, and condom use among college students. *Journal of Applied Social Psychology*, 26: 2076–99.

Sapolsky, R. (1986). Glucocorticoid toxicity in the hippocampus: reversal by supplementation with brain fuels. *Journal of Neuroscience*, 6: 2240–4.

Sapolsky, R.M. (1994). *Why Zebras Don't Get Ulcers*. New York: W.H. Freeman.

Sapolsky, R.M. (1996). Why stress is bad for your brain. *Science*, 273: 749–50.

Sapolsky, R.M., Krey, L.C. and McEwan, B.S. (1986). The neuroendocrinology of stress and ageing: the glucocorticoid cascade hypothesis. *Endocrine Reviews*, 7: 284–301.

Sarason, B.R., Sarason, I.G. and Pierce, G.R. (1990). Traditional views of social support and their impact on assessment. In B.R. Sarason, I.G. Sarason and G.R. Pierce (eds), *Social Support: An Interactional View*. New York: Wiley.

Saremi, A., Hanson, R.L., Tulloch-Reid, M., Williams, D.E. and Knowler, W.C. (2004). Alcohol consumption predicts hypertension but not diabetes. *Journal of Studies of Alcohol*, 65: 184–90.

Sarkisian, C.A., Liu, H.H., Ensrud, K.E., Stone, K.L. and Mangione, C.M. (2001). Correlates of attribution of new disability to 'old age'. *Journal of the American Geriatric Society*, 49: 134–41.

Saunders, C. and Baines, M. (1983). *Living with Dying: The Management of Terminal Disease*. Oxford: Oxford University Press.

Saunders, R.P., Pate, R.R., Felton, G., Dowda, M., Weinrich, M.C., Ward, D.S., Parsons, M.A. and Baranowski, T. (1997). Development of questionnaires to measure psychosocial influences on children's physical activity. *Preventive Medicine*, 26: 241–7.

Sausen, K.P., Lovallo, W.R., Pincomb, G.A. and Wilson, M.F. (1992). Cardiovascular responses to occupational stress in medical students: a paradigm for ambulatory monitoring studies. *Health Psychology*, 11: 55–60.

Savage, R. and Armstrong, D. (1990). Effect of a general practitioner's consulting style on patients' satisfaction: a controlled study. *British Medical Journal*, 301: 968–70.

Scharloo, M. and Kaptein, A. (1997). Measurement of illness perceptions in patients with chronic somatic illness: a review of the literature. In K.J. Petrie and J. Weinman (eds), *Perceptions of Health and Illness: Current Research and Applications*. London: Harwood Academic.

Scharloo, M., Kaptein, A.A., Weinman, J., Hazes, J.M., Willems, L.N.A., Bergman, W., Rooijmans, H.G.M. (1998). Illness perceptions, coping and functioning in patients with rheumatoid arthritis, chronic obstructive pulmonary disease, and psoriasis. *Journal of Psychosomatic Research*, 44: 573–85.

Scheier, M.F. and Carver, C.S. (1985). Optimism, Coping and health: assessment and implications of generalized outcome expectancies. *Health Psychology*, 4: 219–47.

Scheier, M.F. and Carver, C.S. (1992). Effects of optimism on psychological and physical well-being: theoretical overview and empirical update. *Cognitive Therapy Research*, 16: 201–28.

Scheier, M.F., Weintraub, J.K., and Carver, C.S. (1986). coping with stress: divergent strategies of optimists and pessimists. *Journal of Personality and Social Psychology*, 51: 1257–1264.

Scherwitz, L., Perkins, L., Chesney, M., Hughes, G., Sidney, S. and Manolio, T.A. (1992). Hostility and health behaviours in young adults: the CARDIA study. *American Journal of Epidemiology*, 136: 136–45.

Schiaffino, K.M. and Cea, C.D. (1995). Assessing chronic illness representations: the implicit models of illness questionnaire. *Journal of Behavioral Medicine*, 18: 531–48.

Schlenk, E.A., Dunbar-Jacob, J. and Engberg, S. (2004). Medication non-adherence among older adults: a review of strategies and interventions for improvement. *Journal of Gerontological Nursing*, 30: 33–43.

Schmaling, K.B., Smith, W.R. and Buchwald, D.S. (2000). Significant other responses are associated with fatigue and functional status among patients with chronic fatigue syndrome. *Psychosomatic Medicine*, 62: 444–50.

Schneider, R.J., Casey, J. and Kohn, R. (2000). Motivational versus confrontational interviewing: a comparison of substance abuse assessment practices at employee assistance programs. *Journal of Behavioral Health Service Research*, 27: 60–74.

Schneiderman, N., Antoni, M.H. and Saab, P.G. (2001). Health psychology: psychosocial and bio-behavioral aspects of chronic disease management. *Annual Review of Psychology*, 52: 555–80.

Schofield, P.E., Butow, P.N., Thompson, J.F., Tattersall, M.H., Beeney, L.J. and Dunn, S.M. (2003). Psychological responses of patients receiving a diagnosis of cancer. *Annals of Oncology*, 14: 48–56.

Scholte op Reimer, J., de Haan, R.J., Rijners, P.T., Limburg, M. and van den Bos, G.A. (1998). The burden of caregiving in partners of long-term stroke survivors. *Stroke*, 29: 1605–11.

Schulz, R., Bookwala, J., Knapp, J.E., Scheier, M. and Williamson, G.M. (1996). Pessimism, age, and cancer mortality. *Psychology and Aging*, 11: 304–9.

Schulz, R., O'Brien, A., Bookwala, J. and Fleissner, K. (1995). Psychiatric and physical morbidity effects of dementia caregiving: prevalence, correlates and causes. *The Gerontologist*, 35: 771–91.

Schulz, R. and Quittner, A.L. (1998). Caregiving for children and adults with chronic conditions: introduction to the special issue. *Health Psychology*, 17: 107–11.

Schulz, R., Tompkins, C.A., and Rau, M.T. (1988). A longitudinal study of the psychosocial impact of stroke on primary support persons. *Psychology and Aging*, 3: 131–41.

Schulz, U. and Mohamed, N.E. (2004). Turning the tide: benefit finding after cancer surgery. *Social Science and Medicine*, 59: 653–62.

Schur, E.A., Sanders, M. and Steiner, H. (2000). Body dissatisfaction and dieting in young children. *International Journal of Eating Disorders*, 27: 74–82.

Schwartz, B.S., Stewart, W.F., Simon, D. and Lipton, R.B. (1998). Epidemiology of tension-type headache. *Journal of the American Medical Association*, 279: 381–3.

Schwartz, G.E. and Weiss, S. (1977). What is behavioral medicine? *Psychosomatic Medicine*, 36: 377–81.

Schwarzer, R. (1992). Self efficacy in the adoption and maintenance of health behaviours: theoretical approaches and a new model. In R. Schwarzer (ed.), *Self Efficacy: Thought Control of Action*. Washington: Hemisphere.

Schwarzer, R. (1994). Optimism, vulnerability, and self-beliefs as health-related cognitions: a systematic overview. *Psychology and Health*, 9: 161–80.

Scollay, P., Doucett, M., Perry, M. and Winterbottom, B. (1992). AIDS education of college students: the effect of an HIV-positive lecturer. *AIDS Education and Prevention*, 4: 160–71.

Scottish Executive (1999). *Fair Shares for All*. Report of the National Review of Resource Allocation for the NHS in Scotland, chaired by Professor Sir John Arbuthnott, principal and vice-chancellor of Strathclyde University. Edinburgh: HMSO.

Seale, C. (1991). A comparison of hospice and conventional care. *Social Science and Medicine*, 32: 147–52.

Seale, C. and Kelly, M. (1997). A comparison of hospice and hospital care for the spouses of people who die. *Palliative Care*, 11: 101–6.

Searle, A. and Bennett, P. (2001). Psychological factors and inflammatory bowel disease: a review of a decade of literature. *Psychology, Health and Medicine*, 6: 121–35.

Searle, B., Bright, J.E.H. and Bochner, S. (2001). Helping people to sort it out: the role of social support in the Job Strain Model. *Work and Stress*, 15: 328–46.

Segan, C.J., Borland, R. and Greenwood, K.M. (2002). Do transtheoretical model measures predict the transition from preparation to action in smoking cessation? *Psychology and Health*, 17: 417–35.

Segestrom, S.C., Taylor, S.E., Kemeny, M.E. and Fahey, J.L. (1998). Optimism is associated with mood, coping, and immune change in response to stress. *Journal of Personality and Social Psychology*, 74: 1646–55.

Seidman, D.F. and Covey, L.S. (eds) (1999). *Helping the Hard-core Smoker. A Clinician's Guide*. Mahwah, NJ: Lawrence Erlbaum.

Seligman, M.E.P. (2003). Positive psychology: fundamental assumptions. *The Psychologist*, 16: 126–7.

Seligman, M.E.P. and Csikszentmihalyi, M. (2000). Positive psychology: an introduction. *American Psychologist*, 55: 5–14.

Selye, H. (1956). *The Stress of Life*. New York: McGraw-Hill.

Selye, H. (1974). *Stress without Distress*. Philadelphia: Lipincott.

Selye, H. (1991). History and present status of the stress concept. In A. Monat and R.S. Lazarus (eds), *Stress and Coping*. New York: Columbia University Press.

Shaffer, J.W., Graves, P.L., Swank, R.T. and Pearson, T.A. (1987). Clustering of personality traits in youth and the subsequent development of cancer among physicians. *Journal of Behavioral Medicine*, 10: 441–7.

Shakeshaft, A.P., Bowman, J.A. and Sanson-Fisher, R.W. (1999). A comparison of two retrospective measures of weekly alcohol consumption: diary and quantity/frequency index. *Alcohol and Alcoholism*, 34: 636–45.

Shaper, A.G., Wannamethee, G. and Walker, M. (1994). Alcohol and coronary heart disease: a perspective from the British Regional Heart Study. *International Journal of Epidemiology*, 23: 482–94.

Shapiro, F. (1995). *Eye Movement Desensitisation and Reprocessing: Basic Principles.* New York: Guilford Press.

Sharp, T.J. (2001). Chronic pain: a reformulation of the cognitive-behavioural model. *Behaviour Research and Therapy*, 39: 787–800.

Sharpe, P.A., Granner, M.L., Hutto, B. and Ainsworth, B.E. (2004). Association of environmental factors to meeting physical activity recommendations in two South Carolina counties. *American Journal of Health Promotion*, 18: 251–7.

Sheeran, P. (2002). Intention–behaviour relations: a conceptual and empirical review. In M. Hewstone and W. Stroebe (eds), *European Review of Social Psychology*, Vol. 11. Chichester: Wiley.

Sheeran, P. and Abraham, C. (1996). The health belief model. In M. Conner and P. Norman (eds), *Predicting Health Behaviour.* Buckingham: Open University Press.

Sheeran, P., Abraham, C.S. and Orbell, S. (1999). Psychosocial correlates of heterosexual condom use: a meta-analysis. *Psychological Bulletin*, 125: 90–132.

Sheeran, P. and Orbell, S. (1996). How confidently can we infer health beliefs from questionnaire responses? *Psychology and Health*, 11: 273–90.

Sheeran, P. and Orbell, S. (1998). Do intentions predict condom use? Meta-analysis and examination of six moderator variables. *British Journal of Social Psychology*, 37: 231–50.

Sheeran, P. and Orbell, S. (1999). Implementation intentions and repeated behaviour: augmenting the predictive validity of the theory of planned behaviour. *European Journal of Social Psychology*, 29: 349–69.

Sheffield, D., Biles, P.L., Orom, H., Maixner, W. and Sheps, D.S. (2000). Race and sex differences in cutaneous pain perception. *Psychosomatic Medicine*, 62: 517–23.

Sheppard, B.H., Hartwick, J. and Warshaw, P.R. (1988). The theory of reasoned action: a meta-analysis of past research with recommendations for modifications and future research. *Journal of Consumer Research*, 15: 325–43.

Sherbourne, C.D., Hays, R.D., Ordway, L., DiMatteo, M.R. and Kravitz, R.L. (1992). Antecedents of adherence to medical recommendations: results from the Medical Outcomes Study. *Journal of Behavioral Medicine*, 15: 447–68.

Sherr, L. (1987). An evaluation of the UK government health education campaign on AIDS, *Psychology and Health*, 1: 61–72.

Sherwood, A. and Turner, J.R. (1992). A conceptual and methodological overview of cardiovascular reactivity research. In J.R. Turner, A. Sherwood and K.C. Light (eds), *Individual Differences in Cardiovascular Responses to Stress.* New York, Plenum.

Shewchuck, R.M., Richards, J.S. and Elliott, T.R. (1998). Dynamic processes in health outcomes among caregivers of patients with spinal cord injuries. *Health Psychology*, 17: 125–9.

Shifren, K. and Hooker, K. (1995). Stability and change in optimism: a study among spouse caregivers. *Experimental Aging Research*, 21: 59–76.

Shilts, R. (2000). *And the Band Played on: Politics, People and the AIDS Epidemic.* St Martin's Press.

Shinar, D., Schechtman, E. and Compton, R. (1999). Trends in safe driving behaviors and in relation to trends in health maintenance behaviors in the USA: 1985–1995. *Accident Analysis and Prevention*, 31: 497–503.

Siegel, K., Karus, D.G., Raveis, V.H., Christ, G.H. and Mesagno, F.P. (1996). Depressive distress among the spouses of terminally ill cancer patients. *Cancer Practice*, 4: 25–30.

Siegel, K., Schrimshaw, E.W. and Dean, L. (1999). Symptom interpretation and medication adherence among late middle-age and older HIV-infected adults. *Journal of Health Psychology*, 4: 247–57.

Siegrist, J., Peter, R., Junge, A., Cremer, P. and Seidel, D. (1990). Low status control, high effort at work and ischemic heart disease: prospective evidence from blue collar men. *Social Science and Medicine*, 35: 1127–34.

Sikkema, K.J., Kelly, J.A., Winett, R.A., Solomon, L.J., Cargill, V.A., Roffman, R.A., McAuliffe, T.L., Heckman, T.G., Anderson, E.A., Wagstaff, D.A., Norman, A.D., Perry, M.J., Crumble, D.A. and Mercer, M.B. (2000). Outcomes of a randomized community-level HIV-prevention intervention for women living in 18 low-income housing developments. *American Journal of Public Health*, 90: 53–7.

Silverman, D. (1987). *Communication and Medical Practice: Social Relations and the Clinic.* London: Sage.

Simon, J.A., Carmody, T.P., Hudes, E.S., Snyder, E. and Murray, J. (2003). Intensive smoking cessation counseling versus minimal counseling among hospitalized smokers treated with transdermal nicotine replacement: a randomized trial. *American Journal of Medicine*, 114: 555–62.

Singh, R.K., Panday, H.P. and Singh, R.H. (2003). Irritable bowel syndrome: challenges ahead. *Current Science*, 84: 1525–33.

Skarstein, J., Aass, N., Fossa, S.D., Skovlund, E. and Dahl, A.A. (2000). Anxiety and depression in cancer patients: relation between the Hospital Anxiety and Depression Scale and the European Organization for Research and Treatment of Cancer Core Quality of

Life Questionnaire. *Journal of Psychosomatic Research*, 49: 27–34.

Skelton, D.A., Young, A., Walker, A. and Hoinville, E. (1999). *Physical Activity in Later Life: Further Analysis of the Allied Dunbar National Fitness Survey and the Health Education Authority National Survey of Activity and Health*. London: Health Education Authority.

Skevington, S.M. (1990). A standardised scale to measure beliefs about controlling pain (BPCQ): a preliminary study. *Psychology and Health*, 4: 221–32.

Sloper, P. (2000). Predictors of distress in parents of children with cancer: a prospective study. *Journal of Pediatric Psychology*, 25: 79–92.

Smedslund, G. and Rundmo, T. (1999). Is Grossarth-Maticek's coronary prone type II an independent predictor of myocardial infarction? *Personality and Individual Differences*, 27: 1231–42.

Smee, C., Parsonage, M., Anderson, R. and Duckworth, S. (1992). *Effects of tobacco advertising on tobacco consumption: a discussion document reviewing the evidence*. London: Department of Health.

Smith, A. and Roberts, K. (2003). Interventions for post-traumatic stress disorder and psychological distress in emergency ambulance personnel: a review of the literature. *Emergency Medical Journal*, 20: 75–8.

Smith, C., Roberts, J.L. and Pendelton, L.L. (1988). Booze on the box. The portrayal of alcohol on British television: a content analysis. *Health Education Research*, 3: 267–72.

Smith, C.A. and Lazarus, R.S. (1993). Appraisal components, core relational themes, and the emotions. *Cognition and Emotion*, 7: 233–69.

Smith, C.A., Wallston, K.A., Dwyer, K.A. and Dowdy, S.W. (1997). Beyond good or bad coping: a multidimensional examination of coping with pain in persons with rheumatoid arthritis. *Annals of Behavioral Medicine*, 19: 11–21.

Smith, H., Gooding, S., Brown, R. and Frew, A. (1998). Evaluation of readability and accuracy of information leaflets in general practices for patients with asthma. *British Medical Journal*, 317: 264–5.

Smith, M.Y., Redd, W.H., Peyer, C., Peyser, C. and Vogl, D. (1999). Post-traumatic stress disorder in cancer: a review. *Psycho-Oncology*, 8: 521–37.

Smith, T.W. (1994). Concepts and methods on the study of anger, hostility and health. In A.W. Siegman and T.W. Smith (eds), *Anger, Hostility and the Heart*. Hillsdale, NJ: Lawrence Erlbaum.

Smith, T.W., Gallo, L.C. and Ruiz, J.M. (2003). Toward a social psychophysiology of cardiovascular reactivity: interpersonal concepts and methods in the study of stress and coronary disease. In J. Suls and K. Wallston (eds), *Social Psychological Foundations of Health and Illness*. Oxford: Blackwell.

Smyth, J.M., Stone, A.A., Hurewitz, A. and Kaell, A. (1999). Effects of writing about stressful experiences on symptom reduction in patients with asthma or rheumatoid arthritis: a randomized trial. *Journal of the American Medical Association*, 281: 1304–9.

Snell, J.L. and Buck, E.L. (1996). Increasing cancer screening: a meta analysis. *Preventive Medicine*, 25: 702–7.

Soames-Job, R.F. (1988). Effective and ineffective use of fear in health promotion campaigns. *American Journal of Public Health*, 78: 163–7.

Solms, M. and Turnbull, O.H. (2002). *The Brain and the Inner Mind: An Introduction to the Neuroscience of Subjective Wellbeing*. New York: Other Press/Karnac.

Solomon, R.L. (1977). Addiction: an opponent-process theory of acquired motivation. The affective dynamics of addiction. In J.D. Maser (ed.), *Psychopathology: Experimental Models*. San Francisco: W.H. Freeman.

Sorensen, G., Morris, D.M., Hunt, M.K., Herbert, J.R., Harris, D.R., Stoddard, A. and Ockene, J.K. (1992). Work-site nutrition intervention and employees' dietary habits: the Treatwell program. *American Journal of Public Health*, 82: 877–80.

Sorensen, G., Stoddard, A., Hunt, M.K., Hebert, J.R., Ockene, J.K., Avrunin, J.S., Himmelstein, J. and Hammond, S.K. (1998). The effects of a health promotion–health protection intervention on behavior change: the WellWorks Study. *American Journal of Public Health*, 88: 1685–90.

Sorlie, P.D., Backlund, E. and Keller, J.B. (1995). US mortality by economic, demographic, and social characteristics: the National Longitudinal Mortality Study. *American Journal of Public Health*, 85: 949–56.

Sparks, P., Conner, M., James, R., Shepherd, R. and Povey, R. (2001). Ambivalence about health-related behaviours: an exploration in the domain of food choice. *British Journal of Health Psychology*, 6: 53–68.

Sparks, P. and Shepherd, R. (1992). Self-identity and the theory of planned behaviour: assessing the role of identification with green consumerism. *Social Psychology Quarterly*, 55: 388–99.

Speca, M., Carlson, L.E., Goodey, E. and Angen, M. (2000). A randomized wait-list controlled clinical trial: the effect of mindfulness meditation-based stress reduction program on mood and symptoms of stress in cancer patients. *Psychosomatic Medicine*, 62: 613–22.

Speisman, J.C., Lazarus, R.S., Mordkoff, A. and Davison, L. (1964). Experimental reduction of stress based on ego defense theory. *Journal of Abnormal and Social Psychology*, 68: 367–80.

Spiegel, D. (1992). Effects of psychosocial support on patients with metastatic breast cancer. *Journal of Psychosocial Oncology*, 10: 113–20.

Spiegel, D. (2001). Mind matters. Coping and cancer progression. *Journal of Psychosomatic Research*, 50: 287–90.

Spiegel, D., Bloom, J.R. and Yalom, I. (1981). Group support for patients with metastatic cancer. A randomized outcome study. *Archives of General Psychiatry*, 38: 527–33.

Spiegel, D., Bloom, J.R., Kraemer, H.C. and Gottheil, E. (1989). Effect of psychosocial treatment on survival of patients with metastatic breast cancer. *The Lancet*, 14(2): 888–91.

Stansfeld, S.A., Bosma, H., Hemingway, H. and Marmot, M.G. (1998). Psychosocial work characteristics and social support as predictors of SF-36 health functioning: the Whitehall II study. *Psychosomatic Medicine*, 60: 247–55.

Stanton, A.L., Danoff-Burg, S. and Huggins, M.E. (2002). The first year after breast cancer diagnosis: hope and coping strategies as predictors of adjustment. *Psycho-Oncology*, 11: 93–102.

Stanton, A.L., Danoff-Burg, S., Sworowski, L.A., Collins, C.A., Branstetter, A.D., Rodriguez-Hanley, A., Kirk, S.B. and Austenfeld, J.L. (2002). Randomized, controlled trial of written emotional expression and benefit finding in breast cancer patients. *Journal of Clinical Oncology*, 20: 4160–8.

Stanton, A.L., Kirk, K.B., Cameron, C.L. and Danoff-Burg, S. (2000). Coping through emotional approach: Scale construction and validation. *Journal of Personality and Social Psychology*, 78: 1150–69.

Stanton, A.L. and Snider, P.R. (1993). Coping with a breast cancer diagnosis: a prospective study. *Health Psychology*, 12: 16.

Starace, F., Bartoli, L., Aloisi, M.S., Antinori, A., Narciso, P., Ippolito, G., Ravasio, L., Moioli, M.C., Vangi, D., Gennero, L., Coronado, O.V., Giacometti, A., Nappa, S., Perulli, M.L., Montesarchio, V., La Gala, A., Ricci, F., Cristiano, L., De Marco, M., Izzo, C., Pezzotti, P. and D'Arminio Monforte, A. (2000). Cognitive and affective disorders associated to HIV infection in the HAART era: findings from the NeuroICONA study. Cognitive impairment and depression in HIV/AIDS. *Acta Psychiatria Scandinavica*, 106: 20–6.

Stead, M., Hastings, G. and Eadie, D. (2002). The challenge of evaluating complex interventions: a framework for evaluating media advocacy. *Health Education Research*, 17: 351–64.

Steadman, L. and Quine, L. (2004). Encouraging young males to perform testicular self-examination: a simple, but effective, implementations intervention. *British Journal of Health Psychology*, 9: 479–88.

Steadman, L., Rutter, D.R. and Field, S. (2002). Individually elicited versus modal normative beliefs in predicting attendance at breast screening: examining the role of belief salience in the theory of planned behaviour. *British Journal of Health Psychology*, 7: 317–30.

Stenner, P.H.D., Cooper, D. and Skevington, S. (2003). Putting the Q into quality of life: the identification of subjective constructions of health-related quality of life using Q methodology. *Social Science and Medicine*, 57: 2161–72.

Stephens, C., Long, N. and Miller, N. (1997). The impact of trauma and social support on post traumatic stress disorder: a study of New Zealand police officers. *Journal of Criminal Justice*, 25: 303–14.

Stephenson, J., Bauman, A., Armstrong, T., Smith, B. and Bellew, B. (2000). *The Costs of Illness Attributable to Physical Inactivity in Australia: A Preliminary Study*. Canberra: Commonwealth Government of Australia.

Steptoe, A., Pollard, T. and Wardle, J. (1995). Development of a measure of the motives underlying the selection of food: the food choice questionnaire. *Appetite 1995*, 25: 267–84.

Steptoe, A., Wardle, J., Fuller, R., Holte, A., Justo, J., Sanderman, R. and Wicjstrom, L. (1997). Leisure-time physical exercise: prevalence, attitudinal correlates and behavioural correlates among young Europeans from 21 countries. *Preventive Medicine*, 26: 845–54.

Sterne, J.A.C. and Davey-Smith, G. (2001). Sifting the evidence – what's wrong with significance tests? *British Medical Journal*, 322: 226–31.

Stevenson, M., Palamara, P., Rooke, M., Richardson, K., Baker, M. and Baumwol, J. (2001). Drink and drug driving: what's the skipper up to? *Australia and New Zealand Journal of Public Health*, 25: 511–13.

Stewart, A.L. and Ware, J.E. (eds) (1992). *Measuring Functioning and Well-being: The Medical Outcomes Study Approach*. Durham, NC: Duke University Press.

Stewart, M., Davidson, K., Meade, D., Hirth, A. and Makrides, L. (2000). Myocardial infarction: survivors' and spouses' stress, coping, and support. *Journal of Advanced Nursing*, 31: 1351–60.

Stirling, A.M., Wilson, P. and McConnachie, A. (2001). Deprivation, psychological distress, and consultation length in general practice. *British Journal of General Practice*, 51: 456–60.

St Leger, L.H. (1999). The opportunities and effectiveness of the health-promoting school in improving child health – a review of the claims and evidence. *Health Education Research*, 14: 51–69.

Stoate, H.G. (1989). Can health screening damage your health? *Journal of the Royal College of General Practitioners*, 39: 193–5.

Stokols, D. (1992). Establishing and maintaining health environments. *American Psychologist*, 47: 6–22.

Stone, A.A., Bovbjerg, D.H., Neale, J.M., Napoli, A., Valdimarsdottir, H. and Gwaltney, J.M., Jr (1993). Development of common cold symptoms following experimental rhinovirus infection is related to prior stressful life events. *Behavioral Medicine*, 8: 115–20.

Stone, D.H. and Stewart, S. (1996). Screening and the new genetics: a public health perspective on the ethical debate. *Journal of Public Health Medicine*, 18: 3–5.

Stone, G.C. (1979). Health and the health system: a historical overview and conceptual framework. In G.C. Stone, F. Cohen and N.E. Adler (eds), *Health Psychology: A Handbook*. San Francisco: Jossey-Bass.

Stoudemire, A. and Hales, R.E. (1991). Psychological and behavioral factors affecting medical conditions and DSM-IV: an overview. *Psychosomatics*, 32: 5–12.

Strang, S. and Strang, P. (2002). Questions posed to hospital chaplains by palliative care patients. *Journal of Palliative Medicine*, 5: 857–64.

Strauss, R.S. (2000). Childhood obesity and self esteem. *Pediatrics*, 105: e15.

Strecher, V.J., Champion, V.L. and Rosenstock, I.M. (1997). The health belief model and health behaviour. In D.S. Gochman (ed.), *Handbook of Health Behavior Research I: Personal and Social Determinants*. New York: Plenum.

Strecher, V.J. and Rosenstock, I.M. (1997). The health belief model. In A. Baum, S. Newman, J. Weinman, R. West and C. McManus (eds), *Cambridge Handbook of Psychology, Health and Medicine*. Cambridge: Cambridge University Press.

Stronks, K., VandeMheen, H., VandenBos, J. and Mackenbach, J.P. (1997). The interrelationship between income, health and employment status. *International Journal of Epidemiology*, 16: 592–600.

Stuckey, S.J., Jacobs, A. and Goldfarb, J. (1986). EMG biofeedback training, relaxation training, and placebo for the relief of chronic back pain. *Perceptual and Motor Skills*, 63: 1023–36.

Stunkard, A.J. and Wadden, T. (1993). *Obesity: Theory and Therapy*, 2nd edn. New York: Raven Press.

Suarez, E.C., Kuhn, C.M., Schanberg, S.M., Williams, R.B. and Zimmermann, E.A. (1998). Neuroendocrine, cardiovascular, and emotional responses of hostile men: the role of interpersonal challenge. *Psychosomatic Medicine*, 60: 78–88.

Suarez, E.C. and Williams, R.B. (1989). Situational determinants of cardiovascular and emotional reactivity in high and low hostile men. *Psychosomatic Medicine*, 51: 404–18.

Suchman, C.A. (1965). Stages of illness and medical care. *Journal of Health and Social Behavior*, 6: 114–28.

Sullivan, M.J.L., Rodgers, W.M. and Kirsch, I. (2001). Catastrophizing, depression and expectancies for pain and emotional distress. *Pain*, 91: 147–54.

Suls, J. and Rittenhouse, J.D. (eds). (1987). Personality and Physical Health (Special Issue). *Journal of Personality*, 55: 155–393.

Suls, J., Wan, C.K. and Costa, P.T., Jr (1995). Relationship of trait anger to resting blood pressure: a meta-analysis. *Health Psychology*, 14: 444–56.

SuperioCabuslay, E., Ward, M.M. and Lorig, K.R. (1996). Patient education interventions in osteoarthritis and rheumatoid arthritis: a meta-analytic comparison with nonsteroidal antiinflammatory drug treatment. *Arthritis Care and Research*, 9: 292–301.

Surwit, R.S. and Schneider, M.S. (1993). Role of stress in the etiology and treatment of diabetes mellitus. *Psychosomatic Medicine*, 55: 380–93.

Surwit, R.S., van Tilburg, M.A.L., Zucker, N. McCaskill, C.C., Parekh, P., Feinglos, M.N., Edwards, C.L., Williams, P. and Lane, J.D. (2002). Stress management improves long-term glycemic control in type 2 diabetes. *Diabetes Care*, 25: 30–4.

Suter, P.B. (2002). Employment and litigation: improved by work, assisted by verdict. *Pain*, 100: 249–57.

Sutherland, I. and Shepherd, J.P. (2001). Social dimensions of adolescent substance use. *Addiction*, 96: 445–58.

Sutton, S. (1996). Can 'stages of change' provide guidance in the treatment of addictions? A critical examination of Prochaska and DiClemente's model. In: G.E. Edwards and C. Dare (eds). *Psychotherapy, Psychological Treatments and the Addictions*. Cambridge: Cambridge University Press.

Sutton, S. (1998). Predicting and explaining intentions and behaviour: how well are we doing? *Journal of Applied Social Psychology*, 28: 1317–38.

Sutton, S. (2000). A critical review of the transtheoretical model applied to smoking cessation. In P. Norman, C. Abraham and M. Conner (eds), *Understanding and Changing Health Behaviour*. Amsterdam: Harwood Academic.

Sutton, S. (2001). Back to the drawing board? A review of applications of the transtheoretical model to substance use. *Addiction*, 96: 175–86.

Sutton, S. (2002). Using social cognition models to develop health behaviour interventions: problems and assumptions. In D. Rutter and L. Quine (eds), *Changing Health Behaviour*. Buckingham: Open University Press.

Sutton, S., McVey, D. and Glanz, A. (1999). A comparative test of the theory of reasoned action and the theory of planned behaviour in the prediction of condom use intentions in a national sample of English young people. *Health Psychology*, 18: 72–81.

Swartzman, L.C. and Lees, M.C. (1996). Causal dimensions of college students' perceptions of physical symptoms. *Journal of Behavioral Medicine*, 19(2): 85–110.

Taaffe, D.R., Harris, T.B., Ferrucci, L., Rowe, J. and Seeman, T.E. (2000). Cross-sectional and prospective relationships of interleukin-6 and C-reactive protein with physical performance in elderly persons: MacArthur Studies of Successful Aging. *Journal of Gerontology. A: Biological Science and Medical Science*, 55: M709–15.

Tan, P.E.H. and Bishop, G.D. (1996). Disease representations and related behavioural intentions among Chinese Singaporeans. *Psychology and Health*, 11: 671–83.

Tang, P.C. and Newcomb, C. (1998). Informing patients: a guide for providing patient health information. *Journal of the American Medical Informatics Association*, 5: 563–70.

Tapper, K., Horne, P. and Lowe, C.F. (2003). The Food Dudes to the rescue! *The Psychologist*, 16: 18–21.

Targ, E.F. and Levine, E.G. (2002). The efficacy of a mind–body–spirit group for women with breast cancer: a randomized controlled trial. *General Hospital Psychiatry*, 24: 238–48.

Tattersall, M.H., Butow, P.N., Griffin, A.-M. and Dunn, S.M. (1994). The take-home message: patients prefer consultation audiotapes to summary letters. *Journal of Clinical Oncology*, 12: 1305–11.

Taylor, A., Goldberg, D., Hutchinson, S., Cameron, S. and Fox, R. (2001). High risk injecting behaviour among injectors from Glasgow: cross sectional community wide surveys 1990–1999. *Journal of Epidemiology and Community Health*, 55: 766–7.

Taylor, B., Miller, E., Farrington, C.P., Petropoulos, M.C., Favot-Mayaud, I., Li, J. and Waight, P.A. (1999). Autism and measles, mumps and rubella vaccine: no epidemiological evidence for a causal association. *The Lancet*, 2026–9.

Taylor, B., Miller, E., Lingam, R., Andrews, N., Simmons, A. and Stowe, J. (2002). Measles, mumps and rubella vaccination and bowel problems or developmental regression in children with autism: population study. *British Medical Journal*, 324: 393–6.

Taylor, C.B., Bandura, A., Ewart, C.K., Miller, N.H. and DeBusk, R.F. (1985). Exercise testing to enhance wives' confidence in their husbands' cardiac capability soon after clinically uncomplicated acute myocardial infarction. *American Journal of Cardiology*, 55: 635–8.

Taylor, S. (1983). Adjustment to threatening events: a theory of cognitive adaptation. *American Psychologist*, 38: 1161–73.

Taylor, S.E. and Armor, D.A. (1996). Positive illusions and coping with adversity. *Journal of Personality*, 64: 873–98.

Taylor, S.E., Kemeny, M.E., Aspinwall, L.G., Schneider, S.G., Rodriguez, R. and Herbert, M. (1992). Optimism, coping, psychological distress, and high-risk sexual behaviour among men at risk for acquired immunodeficiency syndrome (AIDS). *Journal of Personality and Social Psychology*, 63: 460–73.

Taylor, S.E., Klein, L.C., Grunewald, T.L., Gurung, R.A.R. and Fernandes-Taylor, S. (2003). Affiliation, social support, and biobehavioral responses to stress. In J. Suls and K.A. Wallston (eds), *Social Psychological Foundations of Health and Illness*. Oxford: Blackwell.

Taylor, S.E., Repetti, R.L. and Seeman, T. (1997). Health psychology: What is an unhealthy environment and how does it get under the skin? *Annual Reviews in Psychology*, 48: 411–47.

Taylor, S.E. and Seeman, T.E. (1999). Psychosocial resources and the SES–health relationship. *Annals of the New York Academy of Science*, 896: 210–25.

Temoshok, L. (1987). Personality, coping style, emotion and cancer: towards an integrative model. *Social Science and Medicine*, 20: 833–40.

Temoshok, L. and Dreher, H. (1993). *The Type C connection: The Behavioral Links to Cancer and Your Health*. New York: Penguin.

Temoshok, L. and Fox, B.H. (1984). Coping styles and other psychosocial factors related to medical status and to prognosis in patients with cutaneous malignant melanoma. In: B.H. Fox and B. Newberry (eds), *Impact of Psychoendocrine Systems in Cancer and Immunity*. Toronto: C.J. Hogrefe.

Tennen, H., Affleck, G., Armeli, S. and Carney, M.A. (2000). A daily process approach to coping: linking theory, research, and practice. *American Psychologist*, 55: 620–5.

Terry, D.J. (1992). Stress, coping and coping resources as correlates of adaptation in myocardial infarction patients. *British Journal of Clinical Psychology*, 31: 215–25.

Theisen, M.E., MacNeill, S.E., Lumley, M.A., Ketterer, M.W., Goldberg, A.D. and Borzak, S. (1995). Psychosocial factors related to unrecognized acute myocardial infarction. *American Journal of Cardiology*, 75: 1211–13.

Theorell, T. and Karasek, R.A. (1996). Current issues relating to psychosocial job strain and cardiovascular disease research. *Journal of Occupational Health Psychology*, 1: 9–26.

Theunissen, N.C.M., de Ridder, D.T.D., Bensing, J.M. and Rutten, G.E.H.M. (2003). Manipulation of patient–provider interaction: discussing illness representations or action plans concerning adherence. *Patient Education and Counselling*, 51: 247–58.

Theunissen, N.C.M., Vogels, T.G.C., Koopman, H.M., Verrips, G.H.W., Zwinderman, A.H., Verloove-Vanhorick, S.P. and Wit, J.M. (1998). The proxy problem: child report versus parent report in health-related quality of life research. *Quality of Life Research*, 7: 387–97.

Thoits, P.A. (1995). Stress, coping and social support processes. Where are we? What next? *Journal of Health and Social Behavior* (extra issue), 36: 53–79.

Thomas, D.B., Gao, D.L., Ray, R.M., Wang, W.W., Allison, C.J., Chen, F.L., Porter, P., Hu, Y.W., Zhao, G.L., Pan, L.D., Li, W., Wu, C., Coriaty, Z., Evans, I., Lin, M.G., Stalsberg, H. and Self, S.G. (2002). Randomized trial of breast self-examination in Shanghai – final results. *Journal of the National Cancer Institute*, 94: 1445–57.

Thomas, M., Walker, A., Wilmot, A. and Bennett, N. (1998). *Living in Britain: Results from the 1996 General Household Survey*. London: Stationery Office.

Thompson, S.C. (1981). Will it hurt less if I can control it? A complex answer to a simple question. *Psychological Bulletin*, 90: 89–101.

Thompson, S.C., Galbraith, M., Thomas, C., Swan. J. and Vrungos, S. (2002). Caregivers of stroke patient family members: behavioural and attitudinal indicators of overprotective care. *Psychology and Health*, 17: 297–312.

Thompson, S.C. and Pitts, J.C. (1992). In sickness and in health: chronic illness, marriage and spousal caregiving. In S. Spacapan and S. Oskamp (eds), *Helping and Being Helped: Naturalistic Studies*. Newbury Park, Calif.: Sage.

Thompson, S.C., Sobolew-Shubin, A., Galbraith, M.E., Schwankovsky, L. and Cruzen, D. (1993). Maintaining perceptions of control: finding perceived control in low-control circumstances. *Journal of Personality and Social Psychology*, 64: 293–304.

Thompson, W.G., Longstreth, G. and Drossman, D.A. (2000). Functional bowel disorders and functional abdominal pain. In D.A. Drossman, E. Corazziari, N. Talley, W.G. Thompson and W. Whitehead (eds), *Rome II: The Functional Gastrointestinal Disorders*, 2nd edn. McLean, Va: Degnon Associates.

Thurstone, L.L. (1928). Attitudes can be measured. *American Journal of Sociology*, 33: 529–44.

Timko, C. and Janoff-Bulman, R. (1985). Attributions, vulnerability and psychological adjustment: the case of breast cancer. *Health Psychology*, 4: 521–44.

Tobin, D.L., Holroyd, K.A., Baker, A. Reynolds, R.V.C. and Holm, J.E. (1988). Development and clinical trial of a minimal contact, cognitive-behavioral treatment for tension headache. *Cognitive Therapy and Research*, 12: 325–39.

Toljamo, M. and Hentinen, M. (2001). Adherence to self care and social support. *Journal of Clinical Nursing*, 10: 618–27.

Topf, M. (1989). Sensitivity to noise, personality hardiness, and noise-induced stress in critical care nurses. *Environment and Behaviour*, 21: 717–33.

Triandis, H.C. (1977). *Interpersonal Behavior*. Monterey, Calif.: Brooks/Cole.

Tromp, D.M., Brouha, X.D.R., DeLeeuw, J.R.J., Hordjik, G.J. and Winnubst, J.A.M. (2004). Psychological factors and patient delay in patients with head and neck cancer. *European Journal of Cancer*, 40: 1509–16.

Tschuschke, V., Hertenstein, B., Arnold, R. Arnold, R., Bunjes, D., Denzinger, R. and Kaechele, H. (2001). Associations between coping and survival time of adult leukaemia patients receiving allogenic bone marrow transplantation. Results of a prospective study. *Journal of Psychosomatic Research*, 50: 277–85.

Tubiana-Rufi, N., Moret, L., Czernichow, P. and Chwalow, J. (1998). The association of poor adherence and acute metabolic disorders with low levels of cohesion and adaptability in families with diabetic children. The PEDIAB Collaborative Group. *Acta Paediatrica*, 87: 741–6.

Tudor-Smith, C., Nutbeam, D., Moore, L. and Catford, J. (1998). Effects of the Heartbeat Wales programme over five years on behavioural risks for cardiovascular disease: quasi-experimental comparison of results from Wales and a matched reference area. *British Medical Journal*, 316: 818–22.

Turk, D.C. (1986). Workshop on pain management. Birmingham, UK.

Turk, D.C., Litt, M.D., Salovey, P. and Walker, J. (1985). Seeking urgent pediatric treatment: factors contributing to frequency, delay and appropriateness. *Health Psychology*, 4: 43–59

Turk, D.C. and Okifuji, A. (1999). Assessment of patients' reporting of pain: an integrated perspective. *The Lancet*, 353: 1784–8.

Turk, D.C., Rudy, T.E. and Salovey, P. (1986). Implicit models of illness. *Journal of Behavioral Medicine*, 9: 453–74.

Turner, G. and Shepherd, J. (1999). A method in search of a theory: peer education and health promotion. *Health Education Research*, 14: 235–47.

Turner, J.A. and Clancy, S. (1988). Comparison of operant behavioral and cognitive-behavioral group treatment for chronic low back pain. *Journal of Consulting and Clinical Psychology*, 56: 261–6.

Turner, J., Page-Shafer, K., Chin, D.P., Osmond, D., Mossar, M., Markstein, L., Huitsing, J., Barnes,

S., Clemente, V. and Chesney, M. Pulmonary Complications of HIV Infection Study Group (2001). Adverse impact of cigarette smoking on dimensions of health-related quality of life in persons with HIV infection. *AIDS Patient Care and STDs*, 15: 615–24.

Turner, J.C., Hogg, M.A., Oakes, P.J., Reicher, S.D. and Wetherell, M. (1987). *Rediscovering the Social Group: A Self-categorization Theory*. Oxford: Blackwell.

Turner-Cobb, J.M., Gore-Felton, C., Marouf, F., Koopman, C., Kim, P., Israel, D. and Spiegel, D. (2002). Coping, social adjustment, and attachment style as psychosocial correlates of adjustment in men and women with HIV/AIDS. *Journal of Behavioral Medicine*, 25: 337–53.

Turner-Cobb, J.M., Sephton, S.E., Koopman, C., Blake-Mortimer, J. and Spiegel, D. Social support and salivary cortisol in women with metastatic breast cancer. *Psychosomatic Medicine*, 62: 337–45.

Tversky, A. and Kahneman, D. (1981): The framing of decisions and the psychology of choice. *Science*, 211: 453–8.

Tyas, S.L. and Pederson, L.L. (1998). Psychological factors related to adolescent smoking: a critical review of the literature. *Tobacco Control*, 7: 409–20.

Tyczynski, J.E., Bray, F., Aareleid, T. and Dalmas, M. (2004). Lung cancer mortality patterns in selected Central, Eastern and Southern European countries. *International Journal of Cancer*, 109: 598–610.

Uchino, B.N., Cacioppo, J.T. and Kiecolt-Glaser, J.K. (1996). The relationship between social support and physiological processes: a review with emphasis on underlying mechanisms and implications for health. *Psychological Bulletin*, 119: 488–533.

UK Central Statistics Office (1980). A change in revenue from an indirect tax change. *Economic Trend*, March, 97–107.

UK Health Education Authority and UK Sports Council (1992). *Allied Dunbar National Fitness Survey*. London: Allied Dunbar, Health Education Authority and Sports Council.

United Nations Secretariat (2002). The ageing of the world's population. Population Division, Department of Economic and Social Affairs, United Nations Secretariat. http://www.un.org/esa/socdev/ageing/agewpop.htm

Urquhart-Law, G. (2002). Dissimilarity in adolescent and maternal representations of type 1 diabetes: exploration of relations to adolescent well-being. *Child Health Care and Development*, 28: 369–78.

US Bureau of the Census (1999). *Statistical Abstracts of the United States: 1998* (118th edn). Retrieved (2.10.2002) from http://www.census.gov

US Department of Health and Human Services (1996). *Physical Activity and Health: A Report of the Surgeon General*. US Department of Health and Human Services, Centers for Disease Control and Prevention, National Center for Chronic Disease Prevention and Health Promotion, Atlanta.

US Department of Health and Human Services (1997). *Ninth Special Report to the U.S. Congress on Alcohol and Health, June 1997*. US Department of Health and Human Services, NIH, NIAAA.

United States Preventive Services Task Force (USPSTF) (2003). Routine vitamin supplementation to prevent cancer and cardiovascular disease: recommendations and rationale. *Annals of Internal Medicine*, 139: 51–5.

Vaillant, G.E. (1998). Natural history of male psychological health XIV: relationship of mood disorder, vulnerability and physical health. *American Journal of Psychiatry*, 155: 184–91.

Valente, S.M. (2003). Depression and HIV disease. *Journal of Association of Nurses in AIDS Care*, 14: 41–51.

van den Arend, I.J., Stolk, R.P. and Rutten, G.E. (2000). Education integrated into structured general practice care for Type 2 diabetic patients results in sustained improvement of illness knowledge and self-care. *Diabetes Medicine*, 17: 190–7.

van den Heuvel, E.T.P., de Witte, L.P., Schure, L.M., Sanderman, R. and de Jong, B.M. (2001). Risk factors for burn-out in caregivers of stroke patients, and possibilities for intervention. *Clinical Rehabilitation*, 15: 669–77.

van den Hout, J.H.C., Vlaeyen, J.W.S., Peters, M.L., Engelhard, I.M. and van den Hout, M.A. (2000). Does failure hurt? The effects of failure feedback on pain report, pain tolerance and pain avoidance. *European Journal of Pain*, 4: 335–46.

van der Doef, M. and Maes, S. (1998). The job demand–control(–support) model and physical health outcomes: a review of the strain and buffer hypotheses. *Psychology and Health*, 13: 909–36.

van der Doef, M. and Maes, S. (1999). The job demand–control(–support) model and psychological well-being: a review of 20 years empirical research. *Work and Stress*, 13: 87–114.

van der Geest, S. and Whyte, S. (1989). The charm of medicines: metaphors and metonyms. *Medical Anthropology Quarterly*, 3: 345–67.

van der Heide, A., Deliens, L., Faisst, K., Nilstun, T., Norup, M., Paci, E., van der Wal, G. and van der Maas, P.J. on behalf of the EURELD consortium (2003). End-of-life decision-making in six European countries: descriptive study. *The Lancet*, 361: 345–50.

van der Pligt, J. and de Vries, N.K. (1998). Expectancy-value models of health behaviour: the role of salience and anticipated affect. *Psychology and Health*, 13: 289–305.

van der Pligt, J., Otten, W., Richard, R. and van der Velde, F. (1993). Perceived risk of AIDS: unrealistic optimism and self-protective action. In J.B. Prior and G.D. Reeder (eds), *The Social Psychology of HIV Infection*. Hillsdale, NJ: Lawrence Erlbaum.

van der Velde, F.W., Hooykaas, C. and van der Pligt, J. (1992). Risk perception and behaviour: pessimism, realism and optimism about AIDS-related health behaviour. *Psychology and Health*, 6: 23–38.

van der Vyver, M., Halpern, S. and Joseph, G. (2002). Patient-controlled epidural analgesia versus continuous infusion for labour analgesia: a meta-analysis. *British Journal of Anaesthesia*, 89: 459–65.

van Eck, M., Berkhof, H., Nicolson, N. and Sulon, J. (1996). The effects of perceived stress, traits, mood states, and stressful daily events on salivary cortisol. *Psychosomatic Medicine*, 58: 508–14.

van Tulder, M.W., Ostelo, R.W.J., Vlaeyen, J.W.S., Linton, S.J., Morley, S.J. and Assendelft, W.J. (2003). Behavioural treatment for chronic low back pain. In *The Cochrane Library*, issue 1. Oxford: Update Software.

van Zuuren, F.J. and Dooper, R. (1999). Coping style and self-reported health promotion and disease detection behaviour. *British Journal of Health Psychology*, 4: 81–9.

Vaughan, P.W., Rogers, E.M., Singhal, A. and Swalehe, R.M. (2000). Entertainment-education and HIV/AIDS prevention: a field experiment in Tanzania. *Journal of Health Communication*, 5: 81–100.

Vedhara, K., Cox, N.K.M., Wilcock, G.K., Perks, P., Hunt, M., Anderson, S., Lightman, S.L. and Stancs, N.M. (1999). Chronic stress in elderly carers of dementia patients and antibody responses to influenza vaccination. *The Lancet*, 353: 627–31.

Vedhara, K., McDermott, M.P., Evans, T.G., Treanor, J.J., Plummer, S., Tallon, D., Cruttenden, K.A. and Schifitto, G. (2002). Chronic stress in nonelderly caregivers. Psychological, endocrine and immune implications. *Journal of Psychosomatic Research*, 53: 1153–61.

Vedhara, K., Shanks, N., Anderson, S. and Lightman, S. (2000). The role of stressors and psychosocial variables in the stress process: a study of chronic caregiver stress. *Psychosomatic Medicine*, 62: 374–85.

Vedhara, K., Tallon, D., Gale, L., Dougan, E., Strode, A., Mudge, L. and Weinman, J. (2003). Psychological determinants of wound healing in diabetic patients with foot ulceration. Paper presented at the European Health Psychology conference, Kos, August 2003.

Veenhoven, R. (2003). Happiness. *The Psychologist*, 16: 128–9.

Verbrugge, L.M. and Steiner, R.P. (1985). Prescribing drugs to men and women. *Health Psychology*, 4: 79–98.

Verdugo, R.J. and Ochoa, J.L. (1994). Sympathetically maintained pain. I. Phentolamine block questions the concept. *Neurology*, 44: 1003–10.

Viner, R., McGrath, M. and Trudinger, P. (1996). Family stress and metabolic control in diabetes. *Archives of Diseases of Childhood*, 74: 418–21.

Visser-Meily, A., van Heugten, C., Post, M., Schepers, V. and Lindeman, E. (2005). Intervention studies for caregivers of stroke survivors: a critical review. *Patient Education and Counselling*, 56: 257–67.

Vlaeyen, J.W., Kole-Snijders, A.M., Boeren, R.G. and van Eek, H. (1995). Fear of movement/(re)injury in chronic low back pain and its relation to behavioral performance. *Pain*, 62: 363–72.

Vögele, C. (1998). Serum lipid concentrations, hostility and cardiovascular reactions to mental stress. *International Journal of Psycophysiology*, 28: 167–79.

Vögele, C., Jarvis, A. and Cheeseman, K. (1997). Anger suppression, reactivity, and hypertension risk: gender makes a difference. *Annals of Behavioral Medicine*, 19: 61–9.

Vögele, C. and Steptoe, A. (1993). Anger inhibition and family history as moderators of cardiovascular responses to mental stress in adolescent boys. *Journal of Psychosomatic Research*, 37: 503–14.

Vogt, T.M., Mullooly, J.P., Ernst, D., Pope, C.R. and Hollis, J.F. (1992). Social networks as predictors of ischemic heart disease, cancer, stroke and hypertension: incidence, survival and mortality. *Journal of Clinical Epidemiology*, 45: 659–66.

Vosvick, M., Koopman, C., Gore-Felton, C., Thoresen, X., Krumboltz, J. and Spiegel, D. (2003). Relationship of functional quality of life to strategies for coping with the stress of living with HIV/AIDS. *Psychosomatics*, 44: 51–8.

Wade, D.T. and Halligan, P.W. (2004). Do biomedical models of illness make for good healthcare systems? *British Medical Journal*, 329: 1398–401.

Wakefield, A.J., Murch, S.H., Anthony, A., Linnell, J., Casson, D.M., Malik, M., Berelowitz, M., Dhillon, A.P., Thomson, M.A., Harvey, P., Valentie, A., Davies, S.E. and Walker-Smith, J.A. (1998). Ileal-lymphoid nodular hyperplasia, non-specific colitis and pervasive developmental disorder in children. *The Lancet*, 351: 637–41.

Walker, J.G., Jackson, H.J. and Littlejohn, G.O. (2004). Models of adjustment to chronic illness: using the example of rheumatoid arthritis. *Clinical Psychology Review*, 24: 461–88.

Walker, L.G., Heys, S.D. and Eremin, O. (1999). Surviving cancer: do psychosocial factors count? *Journal of Psychosomatic Research*, 47: 497–503.

Walker, Z.A.K. and Townsend, J. (1999). The role of general practice in promoting teenage health: a review of the literature. *Family Practice*, 16: 164–72.

Wall, P.D. (1979). On the relation of injury to pain. The John J. Bonica Lecture. *Pain*, 6: 253–64.

Wallander, J.L. and Varni, J.W. (1998). Effects of pediatric chronic physical disorders on child and family adjustment. *Journal of Child Psychology and Psychiatry*, 39: 29–46.

Wallston, K.A. (1991). The importance of placing measures of health locus of control beliefs in a theoretical context. *Health Education Research*, 6: 251–2.

Wallston, K.A. and Smith, M.S. (1994). Issues of control and health: the action is in the interaction. In G. Penny, P. Bennett and M. Herbert (eds), *Health Psychology: A Lifespan Perspective*. London: Harwood Academic.

Wallston, K.A., Wallston, B.S. and deVellis, R. (1978). Development of the multidimensional health locus of control (MHLC) scale. *Health Education Monographs*, 6: 160–70.

Walsh, D.A. and Radcliffe, J.C. (2002). Pain beliefs and perceived physical disability of patients with chronic low back pain. *Pain*, 97: 23–31.

Warburton, D.M., Revell, A.D. and Thompson, D.H. (1991). Smokers of the future. Special issue: Future directions in tobacco research, *British Journal of Addiction*, 86: 621–5.

Ward, S.E., Leventhal, H. and Love, R. (1988). Repression revisited: tactics used in coping with a severe health threat. *Personality and Social Psychology Bulletin*, 14: 735–46.

Ward, M.M., Mefford, I.N., Parker, S.D., Chesney, M.A., Taylor, C.B., Keegan, D.L. and Barchas, J.D. (1983). Epinephrine and norepinephrine responses in continuously collected human plasma to a series of stressors. *Psychosomatic Medicine*, 45: 471–86.

Wardle, J., Cooke, L.J., Gibson, E.L., Sapochnik, M., Sheiham, A. and Lawson, M. (in press). Increasing children's acceptance of vegetables; a randomized trial of parent-led exposure. *Appetite*, 40: 155–62.

Wardle, J. and Steptoe, A. (2003). Socioeconomic differences in attitudes and beliefs about healthy lifestyles. *Journal of Epidemiology and Community Health*, 57: 440–3.

Warren, L. and Hixenbaugh, P. (1998). Adherence and diabetes. In L. Myers and K. Midence (eds), *Adherence to Treatment in Medical Conditions*. The Netherlands: Harwood Academic.

Watson, D. and Clark, L.A. (1984). Negative affectivity: the disposition to experience aversive emotional states. *Psychological Bulletin*, 96: 465–90.

Watson, D. and Pennebaker, J.W. (1989). Health complaints, stress and distress: exploring the central role of negative affectivity. *Psychological Review*, 96: 234–54.

Watson, D. and Pennebaker, J.W. (1991). Situational, dispositional and genetic bases of symptom reporting. In J.A. Skelton and R.T. Croyle (eds), *Mental Representation in Health and Illness*. New York: Springer Verlag.

Watson, M., Buck, G., Wheatley, K., Homewood, J.R., Goldstone, A.H., Rees, J.K.H. and Burnett, A.K. (2004). Adverse impact of bone marrow transplantation on quality of life in acute myeloid leukaemia patients: analysis of the UK Medical Research Council AML 10 Trial. *European Journal of Cancer*, 40: 971–8.

Watson, M., Davidson-Homewood, J., Haviland, J. and Bliss, J. (2002). Influence of psychological coping on survival and recurrence: a response to the systematic review, (letter to the editor). *British Medical Journal*, 325: 598.

Watson, M., Haviland, J.S., Greer, S., Davidson, J. and Bliss, J.M. (1999). Influence of psychological response on survival in breast cancer: a population-based cohort study. *The Lancet*, 9187: 1331–6.

Watson, M., Lloyd, S., Davidson, J., Meyer, L., Eeles, R., Ebbs, S. and Murday, V. (1999). The impact of genetic counselling on risk perception and mental health in women with a family history of breast cancer. *British Journal of Cancer*, 79: 868–74.

Weber, A. and Lehnert, G. (1997). Unemployment and cardiovascular diseases: a causal relationship? *International Archives of Occupational and Environmental Health*, 70: 153–60.

Weber, M.A. and Julius, S. (1998). The challenge of very mild hypertension: should treatment be sooner or later? *American Journal of Hypertension*, 11: 1495–6.

Weinman, J., Petrie, K.J., Moss-Morris, R. and Horne, R. (1996). The Illness Perception Questionnaire: A new method for assessing the cognitive representation of illness. *Psychology and Health*, 11: 431–55.

Weinman, J. and Petrie, K.J. (1997). Illness perceptions: a new paradigm for psychosomatics? (editorial). *Journal of Psychosomatic Research*, 42: 113–16.

Weinman, J., Petrie, K.J., Sharpe, N. and Walker, S. (2000). Causal attributions in patients and spouses following first-time myocardial infarction and subsequent life changes. *British Journal of Health Psychology*, 5: 263–74.

Weinstein, N.D. (1982). Unrealistic optimism about susceptibility to health problems. *Journal of Behavioral Medicine*, 2: 125–40.

Weinstein, N. (1984). Why it won't happen to me: perceptions of risk factors and susceptibility. *Health Psychology*, 3: 431–57.

Weinstein, N. (1987). Unrealistic optimism about illness susceptibility: conclusions from a community-wide sample. *Journal of Behavioral Medicine*, 10: 481–500.

Weinstein, N.D. (1988). The precaution adoption process. *Health Psychology*, 7: 355–86.

Weinstein, N.D. (2003). Exploring the links between risk perception and preventive health behaviour. In J. Suls and K.A. Wallston (eds), *Social Psychological Foundations of Health and Illness*. Malden, Mass.: Blackwell.

Weinstein, N.D., Rothman, A.J. and Sutton, S.R. (1998). Stage theories of health behavior: conceptual and methodological issues. *Health Psychology*, 17: 290–9.

Weinstein, N.D. and Klein, W.M. (1996). Unrealistic optimism: present and future. *Journal of Social and Clinical Psychology*, 15: 1–8.

Weinstein, N.D. and Sandman, P.M. (1992). A model of the precaution adoption process: evidence from home radon testing. *Health Psychology*, 11: 170–80.

Weinstein, N. and Sandman, P.M. (2002). Reducing the risk of exposure to radon gas: an application of the Precation Adoption Process model. In D. Rutter and L. Quine (eds). *Changing Health Behaviour* (66–86). Buckingham: Open University Press.

Weisenberg, M., Raz, T. and Hener, T. (1998). The influence of film-induced mood on pain perceptions. *Pain*, 76: 365–75.

Weisse, C.S., Turbiasz, A.A. and Whitney, D.J. (1995). Behavioral training and AIDS risk reduction: overcoming barriers to condom use. *AIDS Education and Prevention*, 7: 50–9.

Weller, D. (2004). Behavioural and social science research in cancer: time for action (editorial comment). *European Journal of Cancer*, 40: 314–15.

Wellings, K., Field, S., Johnson, A.M. and Wadsworth, J. (1994). Studying sexual lifestyles. In K. Wellings, S. Field, A.M. Johnson and J. Wadsworth (eds), *Sexual Behaviour in Britain*. London: Penguin.

Wells, M.E., McQuellon, R.P., Hinkle, J.S. and Cruz, J.M. (1995). Reducing anxiety in newly diagnosed cancer patients: a pilot program. *Cancer Practice*, 3: 100–4.

Wen, L.M., Thomas, M., Jones, H., Orr, N., Moreton, R., King, L., Hawe, P., Bindon, J., Humphries, J., Schicht, K., Corne, S. and Bauman, A. (2002). Promoting physical activity in women: evaluation of a 2-year community-based intervention in Sydney, Australia. *Health Promotion International*, 17: 127–37.

Wessely, S., Rose S. and Bisson, J. (1999). A systematic review of brief psychological interventions ('debriefing') for the treatment of immediate trauma related symptoms and the prevention of post-traumatic stress disorder. In *The Cochrane Library*. Oxford: Update Software.

West, R. (1992). Nicotine addiction: a re-analysis of the arguments. *Psychopharmacology*, 108: 408–10.

West, R., Edwards, M. and Hajek, P.A. (1998). Randomized controlled trial of a 'buddy' system to improve success at giving up smoking in general practice. *Addiction*, 93: 1007–11.

Westman, M., Eden, D. and Shirom, A. (1985). Job stress, cigarette smoking and cessation: conditioning effects of peer support. *Social Science and Medicine*, 20: 637–44.

Whelan, E.M. (1988). The truth about Americans' health. In R. Yarian (ed.), *Annual Editions*: *Health* (9th edition), 25–9.

White, A., Nicolaas, G., Foster, K., Browne, F. and Carey, S. (1993). *Health Survey for England 1991*. London: HMSO.

Whitehead, M., Townsend, P. and Davidson, N. (eds) (1992). *Inequalities in Health*: *The Black Report / The Health Divide*. London: Penguin Social Sciences.

WHOQOL Group (1993). Study protocol for the World Health Organisation project to develop a quality of life assessment instrument (WHOQOL). *Quality of Life Research*, 2: 153–9.

WHOQOL Group (1994). Development of the WHO-QOL: rationale and current status. Monograph on quality of life assessment: cross-cultural issues 2. *International Journal of Mental Health*, 23: 24–56.

WHOQOL Group (1998). The World Health Organization Quality of Life Assessment (WHOQOL): development and psychometric properties. *Social Science and Medicine*, 46: 1569–85.

Widows, M.R., Jacobsen, P.B. and Fields, K.K. (2000). Relation of psychological vulnerability factors to posttraumatic stress disorder symptomatology in bone marrow transplant recipients. *Psychosomatic Medicine*, 62: 873–82.

Wild, S. and McKeigue, P. (1997). Cross sectional analysis of mortality by country of birth in England and Wales, 1970–92. *British Medical Journal*, 314: 705–10.

Wiles, R., Ashburn, A., Payne, S. and Murphy, C. (2004). Discharge from physiotherapy following stroke: the management of disappointment. *Social Science and Medicine*, 59: 1263–73.

Wilkinson, M. (1992). Income distribution and life expectancy. *British Medical Journal*, 304: 165–8.

Wilkinson, R.G. (1990). Income distribution and mortality: a 'natural' experiment. *Sociology of Health and Illness*, 12: 391–412.

Williams, J.E., Paton, C.C., Siegler, I.C., Eigenbrodt, M.L., Nieto, F.J. and Tyroler, H.A. (2000). Anger proneness predicts coronary heart disease risk: prospective analysis from Atherosclerosis Risk in Communities (ARIC) study. *Circulation*, 1010: 2034–9.

Williamson, D., Robinson, M.E. and Melamed, B. (1997). Pain behaviour, spouse responsiveness, and marital satisfaction in patients with rheumatoid arthritis. *Behavioral Modification*, 21: 97–118.

Williamson, G.M., Shaffer, D.R. and Schulz, R. (1998). Activity restriction and prior relationship history as contributors to mental health outcomes among middle-aged and older spousal caregivers. *Health Psychology*, 17: 152–62.

Williamson, S. and Wardle, J. (2002). Increasing participation with colorectal cancer screening: the development of a psychoeducational intervention. In D. Rutter and L. Quine (eds), *Changing Health Behaviour*. Buckingham: Open University Press.

Wilson, J.F. (1981). Behavioral preparation for surgery: benefit or harm? *Journal of Behavioral Medicine*, 4: 79–102.

Wilson, J.F., Moore, R.W., Randolph, S. and Hanson, B.J. (1982). Behavioral preparation of patients for gastrointestinal endoscopy: information, relaxation and coping style. *Journal of Human Stress*, 8: 13–23.

Wilson, P.W.F., D'Agostino, R.B., Sullivan, L., Parise, H. and Kannel, W.B. (2002). Overweight and obesity as determinants of cardiovascular risk, *Archives of Internal Medicine*, 162: 1867–1872.

Wimbush, E., MacGregor, A. and Fraser, E. (1998). Impact of a national mass media campaign on walking in Scotland. *Health Promotion International*, 13: 45–53.

Wing, R.R., Phelan, S. and Tate, D. (2002). The role of adherence in mediating the relationship between depression and health outcomes. *Journal of Psychosomatic Research*, 53: 877–81.

Winkleby, M., Fortmann, S. and Barrett, D. (1990). Social class disparities in risk factors for disease: eight year prevalence patterns by level of education. *Preventive Medicine*, 19: 1–12.

Wise, R.A. (1998). Drug activation of brain reward pathways. *Drug and Alcohol Dependence*, 51: 13–22.

Wollin, S.D. and Jones, P.J. (2001). Alcohol, red wine and cardiovascular disease. *Journal of Nutrition*, 131: 1401–4.

Woods, R.T. (ed.) (1999). *Psychological Problems of Ageing: Assessment, Treatment and Care*. Chichester: Wiley.

Woodward, M., Olpihant, J., Lowe, G. and Tunstall-Pedoe, H. (2003). Contribution of contemporaneous risk factors to social inequality in coronary heart disease and all causes mortality. *Preventive Medicine*, 36: 561–8.

Woolf, S.H. (1996). Immunizations. In S.H. Woolf, S. Jonas and R.S. Lawrence (eds), *Health Promotion and Disease Prevention in Clinical Practice*. Baltimore: Williams & Wilkins.

World Cancer Research Fund (1997). *Food Nutrition and the Prevention of Cancer: A Global Perspective*. Washington: American Institute for Cancer Research.

World Health Organization (1947). Constitution of the World Health Organization. Geneva: WHO.

World Health Organization (1980). *International Classification of Impairments, Disabilities and Handicaps (ICIDH). A Manual of Classification Relating to the Consequences of Disease*. Geneva: WHO.

World Health Organization (1981). *Global Strategy for Health for All by the Year 2000*. Geneva: WHO.

World Health Organization (1988). *Healthy Cities Project: Five Year Planning Framework*. Copenhagen: WHO Regional Office for Europe.

World Health Organization (1995). *World Health Report*. Geneva: WHO.

World Health Organization (1996). *Health Promoting Schools. Report of a WHO Expert Committee on Comprehensive School Health Education and Promotion*. Geneva: WHO.

World Health Organization (1999). *Health 21: Health for All in the 21st Century*. Copenhagen: WHO Regional Office for Europe.

World Health Organization (2002). *The World Health Report: Reducing Risks, Promoting Healthy Life*. Copenhagen: WHO Regional Office for Europe.

World Health Organization (2004). *Young People's Health in Context: Health Behaviour in School-aged Children (HBSC) Study:* International report from the 2001/2002 survey. C. Currie, C. Roberts, A. Morgan, R. Smith, W. Settertobulte, O. Samdal and V.B. Rasmussen (eds). www.euro.who.int

World Health Organization Expert Committee (1990). *Cancer Pain Relief and Palliative Care*, Technical Report Series No. 84. Geneva: WHO.

Wortley, P. and Fleming, P. (1997). AIDS in women in the United States: recent trends. *Journal of the American Medical Association*, 278: 911–16.

Yan, H. and Sellick, K. (2004). Quality of life of Chinese patients newly diagnosed with gastrointestinal cancer: a longitudinal study. *International Journal of Nursing Studies*, 41: 309–19.

Yancy, C. (2002). Online program aids heart patients and their doctors. *Circulation*, 106: 2299.

Yee, J.L. and Schulz, R. (2000). Gender differences in psychiatric morbidity among family caregivers: a review and analysis. *The Gerontologist*, 40: 147–64.

Young, J.M., D'Este, C. and Ward, J.E. (2002). Improving family physicians' use of evidence-based smoking cessation strategies: a cluster randomization trial. *Preventive Medicine*, 35: 572–83.

Yzer, M.C., Fisher, J.D., Bakker, A.B., Siero, F.W. and Misovich, S.J. (1998). The effects of information about AIDS risk and self-efficacy on women's intentions to engage in AIDS preventive behavior. *Journal of Applied Social Psychology*, 28: 1837–52.

Yzer, M.C., Siero, F.W. and Buunk, B.P. (2001). Bringing up condom use and using condoms with new sexual partners: intention or habitual? *Psychology and Health*, 16: 409–21.

Zabora, J., BrintzenhofeSzoc, K., Curbow, B., Hooker, C. and Piantadosi, S. (2001). The prevalence of psychological distress by cancer site. *Psycho-Oncology*, 10: 19–28.

Zachariae, R., Pedersen, C.G., Jensen, A.B., Ehrnrooth, E., Rossen, P.B. and von der Maase, H. (2003). Association of perceived physician communication style with patient satisfaction, distress, cancer-related self-efficacy, and perceived control over the disease. *British Journal of Cancer*, 88: 658–65.

Zakowski, S. (1995). The effects of stressor predictability on lymphocyte proliferation in humans. *Psychology and Health*, 10: 409–25.

Zakowski, S.G., McAllister, C.G., Deal, M. and Baum, A. (1992). Stress, reactivity, and immune function in healthy men. *Health Psychology*, 11: 223–32.

Zarit, S., Reever, K. and Bach-Peterson, J. (1980). Relatives of the impaired elderly: correlates of feelings of burden. *The Gerontologist*, 20: 649–55.

Zaza, C. and Baine, N. (2002). Cancer pain and psychosocial factors: a critical review of the literature. *Journal of Pain and Symptom Management*, 24: 526–42.

Zborowski, M. (1952). Cultural components in response to pain. *Journal of Social Issues*, 8: 16–30.

Zeidner, M. and Saklofske, D. (1996). Adaptive and maladaptive coping. In M. Zeidner and N. Endler (eds), *Handbook of Coping: Theory, Research, Application*. New York: Wiley.

Zelter, L. and LeBaron, S. (1982). Hypnosis and non-hypnotic techniques for reduction of pain and anxiety during painful procedures in children and adolescents with cancer. *Journal of Pediatrics*, 101: 1032–5.

Zervas, I.M., Augustine, A. and Fricchione, G.L. (1993). Patient delay in cancer. A view for the crisis model. *General Hospital Psychiatry*, 15: 9–13.

Zhang, Y., Proenca, R., Maffie, M., Barone, M., Leopold, L. and Friedman, J.M. (1994). Positional cloning of the mouse obese gene and its human homologue. *Nature*, 372: 425–32.

Zimmers, E., Privette, G., Lowe, R.H. and Chappa, F. (1999). Increasing use of the female condom through video instruction. *Perceptual and Motor Skills*, 88: 1071–7.

Zinovieff, F., Morrison, V., Coles, A. and Cartmell, R. (2005). Are the needs of cancer patients and their carers generic? Paper presented to the European Health Psychology Society annual conference, Galway, September.

Zohar, D. and Dayan, I. (1999). Must coping options be severely limited during stressful events: testing the interaction between primary and secondary appraisals. *Anxiety, Stress and Coping*, 12: 191–216.

Zola, I.K. (1973). Pathways to the doctor – from person to patient. *Social Science and Medicine*, 7: 677–89.

Zorrilla, E.P., McKay, J.R., Luborsky, L. and Schmidt, K. (1996). Relation of stressors and depressive symptoms to clinical progression of Viral Illness. *American Journal of Psychiatry*. May, 1996. 153(5): 626–35.

Zuckerman, M. (1979). *Sensation Seeking: Beyond the Optimal Level of Arousal*. Hillsdale, NJ: Lawrence Erlbaum.

Zuckerman, M. (1984). Sensation seeking: a comparative approach to a human trait. *Behavioral and Brain Sciences*, 7: 413–17.

INDEX

Entries in **bold** are defined in the Glossary.